MEDIA IN ASIA

This book is an upper-level student sourcebook for contemporary approaches to media studies in Asia, which will appeal across a wide range of social sciences and humanities subjects including media and communication studies, Asian studies, cultural studies, sociology and anthropology. Drawing on a wide range of perspectives from media and communications, sociology, cultural studies, anthropology and Asian studies, it provides an empirically rich and stimulating tour of key areas of study. The book combines theoretical perspectives with grounded case studies in one up-to-date and accessible volume, going beyond the standard Euro-American view of the evolving and complex dynamics of the media today.

Youna Kim is Professor of Global Communications at the American University of Paris, joined from the London School of Economics and Political Science where she had taught since 2004, after completing her PhD at the University of London, Goldsmiths College. Her books are *Women, Television and Everyday Life in Korea: Journeys of Hope* (Routledge, 2005), *Media Consumption and Everyday Life in Asia* (Routledge, 2008), *Transnational Migration, Media and Identity of Asian Women: Diasporic Daughters* (Routledge, 2011), *Women and the Media in Asia: The Precarious Self* (2012), *The Korean Wave: Korean Media Go Global* (Routledge, 2013), *Routledge Handbook of Korean Culture and Society* (Routledge, 2016), *Childcare Workers, Global Migration and Digital Media* (Routledge, 2017), *South Korean Popular Culture and North Korea* (Routledge, 2019) and *The Soft Power of the Korean Wave: Parasite, BTS and Drama* (Routledge, 2021).

Media, Culture and Social Change in Asia

Series Editor
Stephanie Hemelryk Donald

The aim of this series is to publish original, high-quality work by both new and established scholars in the West and the East, on all aspects of media, culture and social change in Asia.

MEDIA IN ASIA

Global, Digital, Gendered and Mobile

Edited by Youna Kim

Routledge
Taylor & Francis Group

LONDON AND NEW YORK

Cover image: © Getty Images

First published 2022
by Routledge
4 Park Square, Milton Park, Abingdon, Oxon OX14 4RN

and by Routledge
605 Third Avenue, New York, NY 10158

Routledge is an imprint of the Taylor & Francis Group, an informa business

© 2022 selection and editorial matter, Youna Kim; individual chapters, the contributors

The right of Youna Kim to be identified as the author of the editorial material, and of the authors for their individual chapters, has been asserted in accordance with sections 77 and 78 of the Copyright, Designs and Patents Act 1988.

British Library Cataloguing-in-Publication Data
A catalogue record for this book is available from the British Library

Library of Congress Cataloging-in-Publication Data
A catalog record has been requested for this book

ISBN: 978-0-367-65322-4 (hbk)
ISBN: 978-0-367-67285-0 (pbk)
ISBN: 978-1-003-13062-8 (ebk)

DOI: 10.4324/9781003130628

Typeset in Bembo
by Deanta Global Publishing Services, Chennai, India

CONTENTS

ILLUSTRATIONS

Figures

Table

ACKNOWLEDGMENTS

This book is an extension of my previous volume published in 2008, *Media Consumption and Everyday Life in Asia* (Routledge), which was well received by students interested in Asian media, culture and society. Since then, global streaming services, video-sharing websites and social media platforms, as well as mobile smartphones, have been playing a key role in expanding the media landscapes of Asia, offering enormous opportunities and challenges. One of the examples is the rise of digital Hallyu or the Korean Wave, as manifested in the four Academy Awards of film *Parasite*, the global popularity of K-pop band BTS and the visibility of K-drama via Netflix. This evolving phenomenon has been thoroughly documented and analyzed in my three volumes, *The Korean Wave: Korean Media Go Global* (Routledge, 2013), *South Korean Popular Culture and North Korea* (Routledge, 2019) and *The Soft Power of the Korean Wave: Parasite, BTS and Drama* (Routledge, 2021). Back in the 1990s and the 2000s when I worked in the USA and the UK, not many people recognized the Korean media or predicted the Asian media in general would become truly global cultural forces. Now in France and elsewhere, I have noticed surprisingly different responses that would prompt a curious researcher to reflect on the power of transnational media culture and Asia in today's digitally connected mobile world. My publisher Routledge has been continually cooperative and supportive of all my projects since the 2000s, for which I remain grateful. Among many wonderful collaborators at Routledge, special thanks to Peter Sowden and Natalie Foster for their thoughtful understanding and support in all possible ways.

As always, I am grateful to Anthony Giddens for his valuable advice and friendship. I remain appreciative of my colleagues, friends and insightful researchers back in London, now here in Paris and elsewhere, Ien Ang, Joaquin Beltran Antolin, Chris Berry, Michael Delli Carpini, Kathleen Chevalier, Chua Beng Huat, Nick Couldry, James Curran, Rosalind Gill, Jonathan Gray, Dan Hallin,

Christian Joppke, John Lie, Sonia Livingstone, David Morley, Joseph Nye, Terhi Rantanen, Kevin Robins and Daya Thussu, for their inspiring works, intellectual resources, kind invitations and teaching opportunities, delightful meals together and encouraging conversations when much needed. Heartfelt thanks also to my PA and friend Diane Willian for her generous assistance, always remembered and appreciated wherever she is.

I am deeply appreciative of the contributors in this book for collaborating so willingly and delightfully. Thank you all.

Youna Kim
Paris

NOTES ON CONTRIBUTORS

Kalyani Chadha is Associate Professor in the Medill School of Journalism, Northwestern University, USA. Her research is centered on the examination of journalistic practice as well as the societal implications of new media technologies in varied contexts. Informed by critical and sociological theorizing, her scholarship is international in its orientation, with a particular emphasis on journalism-related developments in India and media globalization in Asia. Her work has appeared in a variety of journals such as *Journalism Studies, Journalism Practice, Digital Journalism, Journal of Media Ethics, International Journal of Communication* and *Media, Culture and Society*. She currently serves on the editorial boards of *Journalism Practice* and *Digital Journalism* and is vice-head of AEJMC's Mass Communication and Society Division.

Anandam Kavoori, the co-author, is Professor at the Grady College of Journalism and Mass Communication at the University of Georgia, USA. He works in the field of Transnational Cultural Studies and has written or edited 10 books and over 50 single (or co-authored) journal articles and book chapters on the subject of media and culture in a global context. Among his books are *The Logics of Globalization, Thinking Television* and *Global Bollywood*. He is also the author of a critically acclaimed novel *The Children of Shahida*. He has been a consultant to News Corporation, CNN International and Discovery Channel, among others. He has held visiting positions at Oxford University, UK, the University of Innsbruck, Austria, and Korea University. Before joining academia, he was a journalist with media organizations in India and the United States.

Fabienne Darling-Wolf is Professor in the Journalism Department and the Media and Communication Doctoral Program in the Lew Klein College of Media and Communication at Temple University, USA. A global media scholar, she studies processes of transnational cultural influence and their "local" negotiation in different contexts, including Japan, Europe and the United States. Her books include *Research Methods in Media* – an edited collection published as part of the set of volumes *International Encyclopedia of Media Studies – Imagining the Global: Transnational Media and Popular Culture beyond East and West* and *The Routledge Handbook of Japanese Media.*

Yuiko Fujita is Professor of Sociology at Meiji University in Tokyo, Japan. She holds a PhD in Media and Communications from the University of London, Goldsmiths College, UK, and an MA in Sociology from Columbia University. Her research interests include culture, media, globalization and gender, with a particular focus on international migration of creative workers, youth culture and social media. She is the author of *Cultural Migrants from Japan: Youth, Media and Migration in New York and London* (2009).

Kaoru Takahashi, the co-author, holds a PhD in Sociology from the University of London, Goldsmiths College, UK. She is currently a Visiting Research Fellow in the Sociology Department at Goldsmiths and also teaches at Kogakuin University in Tokyo, Japan. Her ethnographic research focuses on the intersection of gender, ethnicity and migration and specifically explores the Japanese women diaspora in the UK and their gendered life trajectories, digital media use, everyday experiences and social identities.

Anthony Fung is Director of the Hong Kong Institute of Asia Pacific Studies at the Chinese University of Hong Kong. He is also Professor in the School of Journalism and Communication at the Chinese University of Hong Kong and Professor in the School of Art and Communication at Beijing Normal University in Beijing. His research interests focus on popular culture and cultural studies, gender and youth identity, cultural industries and policy, and digital media studies. His recent books are *Cultural Policy and East Asian Rivalry: The Hong Kong Game Industry* (2018) and *Made in Hong Kong: Studies in Popular Music* (Routledge, 2020).

Georgia Chik, the co-author, is a research student and research assistant at the School of Creative Media, City University of Hong Kong. She holds a Juris Doctor from the University of Hong Kong and a BA in Cultural Management from the Chinese University of Hong Kong. Her research interests focus on creative industries, intellectual property and entertainment law.

Xin Gu is Senior Lecturer in Communications and Media Studies at Monash University, Australia. She is an expert appointed by the UNESCO 2005 Convention on the Protection and Promotion of Expression of Cultural Diversity (2019–22). Her research focuses on the transformation of creative cities and the creative economy under different social, economic and political conditions. Her recent books are *Red Creative: Culture and Modernity in China* (2020) and *Re-Imagining Creative Cities in Twenty-First Century Asia* (2020).

Ramaswami Harindranath is Professor of Media at the School of the Arts and Media, University of New South Wales, Sydney, Australia. His research interests include digital cultures, South Asian politics and culture; global media; race, media and identity; postcolonial studies; and media and citizenship. His major publications are *Audience-Citizens* (SAGE), *Perspectives on Global Cultures*, *The Crash Controversy*, *Studying Digital Media Audiences* (Routledge), *Transnational Lives and the Media* and *Approaches to Audiences*. He is one of the editors of the journal *Postcolonial Studies*.

Michelle H. S. Ho is Assistant Professor of Feminist and Queer Cultural Studies in the Department of Communications and New Media at the National University of Singapore. Her research interests lie in issues of gender, sexuality, race/ethnicity; affect and emotion; and media and popular culture in contemporary East Asia. She is currently working on a monograph exploring trans/gender issues through an ethnographic study of *josō* (male-to-female crossdressing) and *dansō* (female-to-male crossdressing) cafe-and-bars in contemporary Tokyo. Outcomes from this project are published in *Sexualities*, *Asian Anthropology* and *Inter-Asia Cultural Studies*.

Koichi Iwabuchi is Professor of Media and Cultural Studies at the School of Sociology and the Director of Research Center for Embracing Diversity of Kwansei Gakuin University in Japan. His recent English publications include *Resilient Borders and Cultural Diversity: Internationalism, Brand Nationalism and Multiculturalism in Japan* and *Global East Asia: Into the 21st Century* (co-edited with Frank Pieke). He has also published *Recentering Globalization: Popular Culture and Japanese Transnationalism* and *East Asian Pop Culture: Analysing the Korean Wave* (co-edited with Chua Beng Huat).

Jayana Jain is currently working as a postdoctoral researcher at the Ludwig Maximilian University of Munich, Germany, within the project ONLINERPOL. She has completed her PhD in English and Cultural Studies at the University of Münster, Germany. She was granted EU's Marie Curie Fellowship and later the DAAD Graduate School Scholarship to conduct research on South Asian diasporas. She is the author of *Thinking Past "Post-9/11": Home, Nation and Transnational Desires in Pakistani English Novels and Hindi Films* (Routledge, 2021). Alongside migration studies, she is interested in digital humanities, law, political theory, gender and disability studies.

Olivia Khoo is Associate Professor in Film and Screen Studies at Monash University, Australia. She holds a PhD in Cultural Studies from the University of Melbourne. She is the author of *Asian Cinema: A Regional View* (2021) and *The Chinese Exotic: Modern Diasporic Femininity* (2007) and co-editor (with Larissa Hjorth) of *The Routledge Handbook of New Media in Asia* (2016). Her articles have appeared in international journals including *Inter-Asia Cultural Studies*, *Asian Studies Review*, *Feminist Media Studies*, *Camera Obscura*, *Screening the Past* and *GLQ*.

Youna Kim is Professor of Global Communications at the American University of Paris, joined from the London School of Economics and Political Science where she had taught since 2004, after completing her PhD at the University of London, Goldsmiths College. Her books are *Women, Television and Everyday Life in Korea: Journeys of Hope* (Routledge, 2005), *Media Consumption and Everyday Life in Asia* (Routledge, 2008), *Transnational Migration, Media and Identity of Asian Women: Diasporic Daughters* (Routledge, 2011), *Women and the Media in Asia: The Precarious Self* (2012), *The Korean Wave: Korean Media Go Global* (Routledge, 2013), *Routledge Handbook of Korean Culture and Society* (Routledge, 2016), *Childcare Workers, Global Migration and Digital Media* (Routledge, 2017), *South Korean Popular Culture and North Korea* (Routledge, 2019) and *The Soft Power of the Korean Wave: Parasite, BTS and Drama* (Routledge, 2021).

Shanti Kumar is Associate Professor in the Department of Radio-Television-Film at the University of Texas – Austin and is affiliated with the Department of Asian Studies and the South Asia Institute. He is the author of *Gandhi Meets Primetime: Globalization and Nationalism in Indian Television* (University of Illinois Press, 2006) and the co-editor of *Global Communication: New Agendas in Communication* (Routledge, 2013), *Television at Large in South Asia* (Routledge, 2012) and *Planet TV: A Global Television Reader* (CNYU Press, 2003). He has published chapters in several edited anthologies and articles in journals such as *BioScope, Jump Cut, Popular Communication, South Asian Popular Culture, Quarterly Review of Film and Video* and *Television and New Media.*

Dorothy Wai Sim Lau is Assistant Professor at the Academy of Film, Hong Kong Baptist University. Her research interests include stardom, fandom, Asian cinema, digital culture and screen culture. She is the author of *Chinese Stardom in Participatory Cyberculture* (2019) and *Reorienting Chinese Stars in Global Polyphonic Networks: Voice, Ethnicity, Power* (2021). She is the managing editor of *Global Storytelling: Journal of Digital and Moving Images.* Her articles are published in journals such as *Positions: Asia Critique, Continuum* and *Journal of Asian Cinema* and several edited volumes.

Tania Lewis is Co-Director of the Digital Ethnography Research Centre and Professor in the School of Media and Communication at RMIT University, Australia. Over the past two decades her work has critically engaged with the politics of lifestyle, sustainability and consumption, with a focus more recently on digital domesticity and ethnographic methods. Her most recent book *Digital Food: From Paddock to Platform* (2020) analyzes how our relationship to food consumption, production and politics is being re-mediated through digitally connected electronic devices, practices and content. She is also the co-author of *Telemodernities: Television and Transforming Lives in Asia* (2016).

Haiqing Yu, the co-author, is Professor of Media and Communication at RMIT University, Australia. She has expertise in Chinese digital media, communication and culture and their socio-political impact in China, Australia and the Asia Pacific.

Her current projects examine the social implications of China's social credit system, technological innovation and digital transformation; China's digital presence in Australia and the Asia Pacific; and Chinese migrants and Chinese language digital social media.

Joanne Lim is Associate Professor in Communications, Media and Cultural Studies at the University of Nottingham, Malaysia. She holds a PhD in Media and Cultural Studies from the University of East London, UK. She was a Visiting Research Fellow at the National University of Singapore and recently a Visiting Senior Fellow at the London School of Economics and Political Science. Her research explores the participatory culture and digital media technology, interculturalism, youth identities and civic and political engagement within the Southeast Asian context. She is an Editorial Board Member of the *Southeast Asian Social Science Review* (IKMAS).

Sheng-mei Ma is Professor of English at Michigan State University in Michigan, USA, specializing in Asian Diaspora and East-West comparative studies. He is the author of over a dozen books, including *On East-West* (2022), *Off-White* (2019), *Sinophone-Anglophone Cultural Duet* (2017), *The Last Isle* (2015), *Alienglish* (2014), *Asian Diaspora and East-West Modernity* (2012), *Diaspora Literature and Visual Culture* (2011), *East-West Montage* (2007), *The Deathly Embrace* (2000), *Immigrant Subjectivities in Asian American and Asian Diaspora Literatures* (1998) and the critical memoir *Immigrant Horse's Mouth: Journey to the West by Bearing East* (2022). Co-editor of four books, *Transnational Narratives in Englishes of Exile* (2018) among them, he also published a collection of poetry in Chinese, *Thirty Left and Right*.

Purnima Mankekar is Professor in the Departments of Anthropology, Asian American Studies and Film, Television and Digital Media at the University of California, Los Angeles, USA. Her areas of expertise are theories of affect, digital media and "virtual" anthropology, transnational media studies, feminist anthropology and South Asian and South Asian American studies. Her most recent book was *Unsettling India: Affect, Temporality, Transnationality* (Duke University Press, 2015). She is currently finishing a monograph with Akhil Gupta on affective labor and futurity, and her next ethnographic project is on algorithmic worlds and governance in India. She is also working on a book project on digital media, race and intimacy.

Kent A. Ono is Professor in the Department of Communication at the University of Utah, USA, and immediate Past President of the National Communication Association. Previously, he was on the faculties of the University of California, Davis, and the University of Illinois, Urbana-Champaign, USA. His research focuses on rhetoric, media and film studies, race, ethnic and cultural studies. Among his six books, his authored/co-authored books are *Contemporary Media Culture and the Remnants of a Colonial Past* (Peter Lang, 2009), *Asian Americans and the Media* (with Vincent Pham) (Polity, 2009) and *Shifting Borders: Rhetoric, Immigration and California's Proposition 187* (with John Sloop) (Temple University Press). He is a past editor of two NCA journals *Critical Studies in Media Communication* and *Communication and Critical/Cultural Studies* and founder and past series co-editor of the book series "Critical Cultural Communication."

Nadja-Christina Schneider is Professor of Gender and Media Studies for the South Asian Region at Humboldt-Universität zu Berlin, Germany. She specializes in Area Media Studies and her background is in South Asian and Islamic Studies as well as Modern and Contemporary History. Her research focuses on cultural and urban studies, mobility and gender, secularism and religion as well as new media configurations. Her books include *Studying Youth, Media and Gender in Post-Liberalization India* (Franke & Timme, 2014). She was a Visiting Professor at Heidelberg University (Chair of Visual and Media Anthropology) in 2016 and a Feodor Lynen Fellow at the University of Delhi in 2015.

Cecilia S. Uy-Tioco is Associate Professor of Media Studies in the Department of Communication at California State University, San Marcos, USA. Her research interrogates the relationships between media, culture and globalization, with a particular focus on digital inequality and the telecommunication industry in the Philippines and digital mobile media and transnational Filipino migrants. She is the co-editor of the book *Mobile Media and Social Intimacies in Asia* (2020). Her work has been published in *Continuum: Journal of Media & Cultural Studies*, *Communication Research and Practice* and various edited volumes.

Cara Wallis is Associate Professor of Media and Communication in the Department of Communication at Texas A&M University, USA. As a critical feminist scholar, she studies the social and cultural implications of communication technologies, especially among marginalized populations in China. She is the author of *Technomobility in China: Young Migrant Women and Mobile Phones* (NYU Press, 2013). She uses qualitative methods, particularly ethnographic fieldwork, to understand how technology use is connected to multiple axes of identity, sociality and forms of individual and collective agency as well as how such usage is shaped by multiple discourses and power relations.

Jing Wang is Professor of Chinese Media and Cultural Studies, S.C. Fang Professor of Chinese language and culture and Director of the New Media Action Lab at MIT, USA. She is also a recipient of the Overseas Distinguished Professor Award, given by China's Ministry of Education. She is the founder and secretary general of NGO2.0, a nonprofit in China specializing in technology-driven and social media-powered activism, and is the author of *The Other Digital China: Nonconfrontational Activism on the Social Web* (2019). Her recent interests include civic technology and digital disruptions of China's entertainment industry.

Luke White is Senior Lecturer in Visual Culture and Fine Art at Middlesex University, London. His research focuses on issues of politics and identity in martial arts cinema. He is the author of *Legacies of the Drunken Master: Politics of the Body in Hong Kong Kung Fu Comedy Films* (2020) and *Fighting without Fighting: Kung Fu Cinema's Journey to the West* (forthcoming). He contributed a chapter to *The Martial Arts Studies Reader* and published articles in journals including *Radical Philosophy*, *Journal of Visual Culture*, *Asian Cinema* and *Journalism*.

Audrey Yue is Professor in the Department of Communications and New Media at the National University of Singapore. Her research interests include Sinophone media cultures, cultural policy and development, and queer Asian studies. Her books include *Promoting Sustainable Living: Sustainability as an Object of Desire* (Routledge, 2015), *Mobile Cultures: New Media in Queer Asia* (2003), *Transnational Australian Cinema: Ethics in the Asian Diasporas* (2013) and *Ann Hui's Song of the Exile* (2010). Her articles appear in journals including *Inter-Asia Cultural Studies*, *Urban Studies*, *International Journal of Cultural Policy* and *Theory, Culture & Society*.

INTRODUCTION

Media in Asia: Global, Digital, Gendered, Mobile Asia

Youna Kim

The pace of change in international media, culture and communication has accelerated today, and a more significant change in the global environment over the past two decades has been the rise of Asia (Thussu 2019). The proliferation of transnational media, online networks and mediated relationships, enabled by sophisticated digital technologies and the deregulation and liberalization of the media, has rapidly created new media landscapes offering enormous challenges and opportunities. Asia, with some of the most wired populations on the globe, is at the very forefront of the consumption, circulation and production of new media in the neoliberal era of networked entertainment. While the rise of satellite broadcast fueled the transnational spread of media culture in the past, streaming platforms and social networking services such as Netflix, YouTube, Facebook and Twitter are now playing a role in expanding Asian digital cultures to a global scene. Social media entertainment constitutes a more radical cultural and content challenge to the established media and regulatory regimes, informing a qualitatively different globalization dynamic that has scaled with great velocity (Cunningham and Craig 2019). The diverse borderless media have penetrated the emerging and lucrative markets of Asia, capturing the imaginations of people who were once accustomed to the national media under government controls. Media culture today is not only a planned flow that originates from nation-states and transnational corporations, but also by accident it is a multi-directional flow and a highly interactive collaborative process that is created by digitally empowered consumer communities. Younger generations are the mediating contributors to the shaping of de-centralizing media flows in neoliberal affective capitalism, given the media field's fun, playful and exuberant nature (Booth 2017), with the Internet's simultaneous place as playground and factory (Scholz 2013) and the ubiquity of popular pleasure on the social web eroding distinction between play and work. The amateurized media universe (Motrescu-Mayes and

DOI: 10.4324/9781003130628-1

Aasman 2019), digital co-creation and spreadability play a key role in enabling the shifts. Audiences, not simply as consumers of pre-constructed content but as co-creative grassroots participants, are playing an active role in shaping the flows of media for their own purposes in an increasingly networked culture of spreadable media (Jenkins et al. 2013). Media content does not remain in fixed borders but circulates in unpredicted and often unpredictable directions, through the bottom-up disruptive practice of creative digital labor, both material and immaterial, which encourages new users to participate in transnationally imagined communities. In today's digitally connected mobile world marked by the expansion of markets, networks, consumers and plurality of cultures, transnational popular media culture can be an important resource for soft power – a cultural weapon to entice, attract and influence people without the use of violence, military or economic force in order to obtain preferred outcomes (Chua 2012; Kim 2013, 2021; Thussu 2013; Voci and Hui 2018; Sakamoto and Epstein 2021). Attractive culture is one of soft power resources creating general influence and long-term diffuse effects in international relations (Nye 2004, 2008). The cultural industry has taken center stage in Asia, with an increased recognition that the transnational spread of popular media culture not only boosts the economy but also potentially creates a nation's dynamic image and soft power. The digital spreadability and symbolic potency of the media is a pronounced case of the crossover of culture, economy and politics.

While not denying the obvious power of Western, particularly American, media infrastructures and dominance over the international media landscape and the continuing significance of Western media influence, this book considers Asian media culture in the global digital age and addresses the social, cultural and political implications in their complexity and paradox within the contexts of global inequalities and uneven power structures. The core issue guiding the book revolves around the concern with power. Recognizing the significance of the media and associated technologies and digital cultures within the existing social structures, it addresses the double capacity of the media with both enabling and disabling consequences that are mediated by profoundly asymmetrical power relations in the multifaceted contexts of Asia and beyond. Its approach to the media and the digital is not technology centric, but directs attention to the dynamic processes and effects of production, representation, circulation and consumption embedded in social structures and power relations in which the globalized technology operates in its complex manifestations. The multi-directional flows of the media and digitally networked communications give rise to the de-territorialization of culture and identity politics transcending national boundaries and engaging with power, cultural difference and diversity in unpredictable ways. The book explores the dynamic and complex place of the media in Asia currently in confrontation with remarkable social change and transition and the need to understand this emerging phenomenon as it intersects with the media. It argues for the centrality of the media to Asian transformations in the neoliberal era of globalization and digitalization. The media involve the complex processes of social change and transition – from the conduct of everyday life, to the reflexive understanding of a global world, to the construction of a new identity and a constant tension in its expression within the everyday. Media culture is creating new connections, new desires and threats, and the identities of people and societies are being reworked at individual, national, regional and global levels. The multiple manifestations of such transformations are under discussion in this volume. New forms of media globalization in Asia need to be recognized as a proliferating, indispensable, yet highly complex and contradictory resource for the construction of identities. The extraordinary profusion of the media today, with new imaginations, new choices and contradictions, generates a critical condition for reflexivity engaging everyday people to have a resource for the learning of self, culture and society in a new light. This book demonstrates the media's centrality to the transforming of contemporary self, culture and society within their historical specificities and contexts of macro–micro processes.

These significant changes as well as the rapid rise of Asian economies are affecting the scale and the manner in which people – especially marginalized and subordinated minorities such as women and youth – engage with the media in the relatively conservative and hierarchical milieu of Asia. Under social controls that deny them the ability to act on their own, individualization can be sought in ever greater participation in media cultural activities and imaginations in relation to global cultural Others (Kim 2012). While there is significant variation in the extent and depth of social change across Asia, gender is not losing its decisive influence; it is still in operation as a powerful category of social stratification and people become more conscious of social exclusion and inequality. Rooted in religion and traditional family practices, gender continues to be a fundamental factor in the way the lives of individuals, families and societies are organized on multiple fronts and spaces (Najafizadeh and Lindsey 2019; Huang and Ruwanpura 2020). Although women of Asia have increasingly become active participants in higher education, employment and media consumption that exposes them to the pluralization of life politics, actual changes to gendered norms, sexuality and body politics have come slower. When real-life situations in Asia are felt to be particularly constrained, mobility in a variety of capacities and forms – imaginary, symbolic, virtual and physical – becomes all the more important. Asia is a region on the move. Globalization has prompted cross-border circulations of the media, ideas, commodities, capital, labor and people, both forging new connections and reinforcing older connections across time and space (Iwabuchi 2015; Liu-Farrer and Yeoh 2018; Tagliacozzo et al. 2019). Multiple mobilities and tensions are expressed in the context of a significantly mobile Asia, between public and private spheres, between online and offline communications. There is an increasing awareness of the possibility of movement, with an increasing tendency toward the inner mobility of an individual's life. The media have transformed the ways in which people imagine themselves and their lives, playing a significant role as a catalyst for the acceleration of transnational migration in a digital age (Kim 2011). Questions of identity are refigured in flows of desire that now

operate transnationally, enacted by Asia's economic growth, digital media technologies and integration into globalization that have enabled new generations of
people to imagine and create a different life trajectory. The plausibly powerful
capacity of the media, deeply ingrained in what people take for granted, should
be recognized in any attempt to understand the phenomenon of transnational
mobility and mobile Asia. This contemporary manifestation has been intensified
by the proliferation of the new media and digital technologies, thereby making
transnational networks and relations available with much greater frequency and
regularity, as well as creating new meanings of being in the world.

The emerging consequences at multiple levels deserve to be analyzed and
explored fully in an increasingly global, digital, gendered and mobile environment of the media. Within historically specific social conditions, this book seeks
to provide a nuanced understanding of the place of the media in Asia acknowledging unique social spaces and contexts. Asia is not a singular and unitary
region nor a geographic category, but a conceptual construct of vast differences –
economically, politically, culturally and historically – and it is being continually
made and re-made over time. Although the process of media globalization does
not take place in a uniform but differential pace and scale from nation to nation,
its interrelated trends have marked significant transformations in the dynamics of
relations within and between nation-states, societies and individuals. Each contextual analysis in this book conveys the diversity of Asia's spaces today when a
future of Asia is being imagined and this imagining is not just a sign of newfound
self-confidence but also a sign of heightened anxiety in a mediated and porous
world. It provides a critical analysis of the dynamics of the media at a time when
the political, economic, socio-cultural and technological contexts in which the
media operate are becoming increasingly global, digital, gendered and mobile.
The book is divided into four thematically coherent parts – Global Asia, Digital
Asia, Gendered Asia, Mobile Asia – demonstrating centrality of the media to
Asian transformations.

Global Asia

The media in Asia transcend national cultural boundaries and are increasingly
regionalized and globalized, while simultaneously protecting national spaces and
contesting cultural identities. Two significant forms of global media flows can
be noted across Asia: First, the dominant flows largely emanating from the West
with the USA at its core; and second, the emergence of transnational Asian
media as new regional and global players alongside the rise of affluent middle
classes, both of which constitute the primary agents of cultural globalization
in the region. Asian media culture is constructing a regional hegemony, but
also co-existing with Western media domination and unequal power relations
that mediate the regulations and representations of media flows. The inequality
and imbalance in the media flow between the West and Asia has not decreased
significantly. Rather, the dominance of the USA has also increased in the Asian

cultural market today through the flows of media products and capital in the forms of joint ventures, direct investment and adaptation. Transnational opportunities for funding and creative collaboration are evident in the high number of film co-productions between Hollywood and regional screen industries such as those in India, China, Japan and Korea (Hill and Kawashima 2018; Jin and Su 2020). Large-scale investments in digital infrastructure from the North to the South are reshaping the economic and social geography of Asia that expresses the force of social change through the emergence of platform economies and a vast series of digital transactions (Athique and Baulch 2020). Powerful multimedia corporations, mostly based in the USA, have widened and strengthened their presence through skillful localization strategies that include producing programs in local languages and outsourcing their work to regional hubs of cultural industries (Thussu 2019). These transnational corporations build up production capacity and distribution networks to generate a reverse global flow from Asia to the rest of the world, resulting in the possibility of cultural connection, reconnection or disconnection in a complex way (Fung 2013). Western streaming services such as Netflix and YouTube have played a role in Asian media's global ascension, expanding production, distribution and consumption in the global market and intensifying the fragmentation of audiences into ever smaller pieces. There is a broader shift to the merging of media, technology and entertainment that produces a new golden age of creativity (McDonald and Smith-Rowsey 2016; Smith and Telang 2016). For Netflix to integrate their business in Asia, collaboration with local media productions is a viable strategy that minimizes opposition and reduces controversy (Anthony Fung and Georgia Chik, Chapter 1 in this volume). The Internet-distributed television service Netflix is significantly changing the spatial dynamics of global television distribution and the fundamental logics through which television travels, introducing new mobilities into the system and challenging the direction of global media flows (Lobato 2019). Netflix's audience-taste-driven narrowcasting appeals to disparate groups of people across the world without a unified cache of content, by using its sophisticated algorithm and seemingly endless resources to buy, develop and distribute as many different types of content to as many micro-targeted audience groups as possible (Barker and Wiatrowski 2017). Audiences in the digital streaming age have more control and choice to self-schedule television online and modify the schedules based on their own desires and needs, although the audience control does not necessarily translate to substantial shifts in power (Jenner 2018). By making the products of small countries more available outside their home markets, Netflix appears to be a facilitator of frictionless digital trade, but nevertheless its cross-border distribution strongly advantages the US origin products (Aguiar and Waldfogel 2018).

The significant expansion of partnerships between Asian media producers and Western media companies and a move away from restrictive media regulation by gate-keeping regimes have transformed media markets, although television audience dynamics in Asia appear to have remained comparatively stable as large majorities of audiences continue to privilege local and regional content tied to their proximate cultures (Kalyani Chadha and Anandam Kavoori, Chapter 2 in this volume). While it has had to borrow and adapt from the West, the region has also developed its own local industries and generated its own more compatible models for production and markets of sufficient size to support local cultural industries (Tay and Turner 2015). Television, as a ubiquitous broadcast and a dynamic technology, occupies a central place in everyday life. Television in Asia, particularly in nations where the levels of literacy and education vary widely, is a crucial instrument for those charged with managing economic, socio-cultural and political transitions. The ability of television as a cultural form represents a whole range of ideas, ideals, ideologies, images and the collective imaginations of its audiences, playing its distinctive role in shaping the terrain of public culture in South Asia (Punathambekar and Kumar 2014). The extensive development of popular media forms, such as TV drama, film, music, reality TV and variety shows, has been a constitutive part of everyday nationhood and remains closely tied to the discursive construction and diverse imaginations of national cultural identity in many spheres of Asia, including Vietnam (Nguyen-Thu 2019), China (Gorfinkel 2018) and India in the interlocking forces of globalization, capitalism, modernism and post-colonialism (Kumar 2006; Kavoori 2009). One of the features that distinguishes significant parts of Asia from much of the world is the direct impact of national politics and policies on cultural production, in particular on television and film, operating differently within the region due to the issues of widespread colonization and subsequent struggles for independence (Chan et al. 2011; Lim 2014; Lim and Lee 2018). Many broadcasters and film production companies are state run or state controlled, and the state continues to play an interventionist and central role in conditioning political and social dynamics in contemporary Asian societies. Inevitable tensions arise between political interests and neoliberal market economies, between the state's intention to maintain control over television broadcasting and the emergence of technological development. New media technologies have impacted not only the regulation and structure of television broadcasting but also the shaping of national media policies in neoliberal East Asia, notably Japan, Hong Kong and Korea (Kwak 2018).

The new media environment in Asia has grown denser, broader, faster and more agile, and trans-Asian and global popular cultural flows and connections continue to develop in uneven and complex ways (Black et al. 2016; Dave et al. 2016). Multi-directional media flows emanate from urban creative cities, the media capitals (Curtin 2007) of Mumbai, Tokyo, Seoul, Hong Kong, Shanghai, Taipei, Bangkok and so on. Traditional companies in film and television and new digital platforms compete and collaborate to deliver individualized entertainment to diverse audiences in post-Bollywoodization (Shanti Kumar, Chapter 3 in this volume). Many of the competing creative hubs are at the heart of the transformation of regional media cultures, capitalizing on the existence of strong regional demand and the explosion of popular fandom that are driven by linguistic, historical and cultural factors across a new Asia on the rise. Regional co-production and collaboration, marketing and intensive circulation of film, television drama, animation, music and derivative products such as games and food generate Asian cultural imaginaries and a new regional economy of transcultural production in East and Southeast Asia (Otmazgin and Ben-Ari 2013). Understanding regional co-production as complex, dynamic and sometimes unpredictable assemblages is particularly imperative in the case of East Asian film and cultural production, as contemporary aspirations toward its market-driven emergence often sit in fraught tensions and uneven negotiations with the legacies of Cold War geopolitics that continue to structure cultural relations and politics in the region (DeBoer 2014). China's global ambitions are linked to its culture, as a system of cultural production, distribution and consumption, and as a new global cultural economy looking to mobilize creativity in strategic ways (Yueming and O'Connor 2018). Many are eager to capitalize on the world's biggest audience, China, and the Chinese government's new ambitions to internationalize its media cultural industries. In practice, collaborating with Chinese partners or working in China entails a willingness to forgo certain freedoms including the expression of ideas that are taken for granted in pluralist societies (Keane et al. 2018). East Asia has become a major hub for transmedia storytelling due to Japanese manga, Korean webtoon and Chinese novels that are re-mediated and transformed into diverse cultural forms such as films, television programs and digital games (Jin 2020).

Asian media have emerged as new players for transnational consumer culture changing the dynamics of the digital city landscape and urbanization in light of the increasing volume and velocity of digital flows (Xin Gu, Chapter 4 in this volume). The appeal of a cultural or creative economy, as a post-manufacturing advanced service economy, would provide the leverage for the wider transformation of the state polity, democracy and modernity in China (O'Connor and Gu 2020). Governments in Asia have increasingly recognized popular media culture as a new economic initiative and sought to reduce their dependence on a manufacturing base by developing a chimney-less industry, digital technology and services. The transformation of Bollywood into a transnational, multimedia cultural industry has been facilitated by increasing levels of technological convergence among the television, advertising, Internet and mobile phone industries, as well as the Indian state's material and symbolic investments in Bollywood and responses to refigure its relationship with the South Asian diaspora and beyond (Punathambekar 2013). Other South Asian nations such as Pakistan, Sri Lanka and Bangladesh are experiencing similar trajectories in popular visual cultures, advancements in digital technology, urban development and a liberalized economy (Varughese and Dudrah 2020). Creativity is emerging as one of the most important sources of economic growth. The value of creative media industries in South Asia is often linked to their ability to stimulate cultural and social development and provide an integral economic resource for national growth (Malik and Dudrah 2020). Nations and global creative cities, or media capitals, are crucial parts of what might be seen as a world system of media (Wilkins et al. 2014). Nations are still the most powerful economic, cultural and political actors in many parts of Asia, in a rapidly evolving world of media pluralism and capitalist power with the formation of a neoliberal economic order. The focus on culture by governments in Asia is the product of a neoliberal ideology espousing a global free market and the linking of globalized consumerism to individual freedom and social well-being (Berry et al. 2009). Popular media and consumer culture transcend national borders with such frequency and intensity as to constitute an irrevocable and irresistible force that regionalizes, globalizes and possibly transforms identity. It is this power that nation-states in Asia seek to promote through the articulation and legislation of cultural policy and the promotion of media cultural industries, with a renewed focus on identity, culture and nation branding as an essential component of international relations and foreign policy thinking.

There is a general shift in the official thinking toward the role of culture in the political life of states as the political economy of global media culture has forced nation-states to consider the possibilities for attaining soft power and persuasive communicative acts that ignore national boundaries (Chua 2012; Hayden 2012; Otmazgin and Ben-Ari 2012; Kim 2013, 2021). Soft power is the ability to make others act in a way that advances desired outcomes through attraction, rather than threat or coercion, in order to achieve general, milieu goals based around long-term diffuse effects rather than short-term immediate effects (Nye 2004, 2008). The soft power of a country rests primarily on three resources – the attractiveness of its culture; its political values, when it lives up to them at home and abroad; and its foreign policies, when they are seen as legitimate and having moral authority (Nye 2004). A country's popular culture, as a soft power resource, can increase its overall attractiveness and its potential influence on the global stage, albeit in unquantifiable, often commercial, capitalistic, unpredictable and even paradoxical ways, involving both state and non-state actors and international networks in a digitalizing world. It may extend to economic interests, national image-making and cultural diplomacy in international relations. Soft power can be "high," directed at elites in a country, or "low," aimed at the general public, and it can stem from governments and non-governmental actors including businesspeople and popular culture celebrities (Kurlantzick 2007). The unintended service performed by popular culture celebrities in mitigating political tensions between Indonesia and Malaysia, for instance, demonstrates the ability of non-state actors, celebrities to win the hearts and minds of the general public in the countries with political animosity toward each other (Heryanto 2008). Although the concept was introduced in the field of international relations focusing on states, soft power is not restricted to states or to international relations but applies to a much wider range of actors and contexts in the new media age. Collaborative creativity "from above" (nation-states, institutions, media industries) and "from below" (digital fans as grassroots intermediaries, producers-consumers, publics), and the combination of top-down and bottom-up forces, generate hybrid, formal and informal networks of circulation and interaction, although the bottom-up actors do not necessarily operate in concert with the top-down actors in a coherent manner. The soft power of attraction is co-determined by the receivers as well as the senders and is socially constructed (Watanabe and McConnell 2008). Universalistic popular culture can attract people and produce soft power in the sense of desired outcomes, depending on the context where it is received and made sense of by people. The globalization of media contents from once subalternized or peripheral nations in Asia is a facet of de-centralizing multiplicity of global cultural flows today, emerging as subversive soft power resources that challenge the Western hegemony of dominant ideas, values and ways of life. Popular culture as a soft power resource has been recognized in India (Thussu 2013), Japan (Iwabuchi 2015; Sakamoto and Epstein 2021), Korea (Kim 2013, 2021) and China (Voci and Hui 2018) as Asian media industries have created visible, regional and global flows of popular film, music, television drama, comics, animation and online games increasingly challenging the dominant power of Western media culture. The rise of the Korean Wave is not just a media cultural phenomenon but fundamentally about the creation of soft power, favorable nation branding and sustainable development (Youna Kim, Chapter 5 in this volume). Popular media culture, which was once considered as emotional and low culture in Korea, has become a potent transnational force providing the significant underpinning for the generation of high value and meaning for the nation since the late 1990s (Kim 2013, 2019, 2021). In Japan with its heavy burden of colonial history and violence, globalized practices of soft power and nation branding have given greater emphasis to the use of popular culture including manga and anime to enhance the image of the nation and promote pop culture public diplomacy (Iwabuchi 2015; Sakamoto and Epstein 2021). Japan's global cultural superpower (Darling-Wolf 2018), the widespread appeal of the narratives, characters and locations of Japanese popular culture, has developed a huge global fan base, driving many people's desire to visit Japan and study about and study in Japan (Seaton and Yamamura 2017). Across much of East Asia, however, intense Japanese influence on cultural forms does not necessarily imply admiration for Japan, and portrayals of Japan in a range of media have become more negative even as the spread of Japanese-inspired consumerism and popular culture has continued apace since the early 1990s (Morris et al. 2013). China's officially promoted soft power has become a key issue in the reform of its media cultural industry and the creation of the image or branding of the nation, following more successful competitors, the USA, Japan and Korea (Voci and Hui 2018). Yet, China has been comparatively deficient because its undemocratic policies are too controlling to unleash the talents of its society, although the ideas of dream and power as imagined by culture cannot be singularly dominated by the state. Throughout Asia, popular media culture becomes competitive resources for soft power with its distinctively national characteristics and different conditions for its operation.

A key feature of the rise of Asian media culture is the active role of nation-states focusing on the creation of a cool national brand, inevitably reinforcing a commercialized pop nationalism or cultural nationalism that appropriates the affective capacities of popular culture to promote political and economic interests. Nationalism has been central to the globalization of media cultural products. Media globalization is thought to weaken the nation, but the nation is still centrally important. While the accelerated transnational processes and connections may appear to negate the significance of national borders, boundaries and national identities, nationalisms have been re-ignited to realign and reconfigure the nation. The media are central to the affective construction and re-construction of national identity, standing for the nation as a means by which the nation can represent itself to its subjects. In a force of globalization, digitalization and interdependence, the transnational flow of Asian media culture is no doubt building a bridge of cultural connectivity and a potential of soft power, or transcultural exercise of "consumer power" (Chua 2012), however with limitations and complexities. With the involvement of governments, such culture has been constructed within nationalistic discourses and policies, and imagined as cultural nationalism – a form of hegemony masked in soft power. This version of nationalistic and expansionistic culture has a tendency to develop into another form of cultural imperialism. A subversive transnational culture, as a resource for soft power that emerged from a postcolonial and somewhat peripheral nation, can ironically generate a new version of cultural imperialism that is deeply embedded in cultural nationalism and an ideological position that undermines cultural diversity and the soft power of attraction (Kim 2013). Implicitly or explicitly, uneven flows of transnational media culture are often perceived as expansionist cultural imperialism, consequently invoking national and cultural protectionism "from above" and "from below" in a neoliberal world order. Nationalistic discourse "from below" is more complex and constructed by young fans as well through the role of fan production and reception of foreign popular culture (Chen 2018) and the formation of affective communities that are not just personal but social and political (Park 2020). Popular culture has played often contradictory roles in either promoting or impeding nationalisms, regional conflicts and reconciliations particularly between countries with colonial relationships of the past (Sakamoto and Epstein 2021). There emerges a call for reciprocal cultural flows and mutual understandings, rather than asymmetrically presenting cultural nationalism based on the market-driven cultural economy. Nevertheless, the re-nationalizing gravity is resilient and flexible enough to overpower such radical possibilities as the cultivation of cross-border dialogues and the sharing of alternative views and hitherto marginalized voices (Koichi Iwabuchi, Chapter 6 in this volume). National identity and attachment to national culture are re-imagined in an Asia where a new politics of multiculturalism unfolds without superseding nationalism, often reformulating nationalism in a distinctive way (Kim and Lee 2018). Seemingly contradictory vectors of globalizing forces of media culture – decentering/recentering, diversifying/homogenizing and transnationalizing/nationalizing – are working simultaneously and inter-constitutively (Iwabuchi 2015). Globalization and its associated digital technologies have made possible new forms of global nationalism which spread far beyond the borders of traditional nation-states (Starrs 2013), and it is important not to underestimate the power of the historical traumas of the past which animate global nationalism today (Kingston 2016). Digital nationalism works affectively and uninhibitedly in the nexus of globalization and postcoloniality, whether it is the hate speech and antiracist protests in Japan, xenophobic rants in Singapore and Hong Kong, or angry Chinese youth showing off their support of China (Wang and Goh 2017). Nationalism in the digital age is not simply a form of "top-down" indoctrination but is actively constructed in an interplay between different stakeholders including not only the authorities but also commercial enterprises and private Internet users, without any single actor directly designing the national narratives that ultimately emerge (Schneider 2018). In today's digital Asia, the dialectic nature of globalizing and nationalizing forces is a key feature of popular culture, given the proliferating yet unpredictable interactions between multiple actors in the mediation and spreadability of media culture across national boundaries.

Digital Asia

The increasing role of digital media and emerging technologies is central to Asian transformations, enabling users to make desired differences in their lives and societies but also continuing to reinforce existing power relations and inequalities well beyond their control. The key issue about the digital media is not that they are "new" media forms in some dramatic break from the past and existing power, but rather they are new ways of configuring issues of production, circulation and consumption of the media and new ways of understanding human–media relations (Kavoori 2010). All aspects of life, not only culture, love, work and politics but also religion, are intimately connected to and transformed by the banal and mundane mediation of the mobilized, de-territorialized digital media to an extent that religion today has become humdrum (Han and Nasir 2016; Radde-Antweiler and Zeiler 2019). Digital technologies potentially alter power and "positionalities," the shifting, asymmetric and path-dependent ways in which the futures of places depend on their interdependencies with other places (Graham 2019). The digitalization of goods, productions and services is crucial to an ever-increasing amount of economic value creation in global production networks, which does not necessarily mean that enterprises can all use digital technologies and connectivity to alter their positionalities or level playing fields in the same ways. The global expansion of Asian media culture has integrated the production, circulation and promotion of the media and celebrity through digital technologies and social media such as YouTube, Twitter, Facebook as well as smartphones. It connects with audiences through social media and streaming services that are less controlled by traditional gatekeepers and that accelerate instantaneous access to content in the post-ownership economy. The digital media not only drive new forms of cultural circulation but also animate new infrastructures, intimacies (Neves and Sarkar 2017), increasingly becoming mainstream as mobile devices afford new access to multimedia tools and networks and further embed within everyday spaces (Hjorth and Khoo 2016). A new form of imagination is built and negotiated through processes of global circulation and consumption of Asian media culture (Fabienne Darling-Wolf, Chapter 7 in this volume). The mediated cosmopolitan imagination (Robertson 2010), not the actual experience of but the imagination of the global through the media in everyday life, intersects with the particularity of local and national conditions and intimately relates to individuals' identities (Darling-Wolf 2015). The appropriation, remixing and redeployment of popular media culture at the grassroots level can offer resources for social change through civic imagination, the capacity to imagine alternatives to current cultural, social, political or economic conditions (Jenkins et al. 2020). Digital technologies have ensured that media content is transnationally shared and discussed in online spaces and that the larger scale of knowledge and information is made available, resulting in unpredictable patterns of identification and reflexive learning of the self at individual, national, regional and global levels. Increased flows and diversity of the media can be seen as important resources for the triggering and operating of everyday reflexivity (Kim 2005, 2008, 2011; Rodrigues and Ranganathan 2015). The media are central to everyday reflexivity – the capacity to monitor action and its contexts to keep in touch with the grounds of everyday life, self-confront uncertainties and understand the relationships between cause and effect, yet never quite control the complex dynamics of everyday life. It is via the increased exposure to global cultural Others and reflexive capacities that people make sense of life conditions which differ from their own and come to question the taken-for-granted social order. What is emerging here can be the problematization of society itself, the increasing awareness of its structural rigidity and discontents as well as the interrogatory attitude toward the surrounding world. Ordinary people may not destabilize the whole system, but the transnational media can prompt them to critically reflect on the legitimacy of their own social system and imagine new possibilities within the multiple constraints of their social context. Popular media culture functions as a "cultural public sphere" (McGuigan 2010), wherein viewers identify with characters and their problems, talk and argue with friends and colleagues about what they should and should not do, and think reflexively about their own lifeworld situations and how to negotiate their way in and through systems. Ideas of a good life and such rising expectations are mediated mundanely through popular media discourse. The media are not the only contributor to the process of reflexivity, but the degree of the media's contribution depends on what other sources of reflexivity might or might not be available and who can access and utilize them as meaningful resources.

Apparently in urban centers of Asia, widespread and mundane imaginations of cultural cosmopolitanism exist as new forms of consumer subjectivity, cultural disposition and practices and cultural transformations invoked by the global forces of the media and networks transcending national boundaries (Kim 2011). It is a world of media use, mediated experience and media talk that generates imagined cultural cosmopolitanism and its multiple articulations as a contested characterization of social reality in question. Media cultural discourses informed by the identification of a vaguely cosmopolitan stance create a multimodal realization of the world, which may allow a particular kind of agency aligned with the world to signify power and competency, a differentiating marker of identity and social mobility in a global order. Digital media fandom and celebrity culture today is increasingly moving from the margins of subcultural celebration to a mainstream identity (Booth 2018; Click and Scott 2018) and potentially decentralizing the global hegemonic cultural market in a seemingly cosmopolitan world. Celebrity capital is influential enough to evoke public scrutiny on morality, body politics and nationalism (Dorothy Wai Sim Lau, Chapter 8 in this volume). The multiple facets of celebrity power as attention capital are manifested in the transformation of identity, emotion, lifestyle choices and participatory culture in the specific contexts of digital Asia (Leung et al. 2017; Cai 2019; Lau 2019). The world today has become a celebrity society with its own distinctive, constantly changing social practices and structures as well as the construction of identity, as social, economic and political life is increasingly organized around celebrities possessing multifaceted celebrity capital (van Krieken 2012; Gunter 2014). Its rise is a result of contemporary socio-political conditions – including an affective deficit in modern life, public data about "statistical" men and women without personalities, the diminution of direct social relations and a loss of community as human relations attenuate and fragment under the pressure of socio-political conditions (Turner 2014; Rojek 2016). The paradox of connection through digital technologies is the consciousness of "alone, together," making people feel at one moment, in possession of a full social life, and in the next, curiously isolated or utterly alone, in tenuous complicity with familiar strangers (Turkle 2011). Greater investment in celebrity culture today can be understood as a compensatory means of constructing para-social interactions, presumed intimacy and a new dimension of community through popular culture (Kim 2021). In the social media age, celebrities are expected to display themselves unedited as "real" people with "real" issues, as the public fame of the celebrities is premised on feelings of connection and interactive responsiveness and is thus co-constructed through a community of interested viewers on the Internet rather than by the mere mechanisms of the traditional entertainment industry (Abidin 2018). Networked political fandom in the domain of popular culture signals a new force for digital activism exercising collaborative cultural power to challenge dominant political power and the dominant media.

Social media appear to be the latest wave of innovation in political communication and campaigning across Asia, with varying levels of market penetration among different user demographics in specific national contexts and local dynamics. People appropriate social media as guerilla tactics for spreading socially conscious messages against divisive rhetoric and action particularly at a time of increased political polarization. Bottom-up participatory media forces are increasingly prevalent, enabling citizens to voice their opinions, distribute reformist messages, or facilitate online activism and social movements that contest the power of corrupted political elites and mass media institutions in neoliberal India (Rodrigues and Ranganathan 2015; Udupa 2015), Indonesia (Tapsell 2017), Malaysia (Leong 2019), Hong Kong (Lee and Chan 2018) and Korea (Lee and Oh 2021). The use of the Internet and always-on connectivity of the mobile phone in everyday life has the potential to trigger informed consumption of public knowledge, civic engagement, political participation and social change in Asia, although most mobile communication may bend toward private chat and comparatively less toward public action (Wei 2016; Wei and Lo 2021). Today's personal relationship to society and public life shows a shift from established structures of representative democracy with group-based identities and mainstream issues toward a wider repertoire of personalized political experience and individually motivated concerns within a digitally networked society (Beaufort 2020). Education is significant not only in terms of literacy, but because it also relates to the processes of imaginings of the state, knowledge of democratic rights and the inbuilt hierarchies that characterize everyday life in both rural and urban areas (Harindranath 2009). It is important to pay attention to the historical and socio–political specificities of national or regional contexts and macro–micro dynamics (Ramaswami Harindranath, Chapter 9 in this volume). Key issues of the media and democracy concern the historically shaped power of the state and commercial corporations versus that of citizens and civil society organizations and the potential of digital platforms to evade state control and create spaces for pluralizing democratic discourses in Southeast Asia (Kenyon et al. 2014; George and Venkiteswaran 2019), South Asia (Udupa and McDowell 2017) and East Asia (Wei 2016). The storytelling infrastructure of digital platforms invites ordinary people to feel their own place in current developing stories, respond affectively, invest their emotion to these stories and contribute to developing narratives, which leads to the formation of "networked affect" and discursively connected "affective publics" (Hillis et al. 2015; Papacharissi 2015). Agency, intent and affect on the network facilitate "soft" structures of engagement, imagination and various forms of civic mobilization.

Everywhere in Asia, the advent of the Internet and mobile connections has been seen, and sometimes uncritically celebrated, as a new catalyst for political freedom and democracy, and as an insurmountable threat to authoritarian regimes. Against the dramatic rise and unprecedented effects of native language-specific or Western social media sites, authoritarian methods are still widespread in the region and compromise the freedom of expression to protect the powerful and to limit the spread of ideas and information harmful to their interests (Burrett and Kingston 2020), as manifested in the democratic transition of Pakistan (Abbas and Sulehria 2021) and China (deLisle et al. 2016; Kent et al. 2018; Hong 2020; Wang 2021). Against the flowering of counter-propaganda narratives, a networked authoritarian regime places digital technologies at the heart of nationalist propaganda – which has become more powerful but less visible – as well as public opinion and social control work in order to strengthen its ability to govern citizens and even create a more closed society (Luqiu 2018; Zhao 2018). Walking around obstacles and navigating tactfully between what is lawful and what is illegitimate, Chinese agents are making social change through non-confrontational activism on their own terms under the surveillance of the authoritarian regime (Jing Wang, Chapter 10 in this volume). Diverse civic actors including grassroots NGOs, the corporate social responsibility sector and young entrepreneurs use social media, form an invisible coalition and bring incremental change to Chinese society – a quiet transformation different from confrontational activism and resistance dominated in Western liberal cultures (Wang 2019). Various instances of fully or partially concealed performative communication – performances of hidden transcripts offstage away from the official public transcript played by authorities – have emerged as alternative, inconclusive and thereby accommodative forms of reflexive political articulation in South Asia (Pathak and Perera 2018). Aesthetic performers and popular media culture such as cross-border music, television dramas and films articulate and negotiate wider societal norms and values, including those of religious piety, in order to improve human conditions and achieve a just society across a globalizing Muslim Southeast Asia (Daniels 2013; Barendregt et al. 2017). The spread of the global media intersected with popular, often capitalist, consumer culture has profoundly influenced the aspirations, attitudes and mobility of citizens inside the tightly controlled closed societies of Asia. Nations with totalitarian regimes cannot be confident any longer of their immunity from the globalized influence of ubiquitous cultural flows and the possibility of bottom-up change. Low-level dissent or criticism against the regimes may emerge as the circulation of outside culture, consumer capitalism and new cultural awareness grow in the digital age. With increasing numbers of people coming online through mobile phones, computers and tablets with a desire to embrace a more open world, monitoring the users' online activities, new cultural connections and broader networks is increasingly difficult for repressive regimes. The growing forces of transnational popular culture via digital media technologies and such "soft power" resources potentially stand a better chance of fostering social change than does more immediate and coercive action (Kim 2019). The effective weapon appears to be the attractive and less formal forces of soft power moving the hearts and minds of people. The rise of cultural weaponization means that in addition to soldiers, tanks, battleships and aircraft deploying violence to impose a political order on people, television, motion pictures and digital media technologies deploy the entertainment to bring about the same goal through long-term cultural engagement (Fattor 2014). Although more constrained North Korea is at a different stage in its digital cultural development, "foreign" and thus "illegal" media contents are smuggled across the border of China into the black market of communist North Korea, and citizens express their discontent toward the young leader and the dynastic rule as the circulation of outside information, new cultural awareness and a more independent way of thinking grow in an emerging digital society (Kim 2019). The regime's control has sometimes appeared tenuous as the socio-political and cultural norms of everyday life so assiduously cultivated by its propaganda are in flux, and the regime confronts challenges to maintaining a rigidly controlled public sphere in a fluid and interconnected world of globalization (Dukalskis 2017). It is wrong to assume that, because its political regime and authoritarian control have not changed significantly, then North Korea must be a static society in which its citizens are devoid of agency or in which socio-cultural change and such imagination are insignificant. North Koreans too, particularly the black market generation of young people, are the agents of change with normal aspirations, hopes and desires, constituting a hidden yet potential force for internal change despite long deep-seated oppression.

Young people across Asia are at the forefront of the digital world of consumer culture and are seen to be agents of social change and transformation. There is a general shift from digital literacy toward digital citizenship promoting youth opportunities, future life chances and embodied engagement in society (Audrey Yue, Chapter 11 in this volume). Youth culture is not a purely physical or locally bounded phenomenon as everyday interactions often embody a merging of offline and online qualities and characteristics in a seamless fashion across the global and the local (Bennett and Robards 2014). Alongside the remarkable expansion of higher education and changing forms of aspirational consumerism in Asia in recent decades (Naafs and Skelton 2019), the potential of mobile digital media develops with the competency and mundane practices of educated, media-savvy users in the new knowledge and creative economy. For instance, contemporary India is an artifact of enterprise culture and the construction of the individual enterprising subject endowed with aspirational capital in the neoliberal economy (Gooptu 2013). Do-it-yourself (DIY) youth culture is manifested among young Indonesians who use DIY fashion, music and digital media technologies to carve out their places in a rapidly changing society, challenging existing conceptions of national and regional identity and asserting themselves onto the world stage (Luvaas 2012). Amid Asia's flourishing media industries and consumption of fashion and beauty, Asian personal style blogs turn their styles of gendered racial embodiment into cultural and economic capital by rearticulating gender and race as aesthetic strategies of value (Pham 2015). The alternative, diversifying and affective forms of identity are manufactured, commodified and marketed to youth culture that is subject to neoliberal consumerism and self-refashioning practices. Soaking up the impact of choice biographies and processes of globalization, contemporary youth cultural practices are more commercialized and more politically ambivalent and display a complex and uneven negotiation between the global and the local (Buckingham et al. 2014). The commodification of alternative subjectivity functions as a new cultural and ideological force for the production of the enterprising self, diversity and inclusivity, or a neoliberal version of inclusive cosmopolitanism that may be broadly accepted and ambiguously celebrated. Active consumers, particularly girls and young women, unwittingly become neoliberal subjects through exercising their purchasing power to acquire commodified ideals of equality, freedom or self-empowerment, however within the confines of the capitalist market that supports the maintenance of systematic, patriarchal gender inequality (Collins and Rothe 2020). Popular media culture is a complex and contradictory space wherein one's imagined empowerment through self-refashioning consumption as a strategy can both subvert and unintentionally reinforce existing inequality and asymmetrical power. Youth in Asia have to comply with the rules of the state, family and local community, as well as negotiate with them through transnational cultural spaces where the imagination of freedom can be transformed into a collective imaginary to subvert official power and regulations (Nasir 2016; Yoon 2020). The social circulations of the young describe the worlds created by previous generations which they inhabit and through which they negotiate the shape of their present and future (Donald et al. 2010). Digital media use has become another element of social distinction, a search for a different future by young generations, who are culturally cosmopolitan and technologically competent, urban-middle and rural-rich classes, linked to global economic and cultural circuits and multiple lifestyle choices as a result of digital communication networks, travel or overseas education.

Currently proliferating in various forms across the Asian media landscape, lifestyle TV and digital lifestyles promote individualized and enterprising modes of selfhood, however within structural constraints and gendered socioeconomic inequities. Lifestyle-themed self-improvement TV programs, from fashion, beauty and career planning to child-rearing, travel and food, instruct audiences, particularly the consumer middle classes, on how to live a good life (Lewis et al. 2016), and borrow heavily from Western makeover formats though combined with regional Asian television conventions. The concept of lifestyle has become an organizing principle for the self and for the structure of everyday life, while the lifestyle media variously present ideals of everyday domestic life to audiences through affect and consumerism (Ryan 2018). Emerging in the context of cultural and economic changes, lifestyle is bound up in the imperatives of consumer capitalism and constitutes a class- and gender-specific public. Taste and class are politically and historically mutable categories. The reinvention of lifestyle genres in China, for instance, through the creation of a post-socialist taste and class culture is an essential part of cultural and affective transformations in contemporary Chinese society (Zheng 2014). Digital lifestyles are created on a daily basis through digital food practices and associated lifestyle choices that are embedded in distinctive socio-cultural, commercial, technological and governmental contexts in Asia (Tania Lewis and Haiqing Yu, Chapter 12 in this volume). The sense of the self and lifestyle, as being a site of constant potential improvement, creativity and optimization, is created in the DIY spaces of online culinary culture (Lewis 2020), as food has become a burgeoning entertainment industry and generated new forms of media engagement (Phillipov 2017). A journey of self-betterment and transformation through a series of emotionally charged choices is made by the active cultural imagination of a past and present self in need of change as well as a future, happy self (Raisborough 2011). The lifestyle media in the digital age continually produce endless desires and anxieties about what ideals of life should look and feel like, within and beyond national cultural boundaries. Audiences, women, in particular, are exposed to a range of transnationally inflected engagements with neoliberal economic and consumerist models of lifestyle and self-monitoring practices. Popular media discourses seemingly produce new models for the empowerment and freedom of women, yet simultaneously continue to deepen gender inequality and existing social oppression by re-stabilizing and regulating the gendered self.

Gendered Asia

The media, not only the global cultural force but also the national and local mediation, is the key cultural mechanism creating the emergence of new yet precarious identities in a gendered Asia (Kim 2012). Women's social roles in many parts of Asia have undergone a rapid transformation from the traditional image of the "good wife and self-sacrificing mother" to the single, career woman working and playing for pleasure. The media have pushed the boundaries of social acceptability with morally controversial views of media production, representation and consumption at the intersectionality of gender, sexuality and power. The multitude of political, socioeconomic, cultural and technological forces is reshaping the meaning of love and intimacy in the popular public culture at the interface between the personal and individual on the one hand and state power and social forces on the other, as the state continues to exercise ideological control and regulates the moral behavior of its citizens (Sun and Yang 2020). The ubiquitous engagements with digital media technologies are reshaping bodies and embodied practices, habits and routines in everyday life, constituting transformations in the realm of virtual intimacy, sexual and gendered life (Nash and Gorman-Murray 2019). People are experiencing a technologically mediated reorganization of the social relations of sexuality, as mobile online life is developing new connections with others whom they may otherwise never meet in real life. Online dating or the cross-border online relationship is a new type of intimate relationship that has emerged and become more and more common in Asia as a result of the spread of the Internet and the changing lifestyle choices of marriage and family (Choi and Chan 2013). Choosing the right love, young people in Southeast Asia seek romantic relationships by engaging with online dating platforms but are also subject to the influence of family and local morality (Joanne Lim, Chapter 13 in this volume). Even in a liberal environment of the West where online dating is replacing traditional methods of dating and the amount of control that family members have over selecting a dating partner for individuals has changed, family and friends are still sought out to provide advice about online profiles and the compatibility of romantic partners (Blue 2020). Online dating has become entangled in wider concerns regarding sexual and emotional marketization, yet simultaneously as a new technology of intimacy it has been an unconventional site of hope for enhancing social equality, specifically for moving beyond the constraints of gendered heteronormativity and advancing gender equality

(Beasley and Holmes 2021). The changing landscape of love and intimacy reveals how social change, with critical reflexivity and desire for more equitable social relations, often arises in the everyday and familiar. Everyday engagement with the digital constitutes a heightened awareness vis-à-vis gender, sexuality and the familiar form of national differences as well as many different forms of cultural difference. Today's proliferating media are implicated in the competing regime of signifiers at socio-cultural and political levels. The re-construction of intimate and public spheres is happening in many Asian societies that experience declining marriage, increasing divorce, family-at-risk and ultra-low fertility, lower than that of Western Europe and North America (Ochiai and Hosoya 2014). In some contexts, the family is no longer the fundamental social unit, but the individual is gradually becoming that unit as the center of sexual politics. Configurations of gender and sexuality are negotiated, contested and at times reproduced in private, intimate experiences that are multiply impinged upon by state policies, economic realities, social hierarchies and cultural ideologies (Zheng 2016). The emerging media trend is impacting the imaginary construction of new "possible" identities, albeit with unresolved tensions and dilemmas embedded in specific local contexts.

The feminization of masculinity is a contesting transformation in gender and sexuality of Asia, with the emergence of young men employing feminine aesthetics and imagining new masculine identities. Despite a nationalist fear and tension over the boundary-crossing practice that challenges the hitherto clearly defined gendered order, the young men distance themselves from conventional masculinity by standing in the position of the feminine, where they can engage ambiguously in the construction of alternative gender identities. Unlike toxic masculinity of American popular culture in the representation of powerful, hypermasculine and aggressive men as influenced by sports and music (Keith 2017), the feminization of masculinity in the Asian media subverts traditional gender politics and Western forms of masculinity defined by physical strength, power and the suppression of emotions. Signifying in-between men and women in the body and affect, the phenomenon of "flower boy" (a young man as delicate and beautiful as a flower) has emerged in Asian popular culture, most visibly in popular music, television drama and manga, since the 1990s. The young generations of women, tired of strongly masculinist and patriarchal men, may desire to project their male fantasy – a soft appearance, caring personality and gender equality – onto the androgynous, non-heterosexual or non-misogynistic male body in their fandom community (Kwon 2019). Gendered socioeconomic and cultural conditions are frustrating everywhere in Asia, in the dualistic labor market, the underemployment of women and the gender gap in female earnings, which increase unevenness in the distribution of life chances and reveal the "illusion of the language of choice and individualization" for women (Kim 2011, 2012). The constructedness of popular culture or celebrity can be interpreted as a desired discursive symptom of cultural change, and the conduit for comprehending cultural values around gender, sexuality, youth and class (Turner

2014; Marshall and Redmond 2016). Popular media culture in the digital age has created spaces for the emergence of inter-Asian queer communities and the proliferation of new modes of eroticized subjectivity (Michelle H. S. Ho, Chapter 14 in this volume). The digital cultures of non-normative sexual identification arise out of the embedded histories of long-established yet invisible, local non-normative sexual identities and practices in Asia, creating spaces for alternative voices to be expressed and heard. "Boys Love" (BL) culture, with male–male romantic and sexual discourse and youthful male beauty, has been expressed in various ways in Japanese popular culture including manga and other cultural contexts, while women have never been passive readers in relation to BL narratives (McLelland et al. 2015). Women are not only readers but also creators, writers and artists in manga cultures and the erotic implications of the female gaze (Hemmann 2020). The transcultural consumption of manga and anime as well as the spread of associated fan culture evokes certain affects and performative practice, swaying between resistance and conformity to patriarchal society (Berndt et al. 2019). Agency is not becoming free or unleashed from social structure and its constraint, but agency is regulated by the structure, operating within broader systems of constraint. The social and cultural fields are not totally restrictive but dialectically positioned; the complexity neither closes the possibilities potentially available for change nor stands completely open for any kind of empowerment.

There is a peculiar trend in Asia, given its collectivistic cultural traditions, in which the engagement with digital media culture becomes a conspicuous means to express social differentiation and a seemingly free-floating move toward individualization, do-it-yourself lifestyle culture that is continually produced and consumed in neoliberal consumer societies (Kim 2012). As producers and consumers of social media culture, young women in particular have increasingly appropriated popular media narratives to fashion new self-narratives of female individualization. New consumption practices of female individualization are constituted by a paradoxical modality that not only creates new modes of self-choosing, self-fashioning life politics but also possibly reproduces gendered subjects and the nature of gendered identity that is resonant with gendered state policies. The family in certain contexts and the growing importance of militarization and national security continue to operate as an important resource in the construction of masculine identity, while global forces and increased transnational media consumption reconfigure traditional institutional structures and resources in such ways that make it difficult to navigate traditional gender and sexual discourses (Lin et al. 2017). As in most societies, power is maintained through the monitoring and disciplining of sexuality in various ways, amid the increased sexual visibility made possible in the public space such as the media and popular culture (Christy 2017). Sexuality is significant because it offers an expression of nationalist anxieties, and queerness is often constructed as an anti-national in the grand narrative of nationalism and belonging (Dasgupta 2017). New queer subjectivities have been fashioned in and through the governance of illiberal pragmatism characterized by the ambivalence between non-liberalism and neoliberalism, rationalism and irrationalism that governs homosexuality in Singapore's media cultures and political economy (Yue and Zubillaga-Pow 2012). The changing representation of subjects and their sexuality in film as possible aggressors, or as active and willing participants in non-marital sexual relations, is viewed as a part of the unwelcome moral deviancy of the West and becomes a contesting site of power by the nation-state, local communities, parents and society across Asia (Pugsley 2016). Hong Kong kung fu film and the politics of the male body offer an insight into how rebellion and resistance might continue at a moment not of political strength and optimism but of weakness and disillusion (White 2020). Popular martial arts media reflect diversified masculinities, anxieties and transformations in Asian experiences of masculinity (Luke White, Chapter 15 in this volume). Global media culture, consumerism and the interaction between local and global forces play an important role in the diverse construction of masculinity and challenge the nationalist, compulsory and unconscious performance of gender and sexuality, as demonstrated in China (Song and Hird 2014) and Southeast Asia (Ford and Lyons 2012).

Young generations of women increasingly assert their right to the body, sexual freedom without condition and rebel against oppression and heteronormative nationalist commodification in South Asia (Jha and Kurian 2018). Social media networks are appropriated and mobilized by urban-middle-class youth to deal with the forces of statist and patriarchal misogyny or the embedded nature of sexual violence against gendered and queer bodies, albeit indifferent to lower castes and classes, as indicated in India (Schneider and Titzmann 2015). The "loitering" female body in the urban city of India and the creation of a mobile public through digital media practice negotiate the restricted participation of women in public spaces (Nadja-Christina Schneider, Chapter 16 in this volume). Various forms of gendered violence – domestic, military, legal and political – are not separate instances of violence, but rather embedded in structural inequalities brought about by colonialism, occupation, state violence, discrimination and cultures of patriarchy in Indonesia (McGregor et al. 2020). Gendered violence is particularly important to recognize in Southeast Asia because of its complex history of armed conflict and authoritarian rule, as well as the complexity of the religious communities involved. Islamic texts significantly influence Muslim women's perceptions and behavior in their relationships with men, particularly in sexual and marital relationships, as the religious teachings tend to suggest marriage as a socio-cultural and religious obligation and sex in marriage as women's duty instead of their right (Riyani 2021). In a multi-ethnic society, the gender dimension is closely linked to ethnicity, religion and class, and representing women's voices on the mainstream media becomes much more complex given the diversity of identity politics. While gender-based violence occurs in all societies irrespective of the level of development or cultural setting, the perpetuation of gendered violence in Asia is often shaped by distinct cultural norms, laws and policies that actively and structurally undermine gender equality (Barrow and

Chia 2016). Young middle-class women across Asia employ the soft power of digital media use to confront the hard power of structural patriarchy to oppose violence and infringement on women's freedom (Brazal and Abraham 2014). Subordinate women, unsatisfied with gendered inequalities and constraints, may find fulfillment through media cultural consumption practices, the often trivialized yet becoming-significant developments for the culturally specific ways in which individualization and de-traditionalization are imagined and searched for, albeit not always accomplished.

The media are situated within a broader process of consumption and modernity wherein the middle class often deploy a new sphere of modern consumer culture to create local cultural distinction and imagine connections to transnational publics. Television in many postcolonial nations of Asia has played a prominent role in managing and representing the cultures of modernity as they have been shaped by political and historical forces (Tay and Turner 2015). What is distinctive about pervasive television in South Asia, both in the traditionally private spaces of the home and in the public spaces of national discourse, is its unique role in shaping the terrain of public culture and staging the modern in the postcolonial context (Punathambekar and Kumar 2014). Asian cinema is the epitome of modernity as a transformative project or altered modernity, emerging from the hegemonic field of Hollywood or Western modernity and representing both the popular and the modern in its own vernacular fashion (Teo 2013). Popular media culture has historically played a key role in negotiating the ongoing and changing internal tensions of gender and modernity, not only for the nation-state but above all for the everyday lives of people, especially women, as cultural participants (Driscoll and Morris 2014). Women's positioning is ambiguous, situated at the crossroads between modernity, tradition and nationalism. Modernity is inescapably gendered and reflexively embodied – often performed by female bodies in transit as a particular site of struggle over identities, unequal power and some degree of control to resist, yet sometimes complicit with, the gendered norms of modernizing and globalizing neoliberal economies of Asia. The global media, consumerism and porous socio-religious boundaries have significantly influenced the current realities of women's lives. The visual realm is a critical component in South Asian modernity because acts of seeing become acts of knowing and such a meaning-making process enables possible change to take place (Varughese and Dudrah 2020). South Asian "new women" are symbolically produced through the challenging of normative practices of gender and sexuality, new aspirations around education, employment and self-construction of their identity as global neoliberal subjects, while negotiating the boundaries of identity around modernity, tradition, religion and class hierarchy (Hussein 2018). In Muslim societies, the cultural presence of Islam has made inroads more insidiously through popular culture including television and music, and women have to negotiate and cope with the ways in which religion, either as politics or as culture, enters the everyday aspects of their lives (Azim 2013). In Indonesia as elsewhere in the Muslim world, the resurgent interest in

Islam and new forms of religious education have resulted in a proliferation of religious authorities and multiple and competing interpretations of Islam, as well as the tensions youth and women face in navigating between the new opportunities offered by popular culture on the shaping of Muslim middle-class subjectivities, modern social change and the increasingly Muslim tenor of society (Smith-Hefner 2019). Transformations of the nation, class, gender and modernity are fundamentally intertwined with media cultural consumption and reflect the specificities of Asian contexts and trans-Asian features of life (Black et al. 2016). Changes at macro–micro levels are increasingly related to digital media technologies, popular cultural markets, digital generations and mobile cultures. Young rural-to-urban migrant women in China use mobile phones to navigate translocal networks, participate in modern consumer culture and constitute an aspirational "modern" self, while struggling with social constructions of identities based on gender, class, age and place (Wallis 2013; Wang 2016). Not only the urban middle class but also the working class in the invisible sphere of society are central to the appropriation of digital media technologies, performing particular socio-techno practices and public forms of self-fashioning in the process of modernization (Cara Wallis, Chapter 17 in this volume). The connectivity, expansion and technologies of the self, albeit in uneven power, manifest more than ever in today's digitally connected world.

Media cultural practices across Asia have seen interrelated forms of modernization, individualization and cosmopolitanization that do not fit a Euro-American model (Kim 2011, 2012). On the one hand, the media's growing emphasis on individualization and lifestyle choices, as well as a process of reflexivity at work, signifies de-traditionalization, individual autonomy and emancipation from traditional social forms including the conventional family and gendered self. The often de-contextualized representation and playful engagement invite individuals to compare experiences, to become free from fixed gender identities and unequal power, and to orientate themselves toward free choices in the consumerist market or further relate to a cosmopolitan outlook transcending national cultural boundaries. Popular feminism with its imagined female empowerment is visible across multiple digital media platforms, while at the same time popular misogyny as a structural force – or the routine and banal operation of gendered hate speech against women – responds to and challenges popular feminism precisely because it has become so spectacularly visible in the de-traditionalized, neoliberal consumerist market (Banet-Weiser 2018; Kang et al. 2020). Simultaneously, there are emerging forms of re-traditionalization, new models of cultural continuity and re-integration replacing ongoing rupture, and the symbolic production of regulative forms of social control over the lives of individuals, women in particular. The pulls of regulative traditions still operate in the competing regime of signifiers, of dialectical relations between gender, work, sexuality and family that are reconstituted in ambiguous and sometimes contradictory ways that both de-traditionalize and re-traditionalize contemporary female subject formation (Kim 2012). There are inevitable tensions between the representation of the ideological images of Asian women and everyday practices that re-contextualize or resist these images (Ijichi et al. 2016). Gendered actors negotiate and subvert the challenges they encounter, whereas local traditions of the past continue to take on new meanings in this process of change (Liu and Yamashita 2020). Various players in the process of modernization and individualization utilize and re-create traditional systems, such as Confucianism in East Asia, to cope with rapidly changing political and economic realities and shape gender politics and family relationships (Tam et al. 2014). The everyday realities of existence in gendered South Asia are shaped by its own traditional division along caste, class and race (Channa 2013). Despite highly varied historical, cultural and socioeconomic backgrounds, women of Asia represent remarkably similar patterns in carrying out their gendered lives (Najafizadeh and Lindsey 2019). A closer examination of the media's role in re-imagining tradition reveals that paradoxical meanings arise in relation to persisting structural power of tradition and the nation in the realm of global media culture. The Korean film *Parasite*, which won the most awards including Best Picture and Best Director at the Academy Awards in 2020, repurposes the familiar traditional image of women and its reductionistic representation re-imagines gender hierarchy and lower-class bodies' limited power (Kent A. Ono, Chapter 18 in this volume). Women and youth – especially those in subordinate positions, discontent with constraints of life politics within the established dominant order – are likely to imagine alternative lifestyles and desire to move out of the national and local forms of life and to seek a more open, more inclusive, alternative life experience elsewhere (Kim 2011, 2012). Media globalization in Asia routinely presents an imaginary of consumer cosmopolitanism that can be commonly shared in the images of something better, seemingly progressive and emancipatory lifestyles. Global media culture, as an extended cultural resource and framework of non-local mediated knowledge, becomes a part of everyday experience and leads to increasing transnational mobility – imaginary, symbolic, virtual and physical.

Mobile Asia

There is a significant intersection between the large-scale mobility of people and media globalization in Asia as people's mediated symbolic encounter with the global cultural Others generates imaginations of alternative lives, lifestyles and work (Kim 2011). This phenomenon has expanded to the everyday lives of the young and middle class who are increasingly becoming mobile transnationals, de-territorialized in their imaginary, virtual and physical existence through regular travels, digital networks and communications across territorial boundaries. Media globalization has reshaped international migration patterns with distinctive features that differentiate them from earlier migration categories of the working class, victim, trade and imperial power. It intersects with new kinds of migration and greater mobility by transient migrants, the highly educated, professionals, guest workers, cultural migrants, lifestyle migrants and large-scale migration of students overwhelmingly from Asia (Fujita 2009; Kell and Vogl 2012; Chan and Koh 2018; Robertson 2021). These new generations of people on the move, many of whom depart from the usual track of marriage, are markers of contemporary transnational mobility, constituting a new kind of diaspora such as a knowledge diaspora. This mobility often forms a prolonged temporary status or diasporic sojourner mentality, "willing to go anywhere for a while" in pursuit of maximal opportunities, potentially entailing an unending sojourn and settlement across national borders. Its unpredictable, temporary and transient nature is precisely one of the unique features that characterize today's transnational mobility, calling for an understanding of a new formation of diasporic subjects. The media play a significant role as symbolic and cultural forms people live by, constituting residual culture that has been accumulated throughout a life history and that is still active as an effective element in the present. The media and communication technologies have redefined the terms and conditions of migrant experiences and identities in an uneven transnational field (Hegde 2016). Diasporic affects of loss and thrill, pain and happiness are embodied in Asian diasporic visual culture including film and television (Ma 2011). Hegemonic racial ideologies and divisive politics are visibly propagated around the world, particularly during the COVID-19 pandemic; bipolar America's love–hate relationship with Asia is a pronounced example (Sheng-mei Ma, Chapter 19 in this volume). The media act as a complex space for the participation of migrants and minorities in a public sphere where they attempt to advance their interests and identities as well as their integration into mainstream institutions including the labor market, schools, social networks and politics (Bleich et al. 2017). White supremacy has historically been maintained through controlling images and stereotypes of people of Asian descent as racialized, gendered and sexualized bodies (Chou 2012). Sexuality is socially shaped in ways that maintain social and political dominance for Whites, particularly White men. Digital assemblages of media culture and erotics enable the reconfiguration of Asia and constitute complex relationships with erotic desire and fantasies on a transnational scale (Mankekar and Schein 2012).

The hypermediation of racial and cultural differences proliferates in the postcolonial era of digital, neoliberal, transnational capitalism (Purnima Mankekar, Chapter 20 in this volume). Whiteness is the epitome of status and beauty, while gendered colorism is often overlooked within the process of racial discrimination but evident in the mainstream media, television and Internet sites (Khanna 2020). Until major shifts in the dominant structure of media cultural production occur, the residual effects of the racialized historical representations of people of Asian descent will continue into the future; in this context it is important to recognize the alternative, independent, ethnic media (Ono and Pham 2009). Minorities have always shown resilience and innovation in their acts of resistance through their own platforms for communication, media networks and activism engaging in a fight for cultural citizenship, or a deeper sense of belonging within a nation that has long rejected them (Lopez 2016). In daily struggles with the reality of being minorities, including banal racism and discrimination, ethnic cultural traditions are not forgotten but re-visited and passed on to the next generations. People's experiences of social exclusion in the lived reality produce paradoxical consequences for media use and new identity positions. The ethnic media – mainly, popular cultural forms – are originally from a national homeland but are circulated transnationally, often reproduced and amplified by digital technologies and the strategic, self-determined use of the Internet generations forming ethnic online communities. The ethnic media are mobilized as key resources to manage the difficulties of everyday life – racial marginalization, self-questioning and eroding confidence, disengagement and disconnection from the host nation, unresolved tensions within it – all remain perpetually unable to be articulated in the dominant language of Europe (Kim 2011, 2017). For individuals and groups at the cultural margins, transnational media forms legitimate and link diasporic members to their perceived homeland, providing symbolic raw materials to cope with feelings of non-belonging and construct identities in ways that resist cultural marginalization in America (Oh 2015; Lee 2020). Skilled migrants tend to move into an expatriate, hybrid diasporic community rather than into a larger national space of the host nation. On the other hand, the state media of the host nation, China, for example, try to forge new forms of collaboration and partnership with its own citizens' diasporic ethnic media all over the world in response to the state's "soft power" push (Sun and Sinclair 2016).

Today's diasporic communities ritualistically appropriate their own ethnic media and digital communication networks to maintain strong ties back to their homeland, while engaging in complex cultural exchanges and negotiations in host societies. Not only food, language and religious rituals that accompanied the itinerant people of Asia (Tagliacozzo et al. 2019), but also increases in the outward flow and hybridization of Asian popular culture, such as transnational music, film, drama, gaming and fashion, create new and expanded sites for Asian diasporic communities (Dave et al. 2016). Ethnic media cultures proliferating in the digital realm have become integral resources that enable people to be simultaneously mobile and connected, leading to new practices and complex consequences in mobile lives. Diasporic media space is a transnational site of contestation, in which nation, race, gender, class, culture and language continuously interrelate to produce complex identities. Today's ubiquitous media flows from Asia to the rest, with greater access through the Internet, create national space and identification within the transnational field, changing the dynamics of diasporic identity in an unpredictable manner. Diasporic nationalism emerges as reactionary ethno-nationalism within global diasporas of those who appear to be bilingual cross-cultural negotiators moving regularly between different cultures and participating in exchanges across national borders (Kim 2011, 2017). Reactionary ethno-nationalism can be caused by the ways in which exclusionary social conditions, ambiguities of racism, marginality and conflictual interaction give rise to a primacy of identification with ethnically defined cultural nationalism – a distinct, highly conscious and sometimes resistive force

— as a defensive strategy in terms of status positioning and affective support in an uneven world of power. Transnational lives and connectivity do not necessarily diminish but rather enhance an essentialist sense of national identity, as expressed by the Japanese digital diaspora in London (Yuiko Fujita and Kaoru Takahashi, Chapter 21 in this volume). Transnational mobility, whether physical or symbolic, is not a sign of the decline of the nation and national identity, or a loosening of national identification in shaping and directing transnational experiences, both lived and mediated. Displaced from their homeland, diasporic subjects attempt to re-create their own imaginative or mythical space of home.

Migration decisions are typically complex, but it is rare for a migration to be undertaken that is not, to some degree, intended to advance the material welfare of oneself or one's family in the homeland (Fielding 2016). The feminization of migration has emerged as a reaction to gendered social constraints, or as a common livelihood strategy to alleviate poverty and improve socioeconomic and familial conditions (Kim 2011, 2017; Rajan 2021). The gendered transnational migrations of domestic care labor and the interplay of the commercialization of the migration industry and precarity (Amrith and Sahraoui 2018; Baas 2020; Huang and Ruwanpura 2020) indicate that lower-class female migrants have little choice about whether or not they live with their family and where they call home as global mobility seems the best livelihood option to earn an income. Both legal and illegal recruitment agencies, as well as informal social networks by the earlier migration of family members and friends and the use of mobile communication technologies, facilitate the flows of undocumented irregular migrants who carry on moving and struggle with multiple mobilities in search of work and stability. Women are significant and active participants in the increased scale, diversity and transition in the nature of international migration in today's digital age. Some of the resources by which migrants manage mobility and attempt to make them feel empowered – albeit temporary, fleeting yet routinized in everyday practices – are the mobile media such as the mobile phone with Internet-enabled multimedia. Because mobile communication devices are disruptive yet deeply personal and vested with emotionality, families must deal with emotional dualities and asymmetries in power and practices (Lim 2016). Mobile media use is central to the experiences and negotiations of mediated, global, family intimacies for transnational Filipino migrants and those they have left behind (Cecilia S. Uy-Tioco, Chapter 22 in this volume). The mobile media have become a crucial site where social intimacies are enacted, reinforced or negotiated between global modernity and local everyday life (Cabanes and Uy-Tioco 2020). New technologies and mobility are seen as offering the potential for a better life and societal improvement and can supposedly empower the marginalized to claim their own space and voice in relation to self-identity, community, home and belonging, but these great expectations are not necessarily met in the lived experiences of racialized, classed and gendered minorities (Kim 2017). Not only race, class and gender but also family dynamics, labor market conditions, political culture and healthcare overlap in intricate ways to shape the structural and quotidian marginalization of migrants and elicit varying styles of negotiation and resistance, among Filipinos in Australia (Aquino 2017), Chinese in Hong Kong (Choi and Fong 2018) and South Asians in the Middle East (Rajan 2021). New technologies arise from existing patterns of hierarchy, while they also enable new practices opening up new spaces of identity politics. Mobile digital technologies can intensify, rather than bridge, differences between the powerful and the disadvantaged by reinforcing the continuity of traditional power structures and enduring patterns of communication, or by producing potential new inequalities (van Dijk, 2012). To realize the dreams and promises of the digital media to empower all users, then there is a need to challenge that context of socioeconomic inequality and asymmetrical power (Curran et al. 2012). While it is worth recognizing any potentialities for self-invention and opportunity structures (e.g. new employment) that the diasporic condition may give rise to, however precarious and secondary they may be, it is equally important to recognize the quiet pain, sufferings, dilemmas and contradictions that it entails, as well as disarticulation that even the most educated diasporic subjects experience (Kim 2011).

The innate characteristics of digital mobile lives are often seen to be able to provide new possibilities for freedom of choice, and the presumption is that those choices, freely made and enhanced by such technological access, will lead to a more equal and liberating life. The production of desire – restlessly internalized in the notion that people can and should live the good life and that the responsibility to achieve this lies with them as individuals – has become a normative aspect of life, circular mobility and accessible technology (Lyttleton 2014). Disavowed and unconscious currents of sexual and erotic energy generate the drive to migrate, although migrants are often represented as asexual accumulators of capital, driven by a rational commitment to the material betterment of themselves or their family, and although governments in migrant-sending countries like Pakistan are keen to project an image of their citizens as pious and patriotic laborers in receiving countries like Europe (Ahmad 2011). Migrants themselves have emotional and sexual lives, personal desires and pleasures which extend beyond the productive sphere. Migrations have separated queer people from their family of origin and changed today's queer kinship structure in China where their sexualities are at odds with the Confucianist family and social order (Wei 2020). Japanese queer individuals have profound reasons to leave the country due to social marginalization and rejection by their parents, but the experiences of Japanese queer migrants in the West reveal their sexual/racial double-minority status and uncertainty (Tamagawa 2020). While historic norms regarding homosexual acts and identities are different in various parts of Asia, gay Asian men's representation in the Western imagination and their shared racial experience frame what it means to be both gay and Asian in the USA as being outside of both gay America and Asian America (Han 2015). The anti-homophobic rhetoric in the mainstream gay and lesbian movement employs the strategy of remasculinization in order to legitimize themselves and gain acceptance from the dominant culture, which is maintained at the cost of marginalizing femininity and feminine embodiment (Nguyen 2014). Embedded in the liberal West or "liquid individualized society" (Bauman 2007) where individuals must plan, produce and accomplish their biographies themselves, migrants and sexual minorities experience new burdens of choice and dilemmas of personal responsibility alongside increased personal freedom, as well as global structures of domination and unspeakable inequalities. A new mode of identity formation is operating in the transnational flow of desire, giving rise to the experience of both increased freedom and increased insecurity and personal responsibility for every move. The mobile digital media enable them to make differences in their lives but also continue to reinforce existing power relations and inequalities well beyond their control in various contexts of use. Digital platforms have reshaped queer cultural production and representation, and diasporic queer cultures have become diverse, fluid and contested on highly mobile web series across national and sexual boundaries (Olivia Khoo, Chapter 23 in this volume).

Cross-border flows of people and media culture serve as a foundational basis to the imagining of a multicultural nation in Asia; however, the goal of preserving social unity is still paramount, discouraging a cosmopolitan outlook and leading to a formulation of multiculturalism without diversity (Lai et al. 2013; Erni and Leung 2014; Iwabuchi 2015). In the USA, the quintessential "nation of immigrants," pluralism is celebrated as a national value, yet the diversity that immigrants carry over the border has been perceived as a threat to the complexion, economy and unity of the nation, and such tensions over identity have surfaced in media culture (Perry 2016). In Europe, the figure of migrants as the threatening "crimmigrant Other" has emerged as a central object of the mainstream media and political discourse (Franko 2020), and the media framing of the crisis presents a friction between the motivations of acceptance and rejection (Krishna-Hensel 2018). Today's migrants, whether of younger generations or older generations, educated or not, follow a broadly similar strategy of rejecting straightforward integration into host societies, but rely to a large extent on their own cultural resources and extensive transnational networks as a means of creating new life-spaces for themselves beyond the direct control of any nation-state (Liu 2016; Nasir 2016; Robins and Aksoy 2016; Yu and Matsaganis 2019). They are able to shape and sustain their distinct cultural identity through their strategic non-assimilation and diasporic media networks and sometimes purposefully enact national selves in everyday transnational lives. National feelings surge in a world increasingly made up of transnational migration and hybridity with the promise of multiculturalism – a promise, however broken – in which competition for resources and economic opportunities is also most intense (Wang and Goh 2017). Europe, despite its awareness of humanitarian ideals and cosmopolitan ethics, is increasingly opting for border closure. Digital youth and diasporas contest emerging "anti-migrant" nationalisms in their transnational practices "from below" (Jayana Jain, Chapter 24 in this volume). Cosmopolitan perspectives deemed vital in a mobile world become a way of imagining ethical life and political responsibilities. With the upsurge in migration into Western countries and the rise of Islamophobia, the social conditions of Muslim youth have become a litmus test to the success of cosmopolitanism in many states around the world (Nasir 2016). The social reality of cosmopolitanism is much more ambiguous, marked by global structures of power and inequality, exclusion and inclusion governing one's relationship to Others and the world. Critically, not all differences have the same value in the global structures of power and hierarchy. In celebrating the supposedly inclusive cosmopolitan consciousness, cultural difference and human pluralism, some forms of cultural difference are seen as more desirable and more valued than others. The hierarchical emphasis on difference and diversity generates a growing ethnic consciousness and a contradictory force for the reinforcing of nationalism within the uneven and highly contested transnational social field (Kim 2011, 2017). The possibility of cosmopolitan identity requires taking account of the uneven social relations of power, ethnic cultural differentiation and situated human contexts in which one defines the self and Others not necessarily in terms of pleasures but in terms of tensions to cope with. Cosmopolitanism as lived experience awaits realization; forms of situated, thin cosmopolitanism, non-cosmopolitanism or anti-cosmopolitanism exist in unexamined sites that should be recognized. Thin cosmopolitans or vulnerable subordinate groups encountering the global structures of exclusionary practices and asymmetries of power seek to express the very specificities of their cultural identities, ways of being and social organization without embracing a strong cosmopolitan aspiration and a further willingness to enter into dialogue. Moving beyond national boundaries and moving freely into other cultures and societies can reveal a sense of contradictions and limitations. Cosmopolitanism in this neoliberal digital age may be limited within the cosmopolitan world of consumption as pop cosmopolitanism, particularly the space of global media culture and hyper-connectivity that has nevertheless generated global consciousness and the current phenomenon of intensely mobile lives and mobile Asia.

References

Abbas, Q. and Sulehria, F. (2021) *From Terrorism to Television: Dynamics of Media, State and Society in Pakistan*, London: Routledge.

Abidin, C. (2018) *Internet Celebrity*, Bingley: Emerald.

Aguiar, L. and Waldfogel, J. (2018) "Netflix," *Journal of Cultural Economics*, 42: 419–45.

Ahmad, A. (2011) *Masculinity, Sexuality and Illegal Migration: Human Smuggling from Pakistan to Europe*, Surrey: Ashgate.

Amrith, M. and Sahraoui, N. (2018) *Gender, Work and Migration*, London: Routledge.

Aquino, K. (2017) *Racism and Resistance among the Filipino Diaspora*, London: Routledge.

Athique, A. and Baulch, E. (2020) *Digital Transactions in Asia*, London: Routledge.

Azim, F. (2013) *Islam, Culture and Women in Asia*, London: Routledge.

Baas, M. (2020) *The Migration Industry in Asia*, Singapore: Palgrave Macmillan.

Banet-Weiser, S. (2018) *Empowered: Popular Feminism and Popular Misogyny*, Durham: Duke University Press.

Barendregt, B., Keppy, P. and Nordholt, H. (2017) *Popular Music in Southeast Asia*, Amsterdam: Amsterdam University Press.

Barker, C. and Wiatrowski, M. (2017) *The Age of Netflix*, Jefferson: McFarland.

Barrow, A. and Chia, J. (2016) *Gender, Violence and the State in Asia*, London: Routledge.

Bauman, Z. (2007) *Liquid Times: Living in an Age of Uncertainty*, Cambridge: Polity.

Beasley, C. and Holmes, M. (2021) *Internet Dating: Intimacy and Social Change*, London: Routledge.

Beaufort, M. (2020) *Digital Media, Political Polarization and Challenges to Democracy*, London: Routledge.

Bennett, A. and Robards, B. (2014) *Mediated Youth Cultures*, London: Palgrave Macmillan.

Berndt, J., Nagaike, K. and Ogi, F. (2019) *Shojo Across Media*, Cham: Palgrave Macmillan.

Berry, C., Liscutin, N. and Mackintosh, J. (2009) *Cultural Studies and Cultural Industries in Northeast Asia*, Hong Kong: Hong Kong University Press.

Black, D., Khoo, O. and Iwabuchi, K. (2016) *Contemporary Culture and Media in Asia*, Lanham: Rowman & Littlefield.

Bleich, E., Bloemraad, I. and de Graauw, E. (2017) *Migrants, Minorities and the Media*, London: Routledge.

Blue, S. (2020) *The Psychology of Modern Dating*, Lanham: Lexington Books.

Booth, P. (2017) *Digital Fandom 2.0*, New York: Peter Lang.

Booth, P. (2018) *A Companion to Media Fandom and Fan Studies*, Hoboken: Wiley.

Brazal, A. and Abraham, K. (2014) *Feminist Cyberethics in Asia*, New York: Palgrave Macmillan.

Buckingham, D., Bragg, S. and Kehily, M. (2014) *Youth Cultures in the Age of Global Media*, London: Palgrave Macmillan.

Burrett, T. and Kingston, J. (2020) *Press Freedom in Contemporary Asia*, London: Routledge.

Cabanes, J. and Uy-Tioco, C.S. (2020) *Mobile Media and Social Intimacies in Asia*, Dordrecht, Springer.

Cai, S. (2019) *Female Celebrities in Contemporary Chinese Society*, Singapore: Palgrave Macmillan.

Chan, F., Karpovich, A. and Zhang, X. (2011) *Genre in Asian Film and Television*, London: Palgrave Macmillan.

Chan, Y.W. and Koh, S.Y. (2018) *New Chinese Migrations*, London: Routledge.

Channa, S. (2013) *Gender in South Asia*, Cambridge: Cambridge University Press.

Chen, L. (2018) *Chinese Fans of Japanese and Korean Pop Culture*, London: Routledge.

Choi, M. and Chan, K.B. (2013) *Online Dating as a Strategic Game*, Berlin: Springer.

Choi, S. and Fong, E. (2018) *Migration in Post-Colonial Hong Kong*, London: Routledge.

Chou, R. (2012) *Asian American Sexual Politics*, Lanham: Rowman & Littlefield.

Christy, C. (2017) *Sexuality and Public Space in India*, London: Routledge.

Chua, B.H. (2012) *Structure, Audience and Soft Power in East Asian Pop Culture*, Hong Kong: Hong Kong University Press.

Click, M. and Scott, S. (2018) *Routledge Companion to Media Fandom*, New York: Routledge.

Collins, V. and Rothe, D. (2020) *The Violence of Neoliberalism*, London: Routledge.

Cunningham, S. and Craig, D. (2019) *Social Media Entertainment*, New York: New York University Press.

Curran, J., Fenton, N. and Freedman, D. (2012) *Misunderstanding the Internet*, London: Routledge.

Curtin, M. (2007) *Playing to the World's Biggest Audience*, Berkeley: University of California Press.

Daniels, T. (2013) *Performance, Popular Culture and Piety in Muslim Southeast Asia*, New York: Palgrave Macmillan.

Darling-Wolf, F. (2015) *Imagining the Global: Transnational Media and Popular Culture Beyond East and West*, Ann Arbor: University of Michigan Press.

Darling-Wolf, F. (2018) *Routledge Handbook of Japanese Media*, London: Routledge.

Dasgupta, R. (2017) *Digital Queer Cultures in India*, London: Routledge.

Dave, S., Nishime, L. and Oren, T. (2016) *Global Asian American Popular Cultures*, New York: New York University Press.

DeBoer, S. (2014) *Coproducing Asia*, Minneapolis: University of Minnesota Press.

deLisle, J., Goldstein, A. and Yang, G. (2016) *The Internet, Social Media and a Changing China*, Philadelphia: University of Pennsylvania Press.

Donald, S., Anderson, T. and Spry, D. (2010) *Youth, Society and Mobile Media in Asia*, London: Routledge.

Driscoll, C. and Morris, M. (2014) *Gender, Media and Modernity in the Asia-Pacific*, London: Routledge.

Dukalskis, A. (2017) *The Authoritarian Public Sphere: Legitimation and Autocratic Power in North Korea, Burma and China*, London: Routledge.

Erni, J. and Leung, L. (2014) *Understanding South Asian Minorities in Hong Kong*, Hong Kong: Hong Kong University Press.

Fattor, E. (2014) *American Empire and the Arsenal of Entertainment*, New York: Palgrave Macmillan.

Fielding, T. (2016) *Asian Migrations*, London: Routledge.

Ford, M. and Lyons, L. (2012) *Men and Masculinities in Southeast Asia*, London: Routledge.

Franko, K. (2020) *The Crimmigrant Other: Migration and Penal Power*, London: Routledge.

Fujita, Y. (2009) *Cultural Migrants from Japan*, Lanham: Lexington Books.

Fung, A. (2013) *Asian Popular Culture: The Global (Dis)continuity*, London: Routledge.

George, C. and Venkiteswaran, G. (2019) *Media and Power in Southeast Asia*, Cambridge: Cambridge University Press.

Gooptu, N. (2013) *Enterprise Culture in Neoliberal India*, London: Routledge.

Gorfinkel, L. (2018) *Chinese Television and National Identity Construction*, London: Routledge.

Graham, M. (2019) *Digital Economies at Global Margins*, Cambridge: MIT Press.

Gunter, B. (2014) *Celebrity Capital*, New York: Bloomsbury.

Han, C.W. (2015) *Geisha of a Different Kind*, New York: New York University Press.

Han, S. and Nasir, K. (2016) *Digital Culture and Religion in Asia*, London: Routledge.

Harindranath, R. (2009) *Audience-Citizens: The Media, Public Knowledge and Interpretive Practice*, Delhi: SAGE.

Hayden, C. (2012) *The Rhetoric of Soft Power*, Lanham: Lexington Books.

Hegde, R. (2016) *Mediating Migration*, Cambridge: Polity.

Hemmann, K. (2020) *Manga Cultures and the Female Gaze*, Cham: Palgrave Macmillan.

Heryanto, A. (2008) *Popular Culture in Indonesia*, London: Routledge.

Hill, J. and Kawashima, N. (2018) *Film Policy in a Globalized Cultural Economy*, London: Routledge.

Hillis, K., Paasonen, S. and Petit, M. (2015) *Networked Affect*, Cambridge: MIT Press.

Hjorth, L. and Khoo, O. (2016) *Routledge Handbook of New Media in Asia*, London: Routledge.

Hong, J. (2020) *China in the Era of Social Media*, Lanham: Lexington Books.

Huang, S. and Ruwanpura, K. (2020) *Handbook on Gender in Asia*, Cheltenham: Edward Elgar.

Hussein, N. (2018) *Rethinking New Womanhood: Practices of Gender, Class, Culture and Religion in South Asia*, Cham: Palgrave Macmillan.

Ijichi, N., Kato, A. and Sakurada, R. (2016) *Rethinking Representations of Asian Women*, London: Palgrave Macmillan.

Iwabuchi, K. (2015) *Resilient Borders and Cultural Diversity: Internationalism, Brand Nationalism and Multiculturalism in Japan*, Lanham: Lexington Books.

Jenkins, H., Ford, S. and Green, J. (2013) *Spreadable Media*, New York: New York University Press.

Jenkins, H., Peters-Lazaro, G. and Shresthova, S. (2020) *Popular Culture and the Civic Imagination*, New York: New York University Press.

Jenner, M. (2018) *Netflix and the Re-Invention of Television*, London: Palgrave Macmillan.

Jha, S. and Kurian, A. (2018) *New Feminisms in South Asia*, New York: Routledge.

Jin, D.Y. (2020) *Transmedia Storytelling in East Asia*, London: Routledge.

Jin, D.Y. and Su, W. (2020) *Asia-Pacific Film Co-Productions*, New York: Routledge.

Kang, M., Rive-Lasan, M., Kim, W. and Hall, P. (2020) *Hate Speech in Asia and Europe*, London: Routledge.

Kavoori, A. (2009) *The Logics of Globalization: Studies in International Communication*, Lanham: Lexington Books.

Kavoori, A. (2010) *Digital Media Criticism*, New York: Peter Lang.

Keane, M., Yecies, B. and Flew, T. (2018) *Willing Collaborators: Foreign Partners in Chinese Media*, Lanham: Rowman & Littlefield.

Keith, T. (2017) *Masculinities in Contemporary American Culture*, New York: Routledge.

Kell, P. and Vogl, G. (2012) *International Students in the Asia Pacific*, Singapore: Springer.

Kent, M., Ellis, K. and Xu, J. (2018) *Chinese Social Media*, New York: Routledge.

Kenyon, A., Marjoribanks, T. and Whiting, A. (2014) *Democracy, Media and Law in Malaysia and Singapore*, London: Routledge.

Khanna, N. (2020) *Whiter: Asian American Women on Skin Color and Colorism*, New York: New York University Press.

Kim, S. and Lee, H.W. (2018) *Reimagining Nation and Nationalism in Multicultural East Asia*, London: Routledge.

Kim, Y. (2005) *Women, Television and Everyday Life in Korea: Journeys of Hope*, London: Routledge.

Kim, Y. (2008) *Media Consumption and Everyday Life in Asia*, London: Routledge.

Kim, Y. (2011) *Transnational Migration, Media and Identity of Asian Women: Diasporic Daughters*, London: Routledge.

Kim, Y. (2012) *Women and the Media in Asia: The Precarious Self*, London: Palgrave Macmillan.

Kim, Y. (2013) *The Korean Wave: Korean Media Go Global*, London: Routledge.

Kim, Y. (2017) *Childcare Workers, Global Migration and Digital Media*, London: Routledge.

Kim, Y. (2019) *South Korean Popular Culture and North Korea*, London: Routledge.

Kim, Y. (2021) *The Soft Power of the Korean Wave: Parasite, BTS and Drama*, London: Routledge.

Kingston, J. (2016) *Nationalism in Asia*, Malden: Wiley.

Krishna-Hensel, S. (2018) *Migrants, Refugees and the Media*, London: Routledge.

Kumar, S. (2006) *Gandhi Meets Primetime: Globalization and Nationalism in Indian Television*, Urbana-Champaign: University of Illinois Press.

Kurlantzick, J. (2007) *Charm Offensive*, New Haven: Yale University Press.

Kwak, K.S. (2018) *Television in Transition in East Asia*, London: Routledge.

Kwon, J. (2019) *Straight Korean Female Fans and Their Gay Fantasies*, Iowa City: University of Iowa Press.

Lai, A., Collins, F. and Yeoh, B. (2013) *Migration and Diversity in Asian Contexts*, Singapore: Institute of Southeast Asian Studies.

Lau, D.W.S. (2019) *Chinese Stardom in Participatory Cyberculture*, Edinburgh: Edinburgh University Press.

Lee, C. (2020) *Mediatized Transient Migrants*, Lanham: Lexington Books.

Lee, F. and Chan, J. (2018) *Media and Protest Logics in the Digital Era*, New York: Oxford University Press.

Lee, H. and Oh, J.H. (2021) *Digital Media, Online Activism and Social Movements in Korea*, Lanham: Lexington Books.

Leong, P. (2019) *Malaysian Politics in the New Media Aga*, Singapore: Springer.

Leung, V., Cheng, K. and Tse, T. (2017) *Celebrity Culture and the Entertainment Industry in Asia*, Bristol: Intellect.

Lewis, T. (2020) *Digital Food: From Paddock to Platform*, London: Bloomsbury.

Lewis, T., Martin, F. and Sun, W. (2016) *Telemodernities: Television and Transforming Lives in Asia*, Durham: Duke University Press.

Lim, L. (2014) *Cultural Policy in East Asia*, London: Routledge.

Lim, L. and Lee, H.K. (2018) *Routledge Handbook of Cultural and Creative Industries in Asia*, London: Routledge.

Lim, S.S. (2016) *Mobile Communication and the Family*, Dordrecht: Springer.

Lin, X., Haywood, C. and Mac an Ghaill, M. (2017) *East Asian Men: Masculinity, Sexuality and Desire*, London: Palgrave Macmillan.

Liu, J. and Yamashita, J. (2020) *Routledge Handbook of East Asian Gender Studies*, London: Routledge.

Liu, L. (2016) *Chinese Student Migration and Selective Citizenship*, London: Routledge.

Liu-Farrer, G. and Yeoh, B. (2018) *Routledge Handbook of Asian Migrations*, London: Routledge.

Lobato, R. (2019) *Netflix Nations*, New York: New York University Press.

Lopez, L. (2016) *Asian American Media Activism*, New York: New York University Press.

Luqiu, L. (2018) *Propaganda, Media and Nationalism in Mainland China and Hong Kong*, Lanham: Lexington Books.

Luvaas, B. (2012) *DIY Style: Fashion, Music and Global Digital Cultures*, London: Berg.

Lyttleton, C. (2014) *Intimate Economies of Development*, London: Routledge.

Ma, S.-M. (2011) *Diaspora Literature and Visual Culture: Asia in Flight*, London: Routledge.

Malik, K. and Dudrah, R. (2020) *South Asian Creative and Cultural Industries*, London: Routledge.

Mankekar, P. and Schein, L. (2012) *Media, Erotics and Transnational Asia*, Durham: Duke University Press.

Marshall, D. and Redmond, S. (2016) *A Companion to Celebrity*, Malden: Wiley.

McDonald, K. and Smith-Rowsey, D. (2016) *The Netflix Effect*, New York: Bloomsbury.

McGregor, K., Dragojlovic, A. and Loney, H. (2020) *Gender, Violence and Power in Indonesia*, London: Routledge.

McGuigan, J. (2010) *Cultural Analysis*, London: SAGE.

McLelland, M., Nagaike, K., Suganuma, K. and Welker, J. (2015) *Boys Love Manga and Beyond*, Jackson: University Press of Mississippi.

Morris, P., Shimazu, N. and Vickers, E. (2013) *Imagining Japan in Post-War East Asia*, London: Routledge.

Motrescu-Mayes, A. and Aasman, S. (2019) *Amateur Media and Participatory Cultures*, London: Routledge.

Naafs, S. and Skelton, T. (2019) *Realities and Aspirations for Asian Youth*, London: Routledge.

Najafizadeh, M. and Lindsey, L. (2019) *Women of Asia: Globalization, Development and Gender Equity*, New York: Routledge.

Nash, C. and Gorman-Murray, A. (2019) *The Geographies of Digital Sexuality*, Singapore: Palgrave Macmillan.

Nasir, K. (2016) *Globalized Muslim Youth in the Asia Pacific*, London: Palgrave Macmillan.

Neves, J. and Sarkar, B. (2017) *Asian Video Cultures*, Durham: Duke University Press.

Nguyen, T.H. (2014) *A View from the Bottom: Asian American Masculinity and Sexual Representation*, Durham: Duke University Press.

Nguyen-Thu, G. (2019) *Television in Post-Reform Vietnam*, London: Routledge.

Nye, J. (2004) *Soft Power: The Means to Success in World Politics*, New York: PublicAffairs.

Nye, J. (2008) *The Powers to Lead*, New York: Oxford University Press.

Ochiai, E. and Hosoya, L. (2014) *Transformation of the Intimate and the Public in Asian Modernity*, Leiden: Brill.

O'Connor, J. and Gu, X. (2020) *Red Creative: Culture and Modernity in China*, Bristol: Intellect.

Oh, D. (2015) *Second-Generation Korean Americans and Transnational Media*, Lanham: Lexington Books.

Ono, K. and Pham, V. (2009) *Asian Americans and the Media*, Cambridge: Polity.

Otmazgin, N. and Ben-Ari, E. (2012) *Popular Culture and the State in East and Southeast Asia*, London: Routledge.

Otmazgin, N. and Ben-Ari, E. (2013) *Popular Culture Co-productions and Collaborations in East and Southeast Asia*, Singapore: National University of Singapore Press.

Papacharissi, Z. (2015) *Affective Publics*, New York: Oxford University Press.

Park, H. (2020) *Media Culture in Transnational Asia*, New Brunswick: Rutgers University Press.

Pathak, D. and Perera, S. (2018) *Culture and Politics in South Asia*, London: Routledge.

Perry, L. (2016) *The Cultural Politics of US Immigration*, New York: New York University Press.

Pham, M.H. (2015) *Asians Wear Clothes on the Internet*, Durham: Duke University Press.

Phillipov, M. (2017) *Media and Food Industries*, Cham: Palgrave Macmillan.

Pugsley, P. (2016) *Exploring Morality and Sexuality in Asian Cinema*, London: Routledge.

Punathambekar, A. (2013) *From Bombay to Bollywood*, New York: New York University Press.

Punathambekar, A. and Kumar, S. (2014) *Television at Large in South Asia*, London: Routledge.

Radde-Antweiler, K. and Zeiler, X. (2019) *Mediatized Religion in Asia*, New York: Routledge.

Raisborough, J. (2011) *Lifestyle Media and the Formation of the Self*, London: Palgrave Macmillan.

Rajan, S.I. (2021) *South Asia Migration Report 2020*, London: Routledge.

Riyani, I. (2021) *Islam, Women's Sexuality and Patriarchy in Indonesia*, London: Routledge.

Robertson, A. (2010) *Mediated Cosmopolitanism*, Cambridge: Polity.

Robertson, S. (2021) *Temporality in Mobile Lives*, Bristol: Bristol University Press.

Robins, K. and Aksoy, A. (2016) *Transnationalism, Migration and the Challenge to Europe*, London: Routledge.

Rodrigues, U. and Ranganathan, M. (2015) *Indian News Media*, Delhi: SAGE.

Rojek, C. (2016) *Presumed Intimacy*, Cambridge: Polity.

Ryan, M. (2018) *Lifestyle Media in American Culture*, New York: Routledge.

Sakamoto, R. and Epstein, S. (2021) *Popular Culture and the Transformations of Japan-Korea Relations*, London: Routledge.

Schneider, F. (2018) *China's Digital Nationalism*, New York: Oxford University Press.

Schneider, N.-C. and Titzmann, F.M. (2015) *Studying Youth, Media and Gender in Post-Liberalization India*, Berlin: Frank & Timme.

Scholz, T. (2013) *Digital Labor*, New York: Routledge.

Seaton, P. and Yamamura, T. (2017) *Japanese Popular Culture and Contents Tourism*, London: Routledge.

Smith, M. and Telang, R. (2016) *Streaming, Sharing, Stealing: Big Data and the Future of Entertainment*, Cambridge: MIT Press.

Smith-Hefner, N. (2019) *Islamizing Intimacies: Youth, Sexuality and Gender in Contemporary Indonesia*, Honolulu: University of Hawaii Press.

Song, G. and Hird, D. (2014) *Men and Masculinities in Contemporary China*, Leiden: Brill.

Starrs, R. (2013) *Asian Nationalism in an Age of Globalization*, London: Routledge.

Sun, W. and Sinclair, J. (2016) *Media and Communication in the Chinese Diaspora*, London: Routledge.

Sun, W. and Yang, L. (2020) *Love Stories in China*, London: Routledge.

Tagliacozzo, E., Siu, H. and Perdue, P. (2019) *Asia Inside Out: Itinerant People*, Cambridge: Harvard University Press.

Tam, S., Ching, W., Wong, A. and Wang, D. (2014) *Gender and Family in East Asia*, London: Routledge.

Tamagawa, M. (2020) *Japanese LGBT Diasporas*, Cham: Palgrave Macmillan.

Tapsell, R. (2017) *Media Power in Indonesia*, Lanham: Rowman & Littlefield.

Tay, J. and Turner, G. (2015) *Television Histories in Asia*, London: Routledge.

Teo, S. (2013) *The Asian Cinema Experience*, London: Routledge.

Thussu, D. (2013) *Communicating India's Soft Power*, New York: Palgrave Macmillan.

Thussu, D. (2019) *International Communication: Continuity and Change*, London: Bloomsbury.

Turkle, S. (2011) *Alone Together*, New York: Basic Books.

Turner, G. (2014) *Understanding Celebrity*, London: SAGE.

Udupa, S. (2015) *Making News in Global India*, Cambridge: Cambridge University Press.

Udupa, S. and McDowell, S. (2017) *Media as Politics in South Asia*, London: Routledge.

van Dijk, J. (2012) *The Network Society*, London: SAGE.

van Krieken, R. (2012) *Celebrity Society*, London: Routledge.

Varughese, E. and Dudrah, R. (2020) *Graphic Novels and Visual Cultures in South Asia*, London: Routledge.

Voci, P. and Hui, L. (2018) *Screening China's Soft Power*, London: Routledge.

Wallis, C. (2013) *Technomobility in China: Young Migrant Women and Mobile Phones*, New York: New York University Press.

Wang, C.M. and Goh, D. (2017) *Precarious Belongings: Affect and Nationalism in Asia*, Lanham: Rowman & Littlefield.

Wang, J. (2019) *The Other Digital China: Nonconfrontational Activism on the Social Web*, Cambridge: Harvard University Press.

Wang, Q. (2021) *The Chinese Internet*, London: Routledge.

Wang, X. (2016) *Social Media in Industrial China*, London: UCL Press.

Watanabe, Y. and McConnell, D. (2008) *Soft Power Superpowers*, New York: M.E. Sharpe.

Wei, J. (2020) *Queer Chinese Cultures and Mobilities*, Hong Kong: Hong Kong University Press.

Wei, R. (2016) *Mobile Media, Political Participation and Civic Activism in Asia*, Dordrecht: Springer.

Wei, R. and Lo, V.H. (2021) *News in Their Pockets*, New York: Oxford University Press.

White, L. (2020) *Legacies of the Drunken Master: Politics of the Body in Hong Kong Kung Fu Comedy Films*, Honolulu: University of Hawaii Press.

Wilkins, K., Straubhaar, J. and Kumar, S. (2014) *Global Communication: New Agendas in Communication*, New York: Routledge.

Yoon, K. (2020) *Digital Mediascapes of Transnational Korean Youth Culture*, New York: Routledge.

Yu, S. and Matsaganis, M. (2019) *Ethnic Media in the Digital Age*, New York: Routledge.

Yue, A. and Zubillaga-Pow, J. (2012) *Queer Singapore: Illiberal Citizenship and Mediated Cultures*, Hong Kong: Hong Kong University Press.

Yueming, R. and O'Connor, J. (2018) *Cultural Industries in Shanghai*, Bristol: Intellect.

Zhao, S. (2018) *Chinese Authoritarianism in the Information Age*, London: Routledge.

Zheng, T. (2016) *Cultural Politics of Gender and Sexuality in Contemporary Asia*, Honolulu: University of Hawaii Press.

Zheng, Y. (2014) *Contemporary Chinese Print Media*, London: Routledge.

PART I

Global Asia

1

NETFLIX, THE DIGITAL WEST IN ASIA

New Models, Challenges and Collaborations

Anthony Fung and Georgia Chik

Asia has always been prone to the influences of Western and Anglo-Saxon entertainment and popular culture. Cultural globalization, if not cultural imperialism, and deglobalization continue to be issues in both academic and industrial debates (Fung 2013). Global popular culture, including Hollywood movies, American TV series and Western pop music, has become a part of Asian popular culture in different degrees of localization. In the present era of digitalization, online entertainment is no exception. From video platforms such as YouTube to music platforms such as Spotify, platformized digital entertainment has been predominant in Asia.

This chapter focuses on the growing number of digital media streaming platforms in Asia, particularly East Asia, including China, Hong Kong, Taiwan, South Korea and Japan. Streaming video-on-demand (SVOD) services have become increasingly popular in the consumption of television content (Lobato 2018). Conglomerate platforms, such as Netflix, Hulu and Amazon Prime, have secured a significant market share in Western nations. In 2019, Netflix became the world's eighth-largest Internet market leader, recording a staggering 266% increase from the previous year (*Applify* 2020). In 2020, Netflix expanded its paid subscriptions in the Asia-Pacific region by 9.3 million, an increase of 65%, which outperformed Europe, the Middle East and Africa. In an interview, the company's chief operating officer and chief product officer, Greg Peters, acknowledged the potential of the Asian market (Iyengar 2021).

An intriguing question is whether Netflix, as a Western digital platform for the dissemination of popular culture and entertainment, could become another dominant form of cultural globalization. Would the presence of Western digital media streaming platforms in Asia become another form of global popular culture that competes with, challenges and overshadows local platforms? Could some forms of localization in which Western streaming platforms would

DOI: 10.4324/9781003130628-3

collaborate with Asian media productions create and advance the global media landscape? Are there variations in terms of willingness for collaboration among Asian cities and nations? As explained below, the presence of Netflix as the globalizing Western media has encountered strong obstacles. This implies that the argument about a simple, Western form of cultural globalization is not likely to happen in Asia. Rather, this chapter argues that a more viable model of cultural globalization/localization would involve collaboration between Western streaming platforms and Asian counterparts in terms of coproduction of content that is conducive to distributing Asian content globally while Western platforms can smoothly integrate their business in Asia.

Western Digital Media: Their Rise and Venture into the East

Streaming digital platforms such as Netflix are generally referred to as over-the-top (OTT) video, video-on-demand (VOD) or online television services that are considered the major competitors of traditional terrestrial (and mainly free) television services. Such platforms are also seen as a creative industry or communication technology that threatens traditional television. However, digital video platforms have also been viewed as bringing new hope to an unequal market because they are expected to operate more "democratically" and hence provide equal distributions of control to producers and distributors (Christian 2012). A theoretical argument concerns whether Netflix or other streaming video platforms can transform the present media ecology, such as in the USA, in which television networks are dominated by a few media giants. This argument could be particularly relevant in Asia, where the media ecology is controlled by either the state or an oligopoly.

OTT platforms provide users with the unique service of easy, fast and affordable access to a massive library of audiovisual content in a single platform. Instead of being bound by a fixed broadcasting schedule, the audience can freely explore the platform's rich library of audiovisual content. In theory, audiences are provided with a greater variety of programs, including those produced in foreign countries. However, "binge-watching," in which several episodes of audiovisual content are consumed in a single session, may be an emerging viewing pattern (Limov 2020). While some scholars have regarded the new viewing pattern as an "insulated flow" that pays tribute to broadcasting schedules (Perks 2015), others have found it to be a reflection of the viewer's autonomy and a fundamental attribute of VOD platforms (Merikivi et al. 2020).

On streaming television platforms, the audience's experience is enhanced by the ability to personally custom content based on recommendation systems that are driven by viewership data in conjunction with the use of algorithms and machine learning (Gomez-Uribe and Hunt 2015). Big data technology enables analyzing and predicting users' preferences based on their previous behavior patterns and peer data on audience taste (Thorson and Wells 2016). Based on viewers' behavior patterns, the production of Netflix's famous series *House of Cards* created a winning combination of actors, producers and themes. Furthermore, these platforms can be viewed on multi-screens so that viewers can access content using different devices, including personal computers, tablets and smartphones. Hence, the audience is not bound by the household television screen. This flexibility also means that streaming television platforms are able to explore a wide range of audience profiles to attract viewers who are not accustomed to watching traditional television at home. Such new consumption patterns also challenge traditional television, the ratings of which have declined in both the East and the West (*Phonetic House* 2020; Adgate 2021).

Nonetheless, the growth and development of Internet platforms are restrained by external factors, particularly the digital infrastructure that delivers the content through the Internet. An increasing number of reports have documented conflicts among Internet service providers (ISPs), carriers that distribute the content, and content providers in the USA (Friden 2015). Among all digital platforms, streaming platforms that require high volumes of data transmission pay huge fees to ISPs. Despite several lawsuits, Google, which is a dominant digital company, laid its own fiber optic cable for data transmission (*CBInsights* 2018). However, when transmissions reach local audiences such as in Asia, the accessibility of telecommunication infrastructures is still controlled by local companies or governments. The most obvious case is in China, where the Great Firewall and its proxy servers forbid the entry of all foreign streaming videos.

Unlike traditional media content, the import of which depends on content copyright, broadcast right, distribution or minimal localization of content to meet local legal regulations, if not censorship, streaming platforms that seek to enter the Asian market are challenged by the lack of accessibility. Moreover, because local audiences have access to a wider diversity of choices beyond their cultural and national geographical regions, OTT video could be perceived as a competitor by local media stakeholders. Thus, it is likely that Netflix's entry has not been without obstacles. Netflix first entered the Asian market in 2015 in Japan, and then in South Korea in 2016. In September 2020, there were 3.3 million paid household subscriptions in South Korea (Choudhury 2020), and in 2021, there were 5 million household subscriptions in Japan (Levy 2021).

Since 2016, Netflix has almost doubled its content catalog annually in South Korea (Choudhury 2020). It has also gained a strong foothold in the anime market in Japan, and it has collaborated with Japanese production companies to produce 40 new animes per year for a global audience (Levy 2021). In the first quarter of 2021, Asia accounted for approximately 10% of Netflix's total revenue (*Statista* 2021). Moreover, Asia has been perceived as the fastest-growing region in the world (Choudhury 2020). In addition to Netflix, HBO GO also has a presence in Asia, either through a direct business to consumer (B2C) subscription model or as a channel for local pay-TV subscriptions.

Competitions and Barriers in Japan, South Korea and China

The initial entry of Netflix into Asia was challenging as it was an external competitor for internal players. The main competition for Western streaming platforms comprises two types of local platforms. The first type was established by traditional television broadcasters as online extensions of their television services, which is prominent in regions. The second type was established by third-party, independent platforms that provide video-on-demand services. Currently, the business model of most Asian streaming video platforms derives income directly from subscriptions and indirectly from advertisements, both of which depend on the size of the viewership. Thus, Western OTT video platforms were perceived as potential competitors that would erode the local market share if the latter were perceived as a zero-sum game.

However, competition is regulated. Because of the lobbying of local incumbent broadcasters, local regulators have remained skeptical of the penetration of Western platforms. In free markets such as South Korea and Japan, the local operators complained that they were not on a level playing field because Asian broadcast regulators in general had stringent regulations on terrestrial TV broadcasting. Hence, programs on the digital platforms of local broadcasters were more restricted than those on Western digital platforms.

Regarding the comparative advantages of streaming video platforms in Western nations, it is likely that the library of television and film content appeals to audiences there. However, the appeal of a global library to audiences with cross-cultural appetites in the Asian market was largely discounted because prior to the emergence of digital platforms, Asian local television channels could have owned the broadcast rights of movies or arranged exclusive licensing agreements with local broadcasters for broadcast rights within a region. Because of existing content and the influence of local broadcasters, the entry of foreign platforms such as Netflix into Asia was not easy. In this research, Japan, South Korea and China, which are the biggest markets in East Asia, have been selected as case studies to facilitate an understanding of the digital media market in this region.

Japan's media scene is dominated by an oligopoly of five major media conglomerates that include both traditional and digital media. These market leaders include Asahi, Fuji, Nikkei, Tokyo Broadcasting System (TBS) and Yomiuri. In recent decades, they have expanded their business from newspaper publishing to television broadcasting. In addition to being the major distributor of media content, these giants are also the major producers and owners of media copyright content. Hence, these major conglomerates occupy a dominant and powerful position in the market. As communication technology advanced, they ventured into digital broadcasting and online delivery before the entry of Western platforms into the Asian market.

In Japan, the digital media trend is mostly a response to changing audience behaviors and preferences (Zhu 2019). The five major conglomerates have developed their respective online presence, providing the audience with access to current and archival audiovisual content. While current content could be viewed for free, a premium structure is adopted for access to older and exclusive material. The market leader of the digital media platform is a digital site called TVer, which was established jointly by the five major media conglomerate groups in Japan, together with the top advertising agencies. Holding the copyright of all local audiovisual content, the platform provides easy and extensive access to the broadcasters' wealth of quality entertainment content. The latter has been a strong battlefront against foreign digital streaming platforms since they came in 2015. Netflix and Amazon Prime both entered Japan in 2015. Disney Plus is the newest addition to the market, entering the country in 2020 at the spike of the COVID-19 lockdown. In general, Western streaming platforms were selling their bulk of English-speaking content to a niche segment of the audience sector. For Western platforms without local content, the strategy is seen as an avoidance of head-on competition.

Similarly, in the case of South Korea, the traditional media industries are dominated by three incumbent broadcasters, namely MBC, SBS and KBS. South Korea is known for a mature and competitive audiovisual market, being home to reportedly some of the earliest OTT platforms, such as Pandora TV and Gom TV (Dwyer et al. 2018). The local digital media landscape was vibrant for a multitude of reasons. South Korea is among the countries with high Internet connectivity that greatly facilitates Internet viewing everywhere. The audience's familiarity with viewing video content on devices has resulted in favorable user habits (Park 2017). In light of their own strong competitiveness of Internet platforms (Hsu et al. 2016), South Korea is less stringent in regulations of OTT business. This has resulted in fierce competition in the OTT service market because of a high number of competitors, none of which has secured a predominant position (KCC 2019). Legacy broadcasters in South Korea have also established their online presence, with the three major terrestrial groups collaborating to establish and operate the video-on-demand platform POOQ in 2012.

As a latecomer, Netflix has had to fight a tough battle in entering the market. On one hand, the company's initial entry into South Korea was met with strong resistance by local filmmakers who feared the competition. In fact, Netflix had approached other major telecommunication carriers, such as SK Telecom and KT Corporation (Song 2019), which were also major providers of Internet Protocol Television (IPTV) services. These platforms were reluctant to collaborate with Netflix, and they objected to its market entry because they were attempting to be "the Netflix of Asia" (Rosati 2019). Eventually, Netflix entered South Korea through licensing agreements with local digital TV providers, such as D'LIVE in 2016 and then LG Uplus in 2018. The alliances were aimed at providing Netflix access to the market while enabling local counterparts to leverage the international platform to deliver services that competed with traditional media service providers (Lee and Kim 2018). Local providers that collaborated with Netflix were denigrated. The Korean Broadcasters Association, which criticized

LG Uplus for collaborating with Netflix because it endangered the local market, urged the government to respond (Kim 2018). Nonetheless, the alliance proceeded, and it became evident that Netflix's presence was not necessarily detrimental to the local market. Instead, in Korea, the number of Netflix users and the number of LG Uplus subscriptions both tripled from 2018 to 2019, which provided clear evidence that the market's demand and potential for SVOD services does not necessarily entail a zero-sum game.

On the other hand, the strong presence of local digital media offerings was also strategized to outwit foreign streaming competitors; bundles of telecommunication plans and OTT subscriptions were offered at lower prices (Dwyer et al. 2018). Hence, Netflix could not successfully enter the market until the successful lobbying and persuasion of local film companies could foster the acceptance of collaborations and coproductions. The shared interests of the international platform and the local film industry overrode the tension among the competitors because Netflix's presence was seen as promoting the general consumption of Korean dramas and movies (Stangarone 2019) which is discussed in the following section.

Western streaming platforms have not been able to enter the Chinese market because, in addition to the commercial pressure from local competitors, the government considers that all audiovisual content is ideological and therefore must be controlled (Fung 2016). First, local SVOD platforms had already gained a significant audience. In 2019, the top three video service platforms in China – Tencent Video, iQiyi and Youku – had secured an active monthly audience of over 40 million users (QuestMobile 2019). In addition, major broadcasters in China ventured into digital media platforms, either through creating their own platforms and applications or through collaboration with conglomerate platforms. Consequently, over 97.1% of central and municipal broadcasters in China had established an online presence (*People.cn* 2019).

Second, foreign streaming platforms are faced with Chinese market regulations. China is known for stringent control over foreign media, both politically and economically (Fung 2016). This is a matter of not only conflict regarding political ideologies but also protection of the country's local players, which are thus sheltered from foreign competition. The Chinese authorities have set a long-established import quota on foreign entertainment content on both private television and public cinema. The State Administration of Press, Publication, Radio, Film and Television (SAPPRFT), which was responsible for censoring media content including digital media, was abolished in 2018 and subordinated to the Communist Party of China Central Committee's Publicity Department. The latter then issued an online streaming quota for foreign audiovisual works; however, the details were not disclosed. Hence, the entry of foreign companies into the Chinese market is difficult, if not *de facto* impossible.

Therefore, foreign streaming companies must rely on local service providers to squeeze into the market. Machkovech (2015) identified two methods used to bypass the blockage – licensing the content to a Chinese distribution platform and establishing a partnership with local counterparts. Netflix initially sought collaboration with Wasu Media Holdings, which is owned by the Internet giant Alibaba's founder Jack Ma. Eventually, in 2017, it sought an alliance with iQiyi, one of China's leading streaming platforms, and then with a subsidiary of the other Internet giant Baidu. However, only two days after the Netflix animated series *BoJack Horseman* began streaming on iQiyi, it was removed by regulators because of its cynical and black humor which was not approved by the Chinese censors (Liu 2017). However, Netflix's reaction to this incident was passive, and it continued to license other content as usual. As Kokas (2020) suggested, the platform company's willingness to comply with Chinese content control demonstrated the tension between upholding creative freedom and meeting the demands of shareholders in expanding into the alluring Chinese market. According to Netflix CEO Reed Hastings, entertainment companies are required to make compromises (Cox 2016) and in practice, apparently, Netflix is willing to follow local regulations, norms and policies.

In summary, the initial entry of Western streaming players was based on a largely unsuccessful "competition strategy" that led to conflicts with local players and regulators. First, local competitors had distinct, long-standing advantages over Western latecomers. Second, China's protective policies and regulations were incontestable barricades to the direct entrance of Netflix. In addition, and perhaps more importantly, the cultural factor of language among Asian audiences weakened the attractiveness of Western content presented in a foreign language. Finally, as Netflix began to blend in with the local media ecology and received the implicit consent of local regulatory authorities, Western streaming platforms such as Netflix sought collaboration with their counterparts in the region.

Toward a Collaborative Partnership

When digital platforms compete in the "red sea," they fight to gain access to a fixed number of audience members. In contrast, Western streaming video platforms explore a "blue ocean" by collaborating with local incumbent broadcasters. In South Korea, at least, the market is expanding. Ted Sarandos, the chief content officer of Netflix, explained that the company did not attempt to distribute Hollywood content worldwide but to bring the content of different countries to a global audience (Spangler 2018). This implies at least two levels of collaboration. The first is the creation of content that targets the audience's interests while leveraging the unique features of the platforms. Second, as a form of partnership or alliance, Western streaming platforms collaborate with local platforms and broadcasters in content distribution.

Netflix has entered into partnership agreements with various local Asian producers, including those in China, Japan, South Korea, Thailand, Taiwan and India, to coproduce localized movies, dramas and animations that are distributed on Netflix. In some cases, the series is screened exclusively or initially on Netflix. Through collaborating with local producers, Netflix creates content that suits the preferences, tastes and languages of local audiences. This strategy also attracts new audiences in addition to audiences that demand English-language content. Some examples include South Korea's television series *Crash Landing on You* (2019), *Sweet Home* (2020) and film *Okja* (2017); Japan's *Alice in Borderland* (2020), *Switched* (2018) and *Erased* (2016); Taiwan's *Nowhere Man* (2019) and *Triad Princess* (2019) and Indonesia's *The Night Comes for Us* (2018). Through such collaborations, Netflix leverages its advantages as a global platform on the local market. Coproductions also enable Netflix to invite the best local talent to create shows that are broadcast worldwide.

In Japan, Netflix's strategy has had an increasing focus on the purchase and commissioning of anime series and motion pictures, taking advantage of the country's fame as the world's animation, comics and games (ACG) powerhouse. This strategy aided the platform company in its ongoing competition with other global SVOD platforms, particularly Disney Plus. As a result, Netflix, the foreign platform, facilitated the reverse flow of Asian content across the globe.

South Korean dramas had already become a widely received genre in Asian countries. Netflix's productions in South Korea also reach audiences in other markets. Between 2015 and 2020, Netflix invested over $700 million in South Korea, including the establishment of two production facilities in proximity to Seoul (James 2021). As previously mentioned, local broadcasting companies in South Korea did not welcome international competitors, whereas Netflix's strategy of coproduction was approved. The influx of capital not only has increased local content production but also has created job opportunities in the local industry. For example, the series *Kingdom*, which was Netflix's first Korean drama, was record-breaking in terms of production costs for non-US original content (Baek 2019). The series has helped to convey Korean content to a global audience through the platform's international reach (Stangarone 2019). Another example is the investment in talent through providing training workshops with local partners in filmmaking and scriptwriting. Previous collaborators include the Korea Animation Producers Association, Thailand's National Federation of Motion Pictures and Malaysia's Digital Economy Corporation. Netflix's experience in Australia provides a parallel example. Despite initial protests against potential competition engendered by Netflix, local producers have benefited from the platforms' commissions and collaborations, which have also provided funding opportunities (Cunningham and Scarlata 2020).

The successful collaboration between Netflix and South Korea's film industry is exemplified by the action-adventure movie *Okja*, which was released in 2017 and directed by South Korean director Bong Joon-Ho, who won an Academy Award for Best Director for *Parasite* (2019). The film was funded by Netflix, created by a transnational production team and distributed internationally on the platform within a month of its premiere at the 2019 Cannes Film Festival, where it competed for the Palme d'Or. When Netflix's logo appeared on the screen, the audience booed to show its disapproval; however, the high quality of the film eventually earned a four-minute standing ovation (Lewis

2020). The audience's initial reaction demonstrated the continuous tension between local media and Netflix productions. Similar reactions occurred in South Korea. *Okja* was boycotted by three major theater chains in South Korea – CGV, Lotte Cinema and Megabox. They considered that Netflix's practice of simultaneously releasing the film online and in theaters was a serious threat to their established business model. The confrontation significantly curtailed the film's local box office receipts, thus shedding light on the local debate regarding the existing monopoly of preexisting players (Lee 2020: 157). At present, based on successful cases in terms of reputation and popularity, it seems that, commercially, Netflix has opened the door for the Korean market. Perhaps it has also taken advantage of the international praise for Korean entertainment by both worldwide distributors and coproducers. However, whether the model of collaboration is acceptable as a long-term strategy for local media and producers remains to be seen.

Last is the tricky case of China. In a context where China retains tight control over foreign cultural content, Netflix's strategic collaboration and licensing of content with Baidu's iQiyi has been akin to walking a tightrope. It seems that the collaboration will continue under a low profile. When Netflix announced its ambitious global expansion strategy in 2016, China was not on the list. More relevant in the long term is China's attitude toward the coproduction of content. This scheme is open to Netflix and many other producers worldwide. In October 2020, the coproduced animation film *Over the Moon* was launched on Netflix and later in China. Although the box office reception in China was not satisfactory, the film was applauded for featuring Chinese culture, which was a very different reception from that of Disney's live-action film *Mulan* (Shen 2020). CNBC wittily commented that Netflix indeed has a strategy in China; it is simply outside China. Instead of attempting to climb over the regulatory barricade, Netflix adopted an expansive strategy to target millions of Mandarin-speaking Chinese audiences outside the country. Netflix has been licensed to distribute popular television series such as *The Untamed* and *Empresses in the Palace*. The series has been well acclaimed internationally, which has contributed to the flow of Asian cultural content into previously unexplored territory.

Digital Entertainment in Unfamiliar Times

Based on the cases of South Korea, Japan and China, evidence suggests that for Netflix and other Western streaming video platforms in Asia, collaboration with local production houses and media is a viable strategy that minimizes opposition and reduces controversy. Coproductions of videos in Asian languages, which are either streamed only on Netflix or shared with incumbent media or platforms, at least in Japan and South Korea, have met with positive audience responses. Although there is no concrete evidence that digital West–Asia coproductions foster diversity or creativity, the ever-increasing popularity of Netflix in Asia implies that new hybrid forms, tastes and aesthetics, to various degrees, have been well received by local audiences who were used to consuming only locally made productions and global cultural products such as Hollywood movies.

From the point of view of local media, in the wake of declining TV viewership in Asia, collaboration with Netflix is a new way of retaining young audiences and increasing viewership and advertising revenues. Hybridized productions also have the potential to open a new avenue for Asian language films to reach Asian and Western audiences in global markets. Such avenues not only create commercial and market value but also possibly enhance Asian cultural values. In shifting from inward-looking strategies, many Asian media could broaden their global reach through Netflix. Hence, as an American platform company, Netflix not only globalizes American culture but also creates "reverse globalization" or contra-flow media, which enables Asian productions to enter the global market.

As a matter of fact, it has been demonstrated that the USA and Britain are driving the phenomenon of "reverse globalization" as a way to tackle the crisis of neoliberalism (Zhang and Gu 2021). It is, however, not a typical case of reverse globalization which people usually refer to – a reverse flow of culture from the East to the West or reverse Americanization (van Elteren 2011). Suffice to say, the East-to-West flow of content is now being seen; it is no longer a one-way flow of content, information or capital. This can be understood as compensation for Asia as a result of Netflix's Asian penetration. But the *de facto* transmission of content is totally in the hands of Netflix with its global platform. Besides, the content made is a hybrid coproduction between Netflix and Asia, not purely Asian-produced cultural content. To be more exact, this "reverse globalization," if anything, should be understood as a reversed flow of cultural content managed by the West or American counterparts without the participation of the East.

Hybrid coproductions have been continued during the global COVID-19 pandemic in 2020 and 2021. While theaters and public performances have been closed, and lockdowns and quarantining have grounded audiences in their homes, the demand for digital streaming entertainment indoors has surged. According to an estimate by Nielsen USA's media team, media consumption had increased by 60%. Statistics in South Korea, Japan, China and Hong Kong indicated strong increases in mobile app use, the need for entertainment and the rise in media advertising revenue (Nielsen 2020; *Nikkei Asia* 2020). In many Asian countries, such as South Korea and Japan, the market requires an increasing amount of content to meet increasing audience demands. Increasing demands for online entertainment, as well as new home-based audiences, have led to an unprecedented opportunity for digital media platforms to invest in innovative collaborations and creative coproductions.

Some nations still have embargoes on Netflix and other Western streaming platforms, although their citizens are exposed to global information. It is likely that these governments will be subjected to pressure "from below." In early 2021, for instance, Chinese authorities cracked down on the country's allegedly largest copyright piracy site, YYeTs. Such sites provide free access to copyrighted video content, and they are financed primarily through advertisements. Despite its illegality, YYeTs attracted a significant amount of traffic because it carried content that was not available elsewhere. Netizens have raised a perceptive question: If foreign content had been legally available in the first place, they would not have to resort to infringing and illegitimate venues. This argument is perhaps a clear call for authorities to allow the distribution of foreign content. Instead of forbidding them, allowing collaboration between Western digital content platforms and their local counterparts might be a temporary, if not a synergic, means of responding to audience needs.

References

Adgate, B. (2021) "As Their Ratings Drop, TV Networks Fault Nielsen. Media Researchers Weigh in," *Forbes*, 20 April.

Applify (2020) "COVID-19: Global Impact & Mobile App Usage Statistics." 13 May.

Baek, B.Y. (2019) "Netflix to Invest More in Korean Content," *Korea Times*, 24 January.

CBInsights (2018) "Google's Growing Prominence in Global Telecommunications," 7 May.

Christian, A. (2012) "Beyond Big Video," *Continuum*, 26(1): 73–87.

Choudhury, S. (2020) "Netflix Bets Big on Asia as It Sees 'Significant Potential' in These Markets," *CNBC*, 8 November.

Cox, J. (2016) "Netflix Won't Commit to Leaving Its Content Uncensored Around the World," *The Verge*, 6 January.

Cunningham, S. and Scarlata, A. (2020) "New Forms of Internationalization? The Impact of Netflix in Australia," *Media International Australia*, 177(1): 149–64.

Dwyer, T., Lee, H. and Hutchinson, J. (2018) "Comparing Digital Media Industries in South Korea and Australia: The Case of Netflix Take-up," *International Journal of Communication*, 12: 4553–72.

Freden, R. (2015) "Conflict in the Networks: How Internet Service Providers Have Shifted from Partners to Adversaries," *Hastings Communications and Entertainment Law Journal*, 38(1): 1 January.

Fung, A. (2013) *Asian Popular Culture: The Global (Dis)continuity*, London: Routledge.

Fung, A. (2016) "Strategizing for Creative Industries in China: Contradictions and Tension in Nation Branding," *International Journal of Communication*, 10: 3004–21.

Gomez-Uribe, C. and Hunt, N. (2015) "The Netflix Recommender System: Algorithms, Business Value and Innovation," *ACM Transactions on Management Information Systems*, 6(4): 1–19.

Hsu, W.Y., Liu, Y.L. and Chen, Y.L. (2016) *The Impact of Newly Emerging Media on the Cable TV Industry*, Taipei: Taiwan Communications Society.

Iyengar, R. (2021) "He May Hold the Winning Ticket in Tech and Silicon Valley Knows It," *CNN Business*, 24 February.

James, S. (2021) "Netflix Ups Production Investment in Korea," *S&P Global Market Intelligence*, 7 January.

KCC (2019) *Annual Report 2018*, Seoul: Korean Communications Commission.

Kim, E.J. (2018) "Korean Broadcasters Pressuring LG U+ to Sever Ties with Netflix," *Business Korea*, 22, November.

Kokas, A. (2020) "Chilling Netflix," *Information, Communication & Society*, 23(3): 407–19.

Lee, D.H. (2020) "Transnational Film Project in the Changing Media Ecology," in D.Y. Jin and W. Su (eds) *Asia-Pacific Film Co-productions*, London: Routledge.

Lee, S.H. and Kim, M. (2018) "Netflix Moves into Korean Living Rooms by Joining Up with LG U+," *Pulse*, 15, November.

Levy, A. (2021) "Netflix is Flexing Its Global Scale in Japan," *The Motley Fool*, 1 April.

Lewis, L. (2020) "Korea Rides Netflix Wave to Win at the Oscars," *Financial Times*, 11 February.

Limov, B. (2020) "Click It, Binge It, Get Hooked: Netflix and the Growing US Audience for Foreign Content," *International Journal of Communication*, 14: 6304–23.

Liu, C. (2017) "How the New-censored 'Bojack Horseman' Became a Voice for a Generation of Disenfranchized Chinese," *Thebeijinger*, 30 June.

Lobato, R. (2018) "Rethinking International TV Flows Research in the Age of Netflix," *Television and New Media*, 19(3): 241–56.

Machkovech, S. (2015) "Netflix Opens Up about Plans to Launch Streaming Video Service in China," *Ars Technica*, 15 May.

Merikivi, J., Bragge, J., Scornavacca, E. and Verhagen, T. (2020) "Binge-Watching Serialized Video Content," *Television and New Media*, 21(7): 697–711.

Nielsen (2020) "The Impact of COVID-19 on Media Consumption across North Asia," 25 March.

Nikkei Asia (2020) "Japan's TV Stations Feel Coronavirus Blow Despite Audience Surge," 19 May.

Park, E.A. (2017) "Why the Networks Can't Beat Netflix," *Digital Policy, Regulation and Governance*, 19(1): 21–23.

People.cn (2019) "2018 Chinese Media Integration Index," 26 March.

Perks, L. (2015) *Media Marathoning: Immersions in Morality*, Lanham: Lexington Books.

Phonetic House (2020) "The Decline in Television," 22 July.

QuestMobile (2019) "QuestMobile Half-yearly Report 2019 on Chinese Mobile Internet," 27 August.

Rosati, A. (2019) "Korean SK Telecom and Leading Broadcasting Firms Gang Up Against Netflix and Launch a New Streaming Platform," *Asian Movie Pulse*, 19 January.

Shen, X. (2020) "Netflix's *Over the Moon* Praised in China But Bigger Box-Office Bomb Than Disney's *Mulan*," *South China Morning Post*, 17 November.

Song, S.H. (2019) "5G to Change Korea's Telecom Industry Landscape in 2019," *Korea Herald*, 1 January.

Spangler, T. (2018) "Netflix Content Boss Ted Sarandos Downplays Looming Threat from Disney, Warner Media," *Variety*, 3 December.

Stangarone, T. (2019) "How Netflix is Reaching South Korean Entertainment," *The Diplomat*, 29 April.

Statista (2021) "Netflix's Global Revenue, by Region," 18 March.

Thorson, K. and Wells, C. (2016) "Curated Flows: A Framework for Mapping Media Exposure in the Digital Age," *Communication Theory*, 26(3): 309–28.

van Elteren, M. (2011) "Cultural Globalization and Transnational Flow of Things American," in P. Pachura (ed) *The Systemic Dimension of Globalization*, London: Intechopen.

Zhang, C. and Gu, H. (2021) "Reverse Globalization – The Crisis of Neoliberalism," a paper in International Political Science Association.

Zhu, Z. (2019) "Mass Media Industry of Japan: Is 'Decline but Not in Recession' Or Trap of Mature Market?," *Contemporary Economy of Japan*, 223(1): 33–44.

2

THE SHIFTING TERRAIN OF ASIA'S TELEVISION LANDSCAPE

Kalyani Chadha and Anandam Kavoori

In our previous work "Media Imperialism Revisited: Some Findings from the Asian Case" (Chadha and Kavoori 2000), we explored the relevance of the concept of media imperialism in Asia against the backdrop provided by the initial emergence of satellite television in the region. Analyzing how nations across the continent engaged with the growth of foreign television content delivered by satellite-based services such as Star TV that had been established in the early 1990s, we made the case that though the forces of media globalization had brought Western media programming into the continent on a large scale for the first time, local media landscapes had resisted being overwhelmed by it due to the workings of a complex trifecta represented by national gate-keeping regimes, competition from local media as well as audience preference for culturally relevant programming. In other words, we argued that even though contemporary political discourse all over Asia was replete with references to the grave dangers posed by Western media, there was little empirical evidence to support pervasive assertions regarding the destruction of indigenous cultural subjectivities and media production.

In this chapter, we revisit this terrain again, justified on the grounds that Asian television landscapes are now more accessible to transborder media flows than ever before, with satellite television service availability and penetration increasing steadily all over the continent, including in countries such as Myanmar, Mongolia and Vietnam that have come to represent the newest frontiers for growth and expansion (Galace 2012). We begin by re-examining the factors – national gate-keeping policies, local competition and audience preferences – that we originally identified as key to limiting foreign, mainly Western, media flows, in order to evaluate their relevance in current Asian mediascapes, followed by tracing larger trends related to media flows in the region.

DOI: 10.4324/9781003130628-4

From Fortress to Sluice Gates? The State of National Gate-Keeping Regimes

The onset of the most recent phase of media globalization that began in the 1990s saw Asian nation-states resolute in their opposition to transnational broadcasting, which they typically sought to limit through an arsenal of "convergent" policy measures aimed at what Schlesinger (1997) has called "communicative boundary maintenance." Typical examples of such measures which included explicit bans on foreign programming and satellite dishes, equity restrictions on foreign media investment, ceilings on media imports, as well as active support of indigenously produced programming, were established all over the continent in response to the incursions of satellite television. However, these regulatory restrictions, so ubiquitous at the turn of the century, are now neither universally manifest nor consistently enforced. Indeed, as things stand, Asian nations that were historically united in their adoption of a fortress-like approach to foreign media inflows now have governments engaging in variable and in many cases, limited degrees of gate-keeping vis-à-vis transnational broadcasting.

While these efforts can be located on a continuum that ranges from a guarded stance to minimal regulation, the *de facto* thrust is in the direction of decontrol, even in countries that are situated on the less open end of the policy spectrum. In Vietnam, for instance, although the government limits the use of satellite dishes and has mandated that all foreign channels on pay-TV be translated into Vietnamese to ensure that content does not violate the country's press and advertising laws (Brummitt 2013), it has made little effort to actually implement these regulations that were introduced in 2011 and later even exempted foreign news channels from the translation requirement altogether (Brown 2013). Similarly, China, while prohibiting private ownership of satellite dishes, has not made a concerted effort to enforce rules against satellite dish ownership at the local level, with the result 56–60 million dishes are being used by Chinese citizens to obtain access to a variety of international channels and programs (Italian Trade Commission 2011). Moreover, although it continues to disallow imported programming during prime time and limits imported content to no more than 25% of a channel's daily offerings (Jacobs 2012), China has not only granted "landing rights" to selected Western media companies but also permitted specific types of joint ventures between domestic and foreign media companies and even allowed the latter to acquire minority ownership stakes in domestic media companies since its entry into the WTO (Huang 2007; Italian Trade Commission 2011).

Parallel trends are visible in Singapore and Malaysia where, despite continuing censorship of content deemed inappropriate by the government (Ang 2007; Wagstaff 2010), there are fewer restrictions on foreign media inflows than at any time in the past. For example, Singapore, which aspires to become a regional media hub, has made a concerted move to encourage foreign direct investment in the media sector, encourage international co-productions and create a "more conducive regulatory culture environment and culture" as a part of the Media Fusion initiative which is aimed at turning Singapore into a global media city (MDA 2012). Neighboring Malaysia where broadcasting was once entirely state controlled, in addition to allowing the expansion of Astro Malaysia, a privately held satellite pay television service which transmits content from transnational broadcasters (Sadiq 2012), now permits some foreign direct investment in cable and satellite operations (US Department of State 2012).

Declines in gate-keeping are also manifest in countries where state control has been less overt in recent years. South Korea, for instance, has committed to decreasing long-standing TV content quotas, increasing the allowable content from a single country and locking all other Korean content requirements at the least restrictive level as a part of a trade agreement with the United States (US Trade Representative 2009). Likewise, Taiwan has reduced subsidies for domestic productions and lowered long-standing domestic content requirements for cable channels (Chang 2013), while in Thailand, international channels will in all likelihood be exempt from the licensing criteria and procedures that are developed by the government (CASBAA 2012a).

Decontrol is also visible in post-reform Indonesia which has not only seen the growth of numerous private broadcasters offering both terrestrial and satellite services that carry a variety of international channels and foreign content but also has emerged as a major potential market for international pay-TV companies (Holmes 2012). According to the Cable and Satellite Broadcasters Association of Asia (CASBAA), the leading trade group for cable and satellite service providers in Asia, Indonesia is in fact characterized by a "positive" regulatory environment in that state subsidies to domestic broadcasters have been reduced and restrictive localization regulations have not been implemented with regard to pay-TV which remains largely unregulated in terms of its business models or program offerings (CASBAA 2012b). Additionally, the government has also agreed to open the terrestrial broadcasting sector to some foreign equity participation (IIPA 2010).

But it is in India that traditional regulatory bulwarks aimed at combating foreign Western media seem to have been most radically undermined. This shift is manifested in new policies aimed at easing previous restrictions on uplinking, service provision and foreign direct investment in the broadcasting sector. Whereas previously only Indian-owned satellite channels could uplink or downlink from within the country itself, now any channel, irrespective of ownership, can do so. Moreover, foreign equity participation in cable networks has been increased from 30% to 49%, with a proposal to increase it to 100% (CASBAA 2013) while 100% foreign equity is permitted in entertainment media companies (Ministry of Commerce and Industry 2013).

The changed regulatory situation in India is perhaps best summed up by the Indian Department of Commerce and Industry website which states that "India has one of the most liberal investment regimes in the world, with a conducive foreign direct investment (FDI) environment and the media and entertainment industry has significantly benefited from this regime" (Ministry of Commerce and Industry 2013). The Indian government has also adopted a low key approach to content regulation so that the content quotas that were once envisaged as limiting foreign programming have never been implemented. In fact, many of the country's 600 channels are owned by international conglomerates and transmit a range of imported programs (Deloitte 2012) – in what would seem to be a comprehensive retreat from the gate-keeping that previously defined the country's broadcasting policy regime.

From Competition to Collaboration?
Changing Media Markets

The wide-ranging move away from restrictive media regulation, reflecting the shifting engagement of Asian nations with the forces of globalization in the post-WTO era, has also had implications for both media markets and entities in Asia. In our previous work (Chadha and Kavoori 2000) we had argued that although Western media organizations sought to gain entry into Asian markets in the 1990s, indigenous media outlets such as Hong Kong-based TVBI or India's ZEE TV, which benefited from access to local and regional markets, connections with political elites and the ability to provide audiences with culturally and linguistically "proximate" programming, had constituted a competitive counterforce to them. This scenario, in which "domestic" media companies appeared to be pitted against "foreign" outlets, has, however, been transformed in recent years with the significant expansion of partnerships between Asian media producers and Western media companies. In China alone, more than 300 deals totaling almost $10.3 billion have been announced since 2009 (Deng 2013).

These growing alliances between global media companies and Asian media organizations – which have gathered considerable momentum in the last decade or so and include a range of countries – have essentially evolved due to changes in the situational calculus of both indigenous and foreign media producers. Originally, transnational corporations had operated on the assumption that their traditional comparative advantage in international media markets would enable them to enter and dominate Asian markets with relative ease. But this goal proved significantly more challenging than anticipated. Indeed, companies like News Corp that were among the early few to look to Asia rapidly discovered that not only were they hampered by a variety of regulatory mechanisms, but also that the very idea of a pan-Asian television, built on economies of scale, was unworkable given the diversity of the continent. Moreover, unlike Eastern Europe, where the comparatively sudden transition to a market system and the absence of established market-oriented media organizations enabled foreign players to leverage their capital and expertise to develop local partnerships and political alliances that facilitated market entry (Sparks 2003), Asia's media trajectory has evolved on different lines. Not only has the transition to the market been significantly slower but also the easing of gate-keeping mechanisms has proved to be an uneven and far more closely managed process. Furthermore, in keeping with their dirigiste roots, national governments in the region have continued to play a role in the market by shaping media policies aimed at supporting local players and developing national creative economies capable of succeeding in global markets (Flew 2013).

Such barriers to market entry in Asia combined with the growing realization that "local knowledge" is essential to successfully negotiating the region's complex political and economic environments and satisfying audience preferences for local/regional content have gradually led Western media organizations to recalibrate their independent stance. The result has been a move away from stand-alone approaches in favor of local partnerships. While some collaborations emerged early such as News Corp's investment in China's Phoenix Satellite TV (Huang 2007), these alliances have since multiplied, involving different players and assuming a variety of organizational and financial forms. These include ventures like the ones between Fremantle Media Asia and Japanese Fuji TV Network and Endemol and Astro Malaysia to co-produce and co-develop new format-based programming for Asian markets; between the Singapore Media Authority and various international media producers or the strategic partnership linking China-based Shanghai Media Group (SMG) and CNBC Asia under which the two companies will exchange content and split advertising revenue from shared programming (O'Neill 2012). In yet another variation, DreamWorks Animation, the Shanghai Media Group and China Conglomerates (in which the Chinese government has a large stake) have teamed up to establish a studio and produce films and content for Chinese television (Verrier 2012). Where possible, some Western companies have also sought to make direct investments in media markets as in the case of India's Colors and ZEE Turner channels, which are jointly owned by local conglomerates and Viacom and Time Warner, respectively (FICCI-KPMG 2011). In India, thus aside from the homegrown ZEE TV, all the major networks in the dominant Hindi language television sector are either owned by or joint ventures with Western media corporations.

For their part, local players who were once deeply wary of being edged out by foreign, notably Western, competitors have come to view such relationships favorably. Indeed, there is a widespread recognition in the region that while local conglomerates possess clear advantages in terms of their ability to produce culturally relevant programming, they often lack adequate financial resources as well as technical and production knowledge. To them, global conglomerates consequently represent not only potential sources of capital but also the opportunity to obtain the critical operational know-how that they require in order to position themselves effectively in regional/global markets. And it is such indigenous players, anxious to turn their content into "tradable culture" (Lim 2005), who have often played a critical role in lobbying Asian governments to introduce policies designed to foster international media partnerships.

Local but Formatted? Audiences and Cultural Consumption

While both gate-keeping regimes and media markets in Asia have come to be characterized by visible shifts over the past two decades, on the surface at least audience dynamics in Asia appear to have remained comparatively stable, in that large majorities of audiences continue to privilege local and regional content as they did following the introduction of satellite television. This is certainly reflected in cultural consumption patterns across the continent, whether in the case of India where Bollywood-related content dominates both large and small screens (Chadha and Kavoori 2012) or China where locally produced reality shows and Korean dramas are among the most-watched shows or the ubiquitous "sinetron" or soap operas in Indonesia (Chua 2012). In other words, television continues to be "tied to local and national cultures" (Waisbord 2004: 360) and there remain various types of barriers or "lacunae" that make foreign content less attractive to audiences (Rohn 2009). Such resistance does not, however, appear to be manifest with regard to imported formats.

As defined by Keane and Moran (2004), formats "constitute processes of systematization of difference within repetition" and involve an adaptive reconfiguring of television programs in which they are localized in ways that combine culturally specific elements with their original structure and visual look and feel. Historically, the rise of formats can be understood in terms of structural shifts such as the deregulation and liberalization of television markets and the emergence of multi-channel environments that created new demands and opportunities for programming. With such changes making television markets increasingly competitive, broadcasters sought ways to avoid the inherent uncertainties of the media market; format-driven programming offered a solution to this problem, both domestically and in the international markets that began to gain significance in the 1970s and 1980s. The recognition of the potential of successful formats as low risk, easily reproducible and saleable programming eventually combined with two globalization-fueled developments. The first was the growing connectivity between television systems that encouraged programming trends and business practices to move beyond national boundaries, while the second was the desire of global media companies to circumvent protectionist audio-visual policies by finding alternatives to the "finished" or "canned" foreign programming that the former sought to limit (Waisbord 2004). The result was the emergence of formats as the basis of an expansive transnational trade valued at over $4 billion (Chalaby 2012).

With programs flowing mainly from the West to the East (albeit with occasional contra-flows, most notably from Japan), Asia has emerged as a major market for formats, complete with industry organizations such as the Singapore-based Asia Television Forum and Market (ATF) as well as impresarios like Michel Rodrigue, all geared to facilitating interactions between local and international media broadcasters and producers. In China alone, 35 new formats have been licensed since 2002 (Waller 2013). Formats have also been licensed in countries ranging from India and Malaysia to Indonesia, Singapore, Thailand and Vietnam. Typically, the formats that tend to find favor in Asia are various types of game and reality shows based on the so-called "super formats" such as *Survivor, Big Brother* and *Idols* that tend to be "culturally odorless," in that they lack distinct cultural or national markers (Iwabuchi 2002). That is to say, they represent a new kind of localization – that one could term "formatization" which moves seamlessly between global (typically Western) genres and local cultural preferences.

Reproduced under licensing deals with local broadcasters or by global format producers like Endemol and Fremantle Media, these shows, which include *Your Face Sounds Familiar, The Money Drop, Step Right Up, Deal or No Deal* and variations of the Idol franchise, have been "domesticated" via the insertion of both linguistic and culturally specific elements. In India, for example, format-based reality shows such as *Indian Idol* or *Kaun Banega Crorepati* (the Indian version of *Who Wants to Be a Millionaire*) draw on Bollywood for hosts, judges and content (Chadha and Kavoori 2012). In China, musical reality shows have been adapted to fulfill the audience interest in results by reducing the number of participants in one-hour programs compared to the original formats (Xi 2011). Similarly, in Indonesia, *Big Brother* avoids sexual themes, focusing instead on emotional issues like the homesickness of participants and in Malaysia, Endemol has only produced *Deal or No Deal* in Chinese, to avoid offending the sensibilities of the Muslim majority who are opposed to the gambling it implies (Miles 2012).

While such "localization" strategies reduce the so-called "cultural discount" of format-based shows and potentially render them open to varied engagement by audiences, such shows, as Waisbord (2004) points out, by no means imply the growth of cultural diversity. In fact, television schedules in many parts of Asia, ranging from India and China to Indonesia and the Philippines, manifest little variety, seemingly colonized by format-driven reality shows, that although culturally and linguistically flavored, nevertheless offer deeply limited representations of social reality, focusing as they do on the values of individual profit and consumption.

Emerging Trends

Mapping contemporary television landscapes in Asia reveals a complex and heterogeneous reality – one that combines national variations (particularly with regard to degrees of integration with the global television system) and calls into question monolithic notions of an "Asian" media system, with more pervasive trends that simultaneously characterize the region. Striking among these emergent trends seems to be the discursive decline of the notion of media imperialism, once the lynchpin of the discourse surrounding transnational media flows in the region. Indeed, previously, governments all over the region defined border-eroding television flows as a serious existential threat to "Asian" identity and culture and political leaders in countries ranging from China and India to Malaysia and Singapore underscored the need to restrict what many at the time dubbed, "the invasion from the skies." Similar concerns were also reflected in the pronouncements of the Association of Southeast Asian Nations (ASEAN), which called for the need to formalize "a united response to the phenomenon of cultural globalization in order to protect and advance cherished Asian values and traditions which are being threatened by the proliferation of Western media content" (Coates 1998).

But whereas a profound cultural anxiety coupled with a desire to safeguard the integrity of closed national spaces from external influences clearly dominated early responses to media globalization, the current discourse in the region represents a decisive pivoting away from this position. In fact, ideas such as "media imperialism" and "cultural pollution," which evolved out of the anti-colonial sentiments that have characterized many Asian nations, find little public expression at present. In fact, statements of the type made by then leaders such as Malaysia's Mahathir Mohamad, Singapore's Lee Kuan Yew or even Indian nationalists, who engaged in persistent polemical attacks against Western media and programming (Chadha and Kavoori 2000), are now rare.

This, of course, is not to say that concerns associated with Western media inflows are wholly absent. China, for example, has argued before the WTO that "cultural goods and services" represent "vectors of cultural identity and values" that "justify the implementation of specific regulatory measures" (Timmer 2009) while its former President Hu Jintao accused "international forces" of trying to Westernize and divide China "by using ideology and culture" (*Bloomberg* 2012). But not only are such rhetorical flourishes infrequent but also perhaps more importantly, they have not become the basis of attempts to mobilize a common "Asian" cultural identity against Western efforts at cultural colonization as they did in the late 1990s when satellite television first emerged (Ang 2001).

Instead, it would appear that Western television programming, once viewed as a key dimension of the cultural contestation that previously defined media globalization debates in Asia, does not appear to be similarly significant in contemporary discussions. In other words, the West vs. the Rest paradigm that previously dominated media globalization debates in Asia seems to have little resonance within public discourse. Certainly, it does not appear to rouse the type of intense moral or cultural concerns that it did at the outset of this current phase of media globalization. Instead, such concerns often tend to be centered regionally. In the Middle East, for instance, it is Lebanese-produced entertainment programs, notably reality television shows, that have raised the ire of religious and political leaders (Kraidy 2012). In countries like Pakistan and Afghanistan, it is Indian programming that inspires moral panics, while in China it is the fear of South Korea's impact on the local television industry that has motivated the government to crack down on television imports (Jacobs 2012). In Asian contexts, arguably, the "Other" is thus no longer automatically Western in nature.

Underpinning this development are clearly larger shifts in the continent's televisual landscapes. For one, the emergence and growth of new media all over the continent has meant that the regulatory center of gravity has shifted.

As a result, the locus of governmental control seems to be increasingly directed online, with states engaged (albeit with questionable success) in monitoring Internet content, both cultural and political. Evidence of such efforts can be seen in governments seeking to ban or limit access to pornography in the case of many South East Asian nations, the Indian government's periodic moves to remove politically objectionable videos from YouTube or the Chinese attempts to censor micro blogs.

Put differently, while new media are perceived as posing a challenge, satellite television, once a threatening novelty, has acquired a taken for granted status with the proliferation of both channels as well as the substantial expansion of regional television flows, fueled by the growth of regional media alliances. Examples of such alliances include Hong Kong-based TVBI's efforts to enter the Chinese domestic market via a joint venture with the Shanghai Media Group (*China Times* 2012); the Smart Alliance between six commercial broadcasters from ASEAN countries to collaborate on the development of content, marketing strategies and technology (MediaCorp 2009) or ZEE TV's sales of dubbed Indian programming to countries in the Middle East (*Deccan Herald* 2012).

Thus, even though media flows continue to be disproportionately dominated by the West, particularly the USA on a global scale, media products developed in "media capitals" based in the South (Curtin 2003) have become increasingly visible in Asia. The growing traffic in such cultural products, which include elements ranging from Bollywood films to dramas produced in South Korea, Hong Kong and Thailand, not only involves a plurality of players, multi-directional flows and regional powerhouses such as India, South Korea and Japan (Thussu 2006), but also reflects the evolution of what have been called "Easternization, or South-South flows" (Nederveen Pieterse 2006). According to Chua (2012), numerous examples of such regionalized media flows are currently visible in Asia, such as those linking Thailand to countries like Myanmar, Cambodia and Laos as well as those connecting India to countries like Pakistan, Afghanistan and the Middle East. In fact, the Middle East constitutes a new and vibrant manifestation of regionalized media flows that have resulted in the creation of a transnational pan-Arab market (Kraidy 2012: 190), of a type that was imagined but never actually materialized in other parts of Asia.

In the Asian context, it is evident that as "capital and cultural products from peripheral countries crisscross and realign in the region, defined by common cultural linguistic and historical connections" (Kim 2008: 4), Western programming has not only been increasingly *de-centered* from television schedules but also evacuated from discourses about television. But though Western program imports have experienced a loss of programmatic and discursive significance, ironically, globalization and the market-oriented media model associated with it have become *normalized*, ideologically speaking, across much of Asia. While this process had begun to develop at the beginning of the millennium in the form of the growing commercialization of broadcasting in Asia and resultant challenges to public broadcasting, they have since gathered powerful momentum.

This is evidenced in the fact that nation-states which previously perceived the broadcast media as key elements of post-colonial nation-building and employed them for purposes ranging from the dissemination of development strategies and educational messages to national integration have moved to adopt a range of neoliberally inclined policy measures (Held et al. 1999). These include the dismantling of state-owned or public broadcasting monopolies, the creation of dual broadcasting systems by opening the broadcast sector to private operators and perhaps most significantly, the easing of restrictions on the presence of foreign media both in the form of direct investment and content provision on a hitherto unprecedented scale (Chadha and Kavoori 2012).

In fact, Asia has come to be characterized by a reworking of the intimate linkages between political and economic power that characterize the present form of capitalism. In this reworking, nation-states recognizing the potential of national media industries as both economic drivers and sources of soft power have backed away from their historic and reflexively protectionist stance toward broadcasting and instead come to play the role of "enablers," moving actively to assist their media industries to succeed in global market places (Flew 2013). Consequently, the region is increasingly marked by a consistent pattern of what we would like to term "state-sponsored marketization" – a role that straddles policy, product development and indirectly audience tastes. This institutionalization of the primacy of the market, embodied in this stance, has put television systems in Asia firmly on the path to greater integration with the global system. An integration that is not predicated on imported content flows, but rather on shifts in terms of media structures, policies and production processes that are being transformed on lines that closely parallel Western trajectories. Lost in this ongoing process are both the discourse of media imperialism and the institutional politics (e.g. policy statements, quotas, gate-keeping) that resonated with the first wave of satellite television – a reflexive reliance on historically grounded post-independence protectionism – and a 1990's resurgent nationalism. But while the old paradigm and policy responses arising out of it are evidently in a state of decline, what is emerging in its place? This remains unclear. Are we witnessing the first wave of a new kind of global media order? One that assumes multiple centers is aggressively "post-Western" (with new "soft power" centers in Mumbai, Seoul and Rio) but nevertheless speaks in a language that is unproblematically grounded in concerns of consumption, access and consumer identity (rather than those focused on the national or third world subject)? If this is indeed a new world media order, its current shape is coming together before our eyes – and while its ultimate shape still indeterminable, the emerging contours may well represent the continued and familiar dominance of capital and market forces.

Acknowledgments

This chapter is an updated version of a previous publication: Chadha, K. and Kavoori, A. (2015) "The New Normal: From Media Imperialism to Market Liberalization – Asia's Shifting Television Landscapes," *Media, Culture and Society*, 37(3): 479–92.

References

Ang, I. (2001) "Desperately Guarding Borders," in S. Yao (ed) *House of Glass: Culture, Modernity and the State in Southeast Asia*, Singapore: Institute of Southeast Asian Studies.

Ang, P.H. (2007) "Singapore Media," a report for Hans Bredow Media Institute, Hamburg.

Bloomberg (2012) "Hu Says West is Trying to Divide China by Using Ideology, Culture," 2 January.

Brown, M. (2013) "Miscommunication: Vietnam's New Rules for TV Channels," *The Diplomat*, 19 May.

Brummitt, C. (2013) "Vietnam Provider Drops Foreign News TV Channels," *Associated Press*, 13 May.

CASBAA (2012a) *Briefing Paper on Landing Rights in Thailand*, Hong Kong: CASBAA – Asia Video Industry Association.

CASBAA (2012b) *Regulating for Growth 2012*, Hong Kong: CASBAA – Asia Video Industry Association.

CASBAA (2013) *Response to the Telecom Regulatory Authority of India: Consultation on Foreign Direct Investment in the Broadcasting Sector in India*, Hong Kong: CASBAA – Asia Video Industry Association.

Chadha, K. and Kavoori, A. (2000) "Media Imperialism Revisited: Some Findings from the Asian Case," *Media, Culture and Society*, 22(4): 415–32.

Chadha, K. and Kavoori, A. (2012) "Mapping India's Television Landscape: Constitutive Dimensions and Emerging Issues," *South Asia History and Culture*, 3(4): 591–602.

Chadha, K. and Kavoori, A. (2015) "The New Normal: From Media Imperialism to Market Liberalization – Asia's Shifting Television Landscapes," *Media, Culture and Society*, 37(3): 479–92.

Chalaby, J. (2012) "Producing TV Content in a Globalized Intellectual Property Market," *Journal of Media Business Studies*, 9(3): 19–39.

Chang, S.C. (2013) "Taiwan's Digital TV Industry Needs Urgent Support," *Taiwan Today*, 3 March.

China Times (2012) "Hong Kong Media Group Targets Chinese Market Through Joint Venture," 26 March.

Chua, B.H. (2012) *Structure, Audience and Soft Power in East Asian Pop Culture*, Hong Kong: Hong Kong University Press.

Coates, S. (1998) "ASEAN Seeks Greater Say in Information Age," *Agence France Presse*, 14 July.

Curtin, M. (2003) "Media Capital," *International Journal of Cultural Studies*, 6(2): 202–28.

Deccan Herald (2012) "ZEE to Invest $100 Million in New Arabic Channel," 11 September.

Deloitte (2012) *White Paper on Media Assets in India*, New York: Deloitte Touche Tohmatsu.

Deng, C. (2013) "Chinese Media Investor Bruno Wu Plans $500 Million Private-Equity Fund," *Wall Street Journal*, 21 August.

FICCI-KPMG (2011) *Hitting the High Notes: Indian Media and Entertainment Industry Report 2011*, New Delhi: FICCI-KPMG.

Flew, T. (2013) "Transforming Policy: Between Media Policy and Digital Content Strategies in East Asia," a paper presented to *Anticipating the Wave: The Transformation of East Asian Media Industries*, Queensland University of Technology.

Galace, P. (2012) "Strong Demand Driving the Asia-Pacific Satellite Market," *Satellite Markets*, 4 June.

Held, D., McGrew, A., Goldblatt, D. and Perraton, J. (1999) *Global Transformations: Politics, Economics and Culture*, Cambridge: Polity.

Holmes, M. (2012) "IMTV CEO Talks Satellite Pay-TV Prospects in Indonesia," *Satellite Today*, 30 October.

Huang, C. (2007) "Trace Stones in Crossing the River: Media Structural Change in Post WTO-China," *International Communication Gazette*, 69: 413–30.

IIPA (2010) *International Intellectual Property Alliance Special 301 Report on Indonesia*, Washington DC: International Intellectual Property Alliance.

Italian Trade Commission (2011) *China Television Industry Market Report*, London: Italian Trade Commission.

Iwabuchi, K. (2002) *Recentering Globalization: Popular Culture and Japanese Transnationalism*, Durham: Duke University Press.

Jacobs, A. (2012) "China Limits Foreign-Made Programs," *New York Times*, 12 February.

Keane, M. and Moran, A. (2004) *Television across Asia: Formats, Television Industries and Globalization*, London: Routledge.

Kim, Y. (2008) *Media Consumption and Everyday Life in Asia*, London: Routledge.

Kraidy, M. (2012) "The Rise of Transnational Media Systems: Implications of Pan-Arab Media for Comparative Research," in D. Hallin and P. Mancini (eds) *Comparing Media Systems beyond the Western World*, Cambridge: Cambridge University Press.

Lim, W. (2005) *Formatting and Change in East Asian Television Industries: Media Globalization and Regional Dynamics*, PhD. Thesis, Queensland University of Technology.

MDA (2012) *Transforming Singapore into a Global Media City*, Singapore: Media Development Authority.

MediaCorp (2009) *ASEAN Broadcasters Form Smart Alliance*, Singapore: MediaCorp.

Miles, E. (2012) *The Future of Television: Linking Local Cultures in a Global World*, Master's Thesis, Drexel University.

Ministry of Commerce and Industry (2013) *Consolidated Circular on FDI*, Delhi: Ministry of Commerce and Industry.

O'Neill, M. (2012) "CNBC Asia and SMG Seal Alliance," *South China Morning Post*, 12 August.

Nederveen Pieterse, J. (2006) "Globalization as Hybridization," in M. Durham and D. Kellner (eds) *Media and Cultural Studies*, Malden: Blackwell.

Rohn, U. (2009) *Cultural Barriers to the Success of Foreign Media Content*, New York: Peter Lang.

Sadiq, J. (2012) "Astro Share Price Falling on Costs: Rules and Future Competition," *The Malaysian Insider*, 26 October.

Schlesinger, P. (1997) "From Cultural Defense to Political Culture," *Media, Culture and Society*, 19(3): 369–91.

Sparks, C. (2003) "Are the Western Media Really That Interested in China?," *Javnost*, 10(4): 93–108.

Thussu, D. (2006) "Contra-Flow in Global Media: An Asian Perspective," a paper presented at *Media in Asia: Aspirations, Choices and Realities*, AMIC Annual Conference, Malaysia.

Timmer, J. (2009) "China's New Media Rules Slammed by WTO as Trade Violations," *Ars Technica*, 12 August.

US Department of State (2012) *2012 Investment Climate Statement – Malaysia*, Washington DC: US Department of State.

US Trade Representative (2009) *Summary of the US – Korea Free Trade Agreement*, Washington DC: Office of the United States Trade Representative.

Verrier, R. (2012) "DreamWorks Animation Unveils Plan to Build Studio in China," *Los Angeles Times*, 18 February.

Wagstaff, J. (2010) "Southeast Asian Media: Patterns of Production and Consumption, A Survey of National Media in 10 Countries of Southeast Asia," Open Society Foundations, 12 February.

Waisbord, S. (2004) "McTV: Understanding the Global Popularity of Television Formats," *Television and New Media*, 5(4): 359–83.

Waller, E. (2013) "China's Demand for Formats Explodes at MIPTV," *The Format People*, 25 April.

Xi, Z. (2011) "TV Stations Gobble Up European Formats," *China Daily*, 10 June.

3

POST-BOLLYWOODIZATION

The Rise of Individualized Entertainment in India

Shanti Kumar

"Digital Platform is the new silver screen," *India Today* (2020), a leading English language magazine, declared on Twitter. The tweet linked to a video featuring five film stars who made big comebacks in 2020 not through the traditional route of blockbusters in popular Hindi film industry, known as Bollywood, but through digital entertainment on streaming platforms such as Amazon, Hotstar, Netflix and ZEE5. The Bollywood stars featured in the video include Sushmita Sen, Abhishek Bachchan, Bobby Deol and Karishma Kapoor. In June 2020, after a ten-year hiatus, former Miss Universe Sen made a successful comeback in a web series on Disney-Hotstar Plus titled *Aarya* that is based on a Dutch crime drama series *Penoza*. In July 2020, Abhishek Bachchan made his digital debut on Amazon Prime in the crime thriller *Breathe: Into the Shadows*. In August 2020, Bobby Deol starred in a Hindi language thriller produced by Shahrukh and Gauri Khan's Red Chillies Entertainment for Netflix. Karishma Kapoor, a superstar of romantic comedies in the 1990s, returned in March 2020 to star in a web series called *Mentalhood* on the streaming platforms ALTBalaji and ZEE5. The fifth actor featured in the *India Today* video, Rahul Bose, appeared in a May 2020 Netflix film set in 1880s Bengal titled *Bulbbul*.

Although male superstars who dominate Bollywood blockbusters, such as Shahrukh Khan, Aamir Khan, Salman Khan and Akshay Kumar, are now well into their fifties, many female stars, especially women past their thirties, are rarely considered for romantic lead roles with the older men. However, in recent years many actors and other talented professionals in India who have been marginalized by the Bollywood industry's traditionalist structures and patriarchal ideologies for a variety of reasons – such as ageism, sexism, colorism, casteism, linguistic chauvinism and hegemonic nationalism – have found newer avenues for their creative talents in terms of acting, producing and directing major films and drama series on digital platforms. Thus, *India Today* and other media outlets

DOI: 10.4324/9781003130628-5

claim that digital platforms are the new silver screens due to their growing potential for countering, and maybe even outcompeting, Bollywood blockbusters by offering a much wider range of cultural representations of gender, class, caste, religions, regions and languages catering to a diversity of viewer interests both within India and around the world (Kaur 2021).

In media industry discourses, terms such as "digital disruption" and "Technology-Media-Telecommunications (TMT) convergence" have become buzzwords to describe the rapid changes taking place in Indian cinema, television, digital media and other allied industries. Describing TMT convergence as a "seismic shift," Girish Menon (2019), the Head of Media and Entertainment (M&E) for the consulting firm KPMG in India, argues that traditional "family TV-viewing" is being both disrupted and complemented by what some industry insiders call "individualistic entertainment." This chapter examines how traditional companies in film and television and new players in the digital arena are competing and collaborating to deliver individualized entertainment to audiences simultaneously at global, national, regional and local levels in multiple languages through multiple delivery platforms. The first section of the chapter situates the rise of individualized entertainment in relation to the historical legacy of "family viewing" as a state-sponsored nationalist ideology in India. The second section outlines the emerging contours of a new debate in the M&E industries about the "seismic shift" toward individualized entertainment. The third section describes some of the new programming, scheduling and distribution strategies used by both major and minor players in the Indian M&E industries in their quest to provide individualized entertainment to audiences across traditionally defined media ecosystems. The final section argues that the shift toward individualized entertainment engendered by digital disruption and TMT convergence is heralding a new phase in Indian M&E industries on global, national, regional and local scales that I describe as post-Bollywoodization. The term Bollywoodization, to recall Ashish Rajadhyaksha's (2003) well-known formulation, refers to the packaging of Indian culture as commercialized commodity images for conspicuous consumption without a blush of shame by upwardly mobile Indians and diasporic Indian audiences who seek to marry their global aspirations to age-old Indian values. On the other hand, post-Bollywoodization, I argue, is marked by a generalized shift away from targeting an imagined Indian "family" of national/diasporic communities toward customization of individualized entertainment for diverse global, national, regional and local audiences.

The State-Sponsored Ideology of "Family Viewing"

Popular advertisements featuring a nuclear family, or an extended family with grandparents and other relatives, watching television together in the darkened space of a living room are now commonplace stereotypical representations of "family TV-viewing" around the world. In India, and in many other developing nations, the term "family TV-viewing" also refers to a time in the second half of the 20th century when the postcolonial ideology of mass programming to a "national family" of viewers governed industry practices, governmental policies and audience perceptions (Rajagopal 2001). The ideological equation of the "national family" with the "television family" in India began with the launch of the state-sponsored network Doordarshan in 1959. Initially, most programs were experimental or educational and broadcast from Delhi in Hindi (the national language). Soon, regional language centers (or *kendras*) were gradually set up across the country in the 1970s and 1980s to cater to non-Hindi-speaking audiences in different states where the political leaders often resented the imposition of Hindi language programming from the centralized broadcasting authority in Delhi. Regional language broadcasts were restricted to specific time slots in the evening and were generally limited to formats like news and film-based shows from regional language cinemas (Kumar 2006).

During the 1990s, the hegemony of Doordarshan's "national family" of audiences was challenged by the growth of the private commercial television channels fueled by the arrival of the Hong Kong-based Star TV network. Soon, many Indian companies such as the Ramoji Group in Hyderabad, the Sun Group in Chennai and ZEE Entertainment Enterprises in Mumbai replicated the Star formula of providing commercially driven entertainment programming in English, Hindi, Hinglish and in other Indian languages. Through the 1990s and continuing well into the late 2000s, there was an explosion of television channels offering a variety of programming in many different languages in genres such as soap operas, prime time dramas, reality television shows, game shows, quiz shows, film- and music-based shows, sports and 24×7 news telecasts. In the 21st century, the globalization of Indian television with the consolidation of transnational media corporations such as Star TV, Disney, Time Warner and others has been accompanied by the rapid growth of domestic companies such as NDTV, UTV and Network 18 as well as the spread of regional language networks like Sun TV, ETV and ZEE TV within and beyond India (Chadha and Kavoori 2012). As various regional language markets emerged as new battlegrounds for increasing market share in the Indian M&E industries, a report in 2018 found that television programming in the four South Indian languages (Tamil, Telugu, Kannada and Malayalam) grew by 7%, while other regional languages such as Bhojpuri, Bangla and Marathi witnessed a 26% growth. While Hindi language programming continued to attract the largest share of audiences, it no longer commanded the attention of a "national family" of viewers as it did in the heyday of state-sponsored broadcasting in the 1980s (Malvania 2019).

In Indian cinema, particularly in the "national" Hindi film industry or Bollywood, the ideology of catering to a "national family" of moviegoers was also the norm in the decades following independence from the British in 1947. Historically, the Indian film industries have been defined in terms of two distinct spheres – the national film industry (dominated by Hindi language films) and regional film industries (comprising all other cinemas in regional languages). In ideological terms, the "uniqueness" of each regional film culture is often celebrated as a powerful indicator of diversity in the "national family," but the cultural uniqueness of regional languages is also contrasted to legitimate their subordinated status to Hindi as the national language, and thus to the hegemony of Bollywood as the "national" film culture. Furthermore, the ideological contrast between the nationally dominant Bollywood and other regionally specific film industries sustained in two ways – minor regional film industries (such as Assamese or Bhojpuri cinema) that cater to distinct regional language audiences and do not compete directly with Bollywood, and major regional film industries (such as Telugu or Tamil cinema) which struggle to compete against the hegemony of Hindi films at the national and international levels with limited or no success (Raghavendra 2017).

The historical distinctions and ideological tensions between regional language film industries and the national hegemony of Bollywood have, of course, not disappeared in the 21st century. However, digital disruption and TMT convergence have complicated the question of "scale" in the relationships among global, national, regional and local film industries in India. Regional film, television and digital media industries now operate on multiple scales and can no longer be subordinated to a sub-national category (on the national scale) or localized to a minor geopolitical category (on a global scale). Instead, the question of scale is now more dynamic and mobile as a result of complex flows between traditional (global and national) media capitals and once peripheral regional (sub-national and supra-national) centers of production and consumption. Occupying a peripheral location in the dominant geopolitical imaginaries of 20th-century nationalism and international relations, regional media producers and consumers were always already in dialogue with their national and global counterparts. Regional language filmmakers and audiences have freely drawn inspiration from Bollywood, Hollywood and other global and national filmmaking traditions that they were constantly exposed to in cinema theaters and on television at home. In a special issue of the journal *BioScope* (2015) on the "region" in Indian cinema, several contributors describe how producers and audiences of regional language films and television channels, who have always been exposed to media in more than one language, have refined their viewing practices by learning to engage with diverse aesthetic styles, political strategies and cultural narratives. For example, Kathryn Hardy (2015) describes how Bhojpuri cinema, a regional film industry in Hindi, complicates the conflation of Hindi cinema with Bollywood. At the same time, Hardy explains that Bhojpuri cinema is so influenced by the conventions of Bollywood filmmaking that Bhojpuri filmmakers have invented a Bhojpuri Hindi dialect that is not spoken anywhere but is only heard in films to create an "authentic" identity for Bhojpuri cinema that is distinct from Bollywood's Hindi cinema.

In terms of transnational connections in Indian cinema, S.V. Srinivas (2005a) describes how Hong Kong cinema clubs and martial arts schools mushroomed in small towns and villages in South India as a result of the growing fandom for kung fu films and martial arts-inspired action sequences in South Indian language films among audiences of Telugu language cinema. "I will rest my case," Srinivas concludes,

> with the Dragon Fist Martial Arts Academy. Not only is the academy named after a Jackie Chan film (*Dragon Fist*, Lo Wei 1978) but its "complete entertainment magazine" *Martial Arts*, features Hong Kong and Indian action film stars on its cover. … The school also has a library of martial arts detective novels and its chief instructor, Satya Shankar made a failed attempt at producing a film called *Karate Fighters*.

As the borders between regions, genres and cultures have always been permeable, filmmakers and audiences, particularly from marginalized film industries, have always been "in the know" about diverse viewing practices of cinematic cultures from other more mainstream and globalized film industries (Srinivas 2005b).

How, then, do we map the complex decentered flows of global, national, regional and local media of the 21st century in media industries still dominated by 20th century thinking about multi-scalar regions in terms of an ideologically defined "national family" of audiences? John Urry (2000) offers the concept of "complex mobilities" to challenge ideological morbidities that prevent scholars and industry practitioners from engaging more fully with the decentered subjectivities and uneven power relations that are horizontally dispersed across multiple scales of social organization at once. Urry writes (2000: 197–8):

> Billions of individual actions occur, each of which is based upon exceptionally localized forms of information. Most people most of the time act iteratively in terms of local information, knowing almost nothing about the global connections or implications of what they are doing. However, these local actions do not remain simply local since they are captured, represented, marketed, circulated and generalized elsewhere. They are carried along the scapes and flows of the emerging global world, transporting ideas, people, images, monies and technologies to potentially everywhere. Indeed, such actions may jump the scapes, since they are fluid-like and difficult to keep within particular channels.

As a consequence of the complex mobilities of individual actors, images, finances and technologies – or human and non-human actants as Urry calls them – media producers and distributors long accustomed to more sedentary notions of "family viewing" in a "national family" are now forced to find new creative strategies to attract and retain the roaming attention of their mobile audiences by catering to the different desires, aspirations, social and familial relationships that can no longer be easily restricted to particular channels. The next section outlines the emerging strategy of Consumer A.R.T. (acquisition, retention and transaction) that traditional and new media organizations alike are embracing to target the complex mobilities of their constantly shifting audiences.

The Era of Consumer A.R.T.

In March 2020, the Federation of Indian Chamber of Commerce and Industry (FICCI) in collaboration with the consulting firm EY (formerly, Ernst Young) released its Annual Report on the M&E industries in India titled *The Era of Consumer A.R.T.* The report defines the era of consumer A.R.T. as a segment-agnostic media landscape with a focus on direct-to-consumer (D2C) products and differential techniques for the acquisition, retention and monetization of customer relationships. Traditionally, media industries have been vertically segmented as radio, TV, film, digital media, with each segment creating and distributing content in its own silo in a predominantly national ecosystem. However, as a result of TMT convergence, media industries are increasingly characterized by horizontal segment-agnostic sections cutting across traditionally defined national, regional and local ecosystems. The EY-FICCI report identifies five horizontal sections in the Indian media industries: (1) content producer or IP owners such as Disney, Balaji and Applause Entertainment which own the license to content; (2) aggregators such as Sony and Hungama which aggregate different elements of content and often repurpose it; (3) distributors such as Telecommunications companies or ISPs such as Jio, Airtel and Tata Sky which build and operate the network for distributing content or services; (4) platforms such as YouTube, Netflix, ZEE5 and Radio Mirchi which offer content-based services by building on their brand identities that end consumers easily recognize; and (5) device/operating system/firmware providers such as Apple OS, Android, Kai and Samsung which may work on any technology with a screen, microphone and/or a speaker (EY-FICCI 2020).

Since the metrics for success in each segment are very different, the EY-FICCI report finds that the segment-agnostic landscape of TMT convergence has forced media companies to operate in multiple segments. For example, many cable and television providers are redefining themselves as content producers while others are transforming into content aggregators. Many print newspapers, telecommunications companies and content production houses have launched direct-to-consumer platforms or invested in theatrical distribution. The findings of the report suggest that digital disruption and TMT convergence are leading to a new era where M&E industries have to pay close attention to individual consumer experiences across segments in diverse contexts in order to acquire new customers and retain existing ones. With the global spread of the COVID-19 pandemic, the report cautions that macroeconomic risks and softening advertising revenues remain major concerns for the M&E industries. Despite a general slowdown in consumption, the EY-FICCI report finds that the number of digital consumers in India tripled in 2019. The report projects double-digit growth for digital media, online gaming, VFX and animation in India. But, unlike many other countries where digital and online media have disrupted the dominance of legacy media, popular Hindi cinema or Bollywood, regional language films and TV and cable industries still take the lion's share of media revenues in India. To date, television remains the largest revenue generator for the M&E industries in India (EY-FICCI 2020).

The release of the much-anticipated EY-FICCI annual report is usually accompanied by a major conference titled FICCI-FRAMES that is attended by several industry leaders from within and beyond India. However, due to COVID-19 restrictions, FICCI-FRAMES scheduled for March 2020 was postponed to a later date. Instead, the EY-FICCI report was released at an online event, and its sponsors invited readers to peruse a few short forewords written by leading figures in the Indian M&E industries about the coming "era of consumer A.R.T." In the first foreword, titled "The world is our stage," leading Bollywood actress and global superstar Priyanka Chopra (2020: 1) confidently proclaims, "If content is queen (yes ... it's 2020), then technology is the golden chariot that is carrying her treasures far and wide." While acknowledging that Indian media content has always had a large global audience, Chopra argues that new distribution channels like streaming platforms and advances in new digital technologies are blurring global boundaries. As a result, she claims that actors, writers, directors, musicians and other artists in the Indian M&E industries are now able to tell different kinds of stories that cater to a "wider audience base in a more niche funnel." Stating that storytelling in varied languages and genres is "decidedly one of India's key soft powers," Chopra (2020) concludes that the formula for success in the Indian media and entertainment industries is no longer "one for all."

In the second foreword, the noted Bollywood director and producer Karan Johar (2020: 2) agrees with Chopra that M&E industries are India's biggest global brand ambassadors because Bollywood is "something that most people on this planet recognize." Claiming that the rise of global Over The Top (OTT) platforms is offering new vistas for Indian content creators, Johar says:

> Our content is being consumed in over 150 countries across television, film and digital originals. Our music resonates across the world. Our events are becoming global IPs. India's animation, VFX and post production facilities have moved up the value chain and the world has recognized their potential as high-quality service providers, with a cost advantage.

Therefore, India's journey in the entertainment world, Johar proudly concludes, has just begun! The final foreword to the EY-FICCI report written by FICCI's senior vice president Uday Shankar (2020) declares that a tectonic shift is underway in India as traditional and new-age media companies in India's M&E industries are now being joined by platforms which were focused on other services. Even as India's economic growth has been lukewarm in the wake of the COVID-19 pandemic, Shankar pointed out that the M&E industries in 2019–20 grew at a healthy rate of 9%. Therefore, he optimistically concludes that with the rapid rise in digital access and adoption, the M&E industries will be a harbinger of a new aspirational India with a billion screens in the next five years.

In other industry reports generated by consulting firms such as Deloitte and KPMG, and in industry conclaves like FICCI-FRAMES, the goal of reaching a billion customers has been a long-cherished goal. In a 2019 report titled "A Billion Screens of Opportunity," EY outlines how media companies are embracing TMT convergence to find new ways of monetizing and targeting every single person in India's 1.3 billion plus population. Google's Next Billion Users division aggressively targets the Indian markets, and Google Search accounts for more than 90% of the search traffic in the country. In its quest to bring every single search user into its ecosystem, Google created Project Navlekha for regional language media in India to provide online content and earn advertising revenues through Google Ad Sense.

In terms of marketing strategies for catering to domestic audiences in India and simultaneously targeting other audiences in the region and beyond, a Deloitte report titled "Connecting the Next Billion" proclaims technology as the key differentiator for businesses that seek to adapt to the changes wrought by digital disruption and TMT convergence. On the other hand, a KPMG report titled "Media Ecosystems: The Walls Fall Down" proclaims that content remains the key differentiator for media companies in their quest to provide individualized entertainment for audiences at the global, national, regional and local levels. In the realm of technologies, there is clear evidence that the digitization of production practices is rapidly changing due to TMT convergence. The report outlines how the use of computer modeling and advances in motion capture technologies have changed the ways in which films, television shows, video games, mobile and online media are produced. The growth of big data has impacted the ways in which media are produced, stored, distributed and exhibited. In the realm of content, digital modes of storytelling are enabling producers and consumers to co-create hybrid media using virtual reality or augmented reality with non-linear storylines that can deliver individualized entertainment. As a result, the state-driven, corporate-sponsored "national family" has become more fragmented as audiences fluidly move across a new segment-agnostic multi-lingual, multi-channel, multiplatform multiverse. In terms of programming in multiple Indian languages, media producers and advertisers recognize that segment-agnostic individualized entertainment can be a lucrative strategy not only for targeting the vast untapped potential of India's urban, semi-urban and rural markets but also for attracting diverse audiences in other national, regional, local and global markets with shared linguistic and cultural affinities.

The Rise of Individualized Entertainment

It is important to note that the concept of individualized entertainment is hardly representative of the current industry practices or of media consumption patterns in India or in other globalized markets today. For instance, while the rate of mobile phone adoption in South Asia has been the fastest in the world, the region also has the widest gender gap in mobile phone usage. In 2018, GSMA, a worldwide association for the mobile industries, conducted a study on "connected women" which revealed that women in South Asia are 26% less likely to own a mobile phone than men and 70% less likely to use mobile Internet. Just as the concept of "family TV-viewing" in the heyday of broadcasting was less about the reality of diverse viewing practices and more about the hegemony of a state-sponsored ideology of one-for-all national programming, the phrase "individualized entertainment" is less about the current state of the media and more indicative of the all-at-once approach to TMT convergence and digital disruption driven by powerful industry interests.

In its Annual Report for 2017–18, the Telecommunications Authority of India (TRAI) (2018) provides a detailed account of, what it calls, stories of "exponential growth" in the telecommunications, broadcasting and cable sectors in India. According to the TRAI report, at the end of 2018, there were 877 private satellite TV channels in India out of which 389 were news channels and 488 were non-news channels. While 300 channels were pay channels, 577 were free-to-air channels. The TRAI report also finds that television distribution is a highly fragmented business in India. There are over 60,000 local cable operators and 6,000 MSOs in the cable industry competing with six Direct-to-Home (DTH) satellite companies, one High Intensity Transit Signals (HITS) distributor and one Internet Protocol Television (IPTV) provider. Doordarshan, the state-sponsored broadcasting service, now also provides a Free Dish satellite service.

Meanwhile, telecommunications companies like Bharat Sanchar Nigam Limited (BSNL), Reliance Jio, Vodafone and Airtel that have for long focused on building their broadband infrastructure to deliver mobile communications are now venturing into delivery of content like web series and short-form videos in collaboration with digital production houses like Amazon, ALTBalaji and Eros Now. Similarly, technology companies like Google, Facebook and WhatsApp which account for distribution of almost two-thirds of total online video consumption in Indian languages are also seeking to produce their own news programming and entertainment content. As a result, consumers can now watch television on their telephone, make phone calls through their IPTV service, or read books and listen to music using an online streaming service.

There are almost 50 OTT platforms in India offering programming services in a variety of languages to audiences within India and beyond. Hotstar is by far the most popular OTT platform in India with an audience base of more than 300 million active subscribers. In 2019, when the Walt Disney Company acquired 21st Century Fox, the parent company of Hotstar, the OTT platform was renamed Disney+Hotstar. The platform provides content in languages such as Marathi, Hindi, Telugu, Malayalam, Tamil, Kannada, Bengali, English and Indonesian. In 2017–18, Reliance Industries entered into content-sharing agreements with Balaji Telefilms and Eros Entertainment so that content from the subscription-based OTT services ALTBalaji and Eros Now would be available for free for users on Reliance Jio's extensive mobile phone network. Soon, Airtel and Vodafone followed suit and partnered with Amazon Prime and Netflix to provide OTT content to their mobile subscribers. At the same time, several OTT players like Amazon Prime, Netflix, Hotstar and JioTV have focused on expanding their digital delivery platforms by building extensive online libraries through acquisition of new films and drama series and the production of new content in Indian languages (Bhattacharya 2019).

The Netflix original series *Sacred Games* brought Indian content in English onto the global stage and it was reported that two of three viewers of *Sacred Games* Season 1 were from outside India. Similarly, *Mighty Little Bheem*, released from India in April 2019, is the most-watched pre-school series on Netflix in 27 million households globally (EY-FICCI 2020: 32). The Tamil language film *Jagame Thandhiram*, featuring South Indian superstar Dhanush, was one of the top ten films watched on Netflix in seven countries, including India, Malaysia and UAE. The film's production house, YNOT Studios, released a poster on Twitter announcing that the film would be available on Netflix to stream in 190 countries in 17 languages including French, German, Italian, Polish, Portuguese, Spanish (Castilian and Neutral), Thai, Indonesian, Vietnamese, Tamil, Telugu, Malayalam, Kannada, Hindi and English (@StudiosYNot 2021).

DishTV, the leading DTH company in India, launched a new "Korean Drama Active" service in August 2020 offering users premium Korean drama content dubbed into Hindi on DishTV and D2H platforms. DishTV promoted the new service as a first on Indian television with the tag line, "Entertainment Videshi, Tadka Desi" (Foreign Entertainment, Indian Spicing) (*Adgully* 2020). Other OTT players like JioTV and Eros Now are seeking to capture a larger share of India's multi-lingual markets by taking their content into rural areas (Bhattacharya 2019). Furthermore, when commercial media companies like ETV, Sun TV and ZEE TV compete for market share of multi-lingual communities, they are not ideologically constrained to operate within national boundaries. For example, when ZEE Entertainment and ETV launched their Bengali language television channels, they targeted audiences not only in West Bengal in India but also in neighboring Bangladesh and in the Bangla diaspora around the world (Ninan 2000). ZEE's OTT platform ZEE5 now offers programming in 12 Indian languages both in India and globally. Its Hindi-Urdu programming is popular in Pakistan, and its Bengali programming is streaming in Bangladesh. ZEE5 also offers Tamil content in Sri Lanka, including popular TV shows from its Indian cable television channel ZEE Tamil (*Exchange4media* 2019). When ZEE Entertainment launched its Zindagi channel in June 2014, it began airing television serials from Pakistan. Although no longer in service, Zindagi was one of the first channels to offer Indian audiences programming content from countries such as Brazil, Pakistan, South Korea, Turkey and Ukraine (Pant 2019). In 2019, Eros International, an Indian film production and distribution company, released a 12-episode Pakistani serial called *Enaaya* as a subscription-based web series on YouTube in Pakistan and also for streaming on its OTT platform Eros

Now in India (Arora 2019). A subscription-based OTT service called Hoichoi offers Bengali language film, TV and music content in West Bengal, Bangladesh and the United Arab Emirates (TVP Bureau 2018). As a result, Bollywood films are no longer the face of entertainment for audiences in India or of Indian entertainment around the world (Jha 2018).

Although the Mumbai-based Bollywood is still the ideologically dominant "national" film industry, it is no longer the predominant center for film production and distribution. The record-breaking box office success of the Marathi language sleeper hit *Sairat* (2016) and the Telugu language film industry's globally successful *Baahubali* franchise (2015, 2017) reveal that other "regional" film industries are becoming not only more integrated with Bollywood but also more integral to the Indian film industry's attempts to reach more diverse and dispersed audiences in India and abroad. *Baahubali 1* and *2*, for example, not only smashed box office records in the traditional strongholds for South Indian films but also became some of the highest-grossing films in North India and in international markets where South Indian films have traditionally not been very popular among moviegoers. While *Baahubali* was a massive global hit in multiple languages and *Sairat* reached many audiences who may not usually watch Marathi language films, it is important to note that many critically acclaimed small-budget films, such as Malayalam language film director Lijo Jose Pellissery's engrossing crime drama *Angamaly Diaries*, do not receive similar visibility or global distribution (Jha 2018).

However, major Bollywood studios and streaming platforms have begun to notice the appeal of low-budget non-blockbuster releases for providing individualized entertainment options to audiences, particularly from smaller regional language film industries where films that do well are not driven by star power and distribution rights but by innovative storytelling. With the rise of digital platforms and streaming services, Bollywoodized blockbusters are not the only avenues to generate significant revenues in the Indian media and entertainment industries (Singh 2019). As smaller budget regional films are being marketed to larger national and international audiences on streaming platforms with good subtitling and dubbing, a small but growing number of multi-lingual productions are catching the attention of major advertisers and sponsors as well. National and international brands such as Airtel, Nestle, Mondelez, Coca-Cola, Pepsico and Oppo have started associating with non-Bollywoodized films made in Tamil, Telugu and other Indian languages (Narasimhan 2017).

From Bollywoodization to Post-Bollywoodization

The shift away from the ideology of a "national family" of audiences toward the delivery of individualized entertainment through digital platforms is clearly challenging the Bollywoodization of the Indian media and entertainment industries. But it is also disrupting other allied industries such as telecommunications, digital software and hardware, consumer products and financial technologies, thus linking old and newer stakeholders in a multi-scalar, segment-agnostic post-Bollywood-ized media ecosystem. As Rajadhyaksha (2003) reminds us, Bollywoodization in the 1990s was the result of the liberalization of financial markets and the emer-gence of mass consumer culture in India that extended from cinema to television, the Internet, glossy print magazines, fashion, clothing and everyday life. As a cul-tural phenomenon, Bollywoodization represented the productive tension between the magical allure of transnational corporate commodities and the ideological appeal of nationalist identity and served as a valuable cultural guide for upwardly mobile Indian consumers. At the same time, for the Indian diaspora particu-larly in the Western capitals of Europe and the United States, Bollywoodization commodified cultural "authenticity" with heavy nationalist overtones and sat-isfied the nostalgic desire for a symbolic "return" to an imagined motherland. Bollywoodization thus created seamless cinematic narratives of a "national fam-ily" of audiences that ideologically extends, as Aswin Punathambekar (2010) puts it, from Bihar in India to Manhattan, New York, in the United States. However, the Bihar-to-Manhattan strategy used in many Bollywood blockbusters of the 1990s and 2000s, such as *Dilwale Dulhania Le Jayenge* (1995), *Kabhi Khushi Kabhie Gham* (2001), *Kal Ho Na Ho* (2003), *Salaam Namaste* (2005), *Namastey London* (2007) and *My Name Is Khan* (2010), featured extremely patriarchal Indian fami-lies globe-trotting between India and New York, London or Melbourne, and often risked alienating audiences in both Bihar and Manhattan.

In the era of individualized consumer A.R.T. (acquisition, retention and transaction), the Manhattanization of Bollywood or the Bollywoodization of Manhattan is no longer the only available strategy for media and entertainment industries in India. The stated goal of the M&E industries in a post-Bollywoo-dized India is to offer individualized entertainment for all viewers from Bihar to Manhattan and everywhere in between. In response to the rapid transforma-tions, TMT convergence and digital disruption in the 21st century, the M&E industries are shifting away from programming for a "national family" toward customizing entertainment for individual consumers. To target the complex mobilities of their target audiences, the M&E industries are seeking to provide individualized entertainment that is simultaneously national, sub-national and supra-national. The concept of post-Bollywoodization as a "contact zone" of national, sub-national and supra-national media ecosystems, I argue, is a useful framework to understand the blurring of traditional distinctions such as Hindi language (national), regional language (sub-national) and English language (supra-national) media in India.

References

Adgully (2020) "In an Industry First, DishTV India Introduces 'Korean Drama Active,'" 6 August.

Arora, A. (2019) "Eros Now Goes International with First Pakistani Original Series *Enaaya*," *Gadgets*, 21 January.

Bhattacharya, A. (2019) "Game On: Netflix and Amazon Prime Aren't the Main Contenders in India's Streaming Wars," *Quartz India*, 16 January.

BioScope (2015) "Special Issue on Regional Cinemas of India," 6(3).

Chadha, K. and Kavoori, A. (2012) "Mapping India's Television Landscape," *South Asian History and Culture*, 3(4): 591–602.

Chopra, P. (2020) "The World Is Our Stage," in *The Era of Consumer A.R.T. – Acquisition, Retention and Transaction*, Delhi: EY-FICCI.

Exchange4media (2019) "ZEE5 Unveils New #ShareTheLove Campaign for Pakistan and Bangladesh Markets," 15 January.

EY-FICCI (Federation of Indian Chambers of Commerce and Industry) (2020) *The Era of Consumer A.R.T. – Acquisition, Retention and Transaction*, Delhi: EY-FICCI.

Hardy, K. (2015) "Constituting a Diffuse Region: Cartographies of Mass-Mediated Bhojpuri Belonging," *BioScope*, 6(2): 145–64.

India Today (2020) "Digital Platform is the New Silver Screen," 29 August.

Jha, L. (2018) "Why Bollywood and Hindi Are No Longer the Face of Indian Entertainment," *Mint*, 24 August.

Johar, K. (2020) "The Indian Media and Entertainment Sector Is the Biggest Global Brand Ambassador for India," in *The Era of Consumer A.R.T. – Acquisition, Retention and Transaction*, Delhi: EY-FICCI.

Kaur, G. (2021) "From Silver Screen to Digital Devices: Indian Actresses above 40 Reclaim their Space," *ZengerNews*, 30 April.

Kumar, S. (2006) *Gandhi Meets Primetime: Globalization and Nationalism in Indian Television*, Urbana-Champaign: University of Illinois Press.

Malvania, U. (2019) "Regional Languages Rule TV!," *Rediff*, 5 January.

Menon, G. (2019) "Tune In: Technology, Media and Telecom (TMT) Convergence – Building Ecosystems," *India Insights: The Indian Economy Newsletter*, KPMG India.

Narasimhan, T.E. (2017) "How Regional Films Are Being Repackaged to Draw Brands Outside Native Sate," *Business Standard*, 3 August.

Ninan, S. (2000) "Channel After Channel," *The Hindu*, 18 June.

Pant, R. (2019) "Televisual Tales from Across the Border," *BioScope*, 10(2): 164–82.

Punathambekar, A. (2010) "From Bihar to Manhattan: Bollywood and the Transnational Indian Family," in M. Curtin and H. Shah (eds) *Re-Orienting Global Communications*, Urbana-Champaign: University of Illinois Press.

Raghavendra, M.K. (2017) *Beyond Bollywood*, Delhi: HarperCollins.

Rajadhyaksha, A. (2003) "The 'Bollywoodization' of the Indian Cinema," *Inter-Asia Cultural Studies*, 4(1): 25–39.

Rajagopal, A. (2001) *Politics after Television: Hindu Nationalism and the Reshaping of the Public in India*, Cambridge: Cambridge University Press.

Shankar, U. (2020) "A Tectonic Shift Underway," in *The Era of Consumer A.R.T. – Acquisition, Retention and Transaction*, Delhi: EY-FICCI.

Singh, A. (2019) "*Sairat* to *Baahubali*: The Coming of Age of Regional Cinema in India," *Financial Express*, 27 September.

Srinivas, S.V. (2005a) "Hong Kong Action Film and the Career of the Telugu Mass Hero," in M. Morris, S.L. Li and S. Chan (eds) *Hong Kong Connections: Transnational Imagination in Action Cinema*, Hong Kong: Hong Kong University Press.

Srinivas, S.V. (2005b) "Kung Fu Hustle: A Note on the Local," *Inter-Asia Cultural Studies*, 6(2): 289–95.

@StudiosYNot (2021) "#JagameThandhiramOnNetflix This Friday! 190 Countries, 17 Languages," Twitter, 15 June.

TRAI (Telecommunications Regulatory Authority of India) (2018) *2017–18 Annual Report*, Delhi: TRAI.

TVP Bureau (2018) "Hoichoi to Ramp Up Original Content Offering: Expands into Bangladesh, Middle East," *Television Post*, 20 September.

Urry, J. (2000) "Mobile Sociology," *British Journal of Sociology*, 51(1): 185–203.

4

MEDIA CAPITAL AND DIGITAL MEDIA CITIES IN ASIA

Xin Gu

The concept of "media capital" considers the multi-directional spatial flows of media content, production and distribution beyond an emphasis on national media systems (Curtin 2003). It focuses on the key role that particular global cities have played – including the rising Asian media capitals. Although the broadcasting media such as television have always provided the loci for addressing national specificities, the idea that the complex nature of media products including popular music and film thrives on the diversity of globally networked labor markets has become ever more prominent (Hesmondhalgh and Baker 2013; Hoyler and Watson 2013). The globalization strategy of media industries has been used as a catalyst for myriad forms of global economy transformation. Such a strategy is at the heart of "the turn to culture" central to post-industrial cities around the world (Garcia 2004). The media industries' predominant business activities entail the production and distribution of "symbolic goods" that place a high value on creativity, originality and innovation with low cost for reproduction and digital circulation; this shift has come to occupy a central place in today's "cultural industries" (Hesmondhalgh 2013). This chapter specifically explores the dynamic flows of media capital in the recent developments of digital media cities in Asia.

Media Capital and Mediated Urbanism

Relatively few studies have considered the intersections between media technology, urbanization and social life. Those working across different disciplines tend to lack a shared culture and history, making it difficult to account for this emerging research agenda which necessarily crosses disciplinary boundaries. As McQuire (2020: 13) suggested:

DOI: 10.4324/9781003130628-6

The complexity of any attempts to address mediated urbanism lies in the fact that the transformation of media platforms and communication practices is tightly implicated in the remaking of urban social experiences.

McQuire (2020) proposed four epochal shifts in the formulation of "media cities," each of which gives rise to different relationships between new forms of mediated communication and urban sociality. In Asia, the evolution of mediated urbanism is underpinned by a shift from the state-centric model to the neoliberal model driven by globalizing media industries (Ang 2001; Kim 2008).

The historical developments of media cities have been attuned to specific national contexts despite the fast global diffusion of media technologies. Sinclair and Harrison (2004) observed how India and China have displayed different local resistance and adaptation to the global television industry. Despite rising pressure on both countries to open up to major global corporations, a multitude of localized cultural choices and routes toward modernization has emerged alongside the global. O'Connor and Gu (2020) revealed China's contemporary cultural economy and creativity as a new path to modernity and entry into global capitalism. This may set to change in the newly minted digital media cities, characterized by the affordance and ubiquity of distributed real-time communication (DRTC) platforms. Thus, India's "Smart Cities" narrative in the context of rising neoliberal imaginary in Asia, prioritizing "efficiency" and "speed," tends to ignore the reality of life on the ground (Dutta 2019). Across Asia, the rising tension between the digital future and new rounds of urban gentrification can be observed (Kuecker and Hartley 2020).

Digital media cities across Asia are becoming embroidered in the neoliberal rhetoric of the state. This includes a realignment of the state interests with business interests, driven primarily by media industries concerned with global trading. Meanwhile, state-led initiatives are replaced by industry-led ones, and the government's responsibilities to civil society have now been channeled as discretionary funds from within digital media corporations. Dressed in the language of "democracy," digital media cities promise to serve the needs of civil society with greater transparency and opportunity for economic prosperity. However, they have increased the level of inequalities in these societies as the commercial sector retains profit rather than contributing to public funds.

The digital media city is believed to have greater potential for democratization through its ability to mobilize public assembly much more efficiently and to be utilized by grassroots organizations in unprecedented ways. However, the actual experiences of digital media cities in China, Singapore and Indonesia, to name a few, cast serious doubts on this (Padawangi et al. 2014). A massive shrinkage of urban public spaces caused by mega urbanization projects in Asian digital media cities has prevented any online democratic potential materializing as offline insurgencies. Far from opposing the logic of "place" and "space," digital media cities are becoming ever more dependent on mobilizing locality if they are to reach their full potential for empowering participation.

There are also concerns over the normalization of surveillance in various urban settings. The rollout of surveillance technology has been met with suspicion and has incurred a new round of public debates over corporatization and platform capitalism in the developed West. In Asia, many authoritarian governments have adopted new surveillance technologies during the COVID-19 crisis, accompanied by very little public consultation. Neither the accountability of those in charge of the regulation of public data nor the potential violation of human rights in those countries has been publicly debated. In the case of China, the merging of facial recognition technology with other forms of urban data streams extrapolated from mobile tracking devices has resulted in "function creep," which is now part of the everyday mediated experiences of urban lives in Chinese cities (Bernot et al. 2021). Instead of empowering public participation, Asian digital media cities have been co-opted by global corporations and authoritarian governments to shape urban mobility and social identity.

These issues require a nuanced approach away from technology-centric determinism to understand the complex impact of media technologies on urban sociality and connections to local urban politics. The following sections focus specifically on three key features of the recent development of Asian digital media cities – first, the process of "worlding" characterized by a particular neoliberal logic and its associated technological utopianism; second, "cultural imperialism" as an underlying logic for global media corporations expanding their influence in Asia; and third, "cultural retrofitting" adopted by governments and civil societies to translate globalizing modernization rhetoric into very different local political and cultural contexts. While developing and developed countries in the region may face very different challenges due to different stages of their development, some common patterns of this rapid urbanization since the late 20th century can be identified. The aim here is to broaden current debates on media cities beyond the examples of European and North American cities. The challenges faced by Asian digital media cities suggest the imbricated relationships between urban structure, media technologies and social life different from those already observed in developed Global North.

Digital Media Cities as "Worlding" Projects

The development of digital media cities was driven by social and economic challenges associated with massive economic restructuring in post-industrial cities (Carter 2013) as well as a process of "worlding" to draw on global urban interventions to solve local problems (Roy and Ong 2011). Digital media cities are a fitting example of "worlding" as they can be taken up by any government aspiring to the status of global cities by investing in a set of technological solutions to variable local problems. As Ong (2006) argued, worlding cities are governed by the neoliberal logic to appropriate a set of economic rationalities in the governing of urban transformations by circumventing ideological questions over class, power and politics.

Digital media cities are exemplary of the new development paradigm known as the "creative economy" (Florida 2002) which entails an emphasis on the knowledge economy, the incorporation of consumption and production, and the re-orientation of local economic development toward the aggregation of cultural and media capital. This process has resulted in many top-down developed digital media cities in Asia, from agglomerations of small media clusters (e.g. animation cluster in Hangzhou, China) to highly capitalized regional initiatives (e.g. Multimedia Super Corridor in Malaysia).

Digital media cities are "entrepreneurial" in neoliberal capitalism (Harvey 1989), where governments, pressured by intercity competitions, become increasingly focused on isolated urban development projects rather than investment in progressive social reforms. These cities emphasize corporatization and the global flow of capital (Cooke and Lazzeretti 2008). The developmental focus on global media corporations thus worked to divert investment away from local creative ecosystems whose "buzz" attracted many of these corporations in the first place (Gu 2020). There is a tendency to prioritize the needs of global media corporations when developing new urban infrastructure. This often includes the building of large media clusters or digital hubs to compete as regional media hubs in countries such as Singapore, Malaysia and Indonesia (Weiss 2014). Heavy investment in the new architectural styles associated with the idea of "generic city" (Koolhaas 1995) is key to uncovering the "dominant discourse" of techno-utopianism in such urban transformations. In China, "a utopian drive to transform skylines and cityscapes, an insistence on instantaneous transformation" (ibid.: 62) has seen the erection of many postmodern architectural behemoths, such as the state media CCTV's new building in the capital, designed by Koolhaas.

From the late 1990s, in Asia there was a race to embrace large-scale infrastructure projects with an emphasis on solving urban problems. Automated urban data systems were increasingly seen as essential to managing urban systems by many digital media cities in Asia. A centralized control hub fed by data from a network of CCTV and cameras around the city was widely adopted, from Jakarta to Mumbai, from Shanghai to Tokyo. It allowed for quick responses to urban problems such as traffic congestion and air pollution. Due to its easily available and clearly defined systemic value, these technological solutions were quickly adopted by many governments in the region. Large media complexes are now rapidly emerging in Asia. The "Tomorrow City" (South Korea) and "Digital Corridors" (Malaysia) are just two examples of this new developmental trend.

This top-down technological utopianism is fueled by postcolonial cultural politics, an attitude of "catching up" with the West. As Datta's (2015) study in India has shown, technological utopianism is the dominant ideology of the government when it comes to urban development in postcolonial India; such an approach is interpreted as "digital solutionism," "entrepreneurial urbanization" and "fast policy," all of which have adversely impacted local life. Sundaram's (2010: 3) study of Delhi further shows how such developments, if they fail to apprehend local specificity, can lead to problems like "infrastructure breakdown, scandal, pollution."

Meanwhile, questions have grown as to the real potential for digital media cities to empower democratic participation. The "universal values" that digital media infrastructures promise to unleash are not always in sync with local customs, norms and experiences. In South Korea, due to different modalities of governance and social mobility, digital media cities have contributed to a development rhetoric based on techno-utopianism, compelled primarily by nation branding rather than empowering the voice of the grassroots (Schwak 2016). Japan's smart city projects have been criticized as having the adverse effect of suppressing existing social reforms (Granier and Kudo 2016). Rather than lessening the power of authoritarian governments in the region, these projects have enhanced forms of control, facilitating a neoliberal incorporation of "discontent" via new technologies and new actors. As Lemke's (2002: 11) critique of governmentality suggested:

> What we observe today is not a diminishment or reduction of state sovereignty and planning capacities but a displacement from formal to informal techniques of government and the appearance of new actors on the scene of government (e.g. nongovernmental organizations) that indicate fundamental transformations in statehood and a new relation between state and civil society actors.

Digital media cities in Asia often assume Western values (e.g. democracy) as a given. They emphasize the potential of networked digital technology in safeguarding democratic cultural participation, but in reality, most are only paying lip service to their potential to stimulate democratic reform. Rather, any subaltern challenge to the ideology of the new technocratic governance model is now deemed a "problem" and a cause for triggering a new round of investment in technological solutions (Kamath 2018).

Digital Media Cities and Cultural Imperialism

Interestingly, the dominant narrative of the digital media city in Asia purports the underlying logic of "media capital" to formulate a system that could counter Western imperialism and hegemony. Writing in the 2000s, Hesmondhalgh (2008) argued that there was a tendency for the developed West to exploit the "indirect" power of its domination of cultural forms in a way that has resulted in a new global hegemony. This tendency has been deepened by the arrival of "platform capitalism" (Srnicek 2017), referring to proprietary practices by global corporations co-operating with governments to extract big data from local markets. Commercial exploitation and political surveillance based on big data has been labeled as "data colonialism" (Couldry and Mejias 2019) and forms one of the defining characteristics of digital media cities in Asia. Cultural hierarchies between the West and the rest are re-enforced rather than diminished with the rapid rise of digital media infrastructures (Jin 2007). Most smart city initiatives have been driven by companies such as IBM, CISCO, Microsoft and Oracle, based in the USA. As Kwet (2019: 17) pointed out, US colonial power has been assimilated into "tech" products, creating a 21st-century form of colonialism: "Western doctrines glorify Big Data, centralized clouds, proprietary systems, smart cities littered with surveillance, automation, predictive analytics and similar inventions."

In Asia, the global expansion of the world's most powerful companies in the development of media city initiatives creates new conditions of cultural colonialism, widening the gap between the developed West and an Asia that is left by the discourses of "creative cities" (Gu 2020). New digital media cities are reliant on the developed West not only for imported cultural content, but also for cultural "exports" in the form of large datasets generated through platform corporations such as Netflix and Amazon. It is in this context that the tendency to maintain cultural imperialism commands critical research attention. Morozov (2019) argued that under the current "Silicon Valley private-ownership model," it is unlikely for any society to bring about democratic transformation in the "age of big data."

The core issue here is the asymmetry of big data in the development of digital media cities. Digital media cities are modeled as data repositories. The present design of digital media cities' data infrastructures relies on a centralization of data streams, giving those corporations in control of the platforms enormous power in shaping local social life (Morozov 2019). In response to the problem, China has invested in a state-controlled system to circumvent "Western influence" under terms of "national cultural security" (Hu 2005). But locking a billion people away from the global techno-cultural infrastructure may be not only unsustainable but also unethical. The reality for most other cities will be to build their infrastructures using training datasets and algorithms developed in whole or in part by global firms. The profiling of local uniqueness via such a global infrastructure will continue to be problematic.

The production of very large datasets about populations is not a recent invention. Governments across the world produce national censuses and businesses are used to collecting information about their customers. What is particularly important in relation to the Asian context is a notable lack of means by which the public could resist automated data collection due to very different attitudes toward privacy and democratic participation. As Lyon (2003) observed, much of the discussion on surveillance measures based on the Western notion of privacy may be inappropriate in Asia because of very different cultural and political practices around privacy. Kostka's (2019) study of people's attitude toward the social credit system in China supports this claim, as the majority of Chinese people believe that surveillance systems can improve the quality of life in cities, unlike survey results in the West.

The asymmetries of cultural power are another issue faced by Asian digital media cities. In recent decades, maintaining a global hegemony has become crucial for Western corporations aiming to extract value and build their legitimacy through the juxtapositions of "us" (the developed West) and "them" (the rest). Dal Maso et al. (2019) uncover how these companies propagate cultural asymmetries to extract value: For instance, the articulation of different cultural discourses is an attempt to re-enforce cultural hierarchies of the Western system as more superior than a Chinese one in order to continuously extract value out of the Chinese market.

Ironically, cities that are most threatened by the process of globalization are more keen to invest in digital media cities. South Korea is an early adopter of digital media cities and has been relatively more successful than others in the region as an ideal destination for global media corporations. The Korean Wave, in particular, has become a testament to a successful peripheral country that has re-imagined and re-positioned itself through the concentration of television, film and subsidiary global media corporations (Ryoo 2009). Nevertheless, studies identify a more sophisticated and hidden model of cultural imperialism, challenging the assumption that the concentration of media corporations would result in the burgeoning local cultural industries reversing global cultural hegemony. US domination has increased during this process of hyper-digital media development as a result of the tendency for conglomeration in media industries and over-dependency of local production on global and vertically integrated supply chains (Jin 2007). Global corporations are unlikely to provide forums or channels for public debate when their core logic embodies a logic of cultural imperialism. Under the influence of such cultural imperialism, the capacity for local communities in these countries to take issues of democracy, sovereignty and privacy into their own hands has been a real challenge, as social reforms are increasingly organized through digital means.

Digital Media Cities and Cultural Retrofitting

The logic by which the digital media city's rhetoric was made operational locally can be understood through the notion of "graduated sovereignty" (Ong 2000), a sophisticated model of "cultural retrofitting" in the development of these modern urban projects. The gap between a globalizing "modern" rhetoric and local cultural imaginaries creates opportunities as well as tensions for knowledge production and social transformation. The focus on different kinds of agency and governmentality has presented new opportunities for many Asian societies to cultivate different urban development paradigms which challenge authoritarian governance. Kusno's (2013) work on how Indonesians in post-Suharto society engaged with social media technology in the spatial reconfiguration of the capital city, Jakarta, is one such example. Here, concerns for environmental degradation, injustice and violence managed to evade the neoliberal development logic in the re-imagining of mediated urbanism. Similar examples suggest that the addition of new technology, mostly conceived in a developed Western urban context, to very different contexts in Asia may result in new development paradigms. Urban infrastructure alone cannot make cities any smarter, but rather it is the marriage between technology and human creativity that counts (Hollands 2008). Graham and Marvin's (2001) "cyber cities" idea further illustrates the potential for mediated urbanism to empower participation, resting not on the technology itself but on "networked urbanism," which is socially defined and is shaping and structuring the social and cultural aspect of cities.

Digital media cities face serious tasks of "cultural retrofitting" in order to function. Media industries increasingly operate outside of national boundaries and are more sensitive to changes in the global marketplace than they are domestic conditions (Deuze 2007). Local industries thrive in milieus that are about long-term trust and shared values between large numbers of very small companies and freelancers; these values may not be shared by media industries operating on short-term contracts and across temporarily linked extra-local media markets (Oakley 2006). Thus, one cannot assume that cultural retrofitting will either work to the benefit of the global media industries that the cities are hoping to attract or answer the requirements of local industries whose "presence" (both symbolic and physical) is increasingly compromised by the arrival of the global footloose.

One such example in Asia is "maker culture," associated with the "open source technology" which emerged first in San Francisco. Maker culture in Asia is far from the individualized counter-cultural revolution depicted in the West. Very different social and cultural practices are at work across maker spaces in Asia. Research on India's *Jugaad* (Murray and Hand 2015) and China's *Shanzhai* (Gu and Shea 2019) suggests that they do not follow protocols of "commons based peer production" nor display any trait of the "gift economy." Instead, they are led by local manufacturing industries adapting to increasing pressure on global supply chains and just-in-time production (Gu and Shea 2019). Most of these local practices emerge out of an attempt to retrofit traditional manufacturing infrastructure and its labor force with new networked technology (e.g. 3D printer) and a new narrative of "creative industries" (Gu 2019). This approach can be termed as "pirate modernity" (Sundaram 2010) – a localized evolution of modernization away from the mainstream development rhetoric but still integrated within it.

Nevertheless, digital media cities often present democracy as a core value without paying attention to the specific social conditions required for sustaining meaningful local participation. As a result, emerging forms of public participation quickly dissipate rather than generate real social transformations. For example, in China's digital media city, Shenzhen, most maker spaces are rapidly institutionalized either by the state or by commercial media corporations such as Tencent. Indeed, maker spaces are blamed for contributing to problems of urban gentrification in Shenzhen by replacing local manufacturing production with highly capitalized real estate property development and consumer-led activities (Gu 2019).

Adding new infrastructures that are attractive to global media firms irrespective of local needs presents particular challenges to cities that do not have an established creative labor market or creative ecosystem able to sustain any resulting growth (Mould 2015). Given the significant size of the investment required to attract such global companies and their requisite personnel, cities may spare investment in the local creative milieu and focus only on flagship media cluster projects (Gu 2020). There is a close correlation between media clusters and gentrification, a process that works at much greater speed and with higher levels of economic and political capital than that traditionally associated with arts-led gentrification (Novy and Colomb 2013).

In many developing states, the ability of individuals to engage with these high-tech infrastructures is limited – most of these infrastructures are underutilized and unable to connect with the broader cultural life in cities because of different cultural attitudes toward "participation" (Brooker 2012). The new identity of digital media cities rarely makes reference to the previous cultural histories of their cities. They are increasingly devoid of any form of history or local "authenticity." In addition to their impact on the local creative ecosystem, digital media cities have been questioned over their false promise to empower democratic movements in cities. Instead, in digital media cities, opportunities for online participation have been undermined by diminishing urban public spaces to make way for new modern infrastructures, as Padawangi et al. (2014: 4) observed:

> Even after successful political reform, displacements and dispossessions of people from land continue unabated through various means, such as global megaprojects presented as symbols of modernity. Encroachments into neighbourhoods, culturally vital sites and social spaces are justified for the sake of competitiveness and progress.

As digital media cities have become increasingly hegemonic across Asia, the likelihood for "urban subversion" to disrupt neoliberal governmentality diminishes. This reflects a deeply rooted relationship between media platforms, communication practices and urban social activities. Culture can act as a tool for encouraging expanded citizenship and as a technology of social control.

Moreover, monitoring and regulating public behaviors mediated by the authoritarian governments and global corporations has become a reality of the cultural life in these cities. Culture is no longer about a way of life to be cherished. Culture has been turned into a mechanism for the effective operation of the new cybernetic environment for a new Asian modernity. Governments are not only able to re-create social hierarchies based on unequal access to the means of participation, but can also disguise a wider intent to control social behavior through the extension of influential use of surveillance technologies to an unprecedented degree. Therefore, cultural retrofitting in the Asian cities that hope to develop digital media cities requires a careful consideration of existing creative milieus, and investment in new digital media infrastructures has to take local social and cultural values as a priority rather than an afterthought. Even with the success of attracting global media corporations, digital media cities risk losing support from the public due to the friction between globalizing aspirations and local imaginaries.

Conclusion

The observation that digital media technologies alone can do very little to ensure the flourishing of the city as a public sphere is core to rethinking the role of public space in different social and cultural contexts (Herold and Marolt 2011). This chapter has offered insights into some of the key dynamics underlying digital media cities in Asia. As suggested in this chapter, neoliberalism has become a governing logic of digital media cities, written under the sign of corporatization and technological utopianism. The focus on developing digital media technologies and attracting global media corporations can only accelerate the spread of the neoliberal imaginary. This is a process of worlding – where cities adopt new cultural forms and technologies to their existing cultural system, involving labeling local places and ways of life as old-fashioned, regressive and resistant to global cultural values. Worlding has clearly motivated many Asian cities to adopt a modernization based on catching up with the West. It is seen to be highly effective in re-branding what appear "non-places" as new creative destinations and locations. It offers, on the surface, a hope that investing heavily in globally standardized cultural, and increasingly technological, infrastructure can be a direct route to a successful global city. Nevertheless, such urban technological utopianism requires what is often a crude cultural retrofitting, creating new conditions for cultural imperialism. By not nurturing a local urban cultural politics and policy, digital media cities in Asia are at risk of entering perpetual catch-up, where Western cultural knowledge, cultural values and ways of life are privileged over local ones.

The experiences of digital media cities in Asia call for nuanced and critical research on culturally specific experiences of mediated urbanism. Firstly, it is important to register the very different historical context within which the Asian digital media city emerges, compared to those in the West. Beneath the mega-media city projects, there is a series of cultural retrofitting, involving the transformation of the socio-political sphere and the fundamental values, beliefs and norms of everyday life in these societies. Secondly, it is necessary to pay more attention to the way rapid urbanization transforms social and political lives in Asian cities and its connection to new digital media communication technologies, such as how citizens' rights to the city trade for "convenience" and "efficacy." Lastly, it is crucial to recognize cultural imperialism which has been normalized by the extended power of global media corporations that control not only the distribution of content but also the big data associated with cultural industries. The extension of corporate power is a route to data colonialism which has become an underlying issue for many emergent digital media cities. Most developing nations in Asia rely on global corporations based elsewhere for developing essential digital media infrastructures. The extent to which local social identity is shaped by a set of algorithms formulated by global platform corporations such as Facebook and YouTube is a critical issue today.

References

Ang, I. (2001) "Desperately Guarding Borders," in S. Yao (ed) *House of Glass: Culture, Modernity and the State in Southeast Asia*, Singapore: ISEAS Publishing.

Bernot, A., Trauth-Goik, A. and Trevaskes, S. (2021) "Handling COVID-19 with Big Data in China," *Australian Journal of International Affairs*, 75(5): 480–486.

Braester, Y. (2013) "The Architecture of Utopia," in J. Kloet and L. Scheen (eds) *Spectacle and the City*, Amsterdam: Amsterdam University Press.

Brooker, D. (2012) "Build it and They Will Come?," *Asian Geographer*, 29(1): 39–56.

Carter, D. (2013) "Urban Regeneration, Digital Development Strategies and the Knowledge Economy," *Journal of the Knowledge Economy*, 4(2): 169–89.

Cooke, P. and Lazzeretti, L. (2008) *Creative Cities, Cultural Clusters and Local Economic Development*, Cheltenham: Edward Elgar.

Couldry, N. and Mejias, U. (2019) "Data Colonialism," *Television & New Media*, 20(4): 336–49.

Curtin, M. (2003) "Media Capital," *International Journal of Cultural Studies*, 6(2): 202–28.

Dal Maso, G., Robertson, S. and Rogers, D. (2019) "Cultural Platform Capitalism," *Social & Cultural Geography*, 22: 565–80.

Datta, A. (2015) "New Urban Utopias of Postcolonial India," *Dialogues in Human Geography*, 5(1): 3–22.

Deuze, M. (2007) "Convergence Culture in the Creative Industries," *International Journal of Cultural Studies*, 10(2): 243–63.

Dutta, M. (2019) "Digital Transformations, Smart Cities and Displacements," *International Journal of Media Studies*, 1(1): 1–21.

Florida, R. (2002) *The Rise of the Creative Class*, New York: Basic Books.

Garcia, B. (2004) "Cultural Policy and Urban Regeneration in Western European Cities," *Local Economy*, 19(4): 312–26.

Graham, S. and Marvin, S. (2001) *Splintering Urbanism: Networked Infrastructures, Technological Mobilities and the Urban Condition*, London: Routledge.

Granier, B. and Kudo, H. (2016) "How are Citizens Involved in Smart Cities?," *Information Polity*, 21(1): 61–76.

Gu, X. (2019) "The Paradox of Maker Movement in China," in J. Hunsinger and A. Schrock (eds) *Making Our World: The Hacker and Maker Movements in Context*, New York: Peter Lang.

Gu, X. (2020) "From Creative Cities to Media Cities," in Z. Krajina and D. Stevenson (eds) *The Routledge Companion to Urban Media and Communication*, New York: Routledge.

Gu, X. and Shea, P. (2019) "Fabbing the Chinese Maker Identity," in L. Bogers and L. Chiappini (eds) *The Critical Makers Reader: (Un)learning Technology*, Amsterdam: Institute of Network Cultures.

Harvey, D. (1989) "From Managerialism to Entrepreneurialism," *Geografiska Annaler: Series B, Human Geography*, 71(1): 3–17.

Herold, D. K. and Marolt, P. (eds) (2011) *Online Society in China: Creating, Celebrating, and Instrumentalizing the Online Carnival*, London and New York: Routledge.

Hesmondhalgh, D. (2008) "Neoliberalism, Imperialism and the Media," in D. Hesmondhalgh and J. Toynbee (eds) *The Media and Social Theory*, London: Routledge.

Hesmondhalgh, D. (2013) *The Cultural Industries*, London: SAGE.

Hesmondhalgh, D. and Baker, S. (2013) *Creative Labour: Media Work in Three Cultural Industries*, London: Routledge.

Hollands, R. (2008) "Will the Real Smart City Please Stand Up?," *City*, 12(3): 303–20.

Hoyler, M. and Watson, A. (2013) "Global Media Cities in Transnational Media Networks," *Tijdschrift Voor Economische en Sociale Geografie*, 104(1): 90–108.

Hu, H. (2005) *Cultural Industries and National Cultural Security*, Guangzhou: Guangdong Renming Publishing House.

Jin, D.Y. (2007) "Reinterpretation of Cultural Imperialism," *Media, Culture and Society*, 29(5): 753–71.

Kamath, A. (2018) "Untouchable Cellphones?," *Critical Asian Studies*, 50(3): 375–94.

Kim, Y. (2008) *Media Consumption and Everyday Life in Asia*, London: Routledge.

Koolhaas, R. (1995) *Generic City*, Rotterdam: Sikkens Foundation.

Kostka, G. (2019) "China's Social Credit Systems and Public Opinion," *New Media and Society*, 21(7): 1565–93.

Kuecker, G. and Hartley, K. (2020) "How Smart Cities Became the Urban Norm," *Annals of the American Association of Geographers*, 110(2): 516–24.

Kusno, A. (2013) *After the New Order: Space, Politics and Jakarta*, Hawaii: University of Hawaii Press.

Kwet, M. (2019) "Digital Colonialism," *Race & Class*, 60(4): 3–26.

Lemke, T. (2002) "Foucault, Governmentality and Critique," *Rethinking Marxism*, 14(3): 49–64.

Lyon, D. (2003) "Cyberspace, Surveillance and Social Control," in K.C. Ho, R. Kluver and C.C. Yang (eds) *Asia.com: Asia Encounters the Internet*, London: Routledge.

McQuire, S. (2016) *Geomedia: Networked Cities and the Future of Public Space*, Cambridge: Polity.

McQuire, S. (2020) "An Archaeology of the Media City," in Z. Krajina and D. Stevenson (eds) *The Routledge Companion to Urban Media and Communication*, New York: Routledge.

Morozov, E. (2019) "Capitalism's New Clothes," *The Baffler*, 4 February.

Mould, O. (2015) *Urban Subversion and the Creative City*, London: Routledge.

Murray, R. and Hand, C. (2015) "Making Culture," *Visible Language*, 49(3): 141–55.

Novy, J. and Colomb, C. (2013) "Struggling for the Right to the (Creative) City in Berlin and Hamburg," *International Journal of Urban and Regional Research*, 37(5): 1816–38.

Oakley, K. (2006) "Include Us Out – Economic Development and Social Policy in the Creative Industries," *Cultural Trends*, 15(4): 255–73.

O'Connor, J. and Gu, X. (2020) *Red Creative: Culture and Modernity in China*, Bristol: Intellect.

Ong, A. (2000) "Graduated Sovereignty in Southeast Asia," *Theory, Culture & Society*, 17(4): 55–75.

Ong, A. (2006) *Neoliberalism as Exception: Mutations in Citizenship and Sovereignty*, Durham: Duke University Press.

Padawangi, R., Marolt, P. and Douglass, M. (2014) "Introduction to the Special Issue: Insurgencies, Social Media and the Public," *IDPR*, 36(1): 1–13.

Roy, A. and Ong, A. (2011) *Worlding Cities: Asian Experiments and the Art of Being Global*, New York: Wiley.

Ryoo, W. (2009) "Globalization, Or the Logic of Cultural Hybridization," *Asian Journal of Communication*, 19(2): 137–51.

Schwak, J. (2016) "Branding South Korea in a Competitive World Order," *Asian Studies Review*, 40(3): 427–44.

Sinclair, J. and Harrison, M. (2004) "Globalization, Nation and Television in Asia," *Television & New Media*, 5(1): 41–54.

Srnicek, N. (2017) *Platform Capitalism*, New York: Wiley.

Sundaram, R. (2010) *Pirate Modernity: Delhi's Media Urbanism*, London: Routledge.

Weiss, M. (2014) "New Media, New Activism," *International Development Planning Review*, 36(1): 91–109.

5

SOFT POWER AND CULTURAL NATIONALISM

Globalization of the Korean Wave

Youna Kim

Since the late 1990s South Korea (hereafter Korea) has emerged as a new center for the globalization of popular culture, referred to as the "Korean Wave" or "Hallyu" – a term first coined by Chinese news media in the middle of 1998 to describe Chinese youth's sudden craze for Korean cultural products. Initiated by the export of television dramas, it now includes a range of cultural products including K-pop music, films, animation, online games, smartphones, fashion, cosmetics, food and lifestyles (Kim 2013, 2019, 2021). Digital generations today look for diverse sources of entertainment, culture and identity, not necessarily American or European. The Korean Wave has become cultural resources for the growing mass-mediated popular imagination, which is situated within a broader process of global consumerism and a new sphere of digital culture. The popularity of the Korean Wave was initially concentrated in neighboring Asian markets but now it reaches the Americas, Europe and the Middle East. This is the first instance of a major global circulation of Korean popular culture in history.

In 2020, the Korean film *Parasite* (2019) won the most awards – Best Picture, Best Director, Best International Feature Film and Best Original Screenplay – at the Academy Awards. Western critics commented that 92 years of Oscars history were shattered when this Korean film became the first non-English language film to win the award for Best Picture, indicating that Hollywood's traditional reliance on White stories by White powers may finally be declining (*New York Times* 2020; *Washington Post* 2020). To the surprise of the director of *Parasite*, Bong Joon-Ho, his collective of global fans, referred to as the BongHive, have championed his movie on social media and made him a viral celebrity. *Parasite*'s unprecedented historic success has attracted attention to Korea, drawing an unfamiliar spotlight on the power and influence of Korean popular culture (Kim 2021). As another historic success, the Korean boyband BTS has topped the Billboard music chart with their popular albums including *Love Yourself*. BTS has

DOI: 10.4324/9781003130628-7

become the first K-pop group to speak at the United Nations, helping to launch the UNICEF's campaign "Generation Unlimited" that promotes education, employment and empowerment for young people globally (BBC 2018; CNN 2019). The UN has stressed the need for the younger generation to get involved, and thus invited this popular K-pop boyband that attracts and influences a global youth community, coupled with fast-moving digital technologies and communications. BTS's devoted fans, called ARMY all over the world, passionately promote and share their idols' stories and values via social media. Earlier in 2012, Korean singer Psy became a global phenomenon with his song *Gangnam Style* and horse-riding dance move – one of the most-watched videos on YouTube. This viral popularity prompted people around the world to seek information on Korea, the sudden attractiveness or sarcastic humor of the singer's culture.

Historically, the Korean Wave was originally initiated by the export of television dramas. In 2004, Korean popular culture became a transnational phenomenon, with a romance drama *Winter Sonata* (2002) featuring beautiful winter scenery, pure love and a hero's unconditional love for a woman that captivated many female audiences in Asia (Kim 2007). The Korean Wave reached another peak with the airing of a historical drama *Jewel in the Palace* (2003), which was sold to over 120 countries. A military romance drama *Descendants of the Sun* (2016) has been translated into 32 different languages, testifying to the widening appeal of Korean dramas (BBC 2016). One unique feature of this drama is its military setting with patriotism as the armed forces play a significant part in South Korean life, with the constant looming threat of war with North Korea. The impact of the Korean Wave has reached into communist North Korea. In 2005, a 20-year-old North Korean soldier defected across the demilitarized zone and the reason given, according to South Korean military officials, was that the soldier had grown to admire and yearn for South Korea after watching its television dramas which had been smuggled across the border from China (*New York Times* 2005). Similar cases have continued to occur, as the means of access to the Korean Wave has expanded through the use of digital technologies and mobile phones among North Koreans (*New York Times* 2016; Kim 2019).

What does the Korean Wave mean socially, culturally and politically in a digital age? This chapter critically explores the development of the Korean Wave and its complex implications with soft power and cultural nationalism. The globalization of the Korean Wave is a facet of de-centralizing multiplicity of global cultural flows and its meanings and significance can be seen as a conscious, and often intentional, way to counter the threat and insensibility of the Western-dominated media market. Cultural flows in the international media landscape are no longer one way from the West to the rest due to the increasing multidirectional and contra-flows emerging from non-Western and non-central contexts. Korea, as a postcolonial and somewhat peripheral nation, has strengthened its national cultural industry to compete against the dominant flow of Western cultural products, while consolidating a relatively rapidly growing position in the regional market and beyond. The Korean Wave, as an important resource for soft power, is becoming a major site for the production, representation, circulation and consumption of global popular culture.

Globalization of Korean Cultural Industry

The Korean cultural industry has been developed for socioeconomic, cultural and political reasons since the late 1990s (Kim 2007, 2013, 2021). Since the 1997 IMF financial crisis, the Korean government has thoroughly re-examined the process of modernization and targeted the export of popular media culture as a new economic initiative, one of the major sources of foreign revenue vital for the country's economic survival and advancement. Korea, with limited natural resources, sought to reduce its dependence on a manufacturing base under competitive threat from China and promote a chimneyless industry. Trade experts have called for the nation to shift its key development strategy to fostering overseas marketing for culture, technology and services, including the popular media and distribution services. The government has striven to capitalize on Korean popular culture and given the same national support in export promotion that was once provided to electronics and cars. The Korean Wave started from the efforts of private sectors, but state-led developmentalist nationalism has played a key role in the speed of growth. Systematic operation by the governmentality of the developmentalist state and institutional strategies by the industry have combined to produce the condition for the rise of the Korean Wave.

The Korean cultural industry has been developed as a national project competing within globalization, not against it. In the late 1990s, the rise of Korean popular culture was facilitated by the opening of the Korean market to global cultural forces. Historically, Korea faced Japanese colonialism (1910–45), the arbitrary division by Western powers into opposed states, North and South (1948), the Korean War (1950–53), and the military rule and successive authoritarian regimes (1961–93) that involved infringements of freedom in political, cultural and artistic expression. Globalization had long been accompanied by the fear of Western cultural invasion, and the fear was amplified by the uncertainty of the competitiveness of Korean popular culture. Japanese popular culture was equally feared and banned in Korea due to the colonial history between the two countries. Only in 1998, more than 50 years after Japanese colonial rule ended, did the Korean government begin to lift a ban on cultural imports from Japan. At the same time, in 1998, the government carried out its first five-year plan to build up the domestic cultural industry and encourage exports. By the time nearly all restrictions on Japanese culture had been lifted in 2004, the Korean Wave had spread across Asia. The sense of crisis coming from the opening of the market to the West and Japan has rather strengthened and benefited the Korean cultural industry.

The first major, yet unplanned and accidental, impact of the Korean Wave started with the export of Korean television dramas that were not produced for international audiences but for domestic audiences (Kim 2013). Dramas have been a major driving force of the Korean Wave, dominating the majority of the television program exports. The one-way flow of American television programs has significantly decreased, as Korea has reduced foreign cultural products since the mid-1990s while increasing its production and exports of domestic media products. In 1999, at the early stage of the Korean Wave, the average price of one Korean drama was $750 per one-hour episode in overseas countries. Only five years later, the range quickly became $15,000–$20,000, more than a 20-fold increase (*Korea Times* 2005). Korean dramas are infused with urban middle-class scenes and embrace the reality of Confucian tradition and alternative modernity. Typically miniseries of 16–20 episodes, they are easily digestible, less sexualized and violent than American dramas, and delicately expose universal themes of love. Korean producers do not pay particular attention to a global formula for the success of drama, but they have nevertheless found its affective form useful to touch the sensibilities of disparate audiences. The rise of Western streaming services such as Netflix has widened the reach and popularity of Korean drama (Kim 2021). Netflix has been co-producing and adding K-drama series, both recent and nostalgic, because of an increase in popular demand from international audiences. As a part of diverse representation, Korean drama becomes a unique producer of modernity and nostalgia. While most drama productions in Korea still value the local market and want to attract more viewers in the home country, some production companies seek to diversify platforms for their works to reach global viewers since Netflix as co-producer covers a large portion of production cost and showcases dramas in more than 190 countries.

Compared to Korean drama, K-pop music is a much more deliberately planned industry targeting international audiences from its start (Kim 2013). The Korean music industry has developed rapidly, making it the sixth largest music market in the world. K-pop has evolved from a niche genre to an elaborate global industry, with the BTS ecosystem contributing $4.9 billion to Korea's GDP (Elberse and Woodham 2020). Most K-pop stars are not accidentally discovered but have been recruited and systematically produced by entertainment management companies and their "star system" that was born in the early 1990s and consolidated in the mid-1990s (Shin 2009). K-pop is not just a random response to neoliberal globalization, but a systematically planned, monitored manifestation of "entrepreneurial self." Young talents have been recruited, sometimes from an age of early teens, and trained to become multi-purpose, transnational performers who "can do everything" through Spartan training. The success of the training regime is driven by Korea's Confucian ethics of hard work, endurance, the disciplined body, obedience to higher authority and affective labor in the neoliberal cultural industry. Like manufacturing cars and televisions, this training regime is criticized as an assembly line of similar, robot-like performers whose every word and move is pre-scheduled, rehearsed and monitored by entertainment companies. As exemplified by BTS, K-pop is not just music but a complete show of sound, fantastical visuals and performance, close to total entertainment that is uniquely appealing to international fans (Kim 2021). K-pop performers exemplify sort of pop perfectionism – catchy tunes, good singing, attractive bodies, cool clothes, mesmerizing movements and other attractive attributes in a non-threatening, pleasant package (Lie 2015). This pleasurable experience can make international fans feel how difficult it is not to enjoy it, even when they may be fully aware of its addictiveness and extremely photogenic, visual illusion. K-pop is perhaps the most hybridized cosmopolitan consumerist form of the Korean Wave, or a futuristic pastiche that sounds like a utopian blending of all contemporary musical genres. K-pop is in essence all things hybrid – a fusion of local, regional and Western cultures, forms, styles, genres, narratives or identities – accelerated by digital technologies and social media, yet without necessarily eliminating the best of Korea's distinctive traditional values, emotional aesthetics and expressive performances.

Korean cinema marked its 100th anniversary in 2019; the global success of *Parasite* stands as the culmination of the centennial development of the film industry into an international cultural powerhouse (Kim 2021). As the fifth biggest film market in the world, Korean cinema is a notable example of non-Western cinematic success in the neoliberal order. The creation of a status comparable to that of Hollywood was enabled by state capital power of the government policy and the capital investment of conglomerates (*chaebol*) such as Samsung and Hyundai in the film industry of the 1990s. The Korean film industry had always been the object of a government focus and historically an extension of its industrial policy. Therefore, Korean films reflected the industry's orientation toward quasi-industrial production, the economy at a critical moment of transition (the post-IMF crisis) and this economy's material embodiment (Jeon 2019). The emergence of the Korean Wave is a story of what happened when filmmakers finally escaped their confinement from the authoritarian regimes, and became autonomous to realize a politically and socially informed cinema, but also to look beyond this to a new era when films were no longer obligated to speak for their nation (Paquet 2010). The Korean Wave films appear to constitute a counter-cinema that seeks to resist the global cultural standardization by Hollywood power and create a unique space. Yet simultaneously, many Korean filmmakers have blended Hollywood styles and genres with characteristically Korean stories and themes, such as the division of the nation, the Korean War, Confucian values and struggles in extraordinarily compressed modernity, which uniquely appeal to international audiences. Korean cinema increasingly faces a dilemma in reconciling issues around the construction of national identity on screen, while at the same time trying to sustain a viable and popular film industry in the face of competition from Hollywood, capitalism and neoliberalism in a digital age.

Digital Power: Digital Fandom

The rise of the Korean Wave is an amalgamation of the strategic export policy at a time when the Asian media market is rapidly growing, fueled by the emergence of the affluent urban middle class and the globalized consumer culture. Younger generations, who were born into the digital netizen era and have grown up with smartphones, YouTube and social media, may have developed a differentiating marker of identity through cosmopolitan consumption practices transcending different languages and cultural prejudices. The rise of social media-oriented, individualized, mobile yet networked generations creates a diverse, outward-looking, eclectic and distinguishable taste for transnational popular culture, deliberately disembedding themselves from the local cultural conventions of previous generations. The phenomenon of the Korean Wave is one of imagined cosmopolitanism in the realm of globalized consumer culture (Kim 2013). The primary site for the development and proliferation of shared global consciousness is located in the mundane, representational domain of popular media culture and digital technologies.

The global expansion of the Korean Wave can be attributed to the power of the Internet and social media – aided by fans' participatory culture and voluntary labor in prompt uploading, forwarding and sharing with wider audiences, while shaping the production, circulation and reception of the Korean Wave (Kim 2013, 2021). It is important to recognize the active role played by marginal, largely invisible yet devoted fans in shaping the Korean Wave's staying power. Fan-subbing, or amateur subtitling, has been critical to the growth of the Korean Wave as dispersed fans contribute their linguistic knowledge and time for the greater work of the collective. Subtitle files are made by fans almost as soon as dramas are aired and songs released. Versions of Korean dramas, and lyrics for songs within the dramas, are available in 15–20 different languages. Digital fandom, as one of the most distinguishing aspects of the Korean Wave, becomes a virtual knowledge community that is encouraged to connect with their celebrity, produce their own vernacular discourses and build the celebrity's brand community on social media. Driven by a desire to help their celebrity, fans do real-time translations of celebrity's performances on social media. This organically formed, collaborative culture of linguistic translations, for a language that holds a peripheral status in the global media industry, is suggestive of fans' voluntary labor and affective investment built around shared values and imaginations.

Fan experiences of Korean popular culture and related social media spaces are performative, co-creative and affective practices that potentially create cracks and fissures in the dominant social imaginaries and competing ideological significations of the way the world is or should be. Unlike the television broadcasting era, in an era of narrowcasting reflected in the rise of digital media technologies, the fan as a specialized yet dedicated consumer has become a centerpiece of foreign niche media producers' marketing strategies. Fan audiences are wooed and championed by niche cultural industries, as long as their activities do not divert from the principles of capitalist exchange and recognize industries' legal ownership of the object of fandom (Gray et al. 2007). The global attraction of the Korean Wave has often grown out of a collective social energy that operates across creative cultural industries and connects official content creators and performers to the multiple non-official hubs of digital fan communities that exist in an elusive liminal state between complicity with, and resistance to, the industries. It represents a distinctive cultural terrain of globalization "from below" based on proliferating digital platforms for dialogic and dynamic interaction that may consciously subvert and challenge enduring structures of power in all spheres of influence (Kim 2021).

Fandom is generally associated with cultural forms that the mainstream, dominant value system denigrates. It is related to the cultural tastes of subordinated formations of people, particularly with those disempowered by race, gender, age and class. The Korean Wave fandom in the West is created largely by Asian diasporas, women and young people of color who occupy marginal subject positions and are interested in other aspects of Asian popular culture as alternatives to the mainstream discourses that privilege White representation (Hubinette 2018; Ohlheiser 2020). Fan communities activate multiple transnational sites of engagement that not only aggregate collective intelligence but also come into conflict with mainstream identities. The Korean Wave may allow fans to reflexively imagine new identities and practices at the heart of their social realities, hierarchies and inequalities (Kim 2013). Digital fan communities can be seen as alternative spaces of identity in which a different voice can be raised and a self can be expressed, contested, re-articulated or re-affirmed in relation to global cultural Others. The Korean Wave and its fandom among digitally connected consumers can be a statement about their dispositions, dis/likings and aspirations, not just reflective of the actual, present self but also formative of the desired, future self (Choi and Maliangkay 2015).

Soft Power and Cultural Nationalism

The success of the Korean Wave overseas is drawing an unfamiliar spotlight on a culture once colonized or overshadowed for centuries by powerful countries. Asia has long been under the influence of Western and Japanese cultural products. In the Western imagination, Korea was once thought to be sandwiched between Japan and China and known only for exporting cars and electronics products, but now Korea has made itself known through its culture. The growth of the Korean Wave has spurred the imagination of the power of Asia, vernacular modernities and modernizing desires (Kim 2013). There is a lingering anti-colonial sentiment lurking in the hearts of people in many parts of the region. Anti-Japanism is a symptom of the historical trauma of the Japanese empire and its legacy, although young people's consumption of Japanese popular culture does not mean that they are becoming Japanese (Ching 2019). The Korean Wave appears to benefit from the sense of solidarity, sympathy more than resentment, which people have toward the country that shared a similar colonial past and continues to struggle in the current postcolonial situation. The Korean Wave is seen to be a less problematic source of power and ideological threat than American media imperialism and Japanese influence. Arising as a part of the historical milieu of decolonization, the significance of the Korean Wave is reflective of a region-wide reassertion or imaginary of Asianism, and a key site of decolonization work that may self-reflexively interrogate and unsettle the global hegemony of Euro-America.

Implicitly, an intriguing reason behind the successful phenomenon of the Korean Wave is the nation's historical colonial victimhood – a combination of Korea's tragic history, the intensity of Korean emotive culture and the perceived non-threatening nature of its people in a current postcolonial situation (Kim 2013). The popularity of the Korean Wave can be understood by the dynamics of global power relations and political sensitivities, while the political conflicts and socio-cultural tensions of the divided nation have been used to good effect to create emotionally powerful content. Korean culture reflects the nation's unique sensibility, *han* – a Korean word for a deeply felt sense of oppression and deep-seated grief. Often, the ambivalent nature of foreignness in imported Western cultural products can be perceived by two extremes – fascination and threat – but the threat is less manifested in the way the Korean Wave is received and affectively invested by audiences and fans across Asia and beyond. In the past, national images of Korea were negatively associated with the demilitarized zone, division and political disturbances, but now such images are giving way to the vitality of trendy, transnational entertainers and cutting-edge technology.

As a participatory pilgrimage practice, the interest in the Korean Wave has triggered an increase in foreign tourists visiting the locations where their favorite dramas, movies and acts have been filmed. Place promotion is mediated through Korean popular culture in fetishized ways, boosting the tourism industry and capitalizing on consumers' emotional engagement (Oh 2018). As each city competes with others for global tourists, national or city identity is reconfigured in the "hyper-spatial," the stretching of space and time to accommodate the accelerating flows of capital, ideas and desires that characterize the world of neoliberal capitalism (King 2018). The Korean Wave has prompted an interest in learning the Korean language, culture and the country, as popular culture is ideal for developing fluid forms of linguistic expression and transmedia storytelling among young people (I. Lee 2018). The global popularity of the Korean Wave has led to heightened market awareness of general Korean products (KBS World 2020). Overseas sales of Korean consumer goods, including televisions, mobile phones, cars, clothing and cosmetics, have risen in the wake of the strategic appropriation of the Korean Wave. The Korean cultural industry is seen to commodify the nation, exporting its popular culture as a cool national brand. The Korean Wave has become an integral part of Korea's affective attention economy built around affective relationships and digital connections with audiences to shape desires, preferences and aspirations.

The Korean government appropriates popular culture as an effective way to create and sell a dynamic image of the nation through "soft power," a cultural weapon to entice, attract and influence international audiences without coercion (Nye 2004, 2008; Kim 2013, 2019, 2021). The nation can be re-invented as a more favorable and lasting brand by the government's cultural policy that global circulations of media cultural products promote the construction of soft power, an attractive image of the nation as a whole. The immediate profits or effects created by the Korean Wave are important, but the improvement of the national image, though intangible, is considered as more important. The Korean Wave's potentiality as soft power may have a significant and complex impact on cultural diplomacy as well as on trade, tourism, academy and other national interests across various contexts. The government, along with private sectors and the academy, has worked on the re-creation of its national image and cultural identity for multiple diffuse effects of soft power by integrating the Korean Wave. Various governmental organizations including the Ministry of Culture, Sports and Tourism (MCST) and the Korea Trade-Investment Promotion Agency (KOTRA) have set aside budgets for programs to promote the national image. This dependency on the Korean Wave to create soft power and develop new markets, such as South America, Southeast Asia and the Middle East, is particularly significant at a time when the world economy shows signs of slowing down. The Korean Wave has heightened the nation's visibility around the world and captured the imagination of a new generation. It has possibly changed foreign perceptions of South Korea, which has dominantly been viewed as an industrial powerhouse and whose achievements have been overshadowed by the military threat of North Korea, or often ignored by more attention paid to the powerful neighboring countries, China and Japan. Likability of the Korean Wave celebrities or emotional engagement with the Korean Wave has a significant influence on the national image of Korea (B. Lee et al. 2015; H. Lee et al. 2020).

Going beyond the traditional state-centric diplomacy, the government has not only promoted the Korean Wave to create positive dispositions toward the nation but also utilized the cultural diplomacy of the Korean Wave celebrities to mobilize the politics of attraction within the commercially driven digital social media that provide a multitude of connections to global audiences and global public spheres (Kim 2021). As a part of the country's statecraft, the Korean Wave celebrities are summoned by the government to play a supporting role in a realm of diplomacy among world leaders and are appointed as honorary ambassadors for the country to use their brand power in cultural promotion abroad. They can help the state to soften diplomatic tensions, re-fashion and re-brand the once colonized nation as a "cool Korea" brand for the global public. Compared to established democracies in the world, Korea shows very low trust in political institutions and politicians (Diamond and Shin 2014). In the context of the public crisis of trust, celebrities are more likely to fill the void in public trust vacated by the political classes, even if their goals remain elusive. The classic definition of diplomats as agents of the state and the national interest excludes celebrities, just as it does all non-state actors; this restrictive view does not reflect the degree to which celebrities have gained recognition as actors in global affairs (Cooper 2016). Celebrity diplomats combine the assertive individualism characteristic of the West with an appreciation of universal or cosmopolitan values, and the mode of operation is decidedly populist. Celebrities generally avoid the hard power issues of security, while concentrating on the soft power issues pertaining to cultural and socioeconomic conditions. Aided by sophisticated experts with whom they surround themselves, celebrities know how to work with the mainstream and social media, and celebrities' cultural diplomacy elicits considerable amounts of press and public attention as well as the global support of digital fans.

In the digital age, collaborative creativity "from above" (nation-states, institutions, media industries) and "from below" (digital fans as grassroots intermediaries, producers-consumers, publics) – albeit the intersections of the two forces are unpredictable – can appropriate popular culture to make its origin nation, language and culture attractive to international audiences and open possibilities for soft power. Not only the top-down approach but also the bottom-up, voluntary and affective participation play a significant role in spreading popular culture and mediating soft power, although the bottom-up actors or their natural, horizontal, cultural influence do not necessarily operate coherently with the top-down governmental or media actors. Digital technologies have ushered in affective politics, new strategies for mobilizing and capturing affect and emotion that have become central engines driving media culture and politics in the digital age, contrary to the traditional dogma of rational political actors (Boler and Davis 2021). The politics of emotion, or propaganda by other "soft" means, are not new but have become strikingly apparent in digital diplomacy especially when a popular culture or the symbolic meaning of celebrity is involved. Today's rapid media globalization and the mundane use of digital technologies present unprecedented opportunities for soft power as well as challenges.

The Korean Wave is now creating Korea's unprecedented strongest form of soft power, however with limitations. Like Japan's popular nationalism, Korea has been among the most successful in propagating its popular culture internationally and is at the forefront of national branding projects (Sakamoto and Epstein 2021). At the heart of this process is the intimacy of global capitalism with national hegemony, as the state intervention in the Korean Wave fits in the globalized market economy. Policy discussions in Korea tend to utilize popular culture as a transnational commodity, taking a neoliberal capitalist approach. The production of popular culture as transnational capital and its symbolic value continues to proliferate in the emergence of the creative cultural economy. Korea's soft power is likely to be an extension of its economic influence, which is a core component of hard power. The Korean Wave, as a complex form of cultural nationalism and soft power, has emerged not only as a core component of the nation's economic competitiveness but also as a powerful resource for social influence and cultural diplomacy at national, regional and global levels in the digital age. Popular culture has become a potentially important resource for soft power diplomacy, transcultural collaborations, dialogues and struggles to win the hearts and minds of people. Such a potentiality is evident in the region of Asia that is still haunted by colonization and violence (Chua 2012). Asian nations are keen to invest in soft power to expand their existing economic influence and acquire more sophisticated politico-cultural leverage (Lee and Melissen 2011; *Korea Herald* 2019).

Amid the national interest in soft power, the issue of unequal cultural flows is pronounced in Asia. For instance, it has been overwhelmingly Korean and Japanese popular cultures such as television dramas that enter China, Taiwan, Hong Kong and Singapore, yet there is very little flow in the reverse direction (Chua 2012). This one-way unilateral flow may serve to disseminate the nation's ideology through attractive transnational culture and not meaningfully lead to inter-Asian dialogues and cross-cultural exchanges. The heightened visibility of the Korean Wave has been criticized by the mass media and the public overseas as a colonial-esque cultural invasion of Korea. Popular culture can be an effective instrument of soft power, yet the meaning or desired outcome of popular culture is contingent upon the appropriation and negotiation by target people or consumer power. What the Korean Wave signifies, what meanings are represented in the Korean Wave and how far these representations map on to established and dominant cultural formations have to be decided by the indeterminacy and fluidity of meaning-making by people under their contexts (Kim 2013). The success or limitation of soft power attraction is highly contextual among different communities (Nye 2004).

The consequences are complex, both intended and unintended. On the one hand, the Korean Wave, as a state-subsidized "soft power" initiative, has changed the dynamics of the media landscape in Asia, challenging the characterization of globalization as a Western-centric cultural force. The growing visibility of the Korean Wave is an example of the subversive contra-flow emerging to service an ever growing diverse consumer market against a one-way flow from the West to the peripheral rest. On the other hand, its increasing volume and velocity have generated a sense of discontent and tension in some local communities of Asia, giving rise to a backlash of anti-Korean sentiment. This tension is evident in anti-Korean Wave movements and xenophobic animosity online in East Asia (Chua 2012; Chen 2017; Park et al. 2019) and the developed Southeast Asian nations of Thailand, Malaysia and the Philippines (Ainslie et al. 2017). It is usually confronted with non-consumer communities reinforcing reactive nationalist discourse with the complicity of local media productions and the state. The Internet has become an influential tool for nationalism, fueling anti-Korean sentiment. Japanese nationalist groups held demonstrations against Fuji Television, demanding that the television company stop excessively broadcasting Korean dramas and other Korean entertainment (*JoongAng Ilbo* 2011). Similarly, in Taiwan, Korean dramas faced negative sentiment for the excessive airing of Korean shows in prime time slots (*Dong-A Ilbo* 2012). In China, the biggest market for the Korean Wave, Chinese interest has naturally prompted a tourism boom. However, in 2017, the Chinese government announced that it would ban all group travel to South Korea as a response to South Korea's decision to deploy the US THAAD (Terminal High Altitude Area Defense) missile system with the sophisticated radar in uncomfortable proximity to Chinese soil, although THAAD was a necessary deterrent to belligerent North Korea from the South Korean government's security perspective (*TIME* 2017).

However, a paradox is that the floating signifier of Korean cultural nationalism – newly expressing self-confidence, pride, imaginary of Koreanness, cultural authenticity, inner passion and energy through popular culture – is also the reason why the Korean Wave has powerful appeal across the rapidly digitalized, porous world today (Jeong et al. 2017; *Forbes* 2019; Park and Lee 2019). This is a reflection of a nation's yearning for an independent cultural force, a particular speaking position in the struggle for national cultural identity amid the threatening presence of the mediated sphere of the West, given that the borders of the nation have increasingly become vulnerable to Western hegemony of globalization (Kim 2008, 2013). Nation-states contend with the erosion of their institutional sovereignty through regulatory regimes as the growth of transnational cultural flows coupled with the rapid dissemination of participatory technologies like social networking platforms alters traditional communication-based foundations for nation-state power and challenges the ideational monopoly once enjoyed by the nation-state (Hayden 2012). The future of a nation and its identity are being re-imagined and re-learned through de-centralizing alternative cultural flows such as the Korean Wave.

References

Ainslie, M., Lipura, S. and Lim, J. (2017) "Understanding the Hallyu Backlash in Southeast Asia," *Kritika Kultura*, 28: 63–91.

BBC (2016) "Descendants of the Sun," 27 March.

BBC (2018) "BTS Will Be First K-pop Group to Speak at the United Nations," 21 September.

Boler, M. and Davis, E. (2021) *Affective Politics of Digital Media*, New York: Routledge.

Chen, L. (2017) "The Emergence of the Anti-Hallyu Movement in China," *Media, Culture & Society*, 39(3): 374–90.

Ching, L. (2019) *Anti-Japan*, Durham: Duke University Press.

Choi, J. and Maliangkay, R. (2015) *K-Pop – The International Rise of the Korean Music Industry*, London: Routledge.

Chua, B.H. (2012) *Structure, Audience and Soft Power*, Hong Kong: Hong Kong University Press.

CNN (2019) "How BTS Became the World's Biggest Boy Band," 9 June.

Cooper, A. (2016) *Celebrity Diplomacy*, London: Routledge.

Diamond, L. and Shin, G. (2014) *New Challenges for Maturing Democracies in Korea and Taiwan*, Stanford: Stanford University Press.

Dong-A Ilbo (2012) "Korean Wave Backlash in Taiwan," 2 January.

Elberse, A. and Woodham, L. (2020) "Big Hit Entertainment and Blockbuster Band BTS," Harvard Business School Case 520–125.

Forbes (2019) "Deciding Which Korean Dramas Will Appeal to US Viewers," 17 May.

Gray, J., Sandvoss, C. and Harrington, L. (2007) *Fandom*, New York: New York University Press.

Hayden, C. (2012) *The Rhetoric of Soft Power*, Lanham: Lexington Books.

Hubinette, T. (2018) "Who are the Swedish K-pop Fans?," *Culture and Empathy*, 1(1–4): 34–48.

Jeon, J. (2019) *Vicious Circuits: Korea's IMF Cinema and the End of the American Century*, Stanford: Stanford University Press.

Jeong, J., Lee, S. and Lee, S. (2017) "Korean Wave: When Indonesians Routinely Consume Korean Pop Culture," *International Journal of Communication*, 11(May): 20.

JoongAng Ilbo (2011) "Hallyu's Popularity Breeds New Wave of Protests in Japan," 7 November.

KBS World (2020) "Economic Effects of Oscar-winning Film Parasite," 17 February.

Kim, Y. (2007) "The Rising East Asian Wave: Korean Media Go Global," in D. Thussu (ed) *Media on the Move: Global Flow and Contra-Flow*, London: Routledge.

Kim, Y. (2008) *Media Consumption and Everyday Life in Asia*, London: Routledge.

Kim, Y. (2013) *The Korean Wave: Korean Media Go Global*, London: Routledge.

Kim, Y. (2019) *South Korean Popular Culture and North Korea*, London: Routledge.

Kim, Y. (2021) *The Soft Power of the Korean Wave: Parasite, BTS and Drama*, London: Routledge.

King, R. (2018) *Seoul: Memory, Reinvention and the Korean Wave*, Honolulu: University of Hawaii Press.

Korea Herald (2019) "ASEAN-Korea Summit: From BTS to Netflix and Beyond," 4 November.

Korea Times (2005) "Is Hallyu a One-way Street?," 22 April.

Lee, B., Ham, S. and Kim, D. (2015) "The Effects of Likability of Korean Celebrities, Dramas and Music on Preferences for Korean Restaurants," *International Journal of Hospitality Management*, 46(April): 200–12.

Lee, H., Chae, M. and Lew, Y. (2020) "The Application of Categorization and Stereotype Content Theories to Country of Origin Image," *Asia Pacific Business Review*, 26(3): 336–61.

Lee, I. (2018) "Effects of Contact with Korean Popular Culture on KFL Learners' Motivation," *The Korean Language in America*, 22(1): 25–45.

Lee, S. and Melissen, J. (2011) *Public Diplomacy and Soft Power in East Asia*, New York: Palgrave Macmillan.

Lie, J. (2015) *K-Pop: Popular Music, Cultural Amnesia and Economic Innovation in South Korea*, Oakland: University of California Press.

New York Times (2005) "Roll Over, Godzilla: Korea Rules," 28 June.

New York Times (2016) "13 North Koreans Working Abroad Defect to the South," 8 April.

New York Times (2020) "Parasite Earns Best-Picture Oscar, First for a Movie Not in English," 9 February.

Nye, J. (2004) *Soft Power: The Means to Success in World Politics*, New York: PublicAffairs.

Nye, J. (2008) *The Powers to Lead*, New York: Oxford University Press.

Oh, Y. (2018) *Pop City*, Ithaca: Cornell University Press.

Ohlheiser, A. (2020) "How K-pop Fans Became Celebrated Online Vigilantes," *MIT Technology Review*, 5 June.

Paquet, D. (2010) *New Korean Cinema*, New York: Wallflower Press.

Park, J. and Lee, A. (2019) *The Rise of K-Dramas*, Jefferson: McFarland.

Park, J., Lee, Y. and Seo, H. (2019) "The Rise and Fall of Korean Drama Export to China," *International Communication Gazette*, 81(2): 139–57.

Sakamoto, R. and Epstein, S. (2021) *Popular Culture and the Transformation of Japan-Korea Relations*, London: Routledge.

Shin, H. (2009) "Have You Ever Seen the *Rain?*," *Inter-Asia Cultural Studies*, 10(4): 507–23.

TIME (2017) "A Row with China over US Missiles is Devastating South Korea's Tourism Industry," 11 April.

Washington Post (2020) "*Parasite*, Bong Joon-Ho and the Golden Age of Korean Cinema," 13 February.

6

BORDER CROSSING AND THE QUESTION OF TRANSGRESSIVE OPENNESS

Koichi Iwabuchi

This chapter considers the rise of transnational circulation and consumption of media culture and discusses what kinds of cross-border connections and exchanges it facilitates, focusing on Japanese and East Asian cases. Transnational circulation and consumption of media culture advances self-reflexive dialogue across borders by encouraging people to rethink the composition of their own societies, transnationally shared socio-cultural issues and historically consti-tuted self–Other relations. However, the facilitation of border crossing of cul-ture and communication does not necessarily accompany the transgression of clearly demarcated national cultural borders. Transnational circulation and con-sumption of media culture also promote "inter-nationalism," which highlights cultural diversity in terms of nation-to-nation relations, disengaging with and disregarding the embracement and inclusion of migrants and ethnically margin-alized groups within national borders.

Media Culture and Transnational Dialogue

In the academic discussion on globalization, "transnationalism" generally refers to a condition in which capital, people, institutions, commodities, information and media images flow across national boundaries, and cross-border activities and connections are engendered. Transnationalism challenges the nation-state's boundary policing in the modern constitution of politics, economy and culture, and the force of transnationalism operates both "from above" (by capital, indus-tries, organizations) and "from below" (by people, activism, grassroots practices). Transnationalism refers to the use of media by migrants and diasporas to main-tain cross-border connections with their homeland. The practice and experience of transnationalism differ according to a person's social positioning, generation and relation to home and host countries. In a hyper-mobile digital age, the rise of

DOI: 10.4324/9781003130628-8

temporary migrants such as international workers, overseas students, long-stayers and expatriates has further complicated the transnational links of "here" and "there" as more mundane, and constant media access to home countries generates a mixed sense of co-presence (Martin and Rizvi 2014). Transnationalism also refers to the generation of mediated cross-border connections among people irrespective of physical movement across borders. Media communication plays a key role in the construction of symbolic communities across distances and over time (Anderson 1983; Carey 1989; Thompson 1995). The modern constitution of national "imagined communities" and the national public through mass media such as newspapers, film, radio and TV is a prominent case. However, media cultures have transcended national boundaries to reach unforeseen audiences via free-to-air channels, cable and satellite channels, pirated VCDs and DVDs, Internet sites and social media. Increasing numbers of media cultures, such as films and TV programs, have come to be produced and internationally co-produced to target those international audiences. The proliferation of media products and information and their cross-border circulation has expanded the various kinds of mediated connections and communications, and the development of digital communication technologies has been intensifying the contact between people at a distance.

Transnationally mediated connections promote people's mutual understandings and self-reflexive dialogues. The abundance of information, ideas and images of various cultures and nations pushes people to take a healthy critical distance from their own life, culture and society as it facilitates "the accentuation of symbolic distancing from the spatial-temporal contexts of everyday life" (Thompson 1995: 175). As media cultures that are produced in various places regularly cross national boundaries, people now have a much wider range of resources to reflect on their own lives and socio-political issues. While the national mass media are still very powerful in this regard, transnational media culture circulation has also gained significant weight in people's public engagement in everyday life.

People's mediated participation in the public realm is not just restricted to a Habermasian public sphere in which people equally partake in deliberation about significant socio-political issues. Media culture also plays a significant role in constituting the cultural public sphere, which "provides vehicles for thought and feeling, for imagination and disputatious argument, which are not necessarily of inherent merit but may be of some consequence" (McGuigan 2005: 435), or affective publics, which is "public formations that are textually rendered into being through emotive expressions that spread virally through networked crowds" (Papacharissi 2014: 133). Transnational media culture flows and connections have significantly amplified such instances. While it is questionable that transnationally mediated connections engender a sense of global citizenship or cosmopolitanism, the consumption of media culture from other parts of the world has created an opportunity in which an understanding of other societies and cultures is dramatically deepened and socio-cultural issues and concerns are compassionately shared by many people across borders. Such occasions might urge people to realize how common experiences of modernization, urbanization, Westernization and globalization are similarly and differently experienced and represented in other social contexts and encourage them to have a fresh view of their own societies through the perception and appreciation of spatio-temporal distance and proximity of other modernities (Iwabuchi 2002). This indicates the possibility of mediated connections engendering cross-border dialogues in the sense of rethinking one's own life, society and culture as well as socio-historically constructed relations and perceptions with others, both critically and self-reflexively. It might lead to transgressive actions and collaborations as an expression and sharing of alternative views and hitherto marginalized voices, the cultivation of open-minded dialogue and the formation of cross-border alliances are transnationally generated.

The National as a Constituent Form of Globalization

Cross-border mediated connections problematize an assumed coherence of the nation and the efficacy of the nation-state's boundary control, so much so that "territoriality is fast becoming an anachronistic delimitation of material functions and cultural identities" (Benhabib 2002: 180). Yet the nation-state still matters. It functions, as Calhoun (2007) argues, as the most important unit of collective organization and plays a significant role in facilitating social solidarity. What is more relevant to this chapter, the national framework, outlook and feeling are not fully or necessarily displaced either, while the flows and connections of capital, people and media/images tend to disregard the boundaries that the nation-states administer. In reality, intensifying transnational connections prompts people to "draw attention what it negates" (Hannerz 1996: 6) by re-highlighting "the continuing significance of borders, state policies, and national identities even as these are often transgressed by transnational communication circuits and social practices" (Smith 2001: 3). The potential of media culture and communication to make a substantial transformation to an exclusive form of national identity, or foster a cosmopolitan outlook (Beck 2006) in terms of openness, togetherness and dialogue within and beyond existing confines, is not unrestricted from a centripetal force to re-demarcate and control national thinking and feeling.

The term "transnational" can be differentiated from "international" in that actors are not confined to the nation-state but range from individuals to various organizations and groups and that cross-border connections are forged to transgress a nation-to-nation framework. However, the pervasiveness of transnational connections and encounters also prompts people to be mindful of nationhood. Transnationalism eventually accompanies "inter-nationalism." Analytically, transnationalism is differentiated from inter-nationalism, but in reality the two might work in conjunction with each other. The national and the international have long been mutually reinforcing each other, but the intensification of cross-border connections and encounters makes their interaction even more significant for the operation of the nation as a mundane cognitive framework. Hence "internationalism" – the hyphen between the "inter" and "national" serves to highlight the reworking and strengthening of the national framework in terms of the governance of cross-border flows and connections.

Since the 1990s, it has been widely argued that market-driven globalization does not simply homogenize the world but heterogenizes it and even generates and organizes cultural diversity (Hannerz 1996). As for media culture, this cultural dynamic is occurring at the site of production as well as consumption. Globally circulating cultural products and images are consumed differently in the specific political, economic and social contexts of each locality and by people of various socio-cultural backgrounds in terms of gender, sexuality, race/ethnicity, class and age. At the same time, in each locality these products and images are reconfigured and mixed with local elements, resulting in the creation of new products that are not just mere replicas of the original. Media and cultural producers are aware of this dynamics of localization process so much so that "local" taste and specificity assumed as such have become well incorporated into their marketing strategy of "glocalization" (Robertson 1995). Transnational corporations that are based in developed countries pursue the profits by tailoring glocal cultures in every corner of the world's markets through transnational tie-ups and partnerships. But the significance of glocalization is not just limited to a business concern but extends to the manners in which a particular kind of diversity is promoted on globally common ground. American and Western cultural influences are always and already inscribed in the formation of media cultures in many parts of the world, but this has become even deeper and more structural. The new configuration of cultural power exploits the locally specific meaning construction process in a globally tailored manner. Glocalization generates an entangled interplay of standardization and diversification whereby, as Wilk (1995: 118) argues, cultural difference is expressed and shown to each other "in ways that are more widely intelligible" through "universal categories and standards by which all cultural differences can be defined." Especially important for the generation of "structure of common difference" is the global diffusion and sharing of cultural formats such as narrative style, visual representation, digitalized special effects, marketing technique and the idea of coolness – most of which "originate" in the USA and other developed countries – through which various differences are articulated in the international arena.

Cultural specificity or particularity being articulated through a common or universal form is a long-standing feature of the modern era. As Robertson (1995: 36) points out, it was during the time of the 19th and early 20th centuries that "'the world' became locked into a particular *form* of a strong shift to unicity" through "the organized attempts to link localities on an international or ecumenical basis." While the locality can take various forms, ranging from a small community to a transnational regional community, it is "the national" that has become a "prototype of the particular," a container form in which cultural specificity is articulated through common cultural formats across the world

(Robertson 1995: 34). Thus, the nation has long been functioning as the most prominent local unit of cultural diversity, a globally shared cultural form through which cultural distinctiveness is expressed and recognized in the international community via common cultural formats.

However, especially since the early 1990s after the end of the Cold War, the market-oriented process of cultural glocalization has been further pushing forward this momentum on a global scale. The key players of this process include international organizations such as UNESCO and IOC and, more significantly, media and cultural industries which transnationally and locally work with/for them. In the last two decades, the number of occasions of international media spectacle and cultural exhibition and festivals has substantially increased, such as sports events, film festivals, TV/music awards, food expo, pageant and tourism, as well as the proliferation of satellite and cable broadcasting and audio-visual Internet sites. These constitute what Urry (2003) calls "global screen," a site through which "localities, cultures and nations appear, to compete and mobilize themselves as international spectacles and consumed by others, compared and evaluated, and turned into a brand" (ibid.: 107). What is crucial here is that the national has functioned as one of the most profitable local markets, as a unit of commercialized cultural diversity in the world, whereby the images of the nation have come to be more and more constituted as a brand through global mass culture formats. They do not just provide the basis for the expression of national cultural distinctiveness but also work as an inter-nationalized interface that highlights the specific nationality of cultures and, as I will discuss later, propagates the idea of the nation as the unit of global cultural encounters, in which people are urged to participate.

Soft Power and Nation Branding

This development makes Urry (2003: 87) apt to say that "the nation has become something of a free-floating signifier relatively detached from the 'state' within the swirling contours of the new global order." However, inter-nationally orchestrated cultural glocalization processes have engendered the increasing interest in the enhancement of the nation's image as a brand and the states have become rather keen to take an initiative by joining forces with media culture industries. The management of the nation's image in the world is an old story, but it has been developing to "a strategically planned, holistic and coherent activity" by incorporating marketing techniques since the late 1990s as British brand consultant Simon Anholt allegedly coined the term "nation branding" in 1996 (Szondi 2008: 4). The international improvement of the nation's brand images via the circulation of media culture has been widely regarded as a serious business for the states to enhance national interests in terms of economy and foreign policy.

The policy concern of nation branding has been widely discussed in relation to creative industries and cultural/public diplomacy, but soft power is the most often used term in Japan as well as other East Asian countries. The term "soft power" was first coined by American political scientist Joseph Nye. In 1990, Nye (1990) argued that "soft co-optic power" was a significant factor in the attainment of the global hegemony by the United States; he defines this as the power to get "others to want what you want" through such symbolic resources as media and consumer culture: "If [a dominant country's] culture and ideology are attractive, others will more willingly follow" (Nye 1990: 32). The US use of media culture for advancing public diplomacy is nothing new. Indeed, the US policy of disseminating the image of liberty, affluence and democracy through media and consumer culture to win the Cold War is all too well known. However, Nye considered it imperative in the post-Cold War context that the US government further develops a soft power policy, the point being to make strategic use, of a globally diffused media and consumer culture, of symbolic icons and positive images and values associated with the United States. A decade later, the concept of soft power attracted renewed attention in the context of the Bush administration's hard-line policies, especially after 9/11. But the discussion of soft power was also extended to other parts of the world. The next part will discuss in detail the rise of such cultural policy discourse in Japan, but it should be noted here that Japan's soft power turn is symptomatic of the globalization of soft power.

In the last two decades, many countries other than the United States have significantly developed the capacity to produce media cultural texts and symbolic images, thanks to the development of digital communication technologies and glocally adoptable cultural formats, and the expansion of media culture markets in previously less developed regions. While Nye deplored the decline of American soft power under the Bush administration, other states began more aggressively to pursue the idea of exploiting the economic and political utility of media culture to win the international competition, although the term "soft power" was not necessarily used. "Cool Britannia" might be the best-known policy and practice of this kind, but in East Asia too, South Korea, Singapore, China, Taiwan and Japan are keen to promote their own cultural products and industries to enhance political and economic national interests. Most famously, the South Korean government has actively promoted its media cultures overseas since the 1990s, thereby contributing to the sweeping popularity of South Korean media cultures, known as the Korean Wave. The Korean success has much stimulated neighboring countries to seriously develop cultural policies to boost the nation's soft power. Indeed, "soft power competition" has been intensifying in 21st-century East Asia (Chua 2012).

While media culture is now publicly recognized as a useful resource for promoting political and economic national interests, the globalization of soft power does in fact diverge from Nye's original argument in significant respects. One such divergence has to do with the uses of media culture as a resource in the context of international image politics. According to Nye (2004), media culture is just one of three possible resources for the enhancement of a nation's soft power, the other two being respectful foreign policy and attractive democratic values established in the relevant society. In particular, Nye clearly warns against conflating the international appeal of media cultures with soft power, stressing that soft power will not be enhanced if the other two resources are not properly developed. What is striking, however, is that this kind of conflation is actually a prevalent operational principle of cultural policy discussions in many parts of the world. Main players, it turns out, are more preoccupied with largely effortless pragmatic uses of media culture for the purposes of enhancing an international image and boosting the economy, the key term here being branding. International relations scholar Peter van Ham (2001), for example, argues for the significance of the state's role in branding the nation, in terms of international politics and the economy, stating that "smart states are building their brands around reputations and attitudes in the same way smart companies do" (ibid.: 3–4). The globalization of the idea of using media cultures as a part of a national foreign policy strategy has given rise to even a shallower policy discourse on the international enhancement of a nation's brand images. Nye's soft power argument shares with nation branding the basic principle of using media culture for the enhancement of a narrow and focused set of national interests and attracting others and making others follow are both instances of unidirectional communication. Yet, a different, more pragmatic, kind of manoeuver for the administration of culture has been pushed forward, which relies on and legitimizes the marketization of culture and sponsors the inter-nationalized glocalization of media culture with a key concern with branding the nation.

We need to be cautious not to take nation branding policy discussion at its face value. What nation branding really means is ambiguous and whether and how the nation can be branded is open to question from the marketing point of view (Fan 2010; Anholt 2013). The academic discussion of nation branding is not limited to the issues of marketing operations. To follow Fan (2010: 101), nation branding can be more broadly defined as "a process by which a nation's images can be created or altered, monitored, evaluated and proactively managed in order to enhance the country's reputation among a target international audience." Nation branding even in this sense is a messy, precarious business. There is no guarantee that the export of media culture enhances national images. Many actors within the states, public relations advisory organizations, and media and cultural industries are involved in the project of nation branding with diverse intentions and approaches, which engender incoherent and contradictory policy actions (Aronczyk 2013). Also, it is rather difficult to judge whether and how nation brand images are enhanced. Only an elaborated ethnography of policy implementation and people's reception process would help us fully understand a complicated process of nation branding.

However, an issue relevant to this chapter is the discursive and performative power of nation branding to socially institute a national outlook. Recently, critical scholarly attention has been paid more to its relevance to the reconstruction of national identity (Jansen 2008; Volcic and Andrejevic 2011; Aronczyk 2013). The international projection of attractive images of the nation eventually necessitates the re-articulation of the selective narratives, symbolic meanings and widely accepted stereotypical images of the nation to be appealingly represented as a coherent entity. The growing interest in nation branding pushes the search for the distinctive cultural assets of the nation and the re-demarcation of "core" national culture that displays nation's distinctive cultural aesthetics, styles and tastes with the metaphor of "cultural gene" or "cultural DNA." Such representation of national culture is eventually projected toward the national citizens (Kaneva 2011; Volcic and Andrejevic 2011; Aronczyk 2013; Varga 2014). While the key aim of nation branding is considered to be the international projection of the attractive images of the nation, it is not just externally oriented but also internally directed. As Jansen (2008: 122) argues, "branding not only explains nations to the world but also reinterprets national identity in market terms and provides new narratives for domestic consumption." This has been accompanied by the extension of the mutually constitutive relationship of the national/internal and the international/external.

The construction of national identity is always closely related to the international appraisal ("how they perceive us") as well as the representation of the foreign ("not like us"), against which the distinctiveness of the nation ("who we are") can be demarcated. Especially, the gaze of significant other, most prevalently Euro-American other, is constitutive of the discursive construction of national identity in non-Western countries such as Japan, where Western Orientalism and self-orientalism function in a complicit manner (Iwabuchi 1994). Euro-American gaze still occupies the dominant position. However, as nationality has come to be "constituted through specific local places, symbols and landscapes, icons of the nation central to that culture's location within the contours of global business, travel, branding" (Urry 2003: 87), wide-ranging and reciprocated international gazes have come to play a key role in the formation of national identity, whereby the idea and practice of nation branding re-highlights the nation-state as the most meaningful cultural entity of collective identification.

Banal Inter-Nationalism

It can be argued that the representation of the nation in market terms is superficial and ahistorical, lacking substantial depth and coherence of national narratives. Furthermore, as Kaneva (2011: 11) argues, while "branded imagination seeks to infiltrate and subsume the symbolic order of nationhood," there is no guarantee that it succeeds in internally getting people's consent over the national narrative with which they are encouraged to identify. Nevertheless, the action of the search for a legitimate content to be filled in the national form itself endorses a given existence of "authentic" national culture: "The mundane practices of nation branding do serve to perpetuate the nation form ... because they perpetuate a conversation about what the nation is *for* in a global context" (Aronczyk 2013: 176). This suggests that the practice of nation branding and people's participation in it themselves work to confirm the nation as a form of collective identification and belonging. In this sense, it can be suggested that nation branding plays a parallel role to the reconstruction of "imagined communities" (Anderson 1983) as it involves a call for people's participation in the mass ritual of nation branding as well as the renewed representation of the nation. Nation branding domestically generates the mobilization of citizens, who are encouraged to join in it as "representatives, stakeholders and customers of the brand": "Citizens are called upon to 'live the brand' and hence to act and think in ways that are well suited to the general contours of the national brand" (Varga 2014: 836). People are thus invited to perform as an ambassador of the nation branding campaign.

Whether such an invitation is really embraced by people is highly questionable, but the coaction of the marketization of media cultures and associated policies of nation branding, to say the least, has broadly propagated an idea among the populace that the promotion of national branding via media culture must be taken seriously as it is of grave importance for national interests. Additionally, there is a more mundane and modest form of mass participation prevalent among the general public. We have observed a rapid development of globally televised spectacles of various kinds in which people are asked to purchase a ticket to become a part of the event and display a particular national symbol (Roche 2000). Moreover, with the amplification of actual or virtual participation in the number of international occasions, people are encouraged to confirm a sense of belonging to a particular nation. Such occasions provoke people to feel a sense of national pride when "our" national cultures do well. Or it might stir up the sense of regret, anger and frustration when others beat "us." In Japan, the international standing of national culture has become even more an important resource for the evocation of national pride due to the decline of the Japanese economy since the early 1990s. A 2010 survey on what aspects of Japan people are proud of showed that while Japan's technology and traditional culture were still conceived as the most significant, 90% of respondents in their twenties and 80% of those in their thirties stated that they were proud of Japanese animation and computer games (*Asahi Shimbun* 2010). This does not just reflect the fact that they have been actually well circulating in the world but also a widely shared perception that they are key cultural commodities for the enhancement of Japan's soft power.

It can be argued that this just displays a trivial transient consumption of and identification with the idea of the nation, lacking substantial meanings of the narrative of the nation and, thus, for the expression of national pride. Fox (2006) argues in his examination of the rise of nationalism sentiment through national holiday commemorations and international football competitions that the participation in such occasions elevates the sense of national belonging but this does not necessarily mean the rise of nationalistic sentiment: "While holidays and sports had the capacity to make the students national, there is little to suggest that they made them nationalist ... any experience of collective belonging neither led to nor followed from heightened nationalist sensitivities" (ibid.: 232). This is rather an important reminder that we should not jump to a conclusion of the rise of nationalism in the age of global interconnectedness without making a close analysis of people's participation in the international cultural event.

Distinguishing between national cohesion and nationalist passion, Fox (2006: 232) further argues that "national content does not follow unambiguously from national form." It can be argued, however, that the increase in the international cultural encounter that "makes people national" also needs to be taken seriously for the firm infiltration of the sense of national belonging and identification eventually takes a non-assertive banal form. Michael Billig (1995) has argued that national feeling is facilitated and displayed by means of such mundane performances as casually showing the national flag in the city. The banal practice of national belonging is further promoted by an increase in encounters with people, goods and images from many parts of the world and a plethora of international events and spectacles, which facilitate a mundane form of people "living the national brand." While this development might open up a possibility of cultivating new kinds of conception and imagination that goes beyond an exclusive framework of the nation, the co-joined operation of market-driven glocalization and nation branding engenders banal inter-nationalism that prompts people to implicitly comprehend cross-cultural encounters as those among mutually exclusive national cultures with the delimited boundaries. With the entrenched permeation of an assumption that the global is the congregation of nations and that cultural diversity is comprehended mostly as that between nations, the conception of the nation as a (brand) form or a container based on the territorial understanding of culture gains wider currency.

Inter-Nationalized Promotion of Cultural Diversity

Pervading the thinking and feeling that the nation is the unit of global cultural exchange, it reinforces the cardinal importance of the nation as a cultural form, which people identify with, belong to and show loyalty to, and newly induces the sense of national belonging and the ownership of national culture. This might take an assertive shape of a nationalistic clash over the ownership of culture. For example, the rise of "soft power competition" has given rise to and added fuel to the flames of the vicious circle of antagonistic nationalism in Asia. Recent Indonesian condemnation of a Malaysian tourism campaign in terms of the ownership of Bali dance culture and Chinese criticism of the distortion of historical representation in the South Korean drama series *Jumong 2* show the increasing role which media culture plays in provoking the disputes over the ownership of national culture and historical narrative in the inter-national arena.

Although not necessarily engendering such xenophobic aggression, banal inter-nationalism implicitly and explicitly engenders exclusionary politics of the nation, as it newly provokes the clear demarcation of "us" and "them" through an inter-nationalized administration of cultural diversity. This is to take seriously Wilk's (1995) argument that the hegemony of the global cultural system is "not of content, but of form." While glocalization organizes cultural diversity through form, it is not inclusive of various kinds of social and cultural differences. The instituting of globally shared container forms and cultural formats generates a certain mode of cultural diversity and this indicates the operation of cultural hegemony that "celebrate(s) particular kinds of diversity while submerging, deflating or suppressing others" (ibid.: 118). Banal inter-nationalism highlights a nation-based cultural diversity of the world, not attending to marginalized differences and multicultural situations within the nation.

While nation branding renders the narration of the nation highly commercialized, de-historicized and incoherent, such narratives are still based on an essentialist conception of the nation as an organic cultural entity and do not pay due attention to the diversity within the nation-state (Kaneva 2011). Nation branding from time to time supports minority groups' traditional culture or promotes tokenized multicultural commodities in an international arena, the kinds of media culture promoted for international circulation are chiefly those which are commercially mainstream in their countries of origin, and there is not much space for socially and culturally marginalized voices within the nation. It fails to bear in mind that national borders are discursively drawn in a way to suppress various socio-cultural differences within and disavow their existence as constitutive of the nation.

It might take the form of the candid suppression by the nation branding policy and the straightforward application of banal inter-nationalism to the media representation of multicultural situation. Or the progression of inter-nationalized media cultural flows and connections further sidelines the recognition of hyphenated subjects such as Asian/Japanese Americans living in the USA or resident Koreans in Japan. This issue of inter-nationalized promotion of cultural diversity deterring the due appreciation of cultural diversity within national borders is never new. It is reminiscent of a crucial point raised by Said's seminal work of *Orientalism* (1978) on how the dichotomized construction of culturally coherent entities exerts symbolic violence onto the lively reality of human society full of cultural diversity. While Western Orientalism has been countered by oriental Occidentalism or self-Orientalism, it is often argued, the two discourses are not in conflict, but in collusion in that they mutually, though unevenly, construct culturally coherent entities in separation (Iwabuchi 1994). The covert victims of an interaction of Orientalism and self-Orientalism are thus those who are excluded, marginalized and silenced in each society as their presence and experience of marginalization themselves are further disregarded.

The operation of intercultural marginalization of this kind also takes more subtle forms with the intensification of cross-border mobility of media culture and people. One complicated case is the impact of inter-nationalized cultural exchange on the social recognition and (dis)empowerment of migrants and diasporas. The key problem here is the oversimplified identification of migrants and diasporas with their home countries. Critical researchers of Asian-Australian studies stated about the enduring stereotypical images of Chinese migrants and diasporas in Australia: "As we become more dependent on the dollars from the economies of Asia, I would hope that the vestige of 19th century orientalism will fade away" (Kwok et al. 2004). This statement refers to an expectation of a positive impact of the rise of the economy and culture of their "home" countries on the social appreciation of migrants and diasporas. The sense of "hope" expressed above is well taken and it might be the case that the rise of the Chinese economy would not just improve international images of China but also enhance social recognition of those diasporas/migrants who identify themselves and are identified as "Chinese" in the host society.

However, there is no guarantee that this is the case. Even if the rise of Asian economy and culture might make a classical mode of Orientalism less relevant, geopolitically driven cultural Othering dies hard. It is well known that the rise of the Japanese economy in the 1970s and 1980s reproduced orientalist images such as "economic animal" or "techno-Orientalism" (Iwabuchi 1994). Likewise, the rise of the Chinese economy actually induces negative reactions in other countries, and this might even lead to a harmful effect on people of Chinese descent living there. A negative effect on migrants and diasporas in the host country can also be exerted by the conspicuous rise of a culture of the home country. Furthermore, even if the rise of media culture of the host country has an empowering impact on the hyphenated subject via the improvement of the images of that nation, this does not guarantee the facilitation of the full recognition of them as a member of the host society. It might further strengthen the perception of their "national" affiliation other than "ours," hence reinforcing the multicultural containment of "their" difference. There is a thin line between the empowerment of diasporas by their association with the images of the home country and the muddling association of their identities and differences through the culture and people of the home country, reinforcing the recognition of migrants and diasporas being in, but not of, "here."

For example, sparked off by the phenomenal hit TV drama *Winter Sonata* in 2003, South Korean films, TV dramas and pop music have come to be widely consumed in Japan. An approving reception of South Korean media culture in Japan generated the improvement in the image of South Korea in self-reflexive manners, which accompanied that of resident Koreans in Japan who had long been suffering from discrimination as ethnic minorities (Iwabuchi 2008). While it empowers some resident Koreans to live in Japan as a citizen of Korean descent, the stress on inter-national cultural exchange between the two countries tends to overlook historically constituted discrimination and identity distress that many resident Koreans have been experiencing in Japan. Moreover, the positive reception of the Korean media culture, which enhances the images of South Korea and promotes the attention to resident Koreans in Japan, tends to make the audiences regard resident Koreans in Japan in the same light as people in South Korea. Such perception disregards the complexity of historically embedded experiences, identification and social positioning of resident Koreans in Japanese society (Iwabuchi 2008).

A crucial point here is an assumption that migrants and diasporas are self-evidently identical with and representative of the nation-state of their descent. And it is this apparent axiom that should be seriously questioned. The sympathetic reception of media culture improves the images of the nation-state that exports it, which might lead to enhancing the social recognition of diasporas/migrants of that country's descent in the host society. However, whether its impact is positive or negative, the presumed identification of hyphenated subjects with their home countries is problematic since it tends to be co-opted by banal inter-nationalism and discourages serious appreciation of cultural diversity and full engagement with multicultural politics within the nation. Banal inter-nationalism precludes a nuanced understanding of the diasporic negotiation of "where one is from" and "where one is at" (Ang 2001) by negating to acknowledge that s/he is a member of "our" society here.

Conclusion

These considerations highlight the way in which transnational media culture connections are implicated in the multicultural questions and the national politics of inclusion and exclusion of ethnic minorities. Multiculturalism is blamed for being too nation centered to take transnationalism into consideration. Its exclusive obsession with multicultural situations "here" in a national society for the purpose of socio-national integration often tends to disregard immigrants' connections with "over there," which is often regarded as detrimental to achieving communal harmony in the multicultural nation (Vertovec 2001). However, transnationalism might not attend to multiculturalism within borders, either. Crossing national cultural borders is much encouraged but chiefly in a non-transgressive manner that mundanely strengthens the clear demarcation of national borders and renders their exclusionary politics inconsequential.

A classical insight of a crucial point of Said's Orientalism is still very suggestive, that is, as Clifford (1988: 273) points out, a "relentless suspicion of totality" about any notions of distinct human groups, cultures and geographical spaces. It is imperative for researchers to strive to make such relentless suspicion part of mundane social praxis if we are to undo the resilience of exclusive national cultural boundaries. Whether and how the development of transnational connections fundamentally challenges uneven media cultural globalization, what sort of cross-border dialogues are promoted and whether and how they encourage socio-culturally marginalized voices expressed, heard and shared in a mediated public space will remain key questions in the study of cultural globalization.

Acknowledgments

This chapter is a revised version of "Banal Internationalism and its Others," in Koichi Iwabuchi (2015) *Resilient Borders and Cultural Diversity: Internationalism, Brand Nationalism and Multiculturalism in Japan*, Lexington Books, pp. 9–24.

References

Anderson, B. (1983) *Imagined Communities*, London: Verso.

Ang, I. (2001) *On Not Speaking Chinese*, London: Routledge.

Anholt, S. (2013) "Beyond the Nation Brand," *Exchange*, 2(1): 6–12.

Aronczyk, M. (2013) *Branding the Nation*, Oxford: Oxford University Press.

Asahi Shimbun (2010) "Poll: 95% Fear for Japan's Future," 12 June.

Beck, U. (2006) *Cosmopolitan Vision*, Cambridge: Polity.

Benhabib, S. (2002) *The Claims of Culture*, Princeton: Princeton University Press.

Billig, M. (1995) *Banal Nationalism*, London: SAGE.

Calhoun, C. (2007) *Nations Matter*, London: Routledge.

Carey, J. (1989) *Communication as Culture*, Boston: Unwin Hyman.

Chua, B.H. (2012) *Structure, Audience and Soft Power in East Asian Pop Culture*, Hong Kong: Hong Kong University Press.

Clifford, J. (1988) *The Predicament of Culture*, Cambridge: Harvard University Press.

Fan, Y. (2010) "Branding the Nation," *Place Branding and Public Diplomacy*, 6(2): 97–103.

Fox, J. (2006) "Consuming the Nation," *Ethnic and Racial Studies*, 29(2): 217–36.

Hannerz, U. (1996) *Transnational Connections*, London: Routledge.

Iwabuchi, K. (1994) "Complicit Exoticism: Japan and its Other," *Continuum*, 8(2): 49–82.

Iwabuchi, K. (2002) *Recentering Globalization: Popular Culture and Japanese Transnationalism*, Durham: Duke University Press.

Iwabuchi, K. (2008) "When Korean Wave Meets Resident Koreans in Japan," in B.H. Chua and K. Iwabuchi (eds) *East Asian Pop Culture: Analysing the Korean Wave*, Hong Kong: Hong Kong University Press.

Jansen, S. (2008) "Designer Nations," *Social Identities*, 14(1): 121–42.

Kaneva, N. (2011) "Nation Branding," *International Journal of Communication*, 5: 117–41.

Kwok, J.T., Khoo, T. and Ling, C. (2004) "Chinese Voices," *Meanjin*, 63(2): 149–60.

Martin, F. and Rizvi, F. (2014) "Making Melbourne," *Media, Culture and Society*, 36(7): 1016–31.

McGuigan, J. (2005) "The Cultural Public Sphere," *European Journal of Cultural Studies*, 8(4): 427–43.

Nye, J. (1990) *Bound to Lead: The Changing Nature of American Power*, New York: Basic Books.

Nye, J. (2004) *Soft Power: The Means to Success in World Politics*, New York: PublicAffairs.

Papacharissi, Z. (2014) *Affective Publics*, New York: Oxford University Press.

Robertson, R. (1995) "Glocalisation," in M. Featherstone (ed) *Global Modernities*, London: SAGE.

Roche, M. (2000) *Mega-events and Modernity*, London: Routledge.

Said, E. (1978) *Orientalism*, London: Routledge.

Smith, M. (2001) *Transnational Urbanism*, Malden: Blackwell.

Szondi, G. (2008) "Public Diplomacy and Nation Branding," *Discussion Papers in Diplomacy*, Clingendael Netherlands Institute of International Relations.

Thompson, J. (1995) *The Media and Modernity*, Cambridge: Polity.

Urry, J. (2003) *Global Complexity*, Cambridge: Polity.

van Ham, P. (2001) "The Rise of the Brand State," *Foreign Affairs*, September/October: 1–6.

Varga, S. (2014) "The Politics of Nation Branding," *Philosophy and Social Criticism*, 39(8): 825–45.

Vertovec, S. (2001) "Transnational Challenges to the 'New' Multiculturalism," Working Paper Series, WPTC-01-06, University of Oxford.

Volcic, Z. and Andrejevic, M. (2011) "Nation Branding in the Era of Commercial Nationalism," *International Journal of Communication*, 5: 598–618.

Wilk, R. (1995) "Learning to be Local in Belize," in D. Miller (ed) *Worlds Apart*, London: Routledge.

PART II

Digital Asia

7

TRANSNATIONAL POPULAR CULTURE AND IMAGINATION IN THE DIGITAL AGE

Fabienne Darling-Wolf

> The biographies of ordinary people are constructions (or fabrications) in which the imagination plays an important role.
>
> (Appadurai 1996: 54)

Despite growing up in rural France without streaming services, the Internet or even a VCR, my childhood imagination was populated by fantastical characters from faraway places. There was Candy, who, as the opening lines of the series told us, spent her childhood in an orphanage "tucked at the bottom of a mountain to the South of lake Michigan," Tom Sawyer, who lived "on the shore of the Mississippi river," Anne, also an orphan but from Prince Edward Island, and Heidi, the "little girl from the Alps" whose experience was much closer to home (I could see the Alps from my bedroom window) but infused with an enchanting quality lacking from my own life. This being the late 1970s and early 1980s, there was also, of course, Actarus (Duke Fleed) who lived on a ranch but transformed into the famous Goldorak (*Grendizer*) to fight invaders from Vega – modeled, incidentally, on the Japanese imperial army (Aumont 1996) – the virile space pirate Albator (*Captain Harlock*), Capitaine Flam (*Captain Future*) and other science fiction heroes too numerous to mention.

This experience, certainly not unique in the European context where people around my age are frequently referred to as the *Goldorak/Grendizer* generation (Pellitteri 2008), illustrates a number of dynamics about the local/global nexus worth critically considering. First, it points to the role of the media in assembling a "complex repertoires of images, narratives and ethnoscapes" through which media consumers can "construct imagined worlds that are chimerical, aesthetic, even fantastic objects, particularly if assessed by the criteria of some other perspective, some other imagined world" (Appadurai 1996: 35). It connects, in other words, mediated texts to the global imagination. Second, it reminds us

DOI: 10.4324/9781003130628-10

that the cultural dynamics of de-territorialization and the related production of a "global imaginary" (Steger 2020: 2) that accompany globalization started long before the spread of more intimately connective digital technologies. Thus, while the digital age may signal a shift in the granular ways in which this imaginary is built and negotiated, as I will argue later in this chapter, this shift must be considered in relationship to this longer trajectory and within the broader context of historically dominant transnational media flows. Finally, the fact that all of the texts mentioned above are works of Japanese animation, including those – such as *Candy Candy*, Tom Sawyer (*Tomu Sōyā no Bōken*), Anne of Green Gables (*Akage no An*) or Heidi (*Arupusu no Shōjo Haiji*) – ostensibly taking place in North American or European settings, points to the Japanese media's complex and long-standing contributions to the database of cultural references available to global media consumers.

Drawing from personal experience and more than a hundred formal interviews and countless informal conversations over the past 25 years with media consumers in Japan, France and the United States, this chapter explores how these dynamics shape individuals' "cultural imagination" (Tomlinson 1999: 119) as well as the related "production of locality" (Appadurai 2013: 66) that takes place through the "temporary negotiations between various globally distributed forms" (ibid.: 68). Identifying the imagination as a key dimension of contemporary experience, it starts with an examination of the role of the media in shaping the awareness of the global. It then more closely examines how engagement with transnational popular culture shapes individuals' sense of place in that imagined global order. Finally, it critically considers how the rise of time- and space-defying digital platforms is transforming the nature of this engagement both at the structural and the individual level.

Imagination, Media and the Global

In his book aptly titled *Imagined Globalization*, Argentinian-Mexican cultural critic Néstor García Canclini notes that "imaginary constructions make the existence of local and national societies possible" (2014: 16). "Our globalized age," he continues, "connects us effectively to many societies; we can situate our fantasy in multiple settings." A complete examination of the vast body of academic literature that, like García Canclini here, connects globalization to the imagination is beyond the scope of this chapter (for "classic" examples, see Appadurai 1996, 2013; Tomlinson 1999; Nederveen Pieterse 2009) but a few points are worth mentioning in a brief sketch. First, globalization scholars identify the "growing *consciousness* of the world as a single whole" that forms individuals' "*global imaginary*" (Steger 2020: 3, emphasis in original) as a distinctive feature of our contemporary era when compared to earlier forms of transnational commercial and even cultural exchange. In other words, while scholars disagree as to whether globalization signals a complete break from the past or simply the continuation of earlier processes (Jones 2010), they agree that the scale, rate and centrality of individuals' collective *awareness* of the global (Chopra 2011) that accompanies the development of globalization as we know it today are at the very least qualitatively different. As Appadurai (1996: 31) concludes, "The imagination is now central to all forms of agency, is itself a social fact and is the key component of the new global order."

Second, starting perhaps most famously with McLuhan's (1962: 31) pronouncement in *The Gutenberg Galaxy* that "the new electronic interdependence recreates the world in the image of a global village," scholars have pointed to globally distributed media as a crucial vector of this "global expansion of imaginaries" (García Canclini 2014: 6; Lule 2015; Jin 2019). As cultural critic Radha Hegde (2011: 5) explains, "In the global context, questions of culture, subjectivity and everyday life have to be situated against the ubiquitous presence and proliferation of communication technologies and their ability to transcend time and space." In other words, mediated global flows of cultural forms provide "a point of departure for elaborating the production of the transnational imaginary" (Shome and Hegde 2002: 182).

The media consumers I talked to over the years readily recognized this fact. With such comments as "Really, the only way to get information [about the world] is through the media," "We are all more or less influenced by something, some images," "The image that is spread [in the media] is what influences us" (France); "I haven't gone to see for myself, but I get sense from TV, or the Internet," "The only information we can get is from the media, television, newspaper, or the Internet" (Japan); "So much of the way that people just operate, whatever culture they're from, is through stories. It's the way that people imagine their world and how they see things" (USA), they clearly acknowledged the role of the media in shaping their awareness of the global. As a young French woman concluded, "we are necessarily tied to the media."

Of course, the exponential growth of digital platforms in the first decades of 21st century has brought renewed attention to the role of media as "part of the infrastructure of globalization" (Nederveen Pietersen 2020: 22). Again, media and globalization may have "partnered throughout the whole of human history" (Lule 2015: 10), but the nature of this partnership experienced a qualitative shift with the arrival of digital technologies allowing for "new forms of personal connection" (Bayme 2010: 1) and a deepening degree of connectivity (Jin 2019) on an increasingly global scale. The implications of this shift will be further discussed later in this chapter.

Third, the "variety of circuits, scales and speeds that characterize the circulation of cultural elements" (Appadurai 2013: 68) under contemporary conditions of globalization simultaneously build our awareness of globality and "create the conditions for the production of locality" (ibid.: 69). In other words, the "local," the "national" and the "global" are mutually constituted through the work of the imagination. Under such conditions, the "local" is not the global's "presumptive victim, its cultural nemesis, or its coerced subordinate" (Kraidy and Murphy 2008: 339). The two are "continuously (re)negotiated in relationship to each other" (Darling-Wolf 2015: 143). Back in 1996, Wilson and Dissanayake defined the "transnational imaginary" as the *"as-yet-unfigured* horizon of contemporary cultural production by which national spaces/identities of political allegiance and economic regulation are being undone and imagined communities of modernity are being reshaped at the macropolitical (global) and micropolitical (cultural) levels of everyday existence" (ibid.: 6, emphasis in original). We now have a better sense of what the configuration looks like – including the fact that rather than being "undone," national spaces and identities are sometimes defensively reasserted in opposition to the global (Chopra 2011; Nederveen Pietersen 2020). We are nevertheless still grappling with its utter complexity.

Indeed, over the past 20 years or so, our "scenarios of global culture" (Kraidy 2005) have become increasingly complex. If 20th century conceptualizations of transnational cultural influence centered on the dominance of Anglo-American capitalism (e.g. McDonaldization, Ritzer 1993) and its perceived concomitant cultural imperialism (Schiller 1989), the 21st century has been characterized by "new" or at least newly (re)acknowledged, regional cultural trends (e.g. the Korean Wave), increasingly multidimensional flows and the simultaneous reassertion of "old" boundaries. The concept of hybridity has emerged as a common lens through which to approach this complexity. While sometimes criticized for its conceptual vagueness or too-cozy relationship to global capitalism – for a detailed assessment of these critiques, see Chapter 6 of Nederveen Pieterse's (2020) *Globalization and Culture* – hybridity provides a useful conceptual tool when understood as a process "shaped by structural and discursive forces" (Kraidy 2005: 153) under global conditions of unequal power. Or, as Nederveen Pieterse (2020) puts it,

> Since "everything is hybrid," discussing examples of hybridity is like drinking from a fire hydrant. It follows that only those forms of hybridity are worth discussing that illuminate the variety, depth and meaning of hybridity or shed light on controversies, past or present.
>
> *(ibid.: 3)*

If that is the case, the role, both past and present, of Asian media in the uneven and contentious process of "globalization as hybridization" (ibid.: 81) is worthy of further investigation.

Asian Media in the (Hybrid) Global Imagination

Flows of culture between "East" and "West" have a long history during which, incidentally, Europe was frequently on the receiving end. The reasons behind the cultural amnesia of "millennia of East-West osmosis" (Nederveen Pieterse 2020: 157) are complex and multidimensional, and they can be attributed to both parties who promoted it in service of their own geopolitical interests at different points in time. For instance, as I have argued elsewhere (Darling-Wolf 2018), the relegation of the revolutionary impact of late 19th-century Japanese visual aesthetics on the global arts scene known as the *Japonisme* movement to mere "Orientalism" served both Europe's and Japan's national imaginaries. Sweeping the fact that the "French" impressionists were imitating Japanese artists under history's carpet simultaneously bolstered Europe's image as an exceptional cultural influencer and Japanese claims of cultural particularism and impenetrability (Iwabuchi 2002). As Iwabuchi (2002: 6) explains, "To put it bluntly, the idea of a Japan lacking in external power has been collusive with a postwar strategy of constructing an exclusive and unique Japanese national identity." Ironically, Iwabuchi himself recognizes having "implicitly accepted the idea of Japan as a faceless economic superpower" (ibid.: 2). Thus, theorizing about media, perhaps particularly in Japan, always necessarily involves the "disarticulation of a national discourse" (Mizuta Lippit 2017: xiii).

As a result of these dynamics, Japan's (and other Asian nations') multifaceted contributions to the "repertoire of 'textual locations' built up out of millions of images in films, TV programmes, books and magazines" (Tomlinson 1999: 119) that form the building blocks of the global imaginary are yet to be fully apprehended. Of course, these contributions are qualitatively different from those of, say, the United States. They were shaped by different chronologies (a relatively later entry on the global stage of popular culture), different positionings in geopolitical power dynamics (in the case of Japan, transitioning from the position of colonizing power to that or neo-colonized war victim) and different national imaginaries (as culturally impenetrable to outsiders). They do not benefit from the unique set of historical circumstances that bolstered "America's" still unrivaled global symbolic power (Darling-Wolf 2015). The trails of their hybridity are particularly sinuous.

In fact, in the case of transnationally distributed Japanese media, one might start by recognizing their contributions to the imagination of *other* cultures. As hinted in the titles mentioned above, my imagination of "America" when growing up in a small French town was profoundly shaped by my consumption of *Japanese* animation. I was not alone. For a generation of French media consumers (and others around the globe), Michigan is where Candy grew up and Tom Sawyer is the (American) main character of a 1980's Nippon Animation series – not a Mark Twain novel. The most frequent reaction when mentioning the latter to French media consumers I interviewed in 2010 was "c'est l'Amérique!" [it's America], in reference to the French version of the show's opening song which starts with the words "Tom Sawyer, it's America, the symbol of freedom." The series evoked images of the Mississippi river – "With the Mississippi" (woman in her 20s); "He lives on the banks of the Mississippi" (man in his 30s) – and of the scary "Joe the Indian" [sic] – "I was traumatized [by Joe the Indian], I was scared to death" (woman in her 20s); "Joe the Indian was so scary. I was shaking" (woman in her 30s). As one viewer concluded, "Tom Sawyer, that was fun, with Huckleberry Finn. They have lots of adventures, it's the very image of freedom, it's true, that's interesting. Tom Sawyer makes you dream" (woman in her 20s). Indeed, Nippon Animation's World Masterpiece Theatre Series (*Sekai Meisaku Gekijō*), of which Tom Sawyer was part, made us dream about all sorts of places as it introduced both Japanese and global audiences to North American and European literature.

Here, the deep impact of these Japanese versions of American life on the European imagination points to a much more complex process of transcultural influence than can be described through theories of cultural hegemony. Indeed, it points to the fact that if the global image of "America" is significantly shaped by the transnational consumption of Hollywood movies or US TV series, this "imagined America" – as I have put it elsewhere (Darling-Wolf 2015: 130) – is also built upon a much more hybrid global media mix that interpellates viewers on different levels. Tom Sawyer and other Japanese animated series located in the USA or Canada – for example, *Princess Sarah* (*Shōkōjo Sēra/Little Princess*), *Anne of Green Gables* (*Akage no An*) or *Tales of Little Women* (*Ai no Wakakusa Monogatari*) – resonated with French viewers in part because of the Japanese-style exoticizing of these "foreign" cultural contexts was in line with French imaginings of "America" as a land of freedom and opportunity, as illustrated in the French expression "c'est l'Amérique!" used to refer to great opulence or a highly positive outcome.

But if the World Masterpiece Theatre Series shaped the European imaginary of North America, it also influenced our visions of places much "closer to home." Shows like *Heidi* (*Arupusu no Shōjo Haiji*), *Remi, Nobody's Boy* (*Ie Naki Ko Remi*), *Les Misérables* (*Re Mizeraburu: Shōjo Kozetto*) or *The Swiss Family Robinson* (*Kazoku Robinson Hyōryūki Fushigi na Shima no Furōne*) represented Europe to European audiences. As a French viewer put it, "Heidi, faithfully represented our lives." Or, as another explained when reminiscing on his childhood engagement with the series:

> Heidi took you into a universe that was almost like your daily life. ... I remember one episode where she arrives at her grandfather's house and she marvels at the crickets and the flowers, and me, I've been lucky enough to share that and to live a bit in the same way, to discover with my uncle where you can dig the cricket, get it to come out a catch it. It's in the same spirit. Rémi was like that too.

In other words, in a process alluded to above and identified by scholars as a key dimension of contemporary globalization, these Japanese texts influenced European viewers' experience of their own locality. As Appadurai (2013: 63) reminds us, "the complexity of global cultural flows has had deep effects on ... the production of local subjectivity."

It is worth noting here that while the novels on which these texts are based are certainly present in other cultural forms in Europe, the Japanese version of their characters often remains the dominant image in Europeans' imagination. As a woman in her 20s commented,

I must admit that if it wasn't for the Japanese animation, I wouldn't even
know the story of Rémi because I never read the Hector Malot novel. …
Same thing with Heidi, I saw the animated series, but I never read the
books.

Nippon Animation's version of Heidi, still omnipresent throughout Europe – she
appeared, for instance, in the "food people" parade at the 2015 World Exposition
in Milan – is indeed a case in point.

The "Western" settings of the World Masterpiece Theatre Series – which
includes dozens of shows and is highly celebrated in Japan – have often resulted
in a lack of interest on the part of scholars of Japanese animation focused on more
straightforwardly "culturally marked" texts (McCarthy 1999; Drazen 2003;
Cooper-Chen 2010). However, the shows were clearly "Japanese" regardless of
where they ostensibly took place. Isao Takahata and Hayao Miyazaki worked on
several of the series' creations before they went off to start Studio Ghibli. *Heidi*,
which was broadcast in some 35 countries around the globe (but, notably, not in
the United States) starting in the late 1970s, was one of their earliest collaborations. It clearly (fore)bears the two celebrated animators' imprint in terms of its
themes – flying, pastoral nostalgia, overcoming adversity – its visual aesthetic, its
use of music and sound, and its characters (Darling-Wolf 2016). The parallels with
Totoro, for instance, are difficult to miss; a bright-eyed motherless five-year-old
moves to the countryside where she lives in an old house discovers the wonders

FIGURE 7.1   Heidi on the cover of the Japanese DVD of the show and at the World
Exposition in Milan.

of nature, plays with large fuzzy animals and talks to a tall tree. The characters of Heidi and Mei, Peter and Kanta are eerily similar. In other words, Heidi and her many companions in the World Masterpiece Theatre Series are Japanese versions of European and North American characters – and this "Japaneseness" is part of their attraction. As a 46-year-old French viewer explained,

> I started to become aware of the origins of cartoons when the Japanese entered the production … Heidi, Tom Sawyer … first of all, it was a different visual aesthetic [un graphisme différent], and it was a new generation of cartoons that was different from what we had before.

Or as a woman in her late 20s explained, "For me, it's the visual aesthetic. There are all these sceneries, you dream of being able to see these kinds of things, it's truly magnificent."

Not surprisingly, these texts and the large amounts of Japanese animation and manga – much of it much more straightforwardly "culturally marked" – that would come to follow this early wave of Japanese animation also shaped individuals' imagination of Asia. (Techno)-orientalist visions of cherry blossoms, samurai, tea ceremony, traditional arts and respect for the elderly mixed in with technological prowess abounded when my conversations with French media consumers turned to Japan: "We have this image of samurai and honor" (14-year-old male); "My image is that of a code of honor, of respect for the elderly … of nature, like the cherry blossoms that are celebrated each year" (woman in her 20s), "They take care of their elderly parents … but there is also a strong dynamism" (woman in her forties); "It's the country of high-technology" (14-year-old male). As one viewer in her twenties concluded, "Westerners are quite fascinated by everything Asian."

Incidentally, French viewers also frequently reflected on how the texts located in Western settings might shape the imagination of Japanese audiences. As one viewer put it, "I think these were made to make the young Japanese dream about the Western world." My conversations with Japanese media consumers confirmed this assessment. Texts from the World Masterpiece Theatre Series, along with *Candy Candy* and *The Rose of Versailles* (*Berusaiyu no bara*), were consistently mentioned as all-time favorites. And they indeed evoked dreamy versions of Western architecture and vistas (the Alps, Prince Edward Island), food – "the cheese and these kinds of things looked good" (33-year-old man) – arts and fashion; "the culture, the history, the tradition, the food, the fashion. The people also are fashionable and very passionate" (41-year-old woman). Of course, it is worth noting here that in the case of both Japanese and European media consumers this imagination was further shaped by other globally distributed media forms, including those coming from Hollywood or Disney.

In other words, the historical case of Japanese animation's global spread points to the need to move beyond an understanding of transnational media flows as vectors of either cultural understanding or cultural imperialism. It forces us to face the more convoluted and subtle ways in which deterritorialized media forms shape "our plurality of imagined worlds" (Appadurai 1996: 5). This work of the imagination has taken on new – and possibly even more complex – dimensions with the rise of digital media technologies.

Imagination in the Digital Age

Indeed, ever since the concept of virtual community entered our collective imagination – due in part to Rheingold's (1993) popularization of the term in his book of the same name – the transformative nature of digital technologies has generated, to borrow Rebillard's (2011: 25) wording, "a genuine discursive and ideological gush" [un véritable bouillonnement discursif et idéologique] in academic and popular culture alike (Shirky 2010; Rheingold 2012; Jenkins et al. 2013). Locating the Internet "at the center of visions for a world made better through connections" (Zuckerman 2015: 29), scholars have pointed to digital media's ability to create a new form of global public sphere predicated on the technology's connective affordances (Benkler 2006; Burgess and Green 2009; Castells 2009). An extensive literature on networked publics (boyd 2011) and their critics (Andrejevic 2011; Fuchs 2014a, 2014b) has developed. Whether concerned over the potentially exploitative nature of digital platforms controlled by powerful US-based corporate entities or seeing networked technologies as offering "a route to new opportunities and to stronger relationships," scholars share "a sense that digital media are changing the nature of our social connections" (Baym 2010: 1). Overall, digital media's ability to connect *individuals* across time and space on an unprecedented global scale and the social and cultural reorganizations generated by this shift have received the bulk of attention. To put it differently, the focus shifted from the *mass* mediated processes that concerned earlier theorists of transcultural exchange, e.g. cultural imperialism, to mediated processes of interpersonal connection, e.g. networked societies (Castells 2004).

The implications of the development of digital technologies in terms of transnational flows of mass media are less frequently acknowledged or explored. Digital platforms, however, have had a significant impact on further consolidating already highly interdependent global cultural markets. As Jin (2019: 2) reminds us,

> On the one hand, some digital platforms have played a key role as *cultural producers*, and on the other hand, other digital platforms have worked as *cultural distributors*, although the boundaries between production and distribution, which were previously clearly separated, are getting blurry. (Emphasis mine)

In other words, digital media not only facilitates communication between people across time and space on a previously unprecedented scale, but it also facilitates the production, distribution and consumption of mass mediated texts across cultural boundaries.

The intensification and diversification of global flows of popular culture that accompanied the rise of digital technologies did receive some well-deserved early attention (Thussu 2007), even if the complete rearrangement of global "soft power" dynamics and decline of US influence heralded in some of these studies (Tunstall 2008) did not fully materialize, especially when one considers patterns of media ownership and conglomeration. Today, as streaming services have increased the availability and visibility of texts from previously underrepresented culture – K-pop and dramas (Kim 2013), Nollywood (Musa 2019), telenovelas (Lee 2015) – the fact that "people around the globe are increasingly consuming culture developed by other countries and therefore are culturally integrated" (Jin 2019: 10) has turned into a taken-for-granted notion. Of course, as I hope to have demonstrated here, for most of the world's population – with the possible exception of the United States – "consuming culture developed by other countries" is not a new thing. Furthermore, ample research has demonstrated that technology alone is not enough to generate a significant shift in patterns of global consumption. The Korean Wave, for instance, happened as the result of a mix of government intervention in the form of powerful cultural diplomacy, K-pop industry efforts, fan engagement (including in physical spaces) and digital networks (Kim 2016, 2021).

What is, perhaps, most significant about the rise of digital platforms is the profound impact the increased *visibility* and perceived *immediate availability* of "the global" has had on our collective imagination. As Internet scholar and founder of the Institute for Digital Public Infrastructure Ethan Zuckerman (2015: 60) explains, the connective affordances of networked communication have led to a new "vision of a globally connected, informed and cosmopolitan world" that is both "a marketing campaign" on the part of the companies building the Internet and "an inevitable consequence of our imagination." "Powerful new infrastructures," Zuckerman concludes, "invite us to imagine profound changes." In other words, an "always out there" global sphere lives in the imagination of even those individuals not actually technologically connected to global digital networks or those choosing not to engage in them, simply because we are aware, and constantly reminded, of its very existence.

This "cosmopolitan imagination" (Delanty 2009) – the digitally enabled strong sense of connection to faraway people and places – frequently transpired in my conversations with media consumers (all names included here are pseudonyms). As Saki (a Japanese woman in her 30s) explained,

> There are people from all over the world who are sharing information on Twitter. For example, on Twitter, in places where there is unrest, there is information from the Arab world or from all sorts of different countries. If someone creates a hashtag from any place in the world, then everyone can see it. … I can instantaneously contact *anyone in the world*.

Or, as Daisuke (a Japanese man in his 70s) put it, "I have communications from Hillary Clinton and Bernie Sanders. I get information from them, they send some news." More generally, people frequently commented feeling "cut off from the world" (Marianne, French woman in her 50s) when unable to access digital networks: "You get the impression that a door, a window onto the world is closed and you find yourself all alone in your little corner" (Carole, 51-year-old French woman).

While these connections may appear to take place at the individual level (even if Daisuke's was not actually having *personal* conversations with the US presidential candidates) they are embedded in the multidimensional dynamics that form our current global media mix – what I have called our contemporary "glocamalgamation" (Darling-Wolf 2015: 142). This data mix is qualitatively different in its diversity, complexity, de-territorialization, intertexuality and form/depth of engagement from its pre-digital iteration. While streaming platforms allow individuals to pick and choose from a variety of globally distributed texts at a level those of us who grew up watching endless re-runs on three terrestrial televisions channels could only dream of, these texts are also embedded in a more complex media ecosystem that generates new forms of global engagement. As deterritorialized cultural references seep into memes or TikTok videos shared quasi instantaneously on a global scale, media consumers are simultaneously constructing, experiencing and imagining the global. Like Hiroki Azuma's "otaku," they are drawing from a fast evolving database of references increasingly disconnected from their "origin" and generating new forms of postmodern subjectivities (Azuma 2001, 2009; Kadobayashi 2017). Perhaps most importantly "the global" is always *potentially* there at individuals' fingertips, even if it remains inaccessible *in practice* to much of the world's population. As Saki (a Japanese woman in her 30s), quoted above, continued, "I can't read English, but if you can read English, you can understand everything that is happening there with just a click."

Old Media Power and New Digital Landscape

In his insightful discussion of Masakazu Nakai's theory of mediation, Akihiro Kitada (2017: 298) suggests that Nakai's work tests our sociological imagination by forcing us to prioritize "the status of the possibilities '*in*' media" rather than approaching meaning-making "'through' media" (emphasis in original). This shift has significantly complicated the power dynamics at work in the development of our collective global imaginary (Stager 2020: 2) and allowed new players to enter the "repertoire of 'textual locations'" (Tomlinson 1999: 119) on which it is built. This does not mean, however, that power relations have necessarily diminished – they are being reorganized along different and constantly shifting axes.

First, it is important to keep in mind that while digital technologies open the field for new players, they also facilitate the continuing influence of old ones. Nostalgia about "classic" texts ran high in my conversation with media consumers. One only needs to look at Hollywood (e.g. Marvels) or television (e.g. *Fuller*

House, Doctor Who) to realize how much of our contemporary global media mix draws on older generations' engagement with popular culture of a pre-digital era when audiences were not fragmented into dozens of niche markets. Digital media not only facilitate continued engagement with these texts on the part of their "original" viewers through greatly facilitated (re)distribution, but also the transmission of these cultural references to future generations. Seven-year-olds in France will still break into song at the mention of *Tom Sawyer, Heidi* or the *Mysterious Cities of Gold* because their parents introduced them to the texts *they* grew up with on YouTube. In other words, the mass-mediated texts that constituted the "original" raw materials of globalized hybridity retain strong symbolic power.

We must also be wary of overly celebratory accounts of the global connective affordances of digital technologies operating from a neoliberal logic on US-based platforms owned by mega-corporations (Jin 2019). As Srinivasan (2017) cogently asks, "Whose global village" are we talking about? We must keep in mind that even for those lucky enough to be among the roughly 60% of the world population with access to technology (*Statista* 2021), the awareness and imagination of the global does not necessarily result in feelings of connection or increased transnational understanding. Recent events, including those surrounding the 2020 presidential elections in the United States, have powerfully demonstrated that digital media can serve as heterogeneous spaces of "discommunication" rather than community-building (Kitana 2017: 297).

Some 20 years ago, postcolonial theorists Raka Shome and Radha Hegde (2002: 186) already observed that "the technologies of transnationalization are proliferating and creating new spaces and locations that are connected, and at the same time disassociated, from one another in remarkably subtle and yet often obvious ways." While operating *in* media can make individuals feel like active participants in global culture, it also heightens their awareness of the ways in which they are "left out" from this imagined "always out there" digitally connected global community. Indeed, feelings of disconnection ran high in my conversations with the many folks who found it difficult, frustrating or impractical to fully engage with digital media for a variety of reasons – language barrier, lack of cultural capital, geographic location (Darling-Wolf 2020). As Arielle, a French woman in her 50s concluded

> The chimera of the digital age is that you have the impression that you can embrace the rest of the world. But no, you simply cannot embrace the rest of the world. Neither time, nor our spirits are wide enough for that. It's impossible.

References

Andrejevic, M. (2011) "Surveillance and Alienation in the Online Economy," *Surveillance & Society*, 8(3): 278–87.

Appadurai, A. (1996) *Modernity at Large*, Minneapolis: University of Minnesota Press.

Appadurai, A. (2013) *The Future as Cultural Fact*, New York: Verso.

Aumont, J. (1996) *À Quoi Pensent les Films*, Paris: Séguier.

Azuma, H. (2001) *Dōbustuka Suru Posutomodam* [Animalizing the Postmodern], Tokyo: Kodansha.

Azuma, H. (2009) *Otaku: Japan's Database Animals*, Minneapolis: University of Minnesota Press.

Baym, N. (2010) *Personal Connections in the Digital Age*, Cambridge: Polity.

Benkler, Y. (2006) *The Wealth of Networks*, New Haven: Yale University Press.

Boyd, D. (2011) "Social Network Sites as Networked Publics," in Z. Papacharissi (ed) *A Networked Self*, New York: Routledge.

Burgess, J. and Green, J. (2009) *YouTube*, Cambridge: Polity.

Castells, M. (2004) *The Network Society*, Northampton: Edward Elgar.

Castells, M. (2009) *Communication Power*, Oxford: Oxford University Press.

Chopra, R. (2011) "Introduction," in R. Chopra and R. Gajjala (eds) *Global Media, Culture and Identity*, New York: Routledge.

Cooper-Chen, A. (2010) *Cartoon Cultures*, New York: Peter Lang.

Darling-Wolf, F. (2015) *Imagining the Global: Transnational Media and Popular Culture beyond East and West*, Ann Arbor: University of Michigan Press.

Darling-Wolf, F. (2016) "The 'Lost' Miyazaki: How a Swiss Girl Can Be Japanese and Why it Matters," *Communication, Culture & Critique*, 9(3): 499–515.

Darling-Wolf, F. (2018) "Who's the 'Great Imitator'? Critical Reflections on Japan's Historical Transcultural Influence," in F. Darling-Wolf (ed) *Routledge Handbook of Japanese Media*, New York: Routledge.

Darling-Wolf, F. (2020) "In the City They Go 'Pit Pit Pit': Digital Media's Affordances and Imagine (Dis)connections in a Rural Japanese Community," *New Media and Society*, 23(7): 1863–81.

Delanty, G. (2009) *The Cosmopolitan Imagination*, Cambridge: Cambridge University Press.

Drazen, P. (2003) *Anime Explosion*, Berkeley: South Bridge Press.

Fuchs, C. (2014a) "Social Media and Public Sphere," *TripleC*, 12(1): 57–101.

Fuchs, C. (2014b) *Digital Labor and Karl Marx*, New York: Routledge.

García Canclini, N. (2014) *Imagined Globalization*, Durham: Duke University Press.

Hegde, R. (2011) *Circuits of Visibility: Gender and Transnational Media Cultures*, New York: New York University Press.

Iwabuchi, K. (2002) *Recentering Globalization: Popular Culture and Japanese Transnationalism*, Durham: Duke University Press.

Jenkins, H., Ford, S. and Green, J. (2013) *Spreadable Media*, New York: New York University Press.

Jin, D.Y. (2019) *Globalization and Media in the Digital Platform Age*, New York: Routledge.

Jones, A. (2010) *Globalization: Key Thinkers*, Malden: Wiley.

Kadobayashi, T. (2017) "The Media Theory and Media Strategy of Azuma Hiroki, 1997–2003," in M. Steinberg and A. Zahlten (eds) *Media Theory in Japan*, Durham: Duke University Press.

Kim, J.O. (2016) "Establishing an Imagined SM Town," *Journal of Popular Culture*, 49(5): 1042–58.

Kim, J.O. (2021) "BTS as Method: A Counter-Hegemonic Culture in the Network Society," *Media, Culture and Society*, 43(6): 1061–1077.

Kim, Y. (2013) *The Korean Wave: Korean Media Go Global*, London: Routledge.

Kitada, A. (2017) "An Assault on 'Meaning': On Nakai Masakuzu's Concept of 'Mediation'," in M. Steinberg and A. Zahlten (eds) *Media Theory in Japan*, Durham: Duke University Press.

Kraidy, M. (2005) *Hybridity or the Cultural Logic of Globalization*, Philadelphia: Temple University Press.

Kraidy, M. and Murphy, P. (2008) "Shifting Geertz: Toward a Theory of Translocalism in Global Communication Studies," *Communication Theory*, 18(3): 335–55.

Lee, A. (2015) "Telenovelas," *Perspectives on Global Development and Technology*, 14(1–2): 193–226.

Lule, J. (2015) *Globalization and Media*, Lanham: Rowan & Littlefield.

McCarthy, H. (1999) *Hayao Miyazami: Master of Japanese Animation*, Berkeley: Stone Bridge Press.

McLuhan, M. (1962/2010) *The Gutenberg Galaxy: The Making of Typographic Man*, Toronto: University of Toronto Press.

Mizuta Lippit, A. (2017) "Preface (Interface)," in N. Steinberg and A. Zahlten (eds) *Media Theory in Japan*, Durham: Duke University Press.

Musa, B. (2019) *Nollywood in Glocal Perspective*, Cham: Palgrave Macmillan.

Nederveen Pieterse, J. (2009) *Globalization and Culture: Global Mélange* (2nd edition), Lanham: Rowman & Littlefield.

Nederveen Pieterse, J. (2020) *Globalization and Culture: Global Mélange* (4th edition), Lanham: Rowan & Littlefield.

Pellitteri, M. (2008) *Mazinga Nostalgia: Storia, Valori e Linguaggi della Goldrake-Generation 1978–1999*, Roma: Coniglio Editore.

Rebillard, F. (2011) "Du Web 2.0 au Web2: Fortunes et Infortunes des Discours D'accompagnement des Réseaux Socionumériques," [From Web2.0 to Web2: Fortunes and Misfortunes of Discourses Accompanying Socio-digital Networks], *Hermès, La Revue*, 59(1): 25–30.

Rheingold, H. (1993) *The Virtual Community*, Boston: Addison-Wesley Longman.

Rheingold, H. (2012) *Net Smart: How to Thrive Online*, Cambridge: MIT Press.

Ritzer, G. (1993) *The McDonaldization of Society*, London: SAGE.

Shirky, C. (2010) *Cognitive Surplus: How Technology Makes Consumers into Collaborators*, New York: Penguin.

Shome, R. and Hegde, R. (2002) "Culture, Communication and the Challenge of Globalization," *Critical Studies in Media Communication*, 19(2): 172–89.

Statista (2021) "Global Digital Population as of January 2021," 7 April.

Steger, M. (2020) *Globalization: A Very Short Introduction*, New York: Oxford University Press.

Tomlinson, J. (1999) *Globalization and Culture*, Chicago: University of Chicago Press.

Thussu, D. (2007) *Media on the Move: Global Flow and Contra-Flow*, London: Routledge.

Tunstall, J. (2008) *The Media Were American: US Mass Media in Decline*, New York: Oxford University Press.

Zuckerman, E. (2015) *Digital Cosmopolitanism: Why We Think the Internet Connects Us, Why it Doesn't and How to Rewire It*, New York: W.W. Norton.

8

ASIAN CELEBRITY CAPITAL IN DIGITAL MEDIA NETWORKS

Scandal, Body Politics and Nationalism

Dorothy Wai Sim Lau

This chapter considers popular culture celebrities as key agents to embody cultural potency and assert influence on Asian societies and beyond. Their image, composed of both onscreen and offscreen presence, works to structure meanings and provides a sense of integrity. In contemporary culture, as David Marshall (1997) posits, celebrity incarnates a tension of signification. On the one hand, famous actors and singers can be heroes who signify ideals of virtue, achievement and self-reliance. The public renown is explicitly part of the celebration and consumption of their power. On the other hand, they can be flawed individuals, representing "the center of false value" (ibid.: xi). In either circumstance, as this chapter will demonstrate, the celebrity sign and power appears imperative in shaping cultural imaginations and ideological impact, underpinning public curiosity and scrutiny of celebrities' private lives and morality.

Scandals can intervene in the process of negotiating the significance of the star image, putting the issues of authenticity and privacy in contestation. Dated back to the early period of the star system in America, as Richard DeCordova (1990: 9–12) notes, knowledge about the private side of stardom is controlled and shown in ways that suggest a performer's offscreen life is a reflection of his or her onscreen roles. In this manner, star narratives achieve moral closure around the identities of performers. By reaching this closure, the star system augmented the marketable value of stars, underscoring the offscreen lifestyles as the core of the consumer aspirations (ibid.: 138). The moral closure is problematized, nonetheless, as scandals emerge and generate a fissure between an actor's public and private existence. Taking cues from DeCordova, Paul McDonald (2003: 30) postulates that star discourses are distributed in the public presence through an array of media conduits including book publishing, photography, the press, radio, television and, most significantly, gossip: Gossip operates in a fashion that the offscreen lives of stars are bifurcated by a publicly promoted sense of the private

DOI: 10.4324/9781003130628-11

(a public–privacy) and an intimate hidden life (the private side of privacy). By employing McDonald's (2003: 36) idea of "intimate transgression," this chapter explores how the private side of privacy of celebrities in Asia is inspected and interrogated at the moment of scandals as intersected with gender, body politics and nationalism. By positioning the scandalous image in the digitally enabled and highly scrutinized spaces co-occupied by media and the public, the chapter examines to what extent such an image potentially unsettles the star profile and evokes fans' affective responses in magnitude and in multitude.

New technology enables a more heightened public scrutiny of stars than before, placing the idea of "celebrity capital" at stake. As Barrie Gunter (2014) argues, celebrity capital reflects the value stars possess and it can be measured in monetary, psychological, consumer/corporate and political terms. Both the growth of newly liberalized media and surveillance culture in recent decades not only valorize fanfare across borders but also destabilize the embodiment of star worth in the global market. Tabloids' paparazzi endeavor to grasp icons' private lives that they can sell to mainstream entertainment news outlets (Cai 2019). The arrival of the Internet, which is a generally less regulated form of media than traditional mass media like television and print, diversifies the production and circulation of star-related materials that were once monopolized by professional institutions. Fans now can circulate news, photographs and videos featuring public figures across promotional websites and fan forums with unprecedented speed and spread. The subsequent emergence of online social networks and the buzzword of user-generated content culminate the decentralized mode of knowledge dissemination. It calibrates not only the aggregation of fan expressions but also an audience-oriented type of star scrutiny beyond the control of studios and agents. Moreover, social media's strong tendencies toward mockery and cynicism facilitate users to post and share materials that cover not only the achievements and virtues but also the incompetence and wrongdoings of celebrities in an open and interactive environment (Humphreys 2020). Torrents of criticism on Twitter and Weibo as well as *e'gao* (a form of online reproofing) or parody videos on YouTube and Bilibili become ubiquitous, vastly challenging previous modes of star knowledge. In addition to audiences' keenness to re-present and comment on famed figures in digital channels, celebrities and their personnel are conscious to manage notoriety by closely monitoring the online "illegitimate" texts and providing timely responses to remedy or salvage the reputation. All these instances have validated that the distribution of "unauthorized" star-related materials is crucial in negotiating the caliber of fame in the volatile media environment, especially at the time that a celebrity's behavior is regarded distasteful by the public.

Recent years have witnessed that Asia has played a leading role in the world's ever-growing media industries and cultures (Park and Dodd 2020). South Korea and Japan have accelerated to be the most wired countries in the world. China and Taiwan have become the major producers of high-end digital products from notebook computers to the iPad (Holroyd and Coates 2012). On top of the proliferation of hardware products, cultural content and soft resources have earned prevalence. Japan has been pioneering and prolific in producing anime, video games and other digital content. Hong Kong cinema's enduring genres like kung fu action and gangster noirs have remained the favorite of countless investors, critics and aficionados worldwide. What is more is the important role of Asian celebrities that are potent cultural exports and influencers in the global entertainment market. Asia has developed a maturation of a celebrity industry. Consider the K-pop sensation in Asia, Europe and North America as well as the appearances of Asian film talents on the Hollywood screen. The ubiquity of digital media, moreover, makes the purportedly less visible "celebrity societies" (van Krieken 2012) such as Bangladesh and the People's Republic of China now become more prominent (Richey 2015: 5). One noteworthy example is China's new breed of influencers, or *wanghong*, which spawns the digital economy (Han 2021).

Celebrity Capital as Soft Power

In Asia, popular culture celebrities, as a form of soft power, are key agents to generate socio-cultural and political capital and bolster ideological dissemination. As Joseph Nye (1990, 2004) defines, soft power refers to the ability to attract and persuade rather than coerce and intimidate people. Soft power strategies have dual functions – first, to improve a country's image abroad and second, to fulfill the goals of propaganda principally at home by mobilizing and heightening national identification and engagement (Nye and Wang 2009; Edney 2012). Government officials of many Asian countries are enthusiastic about inviting globally famous entertainers to high-profile political and cultural events in hopes of attracting a worldwide audienceship and securing a conspicuous public relations payoff (Tomlinson and Young 2006: 6). The presence of these popular personalities functions to celebrate national character, enhance national prestige and provide people with a chance to feel proud of their nation (Dong 2010; Finlay and Xin 2010).

China has been showcasing its growing "soft power" resources, with an effort of fusing the appeal of celebrities into its propagandist agenda. Since its inception in China at the turn of the century, Nye's (1990) concept of soft power has gained currency and potency in China's popular and official discourses (Nye and Wang 2009). In China, the state has been promoting role models for its heroism, patriotism and exemplary role fulfillment (Sullivan and Kehoe 2019: 247). Popular culture stars are expected to comply with normative values like filiality, faithfulness in marriage and the collective good advocated and retained by authorities, businesses and citizens. China's state-run newspaper *People's Daily* once stated, "As public figures, celebrities have a huge influence on society and are often imitated by fans. Although their social responsibility as public figures is not clearly stipulated, it is very much a moral issue" (quoted in Sullivan and Kehoe 2019). In their well-informed essay, Louise Edwards and Elaine Jeffreys

(2010) also pointed out that the Chinese public is ardently concerned about "the moral virtue of prominent individuals": Scandals pertaining to drug use or sexuality feasibly cause immense disgrace, resulting in celebrities being forced to issue public apologies, disqualification from awards or blacklisting from professional and endorsement roles.

By employing scandal as a vantage point of the investigation, this chapter specifically explores the contested Asian female persona in the digital mediascape through tropes of shame, gender, the body and cultural nationalism. It uses the semi-nude beach scandal of China's A-list actress Zhang Ziyi that broke out in 2009 as a point of departure. The scandal involved the exposure of a series of photographs featuring Zhang who sunbathed on a private beach in half nakedness and an intimate exchange with her lover. Once the photographs went live, censure from users proliferated. This chapter probes in what specific ways Zhang's public visibility and cultural identification were evaluated and questioned by viewers. As the analysis unfolds, Zhang's sexualized appeal, mediated in the scandal narratives, was subjected to the scrutinizing-objectifying gaze and the discourse of moral decline, leading to the argument the scandalous female identity operates in a manner, which perpetuates rather than disrupts the gender ideals that are long standing in Asian cultures. In order to better delineate the arguments, the chapter includes a comparison between Zhang and the well-known yet controversial Hong Kong megastar, Jackie Chan, regarding his love affairs and patriotic speeches. By engaging to the "intimately" "transgressive" persona of Zhang in signifying and affective terms, this analysis suggests the importance of the viewers' engagement in the star (re)construction, giving rise to volatile celebrity capital in the socio-political and technological junctures.

Zhang Ziyi and Her Scandalous Persona

As the new face of China at the turn of the century (Leung 2014: 65), Zhang Ziyi epitomizes the rising power of Asian stars in the global arena. Having graduated from the prestigious Central Academy of Drama, Zhang Ziyi had her debut performance in Zhang Yimou's romance drama *The Road Home* (1999). The actress rose to international stardom with her role of a spirited, headstrong swordswoman in *Crouching Tiger, Hidden Dragon* (2000), the martial arts epic directed by Asian American filmmaker Ang Lee. The cinematic hit earned more than US$200 million worldwide, becoming the most successful foreign-language picture in the film history in America (Klein 2004: 18). The success of the film won Zhang subsequent appearances in an array of Chinese-language and Hollywood star vehicles such as *Hero* (2002), *House of Flying Daggers* (2004) and *Memoirs of a Geisha* (2005). Furthermore, the rising actress appeared active in the world's leading international film festivals. She joined the jury at Cannes in 2006 as its youngest member ever (*IndieWire* 2006). Myriad celebrity and fashion magazines, as well as entertainment websites, voted Zhang as one of the "most beautiful Chinese women in the world" or alike titles. Moreover, she was the celebrity endorser of huge brands such as OMEGA Watches and Maybelline for their Asia Pacific markets. In 2011, she was named as a Global Ambassador for the Special Olympics, together with China basketball icon Yao Ming (Tang 2011). On *Forbes*'s (mainland) China Celebrity List in 2009 and 2010, Zhang is ranked number two, immediately following Yao, of China's top 100 power-ranking celebrities (*China Hush* 2010). With such a wide-ranging and robust profile, Zhang has proved herself to be a viable player in the global cultural market.

Whereas Zhang grew increasingly famous, her professional identity and moral status were troubled by the relentless emergence of gossip, rumors and scandals. Zhang's high-profile success in conquering Hollywood fueled the accusation that the actress ignored the entertainment business in her home country (Schwankert 2010). Also, reporters and aficionados have denigrated her accented English and a lack of proficiency in the language (Lau 2019). One may recall Zhang's award presentation for the best editing at the Oscars in 2006 and her Beijing-accented English (*China Daily* 2006) spoken on the stage, or the embarrassing moment that Zhang was wordless in answering the English-speaking press at the 57th Cannes Film Festival on her participation in Wong Kar-Wai's *2046* (2004). Moreover, she was dogged by the offense of charity fraud regarding the 2008 Sichuan earthquake, a disaster that caused approximately 70,000 lives. In 2010, innuendoes surfaced on the Web anonymously accusing Zhang of retracting the full amount she committed to donate to the relief work (Schwankert 2010). Dubbed "donation-gate," her unfulfilled pledge led cyber users to denounce her, engendering "a nationwide crisis of faith" in the goodwill of the famous and the rich (Jeffreys 2011).

Considering the controversies of multiple sorts, Zhang's love life and alleged sexual promiscuity appear to be compelling and perpetual in fan circulations. She had been rumored to have affairs with a cluster of famous men of various geographical, cultural and professional backgrounds including American filmmaker and music video director Brett Ratner, Hong Kong action star Jackie Chan and the Hong Kong tycoon-philanthropist heir Eric Fok Kai-Shan (Lau 2019: 109). Among others, her relationship with Vivi Nevo, an Israeli multi-millionaire and venture capitalist, seems intriguing. Tabloids uncovered that Zhang was to be engaged to Nevo, who was 12 years older than her, in 2008 after an approximately one-year relationship (Arango 2008). Subsequent to Zhang's acknowledgment of the romance, media callously speculate on the actress's intentions with regard to the potential benefits for her career since Nevo is a chief shareholder in Time Warner and a previous patron of The Weinstein Company with whom Zhang is claimed to have a multiple film deal (Lau 2019: 119). Some critics go further, charging that Zhang offered herself to a White man as a stigma to Chinese women or even to Chinese people. The popular discourse surrounding their relationship, hence, was quickly fermented to disputes pertaining to issues like Chinese identity, cultural integrity and national honor.

"Shame on Her!": Zhang Ziyi's Semi-Nudity Scandal

The public attention on the interracial couple reached its peak with the exposure of their semi-nude presence on the beach, which orchestrates the "voyeuristic attraction of seeing a star" (McDonald 2003: 37). In 2009, entertainment news reporters in Chinese media revealed the couple sunbathing on a private beach at St. Barts, supported by a number of secretly taken snapshots. As the paparazzi blowups depicted, Zhang wore a red bikini, removing the top to sunbathe while her lover was lying on top of her body and kissing her at times. Dubbed as "sex photo-gate" (Tan 2009), the scandal immediately appeared in many tabloids' columns and TV entertainment news programs and the materials were later transposed by audiences to Internet forums and video-sharing sites such as YouTube. Arguably, the divulgence of the nearly unclad persona objectified Zhang for a voyeuristic gaze, making her a spectacle for exchange in the popular image circuitry facilitated first by paparazzi and then by cyber users.

The "beach" controversy portrayed Zhang as incarnating a multitude of desires and fantasies in a highly sexualized tenor. Regarding Zhang's established screen persona in martial arts cinema that elevated her to the international stardom, the scandal re-positioned her to the realm inhabited by a sex personality. The snapshots depicted Zhang as erotic and fetishized, unfolding a "hidden star" in front of the public eye while kindling curiosity and a sense of intimacy. The "unsanctioned" persona was facilitated by image (re)production and circulation which is no longer solely manipulated by mainstream media but is undertaken by Web users. In this light, Zhang became an object sexually exploited in the media world and the real world alike. This resonates with Richard DeCordova's (1990: 141) explication that scandal narratives function to make sexuality the ultimate reality of stars' identity.

Zhang's behavior on the beach was considered an honor-or-shame media-scandal event, eliciting affects ranging from sympathy to anger. Certain users consider Zhang worthy of sympathy because Zhang's semi-nude sunbathing took place at a private beach. Also, the lenience extended to the claim that the actress was placed under the paparazzi type of intrusive gaze since she remained oblivious of the presence of the cameras. Yet a more common response was to ridicule her for the "misdeeds" in explicitly moral nuances. Viewers generally regarded the photographs as evidence of the sexual openness of Zhang, who became a sign of disgrace to the Chinese populace (Leung 2014: 73). Consider a YouTube entry, titled in Chinese "Zhang Ziyi: enraged about being spied on the beach," posted by a user on 6 January 2009, soon after the controversy broke out. The entry attracted considerable users' comments and not a few are the nationalistically charged remarks assailing Zhang for devoting herself to a man of another race. For instance, one user disdains, "Shame on you Ms. Zhang, a Chinese slut?" Another explains, "She is a hardcore bitch for all Chinese guys but she becomes a puppy dog for Western billionaire!!! What a shame to all China." Another comment echoes, "She has become another embarrassment for China." As the stream of acute comments indicates, users worried that the entire ethnic group would be stereotypically dishonored (for details, see Lau 2019). According to Eric R. Dodds (1951: 28), in a shame culture, individuals are conditioned by the pressure of social conformity because the estimation of oneself is equated to other people's conceptions. James Lull and Stephen Hinerman (1997: 25) similarly postulate that "the disgrace of scandal lies in the collective willingness of others to impose shame and even bring damage upon the scandalizer." It is true that shame demeans the "integrity of the self" (Gidden 1992: 65). But on top of self-respect, it is also a quintessential social and cultural construct (Lull and Hinerman 1997: 26). As the beach scandal unveiled, the celebrity's deed does not conform to the social standard. It violates the abiding Confucian values *li*, literally meaning propriety, which lies at the kernel of the Chinese culture. It, by and large, perplexed Chinese stars' presumed role to indoctrinate traditional virtues and questioned Zhang's status as a representative of China (MacRitchie 2016).

Female Body Politics in the Discourse of Moral Decline

Alongside the debates that stemmed from the scandalous celebritized presence, Zhang's semi-nudity controversy is telling of how hypervisible bodies of female celebrities become the center of cultural consumption, leaving women "especially vulnerable to scapegoating as the causes and carriers of moral decline" (Donald 2010: 48). According to Lull and Hinerman's (1997: 20–21) typology of media scandals, star scandals are marked by moral contextualization: When the private lives of celebrities enter the public sphere, the personae then become evaluated by the dominant moral code. While Zhang's deeds on the beach, which were forced to go public, were held to a specific type of social accountability (ibid.: 26), her "transgressive" appeal can be interpreted in relation to the female body politics perpetuated in China's socio-cultural landscapes. Scholarship has shown evidence for and assessment of the moral decline of Chinese women in the entertainment industry in relation to the politics of the gendered body. As Mila Zuo (2015: 520) contends, the social construction of gender in China has engendered a sense of anxiety about the female body and sexual desire. Tracing the historical trajectory in the last century, Zuo remarked that "the erasure of gender and sexuality" in the public domain of China was imperative under Mao's communism as it worked to guarantee an active participation of both sexes in revolutionary politics. Women's bodies became masculinized and desexualized, particularly in the Cultural Revolution (1966–76) in which androgynous clothes were strictly practiced (Finnane 1996). In the post-Mao period, China evolved into a market economy and gave rise to the fashion industry, heterogenizing women's dress and spawning the fantasy related to female bodies. Recent decades saw the full-fledged consumer culture and neoliberal capitalism in China. Female celebrities in China can now be seen as the epitome of the "new rich" of which the appeal is interlaced with the fashion and styling industries, serving for the commodifying gaze. The phenomenon purports the potential of the female body in generating novelty and contending to be part of the valuable celebrity presence.

The female body politics, together with stories of the moral deficiency, are often mediated through the terms of prostitution and cultural nationalism, as indicated in the media and popular discourses in Asia. There was hearsay about the actress having been sleeping with Zhang Yimou, who discovered Zhang Ziyi and recommended her to Ang Lee for *Crouching Tiger, Hidden Dragon* (*Asiaone* 2019). She was also under reprimand for her role in Hollywood's *Memoirs of a Geisha* (2006) in the context of intense anti-Japan ethos stemming from the constant refusal of the Japanese government to offer a formal apology for the military mayhem in World War II. Zhang was blamed for "betraying national loyalties" as Internet users mischievously posted naked images of her on set with Japanese co-star Ken Watanabe on China's popular Tianya forum (Sullivan and Kehoe 2019: 241). The dispute not only caused the cancellation of the film's original release in China but also resulted in the open reproach of Zhang selling her virginity to the top Japanese contestant (Bezlova 2006).

The latest controversy informed Zhang having been paid for sex by Bo Xilai, the former Communist Party leader in Chongqing, China. As the senior party official, Bo had been disgraced by a series of scandals such as a murder of a British man who developed espionage ties with his wife, his "playboy" son taking out Jon Huntsman's daughters in an unspecific Porsche, his enormous overseas fortune and the wiretapping of the Chinese president. Zhang's suspicious prostitution seemed to have been brewing for some time but it was first exposed by a controversial US-based Chinese news website called Boxun.com that frequently covers human rights violations and political scandals in China (Taylor 2012). Sources alleged that between 2007 and 2011, Zhang slept with Bo ten times in exchange for more than 700 million yuan, depicting Zhang as a high-end prostitute who had been servicing top Chinese Communist Party (CCP) officials for years (Zuo 2015: 519): However, the actress counter-claimed that the rumors were "contentious lies" intended to stigmatize her reputation.

"It's Acceptable for Men but Not for Women": Controversies about Jackie Chan's Romantic Affairs

Whereas audiences feel strongly scathing toward Zhang's sex scandals, no equivalent response is found toward the parallel controversies of male celebrities. For example, Hong Kong megastar Jackie Chan has his forays into amorous encounters exposed by both Chinese-language and English-language tabloids sporadically. Rumors unveiled that Chan married a Taiwanese actress, Joan Lin Feng-Jiao, in 1982 but it was not made public until 1998 when he published his autobiography *I Am Jackie Chan: My Life in Action*. The incident was seasoned by the "secret" love story between Chan and the well-known Taiwanese singer Teresa Tang prior to his marriage to Lin, as recounted by a former studio executive Du Huidong in his book *Little Stars* (2010). The megastar's name is further piqued by his extramarital affair in 1999 with local beauty queen Elaine Ng, which resulted in a daughter who is nicknamed by Chinese-language media as "little dragon daughter" literally, with "dragon" referring to the Chinese name of Chan. Soon after Ng's pregnancy with Chan broke out, Chan confessed, in an imprudent and arrogant manner, that he had committed a "wrongdoing of which all men on earth commit" (Gan 2020), which provoked public anger and denunciation. Throughout the years, Chan's affair with Ng has resurfaced in entertainment news networks alongside the purported disputes about Chan's financial support to Ng for raising the child, the fortune given by movie mogul Albert Yeung, and the teenage daughter's "coming out" and marriage with her partner in Canada (Lim 2020). In his memoir *Never Grow Up*, written by Zhu Mo (2018), Chan also admitted to gambling, drinking, overspending, visiting prostitutes and exercising domestic violence (Cormack 2018). Revelation of these "hidden truths" (McDonalds 2003: 36) led to negative, particularly domestic, publicity, placing him at the forefront of the discourse of sexual and moral politics.

Notwithstanding media hysteria regarding Chan's deeds lying on the fault line, audiences seem to be more watchful and critical about his political speeches than his romance and sexual life. Well known for his "self-proclaimed patriotism" (Tsui 2012), Chan has been a loyal defender of the Chinese government and holds a hostile attitude toward anybody who is considered to oppose Beijing. On 18 April 2009, during a panel discussion at the annual Boao Forum for Asia, Chan said,

> in the decade after Hong Kong's return to the Chinese sovereignty, as I gradually see, I am not sure if it is good to have freedom or not. … If you are too free, you are like Hong Kong now. It is very much in chaos
>
> *(Jacobs 2009)*

Furthermore, he made a similar reproof to Taiwan, calling Taiwanese democracy "the biggest joke in the world." Chan's diction enraged politicians, journalists and citizens in Taiwan, Hong Kong and the PRC alike. Hong Kong newspaper *Apple Daily* gave the front-page headline "Jackie Chan Is a Knave," followed by the publication's demand for an apology from the superstar on the next day. Indignantly enough, some bloggers lambasted Chan as "fascist," "evil" and "racist" (Ray 2009) and some others urged a boycott of Chan's films, with regard to the impending theatrical release of *Shinjuku Incident* in Asia. Likewise, a discussion group on Facebook called "send Jackie Chan to North Korea," citing the North Korean government's disinclination toward freedom, summoned a signature petition that rapidly earned over 6,600 members in four days (*South China Morning Post* 2009). Chan's comment was later segued into an earlier critique given by Chan, saying that "a television made in China might explode" (Moore 2009), invoking an array of *e'gao* videos that went viral (for details, see Lau 2019).

Chan's "too much freedom" comment was registered in the recent political unrest in Hong Kong, the megastar's hometown. On Weibo, the Chinese version of Twitter, he publicized his view that the protests in the 2014's Umbrella Movement would cost the territory's economy (Tharoor 2014). He also referred to the propagandist song composed by Taiwanese-American Wang Leehom and Hong Kong-based Peter Kam, co-performed with Chinese singer Liu Yuanyuan, to celebrate the 60th anniversary of the founding of the People's Republic of China in 2009. In defense of Chinese nationalism, Chan elicited, "In the song 'Country,' one line goes: 'There is no prosperous home without a strong country.' I am willing to work hard with everyone and return to rationality, to face the future, love our country, love our Hong Kong" (Tharoor 2014). Censure spread among protesters of Hong Kong, who compared Chan with Hong Kong-born celebrated film actor, Chow Yun-Fat, who was assertive to the young spirits' bravery and rationality in the territory's social movements and critical to the police's use of tear gas during demonstrations (Rahman 2014).

Whereas Jackie Chan showed general skepticism to the right to free speech in Hong Kong, he extended his controversial rhetoric to the United States, perplexing his profile as a Hong Kong–Hollywood performer. Chan has pioneered and managed to sustain in the American film market since the influx of Hong Kong film talents in Hollywood in the 1990s. In his 2012 interview with Phoenix TV, a China-based media channel, Chan once ironically opined that the United States is "the most corrupt country in the world" and "there was no reason" (Tsui 2012) for him in making *Rush Hour*, an action film franchise which earned him a fortune and global acclaim: He continued to aver that he refused to play a villain role as he did not "like to be looked [down] upon by foreigners." Though marked by resistance to racial prejudice, Chan's anti-American utterance sounded overtly equivocal. Some online users considered Chan's diction as a strategic remedy with respect to his confession made in 1999 of having fathered an estranged daughter. Some, otherwise, associated his claim with his recent appointment to the Chinese People's Political Consultative Conference (CPPCC), Beijing's top advisory structure, of which the appointment evoked Internet frenzy in Chinese communities (Cheung and Ng 2013). Retweeted and shared, Chan's patriotic remarks, in many ways, sparked local and international castigation more intensely and extensively than that aroused by his sexual life (Tsui 2012).

Conclusion

The argument of this chapter shows no intention to establish the binary of politics-as-masculine and sexuality-as-feminine. Any claim of such polemical should demand efforts of meticulous exploration. Nevertheless, the juxtaposition of the body and the personae of Jackie Chan and Zhang Ziyi tellingly suggests that digital discourse and audiences remain more lenient toward the sexual scandals of male stars than that of female stars, testifying to the imbalance of gender imaginaries receptive to hypersexuality and decency. It also hints at an implicit acceptance of the normative notion of men having the freedom to pursue affairs whereas women should stay within the nationalistic boundaries of the normative heterosexual monogamy and the ideals of femininity.

Specifically, this chapter has analyzed Zhang Ziyi's beach scandal as an example of how the Asian female star publicity is scrutinized and negotiated by the global public in digital media networks. As the analysis has unfolded, scandal ushers the moment that the star image is evaluated against the moral and ideological parameters, risking the celebrity capital in dynamic and capricious fashions. In the instance of Zhang, the semi-nudity photographs invited public condemnation, accusing the icon of national insult and shame. The discourse of moral decline is associated with the politics of the female body, legitimizing rather than problematizing the patriarchal ideals in Asian societies. This claim is further illustrated in the juxtaposition of Zhang's sexuality-induced scandals and Jackie Chan, who has been criticized for his politically induced speeches and patriotic diction more widely than his extramarital affairs. By contending the scandalous imaginaries of Zhang, this chapter has provided insight on how far digital media apparatuses facilitate the private, or "intimate," life of stars going public, unpacking the intricacies of morality, body politics and nationalism as well as digital users' engagement in current Asian celebrity culture.

References

Arango, T. (2008) "Behind the Scenes, A Force in the Media World," *New York Times*, 27 July.

Asiaone (2019) "Zhang Ziyi Might Not Have Acted in Crouching Tiger, Hidden Dragon If Not for Zhang Yimou," 24 May.

Bezlova, A. (2006) "CHINA: 'Memoirs of a Geisha' Lost in Political Din," *Inter Press Service*, 7 February.

China Daily (2006) "Zhang Ziyi has Fans, Not in Hong Kong," 17 March.

China Hush (2010) "2010 Forbes China Celebrity List," 29 April.

Cai, S. (2019) *Female Celebrities in Contemporary Chinese Society*, Singapore: Springer.

Cheung, G. and Ng, K. (2013) "Jackie Chan Appointed to Beijing's Top Advisory Body," *South China Morning Post*, 1 February.

Cormack, M. (2018) "Jackie Chan Shares His Darker Side: Five of the Most Shocking Revelations from His Memoir," *South China Morning Post*, 13 December.

DeCordova, R. (1990) *Picture Personalities: The Emergence of the Star System in America*, Chicago: University of Illinois Press.

Dodds, E. (1951) *The Greeks and the Irrational*, Berkeley: University of California Press.

Donald, S.H. (2010) "Tang Wei: Sex, the City and the Scapegoat," *Theory, Culture & Society*, 27(4): 46–68.

Dong, J. (2010) "The Beijing Games, National Identity and Modernization in China," *International Journal of the History of Sport*, 27: 2798–820.

Du, H. (2010) *Little Stars* [in Chinese], Hong Kong: Wan Li Book.

Edney, K. (2012) "Soft Power and the Chinese Propaganda System," *Journal of Contemporary China*, 21: 899–914.

Edwards, L. and Jeffreys, E. (2010) *Celebrity in China*, Hong Kong: Hong Kong University Press.

Finlay, C.J. and Xi, X. (2010) "Public Diplomacy Games," *Sport in Society*, 13: 876–900.

Finnane, A. (1996) "What Should Chinese Women Wear?," *Modern China*, 22(2): 99–131.

Gan, Z. (2020) "I Have Made a Mistake that All Men in the World Would Make!: Jackie Chan's Confession to His Estranged Daughter" [in Chinese], *Yahoo News*, 5 May.

Giddens, A. (1992) *The Transformation of Intimacy*, Cambridge: Polity.

Gunter, B. (2014) *Celebrity Capital*, New York: Bloomsbury.

Han, X. (2021) "Historicising Wanghong Economy," *Celebrity Studies*, 12(2): 317–25.

Holroyd, C. and Coates, K. (2012) *Digital Media in East Asia*, New York: Cambria.

Humphreys, J. (2020) "Trust No One: The Cynical Logic of Social Media," *Irish Times*, 12 March.

IndieWire (2006) "AFP: Chinese Actress Zhang Ziyi to Join Cannes Jury," 17 April.

Jacobs, A. (2009) "Jackie Chan Strikes a Chinese Nerve," *New York Times*, 23 April.

Jeffreys, E. (2011) "Zhang Ziyi and China's Celebrity-Philanthropy Scandals," *Portal: Journal of Multidisciplinary International Studies*, 8(1): 1–21.

Klein, C. (2004) "Crouching Tiger, Hidden Dragon: A Diasporic Reading," *Cinema Journal*, 43(4): 18–42.

Lau, D.W.S. (2019) *Chinese Stardom in Participatory Cyberculture*, Edinburgh: Edinburgh University Press.

Leung, W. (2014) "Zhang Ziyi: The New Face of Chinese Femininity," in W. Leung and A. Willis (eds) *East Asian Film Stars*, New York: Palgrave Macmillan.

Lim, Y.N. (2020) "Elaine Ng: Jackie Chan Did Not Give Me Money After I Had Given Birth," *Straits Times*, 28 July.

Lull, J. and Hinerman, S. (1997) *Media Scandals*, Cambridge: Polity.

MacRitchie, M. (2016) "Chinese Celebrity and the Soft Power Machine," *LinkedIn*, 7 April.

Marshall, P. (1997) *Celebrity and Power*, Minneapolis: University of Minnesota Press.

McDonald, P. (2003) "Stars in the Online Universe," in T. Austin and M. Barker (eds) *Contemporary Hollywood Stardom*, London: Arnold.

Moore, M. (2009) "Jackie Chan Said Chinese People Need to be Controlled," *Telegraph*, 19 April.

Nye, J. (1990) "Soft Power," *Foreign Policy*, 80: 153–72.

Nye, J. (2004) *Soft Power: The Means to Success in World Politics*, New York: Public Affairs.

Nye, J. and Wang, J. (2009) "Hard Decisions on Soft Power: Opportunities and Difficulties for Chinese Soft Power," *Harvard International Review*, 31: 18–22.

Park, H. and Dodd, M. (2020) "Introduction," in H. Park (ed) *Media Culture in Transnational Asia*, New Brunswick: Rutgers University Press.

Rahman, A. (2014) "Chow Yun-Fat Speaks Out in Support of Hong Kong Democracy Protestors," *Hollywood Reporter*, 2 October.

Ray, K. (2009) "Reactions to Jackie Chan's Views of Freedom in China," *Shanghaiist*, 20 April.

Richey, L. (2015) *Celebrity Humanitarianism and North-South Relations*, London: Routledge.

Schwankert, S. (2010) "Zhang Ziyi Begins to Address Quake Scandal," *Hollywood Reporter*, 9 February.

South China Morning Post (2009) "Row Over Jackie Chan Deepens," 23 April.

Sullivan, J. and Kehoe, S. (2019) "Truth, Good and Beauty: The Politics of Celebrity in China," *China Quarterly*, 237: 241–56.

Tan, L. (2009) "Zhang Ziyi Sexy Beach Photo Scandal," *Chinese-Tool*, 5 January.

Tang, Y. (2011) "Yao and Movie Star Zhang Assist Special Olympics," *China Daily*, 21 June.

Taylor, A. (2012) "The Latest Insane Bo Xilai Rumor is that He was Praying this Chinese Movie Star for Sex," *Business Insider*, 31 May.

Tharoor, I. (2014) "Jackie Chan is No Friend to Hong Kong's Protesters," *Washington Post*, 10 October.

Tomlinson, A. and Young, C. (2006) *National Identity and Global Sports Events*, Albany: State University of New York Press.

Tsui, C. (2012) "Jackie Chan Calls for Curbs on Political Freedom in Hong Kong," *Hollywood Reporter*, 13 December.

van Krieken, R. (2012) *Celebrity Society*, London: Routledge.

Zhu, M. (2018) *Never Grow Up*, New York: Simon and Schuster.

Zuo, M. (2015) "Sensing 'Performance Anxiety': Zhang Ziyi, Tang Wei and Female Film Stardom in the People's Republic of China," *Celebrity Studies*, 6(4): 519–37.

9

DIGITAL ACTIVISM AND PUBLIC PROTEST IN INDIA

Contextualizing Technologies and Cyber-Mobilization

Ramaswami Harindranath

Public events over the past ten years or so have highlighted the contradictions inherent in the role of digital technologies and social media in political and social change. On the one hand, Trump's effective use of Twitter is indicative of how social media platforms have contributed to not only bypassing more traditional forms of mediation and debates over fact and truth but also to the creation of what has been referred to as alternative truths. On the other hand, such platforms have also facilitated social protest movements seeking to address entrenched forms of injustice, from the Arab Spring to #MeToo and Black Lives Matter. Analogously, in the Indian context, digital technologies have arguably enabled the consolidation of right-wing Hindutva power and of Prime Minister Modi as a political brand, as well as to public protests against corruption and sexual violence. This chapter seeks to unpack the complexity that is intrinsic to such developments and how it reveals some of the inadequacies in extant conceptualizations of digital activism.

It is generally acknowledged that one of the main challenges scholars in humanities and social sciences have had to contend with is the relevance, plausibility and explanatory power of theoretical generalizations based on extrapolations from case studies or sample data. This is not the place to engage with the epistemological politics that underpin this issue or with critiques of the structures of power that are inherent in such theoretical enterprises. It is, however, pertinent here to note that such challenges are exacerbated when concepts and insights, generated in the West or Euro-America, are applied directly to other socio-political situations or locations without taking into account the singularities of local contexts. As a consequence, what is achieved is, at best, only a partial understanding, but often the results are a series of misreadings. This is by no means a novel observation but an acknowledgment of the continuing validity of critiques such as Chakrabarty (2008) and Mohanty (2003); the development of alternative

DOI: 10.4324/9781003130628-12

frameworks and approaches more suitable to deal with the non-Euro-American world, such as Chen (2010); the decoloniality framework (Santos 2014; Mignolo and Walsh 2018) and some scholarship in postcolonial studies (Sanyal 2007) and attempts to rethink and redesign research methodologies (Smith 2012).

Such ventures propose useful and important correctives in the form of "provincializing" or "decolonizing" or, at a minimum, adapting Euro-American theoretical formations to other situations, thereby challenging or undermining the latter's universal pretensions and totalizing ambitions. These instances of academic critiques are, more often than not, representative of more than scholarly skirmishes, as they are motivated by the desire to develop a keener understanding of the local and its inter-relations with the global or the transnational. While such epistemological interventions characterize a range of disciplines, scholarship on the political, cultural and social impact of digital technologies and social media exhibits additional problems arising from the over-emphasis on the technological and the neglect of the socio-political. It is reasonable to argue that, until relatively recently, conceptualizations of social and digital media practices, in particular, their relation to public protests, have presented explanatory narratives that, in their eagerness to commemorate the possibilities offered by their various technical affordances to achieve progressive and democratic change, have not paid adequate attention either to their potential to aggravate socially damaging practices or to the historical and political specificities of specific national or regional contexts.

As has been argued recently, at the center of this problem is the conceptualization of "technology." In a manner that recalls the significance that Raymond Williams (1988) accorded to the ways in which the changes in the meaning of fundamental concepts of "culture," "class," "art" revealed changes in broader society and politics, Leo Marx (2010: 576) points to "the hazardous character of *technology* – the word, the concept" (emphasis in the original) which has made it susceptible to a process of reification, enabling its treatment as a causal agent capable of promoting social change by itself. "Technology, as such, makes nothing happen," he declares, "By now, however, the concept has been endowed with a thing-like autonomy and a seemingly magical power of historical agency" (ibid.: 577). His disquiet with such displays of technological determinism is shared by others such as Morozov (2011), who argues that submitting to it

> hinders our awareness of the social and the political, presenting it as the technological instead. Technology as a Kantian category of understanding the world may simply be too expansionist and monopolistic, subsuming anything that has not yet been properly understood and characterized.
>
> *(Morozov 2011: 293)*

Exploring the role of digital technologies and social media platforms in public protest, therefore, requires paying attention to the historical specificities that impinge on a range of relevant issues, including the patterns of use of such technologies in particular locations, the idiosyncrasies of local socio-cultural contexts and the multiple facets that constitute different forms of public protest. In other words, such historical specificities characterize conjunctures that comprise complexities that, in turn, impinge on both the differentiations in the use of technology as well as the possibility of socio-political change. This chapter seeks to explore digital mobilization and social media activism in India, relating it to some of the relevant literature on the subject, while attempting to extend the discussion by locating the contradictions inherent in these practices within a few of the specificities that comprise contemporary social and political formations in India and by extension, other postcolonial countries.

Is the Digital a "Liberation Technology"?

The tarnishing of the image of digital media as a technology of freedom and a facilitator of progressive revolutions and democratic change could arguably be seen as having commenced in 2016, a year which produced convincing counter-evidence of the reprehensible manipulation of the technology by undemocratic forces. In a short essay provocatively entitled "Can liberal democracy survive social media?" published in *The New York Review of Books*, Mounk (2018) locates the Trump 2016 election campaign, in particular the candidate's use of Twitter and the campaign's alleged micro-targeting through Facebook, as one of the main contributors to this recent disillusionment with digital technology:

> In the months that followed the 2016 election, the conventional wisdom flipped. If the Internet had been portrayed as a savior a few short years before, it now had to be the angel of death. Breathless claims about digital technology's liberating potential turned into equally breathless prognostications of doom. Social media was declared the most dangerous foe of liberal democracy.

Despite such prognoses, however, what this highlights is the need to resist conferring agency to technology and accord greater emphasis to the *contexts* in which the technological affordances are put to use. It is possible to see how social media have the potential to close "the technological gap between insiders and outsiders," as Mounk (2018) argues. A significant development to emerge from this has been digital or cyber activism, the utilization of technology to mobilize public protest. On the whole, this seems a relatively unproblematic statement that reflects both publicly held sentiments and academic arguments. As we shall see demonstrated in the case of India, however, such a statement belies the complexities that are inherent in issues such as the urban–rural divide, access to technology, and broader cultural and social factors that impinge on the capacity to use technology.

Recent developments, particularly since 2016, have made the uncritical celebration of social media and new technologies as purely forces of emancipation a more challenging enterprise. Following widely publicized accounts of fake news, the harvesting and nefarious utilization of big data in elections and plebiscites, the revelations on the role of Cambridge Analytica and Pegasus, and the manipulation of Facebook and Twitter, such technologies seem to have both lost their innocence and had their reputation as facilitators of democratic reform and of popular uprisings against dictatorships besmirched. It is possible to conclude that digital and social media can no longer be seen solely as forces for good, an inference that reinforces the concerns about the reification of such technologies as agents for productive change that arises from a lack of engagement with the larger social, cultural and political forces that impinge on their use.

Moreover, should the impact of digital technologies be seen as uniform across the globe or does it take on significant variations in different national, social and cultural contexts? How significant are issues of infrastructure, rates of literacy, state policies, the cost of broadband and mobile connections, and the freedom and the capacity to use the Internet and social media platforms? It is such constantly shifting, but determining and therefore significant, constellations that constitute relevant aspects of the local context that at once reproduce the central logic of digital technology and make available its affordances while manifesting specific socio-cultural and political formations that I want to emphasize here.

The Arab Spring is a paradigmatic instance of the coming together of radical technologies with revolutionary fervor, although other popular protests have also been seen as emblematic of what the Internet and social media can achieve. For instance, Diamond (2010: 70) prefers the term "liberation technology," which he defines as "any form of information and communication technology (ICT) that can expand political, social and economic freedom," to demonstrate its alleged role in mobilizing popular protests in various locations, from Ukraine in 2004, Lebanon in 2005, Egypt in 2008, to Myanmar in 2007. But it is worth noting here Castells's (2001: 275) cautionary observation that the network society is constituted

> in a diversity of shapes, and with considerable differences in its consequences for people's lives, depending on history, culture and institutions. ... The Internet is indeed a technology of freedom – but it can free the powerful to oppress the uninformed, it may lead to the exclusion of the devalued by the conquerors of value.

This, more circumspect, assessment of the potential of the Internet and of the network society touches on several of the issues that will be explored in the rest of this chapter. As noted earlier, one of the primary concerns here is to engage with the issue of digital mobilization and activism not just in terms of what the technology affords but, more importantly, by paying attention to such practices as *situated*, to the socio-cultural and political specificities, in this instance, of India.

In her account of the possibility of multi-centered, cross-border activism facilitated by the affordances of digital technologies that make feasible the circumvention of state jurisdictions to potentially "constitute an incipient global commons," Sassen (2012: 460) emphasizes the importance of the local context in two ways. Firstly, the politics of place-centered, locally significant, issues are "partly embedded in non-digital environments that shape, give meaning to, and to some extent constitute the event" (ibid.: 466). Secondly, it is important to acknowledge "the fact that there is both a digital and a non-digital moment in the often complex processes wherein these new technologies are deployed" (ibid.: 469). Sassen's insistence on the digital and the non-digital as connected-yet-distinct moments is pertinent for our purposes as it underlines the importance of considering the specificities of the broader socio-cultural and political context in which diverse forms of collective digital activism occur. It also draws attention to the differences not only in the political interests and motivations of participants but also in the degrees of access to technology and the capacity to deploy it.

One of the key issues for scholars of digital and social media to bear in mind is that, as Shirky (2011: 32) reminds us, "positive changes in the life of a country, including pro-democratic regime change, *follow, rather than precede*, the development of a strong public sphere" (emphasis added). The degree to which digital tools can amplify or inhibit democratic processes is, for instance, dependent on whether the broader political environment features a healthy and functioning civil society or authoritarian control of the Internet and other media technologies. In postcolonial states such as India, and outside the Euro-American milieu more generally, this is further compounded by the composition of civil society actors and the singular formations of and distinctions between the private and the public spheres.

Digital and Non-digital Spheres in India

It follows that any discussion of digital media and activism should be open to the variety of mobilizations that the technology has been contributing to, and to the impact of specific cultural and political features that societies in which such mobilizations occur. The terrain of social media activism in India retains sets of contradictions, achievements, risks, and as-yet unmet possibilities, that together establish a field of enquiry that refuses to conform to any overarching generalization or totalizing theory that links media practice with specific forms of activism, protest or mobilization, thereby underlining the importance of context-specific understandings of such developments and the need for forms of a grounded theory that acknowledges and builds on locally relevant empirical data. A brief account of a few of the relevant studies reveals some of these key features, the sheer variety of cyber-mobilizations and the diversity of analyses, conclusions and recommendations. While, in some ways, these reiterate and reinforce studies conducted elsewhere, they also disclose aspects that are distinctive to postcolonial states in general and to India in particular.

An editorial in the *New York Times* (2014), bearing the headline "Social media in Indian politics," identified key opportunities offered and challenges posed by new communication technologies and social media, including the successful mobilization of voters by the Electoral Commission and various political parties, smear campaigns, voter fraud, surveillance and censorship of journalists, and the decline in Internet freedom. Overall, while the use of social media to boost voter turnout and registration was considered praiseworthy, on balance the use of technology was seen as contributing to the worsening of democracy and to ethnic and inter-religious violence. The editorial concluded with this advice:

> The Electoral Commission of India has asked social media providers to monitor their sites for fraud in the run-up to the general elections in April this year. That would be helpful. But Indian voters must also demand that their government bring transparency and accountability to electronic surveillance.

It is worth noting that this observation was made before the events of 2016 raised significant and disturbing questions about social media possibly undermining democratic processes in the USA, but digital technologies were considered as having played a significant role in domestic elections in India too.

Writing about the Delhi elections for the World Economic Forum, Mishra (2015) diagnosed the victory of the Aam Aadmi Party as an indication of the fast-changing media terrain in India, in which the affordances of social media were transforming mainstream news: "In the past few months, following close behind YouTube, video roll-outs from both Facebook and Twitter have enabled users to share their video clips. This has made the social platforms a powerful and intimidating tool for public advocacy," enabling "an average citizen" to "have the power to turn the tide through public deliberations and conventional media is opening up to give users a platform for expression." The election campaigns in Delhi 2015 were symptoms of this transformation: "Much of the election – or should we say the battle of perceptions – was fought on Facebook and Twitter." This optimistic estimation of not only the role of social media and online technology in election campaigns but also, even more importantly, its capacity to offer apparently limitless scope for public advocacy and deliberation invokes conceptions of public spheres and communicative action, counter-publics and democracy, media activism and socio-political change.

Building on slightly contradictory statistical data on the use of digital technology and its impact on election campaigns and in mobilizations of voters and political supporters, Narasimhamurthy (2014) identifies a key aspect of the use of the Internet and social media in India, and by extension, in various postcolonial contexts. According to his data, in 2014, among the Internet users in India, totaling 243 million, social media adoption was up to 84%, which represents about 8.5% of the entire population of the country. Up to 31% of this total population, he argues, lives in urban areas, where the use of the Internet and social media is concentrated. The "rest of India, mostly belonging to the rural strata inclusive of smaller townships and villages [is] mostly devoid of any social media usage as of now" (ibid.: 204). In addition, on the age of social media users, "nearly 75% ... are under the age of 35 years and nearly half of them are under 25 years of age" (ibid.: 204). Irrespective of how accurate this data is, social media and Internet use in India appears to be concentrated almost exclusively among the relatively young urban populace. Crucially, Narasimhamurthy (2014: 208) argues that the rapid increase in Internet use

> an unprecedented 14 percent from last year – allowed politicians contesting elections in 2014 and users and voters looking for alternative sources of news other than mainstream media to choose to express themselves on social media. ... In [the] 2014 Lok Sabha elections social media became the choice for people to engage in and consume political content.

Apparently reluctant to engage with the small but interesting inconsistency in the data he presented earlier on social media usage being restricted largely to urban areas, Narasimhamurthy (2014: 208) goes on to propose that the raw numbers show "how Facebook played a major role in the election. Undoubtedly, this was India's first election with such a large-scale usage of technology, open-access Internet platforms to connect, build conversations, share, mobilize opinion and citizen action."

This contradiction highlights the importance of considering the uneven penetration of technologies among the populace in India, which has several contributing factors, ranging from infrastructure, literacy, constraints arising from entrenched socio-cultural factors such as patriarchy and casteism as well as the urban–rural divide (Kumar and Thapa 2015). Such issues characterize the digital and social media terrain in India, which, in turn, reveal the context of use and the specificities of cyber-mobilization and digital activism in the country. For instance, Udupa's (2018) intriguing analysis of "enterprise Hindutva," the mediatization of electorally effective forms of Hindu nationalism through social media, focuses mainly on urban India, presumably due to the constraints on penetration and use of technologies. Rao (2018), in her examination of Modi's political brand that combines apparent contradictions – right-wing Hindu nationalism with neoliberal values; his reputation as a global political leader with that of a "commoner" who has an instinctive camaraderie for Indians belonging to various social and economic hierarchies – argues that one of the features of what she calls Modi's "selfie nationalism" is

> an emphasis on media use rather than access. Tweeting catchwords and phrases such as *digidhan* (digital wealth) and "e-governance" ... do not focus on whether people have access to media – or if people have basic infrastructure to allow connectivity – but rather on the use of media as a potential for profit and growth.

(ibid.: 178)

While Kumar and Thapa (2015) lament the lack of inclusion of rural voices and interests in civil society movements in India inspired by social media, more recent works on protests against sexual violence and #MeTooIndia (Dey 2020; Pain 2020; Nanditha 2021) underscore other patterns of exclusion that can be considered specific to the Indian context. While acknowledging social media's capacity for the creation and maintenance of potentially powerful counter-publics, Dey (2020: 49) argues that the lack of access to digital technology due to financial, educational or linguistic reasons further compounds the existing socio-political hierarchies in India: "The individual countries' power structures further influence the global digital divide." Nanditha's (2021) critique focuses on the use of social media platforms by Bollywood stars, celebrity journalists and media personalities to "come out" as victims of sexual abuse, even while #MeTooIndia leaves out the continuing, everyday sexual targeting of Dalit (lower caste) women, domestic servants and other marginalized communities. In other words, cyber-mobilization of protests against sexual violence excludes women from the traditionally excluded and marginalized. Similarly, Pain (2020) draws attention to the ways in which #MeTooIndia inspired middle and upper class, urban young feminists while largely ignoring the poor and the female domestic workers who continually face sexual harassment. Thus, #MeTooIndia exemplifies the contradictions and paradoxes contained within social media activism in postcolonial countries.

Ilavarasan's (2013) study of youth political participation and use of ICT for civic engagement in India appears, at first glance, to confirm the popular belief about young persons' lack of interest in politics. His conclusions, however, are more nuanced. Seeking to engage with contradictory perceptions of youth either as apolitical or as instigators of popular uprisings, Ilavarasan's project attempts to go beyond the celebration of digital networking by providing the opportunity to share information and mobilize protesters in order to examine "whether ICTs have brought such pluralism and fragmentation to the civic engagement of youth in India" (ibid.: 285). The contradictions evident in the findings from this relatively small qualitative study are revealing: Unlike in Hong Kong, Tunisia or Egypt, youth in India, while they volunteered to contribute to various forms of civic activities and community work, either by donating free labor after school or by working in the NGO sector, appeared less willing to engage in political activity. This apparent inconsistency, Ilavarasan argues, arises from a belief that corruption is far too entrenched in Indian politics for any significant change to occur. This seeming contradiction between, on the one hand, their social awareness and their willingness to actively engage with and participate in civil society and, on the other, a debilitating pessimistic outlook on the possibility of political change is reflected in their use of ICTs: Although mobile telephony and the Internet were part of their everyday lives, such technologies were not used for social or political activism but were recognized as significant for the purposes of entertainment, networking and "for communication needs like coordinating with fellow volunteers or

NGOs" (ibid.: 297). Ilavarasan's explanation for this reluctance "to rise up," despite rising inequality, unemployment and marginalization, and despite endemic corruption which their social engagement indicates they are aware of, is "the level of freedom in India's democratic system, in which the youth can air their frustrations in various ways, including voting" (ibid.: 297), although the youth viewed all professional politicians as corrupt. The study concludes that "youth-driven political upheaval – with or without ICTs – appears unlikely in India for the foreseeable future" (ibid.: 298). This argument runs counter to Shirky's (2011) observation mentioned earlier: While for Shirky democratic processes that retain a healthy public sphere precede positive changes in a country, Ilavarasan argues that Indian youth's faith in the country's functioning democracy inhibits their participation in digital forms of activism. This recalls Oommen's (1990) examination of the centrality of communication to social movements, in which he observes that different phases of development, from the tribal and peasant to the industrial, affect patterns of communication and technological development. The different phases of development that are evident in contemporary India can, in important ways, be linked to developments in technology, more specifically, to access to digital technologies and the capacity to participate in social networking practices. However, Ilavarasan's assessment linking his respondents' incapacity and lack of interest in political protest to democracy is contradicted by other studies that provide evidence of online mobilization and activism.

In her analysis of the use of Twitter by NGOs and activists to mobilize protests against gender-based violence, Losh (2014) argues that, although Twitter and social media platforms afforded the possibility to publicize the widespread incidents of rape, the practice raised questions regarding the privacy of victims through the use of identifying hashtags. In addition to exploring various ethical issues relating to tagging content and the process of choosing identifiers in order to orient and mobilize those participating in protests, Losh also identifies issues that are more specific to the Indian contexts. Using the backlash against the horrific rape and murder of a young physiotherapy student in Delhi as one of her case studies, Losh argues that, while both the street protests and the online mobilization included a diverse group including young female college students, "the demographic characteristics of Twitter users tended to skew toward the opinions of youthful tech-savvy participants and to reflect the views of elites in education, case and class" (ibid.: 13). More problematically, and also significant for our purposes, the involvement of women in public protests and marches and in online activism runs counter to the ideologies of the Hindutva, which, as Chattopadhyay (2011) – in his account of the Pink Chaddi political campaign – points out, idealize women as "mothers, chaste wives and compliant daughters" (ibid.: 66) and attempt to exclude from participating in the public sphere those who do not comply. Therefore, the election of the Hindu nationalist BJP is, Losh (2014: 15) claims, indicative of how "the wired middle classes may still be averse to progressive politics." This identifies yet another culturally and politically important aspect of contemporary India that possibly hinders digital protest and activism.

Also pertinent here are two additional issues. Firstly, to consider digital forms of activism as only pro-democracy or toward progressive social and political change is to overlook the more illiberal forms of digital mobilization. This could take different forms, from "gendered cyberhate" against women (Jane 2017) to mobilization on social media against journalists filing news stories critical of the BJP government in India that take the form of threats of sexual violence and death (Ayub 2018). Secondly, as Harindranath and Khorana (2013) demonstrated in the study of Anna Hazare's Gandhi-inspired public protest against corruption in New Delhi and the digital activism and social movement that followed, analysis of Team Anna's Twitter posts not only revealed the presence of specific political agendas that belied the initial representation of it as a social revolution but also that the Team's use of technology contributed to the particular resonance that the movement had for urban, middle-class youth and to the exclusion of the urban and rural poor, an indication of how social positioning either advances or inhibits participation in the Indian public sphere (Harindranath 2014).

Complexities of Digital Activism in India

In an earlier essay (Harindranath 2000) I made a distinction between two kinds of social movements in 1990's India by way of arguing for different kinds of theoretical interventions: The first, "Chipko," a form of organized collective resistance by rural and tribal women, ostensibly environmental, but containing within it other pertinent and urgent issues such as gender equality, tribal rights, caste and social stratification, and economic independence, was, I argued, indicative of how such activism transcended conceptions of "single-issue" protests and combined the economic, the political and the social and therefore demanded a reconceptualization of social movement theories that were prevalent at that time. On the other hand, the rise and increasing consolidation of ethno-nationalist politics in postcolonial states, which was manifest in India by the "Hindutva" movement, represented the reactionary side of social protest, which had been interpreted and theorized in divergent ways. Social protests in contemporary India too include such potentially emancipatory as well as reactionary elements. In this section, I want to present a tentative set of thoughts by way of a gesture toward theorizing the use of digital media and social networking in India.

One of the most convincing criticisms of the alleged liberatory potential of new media technologies is Dean's (2005, 2009) argument that, on the contrary, they are "profoundly depoliticizing," on the basis that the logic of current political economy is "communicative capitalism," which forecloses politics. Dean's intervention is grounded on what she refers to as three fantasies that constitute communicative capitalism – "the fantasy of abundance," by which "the sheer abundance of messages … is offered as an indication for democratic potential" (2005: 58); the "fantasy of participation," which describes how clicking a button or signing a petition, while it provides the impression of participation, is actually "interpassivity," which "works to prevent actual action, to prevent something from really happening" (ibid.: 60) and finally, the "fantasy of wholeness," which "furthers our sense that our contribution to circulating content matter by locating them in the most significant of possible places – the global" (ibid.: 66). Together, these fantasies work to inhibit what Dean would consider genuine and necessary political engagement, even as they make political change much more difficult to achieve. At the very least, Dean's polemic persuades us to revisit – and possibly, revise – extant arguments that relate the Internet and social media to the enlivening of the public sphere and to democratic change.

Dean (2009) argues that communicative capitalism undermines Habermas's conception of the public sphere by denying communication any orientation toward action, replacing it with a mere contribution to a flow in which understanding and responding to a communication is of less value than circulation of content. It is important to add to this a critique of the public sphere that takes into account the social, cultural and political realities of the worlds outside Euro-America. As Sousa (2012: 48) has argued, it is not possible that

> the "problem" of bringing the concept of the public sphere to bear on the political concerns of non-Eurocentric conceptions of social emancipation might be solved by a new set of adjectives, be they subaltern, plebeian, oppositional, or counter-insurgent public sphere.

For him, such measures are inadequate since theories developed in Euro-America fail to take account of the diversity of the world, and the fact that "the understanding of the world is much broader than the Western understanding of the world" (ibid.: 51). One of the five logics that Sousa identifies as animating this "sociology of absences" is the "logic of the dominant scale," whose forms include universalism, which is "the scale of the entities or realities that prevail regardless of specific contexts" (ibid.: 53). It is possible to argue that the general understanding and conception of the public sphere illustrates this logic, as, in the hands of many scholars, Habermas's concept is or should be applicable to any democratic society regardless of local context. As I have argued elsewhere (Harindranath 2014), Harindranath and Khorana's (2013) analysis of Team Anna's Twitter feeds, and the responses to the spectacle of terrorist violence and the justifications of counter-terrorist measures in India, both indicate the specificities of Indian realities that underline the singularity of the local formations of the public sphere.

To clarify further, it is possible to read Team Anna's mobilization strategies and what they suggested in terms of the links between new technologies and social protests in India as illustrative of Chatterjee's (2004, 2005) distinction between *political* and *civil* societies in post-Independence India. While the former describes subaltern communities that are marginalized by both the state and by civil society and are involved in negotiations with the state that are dependent on contingencies and are therefore constantly changing, civil society he conceives as exclusionary, constituted mainly by urban, middle-class, populations whose interests largely coincide with those of corporate capital. Civil society, "restricted to a small section of culturally equipped citizens, represent in countries like India the high ground of modernity." Political society, on the other hand, encompasses "the relations between governmental agencies and population groups that are the targets of government policy. Political society in this sense consists of a set of practices different from those constituted by relations between civil society and the state" (Chatterjee 2005: 86). The responses to extremist violence and the rise of ethno-nationalism illustrate the consolidation of a kind of affective politics that undermines claims to rationality, one of the characteristics of the public sphere as conceived by Habermas. What they highlight, instead, the contradictions between the private and the public in India, influenced by religious laws and property rights and criminal codes, respectively, which, in turn, fractured the Indian public sphere along religious divides (Ali 2001). Such aspects of the Indian public sphere need to be taken into account for any meaningful discussion of media activism and digital mobilization in India.

Gerbaudo and Treré (2015: 866) underline the significance of a more nuanced approach to the study of digital technologies and social media platforms and the formation of collective identity, which, they contend, "still constitutes a pivotal question for activists and scholars alike; one which is decisive to understand the emergence, persistence and decline of protest movements." Examining the operation of collective identity in digital activism and protest movements, however, requires avoiding certain pitfalls that have hitherto characterized scholarship in this field: Narrow, instrumentalist focus on the technology overlooks the specificities of the discursive and symbolic that carry particular local resonances; the assumption that technologically motivated networks of connection have superseded earlier formations of a collective "we" plays down the significance of the sense of belonging that is crucial to social mobilization and collective action and finally, the over-emphasis on big data for the study of protest movements risks missing the "micro-dynamics" of collective social action. As this chapter shows, such concerns are further augmented in India by a set of complex and context-specific issues.

References

Ali, A. (2001) "Evolution of the Public Sphere in India," *Economic & Political Weekly*, 36(26): 2419–25.

Ayub, R. (2018) "In India, Journalists Face Slut-Shaming and Rape Threats," *New York Times*, 22 May.

Castells, M. (2001) *The Internet Galaxy*, Oxford: Oxford University Press.

Chakrabarty, D. (2008) *Provincializing Europe: Postcolonial Thought and Historical Difference*, Princeton: Princeton University Press.

Chatterjee, P. (2004) *The Politics of the Governed*, New York: Columbia University Press.

Chatterjee, P. (2005) "Sovereign Violence and the Domain of the Political," in T. Hansen and F. Stepputat (eds) *Sovereign Bodies: Citizens, Migrants and States in the Postcolonial World*, Princeton: Princeton University Press.

Chen, K.-S. (2010) *Asia as Method: Toward Deimperialization*, Durham: Duke University Press.

Dean, J. (2005) "Communicative Capitalism: Circulation and the Foreclosure of Politics," *Cultural Politics*, 1(1): 51–74.

Dean, J. (2009) *Democracy and Other Neoliberal Fantasies: Communicative Capitalism and Left Politics*, Durham: Duke University Press.

Dey, S. (2020) "Let There be Clamor: Exploring the Emergence of a New Public Sphere in India and Use of Social Media as an Instrument of Activism," *Journal of Communication Inquiry*, 44(1): 48–68.

Diamond, L. (2010) "Liberation Technology," *Journal of Democracy*, 21(3): 69–83.

Gerbaudo, P. and Treré, E. (2015) "In Search of the 'We' of Social Media Activism," *Information, Communication & Society*, 18(8): 865–71.

Harindranath, R. (2000) "Theorising Protest: The Significance of Social Movements to Metropolitan Academic Theory," *Thamyris*, 7(1&2): 161–78.

Harindranath, R. (2014) "The Indian Public Sphere: Histories, Contradictions and Challenges," *Media International Australia*, 152: 168–75.

Harindranath, R. and Khorana, S. (2013) "Civil Society Movements and the 'Twittering classes' in the Postcolony: An Indian Case Study," *South Asia: Journal of South Asian Studies*, 37(1): 60–71.

Ilavarasan, V. (2013) "Community Work and Limited Online Activism among Indian Youth," *International Communications Gazette*, 75(3): 284–99.

Jane, E. (2017) "Gendered Cyberhate, Victim-Blaming and Why the Internet is More Like Driving a Car on a Road than Being Naked in the Snow," in E. Martellozzo and E. Jane (eds) *Cybercrime and Its Victims*, London: Routledge.

Kumar, R. and Thapa, D. (2015) "Social Media as a Catalyst for Civil Society Movements in India," *New Media & Society*, 17(8): 1299–316.

Losh, E. (2014) "Hashtag Feminism and Twitter Activism in India," *Social Epistemology Review and Reply Collective*, 3(3): 11–22.

Marx, L. (2010) "Technology: The Emergence of a Hazardous Concept," *Technology and Culture*, 51(3): 561–77.

Mignolo, W. and Walsh, C. (2018) *On Decoloniality*, Durham: Duke University Press.

Mishra, P.K. (2015) "How Social Media is Transforming Indian Politics," *World Economic Forum*, 27 February.

Mohanty, C. (2003) *Feminism Without Borders: Decolonizing Theory, Practicing Solidarity*, Durham: Duke University Press.

Morozov, E. (2011) *The Net Delusion: How Not to Liberate the World*, London: Allan Lane.

Mounk, Y. (2018) "Can Liberal Democracy Survive Social Media?," *The New York Review of Books*, 30 April.

Nanditha, N. (2021) "Exclusion in #MeToo India," *Feminist Media Studies*, 13 April.

Narasimhamurthy, N. (2014) "Use and Rise of Social Media as Election Campaign Media in India," *International Journal of Interdisciplinary and Multidisciplinary Studies*, 1(8): 202–9.

Oommen, T.K. (1990) *Protest and Change: Studies in Social Movements*, Delhi: SAGE.

Pain, P. (2020) "'It Took Me Quite a Long Time to Develop a Voice': Examining Feminist Digital Activism in the Indian #MeToo Movement," *New Media & Society*, 3(11): 1–17.

Rao, S. (2018) "Making of Selfie Nationalism: Narendra Modi, the Paradigm Shift to Social Media Governance and Crisis of Democracy," *Journal of Communication Inquiry*, 42(2): 166–83.

Santos, B. (2014) *Epistemologies of the South: Justice Against Epistemicide*, Boulder: Paradigm Publishers.

Sanyal, K. (2007) *Rethinking Capitalist Development*, Delhi: Routledge.

Sassen, S. (2012) "Interactions of the Technical and the Social," *Information, Communication & Society*, 15(4): 455–78.

Shirky, C. (2011) "The Political Power of Social Media," *Foreign Affairs*, 90(1): 28–41.

Smith, L. (2012) *Decolonizing Methodologies*, London: Zed Books.

The New York Times Editorial (2014) "Social Media in Indian Politics," 9 January.

Udupa, S. (2018) "Enterprise Hindutva and Social Media in Urban India," *Contemporary South Asia*, 26(4): 453–67.

Williams, R. (1988) *Keywords: A Vocabulary of Culture and Society*, London: HarperCollins.

10

NGO2.0, NONCONFRONTATIONAL ACTIVISM AND THE FUTURE VILLAGE INITIATIVE

Jing Wang

2020 was a horrendous year. The ravages of COVID-19 spared no continents. During the months when the coronavirus struck China hard, cities were locked down, workplaces deserted and life trapped in the virtual space, but *not* everything was moved online smoothly. One of the sectors heavily impacted by the crisis is the non-governmental organization (NGO) sector where staffers are so used to operational mechanisms that only a physical office can provide that they have been struggling to regain productivity. The organization I founded and run (NGO2.0) and the 2,200 plus grassroots NGOs that completed our Web 2.0 training workshops are exceptions. They had a successful transition.

This chapter will introduce NGO2.0, a super NGO in China that specializes in social media and ICT (information communication technology) powered activism and then discuss the concept and practice of "nonconfrontational activism." Finally, it will elucidate a tech4good project, "Future Village," an experiment that applies bottom-up participatory ethos to the digital efforts of alleviating poverty in disfranchised villages.

NGO2.0 and Social Media Activism

In 2009, during my sabbatical in Beijing, I scouted the ground for collaborators who would join me to set up a project that provides social media literacy training for non-governmental organizations in western and central provinces of China – areas that are technologically backward. Why did I throw myself into a line of work that seems tenuously connected to scholarship and which has drawn me deep into activism since 2009? To answer that question, let us turn to the year 2006 when Creative Commons (henceforth CC) landed in China. CC is a Web 2.0 legal protocol made up of a set of free licenses that enables grassroots

DOI: 10.4324/9781003130628-13

creators of digital content to decide how other netizens can reuse and redistribute it online.

Creative Commons was founded in 2001. Mainland China joined the movement in spring 2006. I got involved as a CC volunteer and later served as the chair of the International Advisory Board of CC China Mainland. That China should join this open content movement was a celebratory event. Lawrence Lessig, the mastermind of CC, came to the inauguration ceremony and made an exuberant remark that "CC's global user community exploded instantaneously with the addition of 1.3 billion Chinese users overnight." As I was watching him speaking, several thoughts raced through my mind: How can we meet the enormous challenges of promoting CC in developing countries where digital elites are a minority? Is CC relevant to those who do not even know how to create digital content?

In short, China's 700 million peasants could be theoretically excluded from the parameters of Creative Commons if we were to be overly obsessed with the promotion of CC licenses alone. It did not take me long to discover the blind spot in the global model of Creative Commons, to wit, its presumption about *universal* digital literacy. The very moment when Lessig congratulated China on its new CC membership marked the beginning of the seeding of NGO2.0 in my mind. It dawned on me that perhaps a professor from a science and technology university could take on the mission of introducing Web 2.0 practices to marginalized communities in China. I chose grassroots NGOs as an entry point not only because they are traditional agents of social change but they have also long suffered from a communication bottleneck due to the party-state's suspicion of grassroots change agents. I was convinced that the skilled use of social media could connect them to the public and make them visible to each other. My next step was to approach Creative Commons and ask for collaboration. After getting rejected by CC China to incorporate my vision about NGO2.0 into its larger agenda (I was informed that creating a project for NGOs is too risky for CC China), I went solo and conceptualized a project that tossed aside CC licenses and focused instead on the fundamental spirit of Web 2.0 thinking and practice that gives life to open content movements like Creative Commons. More precisely, Lessig's remark has led me to envision a master plan that would help the digitally challenged NGOs create spreadable content and have their voices amplified and heard by the public. That was the genesis of NGO2.0.

MIT is a powerful brand name that helped me build my credibility in China at speed. Within two months, I identified three collaborating NGOs and a corporate partner, Ogilvy & Mather, where I did my advertising fieldwork for nearly two years. In 2009 when I founded NGO2.0, the lack of digital infrastructure in west and central China was no longer an issue. What drew the dividing line is the knowledge about how to navigate the Web. NGO2.0 thus started off with a very simple idea – providing grassroots NGOs social media literacy training to enhance their digital and new media literacy, and most importantly, to motivate them to create spreadable content online.

In ten years, NGO2.0 has grown from a small-scale academic project into a full-fledged nonprofit organization registered in Shenzhen. Our workforce expanded from a solo staffer plus 2 part-timers to 7 full-time employees and 15 core volunteers. We have been funded by Ford Foundation in Beijing since 2009, which invited intense scrutiny from both local and national public security bureaus. In the early 2010s, we suffered a series of setbacks probably because our main target area – west China – is a multi-ethnic region and politically ultra-sensitive. Predictably, a Taiwan-born American citizen getting involved in NGO work funded by an American foundation is suspect in the eyes of Chinese authorities, at least at the beginning. I am, however, a headstrong optimist and a true believer of Sun Tzu's motto – the ultimate victory is to win without conflict. That strategic mindset, together with my deep understanding of Chinese culture, helped NGO2.0 navigate through troubled waters. In a word, we practice nonconfrontational activism.

The flagship program we set up in 2009 was designed to help grassroots NGOs in the underdeveloped regions of China to leverage social media to collaborate online, engage in participatory thinking, launch interactive advocacy campaigns, increase the transparency of NGO operation, design online crowdfunding projects and learn human-centered design to create solutions to social problems. To date, we have trained approximately 2,200 organizations across 17 NGO issue areas. Those NGOs are now the least impacted by the pandemic when office work was moved online.

As the project evolved, we have gone beyond literacy training to build a collaborative platform that connects diverse partners committed to transforming China's philanthropy sector through the design and implementation of "social media for social good" and tech4good projects. My book *The Other Digital China: Nonconfrontational Activism on the Social Web* (2019) documents the actions of a wide variety of changemakers that emerged from multiple sectors to form communities both online and offline.

Chinese NGOs and the Obstacle Course

Before I move on to highlight the work accomplished by NGO2.0, we need to reckon with the unique politics of Chinese grassroots NGOs. Paradoxically, they are semi-popular, semi-official and semi-autonomous entities, because all of them, registered or not, maintain a decent and somewhat cordial relationship with the local state even while they identify themselves as grassroots agents. Former Ford Foundation Beijing chief Anthony Saich teases out this paradox most succinctly: "Chinese NGOs' voluntary subordination to the existing state structure should be viewed not as a measure of expediency but a strategic move to enhance their ability to manipulate the official and semi-official institutions for their own advantage" (Saich 2000: 139). Truly, there has been a scholarly consensus characterizing the Chinese NGO–state relationship as nonconflictual (Howell 1994; Perry 1994; Shue 1994). The resistance paradigm that prevails in

Western liberal societies is largely shunned by Chinese NGOs as they are compelled to work within the system. Being strategically minded means you do not collide with the authorities so that you can get your work done with the least disruptions. Paradoxically, although Chinese NGOs are beholden to the state, they enjoy "a remarkable degree of *de facto* autonomy" (Lu 2009: 9). Sometimes the closer an NGO is to the government, the less suspicion it arouses and the more autonomy it gains. A contemporary Chinese saying best captures this paradox: "The most invisible place is the place right underneath the light."

That was exactly the tactic I adopted when local public security bureaus intervened in our literacy workshops held in three provinces. In the early years of 2010s, Web 2.0 was a concept alien to both NGOs and censors. Anxieties about the unknown compelled nervous local governments to resort to the only recourse they were familiar with – shut down the workshops. In 2012, unwilling to handle such harrowing experiences over and again, I made a strategic decision – holding a Web 2.0 workshop right under the nose of the emperor – in Beijing. My reasoning went: If we were shut down by the central government, I would fold our operation. Sure enough, authorities in Beijing were less intimidated by new trends and new experiments than timid provincial governments. The Beijing workshop went extremely well. Since then, NGO2.0 has encountered no interference from authorities. Gradually, we expanded our service from west and central China to the rest of the country.

We introduced to our students Web 2.0 software and platforms, among them tools for multi-person online meeting and collaborative editing that surely came handy during the pandemic. Chinese policy makers have been pushing the industrial sector to digitalize itself, the NGO sector is by no means exempt from the "Internet Plus" initiative (a policy promoting the digitalization of the manufacturing sector economy) championed by Premier Li Keqiang. Now the drawn-out crisis of COVID-19 is making the digital know-hows a competency indispensable to all workers, NGO staffers included.

But however important, digital literacy training is not the only program we rolled out. We built a crowdsourced philanthropy map (www.ngo20map.com) with the goal of linking corporate social responsibility managers to grassroots NGOs; we compiled a field guide of software to NGOs (http://tools.ngo20.org/pages/home), introducing to them a wide variety of Web 2.0 tools that meet the demands of the daily work flow of NGOs; we also established a prototype of civic hackathon, which rounds up NGOs, techie communities, product managers, university students and professors from computer science and interaction design departments to help NGOs solve the problems they encountered.

During my ten years' experience of running NGO2.0, I was exposed, bit by bit, to a gradually unfolding, captivating picture of activism 2.0, in which multiple players from diverse sectors are leveraging the network effect of Web 2.0 to create incremental change in China. The changemakers under discussion include social media savvy free agents, grassroots NGOs and foundations, universities, software developer and maker communities, and IT companies. Those multi-sectoral agents have created memorable ICT-driven philanthropy initiatives. *The Other Digital China* provides a detailed account of how each group of the changemakers I named above contributes to Chinese activism. Most significant, all of them share an approach to change-making that I would characterize as "nonconfrontational."

Nonconfrontational Activism at a Glance

All successful activists in China are nonconfrontationalists. And I urge those noncontentious social actors to stop making apologies simply because the model to which they adhere is not aligned well with the Western liberal paradigm of revolt and resistance. Indeed, when we turn to a country like China or other illiberal societies where open resistance is not the norm but an exception, we as researchers should be called upon to conceptualize beyond the dichotomous mode of thinking (e.g. domination/resistance, state/society, civilized/primitive, mind/body) to unlock the agency of social actors that do not fit squarely into the profile of activists prescribed in the Western liberal tradition. As I argue at length in *The Other Digital China*, Chinese changemakers walk *around* obstacles rather than break through them and they navigate tactfully between what is lawful and what is illegitimate. In short, we practice a typical Chinese mentality – rules are meant to be bent, if not resisted.

Without reckoning with the ways Chinese activists steer themselves in the massive middle ground – the gray zones – where they resort to other means of serving social good than openly defying the political will of Beijing, our understanding of the Chinese "social" and the Chinese style of activism cannot but be one-dimensional. Similarly, focusing digital scholarship about China on censorship alone is problematic because in reality, Chinese people have more options than becoming martyrs or brainwashed dummies. If the activists we study operate mainly in the gray zones, shouldn't we be intrigued by the different shades of gray in which not only activists but also ordinary people in China roam around and get things accomplished? The binary thinking characteristic of Western epistemology – framing reality in bipolar opposites – is a poor analytical tool to decipher China where gray, not white or black, is the ruling color.

James C. Scott (1985) captures the practice of "calculated conformity" most succinctly. He argues that what is missing in scholarly research is the "massive middle ground in which conformity is often a self-conscious strategy." What is understudied is *the continuum of situations* ranging from what Habermas called the ideal speech situation and the public sphere all the way to the concentration camp (ibid.: 285–7). *The Other Digital China* maps out this massive middle ground – China's gray zone – illustrating the kind of social actions that deviates from the playbook for Western NGOs, and in so doing, the book valorizes the powerless and subjugated as savvy political agents. I will not reiterate my discussion of the critical literature revolving around the concept of nonconfrontationalism laid out in my book (Wang 2019: 37–42). Instead, I will count the basic strategies of nonconfrontational activism and provide examples of how it works.

First of all, nonconfrontational activists are anonymous and they remain peripheral to academic discussions of social action even though it prevails in autocratic societies where activists resort to other means of serving social good than openly critiquing and rebelling. In authoritarian countries, NGOs work under great constraints and they experiment with creative ways to effect social change. Indeed, Chinese NGOs are experts in devising strategies to evade censorship while making their footprints visible in the social realm. Some of them created state-sanctioned nonprofit programs such as providing educational assistance to children in poverty-stricken households, promoting HIV-AIDS public health literature and offering social welfare programs to the elderly and other disadvantaged groups. Those pursuing politically sensitive issue areas have to camouflage their missions and activities so as to reduce tension with authorities. For example, Muslim-run organizations in Gansu and Xinjiang typically portray their mission as "cultural preservation" rather than advocacy for religious freedom. A Lanzhou-based Muslim NGO we trained in 2010 runs successful Muslim cooking classes. I doubt that is the only activity they hold but the unequivocal promotion of the tamer aspects of Muslim culture goes a long way of abating the anxieties of suspicious local officials. Camouflage, or hiding in plain sight, is seen as strategic concealment aimed at effacing "the traces of one's own presence from photographic media of surveillance" (Shell 2012: 23). The visual evanescence of camoufleurs should not be seen as a lack or an absence. Instead, it needs to be understood as the productive engagement and calculated performance of the weak and the powerless. We can thus define the agency of nonconfrontational activists in terms of the dual concept of "calculated conformity" and "cultivated subjectivity." Advocates for sensitive NGO issue areas are all practitioners of this tactic.

Strategic positioning is another nonconfrontational strategy that NGO2.0 adopted. NGO2.0 would have invited intense scrutiny if we had framed our literacy training in terms of "media" rather than "technology." That is because the specter of information security hangs over the term "media," while "technology" is culturally and politically neutral. From the very beginning, I took pains to position NGO2.0 as a tech4good project rather than a social media initiative.

Apart from calculated positioning, smart NGOs can resort to the rhetoric of the powerful to curb the exercise of power (O'Brien and Li 2006: 2). Labor NGOs are versatile adopters of this tactic, framing their contention in the context of legitimized official policy discourse and state laws that safeguard the interest of workers, a CCP commitment that can be traced back to Mao's era and the venerable tradition of the proletarian revolution. Those activists excel at tapping into state propaganda to game the system and co-opting concerned party elites for support. NGO2.0 could also resort to this strategy to shield ourselves from political trouble since the nation-state has been trumpeting the mandate of digitalizing rural China. We are thus simply following the state policy.

Finally, regardless of which strategy nonconfrontational activists choose to embrace, it is bound to be associated with incrementalism. In a cultural and political environment that prioritizes harmony over contention, NGOs and other changemakers in China are compelled to make deliberate efforts to ensure that their actions do not appear to effect social change too quickly and too dramatically. A measured step-by-step change agenda is the ultimate amulet Chinese activists can wear for self-protection.

For those who wonder if incremental and nonconfrontational approaches can generate real impact and systemic change, I will share one social media initiative – sociologist Yu Jianrong's "Weibo Attack on Child Traffickers." Launched in 2011, the campaign aims to identify children abducted by human traffickers. Assuming that many underage beggars are abducted children, Yu mobilized netizens all over China to take snapshots of young beggars scavenging in the streets, upload those pictures to their Weibo account and share them with local police stations and national media via the hashtag #WeiboAttackChildAbduction. Those photos were then used for comparison with archived photos of missing children. In less than a month, more than 7,000 photos were collected. In May 2012, the China Social Assistance Foundation and investigative reporter Deng Fei established "The Child Safety Fund" (Wang 2013). Over time, the focus of the campaign was shifted from saving abducted children to in-depth discussions of how society could deliver children from living in poverty. This case illustrates well that microcharity 2.0 – sending a snapshot to identify a missing child or a virtual leave to create a virtual tree for an environmental campaign – can lead to successful advocacy and positive impact offline. Small acts of compassion add up and can trigger a qualitative change on the ground.

Emperor–Subject Relationship and the Two Faces of Paternalism

The case studies of social media activism should make it clear that if we broaden the parameters of "social action" to include incremental nonconfrontational activism, the meaning of "social change" will also mutate. Certainly, the definition of "change-making" varies from culture to culture and from discipline to discipline. Overthrowing the government, I contend, is not the only path for bringing about social transformation. Can a systematic assistance to the socially disadvantaged – a mission articulated by many Chinese NGOs – lead to positive change incrementally? Only the most cynical critic would answer no.

Still, there is a big puzzle to solve – why are the exploited in an authoritarian country like China accept their situation as a normal or even a justifiable part of social order? This is a question for political scientists, but a cultural studies critic has her own analytical tool to crack the nut. Let us return to COVID-19 and scrutinize what the Chinese state has done for its people. Official reports acknowledge that as of 6 April 2020, the Chinese state spent 1.49 billion yuan (US$218,412,466) which included medical expenses for a confirmed diagnosis and suspected patients in all provinces, districts and cities of China (Sina Science & Technology 2020). Another set of statistics about the level of citizen's trust in their own government is equally revealing. The 2020 Edelman Trust Barometer Global Report shows that China topped the chart of the percentages of people's trust in their own government. China scored an index of 82 compared to 47 in the USA (Edelman 2020). Why are Chinese people contradicting the Western perception that the "evil empire" has to collapse so that its subjects can be liberated?

Let us toss aside the conventional wisdom that the Chinese government rules with coercion, which is as true as most Chinese fathers rule their households by instilling fear in the mind of sons and daughters. Indeed, the children are held under the sway of paternalistic authority and complain bitterly about such oppression. However, their reluctant but unconditional subjugation to the tyrannical father constitutes only half of the Chinese story. The other half can only be unveiled by the onslaught of a deadly virus – the father is obliged to take good care of his offspring in times of crisis. In the Confucian hierarchy, the father, the elder son and the husband do not just take from those situated below them on the family ladder, China's cultural ideology dictates that the father/elder son/husband protect his children/younger sibling/wife unconditionally when dire circumstances arise. It is the coronavirus that provides us with a glimpse into the dual nature of the emperor–subject relationship in China – a give-and-take relationship. Scholars dwelling on Chinese paternalism tend to highlight only the negative attributes of the strict autocratic father while ignoring the equally potent resolve of the father to nurture his children in troubled times (Wang 2020). How many governments will spend billions to treat their people? Calling the Chinese government "authoritarian" is therefore shoving under the carpet the cultural equation of the Chinese paternalistic style of governance. In the end, it is not authoritarianism but paternalism and collectivism combined that can shed new light on our understanding of the relationship of Xi Jinping (and his predecessors) and his subjects. Seen in this light, the majority of Chinese people (activists included) do not entertain the idea of revolting against Beijing precisely because their relationship with the ruler is one fraught with complex emotions that are both positive and negative. The presumptive thinking that Chinese "children" should challenge and even kill the "father" can only originate in a culture where the Oedipus complex has a haunting presence and is normalized as an essential developmental phase every Western child is supposed to go through.

The Philanthropy Law and the Promise of "Social Governance"

Lest you think that the Chinese emperor–subject relationship is a permanent fixture that seems to have stifled the growth of the Chinese social, the CCP's recent policy endorsement of "social governance" underpinned the likelihood that the gray zones in President Xi Jinping's China may not have contracted as badly as his critics assumed. Truly, China watchers and NGO researchers in the West take it for granted that Chinese civil society suffered a severe blow after Xi ascended the throne. We tend to assume that Hu Jintao was softer and weaker than Xi in his approach to social control. We also assume that Xi cracked down really hard on the freedom of expression. However, if we study the Philanthropy Law published in 2016 under Xi Jinping's tutelage, we will discover a certain continuity of China's social policy-making between these two regimes. The continuity hinges on the concept and practice of "social governance" (*shehui zhili*). If China's reform is seen as the gradual unfolding of a trilogy, from open economy to open society and onto open politics, then the historical mission of Hu's era can be defined as "open society" with its dual emphasis on "social coordination" and "public participation" – key ingredients that fuel the engine of social governance.

What is an open society? It points to a mode of governance built on collaborative decision making among diverse stakeholders of a community. The shift from social control to social management and onto social governance is seen by policy analysts as a formal invitation of the party-state to NGOs and other grassroots actors to come to the negotiating table and partake in community decision-making processes so as to facilitate what the CCP called "the politics of accommodation" (Chinese People's Political Consultative Committee 2017: 4). Yes, surprisingly, the party itself is increasingly interested in taking a nonconfrontational approach to managing social conflicts.

The earliest occurrence of the slogan "social governance" can be traced back to a speech given by Hu Jintao in 2012 shortly before the country changed stewardship. President Hu might have unveiled the new concept but the experiment with "social governance" continued under Xi's regime. All this indicates a subtle shift of social control in China. Although the Chinese government has never made explicit reference to the term "civil society" in official documents, authorities have now recognized its importance to the making of its social reform agenda. Both Xi and Hu's social policies reflect that recognition.

The Philanthropy Law itself provides a convincing footnote on the state's intended shift from confrontational to nonconfrontational style of governance. The law streamlines the procedures for nonprofit groups to legally register and raise funds in public. The new law also makes it legitimate for groups to exist even without registering, thus theoretically uncorks the expansion of civil society. Other provisions in the law include tax incentives for qualifying organizations, rules for making online donations and establishing a charitable trust, and other measures aimed at professionalizing NGOs, effectively leaving behind the quasi-legal environment where enforcement had been uneven and unpredictable for NGOs and other civic organizations (Kaja and Stratford 2016). Particularly worth noting was the month-long vetting process, an exercise of social governance, through which the government and the unofficial representatives from the nonprofit sector got together, sought and built a consensus on how to revise the draft of the Law (Cishanfa Caoan 2015; An 2016). I myself recall receiving invitations from other NGOs to submit feedback on the first draft. All over China, numerous workshops were held where social stakeholders mulled over details of the new law.

The Philanthropy Law established a new milestone for Chinese civil society in two regards. First, the law made it clear that it will return philanthropy from the government to the people and grassroots organizations (Zhu 2016). In a nutshell, the law aims at gradually transforming "planned charity" in which the government served as the primary player to mobilize citizens to do public good to a new philanthropy in which civic groups will take the lead in shaping philanthropy. This paradigm shift can be characterized as the devolution of power from the official to the social, with the ramification that the government will also transform itself from a top-down controller to the role of facilitator. From then on, professionalized civic groups and organizations will take on the responsibility of driving the development of Chinese philanthropy. A new blueprint for China's nonprofit sector has emerged, with government driven philanthropy, market philanthropy and social philanthropy (which the Philanthropy Law endorsed) forming three parallel ecosystems with the latter two evolving into mainstream practices.

The revamping of the social sector achieved through the phased implementation of the Philanthropy Law can go a long way. If the opening up of planned economy in the past 30 years serves as any indication, the unfolding of China's social reform will follow a similar path characterized by an *incremental* and *voluntary* devolution of state power to social agents. Indeed, the trending slogan for China's social reform is "the separation of government and society," which sounds familiar if we recall the earlier catch phrase that kicked off the economic reform, "the separation of government and enterprise."

Finally, Table 10.1 validates the steady increase of NGOs – an annual incremental growth of approximately 40,000 new registrants each year after 2016. The expansion of China's civil society has been consistent since 2013. This promising scenario further substantiates my observation that while Western civil society was born as the result of the agitating growth of the social, the Chinese civil society can only flourish as a result of the voluntary retreat of the state from society.

TABLE 10.1 Number of NGOs registered between 2013 and 2019 (National Bureau of Statistics 2020)

Year	2019	2018	2017	2016 (Philanthropy Law)	2015	2014	2013 (The start of Xi's regime)
Number of NGOs	487112	444092	400438	360914	329141	292195	254670

The Philanthropy Law, I should note, is by no means perfect. For example, the new law relaxed the dual-management hurdle that prevented many NGOs from getting registered, but the three existing decrees published under the aegis of the State Council still follow the old regulation rule. For the Philanthropy Law to accomplish its goals, those three legislative decrees need to be revised simultaneously. In recent years, difficulties in implementing the new law have been brought to the attention of lawmakers who are now mulling over how to make all NGO-related regulations compatible with each other (Ma 2019).

Civic Hackathons and the "Future Village" Experiment

We now return to NGO2.0 and our ICT practices. Apart from providing social media literacy training, we have also been exploring ways of motivating NGOs to create customized technological solutions to the problems they encountered. Since most NGOs are incapable of conceptualizing such solutions or making tools for themselves, they need to turn to programmers and interaction designers for collaboration.

Right after NGO2.0 was established, we concocted a vision of building local technology expertise to help local NGOs, a vision that had to wait until 2014 to materialize. By then, two missing pieces had fallen in place – a technology-ready nonprofit sector and an emerging critical mass of socially concerned techies working in IT companies in first-tier cities. Transnational IT corporations and design companies in China such as Google, Intel, Frog, Thoughtworks and Microsoft have incentivized employees to leverage their skills to create tech4good projects. Domestic Chinese IT companies like Baidu, Alibaba, Tencent, Kuai and ByteDance followed suit. The civic hackathon program NGO2.0 established has rolled out various activities that appeal directly to the techie volunteers' faith in the transformative potential of technology to build a more just and more equal society. Since 2014, NGO2.0 has kicked off a series of civic hackathons where techies and NGOs come together to design nonprofit technology within 48 hours. Hackathons, in short, are intensive tech marathons, a legacy that originated in Silicon Valley.

What does a typical civic hackathon look like? In each chosen city, we create a local cluster made up of three groups of participants – local NGOs, local techies' communities, and students and professors from the departments of software and interaction design at local universities. We bring together these three groups for a two-day hackathon. The overall goal is to promote the concept and practice of collaborative design that integrates the triple expertise of programmers, NGOs, interaction designers and product managers. The hacker ideals of open source, transparency and preference for horizontal decision-making structures serve as guiding principles through which NGO2.0 implements our tech4good vision.

"Future Village" is a new program built on the civic hackathon model. We identify villages in poverty-stricken areas and mobilize villagers, local NGOs and village leadership to collaborate with our team to improve the lives and live-lihood of villagers. Our manifesto for Future Village is as follows:

> Armed with humanistic spirit, we help poor villages develop into liv-able, ecologically sustainable and scientifically viable villages. We bring together villagers, researchers and practitioners specializing in hardware technology, energy engineering, material science, architecture, bioecol-ogy, design and public art to participate in this undertaking and jointly design a vision for the village.

The vision making of Future Village was inspired by the MIT Fabrication Lab (henceforth Fab Lab) model. In the traditional framework of technologi-cal innovation, scientists call the shots, the physical lab serves as the primary venue for experiment and the end goal is technological development. The Fab Lab paradigm, in contrast, shifts the emphasis from the scientist to the clientele (in our case, villagers) with the implication that the entire village is an organic lab in itself where social innovation takes place. The ultimate goal is thus social development rather than technological advancement. This is not the place for a lengthy discussion of the Fab Lab and the maker move-ment (for details, see Wang 2019: Chapter 5). Suffice it to say that the model explores how an under-served community can be powered by technology and other creative means at the grassroots level. Underlying the Fab Lab model is the vision for one-off, bottom-up innovation and an emphasis on the DIY ethos, open source hardware and maker culture.

NGO2.0 has been implementing this program in several villages. This chapter will highlight one village project – *Shuangtang hezi* (the Shuangtang Box) which used to be performed in the Xiong'an District of Hebei Province. The performing art revolving around the Box can be traced back to the Ming dynasty: Every year during the lantern festival, villagers around Xiong'an gathered at Shuangtang to watch the spectacular show of *Shuangtang hezi*. The Box is a sophisticated amalgam of art and science. A single box can be extended to multiple layers of visual representation that unfold scenes from folk legends. In the old days, fireworks were used to unlock the mecha-nism that triggered each new layer to pop up from the Box. However, since 2009 after fireworks were banned, the performance of *Shuangtang hezi* has been extinct.

We held a civic hackathon to seek solutions to revive the lost cultural heritage. One of the best proposals was an interactive media rendition of the Box. With the goal of preserving the traditional features of the Box while improving its reusability and aesthetics, our team, which was comprised of interactive media artists and electronic engineers, proposed the design of "Shuangtang Impression." The installation is made up of four physical lay-ers, with each layer corresponding to a folktale which the ignited Box would unveil.

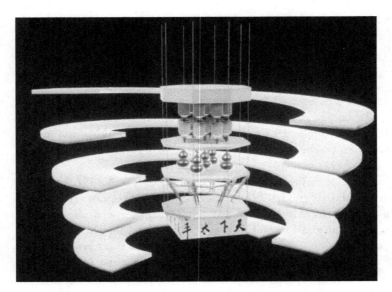

FIGURE 10.1 The Shuangtang Box, created by the author Jing Wang in her NGO2.0.

Layer 1: 3D Hologram display. We replace fireworks with a 3D hologram. The digital content will be collectively designed with the local craftsmen of Shuangtang Box.

Layer 2: Fog Screen/Membrane Screen + 3D Projection Mapping. This layer consists of storytelling scenes featuring folk stories ranging from "Monkey King Romps around the Celestial Palace" to "Eight Immortals Cross the Sea." Our design enables the 3D animation of the content.

Layer 3: LED Rain with Golden Babies. This layer redesigns the "Golden Babies with Golden Pee," a folk tradition that embodies the villagers' wish that every household be blessed with a multitude of descendants. Our design replaces the fireworks with safe LED strings, which create the visual effect of babies taking a leak.

Layer 4: Lotus lantern. Shuangtang Box was traditionally presented during the lantern festival. The fourth layer – the top layer – is a lotus lantern originated in the well-known legend of Chen Xiang, a boy looking for his deceased mother who was punished by gods for marrying a village mortal. The lotus lantern delivers a special meaning because the lighting of the lantern marks the reunion of Chen Xiang and his mother who was freed from Hell thanks to her son's unrelenting fight against divine injustice.

It should now be clear that the Fab Lab model is good at engendering one-off products as the needs articulated by villagers vary from place to place, which fully illustrates the Chinese spatial logic "each according to its geoculture" (Wang 2005: 10–11). There is no single formula for all as each village is unique in its own way. This approach of making customized solutions is in wide demand, especially in recent years, because the state-sanctioned "Village Revitalization Movement" may have lifted many villages out of poverty but it also engenders a dilemma of "a thousand villages looking exactly the same" (*qiancun yimian*) (Wan 2016), a problem reflecting the mainstream, top-down design thinking that emphasizes homogeneous solutions.

NGO2.0 is cautious about falling into the trap of formulaic thinking. We incorporate into Future Village extensive and in-depth fieldwork conducted by teams of students, teachers and other experts who enter the village at regular intervals to explore the needs of individual villagers. One could say that while hackathons respond to the collective needs of the village, the longer-term field-work identifies the varied needs of individuals.

Is this program sustainable? My MIT credentials made it effortless for me to recruit techies in IT companies and university participants. Education goes both ways: We teach techies to recognize that "cool technology" may not be useful technology, and we simultaneously alleviate the villagers' anxiety about techno-logical thinking. The goal is to motivate each group to learn from the other and to design collaboratively.

The practice of NGO2.0 in the past decade yielded both intangible and quantifiable benefits for the grassroots NGOs in our network. The NGOs we train learn how to navigate the social web with a focused purpose, take their place in cyberspace as media creators, understand the importance of self-positioning and self-representation, build online communities to enable scalable collaboration, and in the process, they gradually overcome their fear about new media and technology and become a member of the digital com-mons we set up on Weibo and WeChat. Above all, civic hackathons and a project like Future Village are a fun and effective way for NGO2.0 to build a multi-sectoral platform that mobilizes changemakers from diverse sectors – universities, IT corporations, software developers and maker communities – to come together and make social change incrementally, collaboratively and noncontentiously.

References

An, Z. (2016) "Regarding the Feedback on the Second-round Revision of the Draft of the PRC Philanthropy Law" [in Chinese], *anthonyjspires.weebly.com*, 29 February.

Chinese People's Political Consultative Committee (2017) *The Essentials of the Theory of Consorciagional Democracy* [in Chinese], Beijing: Zhongguo Fazhan Chubanshe.

Cishanfa Caoan (2015) "Public Consultation on the Draft of Philanthropy Law Ends" [in Chinese], *China Youth Daily*, 9 December.

Edelman (2020) *Edelman Trust Report 2020*, New York: Edelman. 19 January.

Howell, J. (1994) "Striking a New Balance," *Capital and Class*, 54: 89–111.

Kaja, A. and Stratford, T. (2016) "China Implements New Charity Law," *Global Policy Watch*, 1 November.

Lu, Y. (2009) *Non-governmental Organizations in China*, London: Routledge.

Ma, J. (2019) "On the Dilemma of Implementing the Philanthropy Law from the Vantage Point of Our Legal Explanatory Framework" [in Chinese], *China Development Brief*, 20 December.

National Bureau of Statistics (2020) https://data.stats.gov.cn/easyquery.htm?cn=C01. Beijing: National Bureau of Statistics of China.

O'Brien, J. and Li, L. (2006) *Rightful Resistance in Rural China*, Cambridge: Cambridge University Press.

Perry, E. (1994) "Trends in the Study of Chinese Politics," *China Quarterly*, 139: 704–13.

Saich, A. (2000) "Negotiating the State," *China Quarterly*, 161: 124–41.

Scott, J.C. (1985) *Weapons of the Weak*, New Haven: Yale University Press.

Shell, H. (2012) *Hide and Seek*, Cambridge: MIT Press.

Shue, V. (1994) "State Power and Social Organization in China," in J. Migdal, A. Kohli and V. Shue (eds) *State Power and Social Forces*, Cambridge: Cambridge University Press.

Sina Science & Technology (2020) "How Much Did China Spend on Curing (Patients of) COVID-19?" [in Chinese], *tech.sina.cn*, 14 April.

Wan, S. (2016) "With a Thousand Villages Looking Exactly the Same, How Could We Save Our Nostalgia for Rural Bygones?" [in Chinese], *views.ce.cn*, 29 November.

Wang, J. (2005) "Introduction: The Politics and Production of Scales in China: How Does Geography Matter to Students of Local, Popular Culture?," in J. Wang (ed) *Locating China: Space, Place and Popular Culture*, London: Routledge.

Wang, J. (2019) *The Other Digital China: Nonconfrontational Activism on the Social Web*, Cambridge: Harvard University Press.

Wang, W. (2020) "Digital Media, State Legitimacy and Chinese Paternalism," *Rowman & Littlefield Blog*, 13 March.

Wang, X. (2013) *Micro Action and Social Good* [in Chinese], Beijing: Peking University Press.

Zhu, J. (2016) "A New Configuration and a Big Transformation: Chinese Philanthropy Entered the Rule-of-Law Era" [in Chinese], *Shanda Net*, 12 September.

11

FROM DIGITAL LITERACY TO DIGITAL CITIZENSHIP

Policies, Assessment Frameworks and Programs for Young People in the Asia Pacific

Audrey Yue

The Asia Pacific is a diverse region housing more than 60% of the world's population of young people aged 15–24 years (UN 2019). It is also home to countries that are at the top and lowest of digital economy developments. Advanced economies enjoy up to 90% of information and communication technology (ICT) uptake compared to 15% in the least developed economies in 2020 (ITU 2021). The Philippines, Thailand, Indonesia, Malaysia and Singapore in Southeast Asia, for example, are among the top 19 countries in the world whose daily Internet use is above the worldwide average of 6.43 hours, with the Philippines clocking the highest at 9.45 hours (We Are Social 2020). Young people are clearly spending much time online engaging in a myriad of activities.

A rising trend in Asia Pacific youth practices, identities and movements is the use of digital media for economic, political, cultural and social empowerment. Emergent transformations have recently surfaced to capture this trend. Young Muslim women (hijabers) in Indonesia have become visible in the male-dominated public culture through their active participation on social media, as religious influencers and via women-run Islamic fashion e-businesses which have allowed them to achieve financial independence and gain political influence (Beta 2019). Progressive young millennial political parties in Thailand have extensively used social media to promote democracy and equality, such as the Future Forward Party (now dissolved and replaced by the Move Forward Party) in the 2019 elections that had successfully changed the course of political campaigns and garnered one-third of the country's votes (Chattharakul 2019). About half of Gen Z in Vietnam regularly use social media instead of school to source career information (Sen 2019).

Digital media policies and programs have nurtured digital youth media production and consumption, and their expression as new agential subjects. These policies and programs cultivate not just digital literacy as "the ability to both

DOI: 10.4324/9781003130628-14

understand and use digitized information" (Gilster 1997: 2) but also digital citizenship as "a practice through which civic activities in the various dimensions of citizenship are conducted" (Yue et al. 2019: 104). With the recent rise in misinformation and digital addiction, governments, international organizations, as well as big techs, have also placed digital well-being high on its agenda. This is made more urgent with the COVID-19 pandemic that has accelerated the digitalization of all aspects of economy and society such that smart (and safe) digital media use is now essential to everyday life, study, work and play. Central to these policies and programs are assessment frameworks that develop common standards to measure and cultivate digital skill competencies.

This chapter critically examines these frameworks to evaluate the intersections between digital literacy and digital citizenship, and their program applications in the Asia Pacific. It demonstrates the changing definitions of digital literacy that have shifted from the instrumental focus on digital skills to a more holistic focus on the critical and creative use of technology (Buckingham 2010) that supports civic participation and empowerment. The first section evaluates the development of global assessment frameworks such as those proposed by the UNESCO (2018), UNICEF (2019), Council of Europe (2019), European Commission (Vuorikari et al. 2016) and the International Telecommunication Union (2020). This focus is significant to the Asia Pacific because these organizations have introduced and endorsed international standards and implemented them through region-specific initiatives. This section conceptually demonstrates how digital citizenship has arisen as a more cogent paradigm to capture the holistic range of competencies to support youth opportunities and future life chances.

The second section tests this paradigm of digital citizenship by critically surveying applications of assessment frameworks in the Asia Pacific through global, regional and local programs such as the UNESCO's (2019) *Digital Kids Asia Pacific* project, Amazon's *Asia Pacific Digital Skills Index* (AlphaBeta 2021) and Singapore's *Digital Readiness Blueprint* (MCI 2021). First, it draws on the baseline data captured in these programs to propose a few emergent key digital citizenship trends in the region – stark digital divide, urban centrism, high digital risk awareness and low digital creativity. Second, it closely examines one Singapore-based program (*Hawkers Go Digital*) to evaluate how digital citizenship is operationalized. Singapore is a unique case study because it has an advanced "smart nation" policy that underpins all aspects of government, business and citizenry, and thus an exemplary site to consider the widespread infusion of digital literacy and the meaningful adoption of technology for citizenry empowerment.

While assessment frameworks are not unproblematic, this chapter argues that they provide common benchmarks to identify digital exclusion and furnish the policy impetus for digital inclusion. Their conceptual shift from digital literacy to digital citizenship promotes an expanded set of indicators to represent the range of foundational, vocational and life skills needed for civic engagement. Through its analyses, this chapter shows how digital citizenship is evident in practices such as responsible digital consumerism, sustainable e-businesses, innovative tech disruption and bridging intergenerational digital divide that further fosters digital, social and economic inclusion.

Digital Literacy and Global Assessment Frameworks

Digital literacy emerged as a concept in education theory and schools and rose to prominence in recent decades with the fourth industrial revolution and its pervasive use of technology in all aspects of life. Over the past five years, in particular, international agencies such as the UN have led the development of common standards and assessment frameworks with the aim of ameliorating the digital divide by identifying digital exclusion and lifting digital access, in particular for young people. A survey of these frameworks reveals that the field is growing with the usage of different related terminologies and there is not a singular globally accepted definition (e.g. BCMOE 2013; ISTE 2020; OECD 2019; Park 2019). In this section, we review four seminal frameworks to identify and elaborate their conceptual shifts from the narrow techno-skills centrism of digital literacy, to the broader and more holistic participatory empowerment objectives of digital citizenship. This broader emphasis is significant because it eschews extant scholarship (Green 2020) which has criticized these frameworks as promoting a top-down policy agenda that solely focuses on online passivity, tech addiction and protection rather than participation. For the Asia Pacific region that does not have established baseline data, these frameworks are important in providing common standards to assess skills gaps in literacy and guide the development of local policies and programs that will lift the digital skills young people need for successful civic engagement including employment in an increasingly technologized world.

One of the most popular is the European Commission's *The European Digital Competence Framework for Citizens* (also known as *the DigCom Framework*), which has been implemented in more than 20 countries in the world (Vuorikari et al. 2016; Kluzer and Priego 2018). It uses the term "digital competence" and identifies 21 competencies under the five key areas of information and data literacy, communication and collaboration, digital content creation, safety and problem solving. These include technical, cognitive and non-cognitive skills, and fit the broader definition of digital skills as the "knowledge and skills required for an individual to be able to use ICTs to accomplish goals in his or her personal and professional life" (Commission on Science and Technology for Development 2018: 4). While this framework uses the term "competency" synonymously with "skill," literacy skills are attributed only to one area, under "data literacy," to refer to the ability to search, filter, evaluate and manage information. Literacy is narrowly defined through the mastery of a technical skill-set. Cognitive and soft skills such as digital citizenship practices are captured in the remaining four areas such as communication and collaboration (e.g. the competency on engaging in citizenship through digital technologies) and safety (e.g. the competency on protecting health and well-being). Despite separating literacy from citizenship, this framework's use of the term "competency" encompasses these foci. Promoted as a common reference tool that allows organizations and individuals to assess digital competencies by conducting online self-assessments, this framework is targeted at those who lack digital skills, including older citizens, low-income families, migrants and especially less-educated young people by enabling them to work with employment agencies to improve job-seeking and career guidance in non-ICT employment that requires digital skills. This framework has also encouraged teachers to develop courses and assess student progress and aid in their own professional development. Indeed, teachers have in turn modified this model for use in European primary and secondary schools (Guitert et al. 2021) and for unemployed people (Guitert et al. 2020).

Another influential framework is the Council of Europe's *Digital Citizenship Education Handbook* (COE 2019). As the title suggests, it uses the term "digital citizenship" for its assessment model to highlight three aspects of online life (being online, well-being online and rights online) that can promote the digital competence of democratic citizenship. These aspects are aimed to develop competent digital citizens who can respond readily to new and everyday challenges in the study, work, employment and leisure in such a way that is inclusive, participatory and respectful of human rights and intercultural differences. Underpinning these aspects are 20 competencies clustered under the indicator sets of value, attitudes, skills, and knowledge and critical understanding, and 10 digital citizenship domains – access and inclusion, learning and creativity, media and information literacy, ethics and empathy, health and well-being, e-presence and communication, active participation, rights and responsibilities, privacy and security and consumer awareness. This model frames digital literacy and digital well-being under the umbrella of digital citizenship and provides a pathway to engage a range of stakeholders from family, school, workplace, private and civil sector actors, regulatory boards and national and international authorities. Through this pathway structure, and by stressing "living digital citizenship," this model highlights digital citizenship as an embodied and continuous practice of responsible engagement in community life.

The International Telecommunication Union, a UN agency, released the *Digital Skills Assessment Guidebook* (ITU 2020) as a self-assessment guide to assist in national strategies, education planning and evaluation. This builds on their earlier *Digital Skills Toolkit* (ITU 2018) developed as a part of their commitment to tackle global youth unemployment. As its title suggests, it uses the term "digital skills" not just to refer to the use of ICTs for life goals but also as a "combination of behaviours, expertise, know-how, work habits, character traits, dispositions and critical understandings" (Broadband Commission for Sustainable Development 2017: 4). This guidebook identifies digital skills across proficiency levels, from basic, intermediate to advanced. Basic skills include technical access skills such as the ability to use a keyboard, download software and apps, and conduct basic online transactions; intermediate skills enable people to use digital technology in more meaningful ways such as the ability to use multimedia across various platforms and advanced skills are those needed in ICT professions. While the term "digital literacy" is not used in this classification, digital skills are considered from the narrowest to the broadest domain of digital literacy, from technical mastery to cognitive and soft skills needed for interpersonal communication and economic empowerment. Similarly, while the term "digital citizenship" is also not used in this classification, its wide skills set definition resonates with digital citizenship as the ability to participate online and as an extension of social and economic inclusion (Yue et al. 2019).

The UNESCO's (2018: 6) Global Literacy Framework defines digital literacy as

> the ability to access, manage, understand, integrate, communicate, evaluate and create information safely and appropriately through digital technologies for employment, decent jobs and entrepreneurship. It includes competencies that are variously referred to as computer literacy, ICT literacy, information literacy and media literacy.

Following this, UNICEF (2019) puts forth a global vision of digital literacy and proposes that "digital literacy" is the most suitable term for its organization as its aim is to "teach digital literacy to keep children informed, engaged and safe online" (UNICEF 2017: 11). UNICEF's framework identifies four sets of interconnected skills that underpin a comprehensive approach to learning and education – foundation skills, which include literacy and numeracy which are necessary for learning, productive employment and civic engagement; transferable skills, which include life and soft skills which are necessary for problem solving, negotiation, self-management, empathy and communication; job-specific skills, which include technical and vocational skills that are necessary for professional occupations; and digital skills, which include skills and knowledge to support the development of digital literacy (UNICEF 2019: 29). In these frameworks, digital literacy is explicitly broad and covers the critical literacy practices of communication, self-management and negotiation, as well as the participatory practices of civic engagement.

These four frameworks reveal how global assessment benchmarks have transformed in their understandings of digital literacy. A myriad of terms including digital skills, digital competence, digital literacy and digital citizenship are used interchangeably. This lack of widely accepted definition is also evident in the corporate tech sector which has also recently promoted these merits, such as the use of "digital literacy" in Microsoft's (2021) *Discover Digital Literacy* resources and the use of "digital citizenship" in Facebook's (2020) *We Think Digital* campaign. Significant to note is not the diversity of terminologies, but the conceptual shift from the narrow confines of technical skills to the broader parameters of civic participation and engagement.

This shift corresponds with the development in literacy studies. Digital literacy's early focus on the acquisition of technical skills mirrors the early autonomous model of literacy which defines literacy as a basic skill where the aim of teaching is about training the acquisition of skills (e.g. reading and writing) through cognitive psychology and logic. This model is rooted in a scientific rationality that uses assessments, standards and classifications to create distinctions between individuals and groups (Street 1984). Similar to Friere's (1971) banking model of education, it has been criticized as instrumentalized and de-contextualized. In the 1980s, the alternative model of new literacies studies emerged to challenge this model by emphasizing the social context of literacy (Street 2013). Influenced by the social semiotics of communication, new literacies studies depart from the narrow confines of acquisition to the broader contexts of how meaning is constructed through social and semiotic processes (Lankshear and Knobel 2008). Rather than thinking about the grammar of language, language becomes the resource for encoding and decoding interpretations of experiences and social interactions. This dialogic process of literacy has since become dominant with the "digital turn" in literacy studies (Mills 2010) that has created the need for multiple literacies, including multimedia, information and data literacies, such as the influential multiliteracies pedagogy (Cope and Kalantzis 2000) developed by the New London Group (1996). New literacies studies' focus on literacy as a social practice underpins the expansion of digital literacy from the ability to use technical skills to the broader contexts of digital citizenship with its Freirean emphasis on the democratic potentials of communication, creativity, participation, collaboration and empowerment. Indeed, this has recently been made more explicit by the rise of social media literacy that views social media not just as a tool, but a process as well as collaboration and participation (Manca et al. 2020). Equally explicit too is the rise of digital citizenship education during COVID-19's remote learning where online classroom experiences are viewed as a form of "crisis management" for students to learn how to be good responsible digital citizens by participating in lesson plans that ask them to examine pandemic-related maps, online articles, hashtags and posted comments to consider how to verify information, use tech for the public good and expose the crisis's unequal impacts across neighborhoods and socioeconomic divides (Buchholz et al. 2020: 12). Digital citizenship is not just a set of digital skills to master, but the goal of the total education experience where young people learn to be personally responsible digital citizens, participatory digital citizens and justice-oriented digital citizens (Westheimer and Kahne 2004; Mattson et al. 2017). These goals and literacies are evident in the impacts of digital citizenship assessment frameworks and programs in the Asia Pacific.

Digital Citizenship and Asia Pacific Programs

Digital citizenship assessment frameworks are emergent in the Asia Pacific. This section evaluates three of these frameworks and their program applications – UNESCO's (2019) *Digital Kids Asia Pacific* project, Amazon's *Asia Pacific Digital Skills Index* (AlphaBeta 2021) and Singapore's *Digital Readiness Blueprint* (MCI

2021). In reviewing these global, regional and local frameworks and programs, the first aim, from the approach of critical program review and synthesis, is to aggregate the data to identify key digital citizenship trends in the region. The second aim, from the approach of media production, is to evaluate how digital creativity is harnessed by young people to develop civic tech that assists marginal groups toward digital inclusion. Through these analyses, this section demonstrates how digital citizenship in Asia has emerged as a concept that brings together the spectrum of digital skills from the narrow to the broadest, and an embodied practice of participatory engagement that achieves social, economic and cultural empowerment.

UNESCO was one of the first international agencies to address the lack of research and data about digital skills standards in the region. In 2017, its Bangkok office initiated the *Digital Kids Asia Pacific* (DKAP) project (UNESCO 2019). The DKAP aims to develop a regional measurement framework for young people's use of technology, create a baseline understanding of their competency, foster youth digital citizenship and enhance national capacity. It uses the concept of digital citizenship for its assessment framework despite the fact that, as discussed earlier, the parent agencies UNESCO and UNICEF have not used this term in their frameworks. The DKAP framework identifies five domains of digital citizenship – digital literacy, digital creativity and innovation, digital safety and resilience, digital emotional intelligence, and digital participation and agency. While these domains are more targeted to digital transactions than the ten digital citizenship domains promoted by the aforementioned *Digital Citizenship Education Handbook* (COE 2019), they nonetheless highlight digital citizenship as a practice that includes not just technical competency but also the creative and critical ability to use and discern digital information for socio-cultural and economic empowerment.

To test this framework, four countries in Asia were surveyed in the pilot phase – Bangladesh, Fiji, South Korea and Vietnam. These countries cross all spectrums in the global ICT Development Index ranking (ITU 2017) which measures infrastructure, access, intensity, capability and outcomes. South Korea, as a developed country, has the second-highest world ranking (2/176), while Vietnam (108/176) and Fiji (107/176), which are in the higher developing countries (HDC) group, are just below the average world ranking, and Bangladesh, which is from the lower developing countries (LDC) group, is the lowest (147/176). The survey was co-supported by South Korea's Ministry of Education, Google and the Institute of School Violence Prevention at Ewha Woman's University, and consisted of 104 questions developed from the five domains. From May to October 2018, 5,219 responses were collected from 15-year-old students.

Survey results reported that all four countries ranked the highest in digital safety and resilience, and the lowest in digital creativity and innovation. They also revealed that young women performed better than men in all countries apart from Vietnam and Fiji. Additionally, young people in urban areas performed better than those in rural areas in all countries except Fiji. The length of time exposed to using digital devices mirrored the global digital divide where 81% in South Korea have more than five years' experience compared to 8% in Bangladesh. These results support the program's assertion that there is a lack of baseline data about young people's digital behavior and capability in Asia, and there is a dominant focus on the instrumentalism of risk and safety compared to other aspects such as creativity that can enhance participation and increase employment opportunities. Policy recommendations include expanding the scope of digital literacy (which focuses only on technical skills and safety) to a more holistic paradigm of digital citizenship to better prepare young people for empowered participation and upwardly mobile life chances. Similar to the COE's (2019) framework, it also advocates for better support systems across family, education and work.

Following the DKAP program, Amazon Web Services commissioned the development of the Asia Pacific (APAC) *Digital Skills Index* (AlphaBeta 2021), which was launched in 2021. Building on existing frameworks most suited for the region such as the UNESCO's (2018) *Global Literacy Framework* and the EU's *Digital Competence Framework* (Vuorikari et al. 2016) to consider emerging digital skills needed for the future of work, this worker-centric framework identified eight competence areas that are grouped into four verticals (devices and software operations, information and data literacy, digital content or product creation, cloud computing competencies) and four horizontals (digital communication and collaborations, digital problem solving, digital security and ethics, digital project management). Similar to the ITU's (2020) *Digital Skills Assessment Guidebook*, it ranked digital skills across a range of proficiency levels from the unskilled learner, the foundational and specialized user to the advanced integrator and innovator. With the aim of projecting the digital skill-sets needed by 2025 and addressing the current digital skills gap, this framework benchmarks the current utilization of digital skills in six countries – Australia, India, Indonesia, Japan, Singapore and South Korea.

Its findings, which mirror DKAP's results, reveal that device and software operations skills are most utilized while digital content or product creation skills are the least utilized across the region. For example, while Australia has the highest rate of digital skills application (64%), its advanced digital skills application is only 20% compared to Singapore which has the highest rate of advanced digital skills application (22%) followed by South Korea (21%). Similarly, while Japan has 54% of workers applying digital skills, half of these use only basic skills. Its findings also reveal that emerging economies such as Indonesia and India are becoming more digitally divisive, with Indonesia having 19% of workers applying digital skills but 58% of these using advanced digital skills, and India having 12% of workers applying digital skills but 70% of these using advanced digital skills (AlphaBeta 2021: 7).

As these two leading frameworks and program reports provide the most current and comprehensive research datasets about baseline competencies in the Asia Pacific, their results furnish a useful profile of current digital citizenship trends for the region, summarized thus: The region has a stark digital divide with the highest to the lowest ICT-ranked countries. Despite the divide, all countries share similar patterns of high digital risk literacy and low digital creative literacy. Young people in urban areas have higher digital literacy levels than those in rural areas. Young women generally have higher digital literacy skills than men. Proficiency levels affect young people's capability. In developed economies, it is not enough to have a high rate of digital skills application as advanced digital skills are increasingly needed for the future of jobs in emerging technologies such as cloud computing and AI automation; in developing countries where the digital divide is most acute, those with digital skills are further advanced than their peers without. These trends reveal country and sector gaps that can be further addressed with local policy recommendations. In Singapore, the *Digital Readiness Blueprint* (DRB) (MCI 2021) demonstrates how focusing on digital citizenship can address these gaps.

The DRB is the latest in Singapore's ICT development planning, which began in concert since the 1980s with its IT Masterplan that introduced computing and broadband (Kong and Woods 2018 and culminated in 2014 with the launch of the Smart Nation (2021) initiative which aimed to transform the country and its citizens through technology. Various digital literacy schemes have supported its ICT development, including Digital Media and Information Literacy Framework (Ministry of Communications and Information), the National Digital Literacy Programme (Ministry of Education), Go Safe Online (Cyber Security Agency) and the Better Internet Campaign (Media Literacy Council). Such developments in digital infrastructure and digital literacy have elevated Singapore as an advanced ICT-developed country, currently ranked 18/176 in the global ICT index (ITU 2017), with 98% of the population having Internet access (IMDA 2020a) and a mobile penetration rate of 150% (IMDA 2021). The DRB is aimed at ensuring all Singaporeans have access to the opportunities and benefits of a digital society. It defines "digital readiness" as having access to technology, having the literacy to use technology and being able to participate in and create with technology (MCI 2021: 10). These three features resonate with the concept of digital citizenship derived in the earlier section as a social and embodied practice of engagement and empowerment through technology. Among the DRB's various programs on digital literacy, technology and inclusion is the *Hawkers Go Digital* (HGD) program.

The HGD program was officially launched in June 2020 at the height of the COVID-19 pandemic to help hawkers adopt e-payment platforms (IMDA 2020b). There are over one hundred hawker centers, wet markets, neighborhood coffee shops and industrial canteens in Singapore that sell cooked food at economical prices. Eating out is a national pastime, hawker culture is distinct to everyday life and hawker centers are now recognized by UNESCO as cultural heritage, but many hawkers are older people with low e-adoption rates. This has been accentuated during the pandemic with social isolation, the ban on dining-in and the rise in the use of food delivery platforms. Stallholders who did not digitalize saw a sharp drop in their businesses. In concert with the COVID-19 economic emergency and recovery plans, Singapore's Smart Nation Digital Office deployed more than one thousand digital ambassadors to raise the digital skills of 18,000 hawkers. More than six months later, 10,000 stalls have adopted e-payments, with more than 1.2 million transactions worth S$14 million (Enterprise Singapore 2021). Some hawkers who have not adopted e-payments complained about the high commission costs (as much as 30%) charged by local popular food delivery platforms such as Grab, Deliveroo and Foodpanda. Others have taken to social media themselves to directly promote their food, often with the support of young tech creators. FoodLeh? is one example.

FoodLeh? is a free online platform designed to connect hawker stalls and restaurant owners to local residents without the need to pay for the "middleman" services of a commercial platform. Created by two university students (Lim Yi Fan and Ng Chee Peng), it is a crowd-sourced, community-based platform where listings can be created and edited by members of the public. Lim, a computing and business student, and Ng, a dentistry student, came together through their love for food and spent five days building the website. They wanted to assist the many food sellers and older hawkers who were struggling with high overheads and having difficulty using technology (Yong 2020). Lim is the main coder while Ng provided the user-experience interaction design skills. To assist with promotion and public relations, a third university student Joyce Sin, also a coder, joined the team. When it started in April 2020, it had 45 listings. Fifteen months later, the site has grown to 605 listings that include neighborhood hawker stalls, small restaurants and home-based food businesses. The platform is simple and easy to use for both sellers and customers. For sellers who are less tech savvy, an online form can be completed in less than five minutes, with the option of also uploading images. Customers, on the other hand, type their postal code to choose listings closest to them, opt for either delivery or takeout, complete the payment via direct e-payment to sellers and can also post a virtual clap to favorably rate the food seller.

This example demonstrates the key features of digital citizenship catalyzed by a smart nation and its digital readiness initiatives. For older hawkers who face technology barriers, their adoption of digital transactions has helped them stay resilient as essential business amid the safety management measures posed by the pandemic. For this marginalized group of seniors, digital skills have afforded digital access, ameliorated digital exclusion and provided sustained economic independence through the continuity of their business enterprise. They are active digital participants and in turn are empowered older working adults. For customers, digital inclusion has widened food consumption choices, allowed them to become digitally smart consumers supportive of the fledging local businesses that maintain the vitality of neighborhood and community, and enabled them to enact responsible citizenship through engaged participation. For tech creators, advanced digital skills have allowed them to become civic-minded digital innovators who use their platforms to bridge the intergenerational digital divide.

Their platform is an example of a civic tech that has the potential to lift the digital capability of seniors, democratize digital consumerism, and in doing so, help nurture existing and create new businesses for themselves and food creators. Across these three cohort groups, digital citizenship is evident in their digital readiness, from having the digital literacy to participate to embodying participation as an engaged practice for socioeconomic empowerment. Digital citizens emerge through responsible digital consumerism, sustainable e-businesses and innovative tech disruption. In a digitally ready society like Singapore, digital citizenship also bridges the intergenerational digital divide that further fosters digital inclusion.

Conclusion

The past five years have seen a marked rise in the development of global assessment frameworks that provide common standards for digital literacy. These have become urgent with the current COVID-19 public health crisis that has accelerated digitalization. From home-based learning to remote working, digital literacy is foundational to participation, connection, empowerment and well-being. With the crisis exposing the abject digital divide across the world and within neighborhoods, it is crucial now to renew calls to lift digital literacy.

This chapter contributes to this call by evaluating the range of assessment frameworks to conceptually map the shift from digital literacy to digital citizenship. It has revealed the departure from the former, which has its roots in the autonomous model of literacy (e.g. digital skill as a tool), to the latter, which is influenced by new literacies studies' focus on the social practice of literacy as embodied engagement in society. Digital citizenship encompasses a range of skills and dispositions that draw on the use of technology which successfully allows people to participate as responsible and empowered citizens.

Further examining the global, regional and local applications of these frameworks in the Asia Pacific, this chapter has revealed how these frameworks are operationalized and through their baseline data, mapped an emerging profile of current digital citizenship trends in the region. These trends are that (1) the region has a stark digital divide, (2) women have higher digital skills compared to men, (3) urban youths have higher digital literacy than rural youths, (4) there is a high awareness of digital risk and (5) a low uptake of digital creativity. Further examining the operationalization of digital citizenship in Singapore, this chapter has demonstrated how digital citizenship has enabled young digital creators to bridge the intergenerational digital divide and introduce responsible digital consumerism, sustainable e-businesses and innovative tech disruption. When assessment frameworks on digital citizenship are accompanied by a comprehensive set of policies and programs, such as that of Singapore's, high digital proficiencies propel a nation toward a more equitable and inclusive society.

References

AlphaBeta (2021) "Unlocking APAC's Digital Potential: Changing Digital Skill Needs and Policy Approaches," 25 February.

Beta, A. (2019) "Commerce, Piety and Politics: Indonesian Young Muslim Women's Groups as Religious Influencers," *New Media & Society*, 21(10): 2140–59.

British Columbia Ministry of Education (BCMOE) (2013) *BC's Digital Literacy Framework*, Victoria: BCMOE.

Broadband Commission for Sustainable Development (2017) *Working Group on Education: Digital Skills for Life and Work*, Paris: UNESCO.

Buchholz, B., DeHart, J. and Moorman, G. (2020) "Digital Citizenship during a Global Pandemic: Moving beyond Digital Literacy," *Journal of Adolescent & Adult Literacy*, 64(11): 11–17.

Buckingham, D. (2010) "Defining Digital Literacy," in B. Bachmair (ed) *Medienbildung in Neuen Kulturräumen*, Wiesbaden: VS Verlag für Sozialwissenschaften.

Chattharakul, A. (2019) "Social Media: Hashtag #Futurista," *Contemporary Southeast Asia: A Journal of International and Strategic Affairs*, 41(2): 170–75.

Commission on Science and Technology for Development (2018) *Building Digital Competencies to Benefit from Existing and Emerging Technologies, with a Special Focus on Gender and Youth Dimensions*, New York: United Nations Economic and Social Council.

Cope, B. and Kalantzis, M. (2000) *Multiliteracies: Literacy Learning and the Design of Social Futures*, London: Routledge.

Council of Europe (COE) (2019) *Digital Citizenship Education Handbook*, Strasbourg: COE.

Enterprise Singapore (2021) "Half of Singapore's Hawkers Now Offering E-payments," 19 February.

Facebook (2020) *We Think Digital*.

Friere, P. (1971) *Pedagogy of the Oppressed*, New York: Herder and Herder.

Gilster, P. (1997) *Digital Literacy*, New York: Wiley.

Green, L. (2020) "Confident, Capable and World Changing: Teenagers and Digital Citizenship," *Communication Research and Practice*, 6(1): 6–19.

Guitert, M., Romeu, T. and Baztan, P. (2021) "The Digital Competence Framework for Primary and Secondary Schools in Europe," *European Journal of Education*, 56: 133–49.

Guitert, M., Romeu, T. and Colas, J. (2020) "Basic Digital Competences for Unemployed Citizens," *Cogent Education*, 7: 1–20.

Infocomm Media Development Authority of Singapore (IMDA) (2020a) *Infocomm Usage – Households and Individuals*, Singapore: IMDA.

Infocomm Media Development Authority of Singapore (IMDA) (2020b) *Hawkers Go Digital*, Singapore: IMDA.

Infocomm Media Development Authority of Singapore (IMDA) (2021) *Statistic on Telecom Service for 2020 Jul–Dec*, Singapore: IMDA.

International Society for Technology in Education (ISTE) (2020) "The 5 Competencies of Digital Citizenship," *ISTE*, 6 October.

International Telecommunication Union (ITU) (2017) *Measuring Information Society*, Geneva: ITU.

International Telecommunication Union (ITU) (2018) *Digital Skills Toolkit*, Geneva: ITU.

International Telecommunication Union (ITU) (2020) *Digital Skills Assessment Guidebook*, Geneva: ITU.

International Telecommunication Union (ITU) (2021) *Digital Trends in Asia and the Pacific 2021: Information and Communication Technology Trends and Developments in the Asia-Pacific Region, 2017–2020*, Geneva: ITU.

Kluzer, S. and Priego, L. (2018) *DigComp into Action – Get Inspired, Make It Happen: A User Guide to the European Digital Competence Framework*, Luxembourg: Publications Office of the European Union.

Kong, L. and Woods, O. (2018) "The Ideological Alignment of Smart Urbanism in Singapore," *Urban Studies*, 55(4): 679–701.

Lankshear, C. and Knobel, M. (2008) *New Literacies*, Maidenhead: Open University Press.

Manca, S., Bocconi, S. and Gleason, B. (2020) "Think Globally, Act Locally: A Glocal Approach to the Development of Social Media Literacy," *Computers & Education*, 160: 104025.

Mattson, K. and Curran, M. (2017) "Digital Citizenship Education," in B. de Abreu, P. Mihailidis, A. Lee, J. Melki and J. McDougall (eds) *International Handbook of Media Literacy Education*, London: Routledge.

Microsoft (2021) *Discover Digital Literacy*.

Mills, K. (2010) "A Review of the 'Digital Turn' in the New Literacy Studies," *Review of Educational Research*, 80(2): 246–71.

Ministry of Communications and Information (MCI) (2021) *Digital Readiness Blueprint*, Singapore: MCI.

New London Group (1996) "A Pedagogy of Multiliteracies," *Harvard Educational Review*, 66(1): 60–92.

Organisation for Economic Co-Operation and Development (OECD) (2019) *How's Life in the Digital Age?: Opportunities and Risks of the Digital Transformation for People's Well-Being*, Paris: OECD.

Park, Y. (2019) "DQ Global Standards Report 2019: Common Framework for Digital Literacy, Skills and Readiness," DQ Institute, March.

Sen (2019) "Young Vietnam Pros Use Social Media to Advance Careers," *VN Express*, 29 June.

Smart Nation (2021) *What is Smart Nation: Initiatives*, Singapore: Smart Nation and Digital Government Office.

Street, B. (1984) *Literacy in Theory and Practice*, Cambridge: Cambridge University Press.

Street, B. (2013) "Literacy in Theory and Practice: Challenges and Debates Over 50 Years," *Theory Into Practice*, 52: 52–62.

United Nations (UN) (2019) *Youth in Asia and the Pacific*, New York: UN.

UNESCO (2018) *A Global Framework of Reference on Digital Literacy Skills for Indicator 4.4.2*, Paris: UNESCO.

UNESCO (2019) *UNESCO Digital Kids Asia-Pacific Report Launch*, Paris: UNESCO.

UNICEF (2017) *UNICEF State of the World's Children: Children in a Digital World*, New York: UNICEF.

UNICEF (2019) *Digital Literacy for Children: Exploring Definitions and Frameworks*, New York: UNICEF.

Vuorikari, R., Punie, Y., Gomez, S. and Brande, G. (2016) *DigComp 2.0: The Digital Competence Framework for Citizens. Update Phase 1: The Conceptual Reference Model*. EUR 27948 EN, Luxembourg: Publications Office of the European Union.

We Are Social (2020) *Digital in 2020*.

Westheimer, J. and Kahne, J. (2004) "What Kind of Citizen? The Politics of Educating for Democracy," *American Educational Research Journal*, 41(2): 237–69.

Yong, C. (2020) "University Students Launch Website to Help Users Order Directly from Hawkers During COVID-19 Circuit Breaker," *Straits Times*, 28 April.

Yue, A., Nekmat, E. and Beta, A. (2019) "Digital Literacy through Digital Citizenship: Online Civic Participation and Public Opinion Evaluation of Youth Minorities in Southeast Asia," *Media and Communication*, 7(2): 100–114.

12

FOOD AND DIGITAL LIFESTYLES IN ASIA

From MasterChef to *Mukbang*

Tania Lewis and Haiqing Yu

This chapter offers an introduction to and overview of some recent transformations in food practices in a digital context in Asia. It uses the complex sociocultural, political, environmental and economic spaces of food to shine a light on broader shifts within digital Asia, including foregrounding the ways in which digital food practices and politics in Asia are embedded in distinctive commercial, social, cultural and governmental contexts. Given the breadth of food domains impacted by the digital turn, from food production, provisioning, politics and consumption to food influencers and food media, it would be impossible to do justice to the complexity and diversity of shifting and emergent digital food practices across the entire Asian region within this space. Instead, this chapter specifically presents an in-depth examination of the phenomenon of *mukbang* (the online livestreaming of eating) as a productive example of the way in which food and digital lifestyles – particularly public performances and practices of eating – have become coarticulated in Asia. The rich practices around and responses to mukbang in the region foreground the complex links between popular and commercialized everyday mediatized practices and governmental concerns around regulating and promoting certain modes of ethical consumption. If just 10 years ago the world of food and media was dominated by reality-style cooking shows like the popular *MasterChef* franchise, today increasingly viewer-consumers are themselves becoming food video producers, sharing food hacks on TikTok or broadcasting cookery tips from their kitchens. Furthermore, consumers more broadly now interact within a culinary landscape where they can review restaurants and share food pictures via apps and order and enjoy their favorite high-end cuisine online, all from the comfort of their homes. This chapter aims to offer some useful insights into the rapidly transforming space of digital food lifestyles and to suggest future research directions.

DOI: 10.4324/9781003130628-15

The topic of food in Asia is in itself a hugely rich one, linked to questions of national and cultural identity, familial ties and social relations and religion, and articulated to a range of other cultural and social practices and rituals. From the role of food in Buddhism and Hinduism to the status and place of the wedding banquet to the centrality of street food in urban life in many Asian countries, food is imbricated into every aspect of social and everyday life. In recent years, the rise of digital technology and mobile media across Asia has gone hand in hand with a complex, multifaceted transformation of food cultures and food practices. The much-discussed growth of the middle classes across the region and the associated rise of consumption alongside the emergence of the Internet and the proliferation of mobile digital devices have seen an intensification and increased mediatization of food practices. Similarly, the explosion of social media use across the region, including global commercial platforms like YouTube and Instagram and "local" ones like AfreecaTV and Douyin (TikTok), has been associated with the proliferation of new digital food practices from online food delivery and the emergence of amateur foodies as online influencers to digital sharing of food photographs and online streaming of live eating. Around the world, these new digital food practices have also been accompanied by the rise of food politics online, with the alternative food movement increasingly powered by online networks and social media and the growth of apps and platforms targeting political and ethical consumers (Lewis 2020). In Asia, the digital mediation of political questions and concerns around food practices both dovetails with these global trends and is also marked by variously distinctive developments across the region.

This chapter uses a particularly rich example of an original South Korean digital food practice – mukbang or the livestreaming of (often) binge eating – as a way of illustrating some of the broader sociocultural, political, technological and governmental forces that are shaping digital culinary culture in East Asia. What is particularly generative about the specific example of young Asian men and women sharing videos of themselves eating live from their homes, often at mealtimes, with a remote audience of other young people is that it foregrounds a range of larger issues in Asian digital media culture. This practice, on the one hand, is tied to and emerges out of Asian social traditions of sharing food in urban contexts where young people are often living alone and away from family. The rise of mukbang also points to the increasingly active role of ordinary people around the world as producers of content and trend influencers in an online environment. Operating in commercial environments in which their relationship to their audience is, for better or for worse, increasingly monetized, mukbangers speak to the broader role of the gig economy in shoring up social media content. In Asia, the digital media landscape is also shaped by nationalist, moral and governmental concerns. As we discuss below, the moral controversy surrounding live eating practices in parts of Asia and, in the case of China, the active government regulation of mukbang illustrates the distinctive role of government in the region in regulating online content and practices. In this chapter, we link the specific ways in which online food practices and food politics are emerging in

Asia to distinctive forms of Asian quasi-capitalist governmentalities and models of citizenship and civility across the region; certain kinds of identity politics, particularly around gender; and the specific social and economic role and status of consumption in Asian countries.

The chapter is structured accordingly. In the first section, we offer a brief overview of the dominant trends around food and digital lifestyles in East Asia. We then turn to discuss the rise of the online phenomenon of mukbang. We outline the ways in which Asian young men and women have developed careers as performative social eaters and discuss their relationship with commercial social media platforms and algorithms, as well as with fans in cross-cultural communication settings, shaped by a range of different food beliefs and values as well as forms of "food nationalism" (King 2019). In turn, as we argue, political and governmental concerns have also come into play. While on the one hand the originally South Korean food phenomenon has become hugely popular not just in the region but globally, it has also provoked a significant backlash and many people are highly critical of the perceived wasteful overconsumption promoted by mukbangers. We end this section with a discussion of China's Operation Empty Plate as an example of a government intervention into mukbang practices.

Digital Food in Asia

In recent years, the rise of digital technology has seen a range of major transformations in Asian culinary culture, from shopping, home cookery and restaurant going to the sphere of food politics, ethical consumption, trust and food safety. Digital automation of everyday practices such as ordering at food outlets and shopping at grocery stores is changing consumer engagement with once traditional forms of retail services (Figure 12.1).

Meanwhile, the online food delivery industry, already a leading market in Asia, is predicted to grow from US$2 billion in 2018 to US$8 billion in 2025 in the region of Southeast Asia such as Malaysia, Singapore and Indonesia (*ASEAN Post* 2020). While pre-pandemic online platforms for meal delivery services were growing across Asia, with people having to self-isolate and stay at home during the COVID-19 outbreak, not surprisingly there was a big surge in the use of online meal apps such as FoodPanda, which started in Singapore in 2012, with claims that the food delivery market has leapt forward as much as 10 years in Asia due to the pandemic (Global Business 2020). Households are now increasingly accessing restaurant quality food in their homes via meal sharing apps (e.g., Ele.me) in Shanghai, supported by an army of largely underpaid, precarious, food delivery workers. China's online food ordering and delivery market reached $65.8 billion in 2018 (Hui 2019) and is growing rapidly, with Shanghai being a significant hub for online meal services. The huge popularity of online food ordering has seen an industry once based on delivering restaurant food increasingly also embracing own delivery-only kitchens, otherwise known as "dark" or "cloud" kitchens. Dahmakan which was founded in Malaysia in 2015 works off

FIGURE 12.1 Customers use touchscreens to order meals at a Yum China Holdings Inc. KFC restaurant in pre-COVID-19 Shanghai, China on 19 March 2019 (Credit: Getty Images/Bloomberg).

this model, promoting itself as providing healthy meals direct to people's homes, with many other food platforms moving toward this model.

Alongside the rise of digitally enabled shifts in food provisioning, the focus and visual content of the digital media realm has become intensely food oriented, with social media apps like TikTok becoming "the food platform of the people" (Makalinta 2020). Indeed, it is hard to imagine social media platforms such as Instagram and Weibo without the highly stylized and curated images of home- and restaurant-cooked meals that circulate daily through people's feeds. Similarly, for many users, going out to eat now habitually involves assessing a café or restaurant's ratings and reviews on food recommendation apps like HaoYouMeiShi ("mei shi" means "good food" in Chinese), a Beijing-based start-up that uses data mining to analyze users' dining experiences and "sentiments" on Weibo to produce a list of recommendations (Wang 2012).

A number of different trends have contributed to this rich digital food culture including the rise of food photography. Sharing food photos was probably one of the earliest markers of the digital culinary turn in Asia. Often referred to as the "camera eats first" phenomenon, a study conducted in Beijing back in 2017 showed that over 85% of young Chinese urbanites had shared food photographs on social media (Peng 2017). In the same year, *Forbes India* observed that, while food photography has a long history, today "photographing food has assumed a proportion that has perhaps never been seen before, thanks to the ubiquitous camera phone" (Banerjee 2017).

In Asia and around the world, we can see this as emerging out of a decade or more of a lifestyle, media and consumer culture increasingly concerned with culinary culture. Here "foodies" on a range of social media platforms have become key influencers or tastemakers and shapers in culinary culture and food practices more broadly. Broadly the tendency here has been to promote cosmopolitan, middle-class forms of taste and consumption around food, with a focus on high-end aesthetics and "culinary capital," but also often on healthy eating (Naccarato and Lebesco 2012). For instance, writing for Kuala Lumpur's *Time Out* back in 2015, Joyce Koh documents the impact of the rise of Instagram's foodie culture on Malaysian food consumption habits (Koh 2015). While young KLers were once content with a low-cost coffee and roti from the local "mamak" stall, early in the 2010s the rise of Instagram along with the influence of international food scenes such as Australia's coffee culture saw a shift over the decade toward a sophisticated, cosmopolitan café scene as well as changes in eating patterns. While Malaysians traditionally used to eat five meals a day, shifting leisure, consumer and lifestyle trends along with the embrace of new eating-out practices like "brunch" marked broader shifts in food habits as well as aspirational tastes, at least for a particular generation with sufficient income. As Koh (2015) puts it:

> Call it keeping up with the Joneses, call it curiosity, but if someone has had a good latte and we see it on social media, we'd (consciously or subconsciously) want to try it too. If we ended up liking it, somewhere along the line paying RM15 for coffee or a slice of cake became acceptable – because we'd get a nice photo out of it, which could lead to validation on social media.

Asian online foodie culture has also more recently increasingly been shaped by the rise of amateur cookery videos, offering arguably a much more diverse and unruly array of content compared with the largely middle-class, digitally "gentrified" fodder on Instagram (Lewis 2020). YouTube, AfreecaTV and TikTok/Douyin would not be what they are today without the huge range of cooking and food channels, from creative food hacks and how-to cookery shows shot in people's homes around the world to the live, interactive broadcasts (or *mukbang*) popular in South Korea and beyond where the video's "host" noisily ingests large amounts of food for our viewing pleasure. The rise of food videos made by ordinary people and broadcast from their homes has contributed to a rich and diverse culinary community in Asia and globally. Chris Crowley, a writer for the high-end culinary website *Saveur*, argues that YouTube has become a huge repository of food knowledge via video "tutorials on everything from Southern fried turkey necks to homemade Korean condiments, with hosts from India, Ghana, Vietnam and other countries well outside the usual hubs of Western media attention" (Crowley 2018). This online video ecology includes a range of challenging, experimental food-related content that is a far cry from the conventional *MasterChef*-style world of cooking shows.

Mukbang: Broadcast Eating and Participatory Culture

This section explores a very specific though highly popular example of online food practice that has emerged in East Asia in recent years, the live streaming of "ordinary" people eating their meal usually in their own home. Originating in South Korea around 2010, the practice of *mukbang* (a portmanteau of the Korean words for "eating" and "broadcast") involves live broadcasts of people eating food, often in excess. In the case of autonomous sensory meridian response (ASMR)-oriented food videos, the key focus is on the sensory buzz that one can get from listening to and somatically experiencing the auditory and visual stimuli associated with mukbangers cooking, handling and slurping and crunching their way through certain kinds of sensual, noisy foods, from crispy deep-fried prawns to an abundance of thick sauce-laden noodles (Lewis 2020).

While at first glance this example might seem rather idiosyncratic, it offers a range of insights into shifts and tensions around digital media practices and politics in Asia, particularly in relation to what might be seen as the aberrant, excessive and/or irresponsible forms of consumption promoted by mukbang. Indeed, as we will see, while it emerged specifically from South Korea, the practice has become a source of much debate and controversy across the region, particularly in China where the government has even sought to regulate the viewing of mukbang. How might we understand the emergence of this phenomenon of eating (and often binge eating) for a paying live audience? How does it relate to broader shifts around digital media and consumption and in particular the regulation of consumer-citizens, the rise of ordinary people as influencers, and the tensions between commercial and governmental logics online?

Mukbang or online eating shows first emerged a decade ago in South Korea and were particularly associated with interactive peer-to-peer video streaming services like Twitch and AfreecaTV. Korean mukbang hosts, or "broadcast jockeys" as they are known, often time their online eating with conventional dinner time in South Korea, with the idea that they are sharing and reacting with and alongside a community of viewers and fellow eaters. Often involving eating (and sometimes, as in the Cookbang genre, including cooking and then eating) traditional Korean food for a live audience, Korean eating shows also often involve a challenging dimension such as eating a large amount of food and/or eating super spicy or fatty food, or even live animals. The "genre", if we can call it that, is a highly unique one that seems to be quite distinct from the rise of more conventional "how to" online cooking shows and food hacks, which now make up a substantial proportion of the amateur video content shared on platforms like YouTube.

Much of the critical scholarship on the topic suggests that mukbang watching is about social connection (Donnar 2017). Eating together with family is an important tradition in Asian societies that have been challenged as more and more young people leave their family home to pursue education and career in other cities or countries. In the context of growing numbers of young singles living alone, Hakimey and Yazdanifard (2015) argue that mukbang enables them to overcome loneliness, alleviate social isolation and forge an emotional connection and a sense of community with mukbangers and fellow viewers, while Spence et al. (2019) term this kind of collective (virtual) dining "digital commensality." Mukbang can be seen as a late modern version of shared, parasocial eating, acting as a kind of surrogate for family meals and everyday culinary intimacy.

Watching mukbang has also been read as a form of escapism from the everyday realities of eating and dieting (Hakimey and Yazdanifard 2015; Bruno and Chung 2017). There are clearly pleasures for certain female viewers in watching often slim, young mukbangers, many of them women, bingeing on excessive amounts of greasy, calorific food, potentially challenging normative conceptions of Asian feminine food propriety as well as norms around healthy eating. For viewers, especially those with eating disorders, watching mukbangers eating excessively on their behalf offers a vicarious form of pleasure (Choe 2019).

The mukbang form or genre, like other online cooking shows in Asia and around the world, can also be seen as emerging – originally at least – out of an online sharing environment or what Henry Jenkins (2006: 3) broadly termed "participatory culture," that is "a culture with low barriers to artistic expression and civic engagement, a strong support of sharing one's creations, in which members believe their contributions matter, and feel some social connection." Enabled by the affordances of Web 2.0 and by video conversion and sharing technology and platforms like Twitch and YouTube, the 2000s saw a transition around the world from the digital consumer as passive downloader to an upload and peer-to-peer culture of creativity and prosumerism. In the food space, this culture of active engagement, interactivity and connection with community has been evidenced by the sheer number of amateur cooks and foodies expending considerable time and energy producing and sharing pictures and videos of themselves eating and cooking often in their own homes. While much of this content is very much at the lo-fi amateur end of the video production spectrum, Asia's obsession with culinary culture has not surprisingly seen the growing monetization and professionalization of online food videos, as part of the broader emergence of what Cunningham and Craig (2019) term "social media entertainment" and the commercial platformization of the Internet more broadly (Gillespie 2010; Helmond 2015). As we discuss in the next section, this space has become increasingly monetized as YouTube and others have sought to profit from the sometimes huge, often cross platform, cross-cultural popularity of online cooking and eating shows, integrating financial logics and rewards into the online sharing and exchange system (Lobato 2016; Burgess and Green 2018; Cunningham and Craig 2019).

Mukbang and the Precarity of the Platform Economy

Mukbang is also a new genre in the online food influencer economy. The influencers here refer to live-streamers and vloggers who have numerous followers on social media platforms, interact with followers in a parasocial relationship and hence become an important digital marketing tool for new and/or small companies to reach large numbers of consumers quickly (Taneja and Toombs 2014; Gong and Li 2018; Parson and Lepkowska-White 2018). Mukbangers can be seen as micro celebrities (Khamis 2017), appealing to a particular niche though in some cases they may have very sizable audiences. Some recent examples of popular mukbangers provide a glimpse into the large viewer numbers and potential profits involved. For instance, Mizi Jun, a female Chinese mukbanger, has 2.7 million followers on the video-sharing site Bilibili, while a video of Japanese YouTuber Yuka Kinoshita eating noodles attracted nearly 5 million views. South Korean mukbangers are similarly highly successful not only locally but also on Chinese social media platforms and more globally. For instance, South Korean mukbang star Banzz, who has 2.3 million fans on YouTube, has recently made the move to Bilibili. However, in contrast to glossier Internet stars, these popular mukbangers present themselves as common consumers or friendly would-be neighbors who happen to like food and sharing their eating practices. As noted, their popularity is linked not only to performing and sharing meals, but also to bingeing and eating unusual or irritating foods, with some mukbangers using more and more extreme food practices to attract viewers.

Tied to the commercial logic of platform capitalism, popularity becomes a product of entrepreneurialism through self-branding (Marwick 2013; Srnicek 2016), potentially translating into fame and financial gains. Many young men and women take on mukbang as a career because of entrepreneurial opportunities and affordances that social media platforms like YouTube, AfreecaTV, Douyin or Bilibili provide through their algorithmic relations with digital content producers and users. Mukbang influencers are acutely aware of the algorithmic power of platforms, for instance, how their videos are ranked or recommended around relevancy and engagement. To remain popular (and hence economically viable), they actively participate in "algorithmic circulation" (Glotfelter 2019) or the "production of calculated publics" (Gilliespie 2019), a process by which algorithms mediate and distribute content to shape public engagement with the platform. Mukbangers as content creators also actively navigate, adapt and develop content strategies and engagement tactics (with their followers/fans and the platform) to stay on top of "the visibility game" (Cotter 2019).

Platform algorithms impact popularity (of both videos and video creators) and hence business deals through advertising and sponsorship. Viewer engagement – interaction with mukbangers through textual or verbal forms and monetary encouragement through gifting – is important to platform algorithms. This is where the challenge lies for many mukbang influencers. While Choe (2019: 204) proclaims that mukbang "re-imagines collaborative eating, challenges the traditional social stigma of eating alone and demonstrates how agency can be collaboratively achieved on the Internet," powerful but in many ways invisible actors such as platform algorithms complicate such celebratory claims. With the growing commercialization of "sharing" platforms, the agency of both muk-bangers and their audience is limited and contingent on a number of factors, including the mutually constitutive but unbalanced power between mukbang influencers and platform companies. Content analysis of mukbang videos by Kang et al. (2020) shows that mukbang videos featuring overeating or unhealthy eating habits, e.g., food consumption within a time limit and consumption of irritating food, have a higher number of views. The number of views and level of engagement between mukbangers and their viewers constitutes crucial data that is fed into platform algorithms, in turn determining how mukbang videos are ranked and recommended. Under the disciplinary apparatus of algorithms, many mukbangers turn to challenging eating practices to increase views and viewer engagement, and indirectly through algorithmic ranking. Choe (2019), who likens online eating to busking, discusses how mukbangers interact with viewers via audiovisual effects, spoken commentary, humor and physical actions, often responding to viewer requests to eat differently and receiving monetary rewards from viewers through gifting.

Having discussed the growing role of predictive analytics and other forms of data-driven popularity, it is important to note that the social and cultural norms and values in which technological objects and systems are embedded are also powerful players in social media economies. This is shown in the case of Hamzy, a South Korean female mukbang influencer who hosts mukbang channels on YouTube (with over 5 million followers), Bilibili (with over 3 million followers) and Weibo. Hamzy is known as an ASMR mukbanger who posts videos of her-self cooking and eating while making loud chewing and swallowing noises. She was one of many foreign (mostly South Korean and Japanese) mukbangers who became popular on Chinese social media platforms (Bilibili and Weibo), earning a large amount of money through mukbang videos and eating live on screen.

In January 2021, Hamzy found herself in the middle of a controversy between South Korean and Chinese nationalists over the national identity of kimchi (a fermented cabbage side dish). It started when Hamzy posted a video on YouTube of her eating a super spicy octopus bibimbap (featuring fried eggs, kimchi and lettuce), which she described as Korean food. This was picked up by one of her followers who commended her for saying that kimchi and ssam (leafy vegetable wrap) were Korean instead of Chinese food as claimed by some Chinese people. Her positive response to the post infuriated her Chinese fans on YouTube, who left harsh comments on her videos. This also resulted in a heavy backlash against her on Weibo and Bilibili, where Chinese fans started to unfollow her, and her Chinese agency terminated her contract on the grounds that she had disrespected China and offended the Chinese people (*Tech Times* 2021).

The case illustrates the precarity of the "fame" associated with the platform-based mukbang economy. While proactive online fans can make a mukbanger a star, their data activism can also lead to public opinion wars against idols or influencers for crossing political or cultural red lines as seemingly mundane and innocuous as branding kimchi "Korean" rather than "Chinese." Such online fan nationalism (Liu 2019) goes beyond food nationalism – food as an essential part of national identity and national branding – to reshape platform-based creative industries or forms of social media entertainment, of which mukbang is a popular genre. Cross-cultural mukbang influencers and their agencies/representatives must internalize the unofficial norms of different national markets, as well as the official rules of country – and linguistic-focused social media platforms, in order to stay on top of the game (Chen 2021): Chinese fans are regarded as the most nationalistic and their globalized fan nationalism is reshaping norms in the global cultural and creative industry.

Government Intervention: "Operation Empty Plate"

The huge popularity and prominence of mukbang have meant that its at times challenging content has also come to the attention of government and media regulators, pointing to the distinctive status of social media practices in more authoritarian Asian governmental contexts where commercial media spaces are highly monitored and regulated. For instance, in 2018, China used anti-porn regulations to implement a ban on ASMR, including ordering those sites such as Youku and Bilibili to remove ASMR videos, which the government argued might be potentially harmful to the young viewers who dominate its fan base (Abraham 2018).

More recently, mukbang in general has been targeted as part of a civic campaign around responsible consumption, frugality and waste minimization. On 11 August 2020, Chinese President Xi Jinping urged the country to curb food wastage and announced a set of rules and regulations for what he called "Operation Empty Plate." On the same day, China Central Television (CCTV) initiated a media campaign against binge-eating mukbangers known as big-stomach stars (*daweiwang*) while also attacking binge-eating mukbang streamers via its Weibo account. These prominent interventions saw social media platforms and local governments follow suit. The clean-up campaign involved 13,600 mukbang shows being shut down by social media and livestreaming platforms at the instruction of the Cyberspace Administration of China by the end of August 2020 for violating public order and corrupting morality (BBC 2020). Leading livestreaming platforms including Douyin, Douyu, Kuaishou, Weibo and Bilibili all made public announcements that they would be tightening rules on mukbangers and shutting down any accounts deemed to be operating illegally or violating regulations.

The mukbang community in turn responded in a range of creative ways to these incursions on their streaming freedoms including adopting four strategies: Firstly, streamers strategically changed account nicknames to avoid using terms like "big stomach," adopting names like "foodie pussycat" (instead of "big-stomach pussycat") or switching from "big-stomach Duoyi" to simply "Duoyi"; secondly, binge eaters transitioned to become more conventional culinary vloggers, introducing local gourmet and delicacies or livestreaming their regular daily meals; thirdly, some mukbangers took a "buyer beware" approach, including a "consume moderate amounts of food" message in their livestream and/or a "clean your plate" byline under their videos; and fourthly, and perhaps most creatively, some streamers performed a quite literally "virtual" culinary or "eating air" experience, pretending to be consuming a delicious meal.

The Chinese government was not in fact the first in the region to take action against food-related videos on social media platforms that it saw as potentially contributing to social problems like food waste and obesity. In 2018, the South Korean government considered a crackdown on mukbang as part of a broader government initiative to try and curb rising obesity rates in the country (Park 2018). At the time many mukbangers opposed the plan, calling it dictatorial, though some netizens including parents defended the plan, arguing that mukbang might have a negative impact on teenagers and their consumption habits.

While the South Korean government's planned intervention was a relatively mild one compared to China, looking to set media guidelines rather than directly banning mukbang, these developments point to the challenges faced by Asian Internet users and streamers in using social media spaces that are commercialized, scrutinized by the government and also framed as moral civic spaces. The "Operation Empty Plate" movement in China is often used to illustrate the Chinese government's intrusion into everyday life in the name of traditional values and morality discourses. It further illustrates how digital food practices like mukbang cannot be fully understood outside of their technological, socio-cultural and political contexts.

Conclusion

While a far cry from the world of conventional *MasterChef*-style cooking shows and glossy Instagram feeds, we have argued that the example of mukbang – a popular and yet highly contested online food-related practice – is a useful and productive one for thinking about the complexities of shifting and emergent digital lifestyles in Asia. The growth of the middle classes in Asia and the growing penetration of the Internet and particularly mobile access into Asian markets have seen some interesting challenges to traditional food practices and also the evolution of new and emergent practices. Households and individual consumers can now access a huge array of online food products that can be delivered to their door, thanks to a growing often precarious gig economy of drivers and cooks in dark kitchens. Foodies can engage with the latest dishes from their favorite street vendor via Instagram without even having to venture outdoors while mediated food content has wildly proliferated in a digital environment, largely due to the huge number of people now sharing their food experiences and cooking via social media and video platforms. What we are seeing in the burgeoning food video space are a range of new and experimental practices, some of which extend upon traditional cookery television while others such as live overeating videos watched (virtually) with a group of others challenge the ways in which we have conventionally understood the role and status of media and technologies in the home.

These transgressive, "carnal" videos (Kim 2021) also offer challenges to the broader public, media and governmental apparatuses. As we have seen, these shifting and evolving digital food practices are producing an array of often paradoxical responses – a kind of ripple effect – across digital publics and in political, economic and governance contexts that speak to some of the broader complexities of contemporary digital practices. The significant status and impact of "ordinary" mukbangers and others who livestream from their private homes have been brought home by direct governmental interventions such as China's clean-up campaign on mukbang, which while framed in terms of food waste and responsible consumption is surely also in part a reaction to the sheer viral popularity of these young performative influencers. While increasingly driven by commercial logics, new media platforms have opened up spaces of experimentation and social connection around food and consumption practices for a younger generation. The intense political and moral debates that have accompanied the rise and popularity of mukbang speak then to a shifting landscape of digital lifestyle practices, marked by increasingly complex relationships between civic players, commercial actors, technological innovation and forms of governance.

References

Abraham, A. (2018) "Why China Has Banned Videos of People Whispering," *The Guardian*, 22 June.

ASEAN Post (2020) "Food Delivery on the Rise in ASEAN," 4 May.

Banerjee, J. (2017) "Shoots, Eats and Leaves: The Changing Frames of Food Photography," *Forbes India*, 28 March.

BBC (2020) "China Shuts 13,600 Mukbang in Ongoing Internet Clean-up Campaign," 4 September.

Bruno, A. and Chung, S. (2017) "Mokpang: Pay Me and I'll Show You How Much I Can Eat for Your Pleasure," *Journal of Japanese and Korean Cinema*, 9: 155–71.

Burgess, J. and Green, J. (2019) *YouTube*, Cambridge: Polity.

Chen, S. (2021) "How Chinese Fans Enforce Chinese Nationalism on the World," *The Diplomat*, 8 May.

Choe, H. (2019) "Eating Together Multimodally: Collaborative Eating in Mukbang, a Korean Livestream of Eating," *Language in Society*, 48: 171–208.

Cotter, K. (2019) "Playing the Visibility Game: How Digital Influencers and Algorithms Negotiate Influence on Instagram," *New Media & Society*, 21(4), 895–913.

Crowley, C. (2018) "The World's Best Cookbook is Actually YouTube," *Saveur*, 10 January.

Cunningham, S. and Craig, D. (2019) "Creator Governance in Social Media Entertainment," *Social Media and Society*, 5(4): 1–11.

Donnar, G. (2017) "'Food Porn' or Intimate Sociality: Committed Celebrity and Cultural Performances of Overeating in Meokbang," *Celebrity Studies*, 8: 122–7.

Gillespie, T. (2010) "The Politics of Platforms," *New Media & Society*, 12(3): 347–64.

Global Business (2020) "Research Firm: Asian Food Delivery Industry Growth Ahead by 10 Years," *CGTN*, 22 July.

Glotfelter, A. (2019) "Algorithmic Circulation: How Content Creators Navigate the Effects of Algorithms on Their Work," *Computers and Composition*, 54(11): 102521.

Gong, W. and Li, X. (2018) "Microblogging Reactions to Celebrity Endorsement: Effects of Parasocial Relationship and Source Factors," *Chinese Journal of Communication*, 11(4): 185–203.

Hakimey, H. and Yazdanifard, R. (2015) "The Review of Mokbang (Broadcast Eating) Phenomena and Its Relations with South Korean Culture and Society," *International Journal of Management, Accounting and Economics*, 2: 443–55.

Helmond, A. (2015) "The Platformization of the Web: Making Web Data Platform Ready," *Social Media and Society*, 1(2): 1–11.

Hui, L. (2019) "China Online Food Delivery Market Volume Doubles in 2018: Report," *China Daily*, 10 April.

Kang, E., Lee, J., Kim, K. and Yun, Y. (2020) "The Popularity of Eating Broadcast: Content Analysis of 'Mukbang' YouTube Videos, Media Coverage, and the Health Impact of 'Mukbang' on Public," *Health Informatics Journal*, 26(3): 2237–48.

Khamis, S., Ang, L. and Welling, R. (2017) "Self-Branding, 'Micro-Celebrity' and the Rise of Social Media Influencers," *Celebrity Studies*, 8(2): 191–208.

Kim, Y. (2021) "Eating as a Transgression," *International Journal of Cultural Studies*, 24(1): 107–22.

King, M.T. (2019) *Culinary Nationalism in Asia*, London: Bloomsbury.

Koh, J. (2015) "Camera Eats First: Is Instagram Changing the Way We Eat?," *Time Out*, 22 December.

Lewis, T. (2020) *Digital Food: From Paddock to Platform*, London: Bloomsbury.

Liu, H. (2019) *From Cyber-Nationalism to Fandom Nationalism: The Case of Diba Expedition in China*, London: Routledge.

Lobato, R. (2016) "Creator Governance in Social Media Entertainment," *Convergence: The International Journal of Research into New Media Technologies*, 22(4): 348–60.

Makalintal, B. (2020) "TikTok is the Food Platform of the People," *Vice*, 29 May.

Marwick, A. (2013) *Status Update: Celebrity, Publicity and Branding in the Social Media Age*, New Haven: Yale University Press.

Naccarato, P. and Lebesco, K. (2012) *Culinary Capital*, London: Bloomsbury.

Park, K. (2018) "South Korea to Clamp Down on Binge-Eating Trend amid Obesity Fears," *Daily Telegraph*, 25 October.

Parsons, A. and Lepkowska-White, E. (2018) "Social Media Marketing Management," *Journal of Internet Commerce*, 17(2): 81–95.

Peng, Y. (2017) "Sharing Food Photographs on Social Media," *Social Identities*, 25(2): 269–87.

Spence, C., Mancini, M. and Huisman, G. (2019) "Digital Commensality: Eating and Drinking in the Company of Technology," *Frontiers in Psychology*, 9 October.

Srnicek, N. (2017) *Platform Capitalism*, Cambridge: Polity.

Taneja, S. and Toombs, L. (2014) "Putting a Face on Small Businesses," *Academy of Marketing Studies Journal*, 18(1): 249–58.

Tech Times (2021) "Who is Hamzy? Mukbang Vlogger Fired by Chinese Agency over Kimchi," 21 January.

Wang, A. (2012) "Food Recommendation App Mines Weibo Data for Restaurant Tips," *TechInAsia*, 16 October.

PART III
Gendered Asia

13

CHOOSING THE RIGHT LOVE

Online Dating Platforms and Gender Inequality in Southeast Asia

Joanne Lim

Since the inception of Grindr in 2009, the vast global industry for choosing the right love has found its way into the daily lives of Southeast Asian societies where sex and sexuality have long been taboo or *haram* subjects, parallel to shame and religious wrongdoings (Misra and Chandiramani 2005; Schröter 2013). Online dating platforms such as Tinder excluded some parts of Asia as their target market, given that premarital sex and hookups were strongly condemned by conservative societies such as Malaysia, Brunei and Indonesia. Popular culture products originating from this region further affirm the taboo, citing moral and religious offensiveness, despite the rise in prostitution, same-sex relationships and free-dating in local communities. Unsurprisingly, negative perceptions of online dating continue to linger and dating app owners have adapted and embedded unique functions (e.g., Bumble and Eshq where only female users can make the first contact) to accommodate the different levels of acceptance, stigma and contentions around online dating. Muzmatch and Salams (formerly Minder) cater to Muslim millennials, while also adopting the function of allowing only females to make the first move. Their unique "Chaperone" feature allows users, who are uncomfortable having a conversation with strangers, to invite a friend or family member to follow their chats because the presence of a "third person" can possibly help to ease the use of online dating platforms in such conservative societies. In Muzmatch, users are asked to indicate their ethnicity and languages spoken, as well as their level of religiosity, from "Not Practicing" to "Very Religious." They are also asked for their "Flavor," which is essentially a question meant to describe which sect of Islam they belong to. Here, users are subjugated by the request to state their position/preference of ethnicity/ religiosity, which is masked by other elements that appear to be liberating or empowering (e.g., females as initiators, the chaperone feature).

DOI: 10.4324/9781003130628-17

Content creators and app designers in Southeast Asia have seen the potential for dating apps in the region and are thus motivated to launch their own versions and platforms, claiming to better understand the psychology of Asians when it comes to love and romance. They try to find a distinction and differentiation from Western dating apps, as expressed by the co-founder of Paktor, a dating app founded in Singapore:

> We found that successful tactics used by the US and European dating apps just didn't translate to Asian societies, because of our more conservative dating norms … Our approach had to be about thinking local, and Paktor started differentiating itself by tapping into our own knowledge of local culture and people.
>
> *(Twigg 2019)*

In addition to the region-specific features mentioned above, localized apps entice Southeast Asian users with more safety features claiming to better protect users' identity. Paktor, known as Asia's Tinder rival (Singh 2018), has grown to become one of the biggest dating apps in Asia, with over 16 million users across Taiwan, Singapore, Malaysia, Indonesia, Vietnam and Thailand. Their secret to success has been ascribed to tapping into a need for discretion which addresses the concern of more conservative, Muslim, Southeast Asian users. Membership soared when the producers changed the rules by ensuring that people simply needed to enter a phone number to join, rather than link their membership to a social media account. The app also introduced "Paktor Group Chat" where shy daters can get to know each other more informally. It has another feature "Send Winks" which enables the system to automatically send messages to users that the system identifies to be compatible. A crucial element in ensuring the success of apps in Southeast Asian countries is the ability to manipulate the masses to believe that they are "safe" and "secure" when participating in online dating. Apps such as Paktor allow users to report others who are fake or who engage in spamming, resulting in banning of such wrongdoers. Tantan also functions to police relationships; users get a warning via a text message if vulgarities are used or words imply that users are looking for a hookup.

Overall, the popularity of dating apps in Southeast Asia is reflected in the increase of expenditure on dating apps by 260% in 2019 (Hetherington 2020), with Thailand having spent the most ($648 million) compared to other Southeast Asian countries, Singapore ($466 million), Indonesia ($386 million), Malaysia ($379 million), the Philippines ($225 million) and Vietnam ($208 million). While research on online dating tends to focus on examining the general usage of online dating sites (Potarca 2020), it is important to consider the manifestations of the self within these dating networks, and what it ultimately reveals about gender inequality and social exclusion amidst seemingly liberating platforms, particularly for the more conservative societies in Southeast Asia. Online dating apps are also increasingly being repositioned and repackaged by app producers in response to the needs of society and to leverage this time of social and physical distancing during the pandemic.

Through a collection of stories, sentiments and an analysis of the platforms' user interfaces, this chapter critically explores how these networked acts of finding the right love not only perpetuate differences between users but also project, in a paradoxical way, autonomy as an alienating factor that creates distance between users while at the same time crucial to attaining self-fulfillment. Although empowering for users in some ways through the freedom to swipe left or right and to portray a particular persona of oneself, the very structures of dating platforms that connect and matchmake these profiles (mis)use the information to filter, differentiate and discriminate users to offer only the "right" ones to another. Thus, the more users swipe left indicating differences in character and preference, the more the system sieves out and alienates similar, undesired profiles. As will be demonstrated in this chapter, users are generally aware that their choices and self-portrayal are crucial in determining to whom they are matched, and this determination is meant to ensure the desired outcome.

This chapter draws on the multi-phase research on online dating sites, conducted with online dating users from six Southeast Asian countries – Malaysia, Singapore, Thailand, Vietnam, Indonesia and the Philippines. Phase 1 examined the general discourse, marketing and regulatory mechanisms of online dating sites. Phase 2 was exploratory in nature and involved a survey which garnered over 660 responses between February 2021 and April 2021. The survey link was posted on popular Facebook groups that contained discussions on love and dating in the respective countries, and also disseminated via WhatsApp, WeChat, Telegram and other social networking apps. Based on the findings from the survey, key questions were formulated for in-depth focus group interviews (Phase 3). Five focus group sessions, consisting six participants in each group, were carried out online via Zoom due to the pandemic. Two gender-specific groups and three mixed groups consisted of representation from the six countries. Focus group participants were recruited from an advert that was circulated via personal social media networks in these countries. Those who responded were mainly from the 18–35 age group, with a mix of students and working professionals possessing diverse educational qualifications. Questions were focused on general dating app usage; expectations, motivations and personal experiences; and perceptions with regard to bias, inequality and algorithms. The participants have experience of using one or more dating apps for over two years. To protect privacy and confidentiality, the participants' names are replaced with codes in the interview data.

Online Dating: Enticement or Chastisement?

With over 1,500 dating apps or websites in the world looking to match people via the "swiping right" model, two individuals are able to find a match, text and initiate a date. OkCupid (2020a) and Tinder (2020) have reported an increase of

50% and 52%, respectively, in connections and conversations across geographical borders since the pandemic began, while Tinder noted up to seven times increase in members' use of the "Passport" feature. There is a larger percentage of males who use the dating apps compared to their female counterparts, while the age group varies according to the apps; OkCupid and Bumble have a majority of 18- to 29-year-olds and Tinder has a majority of 30- to 44-year-olds. As people increasingly find it more convenient to start conversations online than in person, the majority of users believe that common dangers on online dating sites include "people lying to make themselves more attractive" (71%) and "people setting up fake accounts to scam others" (50%). As such, 68% of men and 74% of women find it important to include photos of themselves, while 48% of women and 43% of men claim it is important for profiles to also include whether or not they have children (Vogels 2020). Other information deemed important includes posting hobbies and interests, religious beliefs, racial/ethnic background, occupation, height and political affiliation. To better their chances, users would include TikTok mentions for showing moves, sharing tastes and "some bragging" (Tinder 2020), along with using smiling selfies as profile pictures (OkCupid 2020b). While users seem to understand how the game is played on dating sites and strive to find their match by optimizing their profiles' attractiveness, the task of self-profiling proliferates the act of profiling others as well, the cause of societal degradation. By carefully curating what information to reveal or exclude about themselves, some users consciously manipulate their self-image and send a message about ideals and preferences in terms of gender, religious belief, political affiliation and socioeconomic markers of differentiation including educational levels, all of which stem from and further generate the issues of polarization, social and gender inequality, injustice and exclusion embedded in Southeast Asian societies today.

> I didn't get many guys swiping right on me initially … Then, I made a few changes to my profile, uploaded a better picture and it made a huge difference.
>
> *(E1, age 24, female, Thailand)*

> I don't think anyone expects that what is posted in a profile is the whole truth … Especially if the aim is to get swiped right, there will be a fair bit of manipulation.
>
> *(C4, age 35, male, Singapore)*

> Sometimes you get the feeling like it's a university or job application, like how people judge you.
>
> *(E4, age 23, female, Malaysia)*

Although it may seem reasonable and perhaps expected of a dating app to encourage the profiling of individuals and personal information that is otherwise not often readily available nor easily accessible on other platforms, the current discourse on dating is nonetheless intelligible in terms of "biopower" (Foucault 1990), which is a useful framework to understand modern-day dating alongside gender and sexuality. The first sign of biopolitical adherence is by accepting a statement or an enticement that emerges on the registration page of dating apps although users are usually aware that such a statement is far from the truth, as revealed in this research. Seemingly decontextualized dating apps use tactical and elusive phrases such as: "Dating isn't about data. It isn't about algorithms;" "It isn't about whether you want a boy or a girl or no kids ... how tall someone is or the color of their hair;" "Dating is a chance ... the chance to spend time together, maybe a lifetime." This kind of statement acts as an inclusion–exclusion mechanism that entices users to subscribe and reveal personal information. This is followed by a disclaimer: "It's the chance that you won't like them and they won't like you." Hoping that there is a chance that a dating app offers something beyond imagination, users are usurped through a biopolitical exercise. The deception works through two mechanisms: (1) the politically profiled individual concerned with the *disciplining* of the self in manipulating his/her dating opportunities via the app's demands, functions and features, and (2) biopolitics concerned with the *regulation* of other users on the site by taking a form of population management through the control of what constitutes as sexually/ physically attractive, exotic or unique. These two mechanisms are not mutually exclusive; both the disciplinary and the regulatory means are interconnected (Foucault 1997). It can be said that the dating site becomes a biopolitical intervention technique with specific power effects that may affect the participating body through discipline and regulation.

Profiling demands made via the app interface can be regarded as an exercise of disciplinary power. By requiring users to declare personal information, submit photos that showcase their personality, write a self-summary, perform particular (swiping) acts and conform to the norms and processes associated with modern-day online dating, the act of self-profiling serves as a form of taming and docilization of users. To be recommended compatible matches, users are also required to answer questions such as: "How important is religion/God in your life?"; "Are you ready to settle down and get married right now?"; "Do you care about your parents' opinion of your partner?" Furthermore, the combination of technology and dating establishes a relationship between agents of biopower – the individual and the population of users. By withholding intimate information such as being able to see who liked them unless users upgrade and pay for premium membership, a further method of regulation and control is imposed. Made available only to VIP premium members, such users are able to view all introductions sent to them rather than one at a time. Here, regulation and control are exercised and imposed through enticement to upgrade one's membership.

While these basic functions, features and platform regulations are generally embedded in most if not all dating apps, it is important to consider three key questions that may tell a different story of the online dating phenomena in Southeast Asia: How have globally popular apps been repackaged (in terms of changes to the app interface, or to the way it is marketed) to suit Southeast Asian cultures? What is the appeal of locally or regionally created dating apps to cater to the needs and desires of users? How do experiences of an online dating user differ in Southeast Asia? In addressing these questions alongside Foucault's (1990) notion of biopolitics, it is necessary to observe the underlying forms of power and control through subtle yet strict discipline and regulatory processes in online dating sites as well as their implications on the larger societal issue of biopolitical exclusion.

Marketing efforts for both local and international online dating platforms have been crafted with the Southeast Asian audience in mind by localizing the apps to satisfy the needs and desires of users. The first marketing push by Tinder in Southeast Asia (particularly localized for its market in Indonesia) uses the hashtag #CariJodohApaAja ("Find a Match"). It encourages young adults to find a surfing, silent disco or "Carpool Karaoke" partner using the app, thereby diverting the focus on sex and romance to fun and play. Tinder Indonesia says that the company tries to change the negative perception of online dating by adding a lot of "Southeast Asia flavors" (Whitlock 2019). To further aid its Asia expansion, Tinder Lite was designed to target people in more rural areas with slower Internet connection. Collaborations with consumer brands that are popular among users in specific countries have also been a part of the marketing strategy to entice more downloads of the dating app. Tinder partnered with Oppo, Shopee and Pomelo to capitalize on the young and trendy market and align the dating app with sports, dancing, music and fashion. For dating apps to thrive in this region, they need to be regarded as culturally fitting or at least culturally sensitive. App producers pay particular attention to ensure heightened localization in the user interface and user experiences in order for culture-specific dating nuances to be met. This is offered via localized content including language and featuring Asian models in the app's interface and promotional materials. More recently, app producers engage local YouTuber influencers to introduce the features and methods of usage as well as local celebrities to share their personal success stories in using the dating app.

Illusion of Inclusivity: The Echo-Chamber Effect of Online Dating

Dating apps have often been regarded as misogynist (Shaw 2016; Hess and Flores 2018) and racist (Mason 2016; Carlson 2020). Nevertheless, users of diverse gender and sexual identities have reported their feelings of empowerment and freedom to meet like-minded people, explore their sexuality and facilitate intimacy and sexual encounters that dating apps can offer them (Tziallas 2015; Hobbs et al. 2017; Ferris and Duguay 2019). Studies on social media and the echo-chamber effect have pointed to the increase in social and political polarization and extremism in societies (Yusuf and Banawi 2014; Quattrociocchi 2017;

Dubois and Blank 2018; Giliani et al. 2018; Nyugen and Vu 2019; Cinelli et al. 2021). While existing studies tend to focus on social media such as Facebook and Twitter to explore the influence of information diffusion, and the framing and reinforcement of shared narratives, it is important to consider similar online interaction paradigms that exist within dating sites and how such interactions reinforce the formation of echo chambers that perpetuate polarization and extremism online. Here, the echo-chamber effect can be read as a form of biopolitics that affects how people swipe left or right, thereby altering the way an individual perceives and chooses to connect with others within a closed system; the individual is firstly required to self-regulate by actively manipulating his/her dating persona on the app, and in turn profiling whom he/she will be matched with, and subsequently whom he/she chooses to connect with. Dating apps that allow for group chats may be an added catalyst for this, as the echo-chamber effect is further extended to include like-minded users. The algorithmic structure of dating apps serves as a mechanism dominating how users inadvertently adhere to the processes of self-profiling, othering and forming preexisting opinions of users on the site. The selection process of like-minded candidates for a match via the dating app is the result of the information fed by the user into an algorithm. This suggests that while there is a tendency for the individual to be biased based on his/her opinions, political leanings, religious beliefs and so on, this bias is also conditioned by the dating app. This bias gets reinforced due to repeated interactions with matches, thereby creating an echo-chamber environment based on selective exposure, contagion and group polarization.

While dating platforms offer different interaction features to users, such as "Send Winks" on Paktor and "Friend Moments" on Tantan where users can post pictures or statuses and allow interaction between previously matched users through these posts, the dating app mechanism is a closed system insulated from rebuttal, which allows for the amplification and reinforcement of racism, polarization and extremism within a seemingly secure and liberal environment. Homophilic clusters of users form the basis of attitudes and social dynamics operating within the dating site and beyond. This is evident in the way user profiles are created (mostly similar across all platforms), which requires a user to suggest not only his/her own leanings but also subconsciously the profile of a "match" in mind. In such an interaction network, two users are connected because they are aligned according to similar leanings, following an algorithmic level of filtering often known to the users. When asked about whether there was a sense of bias in the matchmaking process, the general reply in this research was as follows:

> Some applications provide a "boost" to put up your profile for people who are swiping for a certain period of time, so I believe the algorithm allows the matches to be manipulated in certain situations.
>
> *(A2, age 23, male, Malaysia)*

Generally, most dating applications work by recommending you/users that have swiped right on you; system algorithm thinks you are compatible with the user, and if both users swipe right they will be matched together.

(A4, age 21, female, Vietnam)

Users express a common view that despite systemic manipulations, users ultimately have the power to decide if the match is successful.

The system basically recommends users with mutual interest. Whether or not the match is successful is decided by the users, instead of the matching system.

(A1, age 27, male, Thailand)

What is apparent in the responses is the perception that there is an underlying knowledge about how self-profiling implicates who users are matched with, thereby creating an ideal environment for the echo-chamber effect to take place. The interaction network is then reconstructed as the user proceeds to "level up" on the platform by providing more information through VIP premium memberships (e.g., Tinder Gold) and subscribing to extended features. Once individual leanings are inferred, polarization can take place as one swipes right or left, creating positive or negative opinions of others. Homophily can be observed as these social relationships or interactions evolve, further affirming that a "match" happens because two people share similar characteristics or similar opinions and leanings in terms of race/ethnicity, age, religion, education, occupation and so on, the attributes that create strong divides in societies.

To some extent, it helps me to identify and decide whether or not I should try and connect with the person. Such information gives me a brief idea of what the person may be like.

(A4, age 21, female, Vietnam)

The application will recommend users who have a higher similarity to my responses on questionnaires or preference of music, food, etc. The application will also show me if there are any similar hobbies and traits between me and the user.

(A5, age 31, male, Indonesia)

While online dating may appear to be a personal encounter with another user, or with like-minded users on group chats, the presence of echo chambers is primarily rooted in individual leanings that feed algorithms in order to mediate and influence the content and matchmaking results based on users' self-profiling and preferences. The focus group interviews and survey responses also reveal that the percentage of people who use dating apps for romantic and sexual relationships (48%) is slightly lower than the percentage of those who use dating apps for platonic friendships and networking purposes (52%). Matches that are not focused on romantic and sexual relationship-building function almost in the same way as relationships formed on other social media platforms that arguably spread polarization through interaction and information sharing between like-minded users and the proliferation of homophily (Dubois and Blank 2018; Cinelli et al. 2021). Online dating sites have similarly amplified the production of echo chambers through the manipulation of mindsets that may influence users' subsequent beliefs and actions of deciding whether to swipe right or left.

> I mainly still regard it as a dating application, but personally I am not using it to look for hook-ups. My main focus was to meet new people, so I would say my methods of usage ended up leaning toward using it as a networking application.
>
> *(B1, age 32, female, Singapore)*

> I use the application to look for long-term relationships, hook-ups, depending on what the other party is looking for … But I mainly use it for networking and broadening my social circle, too.
>
> *(A2, age 23, male, Malaysia)*

The workings of biopolitics may be prevalent when people believe that power and control lie in their hands. In line with the focus group responses below that reflect this sentiment, the survey respondents who engage in online dating label themselves mainly as "liberal" (76%) compared to "conservative" (19%).

> Users mainly decide whether or not the matches work – not the system.
>
> *(A1, age 27, male, Thailand)*

> I do not feel manipulated or controlled by the application. I generally feel that I am given the opportunity to decide on who I am matched to, who I do not want to match with.
>
> *(B4, age 30, male, Malaysia)*

The issue of power and control is recognized and articulated, particularly by male users more than female users, alongside perceived liberation and further fueled by a sense of safety and security while using these dating platforms.

> I tend not to give out too much information about myself, even after starting a conversation. You don't really know who's behind the profile.
>
> *(A4, age 21, female, Vietnam)*

> I've not gone on any dates yet even after using the app for over 3 years. Maybe I'm comfortable connecting online but I can't bring myself to meet

him in person. What if he doesn't turn out to be who he says he is ... or worse if he thinks I'm not good enough.

(E2, age 30, female, Singapore)

I'm sure a prettier, sexier girl will have more matches. People are mostly judged by their looks especially on these apps.

(E5, age 27, female, Indonesia)

Given the findings revealed above, it is pertinent to ask how these experiences possibly present deeper concerns about inequality, exclusion and marginalization, compared to other social media platforms. Unlike other platforms where network interactions remain largely online, at least half the users of dating apps connect online for the sole purpose of subsequently meeting offline. Herein lies the complexity of synergizing the online with the offline experience, negotiating a "mismatch."

I had two bad encounters, whereby the person didn't turn out looking like the person I was matched with. I made an excuse and left the scene within 20 minutes, on both occasions.

(D1, age 26, male, Philippines)

A homosexual user has faked his identity as a female to ask me on a date ... I had to block and ghost the person to stop the situation from extending further.

(B4, age 30, male, Malaysia)

While the probability of a mismatch would be normally expected in any dating encounter, the online practice of being able to block, swipe left and ghost an individual before a physical encounter provides relatively easy and ample opportunities for users to perpetuate acts of exclusion and reproduce inequality, wittingly or unwittingly. Furthermore, this kind of online dating practice can be perceived as acceptable and justified on the basis of power, control, liberalism and empowerment afforded by highly popular yet problematic online social networking platforms.

Reproducing Inequality: Biopolitical Exclusion and Marginalization

In 2018, Bumble rebranded itself from a dating app to a networking app and launched a series of face-to-face experiential events. Tantan collaborated with BigoLive Malaysia to host a series of speed-dating events which allowed Malaysian users to meet with each other and engage in so-called "fun" games. Paktor was awarded a Guinness Record in 2013 for hosting the largest speed-dating event which was held in Vietnam, involving 600 participants. Indeed, the element of mystery found in connecting with strangers on a dating app as opposed to connecting with familiar people (e.g., through Facebook) is what makes the difference – an inverse experience from other social media apps (Bennett 2018).

The re-positioning of dating apps for social networking presents a myriad of issues, despite seemingly opening-up opportunities for networking precisely because of self-profiling requirements and algorithm matching systems. Returning to the notion of biopower (Foucault 1990), what appears even more decontextualized based on the assumption that two strangers meet by chance on a dating app (unlike LinkedIn or Facebook where connections are mostly made on the basis of a preexisting relationship or friendship) serves as an underlying means of biopolitically profiling and regulating users through this unassuming form of user management, thereby defining (as a means of control) what is deemed attractive, exotic or unique. As a consequence, users in this research tend to feel alienated, judged or unworthy when they do not receive swipes often enough. Furthermore, some respondents explicitly express inequality in this context. On the other hand, several others share a different viewpoint that being able to package and present oneself to appear more attractive on dating apps accounts for equality.

> On dating applications, there is even more inequality. People will judge you based on your looks or your wealth status, which they grasp through the photos and moments you feature on the application. The possibility of getting good matches is low if you are not attractive enough, if you are not able to show your personality within a short conversation.
>
> *(A1, age 27, male, Thailand)*

> I have met some users who are demanding and feel like they equate to a higher standard, so I do not feel like the inequality or social hierarchy is removed just because it is a dating application.
>
> *(B2, age 28, female, Vietnam)*

> I think that the inequality is very obvious as online dating applications are very dependent on looks and short profiles that you can leave in your biography. Which means, on the application people are even faster at judging you.
>
> *(C4, age 35, male, Singapore)*

> I think in some ways you are able to "package" yourself into a more presentable image, so I think to some extent, it does feel more equal.
>
> *(A5, age 31, male, Indonesia)*

Coupled with new strategies embedded in the design of dating apps such as Tinder, elements of gamification (Tziallas 2015; Hobbs et al. 2017) and ludification (Frissen et al. 2015) transform non-game activities and interactions into play. Thus, the quest for romantic or platonic relationships packaged as a form of competition based on physical attractiveness adds a further element of play, fun and excitement to the quest. This, however, serves to perpetuate highly gendered practices that present users with different sets of risks. Despite the obvious gaming practices that people may incorporate into dating either through the apps or in real life, the gamification of dating stimulates risks such as being shamed, humiliated or made to feel guilty, while also stimulating pleasure, pride, achievement and control from having gained "rewards" for being swiped right by another user or answering a series of questions accurately.

> It's fun swiping right or left. I don't take this too seriously. But some people do ... So I just tell them to take it easy. One girl got quite upset.
>
> *(D5, age 25, male, Philippines)*

> I started out just curious if I could find a date online. It ended up becoming more like a game ... It was exciting to see how many people swiped right on me especially when I changed my profile or added a link to my TikTok account.
>
> *(E5, age 27, female, Indonesia)*

> This swiping "right" thing can be very addictive especially when you're on the receiving end of the swipe. What a boost of ego!
>
> *(C2, age 25, male, Malaysia)*

The motivation to succeed or emerge as a winner in dating games lends to biopolitics, whereby users try to avoid disappointments and frustrations and are sometimes forced into changing their bodies, activities and personas. Self-surveillance and self-regulation alongside disciplinary practices, such as determining if one is too fat or too ugly, serve as new levels of expectations for society. This kind of biopolitics consists of a combination of "raw" power (exercised by the dating app system which is top-down in nature, making it mandatory to complete the user profile before gaining membership and paying a subscription fee to access more features) and a more subtle "soft" power (involving voluntary actions from users who are encouraged by the dating app to make oneself appear attractive to increase the chances of finding a right match). Evoking these feelings can inspire users to adhere to the ideals of self-monitoring and self-policing. For Southeast Asian users, this becomes a counter-culture that seemingly offers conservative societies a rare opportunity to experience a form of liberalization and counter-taboo via dating sites, which however reproduces the same inequality and marginalization that take the form of power and control embedded in the structure of the dating apps. Sometimes, the excitement from playing the game takes precedence over the outcome of using the dating apps as originally intended for romantic or sexual relationships.

The survey outcome in this research reveals that the majority of users (67%) have not gone on a date since they started using a dating app, compared to those who went on 1–2 dates (16%), 3–4 dates (5%), 5 or more dates (12%). This finding provides an insight into the motivation of dating app usage and affirms that game-like dating experience speaks to those seeking entertainment rather than actual relationships as a core motivation for mobile dating app usage (Sobieraj and Humphreys 2021). Users have often described dating apps as entertaining and fun (Timmermans and De Caluwe 2017). However, the perpetuation of gender norms amidst the fun in dating apps suggests that men and women continue to reproduce gender-normative behavior, even with features that allow only women to make the first move or initiate conversations.

> I think it's the role of the woman to keep the guy interested, so although I start the conversation first, I keep it going by sending him messages and jokes … excite him.
>
> *(E5, age 27, female, Indonesia)*

> Everything was going well until we started chatting about sex … I tried to refuse initially and then he said things like oh! it must be because you're too young and have no experience.
>
> *(D2, age 20, female, Malaysia)*

> One guy was so insulting. He said I don't do sex-talk very well because I'm Malay … How racist is that?
>
> *(E4, age 23, female, Malaysia)*

While men are normatively expected to initiate relationships, women who act like aggressors tend to increase the fun in dating sites as the script returns to gender normalcy – men being more sexually driven and women functioning as sexual objects. Women continue to risk being predated and being the object of the male gaze. While it can be argued that women, too, can play the dating game, experience fun and control how she is perceived, this is only true for as long as she does not make herself "available." The normativity regarding gender, sexuality, age, race and class can be amplified once a woman engages in sexual interaction and puts herself at risk of punishment and marginalization (Christensen 2020). The gamified practices propagate male masculinity, and those who face rejection, men or women, continue to struggle with the punishment of being seen as lacking in either masculine/feminine values or desirability.

Conclusion

Online dating platforms in Southeast Asia can be regarded as seemingly liberating modern-day sites for connecting with many unknown people in an effort to find the right love. For Southeast Asian users, localized sites offer a sense of safety and security as well as a sense of freedom to participate in social networking that is more about the quest and less about the outcome. While the use of dating apps has increasingly become popular in the region, the disciplinary and regulatory nature of the apps is seen to serve as echo chambers and possibly perpetuate gender norms including patriarchy and masculinity, despite the various localized strategies made to the dating apps that appear to empower female users. In the typical marketing statement of dating apps, marginalization is repackaged into a simple message to suggest that attraction happens by "chance" and is not dependent on physical appearances or gender preferences. Rejection and exclusion are expected when users are deemed inadequate or not at all the preferred choice. Biopolitical power and control continue to be at play in what has now taken on a game-like format, while simultaneously taming and managing the users through the means of self-profiling and self-policing. Regulatory practices are prevalent in a way that is more subtle, through the withholding of features and functions until the users conform to the conditions set by the dating system, and the users are further enticed into paying for VIP premium features to partake in what is otherwise forbidden to the socioeconomically non-privileged. Whether online dating platforms are used for social networking, advice seeking, sexual conquest, or simply individual/collective gaming, the stigma and taboo attached to online dating in Southeast Asia continues to linger in conservative societies. Younger generations seem more willing to search for diverse choices on online dating sites and risk being exposed to discriminatory practice and inequality. They are subject to implicit forms of gendered moral punishment, while attempting to find rare opportunities that may arise from a seemingly decontextualized online environment in order to feel liberated, to have some fun and maybe to eventually choose the right love.

References

Bennett, L. (2018) "The New LinkedIn for Women?," *ADNews*, 21 March.

Carlson, B. (2020) "Love and Hate at the Cultural Interface," *Journal of Sociology*, 56(2): 133–50.

Christensen, M. (2020) "Tindersluts and Tinderellas," *Sociological Perspectives*, 64(3): 432–49.

Cinelli, M., Morales, G., Galeazzi, A., Quattrociocchi, W. and Starnini, M. (2021) "The Echo Chamber Effect on Social Media," *Proceedings of the National Academy of Sciences*, 118(9).

Dubois, E. and Blank, G. (2018) "The Echo Chamber is Overstated," *Information, Communication & Society*, 21(5): 729–45.

Ferris, L. and Duguay, S. (2019) "Tinder's Lesbian Digital Imaginary: Investigating (im)permeable Boundaries of Sexual Identity on a Popular Dating App," *New Media & Society,* 22(3): 489–506.

Foucault, M. (1990) *The History of Sexuality*, New York: Vintage.

Foucault, M. (1997) *Society Must Be Defended*, New York: Picador.

Frissen, V., Lammes, S., de Lange, M., de Mul, J. and Raessens, J. (2015) "Homo Ludens 2.0," in V. Frissen, S. Lammes, M. de Lange, J. de Mul and J. Raessens (eds) *Playful Identities*, Amsterdam: University of Amsterdam Press.

Gillani, N., Yuan, A., Saveski, M., Vosoughi, S. and Roy, D. (2018) "Me, My Echo Chamber and I," a paper in Proceedings of the 2018 World Wide Web Conference.

Hess, A. and Flores, C. (2018) "Simply More Than Swiping Left," *New Media & Society*, 20(3): 1085–102.

Hetherington, A. (2020) "Dating App Spend in Southeast Asia Rises by 260%," *GDI*, 2 March.

Hobbs, M., Owen, S. and Gerber, L. (2017) "Liquid Love?," *Journal of Sociology*, 53(2): 271–84.

Mason, C. (2016) "Tinder and Humanitarian Hook-Ups," *Feminist Media Studies*, 16(5): 822–37.

Misra, G. and Chandiramani, R. (2005) *Sexuality, Gender and Rights*, London: Sage.

Nguyen, A. and Vu, H. (2019) "Testing Popular News Discourse on the Echo Chamber Effect," *First Monday*, 24(6).

OkCupid (2020a) "Love in the Time of Corona," 15 April.

OkCupid (2020b) "The Future of Dating," 8 November.

Potarca, G. (2020) "The Demography of Swiping Right," *PLoS ONE*, 15(12).

Quattrociocchi, W. (2017) "Inside the Echo Chamber," *Scientific American*, 316(4): 60–63.

Schröter, S. (2013) *Gender and Islam in Southeast Asia*, Leiden: Brill.

Shaw, F. (2016) "Bitch I Said Hi," *Social Media & Society*, 2(4): 1–10.

Singh, P. (2018) "How This App is Helping People in Asia Find Love, One Swipe At A Time," *Entrepreneur*, 11 December.

Sobieraj, S. and Humphreys, L. (2021) "The Tinder Games," *Mobile Media & Communication*, 10(1): 57–75.

Timmermans, E. and de Caluwé, E. (2017) "Development and Validation of the Tinder Motives Scale," *Computers in Human Behavior*, 70: 341–50.

Tinder (2020) "Gen Z Never Stopped Dating in 2020," 7 December.

Twigg, M. (2019) "Asian Dating Apps are Hungry for Your Love," *Gen.T*, 3 April.

Tziallas, E. (2015) "Gamified Eroticism," *Sexuality & Culture*, 19(4): 759–75.

Vogels, E. (2020) "10 Facts About Americans and Online Dating," *Pew Research* Centre, 6 February.

Whitlock, D. (2019) "Tinder Rolls Out Major Marketing Campaign in Southeast Asia," *GDI*, 8 July.

Yusuf, N., Al-Banawi, N. and Al-Imam, H. (2014) "The Social Media as Echo Chamber," *Journal of Business & Economics Research*, 12(1): 1–10.

14

"QUEER" MEDIA IN INTER-ASIA

Thinking Gender and Sexuality Transnationally

Michelle H. S. Ho

This chapter explores how thinking gender and sexuality transnationally can help us make sense of "queer" media, practices and performances proliferating across East Asia and Southeast Asia through two prominent examples – South Korean popular music (K-pop) and "boys love" (BL) media. K-pop might be characterized as a distinct genre of idol music coming out of South Korea, whereas BL media refer to a narrative genre originating from Japan featuring homoerotic relationships between *bishōnen* (beautiful boys). Much scholarship on the inter-Asian circulation of popular culture has examined uneven cultural and economic exchanges (Chua and Iwabuchi 2008), recentering and de-Westernization of global media markets (Iwabuchi 2002; Kim 2008), soft power (Kim 2013) and cultural and postcolonial hybridity (Shim 2006; Yoon 2017). Although this body of work is important, less has been written about its queer inter-Asian flows, such as K-pop cover dances in which the choreography of K-pop artists is imitated and performed by Thai feminine gay groups (Kang 2015) and BL fan practices and production by Chinese *danmei* (translation of the Japanese *tanbi* or aesthete to index BL) creators (Yang and Xu 2017). By bringing the approaches of inter-Asia referencing, transnational feminism and transnational sexualities to bear on one another, this chapter theorizes these queer flows as a form of solidarity among individuals living in the margins of Asian societies, notably gender and sexual minorities.

Inter-Asia referencing is a critical approach that compares and builds upon Asian sources, locations, experiences, understandings and conceptualizations to promote theorization of and "making reference to other Asian modernities" (Iwabuchi 2014: 47). However, this is not a parochial call to essentialize Asia or endorse so-called "Asian theories" over "Western theories," but a form of critical regionality that takes into account regions' historicity and "diverse inter-connections and inter-cultural comings and goings" as "imagined communities"

DOI: 10.4324/9781003130628-18

(Johnson et al. 2000: 362). By challenging the West's intellectual domination of scholarship, the impetus of the "inter-Asia" framework is to advance knowledge production from within Asia. In his reworking of Japanese sinologist Yoshimi Takeuchi's notion "Asia as method," Chen (2010: xv) suggests that we use Asia as an "imaginary anchoring point ... to become one another's reference points, so that the understanding of the self can be transformed and subjectivity rebuilt."

Although inter-Asia referencing, transnational feminisms and transnational sexualities emerged separately, they have overlapping goals to de-Westernize knowledges and movements, particularly queer and feminist scholarship privileging the lives, writings and experiences of White middle-class Euro-American women and sexual minorities. In the mid-1990s, transnational feminisms originated as a diverse field of inquiry in the US academia to de-center Euro-American discourses and stress the asymmetrical relations between culture, capital, nation-state and globalization (Kaplan and Grewal 1999). Moving beyond the local–global binary, scholars of transnational feminisms advocate alternative approaches to US feminism, much in the same ways scholars advance the inter-Asia framework to intervene in the study of Asian peoples, cultures and languages in the USA, Europe and Australia. Transnational feminisms might therefore be said to simultaneously build on and diverge from the "intellectual and political legacies of women of color/third world/multicultural/international/global feminisms" (Nagar and Swarr 2010: 4).

Coming out of transnational feminisms, transnational sexuality studies similarly traverses multiple disciplines to underscore inequalities and uneven power relations and knowledge production constructions of sexual subjectivities across national contexts (Grewal and Kaplan 2001). Transnational sexuality studies is an interdisciplinary field engaging "both the role sexuality plays in transnational relations and formations in an era of globalization, and the complex discourses of nation, gender, sexuality and ethnicity that make this intervention so essential" (Hemmings 2007: 15). Despite this, Blackwood (2005: 222) argues it is "extremely difficult not to rely on and privilege Western understandings of sexualities," but at the same time, we should not fall back on indigenous premodern discourses of sexualities. Blackwood (2005: 238) demonstrates how the subjectivities of Indonesian *lesbi* (women who desire women) are "neither traditional nor backward but a product of modern national and transnational processes." Complicating this dichotomy is how genders and sexualities in Asian contexts are not always disentangled from one another (Chiang et al. 2018).

Although inter-Asia referencing, transnational feminisms and transnational sexualities are distinct approaches, this chapter brings them together to productively discuss the queer flows of media, practices and performances across East Asia and Southeast Asia. Drawing on existing research on K-pop and BL media, it (re)reads these works through the analytical lens of inter-Asia referencing, transnational feminisms and transnational sexualities to make broader connections between them. This follows scholars' call for more "transborder projects" and "inter-connectivity across different subregions" in the study of queer Asia (Martin et al. 2008: 9; Chiang and Wong 2017: 123). The chapter argues that thinking gender and sexuality transnationally remains important for understanding how K-pop and BL media fandom, consumption and (re)production simultaneously enable more visibility and inclusion of gender and sexual minorities and operate to obscure and exclude them. The processes of fandom, consumption and (re)production are not limited to gender and sexual minorities but can include queer interpretations of K-pop and BL media. That is, regardless of how a consumer identifies, they may occupy "queer positions" during their consumption of media and popular culture (Doty 1993: 3), such as when cisgender straight women develop queer readings of BL media. This chapter employs "queer" as an analytic, drawing on Sedgwick's (1994: 7) definition of queer as "the open mesh of possibilities, gaps, overlaps, dissonances and resonances, lapses and excesses of meaning."

The chapter will first introduce the BL genre in Japan in relation to its gender-bending characteristics and survey its diverse fandom and production in Thailand, Indonesia, Singapore and the Philippines. Subsequently, after situating K-pop within the spread and global phenomenon of the Korean Wave (*Hallyu*) and its androgynous elements, this chapter will provide an overview of queer K-pop consumption and performance in Thailand, Indonesia, Singapore and the Philippines. Finally, it concludes with some observations for future research.

"Boys Love" Media Fandom and Production beyond Japan

In the early 1970s, BL narratives originated from commercial *shōjo* (for girls) manga when women artists developed a new subgenre called *shōnen-ai* (love between adolescent boys) to negotiate sexuality – a taboo subject in Japanese society at the time (McLelland and Welker 2015): Since then, various categories have emerged as a result of exchanges between readers, amateur *dōjinshi* (self-published) creators and commercial channels to index diverse forms of BL media, such as *yaoi*, an acronym for *yama nashi, ochi nashi, imi nashi* (no climax, no point, no meaning) to denote noncommercial works. Outside Japan, similar categories have been adopted by BL fans and creators but with different meanings specific to their sociocultural contexts. Despite the proliferation of categories and meanings, BL media – which span across manga, anime, light novels, films, video games and television series – can be collectively characterized by often explicit narratives of romantic and sexual relations between *bishōnen*, which are purportedly by and for cisgender straight women. Such BL fans are called *fujoshi* (rotten girls) – a derogatory term they have since reclaimed – for fantasizing about male–male eroticism (Nagaike 2012). This is not to say that men or lesbian women cannot be consumers of BL; allegedly cis-heterosexual male fans have self-identified as *fudanshi* (rotten boys).

The gender-bending characteristics of BL media can be gleaned from their overtly homoerotic content, non-normative sex/gender transgression, and fans' consumption and meanings they generate. The *bishōnen* in BL media might be described as "neither male nor female" (Welker 2006: 842) and "can be mistaken for a girl (and who sometimes dresses as one)" (Fujimoto et al. 2004: 81) who blur gender boundaries and unsettle "any kind of monolithic understanding of gendered or sexual identity" (Wood 2006: 397) for readers. Granted, following Doty (1993), enacting a potentially queer reading also depends on who consumes these texts and how they interpret the characters' gender and sexually ambiguous presentation. Scholars have argued that BL manga serves the role of "liberating readers not just from patriarchy but from gender dualism and heteronormativity" (Welker 2006: 843; Nagaike 2012). Women reading BL manga could escape the norms defining their social positions and heterosexual relationships as these narratives offer them a productive space to reimagine their identities; for some, this process could entail shaping their gender identity and sexual orientation. This should also be understood within the context of the 1990s *yaoi ronsō* (debate) when a gay activist criticized BL manga, readers and creators for discriminating against real gay men. This led to a dispute with several women fans who contended that because such narratives are created by and for women – not gay men – *bishōnen* are neither supposed to represent real gay men nor their interests (McLelland 2001; Mizoguchi 2003). Lunsing (2006) offers a different perspective, describing BL manga as having a positively queer influence on male sexuality because the whole debate reveals the danger of prescribing how male homosexuality should be portrayed.

Beyond Japan, transnational BL fan cultures are situated in specific cultural, historical and geographical contexts and need to be interpreted differently from Japanese BL fandom (Nagaike and Suganuma 2013). For example, Chinese *danmei* can be said to depart from Japanese popular culture and engender its own distinct Chinese-speaking fan cultures and productions (Yang and Xu 2017). Transnational BL consumption is not new; as early as the 1970s, Taiwanese readers were consuming Japanese BL manga as pirated content (Martin 2012). However, only in the last two decades did BL media spread globally as the Internet made BL media accessible to online fan communities. In the USA, this boom is attributed to the 1994 distribution of *Kizuna* ("Bonds"), a BL manga marketed to a "gay male audience," and "slash," a fan fiction genre written by featuring the homoerotic relations of two male characters from popular culture (Levi 2008: 3). Despite similarities between slash and BL media, one main difference is BL media's "greater lability of gender and sex," such as the presumed depictions of gender shifting and same-sex relationships (ibid.: 4). Other comparisons have also been made, such as Bauwens-Sugimoto's (2011) study on some US slash fans' criticisms of Japanese *yaoi* as "ideologically inferior" to slash for being more racist, misogynistic and homophobic. Scholars have demonstrated the importance of BL narratives for developing a "distinct sexual/gender subculture" and the empowerment and subject-making of transnational LGBTQ (Lesbian, Gay, Bisexual, Transgender, Queer) fans and creators (Meyer 2008; Lavin et al. 2017). Note though that not all BL fans and creators identify as gender and sexual minorities and consumption can also encompass queer readings of BL media.

In her ethnographic study of primarily women BL fans in Indonesia, Singapore and the Philippines, Fermin (2014) posits that consuming BL allows them to question and shift dominant ideological discourses of gender and sexuality in their respective patriarchal societies. Although the majority of these BL fans are urban middle-class cis-heterosexual women (only a handful are men or lesbian and bisexual women), they "develop at least an open or permissive attitude toward non-heteronormative sexualities" (ibid.: 171). Unlike Japanese BL fans, these Southeast Asian BL fans tend to make connections between homosexuality and the male homoerotic relations they encounter in BL media. However, they are reluctant to advocate for LGBTQ issues or engage directly in activism and instead interpret their queer readings of BL media mostly in terms of their own pleasure and entertainment. That said, Fermin (2013) also noticed how Filipino BL fans' consumption was shaped by an imaginary of Japan as an "exotic," "liberal" and "gender-open" culture and society in sharp contrast with their conservative country. This imaginary fits into a progress narrative of Japan as more modern due to the sexual and gender-bending discourses BL media elicit for Filipino/Southeast Asian readers. Yet, if we adopt a transnational feminist and sexuality lens, we might say that the consumption of Filipino/Southeast Asian BL fans highlights precisely the unevenness of inter-Asia capital and cultural flows and complexities of negotiating localized and Japanese genders and sexualities. On the one hand, BL media appear to circulate unidirectionally from Japan to Southeast Asia where its fans look to Japan as more liberal. On the other hand, Southeast Asian BL fans' consumption also deviates from that of Japanese fans by not disassociating the content they consume from gay desires in real life; this has the potential for shaping more open attitudes to LGBTQ issues in Southeast Asia.

More recently, the rise of "Thai BL," a narrative genre produced in Thailand featuring homoerotic relations between two attractive men, manifests queer inter-Asian flows of transnational BL fan cultures in radically different ways. Thai BL is distinct from Japanese BL, which caught on among gay men and young women after it was first introduced to the Thai market in the 1990s (Keenapan 2001). Thai BL emerged in the 2010s when television producers began making BL drama series fan-subbed into many languages, which became popular among audiences in China, Vietnam and Indonesia (Jirattikorn 2018; Baudinette 2020). In his digital ethnography of a Thai BL Facebook fan page, Baudinette (2020: 106) finds that most of the Filipino gay male participants use Thai BL – which they believe is "specifically and fundamentally Thai" – as an empowering space for exploring their same-sex desiring subjectivity. Thai BL fandom is also informed by these participants' discussions in English – they are not fluent in Thai – and understandings of Thailand as a "gay paradise" and of Japan and the Philippines as heteronormative and homophobic societies (Baudinette 2020). Baudinette's study demonstrates why thinking gender and sexuality transnationally is important for making sense of sexual minorities' consumption in an inter-Asia context and showing how their queer positions may travel far beyond the genre's origins and the text's intended use. BL media, which are dislocated or decentered from Japan, produced in Thailand, fronted by handsome actors and presumably target women, become consumed by Filipino gay men who creatively use these media and their fandom to negotiate their same-sex desires. A similar phenomenon among Indonesian gay men who consume Thai BL due to the lack of LGBTQ representation in local television series (Nugroho 2020) has emerged, but more research needs to be done to understand how their queer fandoms may overlap or not. What this does point to is the generative potential of a phenomenon like Thai BL for (re)configuring inter-Asia referencing, transnational feminisms and transnational sexualities. Instead of looking to Japan or the West, Thai BL becomes a site of reference for Filipino and Indonesian gay men and young women to simultaneously develop their subjectivities and disrupt practices in their own cultural contexts.

Queer K-Pop Consumption and Performance in Southeast Asia

The Korean Wave (*Hallyu*) originated in the late 1990s as cultural products such as television dramas and movies were exported, first to Asian countries and subsequently K-pop became popular in other parts of the world including the Americas and Europe (Kim 2013). These transnational flows have been attributed to the export imperative – the belief that a small domestic market demanded the exporting of goods and services – which was exacerbated by the recession following the 1997 International Monetary Fund (IMF) crisis (Chua and Iwabuchi 2008; Lie 2015). However, the desire to develop new markets abroad is not enough to explain Korean popular culture's transnational success; it also depended on other factors like having K-pop musicians take the lead in an often unpredictable industry (Lie 2015). Similar in some ways to transnational BL consumption, *Hallyu* – or *Hallyu* 2.0 or New Korean Wave as some scholars have called to denote differences in fan bases, cultural products and policies, and technological developments – spread across the world through video-sharing platforms and social networking services, relying on fans' labor to upload, subtitle, translate and review K-pop and Korean dramas (Kim 2013; Jin 2016). Contemporary K-pop since the 2000s is known for its upbeat melody, devoted fan base, integration of music and choreography – albeit borrowing from diverse influences – and polished "body beautiful" visual presentation of mostly group acts (Lie 2015). K-pop has become a global cultural phenomenon not only because it has traveled all over the world but also because of its "glocalization of production, coproduction of K-pop with foreign producers and composers, and English mixed into the lyrics" (Jin 2016: 122).

Scholars have also discussed aspects of androgyny, crossdressing, gender-bending and "soft masculinity" in Korean popular culture. In what Jung (2010) calls "*chogukjeok* (transnational) pan-East Asian soft masculinity," *kkonminam* (flower pretty boy) male idols exhibit a different form of masculinity characterized by being gentle and feminine-looking – a combination of attractive characteristics that overlaps with Japanese *bishōnen* characters and Chinese Confucian *wen* masculinity. Soft masculinity has the potential to transgress social norms of gender and sexuality but as Oh and Oh (2017) have noted, K-pop male idols' crossdressing and androgynous presentation neither index homosexuality nor a lack of masculinity. Yet, other scholars have argued that consumers nevertheless "queer" such crossdressing and androgynous performances through online "fanfic" (fan-produced fiction) and "vidding" – the act of fans making compilation videos on YouTube – where male idols are often depicted as dancing, behaving sensually, or being romantically involved with each other (Oh 2015; Kwon 2019). Soft masculinity also takes on a queer turn when embodied by "tomboy" characters like Eun-Chan in the Korean drama *First Shop of Coffee Prince* (2007) and androgynous K-pop idols like Amber Liu, a member of the disbanded girl group f(x) (Lavin 2015; Laurie 2016). Aside from encouraging queer interpretations of these figures, such representations can provide a site for fans' cross-gender female identification and exploration of their gender and sexual identities, such as in the case of *fancos* (fan "cosplay" or costume-play) in Korea (Shin 2018). In her ethnography of *fancos* communities in the 2000s, Shin (2018: 92) finds that K-pop has had "unexpected influence" on *iban* (queer) women fans who emulated the soft masculinity of male idols or fanfic characters and even engaged in same-gender pairing – for instance, two masculine-presenting women taking the roles of *gonggyeok* (offense) and *subi* (defense), which resemble *seme* (penetrator) and *uke* (penetrated) roles in BL media.

A growing body of scholarship on transnational queer K-pop consumption and performance has discussed how fans connect their LGBTQ identities to their fandom and participation in "reverse cover groups," where gender-crossing performers reenact the original music video from choreography, makeup, to costumes. In one study, although LGBTQ Asian American fans recognized that K-pop idols' queer performance and representation can be problematic for being disingenuous, they negotiated this through singing K-pop, making and consuming fan art and videos, performing or choreographing K-pop dances, and writing fanfic or cosplaying as one of its characters (Kuo et al. 2020). These forms of fan labor are vital for providing "alternative narratives of sexuality, gender and Asian identity," particularly for young LGBTQ Asian Americans who are doubly discriminated in the USA (ibid.: 19). Such sentiments appear to be similar for young LGBTQ K-pop fans living in Southeast Asia. For example, queer teen K-pop cover groups in the Philippines provide an "accepting and supportive community" for young fans to freely express their gender and sexuality (Guevarra 2014: 114). Situated within the context of tolerance for LGBTQ people in the Philippines, K-pop reverse cover groups and performances are considered empowering for those who partake in this fandom. In the Indonesian context, through their reverse cover dances of K-pop boy bands, female-assigned fans dismantle normative gender representations, which reinforces the construction of a new Indonesian femininity (Jung 2011). From a transnational feminist and sexuality perspective, we might also argue that these Indonesian reverse cover groups shape and are shaped by soft masculinity, queering this alternative form of masculinity.

Extending from discourses of empowerment, Kang (2015: 287) characterizes Thai K-pop reverse cover groups as "demi-idols," "hyper-fans" and semi-professional dancers who are often effeminate (gay) men materializing as local idols to "fan followings in their own right." One prominent example Kang discusses is Wonder Gay, a group of male high school students who identify as *tut* (sissy or queen) and rose in popularity in 2009 after releasing a YouTube video of them dancing to the now-disbanded K-pop girl band Wonder Girls' hit song *Nobody* (Kang 2014). After their YouTube video went viral, achieving 1.3 million hits by June 2009, Wonder Gay became the first cover group to attain national celebrity and inspired the phenomenon of Thai K-pop cover dances (Kang 2015). Epitomizing queer inter-Asian flows of transnational K-pop fandom, Thai K-pop demi-idols offer a site for fans – who are predominantly young Thai women but also include LGBTQ individuals – to make sense of their gender and sexuality. Overlapping in some ways with Thai BL, Wonder Gay fans appear to consume their performances – mimicries of the Wonder Girls – as "Thai K-pop," indicating a kind of dislocation from the original K-pop. Of course, as Kang (2018) points out, K-pop itself draws on diverse music and aesthetic forms from the USA and Japan, which raises questions about K-pop's authenticity in the first place. The Wonder Gay example demands thinking gender and sexuality transnationally precisely because K-pop is in and of itself unstable; Wonder Gay's reverse cover dances complicate K-pop performance and consumption in Thailand and other countries like Malaysia and the Philippines where similar groups have emerged (e.g., a quick search on YouTube for "Wonder Gay" reveals video performances by the Filipino Wonder Gays). Moreover, Wonder Gay performances appeal to fans because of their "queer difference," which is similar to cis-heterosexual women's BL fandom in which fans imagine K-pop demi-idols as *khu-wai* (Y couple; Y is short for *yaoi*) or in homoerotic relationships with one another (Kang 2014: 566). Perhaps we might say that cis-straight women's appropriation of Wonder Gay's queer performances operates to exclude LGBTQ people. Yet, cis-straight women's queer interpretations also enable LGBTQ people to imagine otherwise, such as developing different meanings through embodying Korean femininity and Asian middle-class lifestyle (Kang 2014).

K-pop's influence in Southeast Asia has also manifested in women's alternative forms of masculinity – or what Halberstam (1998) called "female masculinity." Emerging in Singapore in the 2010s are tomboy boybands comprising young butches who model, sing and dance, inspired by the aesthetics and performances of K-pop, Asian *T* or *tom* cultures in Taiwan and Thailand, and the local Butch Hunt competition, an annual pageant for crowning the most talented butches (Yue 2017). *Tom* and *T* – derived from the English "tomboy" – refer to masculine women in Thailand and Taiwan, respectively, who are sexually attracted to their feminine women counterparts, *dee* and *po* (wife) (Chao 2001;

Sinnott 2012). One example Yue (2017) discusses is SMZ Tomboy Crew, comprising young Singaporeans who adopt the androgynous appearances of K-pop male idols, such as dyed hair, long fringe, eye makeup and hip-hop street wear, and perform a repertoire of K-pop and Mandopop (Mandarin popular music) accompanied by an elaborate choreography. Characterizing tomboy boybands' "soft butch masculinity" as inter-Asian for referencing models from East Asia and Southeast Asia instead of the West, Yue (2017: 19) argues that their trans-embodiment "opens up alternative pathways of life-making." Advancing queer inter-Asian referencing is also how K-pop has shaped *tom* culture in Thailand since the early 2000s, departing from the belief that gender and sexual identity categories are derived from the West (Sinnott 2012). K-pop's gender ambiguity and soft masculinity encouraged *toms* to experiment with various categories and one prominent example is *tom gay*, a *tom* sexually partnered with another *tom*. This is unlike the usual *tom–dee* pairing – that is a masculine–feminine pairing between *tom* and *dee* based on the gender binary – but similar to Shin's (2018) observation of same-gender pairing among Korean *fancos iban* women. Although both wear Korean fashion, *tom gays* are regarded as embodying more "campy" and feminized masculine aesthetics than *toms*, who have short hair and little to no makeup (Sinnott 2012: 471). Korean dramas, notably *First Shop of Coffee Prince*, heavily influenced *toms* and *tom gays* who identified with Eun-Chan and assumed from watching these dramas that masculine women were widespread in Korea (Kang-Nguyen 2019). From a transnational sexuality studies lens, the transnational circulation and consumption of K-pop enabled *tom gays* and tomboy boybands in Thailand and Singapore, respectively, to actively express new categories and (re)configure their subjectivities.

Conclusion: What's Next?

Thinking gender and sexuality transnationally is useful for making sense of the overlapping processes of queer K-pop and BL media fandom, consumption and (re)production, whether this means fans identify as LGBTQ or cis-heterosexual. This chapter brings together the approaches of inter-Asia referencing, transnational feminisms and transnational sexualities in order to discuss the queer circulation of K-pop and BL media from East Asia to Southeast Asia and the flows within Southeast Asia. For instance, Filipino gay men's consumption of Thai BL – which is distinct and thus removed from Japanese BL – is an interesting example of how LGBTQ people creatively use media to negotiate their own subjectivity. Similarly, the potential of Wonder Gay's K-pop cover dances to engender a successful demi-idol fan following and spawn imitations by other reverse cover groups, such as in Thailand, Malaysia and the Philippines, demonstrates a dislocation from Korean K-pop. These examples of decentering are particularly productive for imagining new queer practices, categories and configurations for fans who actively consume BL and K-pop. Granted, because BL and K-pop typically target cis-heterosexual women as their main consumers, such media can still operate to obscure and exclude LGBTQ individuals. However, it can be argued that despite this, fans' consumption – which depends on what they themselves make out of BL and K-pop – nevertheless functions to empower them in diverse and unexpected ways.

Future directions in research can include consumption, appropriation and inter-Asia queer flows of K-pop and BL media by LGBTQ fans in different parts of Asia. For instance, Japanese anime and manga first entered the Indian market in the 2000s and appeal to young Indian audiences (Bryce et al. 2010). As the popularity of Japanese anime and manga continues to grow in India, it would be necessary to study Indian gender and sexual minorities' fandom of BL media, including fanfic and art – a subject on which little has been written. More attention can also be paid to the flows of indigenous forms of popular culture arising from other parts of Asia. For example, since the mid-2010s, Q-pop (Qazaq pop), referring to Kazakhstani popular music that draws influences from K-pop and Western music, has arrived in the international pop music scene. Q-pop is characterized by "energetic music, combining different genres, a vivid style in clothes and defiant behavior," epitomized by Ninety One, a boy band comprising five young men clad in bright clothes with makeup, pierced ears and dyed hair, who rap, dance and sing songs in a "modern style in the Kazakh language" on the subject of love (Danabayev and Park 2020: 95–6). Unlike Wonder Gay, Ninety One is further removed from K-pop and yet still draws inspiration from the latter, but what they do have in common are domestic and international fan followings in their own right. Ninety One's fans hail from various countries including Korea, Uzbekistan, the USA and Latin America (Danabayev and Park 2020). Given this background, it would be interesting to observe inter-Asia and transnational queer fandoms of Q-pop including fans' queer readings and consumption of Q-pop idols.

References

Baudinette, T. (2020) "Creative Misreadings of 'Thai BL' by a Filipino Fan Community," *Mechademia: Second Arc*, 13(1): 101–18.

Bauwens-Sugimoto, J. (2011) "Subverting Masculinity, Misogyny and Reproductive Technology in Sex Pistols," *Image & Narrative*, 12(1).

Blackwood, E. (2005) "Transnational Sexualities in One Place," *Gender & Society*, 19(2): 221–42.

Bryce, M., Barber, C., Kelly, J., Kunwar, S. and Plumb, A. (2010) "Manga and Anime: Fluidity and Hybridity in Global Imagery," *Electronic Journal of Contemporary Japanese Studies*, 10(1).

Chao, Y.A. (2001) "Drink, Stories, Penis and Breasts: Lesbian Tomboys in Taiwan from the 1960s to the 1990s," *Journal of Homosexuality*, 40(3–4): 185–209.

Chen, K.H. (2010) *Asia as Method: Toward Deimperialization*, Durham: Duke University Press.

Chiang, H., Henry, T. and Leung, H. (2018) "Trans-in-Asia, Asia-in-Trans," *Transgender Studies Quarterly*, 5(3): 298–310.

Chiang, H. and Wong, A.K. (2017) "Asia is Burning: Queer Asia as Critique," *Culture, Theory and Critique*, 58(2): 121–6.

Chua, B.H. and Iwabuchi, K. (2008) *East Asian Pop Culture: Analysing the Korean Wave*, Hong Kong: Hong Kong University Press.

Danabayev, K. and Park, J. (2020) "Q-pop as a Phenomenon to Enhance New Nationalism in Post-Soviet Kazakhstan," *Asia Review*, 9(2): 85–129.

Doty, A. (1993) *Making Things Perfectly Queer*, Minneapolis: University of Minnesota Press.

Fermin, T.A.S. (2013) "Appropriating Yaoi and Boys Love in the Philippines: Conflict, Resistance and Imaginations through and beyond Japan," *Electronic Journal of Contemporary Japanese Studies*, 13(3).

Fermin, T.A.S. (2014) *Uncovering Hidden Transcripts of Resistance of Yaoi and Boys Love Fans in Indonesia, Singapore and the Philippines*, Ph.D. Thesis, Osaka: Osaka University.

Fujimoto, Y., Flores, L., Nagaike, K. and Orbaugh, S. (2004) "Transgender: Female Hermaphrodites and Male Androgynes," *US-Japan Women's Journal*, 27: 76–117.

Grewal, I. and Kaplan, C. (2001) "Global Identities: Theorizing Transnational Studies of Sexuality," *GLQ*, 7(4): 663–79.

Guevarra, A.U. (2014) "Creating a Safe Space for Queer Teens?," *AIKS Korean Studies Conference Proceedings*, 1: 102–19.

Halberstam, J. (1998) *Female Masculinity*, Durham: Duke University Press.

Hemmings, C. (2007) "What's in a Name? Bisexuality, Transnational Sexuality Studies and Western Colonial Legacies," *International Journal of Human Rights*, 11(1–2): 13–32.

Iwabuchi, K. (2002) *Recentering Globalization: Popular Culture and Japanese Transnationalism*, Durham: Duke University Press.

Iwabuchi, K. (2014) "De-Westernisation, Inter-Asian Referencing and Beyond," *European Journal of Cultural Studies*, 17(1): 44–57.

Jin, D.Y. (2016) *New Korean Wave: Transnational Cultural Power in the Age of Social Media*, Urbana-Champaign: University of Illinois Press.

Jirattikorn, A. (2018) "Thai Popular Culture: A New Player in Asia Media Circulation and Chinese Censorship," a paper in Center for Southeast Asian Studies, Kyoto: Kyoto University.

Johnson, M., Jackson, P. and Herdt, G. (2000) "Critical Regionalities and the Study of Gender and Sexual Diversity in South East and East Asia," *Culture, Health & Sexuality*, 2(4): 361–75.

Jung, S. (2010) "Chogukjeok Pan-East Asian Soft Masculinity," in D. Black, S. Epstein and A. Tokita (eds) *Complicated Currents: Media Flows, Soft Power and East Asia*, Melbourne: Monash University ePress.

Jung, S. (2011) "K-pop, Indonesian Fandom and Social Media," *Transformative Works and Cultures*, 8(1).

Kang, D.B.C. (2014) "Idols of Development," *TSQ: Transgender Studies Quarterly*, 1(4): 449–571.

Kang, D.B.C. (2015) "Cultivating Demi-Idols," in N.C. Schneider and C. Richter (eds) *New Media Configurations and Socio-Cultural Dynamics in Asia and the Arab World*, Baden-Baden: Nomos.

Kang, D.B.C. (2018) "Surfing the Korean Wave: Wonder Gays and the Crisis of Thai Masculinity," *Visual Anthropology*, 31(1–2): 45–65.

Kang-Nguyen, D.B.C. (2019) "The Softening of Butches," in S. Lee, M. Mehta and R. Ku (eds) *Pop Empires: Transnational and Diasporic Flows of India and Korea*, Honolulu: Hawaii University Press.

Kaplan, C. and Grewal, I. (1999) "Transnational Feminist Cultural Studies," in C. Kaplan, N. Alarcón and M. Moallem (eds) *Between Woman and Nation: Nationalisms, Transnational Feminisms and the State*, Durham: Duke University Press.

Keenapan, N. (2001) "Japanese 'Boy-Love' Comics a Hit among Thais," *Kyodo News*, 31 August.

Kim, Y. (2008) *Media Consumption and Everyday Life in Asia*, London: Routledge.

Kim, Y. (2013) *The Korean Wave: Korean Media Go Global*, London: Routledge.

Kuo, L., Perez-Garcia, S., Burke, L., Yamasaki, V. and Le, T. (2022) "Performance, Fantasy or Narrative: LGBTQ+ Asian American Identity through K-pop Media and Fandom," *Journal of Homosexuality*, 69(1): 145–68.

Kwon, J. (2019) *Straight Korean Female Fans and their Gay Fantasies*, Iowa City: University of Iowa Press.

Laurie, T. (2016) "Toward a Gendered Aesthetics of K-pop," in I. Chapman and H. Johnson (eds) *Global Glam and Popular Music*, New York: Routledge.

Lavin, M. (2015) "Tomboy in Love: Korean and US Views of Heterosexual Eroticism in the K-drama First Shop of Coffee Prince," *Situations*, 8(1): 45–69.

Lavin, M., Yang, L. and Zhao, J. (2017) *Boys' Love, Cosplay and Androgynous Idols: Queer Fan Cultures in Mainland China*, Hong Kong: Hong Kong University Press.

Levi, A. (2008) "Introduction," in A. Levi, D. Pagliassotti and M. McHarry (eds) *Boys' Love Manga: Essays on the Sexual Ambiguity and Cross-Cultural Fandom of the Genre*, Jefferson: McFarland.

Lie, J. (2015) *K-pop: Popular Music, Cultural Amnesia and Economic Innovation in South Korea*, Berkeley: University of California Press.

Lunsing, W. (2006) "Yaoi Ronsō: Discussing Depictions of Male Homosexuality in Japanese Girls' Comics, Gay Comics and Gay Pornography," *Intersections: Gender and Sexuality in Asia and the Pacific*, 12.

Martin, F. (2012) "Girls Who Love Boys' Love: Japanese Homoerotic Manga as Trans-National Taiwan Culture," *Inter-Asia Cultural Studies*, 13(3): 365–83.

Martin, F., Jackson, J., McLelland, M. and Yue, A. (2008) *AsiaPacifiQueer: Rethinking Genders and Sexualities*, Urbana-Champaign: University of Illinois Press.

McLelland, M. (2001) "Why are Japanese Girls' Comics Full of Boys Bonking?," *Intensities: The Journal of Cult Media*, 1.

McLelland, M. and Welker, J. (2015) "An Introduction to 'Boys Love' in Japan," in M. McLelland, K. Nagaike, K. Suganuma and J. Welker (eds) *Boys Love Manga and Beyond: History, Culture and Community in Japan*, Jackson: University of Mississippi Press.

Meyer, U. (2008) "Hidden in Straight Sight," in A. Levi, D. Pagliassotti and M. McHarry (eds) *Boys' Love Manga: Essays on the Sexual Ambiguity and Cross-Cultural Fandom of the Genre*, Jefferson: McFarland.

Mizoguchi, A. (2003) "Male-Male Romance by and for Women in Japan," *US-Japan Women's Journal*, 25: 49–75.

Nagaike, K. (2012) *Fantasies of Cross-Dressing: Japanese Women Write Male-Male Erotica*, Leiden: Brill.

Nagaike, K. and Suganuma, K. (2013) "Transnational Boys' Love Fan Studies," *Transformative Works and Cultures*, 12.

Nagar, R. and Swarr, A. (2010) "Theorizing Transnational Feminist Praxis," in A. Swarr and R. Nagar (eds) *Critical Transnational Feminist Praxis*, Albany: SUNY Press.

Nugroho, J. (2020) "Thailand's Erotic Boys Love TV Dramas are a Hit with Indonesians Both Gay and Straight," *South China Morning Post*, 11 October.

Oh, C. (2015) "Queering Spectatorship in K-pop," *Journal of Fandom Studies*, 3(1): 59–78.

Oh, C. and Oh, D.C. (2017) "Unmasking Queerness," *Journal of Popular Culture*, 50(1): 9–29.

Sedgwick, E. (1994) *Tendencies*, New York: Routledge.

Shim, D. (2006) "Hybridity and the Rise of Korean Popular Culture in Asia," *Media, Culture and Society*, 28(1): 25–44.

Shin, L. (2018) "Queer Eye for K-pop Fandom," *Korea Journal*, 58(4): 87–113.

Sinnott, M. (2012) "Korean-Pop, Tom Gay Kings, Les Queens and the Capitalist Transformation of Sex/Gender Categories in Thailand," *Asian Studies Review*, 36(4): 453–74.

Welker, J. (2006) "Beautiful, Borrowed and Bent: 'Boys' Love' as Girls' Love in Shōjo Manga," *Signs*, 31(3): 841–70.

Wood, A. (2006) "Straight Women, Queer Texts: Boy-Love Manga and the Rise of a Global Counterpublic," *Women's Studies Quarterly*, 34(1–2): 394–414.

Yang, L. and Xu, Y. (2017) "Chinese Danmei Fandom and Cultural Globalization from Below," in M. Lavin, L. Yang and J. Zhao (eds) *Boys' Love, Cosplay and Androgynous Idols: Queer Fan Cultures in Mainland China*, Hong Kong: Hong Kong University Press.

Yoon, K. (2017) "Postcolonial Production and Consumption of Global K-pop," in T.J. Yoon and D.Y. Jin (eds) *The Korean Wave: Evolution, Fandom and Transnationality*, Lanham: Rowman & Littlefield.

Yue, A. (2017) "Trans-Singapore: Some Notes Towards Queer Asia as Method," *Inter-Asia Cultural Studies*, 18(1): 10–24.

15

CRIPPLED WARRIORS

Masculinities and Martial Arts Media in Asia

Luke White

This chapter explores a body of martial arts filmmaking and its intersection with complex masculinities, gender and colonial histories in Asia. The chapter starts with a film released close to the present in a former British colony: It is one which pays extensive homage to the kung fu genre. Surya, the hero of the Hindi action comedy film *The Man Who Feels No Pain* (2018, India, dir. Vasan Bala), is born with congenital analgesia, and while this constitutes a kind of superpower, the film also emphasizes, from the outset, that this is a dangerous medical condition. Surya's neurotic father locks him away from the hazards of the world, but under the guidance of his grandfather, an idealistic but impractical fantasist, he attempts to learn about it by watching old VHS tapes of kung fu movies. It is through these that his sense of identity and his idea of reality and the proper way to act in it are formed, along with his ability to fight injustice through martial arts movements imitated from the on-screen antics of role models such as Bruce Lee. The intertwining of the film's nostalgic depiction of its Mumbai setting with Surya's imitation of Hong Kong media might remind us of the intensely transnational nature of Asian action cinema, both as consumed and as produced, and of the images that circulate across it. Echoing its protagonist's obsessions, the film's narrative and its action sequences are constructed through a loving pastiche of movie tropes from Hollywood, Bollywood and – above all – Hong Kong.

It might also remind us of the importance of the "kung fu craze" in the 1970s in molding the pan-Asian and transnational landscape of popular media on which the film draws. In an era of anticolonial unrest across the world, the global stardom of figures such as Bruce Lee seemed for a brief while to reverse the dominance of Hollywood, offering affirmative images of Asia on the world's stage. The kung fu craze did not just entail Hong Kong cinema breaking into the American and European markets, but also across Asia, Africa, the Middle East and Latin America. Fore-echoing Surya's enthusiasms, the cultural theorist

DOI: 10.4324/9781003130628-19

Vijay Prashad has written of his youth in Calcutta in 1974 as a Marxist and anti-imperialist activist, and of a Bruce Lee poster that adorned his bedroom wall as an icon of Asian pride and proof that "we, like the Vietnamese, could be victorious against the virulence of international capitalism" (Prashad 2001: 127). For people across Asia and its diasporas, Lee was "the brother who showed Asians can kick some ass" (Pang 1991: 44, quoted in Prashad 2001: 140). Since then, of course, martial arts have become a highly visible aspect of Asian popular cinemas – a part of the "brand" as it were. We are now faced not only with Chinese stars such as Bruce Lee, Jackie Chan, Jet Li and Donnie Yen, or equivalents from Japan (Sonny Chiba or Estuko Shihomi), but also, for example, Thailand (Tony Jaa), Indonesia (Iko Uwais) and India (Vidyut Jammwal).

In this chapter, my focus in thinking about this phenomenon will be the question of how masculinity is at stake within it. Many writers (Hunt 2003: 117–39; Lo 2010: 107–40; Funnell 2014; Yip 2017: 115–44) have also discussed kung fu cinema in terms of representations of fighting women, and there is certainly a strong tradition of female martial arts stars. However, my focus here will be the ways that the kung fu phenomenon entailed transformations in Chinese or Asian experiences of masculinity. This issue is evident in the example with which I started this chapter. Highlighting the link of its thematic concerns to manliness, the title *The Man Who Feels No Pain* was drawn from a line in the Hindi blockbuster *Macho* (1985, India, dir. Manmohan Desai) (see Dalton 2018), and in the film's trailer, Surya, outlining its premise to the camera, explains, "You must have heard … Men feel no pain. That is my disease."

The Man Who Feels No Pain is also a useful example for my purposes here in that it allows me to introduce the motif, which it draws from innumerable martial arts films, of the crippled or impaired martial artist. Surya's analgesia is itself such a disability, but even his identification with the hyperathletic Bruce

FIGURE 15.1 The one-legged "Karate Man" (Gulshan Devaiah) of *The Man Who Feels No Pain*.

Lee is marked by the (probably apocryphal) fact, which he brings up in his voiceover, of the star's childhood epilepsy. Furthermore, Surya idolizes a one-legged Mumbai karate practitioner, Mani Kamraj (aka Karate Man), who he watches on video emerging victorious from a hundred-man tournament. The comical hopping karate that Mani performs is clearly a joke on classic martial arts movies featuring amputee heroes such as *The One-Armed Swordsman* (1967, HK, dir. Chang Cheh) or *One Armed Boxer* (1971, HK, dir. Wang Yu). As this chapter unfolds, I shall return to the recurrence of such images of impairment throughout the history of kung fu cinema in order to explore the ways that it has registered the anxieties of masculinity and of Asian masculinities in particular.

"Staunch Masculinity": The Rise of the Hong Kong Martial Arts Film

To begin this task, it seems important to trace the rise of kung fu cinema and the ways that this entailed changes in the balance of gender in the Hong Kong industry. The roots of Chinese martial arts filmmaking lie in Shanghai's silent era. The 1920s saw an explosion of *wuxia* (swordplay) movies, in part setting out to rival American swashbucklers and in part showcasing the local performance traditions of Beijing opera acrobatics and martial arts (Teo 2009: 6–11). The popularity of the genre was such that between 1828 and 1931, when it was banned by the Nationalist government, a staggering 250 martial arts pictures were made, constituting 60% of the industry's output (Desser 2000: 31). With the Japanese occupation, the civil war that followed, and the communist takeover of the mainland, cinematic production shifted to the British colony of Hong Kong. Though denied access to the strictly censored screens of the mainland, Hong Kong moguls sought to build not just a local entertainment empire, but one that spanned the Chinese diaspora across East Asia and Southeast Asia. The studio that was particularly effective in this, and which soon came to dominate Mandarin-language cinema, was Shaw Brothers, who churned out lavish and colorful pictures in their vast studios at a level of technical production beyond the reach of their competitors, often drawing on expertise from the neighboring industries in Japan and South Korea (Fu 2008).

However, during the late 1950s and early 1960s, martial arts and action pictures played a relatively marginal place in Shaw's formula, which focused instead on musicals, romance and opera adaptations in the Huangmei style that was popular in Taiwan, Shaw's most lucrative market. Hong Kong's star system was centered primarily around female rather than male leads, and this was even the case in many of the swordplays of the era, to the extent that actresses would be cast in drag to play the male hero of a film. Audiences would flock, for example, to see Connie Chan and Josephine Siao play alongside each other, the former usually taking the role of the male lead and the latter his love interest or "martial sister," a swashbuckling heroine.

This would change with the announcement in the October 1965 issue of Shaw's publicity magazine *Southern Screen* of a "new action era" and a "new *wuxia* century." The article promised a newly gritty martial arts cinema, which would put fighting front and center, amp up the level of violence and reduce the dance-like "theatricality" of opera-influenced combat in favor of a new "realism" (Gravestock 2006). Driving this agenda was the critic and screenwriter Chang Cheh, who Shaw's executive had taken on as an advisor and who would soon become one of the foremost directors of Shaw's new brand of ultraviolent martial arts movies and one of the progenitors of the kung fu genre itself as it arose in the early 1970s.

Chang's vision for the new action era revolved around a transformation in gender roles in Hong Kong cinema. Chang saw the local industry as being out of step with broader global trends, and he considered that in order to compete both at home and abroad, studios such as Shaw Brothers would have to modernize. Japanese samurai movies and American Westerns – both globally popular genres offering strong competition in Shaw's markets – revolved around toughly masculine stars. Hong Kong, Chang argued, would have to follow suit. He thus promoted a program of what he called *yanggang* – "staunch masculinity" – in the new action era, seeking to cultivate a stable of youthful, handsome, muscular and rugged male leads (Teo 2007: 93–7). The actor that Chang initially chose for his own pictures was Jimmy Wang Yu, a champion swimmer who had only a modicum of martial arts training but, thought Chang, looked good holding a sword (Hunt 2003: 23). Wang Yu's athletic torso was frequently displayed in shirtless scenes, and he provided the blueprint for a wave of young martial arts stars such as Lo Lieh, Chen Kuan-Tai, Ti Lung and, of course, Bruce Lee, who rose to prominence with *The Big Boss* (1971, HK, dir. Lo Wei).

Kung Fu Masculinity, Orientalism and the Global Context

To make sense of the ways that Hong Kong cinema's images of martial masculinity were new, and to make better sense of them, we need to place them within their broader contexts. The first of these that I will address is the global field of representations and ideas of identity. Kung fu films arose in a transnational media landscape dominated, of course, by Hollywood. Moreover, in the longer term, European and American cultures had long-held sway across the world, their hegemony rooted in the imperial and colonial projects of the 18th and 19th centuries, which established material power in political, economic and military terms. As a result, it was Westerners who were able to define the ground of "modernity" in their own image and to set the norms and standards by which other cultures should be measured – and by which the modernizing and Westernizing elites of many Asian countries often sought to measure and understand themselves.

Literary critic Edward Said (1978) famously named the discourse through which this dominant Western gaze defined and came to know and control its

FIGURE 15.2 An "excess" of masculinity? Bruce Lee flexes his muscles in *Way of the Dragon.*

non-Western others — and to justify their subjugation — "Orientalism." Orientalist discourse was deeply gendered, defining the West as normatively active and masculine in opposition to a fantasied passive and feminine Orient. Within the hierarchies of race set up by White culture, Chinese men were accorded a particular place. Asian males more generally were imagined as feminized (Loomba 2015: 154), in contrast both to ideas of Black men as primitive and hypermasculine and to an ideal White masculinity understood as virile yet controlled by reason (Dyer 2017). Chinese men in Western media, before the 1970s kung fu craze, were imagined through two opposing archetypes encapsulated by two popular screen characters — first, the perverse and sadistic Fu Manchu, evocative of "yellow peril" anxieties and second, the subservient, emasculated and unthreatening "model minority" Charlie Chan. Above all else, the scintillating muscularity and heroism of stars such as Wang Yu and Bruce Lee were a rejoinder to these stereotypes, offering new and glamorous images of Chinese and Asian muscularity on the world stage and on the territory laid out by the West and its cultural models. As Kwai-Cheung Lo (2010: 107–11) has argued, with Asian masculinity defined in terms of "lack," Hong Kong cinema offered us, as a rejoinder, the spectacle of its potential for troubling "excess," replaying Hollywood tropes of violence and muscularity in the register of hyperbole.

Chinese Masculinities: *Wen* and *Wu*

Masculinity, of course, is not cut of a single cloth, but is plural and is constructed differently across time and space, and according to a multitude of factors such as class, ethnicity and sexuality (Connell 2005). Thus, the picture of the gendering of Hong Kong cinema's martial arts stars is made more complicated when we approach it from the perspective of the specific history of Chinese masculinities and the ways that these have interacted with the Western models discussed above.

As Kam Louie and Louise Edwards (1994) have argued, traditional conceptions of masculinity in China present two systematically opposite versions – the
scholarly (*wen*) and the martial (*wu*). In late imperial China, it was the scholarly
version that was privileged; rather than constituting a warrior caste, the ruling
elite was defined by the education necessary for success in the civil service exam-
inations and thus a post in government. Furthermore, when we think about
the *wen/wu* distinction in the familiar terms of yin and yang (with yin usually
understood as embodying the feminine principle and yang the masculine), it
is the scholar, posited around the transcendent principles of reason and order,
who most closely represents the "yang" pole, rather than the warrior, associated instead with the "yin" qualities of the body and with all the disorder that
comes with violence. While China's literary warriors are tough and rugged in
ways more recognizable in the West as "masculine," it is notable that they are
usually imagined as somewhat asexual and less concerned with romantic love
than the homosocial bonding of martial brotherhood – which would, of course,
develop as a core theme in the movies of Chang Cheh (Yip 2017: 85). Instead, it
is the delicate and refined scholar, sensitive though often passive and bumbling,
who is the focus of love stories and who ultimately represents a "sexy" version
of masculinity (Louie and Edwards 1994: 146–7). A prime example of such a
scholar hero from Hong Kong cinema is Leslie Cheung's role as the hapless but
good-hearted tax collector who falls in love with a ghost in the romantic horror
comedy *A Chinese Ghost Story* (1987, HK, dir. Ching Siu-Tung). The androgynous Cheung himself was voted "Asia's Biggest Superstar" in the 2000 CCTV/
MTV music awards in mainland China (Chan 2000) and was named "The Most

FIGURE 15.3 A striking contrast to Bruce Lee: Heartthrob Leslie Cheung's "soft,"
scholarly masculinity in *A Chinese Ghost Story*.

Beautiful Man in Hong Kong Cinema" by CNN (Yan 2018). These facts should remind us that the martial masculinities discussed here are only one half of the story. Similar "scholar" masculinities are, of course, influential in the broader rise of what Sun Jung (2009) has discussed as the "soft masculinities" that span contemporary East Asian popular culture, from the *bishōnen* aesthetic in manga through to K-pop boy bands and *danmei* ("indulging [male] beauty") dramas in China.

If these seem to offer a striking contrast to the martial masculinity of Bruce Lee and his ilk, their rise to global prominence is, perhaps, nonetheless unthinkable without the ways that kung fu stars had previously redefined Asian men as objects of desire and emulation. Establishing this required an amalgamation of Western and Chinese codes of masculinity, and in terms of the latter a revaluation of its martial variant.

In Hong Kong itself, this reprivileging of martial masculinities was also a matter of class. Louie and Edwards (1994: 146) note that though the opposition of *wen* and *wu* cannot simply be ahistorically mapped onto the division between elite/lower socioeconomic groups, nonetheless at various junctures where *wen* was inaccessible to the socially inferior, *wu* became their primary path to masculinity. Avron Boretz (2010), for example, has made an ethnographic study of how this is the case today among some of the most marginal social groups in Taiwan and China.

Furthermore, Man-Fung Yip (2017: 31) has noted how the conditions of Hong Kong in the 1960s and 1970s as a burgeoning manufacturing economy reliant on unskilled workers meant that for many men their laboring bodies were the source of their economic power and thus their masculinity. For Yip, kung fu cinema's images of the martial body as a source of power chimed with the corporeal nature of this experience. They offered an affirmation of the power of such laboring male bodies in terms of *wu*. Through cinematic fantasies of heroism, these were imagined in terms of "liberated labor," disavowing the actual conditions of exploitation which factory work entailed. The working-class heroes of kung fu pictures with modern-day settings such as *The Big Boss* and *Way of the Dragon* (1973, HK, dir. Bruce Lee) and the more general tendency of even historical movies such as *The One-Armed Swordsman* to focus on rebels and outsiders cement this association between the body in kung fu cinema and the laboring men who formed its core audience.

Kung Fu, Physical Culture and Modernity

Beyond the cinema, these new images of Chinese manhood also had their context within 20th-century discourses on the role of physical culture within the modern nation-state, and in particular the place of the martial arts within these.

China had suffered a tumultuous 19th century, witnessing the gradual collapse of the Qing dynasty, which had ruled since 1644. After centuries in which China had been a world power both economically and militarily, challenges from the West – in particular in the form of the Opium Wars (1839–60) and the "unequal treaties" enacted in their wake – had left China militarily humiliated and subject to a form of semicolonialism. China was also beaten in the Sino-Japanese War of 1894–5. A collapsing economy further undermined the "mandate of heaven" of the Qing, leading to a period in which civil war and rebellion were rife. Failures to institute adequate reforms led to the final fall of the dynasty and the institution of republican government in 1911.

Within the new republic, the question of the ways that China should "modernize" and "Westernize" in order to compete within the cut-throat world of international commerce, politics and war – but also how to retain culture and identity in the face of this modernization – were taken up as urgent ones. As Andrew Morris (2004) has argued, sporting or physical cultures – and within these the martial arts – constituted a prominent domain within which these debates were played out. Joseph Alter notes in his foreword to Morris's book that these debates were part of a broader discourse on health, physical culture and the nation-state that swept the world in the late 19th and early 20th centuries, from ideas of "muscular Christianity" to the cult of the body in Nazi Germany. Governments and reformers across the globe – whether involved with imperial projects or bolstering the nationalism that might resist these – concerned themselves with the strengthening of individual physiques as a means to fortify the body politic. Comparing the Chinese experience with that of Indian wrestling, Alter argues that across the colonized world this entailed the "gendered anxiety of empire itself," with exercise serving as a "mechanism for transforming effete self-serving subjects into manly citizens with a single, common purpose" (Morris 2004: xvii).

In China, it was Western calisthenics and sports – with their "scientific" credentials – which initially dominated, and local martial arts were looked on with suspicion as backward and superstitious, a part of what held China back from modernity rather than something that might help in the modernizing task (Morris 2004: 17). However, by the 1920s, modernized and rationalized versions of the martial arts were increasingly being located at the heart of China's physical culture (ibid.: 185–229). The success of Japan in building a technologically and militarily advanced society, able to go toe to toe with Western competitors, meant that its example was taken as a blueprint here (ibid.: 130–31). Japan had leveraged the mythology of the samurai to bolster a militarist ethos, and its transformation of its traditional fighting arts into modernized and sporting versions such as judo or jujitsu had made them successful exports across the world. With this example in mind, Chinese reformers recognized that the martial arts had the advantage of allowing the assertion of an image of the nation having within itself a source of health, strength and power, rather than relying on something alien. By the end of the decade, the officially recognized term for Chinese combat systems was *guoshu* – "national arts" (ibid.: 220). Within the increasingly militaristic terms of the Nationalist government, they also had the virtue of being explicitly arts of war, with fitness culture increasingly tied to the creation of a muscular, drilled and disciplined body of – implicitly male – workers and soldiers, ready for mobilization (ibid.: 223). Though fitness movements often included women as a part of their progressive credentials, it was increasingly the bodies of men which were its fundamental stake (ibid.: 86–95). Within the Orientalizing Western optic which structured these reform debates, the more traditional ideals of *wen* and the ruling scholar classes who embodied them looked problematically effeminate, and their lack of *wu* masculinity was seen as a reason for imperial China's political and economic weakness and collapse.

The closeness of this link between health, masculinity and the nation is evidenced in the famous phrase, probably first coined by Yan Fu in 1895 and taken up by a generation of reforming intellectuals in his wake, naming China *dongya bingfu* – "the sick man of East Asia." Echoing Orientalist imagery, it defined the nation in terms of decrepitude, impotence and lack of masculine virtue.

These themes and histories would be taken up in the kung fu craze and the images of the masculine body that it entailed. They are perhaps most explicitly and directly imagined in Bruce Lee's *Fist of Fury* (1972, HK, dir. Lo Wei), set in 1910 in the foreign-occupied Shanghai International Settlement, in the wake of the death of Huo Yuanjia, one of the real-life pioneers of the patriotic martial arts reform movement discussed above. Lee plays Chen Zhen, a fictional student of Huo who has returned home to mourn the death of his teacher, which turns out to be due to poison at the hand of Japanese antagonists. In an early scene, these Japanese enemies crash Huo's funeral and "gift" his school a calligraphic sign with the words "Sick Men of East Asia" on it, an insult not just to their national pride but also to their masculinity. Reclaiming both of these things, Lee visits the Japanese dojo, takes off his shirt to reveal his ripped muscular physique, and single-handedly beats and subdues the whole of the school, forcing its senior students, literally, to eat the paper on which their insult was written. "Now you listen to me, I'll say this only once," he tells them. "We are not sick men!"

Crippled Kung Fu

The images in *The Man Who Feels No Pain* of illness and disability, associated as they remain with the martial artist's body, make their sense precisely in relation to this longer and deeper concern with a relation between kung fu, health and manliness. This is to say, of course, that Surya and Mani are, rather literally, "sick men of Asia." They are also far from alone in this within the realm of contemporary martial arts cinema and media (from both Asia and the West). In the Netflix series *Marco Polo* (2014–16), Marco is taught martial arts by the blind Wudang swordsman Hundred Eyes (whose backstory is told in a standalone Christmas special). In the Star Wars spinoff *Rogue One* (2016, USA, dir. Gareth Edwards), Donnie Yen plays a similarly blind, monk-like character, Chirrut Imwe. Zhang Ziyi spent months living with an unsighted woman to prepare for her role as Xiao Mei in *House of Flying Daggers* (2004, China, dir. Zhang Yimou). In the film *Dragon* (2011, HK, dir. Peter Chan), Liu Jinxi (Donnie Yen) severs his arm to break ties with the criminal gang he was a part of but is nonetheless forced to fight its boss one-handed. That the role of this villain is taken up by Wang Yu, the original "One-Armed Swordsman," underlines the relation to the classic film of that name, which, quite aside from the innumerable sequels and reboots of the 1970s, was also remade by Tsui Hark as *The Blade* (1995, HK). In *Shaolin Soccer* (2001, HK, dir. Stephen Chow), Ng Man-Tat plays an ex-soccer star whose leg was crippled by rampaging fans after he deliberately threw a match. He seeks redemption by coaching a new squad of kung fu-enhanced players. The list would rapidly expand if we were to include mental as well as physical impairments, such as the autism of Zen (Jeeja Yanin) in *Chocolate* (2008, Thailand, dir. Prachya Pinkaew) or the madness and alcoholism of Su Can (Vincent Zhao) in *True Legend* (2010, China/HK, dir. Yuen Woo-Ping). In all these examples, the image of the sick or deficient body seems to haunt the ideals of masculine perfection and strength upon which martial arts cinema is so strongly premised, insistently returning like a Freudian symptom.

The trope has its roots in the newly violent martial arts cinema of the 1960s and 1970s, not only in Hong Kong but across East Asia. Above all, it was established in the hugely popular series of films featuring Zatoichi (played by Shintaro Katsu), a blind master swordsman who wanders the landscape of 19th-century Japan in the disguise of a lowly masseur, protecting the weak and innocent against gangsters and officials who seek to exploit them. Between 1962 and 1973 some 25 Zatoichi movies were made, followed by a TV series that ran from 1974 to 1979. Zatoichi's enduring appeal is evidenced by the resurrection of the character, this time played by Takeshi "Beat" Kitano, in *Zatoichi* (2003, Japan, dir. Takeshi Kitano). This was followed by *Ichi* (2008, Japan, dir. Fumihiko Sori), which featured a blind swordswoman who was once rescued by Zatoichi, now searching for her mentor. Two years later, *Zatoichi: The Last* (2010, Japan, dir. Junji Sakamoto) sought to provide the saga an ending.

In the 1960s, this series was not just popular in Japan but also across East Asia and was rapidly imitated by filmmakers there. The publicity for Taiwan's *Three Blind Spies* (1965, dir. Chin Han) made explicit comparison to Zatoichi (Yip 2107: 169). Though the influence of Japanese cinema was probably indirect in the case of South Korea, *Returned One-Legged Man* (1974, dir. Lee Doo-Yong) was just one of a spate of films made there featuring impaired heroes. Its motif of a leg injury had special resonance with regard to the importance of kicking in Korea's iconic national martial art, taekwondo (Yip 2017: 170).

Zatoichi, furthermore, was a key reference for the genre-defining "new action era" *wuxia* film *The One-Armed Swordsman*, which launched the martial arts craze in earnest by becoming the first Hong Kong film to bank $1 million at the box office, in 1967. This tells the story of Fang Kang (Wang Yu), whose father, a servant, dies defending the life of his master, the upright swordsman Qi Rufeng. Qi adopts the child but his other, more privileged, students bully Fang as an outsider, and he ultimately has his arm chopped off by Qi's daughter. He restores his broken sense of masculine self-worth by training in a special style of left-handed swordsmanship he learns from a partially destroyed manuscript given to him by his savior, a kindly peasant girl. His father's broken sword (the only heirloom he possesses) turns out to be peculiarly effective in performing this. The manual and sword each serve as analogues of Fang's amputation and reinforce the Freudian metaphor of castration. However, of course, what seem to be disadvantages are turned into advantage when Fang comes to the rescue of his master against the same villain who had killed Fang's father and who has in the meantime developed a special weapon and style of fighting designed to trap and defeat Qi's "Golden Sword" technique. In his final victory, it is not only the emasculation caused by his amputation that is reversed but also that of his lowly birth and lack of paternal legacy.

In the wake of *The One-Armed Swordsman*, impaired heroes and heroines proliferated – in, for example, *The One-Armed Magic Nun* (1969, HK, dir. Chan Lit-Ban), *Deaf and Mute Heroine* (1971, HK, dir. Wu Ma), *Vengeance of a Snowgirl* (1971, HK, dir. Lo Wei), or, once the kung fu craze appeared, *One Armed Boxer* and its sequel *Master of the Flying Guillotine* (1976, HK/Taiwan, dir. Wang Yu). *One Armed Boxer* returned to the nationalist dimension of the discourse on martial masculinity, setting its hero against Japanese antagonists. Chang Cheh's *Crippled Avengers* (1978, HK) features not one but four protagonists who are variously maimed by the film's tyrannical villain, before being trained in kung fu in order to overcome their disabilities and seek justice. In the kung fu comedy era of the late 1970s, such images of impairment exploded with films such as *Dance of the Drunk Mantis* (1979, HK, dir. Yuen Woo-Ping), which includes a specially deadly "sickness kung fu," or *Drunken Arts and Crippled Fist* (1979, HK, dir. Ti Tang). I have argued elsewhere (White 2020: 30–58) that such images take their place here within a general "carnival" aesthetic that rejected the purity and order of the early 20th-century nationalist visions of the martial body, and perhaps its more "fascist" or militant modes of masculinity too, for a more anarchic ethos of excess and play.

Yip (2017: 170–4), in any case, traces the origin and meaning of the motif of the impaired martial artist in the broader trauma of Asian social and political experiences of the 20th century. There are specific national circumstances that inflect this trauma – the atomic bomb, American occupation and a feeling of alienation among the young in Japan; the increasing distance from China of Hong Kong identity and the experience of capitalist exploitation within its sweatshops; and the split of Korea into two warring nations. However, overall, we might well read in the way that such images resonated across a range of contexts – including, of course, the contemporary India of *The Man Who Feels No Pain* – a shared Asian experience with roots in the encounter with the imperial projects of the West. For Yip (2017: 172), disability becomes a tangible sign for a "sense of lack and disenfranchisement," while the fact "that this handicapped character is also a superb fighter no doubt also signals a desire to be healed and restrengthened." While Yip's interpretation foregrounds national or local identities, these are, of course, closely intertwined with gender, and the "lack" he points to is also the emasculation brought about through imperial domination and the hegemony of Orientalist discourses on "Asian masculinity." Although the twist is that illness has now paradoxically become a source of power, rather than something to be eliminated to achieve it, the transcendence of the sick and disempowered body in these films is similar to that commonly promised in early 20th-century martial arts manuals, which often began with a foreword telling the story of the author's own transformation from sickly youth to vigorous martial master (Cheng 1985: 9).

Indeed, the crippled fighters discussed here share a lot with the women warriors discussed by Kwai-Cheung Lo (2010: 107–40): Lo notes that the most "stable" and privileged masculinities are usually reserved for the villains of Hong Kong movies. The woman warrior and the impaired martial artist alike must struggle to attain a masculine position from a fragile position, which makes them more compelling narratively and as objects for identification. Such characters address insecurities that perhaps have a specially potent force in post-colonial societies, but are, after all, more globally structural to patriarchal masculinity itself.

Conclusion: The Man Who Feels No Pain

It is, I would argue, this cross-Asian significance in terms of the intersection between colonial histories and experiences of masculinity that draws the nostalgic gaze of *The Man Who Feels No Pain* back to the consumption of kung fu films from the 1970s on VHS tapes in India in the 1990s. Though the film was often treated by critics as an uncomplicated piece of frippery – "a fun ride ... eager to please" and "undemanding, mindless enjoyment" (Dalton 2018) – it seems to have much to say about Indian history, both in the period of its young protagonist's lifespan and in terms of its longer past under colonial rule and its aftermath. At one point, driving through the contemporary landscape of the skyscraping redevelopments of Mumbai that he has not seen since his early childhood in the 1990s, Surya wonders aloud, "What did India achieve in 70 years since independence?" His question is never answered, but this seems, in any case, something the film is quietly setting out to explore through its evocation of both urban and pop-cultural pasts. When Surya starts his martial arts training to heroically defend the weak against injustice, this is framed by his grandfather in terms of the story of his own youthful journey to Japan to join up with the nationalist hero Netaji to fight the British occupation. (Surya only realizes later in life that the discrepancy between Netaji's death and his grandfather's birth means that the story is clearly a fabrication). All this makes Surya's peculiar life and illness seem allegorical of a national condition, and as with my analysis of Hong Kong movies (and Chinese martial arts culture) questions of national strength are folded onto experiences of what masculinity means at the level of the individual.

Characters in the film often function as "types" rather than in psychological depth, standing in for broader phenomena. The film's father figures, in particular, seem to indicate aspects of masculine lack within the cultural landscape.

Surya's father is weak, unadventurous and unimaginative (desiring his son to become an accountant), while his grandfather is a hopeless dreamer of grand political dreams. Neither is effectual enough to stop Surya's mother from being killed, and failing to do so they become symbolically "feminized" by the role of caring for her child. Surya's childhood friend and his love interest in adult life, Supri, has a father who is an even less attractive figure for identification; he is an alcoholic, wife-beating tyrant. Karate Mani's stern and demanding father sets an impossible ideal and dies leaving his two sons locked in a feud over his approval and respect. In many ways it is the film's women who are strong and liberated (like Hong Kong cinema's prominent female warriors), and this further highlights the inadequacy of its men. However, Surya's mother dies because of her eagerness for conflict, and Supri – who fiercely protects Surya as a child when he is bullied and whom we meet again as an adult in the process of beating up a gang who are drugging and raping a young woman – is, until the end of the film, unable to stand up for herself in the way she stands up for others. The film seems to propose that it is only through the substitute father figures of East Asian martial arts cinema – blind, one-armed or even one-legged though they may be – that Surya can transform himself into the kind of man adequate to them, and to the task of reimagining Indian masculinity within the transnational flows of contemporary representation.

That this task of regeneration lies so squarely on Surya's shoulders as the film's male protagonist spotlights the ways in which it remains well within a patriarchal and phallocentric worldview that persists across the history of martial arts cinema that I have been tracing here. However, what is interesting in Surya is that the masculinity he performs is certainly not the invulnerable, "hard" machismo that the title of the film seems to allude to, and with which we might associate martial arts and action heroes more generally. He is slight, bookish, "nerdy": One character teasingly names him "Indie Avenger" and "Mumblecore Justice League." In all this, he seems to echo the "soft masculinities" of East Asian pop culture. That kung fu cinema's many images of "crippled avengers" and "sick men" can serve as material for this construction suggests that the resources it offers for imagining masculinity are far more complex than perfectly sculpted and invincible "men who feel no pain."

References

Boretz, A. (2010) *Gods, Ghosts and Gangsters*, Honolulu: University of Hawai'i Press.

Chan, J. (2000) "Trouble-Free 2nd Year for CCTV/MTV Show," *Billboard*, 1 July.

Cheng, M.C. (1985) *Cheng Tzu's Thirteen Treatises on T'ai Chi Ch'uan*, Berkeley: North Atlantic Books.

Connell, R.W. (2005) *Masculinities*, Cambridge: Polity.

Dalton, S. (2018) "The Man Who Feels No Pain," *Hollywood Reporter*, 1 September.

Desser, D. (2000) "The Kung Fu Craze," in P. Fu and D. Desser (eds) *The Cinema of Hong Kong*, Cambridge: Cambridge University Press.

Dyer, R. (2017) *White*, London: Routledge.

Fu, P. (2008) *China Forever*, Urbana-Champaign: University of Illinois Press.

Funnell, L. (2014) *Warrior Women*, Albany: SUNY Press.

Gravestock, P. (2006) "The Real and the Fantastic in the Wuxia Pian," *Metro Magazine*, 148: 106–11.

Hunt, L. (2003) *Kung Fu Cult Masters*, London: Wallflower.

Jung, S. (2009) "The Shared Imagination of *Bishōnen*, Pan-East Asian Soft Masculinity," *Intersections: Gender and Sexuality in Asia and the Pacific*, 20.

Lo, K.C. (2010) *Excess and Masculinity in Asian Cultural Productions*, Albany: SUNY Press.

Loomba, A. (2015) *Colonialism/Postcolonialism*, London: Routledge.

Louie, K. and Edwards, L. (1994) "Chinese Masculinity," *East Asian History*, 8: 135–48.

Morris, A.D. (2004) *Marrow of the Nation*, Berkeley: University of California Press.

Pang, V. T. (1991) "To Commemorate My Grandfather," in R. Leong (ed) *Moving the Image*, Los Angeles: UCLA Asian American Studies Center.

Prashad, V. (2001) *Everybody Was Kung Fu Fighting*, Boston: Beacon Street.

Said, E. (1978) *Orientalism*, London: Routledge.

Teo, S. (2009) *Chinese Martial Arts Cinema*, Edinburgh: Edinburgh University Press.

White, L. (2020) *Legacies of the Drunken Master: Politics of the Body in Hong Kong Kung Fu Comedy Films*, Honolulu: University of Hawai'i Press.

Yan, V. (2018) "Andy Lau, Leslie Cheung, Carina Lau, Brigitte Lin, Maggie Cheung," *South China Morning Post*, 4 December.

Yip, M.F. (2017) *Martial Arts Cinema and Hong Kong Modernity*, Hong Kong: Hong Kong University Press.

16

FEMINIST LOITERING IN THE CITY

Transmedia Practice and Imagination

Nadja-Christina Schneider

In the wake of economic liberalization since the 1980s, India has witnessed profound societal changes which became especially visible in the negotiation of gender roles and relationships. These changes are closely interwoven with the rapid growth and expansion of media and communication technologies. With increasing digitalization, and particularly with the arrival of mobile technologies in India, new spheres of visibility, debate and participation have emerged for many individuals and collectives. The convergence of media technologies and changing communicative practices require an approach which is less centered on the study of single media forms or technologies but more focused on what people actually do with these convergent media (Couldry 2012; M. Lim 2012). Focusing on the "loitering" movement in urban India which strives to negotiate the hitherto restricted access to and participation of women in urban public spaces, this chapter explores the mutual constitution of material urban spaces and new mobile publics (Sheller 2004). The chapter builds on the assumption that the interlocking of preplanned bodily performances such as "sauntering" or "hanging around" in the city and concurrent creation of a mobile public through digital media practice and circulation can be seen as a context-specific response to three interrelated and ongoing processes – urban transformation in the course of economic liberalization; the repercussions of the discourse of risk and gendered safety in Indian cites (Phadke 2013, 2020); and changing media environments and performative practices of protest and dissent (M. Lim 2014; Schneider and Titzmann 2014).

Globalizing Cities in India: Urban Transformation, Sociospatial Segmentation and Intersectional Im/Mobility

A growing body of academic literature focuses on the profound transformation and expansion that Indian megacities have witnessed in the wake of economic

DOI: 10.4324/9781003130628-20

liberalization from the mid-1980s onwards (Anjaria and McFarlane 2011). One of the major themes in this research area is the aspired status of "world-class-ness" and international recognition as cosmopolitan, "well-ordered" global cities by national and state governments and by the political and economic elites (Sassen 2005; Brosius 2010; Schindler 2014). By referring to terms such as "Americanization" or "Westernization" of cities in India, it is often suggested in academic and journalistic discussions that urban megaprojects and restructuring, or the metropolitan aspiration per se follow an imported, global Western model of urban planning and city modeling. However, and specifically regarding the meta-level discussion about metropolitan and urban studies with a geographical focus on Asia, Ong and Roy (2011) have put forth an influential critique of the prevailing assumption that cities in the "West" or the Global North are always taken as an "unproblematic benchmark of an apparently unsituated urban ideal" in the Global South, despite the fact that the "critical mass and vitality of urban projects in Asian centers, especially, are destabilizing established criteria of global urban modernity" (ibid.: 5). Notwithstanding the question whether the hegemonic project of "world-class" or "global" city-making emerged primarily from an "inter-Asian, " "South–South" or "transregional" horizon of metropolitan and global aspirations, a central element of it is the transition of urban industries to an information and service economy, and this process has generated entirely new urban lifestyles of an emerging new middle class in India (Srivastava 2015). The rising level of social segmentation in rapidly transforming cityscapes becomes also manifest in the creation of entirely new residential areas, such as gated communities (Roy Chaudhuri and Jagadale 2021) or satellite towns as well as recreational spaces, for instance, theme parks or sports architecture built exclusively for the upper strata of this new middle class, as shown in seminal ethnographic studies and related research publications (Fernandes 2006; Brosius 2010; Baviskar and Ray 2011; Donner 2011; Dickey 2012).

On the other side of the social spectrum, informal settlements very often have to make way to new large-scale projects, so that lower middle classes and poorer sections of society are literally driven out of the city centers and surrounding areas and into the newly emerging "peripheries" of the cities. This has been an ongoing process since the 1990s, despite the fact that the "functioning" of an Indian city heavily depends on the permanent availability of their workforce and participation in the informal sector (Baviskar 2002; Dupont 2008, 2011; Schindler 2014). This has recently become painfully clear to many urban middle-class residents during the severe COVID lockdown in India in 2020. Accordingly, the accelerated sociospatial segmentation and segregation of metropolitan or megacities in India can be traced both in the materiality of the new urban architecture and in the visual representation and imagination of the new "global" or "world-class city," especially in city- or place-branding campaigns (Rao 2010). The groups, however, who benefit most from the recent restructuring toward automobile cities or new infrastructural large-scale projects, such as the prestigious Delhi Metro, belong mostly to the upwardly mobile middle class (Sadana 2012).

Although large sections of society clearly aspire to "become" middle class or already claim to belong to this stratum, "being" middle class in India cannot be seen as a secure status position at all. In view of the differences in education, cultural and social capital as well as the vast disparities between lower- and upper-income groups, it can be argued that the Eurocentric concept of a "class" may not be fully fitting in the Indian context in order to grasp the heterogeneity of the middle stratum of society. Especially, the lower and lower middle-income groups are constantly faced with the risk of falling back into poverty (Krishna and Bajpai 2015). Contrary to the inference, however, that this recognizable fluidity would make it difficult to draw clear class boundaries in India, precisely the constant risk of downward mobility can be seen to increase the sharp distinction many middle-class groups draw between them and "the poor" in India. Therefore, in addition to caste-based and communalist (religion-based) discrimination and marginalization which are often seen as the root cause of growing social inequality in India, the rise of classism also has to be seen as a major repercussion of economic liberalization in India that significantly impacts on urban life and politics.

Contemporary urban processes in India thus seem to exemplify in an almost paradigmatic way Sheller and Urry's (2006: 211) argument that the increased mobility of some may simultaneously "immobilize" other groups and that the (visual) representation of im/mobility is centrally linked to socioeconomic power relations in the city. It is perhaps no coincidence that mobility has become the central metaphor in post-liberalization urban society in India (Chakravarty and Gooptu 2000), while those who are increasingly represented as "immobile others" (poorer sections of society or religious minorities) are often seen as bearing the responsibility for their "failed" development and marginalization (Appadurai 2005; Schneider 2015).

In sum, cities in India just like in other regions of the so-called Global South continue to experience an elite-oriented urban transformation, growing social inequality as well as intersectional immobility/mobility – but simultaneously the articulation of dissent and protest against these ongoing processes. The multidisciplinary research area of urban studies in India provides the contextual background to grasp how multiple inequalities exactly intersect in regional and local contexts, and more specifically in metropolitan cities and regions. In the course of economic liberalization, these inequalities have added to the ongoing privatization or "shrinking" as well as to an intensified social exclusion of marginalized groups from public spaces. An aspect which had gained comparatively little attention until the beginning of the 2010s in this context is the question of women's im/mobility, access to and participation in urban public life. At least since the globally mediated incident of massive, sexualized violence in December 2012, which came to be known as the "Nirbhaya case" in India or as the "Delhi gang-rape case" in international media (Schneider 2014), it became very clear that an intersectional gender perspective in Indian urban studies is vitally needed. One year before this critical event, in 2011,

Shilpa Phadke, Sameera Khan and Shilpa Ranade published their coauthored book *Why Loiter? Women and Risk on Mumbai Streets.* Ten years later, in 2021, it can be safely said – and observed with a view to several special events and newspaper articles which were published on the occasion of its 10th anniversary – that this critically acclaimed book hit a nerve especially with a young generation of readers in India, among them many students. The book also continues to inspire lively discussions in university seminars worldwide, already existing, or emerging collectives as well as feminist authors who write autobiographical texts about the individual experience and pleasure of walking the city. In addition to that, many small-scale or local movements grew out of the book or have been in conversation with the authors since 2011 (Phadke 2020), not only in India but also in the neighboring country Pakistan where a collective called Girls at Dhabas strives for gender-inclusive cities.

Gendered Exclusion from the City: The Discourse of Risk and Gendered Safety

Phadke, Khan and Ranade (2009, 2011) show that women from all castes and strata of society are permanently confronted with multiple and sometimes even violent exclusions from and repressions in the city. They argue that the presence of women in the city is not per se unwanted or contested (at least during daytime), but women who do not want to lose their own "respectability" or harm their family's moral reputation are expected to constantly display a clearly recognizable and socially accepted purpose of their "transition" of urban space and that they remain primarily attached to the private space of their family's home. The "good little women" do so in a performative sense by emphasizing that they are either "rushing" to their children's kindergarten, school or back home with them or that they are very active citizen-consumers (carrying shopping bags), and hence allowed to be temporarily located in the semi-public or privatized space of the shopping mall; or they stress their professional affiliation to the private sector, for instance, by following the global business dress code. On the other hand, women who do not follow these "unwritten rules" and dare to saunter or "loiter" in the city without a clearly recognizable and socially accepted purpose – a practice which the authors see as holding a huge transformative for women, other marginalized groups and cities alike – are severely criticized for taking unnecessary and self-imposed risks (Phadke 2013).

Loitering is perceived to be risky because it is often cast as dangerous and antisocial in some way. Interestingly, it is also illegal in many countries; good citizens are expected not to loiter, but to go about their work in an orderly fashion. Good citizens are then rewarded with the promise of protection in public space which is denied to those who loiter. This is even more stringently applicable to women who are forbidden from taking risks of any kind. When women demand the freedom to take risks instead of the guarantee of safety, we are implicitly rejecting this conditional protection in favor of the unqualified right to public space (Phadke, Khan and Ranade 2011: 180).

The three authors (ibid.: 179) mention that "the loiterer maps her own path, often errant, arbitrary and circuitous, marking out a dynamic personal map of pleasure. The loiterer is independent, free-spirited and carries only the responsibility for herself." Perhaps these sentences led some readers to the impression that not only the act of loitering but also the way the authors imagined loitering women in the city represented a rather exclusive middle-class vision "steeped in individuality and neoliberal desires" (Phadke 2020: 282). Phadke responds to this critique in her article "Defending Frivolous Fun: Feminist Acts of Claiming Public Spaces in South Asia" by arguing that "loitering assumes valency only when performed in community with others. Claims to loitering are fundamentally imagined as collective rather than individual. This sense of the collective is often missed by arguments that understand such protests as individualistic and neo-liberal" (ibid.: 289). It is a very interesting question – how we understand the term collective in this context. Does it necessarily imply that (large numbers of) bodies are visibly "in alliance" in the street (Butler 2011), or is it possible to think of a different conceptualization, perhaps more in terms of a shared feeling or sense of collectiveness that is connected to the individually or collectively exerted act of loitering in the street, but even more so to the digital (re)mediation or mediated communication about it? We have seen in so many instances since 2011 how the digital mediation or multimedia transmission of emphatically local events and locally situated practices to digital and translocal spaces helps those who are elsewhere to "have the sense that they are getting some direct access through the images and sounds they receive" (Butler 2011). Does this mean, however, that digital space is primarily a "channel of mediation" or are digital or related media practices co-constitutive for new ways of seeing and *feeling* collective solidarity (see on the question of mediated solidarity, Titzmann 2021)?

Changing Configurations of "Non-Technological" and "Digital" Media in the Practice of Urban Protest and Dissent

The increasing convergence of media technologies and changing communicative practices have led to an interrelatedness of various forms of media on a local and translocal level (M. Lim 2012), requiring an approach which focuses less on single media but more on people's engagement with convergent media forms (Couldry 2012). Furthermore, it is not so much singular media forms or communication technologies but rather context-specific new formations or communicative figurations which seem to be closely interrelated with changing practices, actions and spatial relations in contemporary societies (Hepp 2010; Rajagopal 2011). The rise of candlelight demonstrations and vigils in India (Schneider 2014) and in other Asian countries (Pang 2013) may serve as a good example to illustrate this aspect of changing spatial relations in the city and closely related to it, of access to public spaces and places to demonstrate peacefully. Theoretical discussions in the field of choreography and theater studies provide very helpful insights into the question – what these demonstrating bodies, or in the context of this chapter loitering bodies, are actually doing in public places. And linked to this question, how they are related to an emerging public, precisely because the focus is laid on the interlocking of body techniques and media practices which are involved in the new choreographies of nonviolent protests, as Susan Leigh Foster (2003) calls them. In this perspective, demonstrating or loitering bodies are learning to "trust public space and what one might encounter in it" (ibid.: 410) and actively reconfigure or refunction their material environments (Butler 2011; Glass and Ross-Redwood 2014). Candles as much as bodies can hence also be argued to be "reactivated" as important nontechnological media which, due to their specific interrelationship with visual media, are as important to look at in the context of performative practice as technological media are. Graffiti and street art can be understood as a third "old" or nontechnological medium which has gained a new prominence and visibility worldwide in recent years, especially in the context of protests in the Arab world or against the financial crisis in Greece. Introducing and focusing on this old media form as a "media modality to be examined in conjunction with others (television, social media etc.) ... may provide a corrective to celebrations of the centrality of new media to social and political processes" (Kraidy 2015: 320).

Conceptually, however, the loitering movement which is focused on the negotiation of access for women to, and new articulation or creation of, public space in the city, has to be distinguished from protest movements which may also use physical urban places in Indian cities for their demonstrations (e.g., in the context of the anti-corruption movement in 2011 and more recently, of the farmers' protests in 2020/21) but whose objectives are not primarily directed toward the city itself (Schneider 2014; Blokland et al. 2015). This distinction is based on the assumption that the loitering movement has a lot in common with other trans/local urban movements in many other countries that have been discussed under labels such as the right to the city, grassroots urbanism or do-it-yourself urbanism, either with regard to a shared theoretical foundation, conceptual references and language they use or the practices with which they draw attention to the materiality of urban space (Iveson 2013; W. Lim 2014). As Iveson argues, the actual societal relevance and political potential of these urban movements depend largely on the successful remediation (Bolter and Grusin 2000) of their performative practice and addressing or forming of a new public. He uses the term "making the city public" for this process, "not just through physically occupying its public spaces, but also through making those occupations a matter of public interest and debate in a procedural sense" (Iveson 2013: 947).

Is Loitering a Performative Practice, a New Form of Urban Protest – or Both?

It is arguably no coincidence that Phadke, Khan and Ranade's (2011) coauthored study, which is simultaneously read as a manifesto in India (and beyond), has been even more widely circulated and discussed after the wave of protests against sexualized violence in Delhi and other Indian cities in the winter of 2012–13. Security forces reacted with disproportionate harshness against these peaceful demonstrations and some Indian politicians displayed a kind of machismo which made many citizens in the country feel that the gap between the political class and the citizens, especially the younger generation, had widened even further (Chaudhuri 2014; Schneider 2014). As a result, many feminists who had participated in these large demonstrations wondered what could bring about change in their society and if protests were really the appropriate means to counter a serious societal problem which manifests itself in myriad everyday interactions in the cities that are very often "unspectacular" and sometimes hardly visible. The performative practice of "loitering," "sauntering" or "hanging out" (e.g., having a picnic in a park, taking a nap on a park bench, drinking chai at tea stalls which are perceived as male spaces, taking a walk on the street in the night, or cycling in the city) is defined by Phadke, Khan and Ranade (2011) as a "radical act" by women who thereby articulate their right to the city and at the same time strive to create an inclusive public space. Interestingly, however, these acts are emphatically understood and described by the authors as *everyday practices* and not as organized protest events. It may nevertheless be helpful to complicate the notion of "everydayness" or "everyday life" in this context for two reasons: (1) Even though the performed everydayness of loitering is meant to suggest a normalcy and legitimacy of women's equal right to urban public space, exactly this has not been established yet in India. The aspired inclusion into public everyday life is therefore actually anticipated through the performative practice and theorizing of it (Lieder 2018). (2) Simultaneously, and despite the emphatic reference to everyday practice, the immediate (re)mediatization of the loitering events is precisely meant to contribute to an emerging transmedia public and they are therefore sometimes turned into "small media events." As such, they require careful preparation and labor (often by more than one person) that is intrinsically related to the practice of public loitering and has to cater to a lot of different media forms, technologies and media environments in India, e.g., the announcing of happenings via social media; the (self-)filming of "loitering bodies in action"; the editing and uploading of videos and photos; tweeting, sharing of (mass) media coverage of loitering events; posting or liking of comments and conversation threads; commenting on social media content and publication of newspaper articles and so on. Nevertheless, event-oriented emerging publics cannot be expected to be long-lasting or stable, but should rather be seen as temporary, fluid or mobile and hence changeable (Sheller 2004; Volkmer 2014). On the other hand, precisely as these emerging publics are changeable, the transition from a focus on "everyday actions" to the non-ordinary reality of a new protest moment is also possible – and indeed took place only a few years after the publication of *Why Loiter?* when the Pinjra Tod (Break the Cage) protest movement was created and became publicly visible in 2015.

The discourse of self-imposed risks and gendered safety in urban spaces of India gained even more prominence and legitimacy in the wake of the Delhi gang rape case in 2012 and therefore added in many ways to an increased "immobilization" of many women across caste, class, religion and generation in Indian cities (Schneider and Titzmann 2014). In a number of incidents, especially young women who were visibly not willing to accept their exclusion from urban life and public spaces any longer were targeted by a self-appointed "moral police" which aggressively asserted the domination of urban spaces by hegemonic masculinity (Connell and Messerschmidt 2005) so that stories about the beating up of single women or couples in parks, bars or restaurants made headlines in Indian media during the last decade and generated a lot of debate as well as activism against it (Brosius 2013 and 2011). On the other hand, precisely as women's presence in urban spaces at night or without a recognizable purpose is seen as careless and risky behavior, they were often blamed to bear the responsibility for the aggressiveness or violence they may experience there (Phadke 2013). As many parents felt that they cannot "protect" their daughters any longer – by restricting their self-determined mobility, for instance, when they join a university or workplace (Patel 2010) in another city – they increasingly demanded that university administrations do the same. This resulted in a scenario where on many campuses in India, students read as male were allowed to move freely on the campus or outside after sunset, whereas students read as female were confined to the hostels. "Pinjra Tod – Break the Hostel Locks" emerged as a new movement of young feminist students against these restrictions and their exclusion from public life in the cities in general. It was started by students from several university colleges in Delhi in 2015 but soon gained momentum in other cities, too (Oechslen 2019). Much like a growing number of similar and digitally interconnected urban movements in other regions of Asia (M. Lim 2014), Pinjra Tod is linked in many ways to the book *Why Loiter?* and to the movement which crystallized around the idea and call to loiter in the city with the stated aim of making it more inclusive and gender democratic. As the movement's actions included both performative "everyday like" practices and the repertoire of non-violent protests, the example of Pinjra Tod shows that instead of a distinction between performative practice or protest, it may make more sense to think of a continuum of practices that are interrelated and can take on various forms in response to specific contexts and phases.

Imagination of the "Wandering Women" in Digital Literary and Autobiographical Writing

Another interrelated development that can be recognized in this chapter is the remarkable number of autobiographical texts, visual essays, journal articles and interviews with "loitering women" that have been published in Indian newspapers, magazines and digital literary journals (mostly in English, but some of them also in Hindi and other Indian languages). Maya Sorabjee's (2016) long and widely circulated essay "The Wandering Women," which won the Architectural League's Urban Omnibus (USA) writing award, is an illustrative example of this emerging genre. As a young scholar in urban studies and architecture, Sorabjee was at that time based in the United States, but through her articles, website and especially through her award-winning essay she also helped to increase the visibility and interest in the loitering movement beyond India and South Asia. Although generally (or at least temporarily) more loosely connected to the performative loitering practice in physical urban spaces or to the interrelated remediation of these actions, it can be argued that this emerging genre contributes to the formation of this public and to the establishing of translocal cross-connections with other publics dedicated to the idea and experience of feminist loitering in the city as a potentially transformative practice. It seems that many of the authors contributing to this new digital literary and/or autobiographical genre were trained as journalists and now extend their writing practices to various media forms, beyond online and print journals or newspapers; others come from different educational and professional backgrounds and many of them have spent a formative part of their lives in big cities in India, but later on also lived and worked in other geographical regions, similar to Sorabjee's own experience. It would be particularly interesting to see more research on the meaning that these authors attach to their digital writing practice, both in their everyday life and in the context of their (professional) publishing and sharing of texts with others.

Another question awaiting further exploration concerns the relationship between these newly emerging literary and transmedia writings about loitering women and earlier literary and/or visual imaginations of female flânerie in 19th- and 20th-century European metropolises: Can the contemporary figure of the loiterer in Delhi, Mumbai or Lahore be seen as a 21st-century version of the flâneuse in 19th-century Paris, London, or the early 20th-century flâneuse in Berlin? Or, are the two phenomena not as comparable and connected as the central idea of women's unrestricted mobility and performative "nonproductivity" of women's movements in urban public space would suggest? The discussion on the female flâneur initially emerged as an offshoot of scholarship about the male counterpart, the "nineteenth century Parisian man, whose chief occupation was mastering the city with idle walking and detached looking" (Iskin 2006: 113). Especially since the mid-1980s, a growing number of studies have shifted the focus from the supposed exclusion of women from, to their presence in, the European metropolises (Wolff 1985; Buck-Morss 1986; D'Souza and McDonough 2006). They have also demonstrated that the feminine stroller or flâneur "emerged both in historical practices and in literary representations by the late nineteenth century" (Iskin 2006: 113). In her conceptualization of the contemporary figure and practices of the cyberflâneuse, Hartmann (2004) offered a very useful model for the linking of the offline and online practices of strolling women which could be taken up and extended geographically to a region in Asia which has hitherto not really been included in this transdisciplinary debate. Even Elkin's (2016) latest addition to the literature on women's imagined and real flânerie largely reproduces the Eurocentric idea that "a cultural history of women writers and artists who have found personal freedom as well as inspiration by engaging with cities on foot and on their own terms" can be written by looking more or less exclusively at cities in the Global North.

Critique and Outlook

The book *Why Loiter?* and many of the small-scale and local movements in South Asia that either grew out or have been in conversation with the three coauthors are highly sensitive to and recognize intersectional differences. In view of the multiple and intersecting forms of discrimination and exclusion that so many people in India are faced with on a daily basis, it would indeed be deeply problematic to talk about (cis-) "women's experiences and perceptions" irrespective of caste, religion, gender or sexual identity, among many other categories. Despite this recognition of intersectional differences, and by drawing on Spivak's concept of strategic essentialism, Phadke argued in an event on the occasion of the 10th anniversary of the publication of *Why Loiter?* that exactly such a collective response "as women" is required in the increasingly repressive situation that India has experienced during the last decade. Another aspect which requires more critical attention is perhaps the role of caste-based discrimination and marginalization in urban spaces as well as the intersection of gender and caste. Although discrimination and violence against less privileged and marginalized caste groups is mentioned in the book, its intersectional analytical perspective focuses mostly on class and gender, especially on how men of lower-class backgrounds are being portrayed as a major threat to the "safety" or "sexual security" particularly of middle-class women. However, the notion that caste matters less or perhaps less than class in urban India has been increasingly questioned during the last decade. In a personal conversation with Shilpa Phadke that we recorded for a conference on the question of "How to Live Together? Circulations, Practices and Spaces in Indian Contexts" in August 2021 (available via www.replito.de), she acknowledges that caste has been "a blind spot of the book in many ways," not least because many of their interlocutors for the study were reluctant to talk about caste and so the focus of discussions was much more on the way urban society in Mumbai had become fractured along class and religious lines. But the public perception has changed significantly during the last decade and once again, the debate on caste-based discrimination and on the intersection of marginalization and inequality has been renewed. Accordingly, Phadke says that if the three coauthors were writing the book *Why Loiter?* today, they would engage far more centrally with caste.

My final question in our conversation was about her hope for positive change in this decade. In her response, Phadke draws our attention once again to the necessity of public urban infrastructure to overcome gendered, intersectional immobility and exclusion in cities of India:

> If we imagine that our worlds will no longer be patriarchal or misogynist, I'm not sure that's something one can really imagine. But I think that if we imagine that our cities will have built more public infrastructure,

more transport, more public toilets, including gender-neutral toilets, that our cities would have reimagined public space in ways that invites people rather than excludes them, rather than closing off parks, to open them ... If we could imagine a different infrastructure in which we work, that would be a huge gain.

(personal conversation with Phadke on
20 August 2021)

References

Anjaria, J. and McFarlane, C. (2011) *Urban Navigations: Politics, Space and the City in South Asia*, London: Routledge.

Appadurai, A. (2005) "Cosmopolitanism from Below," *The Salon*, 4: 32–43.

Baviskar, A. (2002) "The Politics of the City," *Seminar*, 516: 40–42.

Baviskar, A. and Ray, R. (2011) *Elite and Everyman: The Cultural Politics of the Indian Middle Classes*, Delhi: Routledge.

Blokland, T., Hentschel, C., Holm, A., Lebuhn, H. and Margalit, T. (2015) "Urban Citizenship and the Right to the City," *International Journal of Urban and Regional Research*, 39(4): 655–65.

Bolter, J. and Grusin, R. (2000) *Remediation: Understanding New Media*, Cambridge: MIT Press.

Brosius, C. (2010) *India's Middle Class*, Delhi: Routledge.

Brosius, C. (2011) "Love in the Age of Valentine and Pink Underwear," in C. Brosius and E. Ambos (eds) *Transcultural Turbulences*, Berlin: Springer.

Brosius, C. (2013) "Love Attacks," in S. Srivastava (ed) *Sexuality Studies*, Delhi: Oxford University Press.

Buck-Morss, S. (1986) "The Flâneur, the Sandwichman and the Whore," *New German Critique*, 39: 99–140.

Butler, J. (2011) "Bodies in Alliance and the Politics of the Street," *Transversal*, 7 September.

Chakravarty, R. and Gooptu, N. (2000) "Imagi-nation," in E. Hallam and B. Street (eds) *Cultural Encounters*, London: Routledge.

Chaudhuri, M. (2014) "National and Global Media Discourse after the Savage Death of Nirbhaya," in N.C. Schneider and F.M. Titzmann (eds) *Studying Youth, Media and Gender in Post-Liberalisation India*, Berlin: Frank & Timme.

Connell, R. and Messerschmidt, J. (2005) "Hegemonic Masculinity," *Gender & Society*, 19(6): 829–59.

Couldry, N. (2012) *Media, Society, World*, Cambridge: Polity.

Dickey, S. (2012) "The Pleasures and Anxieties of Being in the Middle," *Modern Asian Studies*, 46(3): 559–99.

Donner, H. (2011) *Being Middle-Class in India*, London: Routledge.

D'Souza, A. and McDonough, T. (2006) *The Invisible Flâneuse?*, Manchester: Manchester University Press.

Dupont, V. (2008) "Slum Demolition in Delhi since the 1990s," *Economic and Political Weekly*, 43(28): 79–87.

Dupont, V. (2011) "Which Place for the Homeless in Delhi?," *South Asia Multidisciplinary Academic Journal*, 8.

Elkin, L. (2016) *Flâneuse*, London: Chatto & Windus.

Fernandes, L. (2006) *India's New Middle Class*, Minneapolis: University of Minnesota Press.

Foster, S.L. (2003) "Choreographies of Protest," *Theatre Journal*, 55(3): 395–412.

Glass, M. and Rose-Redwood, R. (2014) *Performativity, Politics and the Production of Social Space*, New York: Routledge.

Hartmann, M. (2004) *Technologies and Utopias*, Ph.D. thesis, London: University of Westminster.

Hepp, A. (2010) "Researching Mediatized Worlds," in N. Carpentier (ed) *Media and Communication Studies*, Tartu: University of Tartu Press.

Iskin, R. (2006) "The Flâneuse in French Fin-de-Siècle Posters," in A. D'Souza and T. McDonough (eds) *The Invisible Flâneuse?*, Manchester: Manchester University Press.

Iveson, K. (2013) "Cities within the City," *International Journal of Urban and Regional Research*, 37(3): 941–56.

Kraidy, M. (2015) "Graffiti, Hypermedia and Heterotopia after the Arab Uprisings," in N.C. Schneider and C. Richter (eds) *New Media Configurations and Socio-Cultural Dynamics in Asia and the Arab World*, Baden-Baden: Bloomsbury.

Krishna, A. and Bajpai, D. (2015) "Layers in Globalising Society and the New Middle Class in India," *Economic and Political Weekly*, 50(5): 69–77.

Lieder, K. (2018) "Performing Loitering," *TDR: Drama Review*, 62(3): 145–61.

Lim, M. (2012) "Clicks, Cabs and Coffee Houses," *Journal of Communication*, 62(2): 231–48.

Lim, M. (2014) "Seeing Spatially," *International Development Planning Review*, 36(1): 51–72.

Lim, W. (2014) *Public Space in Urban Asia*, Singapore: World Scientific Publishing.

Oechslen, A. (2019) "Rage against the Cage," *Gender Bulletin*, 45: 27–45.

Ong, A. and Roy, A. (2011) *Worlding Cities*, Oxford: Wiley.

Pang, H. (2013) *The 2008 Candlelight Protest in South Korea*, Ph.D. Thesis, Tampa: University of South Florida.

Patel, R. (2010) *Working the Night Shift*, Delhi: Orient Blackswan.

Phadke, S. (2013) "Unfriendly Bodies, Hostile Cities," *Economic and Political Weekly*, 48(39): 51.

Phadke, S. (2020) "Defending Frivolous Fun," *South Asia: Journal of South Asian Studies*, 43(2): 281–93.

Phadke, S., Ranade, S. and Khan, S. (2009) "Why Loiter?," in M. Butcher and S. Velayutham (eds) *Dissent and Cultural Resistance in Asia's Cities*, London: Routledge.

Phadke, S., Khan, S. and Ranade, S. (2011) *Why Loiter? Women and Risk on Mumbai Streets*, Delhi: Penguin.

Rajagopal, A. (2011) "Notes on Postcolonial Visual Culture," *BioScope: South Asian Screen Studies*, 2(1): 11–22.

Rao, U. (2010) "Making the Global City," *Ethnos*, 75(4): 402–24.

Roy Chaudhuri, H. and Jagadale, S. (2021) "Normalized Heterotopia as a Market Failure in a Spatial Marketing System," *Journal of Micromarketing*, 41(2): 297–314.

Sadana, R. (2012) "The Metro and the Street," *Seminar*, August.

Sassen, S. (2005) "The Global City," *Brown Journal of World Affairs*, 11(2): 27–43.

Schindler, S. (2014) "The Making of World-Class Delhi," *Antipode*, 46(2): 557–73.

Schneider, N.C. (2014) "Medialised Delhi: Youth, Protest and an Emerging Genre of Urban Films," *South Asia Chronicle*, 3: 86–110.

Schneider, N.C. (2015) "Applying the Lens of Mobility to Media and Gender Studies," in N.C. Schneider and C. Richter (eds) *New Media Configurations and Socio-Cultural Dynamics in Asia and the Arab World*, Baden-Baden: Bloomsbury.

Schneider, N.C. and Titzman, F.M. (2014) *Studying Youth, Media and Gender in Post-Liberalisation India*, Berlin: Frank & Timme.

Sheller, M. (2004) "Mobile Publics," *Environment and Planning D*, 22(1): 39–52.

Sheller, M. and Urry, J. (2006) "The New Mobilities Paradigm," *Environment and Planning A*, 38(2): 207–26.

Sorabjee, M. (2016) "The Wandering Women," *Urban Omnibus*, 13 January.

Srivastava, S. (2015) *Entangled Urbanism*, Delhi: Oxford University Press.

Titzmann, F.M. (2021) "Solidarity," *RePLITO*, 20 July.

Volkmer, I. (2014) *The Global Public Sphere*, Cambridge: Polity.

Wolff, J. (1985) "The Invisible Flâneuse," *Theory, Culture & Society*, 2(3): 37–46.

17

DOMESTIC WORKERS AND IMMOBILE MOBILITY VIA WECHAT

Performative Motherhood and Modernity in Beijing

Cara Wallis

It is a Sunday afternoon in the fall of 2015, and I am sitting on a low stool around a table in a cramped room in the basement of a high-rise apartment building on what used to be the edge of the ever-expanding Beijing metropolis. About a dozen female domestic workers have gathered for a weekly workshop/hangout hosted by a non-governmental organization (NGO) that serves the needs of domestic workers, who are some of China's most exploited working-class laborers. The topic on this day is domestic workers' legal rights. A woman I will call Ms. Wang (all names are pseudonyms), who is the cofounder of the NGO, begins with a rapid-fire series of questions: "How many hours a week do you have to work? How many days off a month should you get? If you work on a holiday, how much overtime pay should you receive?" Several domestic workers answer, but at the end of this interaction, Ms. Wang tells them that most of their answers are incorrect. The workshop then proceeds as she tries to impart a sense of their rights – "Are you workers? Are you citizens?" – even though, as domestic workers, they are not covered by China's Contract Labor Law. When the workshop ends one hour later, a couple of women stay at the table, asking further questions, but most move to an adjacent room where there are pillows and mats and ample space to relax. A few women nap while others chat in pairs or small groups, with certain topics becoming conversation fodder for everyone. A consistent feature of all these interactions is the women engaging simultaneously with each other and their mobile phones – sharing pictures, watching short humorous videos, playing a song. They also place and take calls, sometimes discreetly and other times in the middle of all the action.

This chapter explores how "older" (over age 35) female domestic workers in Beijing navigate their dual roles as "workers" and "citizens," focusing specifically on how they use mobile phones and social media to perform caring labor for their own children and, in some cases, grandchildren. In popular discourse

DOI: 10.4324/9781003130628-21

and government policy documents, rural-to-urban migrant workers who move to towns and cities to seek jobs and a "modern" lifestyle are often constructed as having low *suzhi*, or "quality" (physical, moral, spiritual) due to their rural background and class status. Older female domestic workers are viewed as some of the most "backward" and "vulnerable" because of their gender, age and low education level and because they often come from China's most impoverished rural areas. Moreover, even as their labor is a sacrifice for their families, they carry the social stigma of having contributed to the "left-behind" problem, whereby millions of rural youth are looked after by other relatives, usually grandparents, because their parents are out laboring. This phenomenon has raised much societal concern about the mental health of these children and about moral decay in the countryside (Ye 2011). Domestic workers, perhaps even more so than other female migrant workers, bear the heavy weight of this burden because they are viewed as having forsaken their own parenting duties while caring for urban children. Thus, for many, rejecting these stereotypes and demonstrating their moral uprightness and modern training in caring for their own and their employer's children are paramount.

This chapter examines how social media and access to low-end smartphones have enabled new ways for domestic workers to negotiate and manage these tensions. More specifically, it interrogates whether smartphones and social media allow them access to what I call "immobile mobility," or how a mobile phone can enable those who are marginalized to overcome but not surpass certain barriers (Wallis 2013). It focuses on how immobile mobility is articulated to the women's mediated public practices of what Chin (2018), drawing on Butler (1999), calls "performative motherhood," or the discursive construction of rules and embodied practices that regulate and discipline the gendered, maternal body. It also shows how these practices are constitutive of how a "modern" subjectivity has been constructed for older migrant women.

As China's rural-to-urban migrant workers have gained access to communication technologies, scholarship has focused on how "young" adult migrant workers initially used mobile phones and more recently smartphones and social media to maintain social networks and resist their limited circumstances (Law and Peng 2006; Qiu 2009; Wallis 2013; Wang 2016). However, with few exceptions, the use of these technologies by female domestic workers who are "older" and viewed as more traditional has received little attention even though most of them use smartphones for a myriad of reasons (Wallis 2018). In contrast, a large body of research has examined how domestic workers in transnational contexts use communication technologies in their jobs and for caring for their children, who are separated by thousands of miles and often several time zones (Parreñas 2005; Thomas and Lim 2011). The bulk of this research relies on surveys, focus groups and interviews, with little attention to virtual ethnography (Madianou 2012; Madianou and Miller 2012, for exceptions). Through focusing on older domestic workers' digital media practices and deploying qualitative methods that include participant observation and analysis of social media posts, this chapter builds upon and fills gaps in both studies of China's female migrant workers and the broader scholarship on domestic workers globally.

In what follows, the chapter first sets the context by discussing what I call "neo/non-liberal China." It next reviews scholarship on migrant workers' use of communication technologies, including domestic workers, mobile phones and "remote mothering," and then elaborates on immobile mobility as a theoretical framework. The analysis focuses on how domestic workers use smartphones and social media for performative motherhood and grandmotherhood in ways that demonstrate varying degrees of publicness. The chapter argues that through these performative modes of caretaking, domestic workers use digital media to achieve immobile mobility, displaying their modernity and affirming their roles as workers and citizens, embodied in their self-sacrificial physical and affective labor for their families. Still, this immobile mobility is circumscribed by the gendered, placed (rural), classed and aged parameters set for them.

Neo/Non-Liberal China

The domestic workers in this chapter are situated in a contemporary context I call "neo/non-liberal China," a term meant to capture the intersection of deeply engrained patriarchal ideologies, the economization of social life, and the party-state's harnessing of emotions and feelings as part of its authoritarian governance of the populace (Wallis and Shen 2018). These processes began during prior decades of reform, yet since Chinese President Xi Jinping's ascent to power in 2012 they have become intensified.

As the term implies, neo/non-liberal China is constitutive of several phenomena associated with neoliberal capitalism – greater marketization and privatization of certain enterprises, the shrinking of the urban social safety net, increased commodification of social life and an emphasis on the self as a project for perpetual work and upgrade (Harvey 2005; Ong and Zhang 2008; Dean 2010). These shifts are evident in how domestic work has transformed since it emerged in the early 1980s at the beginning of the reform era as part of China's modernization drive. At the time, domestic work was seen as a way not only for rural women to earn money by working in private homes but also for them to improve their "quality" by learning "modern" skills (e.g., hygiene, "scientific" child-rearing techniques). It was also viewed by middle-class urban families as a way to assert their modernity and thereby gain distinction (Yan 2008). In recent years, domestic work has become increasingly commodified and is now a booming industry, with a growing number of domestic worker agencies and services along with professional standards, which potential domestic workers must meet to ensure their value in the marketplace (Fu et al. 2018; Tong 2018). This entire domestic service ecosystem tends to benefit employers rather than domestic workers, who currently number more than 30 million, a figure expected to increase to 50 million by 2025 (Ye 2018).

The commodification of domestic work intersects with another facet of neo/non-liberal China, namely patriarchal views regarding gender. Most domestic workers globally are women due to the common perception that women are "natural" caregivers. However, China's emphasis on innate biological sex differences, which were embraced in the 1980s as "modern" and "scientific," in contrast to the "de-gendered" Mao era (Wu 2010), and the contemporary revival of Confucianism produces notions of essentialized gender that manifest in distinct ways in family relationships and in the marketplace. Traditional Confucian ideology stresses women's subordinate role to men in the family and that they should be virtuous wives and good mothers, and President Xi Jinping has supported this role for women as part of a "harmonious" family (*Study Times* 2015). As commodified, gendered laborers, domestic workers expend a large degree of emotional and affective labor in the urban home. Somewhat ironically, they are taught in training programs that through acquiring caretaking skills, purportedly based on science, they can demonstrate that they are "modern" subjects, yet they are often derided as backward and lacking by their urban employers (Yan 2008; Fu et al. 2018).

A final tenet of neo/non-liberal China relevant to this discussion is how the current regime has elevated its mode of "therapeutic governance," or the way the state mobilizes affect – or bodily sensations, passions and forces – and emotion among ordinary people so that their personal aspirations are in line with state goals (Yang 2015). Xi Jinping's emphasis on "positive energy" is one example, as is state-led reemployment training programs, including those for domestic workers, that invoke affect as a means of value extraction and ensuring social stability through trying to channel workers' "positive" rather than "negative" potential (Yang 2015). The state's mobilization of affect also accords with the broader "psychologization" of society, as seen in various modes of "self-help" and a related "happiness craze" diffused throughout popular culture including television, radio, books and online videos (Zhang 2017). Domestic worker service agencies also train domestic workers to be positive and cheerful and that even in times of conflict, their role is to maintain harmony and be caring, devoted (surrogate) mothers (Fu et al. 2018).

Domestic Workers, Communication Technologies and Immobile Mobility

Chinese domestic workers, like transnational domestic workers, experience exploitation, alienation and discrimination (Parreñas 2005; Hondagneu-Sotelo 2001; Yan 2008). However, the structural and cultural constraints they face are also somewhat unique. For example, unlike many Filipina domestic workers in Hong Kong, Singapore or the United Kingdom, who tend to be comparatively educated and middle class back home (Constable 2007; Thomas and Lim 2011; Madianou 2012), most domestic workers in China are internal migrants who come from relatively impoverished areas that have historically been left out of the government's reform-era development focus. Because they hold a rural, not urban, *hukou* (household registration), they are treated as second-class citizens in the city. Although less rigid than in the past, the *hukou* marks insiders and outsiders, urban and rural, privileged and deprived, and "modern" and "backward." Despite reforms to the *hukou* system over the years, all migrant workers still have limited access to any type of social welfare provision, including health insurance or a pension. However, because domestic workers are employed in private homes, most are not covered by China's Labor Contract Law; thus, they often have little recourse if they are denied wages or experience physical harm (Hu 2011; Fu et al. 2018; Tong 2018).

Over the years, the Chinese government has created certain policies that in theory should offer greater protection for domestic workers; however, in reality these are difficult to implement and they tend to serve the needs of the market, not workers (Liu 2017; Fu et al. 2018; Tong 2018). Laboring long hours in private homes, where often the cultural differences between them and their employers are large, domestic workers are "intimate strangers" with "ubiquitous invisibility" (Sun 2009). Still, a consistent theme in scholarship on Chinese domestic workers has been whether migration offers opportunities for their empowerment and to exercise agency, the latter defined broadly as the ability to act on and achieve one's goals. The findings show that migration brings mixed outcomes – the learning of new skills and greater personal autonomy away from the rural village, especially for younger women, yet also subjugation and control (Gaetano 2004; Yan 2008; Sun 2009).

With the widespread diffusion of communication technologies, especially mobile phones, among the rural-to-urban migrant worker population, there has been much interest in how young adult workers use these for maintaining and expanding social networks, finding romantic partners and forging a "modern" identity (Law and Peng 2006; Wallis 2010, 2013; Wang 2016). The gendered dimensions of these processes have been especially highlighted in research on young female migrant workers (Wallis 2010, 2013; Cao and Li 2018; Pei 2021). In contrast, analyses of Chinese domestic workers' use of such communication technologies are sparse although they too use smartphones and social media for informal learning, social support and venting grievances (Wallis 2018). In contexts outside of China, studies have shown how domestic workers use communication technologies, especially for "remote mothering" (Rakow and Navarro 1993), or caring for one's children via voice calls and text messaging (Parreñas 2005; Thomas and Sun 2011). Not only mobile phones, but also webcams and social media enable "intensive mothering," that is, long video calls, text messages throughout the day and night, and engaging with social media platforms such as Facebook to care for (and surveil) one's children (Madianou 2012; Chib et al. 2014; Platt et al. 2016). These studies for the most part have focused on relatively private interactions between domestic workers and their families back home. This chapter adds to this body of research by highlighting how domestic workers in neo/non-liberal China use social media for very public performances of virtual mothering and how this potentially enables immobile mobility.

Immobile Mobility Revisited: Context and Method

In prior research on how young rural-to-urban migrant women working in the low-level service sector navigated their lives in Beijing, where they were (and are still) extremely marginalized, I theorized the mobile phone as enabling immobile mobility, which I define as "a socio-techno means of surpassing spatial, temporal, physical and structural boundaries" (Wallis 2013: 6). Emerging from, and grounded in, the constraints of the women's everyday lives and their own socio-techno practices, immobile mobility through a mobile phone offered young migrant women opportunities for agency and empowerment. Many lived very socially isolated lives and used the phone to expand and enrich their social networks, which was extremely important for their mental health; date outside the constraints of parents and relatives back in the village; search for jobs; and learn new skills. However, immobile mobility has a dual logic because it is not a bounded phenomenon; that is, those who are marginalized can engage in practices that reify their own marginalization, and those in power can mobilize immobile mobility to exploit and disempower those under their control.

Older female domestic workers face even more constraints than the young migrant women featured in my prior research. Domestic workers who live with employers have minimal downtime and bear constant pressure as laborers to prove their worthiness (e.g., to show they are industrious, have a "modern" mindset and are trained in scientific techniques) and by extension, as citizens, to show their contribution to China's development. In the urban home, their focus is expected to be on their employer's children and/or elderly family member who needs care. Given their situation, what modes of immobile mobility are articulated to their use of social media and smartphones in their desire to care for their own families?

This chapter is based on fieldwork conducted on the ground in Beijing and virtual ethnography for extended periods between 2013 and 2017. The participants were 23 female domestic workers who ranged in age from 35 to 55 and who had been in Beijing anywhere from 2 to 21 years. All had children, and in some cases grandchildren. Depending on their age, the children were either at home in their village, in a vocational school or in a few cases university or out laboring. I met 14 of the women in 2013 and the other nine in 2015 through attending workshops and other activities hosted by three different NGOs that serve the needs of domestic workers in Beijing. I conducted extensive participant observation, interviews and focus groups with the women, and engaged in numerous informal conversations during the NGO-sponsored activities that I attended.

At the beginning of the research period, some women had basic mobile phones while others had low-end smartphones. Several were using QQ (for text chatting) and Qzone (a social networking platform similar to MySpace), which were popular with both migrant workers and rural residents at the time. Others had switched entirely to WeChat, a newer social media platform favored by urban residents, and still others were using both QQ and WeChat. However, by 2017, all of the women had some type of smartphone and were using WeChat only. By this time WeChat had become the do-everything platform used by nearly everyone in China for everything (chat, video, games, shopping, mobile payments, etc.). WeChat's "friends circle" (translated as "Moments" in English), which is akin to Facebook's "wall" function, enables users to post comments, pictures, videos and articles. Users can also create separate "friend circles" and thereby place friends, family, colleagues and others into distinct groups. I analyzed the women's QQ and WeChat posts (Wallis 2018) and was a member of the WeChat group chats of two of the organizations. The following analysis focuses on how women used WeChat for performative motherhood, or to publicly perform their "modern" identities as nurturing distant caregivers.

WeChat, Performative Motherhood and Immobile Mobility

Domestic workers' identity as caregivers encompasses their roles as workers and as gendered, classed and placed (rural) citizens. They are also situated as daughters, sisters, aunts, mothers and/or grandmothers in their rural families. When the women were copresent with each other during weekend activities, these roles, especially that of mother and/or grandmother, often took front stage in their use of smartphones and social media. This is not to say they did not spend time socializing, complaining or seeking advice from other "sisters" (as they called each other) about how to manage difficult employers, unscrupulous placement agencies or other hardships they faced. They indeed did, but in keeping with the government and employment training discourses of positivity, in their public social media use and in what they posted on WeChat, for the most part they maintained a positive demeanor. Thus, in these interactions, performative motherhood blended with what I call "performative positivity," in which they inverted the discourse placed upon them by others as backward or neglectful of their own families and also downplayed sadness and pain. Smartphones allowed for immobile mobility and were articulated to this inversion in several ways that displayed various degrees of publicness. I discuss three of these here – the private becoming semipublic, the synchronous public performative and the asynchronous public performative.

From Private to Semipublic

Like domestic workers in transnational contexts who use text messaging for intensive mothering, the domestic workers featured here similarly used WeChat for chatting (typing or voice messages) with their children and other family members. These chats were private conversations, often conducted early in the morning before work began or at night after work ended, or depending on the woman, clandestinely for a few moments here and there while at work during the day. Any of these private chats could in turn be used as a public record of the women's caring labor for their families. At the NGO gatherings during downtime, it was common to see women in small groups scrolling through their WeChat conversations to find pictures or short videos of children or grandchildren that had been sent to them and then sharing these with other women. In the private realm, these were modes of emotional support and connection, yet in public they served as testaments that the women's sacrifices were appreciated regardless of the distance.

A memorable example of this type of conversion occurred one Saturday when Ms. Chen, a woman in her late thirties, beckoned to me to come over and look at her phone. She then opened her most recent WeChat conversation, which was between her and her son, so that she could show me pictures he had just sent her. He had recently finished senior middle school in the town adjacent to the village where her home was located (many rural children attend boarding school after elementary school because their villages are too small to have their own junior or senior middle schools). "This is my son," she said, beaming with pride as we gazed at a tall, thin young man dressed in jeans, a button-down shirt and stylish tennis shoes. I commented on how handsome he was, and she asked, "Really?" with a smile, a common reply to a compliment and meant to demonstrate humility. She had told me before that she was working in Beijing so that he could eventually attend university and that dream was now drawing closer. Other domestic workers also looked on and offered approving remarks and soon a round of sharing pictures of children ensued.

The most attention and praise, however, was given to shared images and videos of grandchildren. Seemingly every new experience, no matter how mundane, could be captured in a picture or short video — a toddler puckering his lips after tasting an orange, a preschool-aged girl skipping in a new frilly dress — and sent to the proud grandmother. On these occasions, the other domestic workers would affirm the cuteness, smartness or other positive qualities revealed in the images. I do not ever recall seeing a picture or video with only the adult son or daughter; rather, the grandchild, in which all the hopes were placed, was the focus.

In many ways, parents and grandparents sharing images and videos with copresent friends and family is not unique. However, the ritual quality in the group setting and the ability to publicly document over time a distant child or grandchild's growth and success reveal the particular significance of the immobile mobility enabled by mobile phones for marginalized domestic workers. In using technology, they also asserted their modern identity and transformed these digital artifacts into embodiments of their own embodied caring labor.

The Synchronous Public Performative

The scenario which opened this chapter, of domestic workers attending a weekend activity organized by an NGO, with a mixture of structured activities and downtime for women to relax and socialize was common in the different organizations where I conducted research. Despite their limited budgets and lack of resources, the NGOs strive to make these spaces feel like a "home," or at least a place where the women can feel comfortable and make the space their own through chatting, listening to music and occasionally even bursting out into song, all away from the watchful eye, and often scorn, of their urban employers. Being in a "home," and as this was their one day off a week, many women also took the opportunity to engage with family members, usually teenaged children and their caregivers, or, if the children were older, the children and grandchildren. Sometimes these were private conversations, where a woman would stand away from others or go outside. However, unlike the photos and short videos discussed above that were private, asynchronous interactions made public, during the weekend activities women also engaged in synchronous performative motherhood. These interactions were most often accomplished through WeChat video calls with younger children and/or their caretakers, older children and grandchildren in the village. An example from my fieldnotes written in September 2015 is quite illustrative:

> During the break Ms. Fan was using a karaoke app on her phone and watching someone singing traditional Chinese folk songs. The volume was turned up so that everyone could hear, and she and others periodically sang along or commented on the skill of the singer. Suddenly she received a video call from her daughter who was at home in their village. She was holding an adorable small boy, Ms. Fan's grandson. Rather than turning off the speaker of her phone, she left it on and their entire conversation became a public event, with Ms. Fan occasionally inviting other domestic workers to say hello. While I was observing, she told the little boy to say hi to the "foreign auntie" (me) and turned the screen of the phone in my direction. When I waved and said "nihao" (hello), he looked at me and instantly burst into tears. Everyone, including Ms. Fan and her daughter, thought this was hilarious and burst out laughing. I thought it was funny as well. Ms. Fan then turned the phone back toward herself and continued the conversation with her daughter.

On the one hand, the historically more collective focus of Chinese society, especially rural China, could explain why I witnessed so many "private" conversations conducted in public among the domestic workers. Or, one might attribute it as just one more example of how mobile phones have broken down public/private boundaries. Once when I remarked upon these public shared video calls, Ms. Li said they were "fun" (*hao wan*). On another occasion at a different locale, Ms. Xie commented on the good feeling they brought. They were never viewed as obtrusive, at least not to my knowledge. It can be argued that they exemplify the phone enabling immobile mobility; however, it was not just that temporal and spatial barriers were broken down. By bringing everyone into the conversation, the affective dimensions of Ms. Fan's (and other's) performative motherhood and grandmotherhood flowed through the room, creating feelings that confirmed that the sacrifices of all the domestic workers' present were worthwhile.

The Asynchronous Public Performative

Another way that domestic workers used social media to demonstrate their love and sacrifice for their families was by posting photos on WeChat "Moments." Because most of the women rarely went back home, images and short videos of family members that were posted on WeChat were often those that had been sent to them. Most women did not post many of these types of photos, however. As I have discussed elsewhere, their imaging practices tended to focus on the group activities organized by the NGOs (Wallis 2018). Some women had adult children who were also migrant workers out laboring, and who sent few pictures, except when a daughter or daughter-in-law was home in the village caring for a baby or very young child, as in the case of Ms. Fan. However, women with children still in senior middle school often did not want their children to grow up as laborers; like most parents everywhere, they wanted their children to have a better life.

Thus, it is notable that four of the women had children attending university. Other than the location of the school and their child's major, they knew little detail about what college entailed except that it was seen as a path to betterment. However, because the women did not have the time or money to visit their son or daughter at college, they could only rely on the conversations they had with them, photos sent or viewing their WeChat Moments (if their child did not block them, which many university students do). Nonetheless, occasionally a picture of a woman's child on a college campus appeared on her WeChat Moments with a short comment denoting the location or activity, usually some sort of achievement or opportunity that showed success or learning. In this way, women could present themselves not only as modern parents valuing education but also giving their children a modern lifestyle.

I present one specific example here: Ms. Hu, more so than others, expressed discontent with her employers. She felt like they did not appreciate or trust her, no matter how long she had been with the family. In one early conversation, she told me that she was doing domestic work to support her daughter, who was studying at a provincial university. I later saw pictures of her daughter's graduation on Ms. Hu's WeChat Moments. After graduating, her daughter got accepted to a Master's degree program in Hong Kong, and again would be supported primarily by her mother. This was seen as a huge accomplishment and Ms. Hu accompanied her daughter to Hong Kong at the beginning of the new school term. This rare mother–daughter reunion, in a place far from their village and far from Beijing, warranted several pictures on WeChat of them together – on cliffs overlooking the bay, at a nice restaurant and so on. These images were not only documenting an enjoyable and special holiday but also showed that Ms. Hu's sacrifices for her daughter's education were worth it.

A year later, I was surprised when Ms. Hu's WeChat Moments showed photos of her daughter traveling on a holiday in the United States. I had assumed that her daughter would work during breaks from school in order to contribute to her education. However, on reflection, this trip and the photos that documented it performed an important function. Similar to McDonald's (2016) assertion that rural families' posts of idealized images of the family, especially of babies, operate as a moral discourse, affirming what good family relations should be, the pictures of Ms. Hu's daughter in the USA also showed her care and sacrifice as a mother. Such a trip was another way that she was giving her daughter modern experiences that she had never dreamed of and would probably never have.

In all these examples of performative motherhood, the immobile mobility enabled by the phone could overcome, at least somewhat, the women's separation from their families and counter the discourse of "left-behind" children. Images shared were meant to reassure the viewer, including the women themselves, that these children were not neglected but were receiving love and care. I have focused on images of children and grandchildren, but this was also accomplished through sharing pictures of recently built two-story homes, cars, modern appliances and other material goods after a visit to one's village.

Conclusion

Within the context of neo/non-liberal China, marked by heightened commodification, retrenched patriarchal gender roles and modes of affective governance in which the state and its related entities emphasize positivity regardless of the rural–urban divide, increasing economic inequality, social stratification and authoritarian control, these domestic workers occupy a particular place. They are discursively constructed as the most traditional and "backward" of the rural populace due to their gender, older age and low socioeconomic status. Even as their physical and affective labor is commodified to meet the needs of urban middle-class families, they are urged to work on themselves and demonstrate that they are modern, disciplined citizens and morally upright workers who are "naturally" nurturing. They are also supposed to show a positive public face despite numerous hardships. Although their commodified reproductive labor is focused on the urban household, their sacrifices are ultimately for their family members, who are back home in the village or scattered around various locales in China.

This chapter has analyzed how older domestic workers in Beijing use smartphones and social media for performative motherhood and grandmotherhood in ways demonstrating varying degrees of publicness – through sharing privately received images and videos, engaging in synchronous video chats where all who are copresent become part of the interaction and finally through images posted on WeChat. Such performative motherhood often intersected with performative positivity. This analysis thus reveals another layer of immobile mobility; that is, the use of digital technologies does not merely allow domestic workers to overcome constraints of time, spatial distance, physical locale and structural barriers so that they can communicate with family members. Equally significant, in the women's communicative practices, they highlight the "positive" aspects of their roles as caring, nurturing workers and gendered citizen-subjects to claim or imply a new, modern identity in which their sacrifices are affirmed and valued – by their families, training agencies, other domestic workers and ultimately themselves, as well as by the neo/non-liberal state. The way that performative motherhood and grandmotherhood blended with performative positivity does not in any way imply that the women do not have a critical consciousness of their marginalization in society. Rather, in private and in public, this particular assemblage of technology, practices, laboring bodies, feelings and emotions generates affective flows that, at least momentarily, help them to navigate and counter the hardships of their daily lives.

References

Butler, J. (1999) *Gender Trouble: Feminism and the Subversion of Identity*, New York: Routledge.

Cao, A. and Li, P. (2018) "We Are Not Machines," *Chinese Journal of Communication*, 11(3): 289–305.

Chib, A., Malik, S., Aricat, R. and Kadir, S. (2014) "Migrant Mothering and Mobile Phones," *Mobile Media & Communication*, 2(1): 73–93.

Chin, G.V. (2018) "Between Danger and Pleasure," *KEMANUSIAAN: The Asian Journal of Humanities*, 25: 121–42.

Constable, N. (2007) *Maid to Order in Hong Kong*, Ithaca: Cornell University Press.

Dean, M. (2010) *Governmentality: Power and Rule in Modern Society*, Thousand Oaks: SAGE.

Fu, H., Su, Y. and Ni, A. (2018) "Selling Motherhood," *Gender & Society*, 32(6): 814–36.

Gaetano, A.M. (2004) "Filial Daughters, Modern Women," in A.M. Gaetano and T. Jacka (eds) *On the Move: Women and Rural-to-Urban Migration in Contemporary China*, New York: Columbia University Press.

Harvey, D. (2005) *A Brief History of Neoliberalism*, New York: Oxford University Press.

Hondagneu-Sotelo, P. (2001) *Doméstica: Immigrant Workers Cleaning and Caring in the Shadows of Affluence*, Berkeley: University of California Press.

Hu, D. (2011) "Analysis of the Legal Protection for Domestic Workers in Developed Regions of China" [in Chinese], *Journal of Henan Administrative Institute of Politics and Law*, 128(5–6): 135–41.

Law, P.L. and Peng, Y. (2006) "The Use of Mobile Phones among Migrant Workers in Southern China," in P.L. Law, L. Fortunati and S. Yang (eds) *New Technologies in Global Societies*, Singapore: World Scientific Press.

Liu, M. (2017) *Migrants and Cities: Research Report on Recruitment, Employment and Working Conditions of Domestic Workers in China*, Geneva: ILO.

Madianou, M. (2012) "Migration and the Accentuated Ambivalence of Motherhood," *Global Networks*, 12(3): 277–95.

Madianou, M. and Miller, D. (2012) *Migration and New Media: Transnational Families and Polymedia*, London: Routledge.

McDonald, T. (2016) *Social Media in Rural China: Social Networks and Moral Frameworks*, London: UCL Press.

Ong, A. and Zhang, L. (2008) *Privatizing China: Socialism from Afar*, Ithaca: Cornell University Press.

Parreñas, R. (2005) "Long Distance Intimacy," *Global Networks*, 5(4): 317–36.

Pei, X. (2021) "Reshaping Co-existence of Tradition and Modernity," *Journal of Ethnic and Migration Studies*, 47(13): 3114–30.

Platt, M., Yeoh, B., Acedera, K., Yen, K., Baey, G. and Lam, T. (2016) "Renegotiating Migration Experiences," *New Media & Society*, 18(10): 2207–23.

Qiu, J. L. (2009). *Working-class Network Society: Communication Technology and the Information Have-less in Urban China*. Cambridge, MA: MIT press.

Rakow, L. and Navarro, V. (1993) "Remote Mothering and the Parallel Shift," *Critical Studies in Media Communication*, 10(2): 144–57.

Study Times (2015) "We Should Give Full Play to Women's Initiatives in the Construction of Family Civilization" [in Chinese], 18 May.

Sun, W. (2009) *Maid in China: Media, Morality and the Cultural Politics of Boundaries*, New York: Routledge.

Thomas, M. and Lim, S. (2011) "ICT Use and Female Migrant Workers in Singapore," in J. Katz (ed) *Mobile Communication*, New Brunswick: Transaction.

Tong, X. (2018) "Gendered Labour Regimes," *Asian Journal of German and European Studies*, 3(1): 1–16.

Wallis, C. (2010) "The Traditional Meets the Technological: Mobile Navigations of Desire and Intimacy," in S. Donald, T. Anderson and D. Spry (eds) *Youth, Society and Mobile Media in Asia*, London: Routledge.

Wallis, C. (2013) *Technomobility in China: Young Migrant Women and Mobile Phones*, New York: NYU Press.

Wallis, C. (2018) "Domestic Workers and the Affective Dimensions of Communicative Empowerment," *Communication, Culture and Critique*, 11(2): 213–30.

Wallis, C. and Shen, Y. (2018) "The SK-II #changedestiny Campaign and the Limits of Commodity Activism for Women's Equality in Neo/Non-Liberal China," *Critical Studies in Media Communication*, 35(4): 376–89.

Wang, X. (2016) *Social Media in Industrial China*, London: UCL Press.

Wu, X.-Y. (2010) "From State Dominance to Market Orientation," *Social Sciences in China*, 31(2): 150–64.

Yan, H. (2008) *New Masters, New Servants: Migration, Development and Women Workers in China*, Durham: Duke University Press.

Yang, J. (2015) *Unknotting the Heart: Unemployment and Therapeutic Governance in China*, Ithaca: Cornell University Press.

Ye, H. (2018) "Our Country's Domestic Service Industry Has Continuously Maintained an Annual Growth Rate of More than 20%," *gov.cn/xinwen*, 16 July.

Ye, J. (2011) "Left-behind Children: The Social Price of China's Economic Boom," *Journal of Peasant Studies*, 38(3): 613–650.

Zhang, L. (2017) "The Rise of Therapeutic Governing in Postsocialist China," *Medical Anthropology*, 36(1): 6–18.

18

NECROPOLITICAL GENDER POLITICS

Parasite's Figuring of Women's Sacrificial Disposability

Kent A. Ono

The Cannes (Palme d'Or Award) and Academy Award winning film, *Parasite* (2019), does more than just draw attention to and remark on class politics in Korea. It does more than draw an allegorical connection between minute creatures living off of the discards, crumbs and excesses of other living beings and poor people conspiring to live off of the rich, as the title of the film so powerfully signals. It does more than contrast the aspirations and ideals of modernity to modernity's underbelly, juxtaposing the haves against the have-nots along myriad dividing lines. Even though critics almost to a one concentrate on class politics in the film, gender is also critical to the narrative and thus it behooves us to look at both gender and class simultaneously, noting the many ways in which there is slippage between class and gender throughout *Parasite*. This chapter develops a theoretical lens through which to understand the relationships between gender and class in the film; surveys film reviews in the United States written by media critics, noting the focus on class issues; and then offers a study of the film, primarily employing close textual analysis to do so. Ultimately, the chapter argues that by engaging in a layered reading of the film in terms of gender, the film's narrative trajectory is repositioned.

Anyone who knows of Michel Foucault's (2007) theorization of "biopower" in the late 1970s and the many conversations it has spurred until the current global pandemic may find themselves thinking about biopower when watching the film. Indeed, from the very beginning of the film, the metaphor of humans as insects (stink bugs and cockroaches) and sewage (a man urinating outside the Kims' basement apartment window and their apartment flooded by sewage) makes consideration of Foucault's idea natural. Biopower is the idea that, for nation-states (and for capitalism), people matter more in terms of their productive potential in society than their status as human beings, members of society or citizens. The theory of biopower has stimulated much thinking about

DOI: 10.4324/9781003130628-22

the way governments and corporations manage whole populations by making strategic decisions based on the desirability of life for some and for others death (Foucault 2007). The management and regulation of populations according to the assessment of the desirability of their survival versus extinguishment is, as Foucault has it, contemporary statecraft's strategic value balancing. Building on this approach, Giorgio Agamben (1998) described the way contemporary governmentality operates to reduce humans to the most minimal existence of "bare life." Bare life is a pathetic state of rightlessness, where humans experience a world of deprivation and precarity, existing almost entirely to serve the machinery of geopolitical economic and political maneuvering (Agamben 1998). Achille Mbembe's (2003) work extended that of Foucault and Agamben to include the notion of "necropolitics," which not only reiterates biopower's assertion that governmentality divides populations according to humans' eligibility to live or die, but also concentrates on the role of political violence, of the acceptance of social and civil death, and of the larger production of precarities of life as political strategy (Butler 2004).

While compelling, theoretical work on biopower tends to concentrate on race and class, and sometimes religion, citizenship, nationalism and ethnocentrism glancingly, but rarely considers gender important in calibrating global power politics (Repo 2016; Cox-Palmer-White 2021). One way to study power in terms of gender, especially in terms of powerlessness, can be through Julia Kristeva's (1982) conceptualization of abjection. As Kristeva writes, "There is nothing like the abjection of self to show that all abjection is in fact recognition of the want on which any being, meaning, language, or desire is founded" (ibid.: 5). For Kristeva, gender is critical to abjection; to be abject is to stand on the outside looking in and to have little power or control over the role one is scripted to play, let alone the drama unfolding, regardless of one's own interests or desires, and the consequences a subject experiences as a result. Thus, the concept of abjection can extend the work of biopower by requiring an understanding of the instrumentalization of gender in statecraft and power balancing equations. *Parasite* is an apt text with which to study gendered biopower, because women exist on the periphery of a narrative principally about men's bare life. Thus, by closely examining the film, we can chart the scripted roles women play in the film's organization of power. Their abject status, their positionality on the outside of power looking in, is guaranteed, taken for granted, hardly an afterthought. The abject state of women in the film is characterized thoroughly by their *epiphenomenality*, their *incidentality* and the necessity of their *existence in relation*. As well, by its end and despite men's substantial resistance, the film moves those men toward this feminized/emasculated space. It is here in biopower's consideration of the disposability of human life, the rationale for regarding some lives as worthy and others as tangential and sacrificable, where we can consider the representation of gender in relation to class in *Parasite*.

And yet, critics of the film overwhelmingly focus only on class, rarely addressing gender as an important element of the film. Before *Parasite*'s theatrical release in the United States on 5 October 2019, media critics and reviewers understood the film as a piece of social criticism. They emphasized the film's critique of class within South Korean society, noting how the film highlights South Korea's "systemic inequality" (Ranjith 2019), "class rigidity" (Chen 2019) and "structural inequity" (Tallerico 2019). After its release, Eve Tushnet (2019), for example, went so far as to conceive of the film as a "counternarrative written by the subordinate classes," the poor denizens of South Korean urban space. Making note of the fact that the Kims live below ground, have to move around their home to find enough bandwidth for free Wi-Fi, have a stinkbug infestation and fold pizza boxes for money (sometimes unsuccessfully), Tushnet suggests, "The more severe the society's repression of its underclass, the more violent the fantasies of that subjugated class ... the more carefully they must disguise their true emotions and thoughts in order to survive."

So central was the theme of class to reviews of the film that the BBC compared real-life South Korean poverty to poverty as depicted in the film, eschewing the fantastical horror aspects of the film as a metaphor for class relations and instead reading the film as realistic (Yoon 2020). The article notes that the kind of apartment the Kims live in is called a *banjiha* in Korean, a kind of dwelling that "thousands of people live in ... in South Korea's capital, Seoul." The article goes on to describe how one person's apartment gets so little light that "his little succulent plant couldn't survive." Like the Kims' apartment, "People can peer into his apartment through the windows." People also smoke outside near his windows and sometimes spit on the ground. In the summer, the apartment is unbearably humid and the tenant has to fight mold that grows. Like the story of actual inhabitants of South Korea's existent low-income apartments, *Parasite* "is a twisted tale of the haves and have-nots." The article draws attention to the dichotomous representation of the extreme wealth of the Parks and the extreme poverty of the Kims, geographically dramatized by the Park's house on the hill and the Kims' basement apartment, a gutter dwelling, which is figuratively represented by what the daughter, Gi-Jeong, calls the "basement smell. The smell won't go away unless we leave this place," a smell so characteristic of poverty that the Parks cannot stop associating it with Mr. Kim's identity (Gi-Taek).

Even as the film (as a genre) does consider social issues, and even though the film certainly does address class, it also depends on a juxtaposition of the role of women contra that of men in the narrative. Here, I argue that gender plays a highly significant role in the film, not only by helping to define class relations but also by significantly affecting the representation of power, specifically through the depiction of the characters' gullibility, humiliation and dignity. For an understanding of how the film represents gender, I use an intersectional critical lens that takes into consideration both gender and class, while also understanding the unevenness of social power, as well as the larger panoply of social injustices that go beyond gender and class.

In that vein, I keep in mind Dean Spade's (2010) notion that vulnerability is distributed unevenly, that not everyone is equally vulnerable. Furthermore, dignifying one person can come at the expense of the dignities of another, and dignity may only be made possible within a system of power relations that require another's abjection and indignity. Thus, vulnerability is not zero sum; in this film, for instance, class and gender are in relation to one another, one informing the other, not one taking precedence over the other. This chapter, then, explores the gendered representation in the film by discussing the gendered role of Gi-Taek's *bildungsroman*, the hierarchical role of women in the film and the process by which Gi-Taek becomes emasculated, and how his coming to terms with his classed identity ultimately results in cathartic acts of masculine violence that ultimately reinscribe his subordination.

One way of thinking about gender in the film is by acknowledging that, while the film tells stories within stories, the primary story is that of a *bildungsroman*, a story of a character's development over the temporal period depicted in the narrative (Bakhtin 1996). Kim Gi-Taek, the poor father, is the central character in *Parasite*, and the film can be understood through his point of view. Popular criticism focuses on Gi-Taek's classed identity, but one can read his gendered identity as well, and indeed, his gendered identity comes to make sense through his classed identity. From this perspective, his emasculation − the diminishment of his masculinity − leads to his feminization, and while his status as a poor person nevertheless marks him as without power, he is characterized through humiliation as attaining the ultimate powerlessness when he is emasculated and thereby feminized. Thus, his loss of power as a man means his becoming more like a woman. And, in this context, his class status is closely intertwined with the humiliating experiences he endures.

My argument is that, being aware of the way the film unfolds for spectators, within a filmic context of visual and narrative desire and pleasure, it becomes clear that cultural capital is gained through masculine characters' incremental responses to class/gender humiliation and humiliation's contrast with dignity. For example, the Kims' son, Gi-Woo, has a friend, Min-Hyuk, who represents the pinnacle of masculinity; Min-Hyuk chastises the man urinating in the streets outside the Kims' apartment, an action that the Kim family labels as Min-Hyuk having "vigor." As well, Min-Hyuk brings a large and heavy rock as a gift for Gi-Woo. Min-Hyuk also has a plan to protect his girlfriend while he is away. The mother of the Park family, Yeon-Gyo, sees Min-Hyuk as the epitome of a great tutor. And, when Gi-Taek does not have a plan, Gi-Woo asks what Min-Hyuk would do. The restoration of dignity, the salve for humiliation, is ostensibly for the benefit of Gi-Taek. But, as Mimi Nguyen (2011: 369) notes, although dignity "is understood as the foundation of all human rights, dignity is unstable." In the case of this film, dignity's instability ultimately calls for Gi-Taek's dignity to be reestablished (which it never is) at the cost of the indignity of women, which the narrative requires.

Geography, specifically altitude, plays a key visual role in establishing both class and gender hierarchies. For instance, as Gi-Woo is leaving his apartment for the interview with Yeon-Gyo, he walks toward the viewer, with his mother,

Chung-Suk, doing laundry at the bottom of the cement stairs he has just climbed. She is looking up at him, while working, and is located below both him and the spectator. With clothing hung on laundry lines, we gaze on her at not only the lowest level, in the basement, but also crouching, hence occupying this lowest space. Of course, since Gi-Woo is walking at the level of working humans, he is on his way up in an effort to become equivalent with the rich, while his mother remains at the lowest level of poor people, with the other basement dwellers, insects. In this way, the film visually associates working women with the lowest register of basement dwellers and Gi-Woo's departure from this space as his possible climb out of it.

To understand the function of women in the film, one must understand the roles they play. Prototypically, women play the role of wives, mothers, housekeepers and daughters. They make sacrifices for men and for their families and do so largely without complaint. They play support roles, act as caretakers, and while the rich wife, Yeon-Gyo, for instance, has power over the Kims, she is also, in turn, nevertheless subservient to men, put in humiliating circumstances, herself made to squat down low when forced to tend the dishwasher after her housekeeper is dismissed. She experiences dominance and plays the prototypical role as an object of heterosexual romantic affection.

Throughout the film, women function stereotypically as love interests. Gi-Woo's tutorship of the Parks' daughter, Da-Hye, plays on stereotypical heterosexual male fantasies about student–teacher romances and boundary-breaking intimate relationships, as their romantic interludes often take place in Da-Hye's bedroom, a prohibited space for sexual activity. Risky sexual encounters not only occur between them but also between Da-Hye's parents. In one night scene, Yeon-Gyo and Dong-Ik are laying on the couch monitoring their son, whose glowing teepee we see through the living room picture window. Dong-Ik begins to caress Yeon-Gyo's breast through her pajama top, and while she initially protests, afraid her son might see them, the father persists saying that if their son comes out of the teepee, he will take his hand away. The scene's titillation is in part based on the thrill of exhibitionism and the danger of exposure, not only because the son might come out of the teepee, but also because, unknown by the Parks, Gi-Taek, Gi-Woo and Gi-Jeong are stuck hiding underneath the living room coffee table, with multiple intercuts emphasizing that they must stay absolutely silent so as not to be discovered, and that they have no choice but to listen to the entire sex scene. In this scene, the woman's body is positioned in front of the man's for the camera, and while she, in turn, does caress Dong-Ik's groin through his pajama bottoms, the primary action that appears for the spectator is the fondling of her body, her moaning and the filmic visualization of her pleasure.

In addition to the film assuaging Yeon-Gyo's discomfort at her son's possible discovery of them, and despite the foregrounding of her body as being acted on by her husband, the sex scene also produces titillation by centering the ostensible sexualization of Gi-Jeong. During this scene, Dong-Ik asks Yeon-Gyo if she still has the underwear that he found in the back of their first chauffeur's car (under-wear spectators, but not the Parks, known to be Gi-Jeong's), which led to that chauffeur's firing and the hiring of Gi-Taek as the Park's second chauffeur. The prurient nature of his question, and Yeon-Gyo's subsequent comment imagin-ing their sexual encounter as if in the backseat of her husband's car, where their former chauffeur, they imagine, had sex, not only centers Yeon-Gyo's fondled body at risk of being seen by her son, and actually heard being fondled (albeit unknowingly) by members of the Kim family, but also centers on Gi-Jeong and her underwear, positioning her, indirectly, as a sexual object for Dong-Ik's fas-cination and imagination.

This scene follows earlier scenes where viewers learn of the grotesque and illicit story behind Gi-Jeong's underwear. In the back of the first chauffeur, Yoon's, car, while Yoon is taking Gi-Jeong home from the Park's house at night, the camera shows Gi-Jeong reaching under her skirt and slipping off her under-wear, without Yoon seeing, and dropping it on the floor of the car. Following that scene, Dong-Ik is riding in the back of the car, while Yoon drives, and spots the underwear below the seat. We see him look at them, then we see the disgust on his face, before we see him look at the back of Yoon's head. Then, after Dong-Ik arrives home, he shows the underwear to Yeon-Gyo, who is also horrified. The Parks initially imagine Gi-Jeong willingly or unwillingly had sex with Yoon. But, then, when Yeon-Gyo confronts Gi-Jeong, asking her if anything happened on the ride home from their house, Gi-Jeong says no and acts like nothing hap-pened. The Parks then assume Yoon is having sex with other women in the back of Dong-Ik's car and the underwear is not Gi-Jeong's, after all. The illicit nature of Yoon's having sex in his boss's car, the "crossing the line" this implies, and the assumed risk Yoon seems willing to take in order to have sexual pleasure leads to the class masquerade of the Parks's sexual scene on the couch, where both Yeon-Gyo and Dong-Ik fantasize about being members of the lower class in order to enhance their sexual experience. In both scenes, the film increases the titillating sexual energy through omniscient narration that makes Gi-Jeong the central object of sexual desire, a girl significantly younger than Dong-Ik, yet someone about whom he fantasizes. Both scenes then direct attention to women as sexual objects and illicit, exhibitionist sexual behavior, but also suggest women will and do use their sexuality to manipulate circumstances, to trick men into getting what they want, and as an instrument of power. In all three cases, women's sexu-ality is central to the development of heterosexual masculine fantasies in the film.

Gullibility as Gendered Trope

In addition to the stereotypical roles women play, such as sexual objects and objects of romantic possibility, one of the film's tropes, or rhetorical strategies, also used to convey power, is that of gullibility. Gullibility is established as a conceit by which spectators come to understand the film's assumed hierarchies, to know how power is to be negotiated. Gullibility betrays an understanding of class. As Dargis (2020) writes, the rich Parks are not gullible, as Gi-Taek believes, but are instead defined by "cultivated helplessness, the near-infantilization that money affords." Women and men play particular roles in the narrative about gullibility, and the character relations to gullibility are established narratively in the film prior to building the story of class humiliation as a gendered affront to violent, gender retribution and secret/shadow class rearrangement as recompense.

Gullibility is staged through a series of deceptions, and it is primarily shown to us through the trope of innocent acceptance of human earnestness, which women are characterized as demonstrating most effectively. For instance, early in the film we see Gi-Woo manipulate the female owner of the pizza box company by shifting focus away from the Kim's inadequate box folding to one of her employees who recently quit. In part, he manipulates her through seductive charm, as she appears flattered by his attention. So suave and manipulative is he that he talks her into hiring him as a new employee on the spot.

In another scene, Gi-Woo and his friend, Min-Hyuk, hatch a plan to trick the Parks into allowing Gi-Woo to be a high paid tutor of the Parks' daughter, Da-Hye. Gi-Jeong uses composition technology to craft a seemingly authentic admissions document to university to fool Yeon-Gyo, whom Min-Hyuk tells Gi-Woo is "simple." The rich mother, Yeon-Gyo, in turn, is deceived by Gi-Woo and his ability, which in part is based on the masculine power he shows her by grabbing her daughter's wrist and teaching her that she needs to attack her exams, and thus, she hires him. Gi-Woo then hatches a plan to deceive Yeon-Gyo again so as to help Gi-Jeong become employed as an expert art instructor/child psychologist for the Parks' son, Da-Song. Yeon-Gyo is also deceived in multiple steps to hire Chung-Suk to replace Mun-Gwang as housekeeper. And, finally, the Park father, Dong-Ik, is deceived in multiple steps to hire Gi-Taek to replace Yoon as chauffeur. The ease of these deceptions, at times comical, function (prototypically in film) to assuage class stress, as they are fantastical imaginings of the power of working-class people and the wealthy people's stupidity, gullibility and class-based obliviousness to the world and associated trust in class protections. This gullibility suggests the lack of consciousness, an agential incapacity and a lack of intentionality about power that is centered in the film as, in part, the rationale for the classed shift in power to take place.

Humiliation, Emasculation, Redignification and Violence

While the Park family's gullibility and the Kim family's deceptions of the Parks come without a corollary feeling of angst or humiliation by the Parks, the narrative of class and gender retribution requires this affective register. Hence, the process by which Gi-Taek's humiliations take place, prior to his exacting retribution on the Parks, develops over time. Multiple scenes tell the story of the Parks regarding Gi-Taek as smelling bad, sedimenting his status physiologically and categorically as a member of the "poor." For instance, at one point Da-Song notices that Gi-Taek and Chung-Suk smell the same and tells his parents in front of the Kims. Then, Gi-Jeong tells us that the smell of their clothes, which comes from their basement apartment, won't go away until they leave the apartment. Then, before having sex with Yeon-Gyo, Dong-Ik, not knowing Gi-Taek is under the coffee table, smells something and attributes it to Mr. Kim. They discuss it and agree that it is the smell of poor people, people on the subway, who smell like an old radish. Then, when Gi-Taek is driving Yeon-Gyo, we see her hold her nose and roll down the window. And, in the most violent scene of the film, Dong-Ik, trying to get the keys to the car so that he can flee the scene of violence, smells Geun-Sae, who has been living in the basement for a long time, and frowns in disgust. Importantly, it is seeing Dong-Ik react to Geun-Sae's smell that leads Gi-Taek to pick up the toy axe from the ground and use it to kill Dong-Ik; it is that moment of humiliation that causes the radical change in the development of Gi-Taek's *bildungsroman*.

The physiological register of poverty, then, is mapped onto the sociological one isometrically, as if Mr. Park has been so socially conditioned to regard poverty with disgust that his nose chemically and biologically cannot tolerate the smells he associates with it. Gi-Taek overhears the Parks talking about how badly he smells, but correspondingly praising him for not "crossing the line," which implies he stays in his place, does not act uppity, and respects and does not upset class hierarchies. When he is beckoned by Yeon-Gyo to go to the grocery store with her, she keeps handing him heavier and heavier items, apparently oblivious to the impact the accumulated weight of the goods she is purchasing has on him as a mortal human being. He tags along behind her, serving at her beck and call, while she gleefully chats on the phone about the upcoming birthday party for her son, Da-Song. Less is made of Chung-Suk's humiliation, who is asked by Yeon-Gyo to arrange the tables in the backyard for the birthday party like a Japanese boat formation. And, then, when Chung-Suk is working hard to move the tables as Yeon-Gyo instructed, hefting the tables like a weightlifter, Dong-Ik asks her to keep it down, because Da-Song is sleeping in his tent. The various emasculating events build, and both the Kims as a family, and Gi-Taek, in particular, experience a feminization, a loss of power that impacts the family and him, as the family's representative patriarch, in terms of an affront to his masculinity.

Thus, for Gi-Taek, the father, provider and central Kim power figure, to have his loss of power staged, and his humiliation publicized, requires a narrative response. This is the exigence leading to a series of retributive acts of ostensible justice that generate the action for the rest of the film. How does the film show that connection between humiliation and retributive justice? Are we brought along as spectators with Gi-Taek's experience, for example? How does this relate to the ways in which the spectator is excluded from knowledge at the beginning of the film?

Gi-Taek becomes emasculated through the series of humiliating circumstances, many surrounding the Parks' reaction to Gi-Taek's smell. But, in addition to the representation of smell and poverty, the film documents the emasculation and humiliation of Gi-Taek in other ways. In addition, his devolution from power is accompanied by Geun-Sae's emasculation in parallel fashion. It is through the combination of both of their falls from masculine power that the narrative sets up a violent retributive justice, based on masculine dissatisfaction and disempowerment, a violence justified by the violence enacted upon them as subordinate denizens of South Korean society by members of the upper class.

The fall from Grace for the Kim family begins when, in the basement of the Park home, while the Parks are camping, Mun-Gwang realizes the coordinated deception the Kims have perpetrated and takes a picture of them all together in the Parks' house as evidence, which she threatens to send via text to the Parks, and in this way replaces the Kims as servant-masters of the house, if but temporarily. Up until this point, the film has primarily focused in a relatively upbeat way on the Kims' status and economic climb up the myriad literal and figurative stairs from their meager basement dwelling, which a heavy rain later floods, up the interminable climb of stairs to the geographical pinnacle, where the Parks live. Little discussed in the published reviews of the film, the fantasy of becoming wealthy begins to fall apart for the Kims when they subjugate Mun-Gwang and her husband Geun-Sae. Having reached the pinnacle of success, partying in the Parks' home while they are away, eating and drinking lavishly, taking a luxurious bath, drunkenly and laughingly fantasizing about a marriage between Gi-Woo and Da-Hye, which would result in Gi-Woo becoming a legal member of the Park family, and Gi-Woo's family legitimate, they experience a fall.

Mun-Gwang interrupts their frivolity by ringing the doorbell and asking to be let in; then, once inside she hurries past the false vegetable cellar shelves down to the basement to give milk to her husband, Geun-Sae. This is how the Kims (and the spectator) discover that Geun-Sae has been living in the sub-basement, and Mun-Gwang, the former housekeeper, has been taking care of him by bringing him food she has purchased. Geun-Sae represents, then, what Gi-Taek will ultimately become. Geun-Sae, too, experienced humiliation at the hands of a loan shark, not having enough money to pay back the loan, and having to live in a basement in order not to be found, subsisting off of canned food and the bits of food his wife brings him. Geun-Sae is indicative of the lowest class and gender status; unable to work or pay his debts, indeed trapped in a basement, his wife nurses him; without her, he is entirely helpless. He represents the status toward which Gi-Taek is moving. He is a prisoner in the basement of a rich family's home, unable, even, to communicate successfully through Morse code, a code boys (who are not men) learn in boy scouts, simple information to the outside world. The Kims decide to keep him in the basement; but, this character flaw of desiring what rich people have and being willing to subjugate other "parasites" in the process is the Kim family's ultimate undoing, and Mun-Gwang and Geun-Sae's willingness to lord over the Kims, once they take control, is, in turn, their undoing.

After Gi-Woo drops the stone Min gave him down the staircase, scheming to kill Mun-Gwang and Geun-Sae, Geun-Sae surprises him, screams crazily and chases Gi-Woo up the stairs hitting him with tremendous force with the stone twice. The apparent death of Mun-Gwang, and thus Geun-Sae's loss of a wife, as well as retribution for the Kims having subordinated them, precipitates this violence, which begins a series of violent acts, including Geun-Sae's murder of Gi-Jeong, Chung-Suk's retributive murder of Geun-Sae, and finally Gi-Taek's murder of Dong-Ik. Once toppled from their perch, Gi-Jeong dead and Gi-Woo essentially brain dead, from which he seems later to recover, Gi-Taek returns to below ground, occupying the sub-basement and living a "bare life," powerless, emasculated, family-less and without hope.

Conclusion

By way of conclusion, two particularly powerful illustrations of the way gender operates in the film to enhance and define the role of class and bare life are worth considering. The first demonstrates the degree to which women are positioned abjectly. After his sister, Gi-Jeong, dies, Gi-Woo goes to the cinerarium and, looking at rows of white urns with ashes in them, sees her urn for the first time, laughs and then murmurs, "I laughed then, too." This perplexing response can be read as resulting from his brain injury and surgery, but it is also symptomatic of the role women play in the film, and it gives insight into the complex way gender functions in the film. The memory of his sister is humorous, or perhaps he is humored at her being dead while he is now the dead living. Nevertheless, while she and her memory are central to the narrative and to the scene, the scene draws attention to her agential absence, indicating the overarching irrelevance of her presence, except as trace memory. It also puts into question the significance of her very existence.

I conclude with a second illustration of the way gender operates in the film – Gi-Taek and the film's representation of him as a father with a plan. Early in the film, when the phones are not working and the Internet is dead, Chung-Suk kicks him in the butt with her foot and asks, "What's your plan?" Later, after they have tied up Mun-Gwang and Geun-Sae and descended myriad stairs during the rainstorm trying to get home, Gi-Jeong asks Gi-Taek what his plan is. Gi-Taek then responds that he does have a plan and tells them to forget about the people they have trapped in the basement. Finally, after the flood has forced them out of the apartment and they wind up at a disaster relief site with hundreds of other displaced people, Gi-Woo again asks him what his plan is. Gi-Taek takes his time, considers the question and then says that he has no plan, and that sometimes the best plan is to have no plan at all. This philosophical stance that, if you have no plan, you cannot fail suggests that, for Gi-Taek, being a father is a hopeless state of disempowerment; even his one act of masculine bravado in the film, killing Dong-Ik, leads to his perpetual imprisonment in the Park basement. Gi-Taek tries to be a masculine father in one way to his daughter and in a different way to his son, but in both instances, he cannot actually *do* anything; he is powerless.

In this way, the multiple humiliations and acts of emasculation are slights to Gi-Taek's masculinity. They hit at his role as a father, provider and husband.

They certainly affect his status as having and not having capital. Thus, this story – which critics portend to be about class and the logic of class subordination and existence – is, in turn, also about gender, about the humiliation of men and men's loss of power and control, about women's lowest social status, about the metaphorical way women's abjection is utilized to explain men's indignities, and ultimately about women's lack of meaningfulness within the narrative. When Geun-Sae reaches the end of his rope, he can't help himself. He kills Gi-Jeong in a cathartic act of violent masculine aggression, as if this will release him from his classed and gendered positionality. Similarly, too, Gi-Taek, having seen this act, mimics it, killing Dong-Ik. Their symmetry, their mirrored behavior, was presaged in the film when Mun-Gwang repeatedly told Chung-Suk they were the same, trying to get her to realize their common lot, and yet the dramatic conclusion is not about the women/wives/mothers/housekeepers' similar abjection. It is about the men/husbands/fathers/chauffeurs' similar central emasculation.

Considering the film through the lens of gendered biopower allows us to see that power not only operates via class, as both critics and the film itself foreground. Power also operates through gender and does so by analogizing poverty with gendered identity and experiences. With this lens, the humiliations and indignities the characters experience can be understood not only as classed experiences but also as gendered ones. We can chart the way power is conceptualized by the film not only by the way it corresponds with the social position of rich and poor people, but with men and women, too. Furthermore, this analysis allows us to see that the film considers gender a useful metaphor to help explain poverty as a social phenomenon – strategically using one social condition to make sense of another. This suggests that the film cannot explain the bare life of poor people fully without understanding it in terms of the bare life of poor women, leaving women and women's class position as rhetorical modifiers of men's subjective experiences of oppression.

References

Agamben, G. (1998) *Homo Sacer: Sovereign Power and Bare Life*, Stanford: Stanford University Press.

Bakhtin, M. (1996) "The Bildungsroman and Its Significance in the History of Realism," in C. Emerson and M. Holquist (eds) *Speech Genres and Other Late Essays*, Austin: University of Texas Press.

Butler, J. (2004) *Precarious Life: The Powers of Mourning and Violence*, London: Verso.

Chen, X. (2019) "Bong Joon-Ho's 'Parasite' Sparks Discussion in Chinese Mainland," *Global Times*, 14 August.

Cox-Palmer-White, E. (2021) *The Biopolitics of Gender in Science Fiction*, New York: Routledge.

Dargis, M. (2020) "'Parasite' Review: The Lower Depths Rise with a Vengeance," *New York Times*, 10 February.

Foucault, M. (2007) *Security, Territory, Population: Lectures at the Collège de France 1977–1978*, London: Palgrave Macmillan.

Kristeva, J. (1982) *Powers of Horror: An Essay on Abjection*, New York: Columbia University Press.

Mbembe, A. (2003) "Necropolitics," *Public Culture*, 15(1): 11–40.

Nguyen, M.T. (2011) "The Biopower of Beauty: Humanitarian Imperialisms and Global Feminisms in an Age of Terror," *Signs*, 36(2): 359–83.

Ranjith, P. (2019) "Pa. Ranjith Praises 'Parasite,' Calls Korean Film Representative of Systemic Inequality," *The Hindu*, 13 December.

Repo, J. (2016) *The Biopolitics of Gender*, New York: Oxford University Press.

Spade, D. (2010) "Introduction: Transgender Issues and the Law," *Seattle Journal for Social Justice*, 8(2): 445–53.

Tallerico, B. (2019) "Reviews: Parasite," *Rogerebert*, 7 September.

Tushnet, E. (2019) "Upstairs, Downstairs: I Review Parasite," *Patheos*, 4 December.

Yoon, J. (2020) "Parasite: The Real People Living in Seoul's Basement Apartments," *BBC News*, 10 February.

PART IV
Mobile Asia

19

BIPOLAR AMERICA

Anti-Asian versus Hollywood's *Minari*

Sheng-mei Ma

In this new millennium, America suffers from the bipolar syndrome toward Asia, hating and loving it at the same time. This psychotic split within America manifests itself in media and popular culture with respect to Asia or putative Asianness. Media representations become the window to America's soul, projecting conservative, xenophobic loathing spearheaded by Trump as well as liberal, progressive love radiating from Hollywood. The far right and the far left, however, are mirror images of each other in their extremities. Trumpian loathing stems from self-loathing; Hollywood smooches from self-cuddling.

Goaded by Trumpian populism and nativism, half of America scapegoats Asians, among other peoples of color, on account of the paranoia of White replacement. This fear of dispossession is intensified by the ascent of China in the "Chinese Century," which challenges American exceptionalism and supremacy in what has been the "American Century," particularly during the Cold War and beyond. With its presumed origin in Wuhan, China, the global pandemic of COVID-19 has only exacerbated the tension. China's lack of transparency in sharing data and assisting the WHO investigators in locating the source or even the index patient has increased suspicion and resentment against China. The list of patients and the course of their illness should have been published for the sake of humanity in preventing another global outbreak.

Against Trump's America, the other half of this bipolar collective psyche overcompensates by valorizing things Oriental. For instance, in 2021, the liberal forces, encapsulated by Hollywood, pick this hate-filled moment to bestow praise and awards upon Lee Isaac Chung's *Minari* (2020), as though the Korean immigrant family drama counterbalances anti-Asian hate crimes and sentiments. That *Minari* is a softball of an understated melodrama fits the bill for a feel-good breather to escape from the anti-Asian reality. Which is the real and which the dreamscape? Which is a real/reel dream and which a fake reality? The

DOI: 10.4324/9781003130628-24

crimes committed by the Atlanta shooter Robert Aaron Long and the New York "kicker" Brandon Elliot and the unidentified anti-masker-cum-hammerer and the San Francisco stabber Patrick Thompson, just to name the most recent and most atrocious, are the reality both Asians in America and Americans of Asian descent are forced to inhabit, a reality born out of twisted minds and crazed delusions. Asians live and die in accordance with Americans' sick hallucination. The exact number of these Americans remains to be determined.

On the other hand, *Minari* purports to be largely autobiographical, where immigrant (grand)parents' life experiences are, nevertheless, adapted for the genre of family melodrama from the perspective of the filmmaker Chung's alter ego, an American-born Korean boy growing up in rural Arkansas. Where is the immigrant's shared American nightmare of being the perennial alien? Is the Ozarks the Promised Land sans bigotry and racism? This chapter follows the trajectory of American bipolarization, swinging from hate at one end of the spectrum, manifested by AAA or Anti-Asian Anonymous to, at the other end, love showered on *Minari*, named after water celery or Chinese celery, which is practically an invasive species to conservationists of native plants, reminiscent of the nativist rhetoric against the racial other.

AAA: Anti-Asian Anonymous of Atlanta and America

COVID-19 has so sickened America's body politic that the latent frailty of its composition exposes itself, triggered by Trump's racist "Chinese virus" and "kung flu" to shirk the commander-in-chief's pandemic-fighting responsibility. Amidst Trump's flurry of activities casting blame of America's death tolls on the Chinese, *The Washington Post* published on 19 March 2020 Anne Gearan's reporting with a close-up photograph by Jabin Botsford. The picture is a blow-up of Trump's briefing notes, where "corona" in coronavirus was crossed out and replaced by "CHINESE" in caps with the infamous sharpie (Ma 2020, 2022; Figure 19.1).

An extension of Trumpian discursive and political violence, on 16 March 2021, the Atlanta shooter Robert Aaron Long took eight lives, six of whom were Asian immigrant women, at three massage parlors. In the press conference at the Police Department headquarters in Atlanta the following day, "backed" by Mayor Keisha Lance Bottoms and two other African American police officers arrayed behind him, spokesperson Jay Baker described Long's "sex addiction". To rid himself of such temptations on a particularly "bad day," Baker alleged, the mass murder was committed. By parroting Long, Baker damned, in one fell swoop, the six deceased, ranging in age from 33 to 74, as sex workers.

Baker was later revealed to have uploaded on his website a Sinophobic T-shirt brandishing "Covid 19/IMPORTED VIRUS FROM CHY-NA" under a biological warfare logo (Figure 19.2). As deafeningly silent as the military colors raised at a battlefield, the logo accuses "CHY-NA" of waging a biological warfare linked to the yet-to-be-proven theory of leaked virus from Wuhan Institute of

FIGURE 19.1   Trump's briefing notes, where "corona" in coronavirus was crossed out and replaced by "CHINESE".

FIGURE 19.2   Jay Baker's Facebook page with the image of a Sinophobic T-shirt brandishing "Covid 19/IMPORTED VIRUS FROM CHY-NA" under a biological warfare logo.

Virology in the Chinese city. The Gothic, Germanic script for "Covid 19" comprises dagger-like strokes with sharp, jagged points and hooks, as though hailing from menacing dark forces, if not straight from hell, the Third Reich. The apparel's fascist rhetoric borrowed from Nazi Blackletter to portend peril. The T-shirt designer also captured well Trump's compulsive butchering of "China" into a misshapen "CHY-NA," its first diminutive syllable associated subliminally with "Chink," followed by the hyphen for a space, a chink. Traumatic enough it is to learn once again of an active shooter from AAA, not Alcoholics Anonymous, but Anti-Asian Anonymous of Atlanta, America! Furthermore, secondary trauma was afflicted by the criminal justice system, the Atlanta authority of the police backed by the mayor, giving voice to the reprehensible killer.

One of which was Brandon Elliot's 29 March assault of a petite 65-year-old Filipino American woman at the front door of Midtown luxury apartments at 360 West 43rd Street, a few blocks from Times Square, while shouting racial slurs and "You don't belong here!" (see CCTV footage released by NYPD: https://www.youtube.com/watch?v=Xswt73F9gUY). Throughout the kicking and stomping in plain view of the apartment staff, a security guard walked over to shut the front door, and at least two apartment personnel and one delivery man stood by, watching the street show. The assault was captured by the security camera of the apartments. The spectators' indifference added a new wrinkle to the good ol' USA's AAA: Anti-Asian Accomplice.

Long's "sex addiction" stems from the even longer Orientalist addiction of Anglo-America that stigmatizes Asian males as racially castrated and Asian females as hypersexualized (Eng 2001; Shimizu 2007). A long tradition lies at the heart of White masculinity silhouetted against Asian femininity from popular culture of Hollywood and Broadway, including *Madame Chrysantheme*, *Madame Butterfly*, *M. Butterfly*, *Love Is a Many-Splendored Thing*, *The World of Suzie Wong*, *The Teahouse of the August Moon*, *Sayonara*, *The Quiet American*, *Miss Saigon*, *Girl by the Road at Night* and more. To occupy the centrality of humanity, White maleness bumps other races to the opposite ends of the gender spectrum: Blackness is made to gravitate to aggressive, primitive masculinity; Asianness to passive, decadent femininity. Hence, Asian man turns effeminate, Asian woman superfeminine. Very much a White game, the US entertainment industry realizes this masturbatory fallacy with yellowface in the vein of blackface. To rephrase Frantz Fanon's (1967) *Black Skin, White Masks*, the yellow mask was worn by White skin, including mixed-race actors. The aforementioned films feature, for instance, Jennifer Jones in *Love Is a Many-Splendored Thing* and Nancy Kwan – half Chinese and half English – in *The World of Suzie Wong*. The Japanese geishas and Vietnamese bargirls of the other films suggest the eroticized stereotypes and roles into which Asian performers must have contorted themselves to fit. It goes without saying that Asian, mixed-race and White female leads comprise the love interest of White male leads, oftentimes ending in tragic deaths from *Madame Butterfly* to *Miss Saigon* onscreen to Atlanta massage parlor off-screen.

Also in real life outside the celluloid frame, fetishization of Asian women prompted a predator like the University of Southern California gynecologist George Tyndall to specifically prey upon Asian and Asian American female students from 1989 to 2016. Plenty to pick from: USC, after all, is facetiously dubbed the University of Southern Chinese. It matters little that these films and sexual assaults have been set across the globe, in Japan, "CHY-NA," erstwhile Saigon, Atlanta or Los Angeles, for Asian women everywhere are, as they like to say, "all alike" in reputedly dedicated as a body, pun intended, to White male pleasure.

Beyond White supremacy on the back of Asian gender roles, what does it say about Asian American citizenship when we use derogatory terms like "Chink" in public, while shunning the N-word, as Randall Kennedy expostulates in his 2002 book? Name-calling Asians is but being "factual," more acceptable than name-calling African Americans. Whereas the N-word has been tabooed as the unsayable, other racial epithets remain as part of the public discourse. Racism comes in gradations, depending on the political clout of the group being discriminated against. That we are saying "Asians" but never "Africans" for "African Americans" suggests grouping Asians, that is, Asian Asians, with Asian Americans. The American Self, White or Black, defines itself vis-à-vis the Asian Other. As such, America continues to be addicted to an externalized AlieNation, aka, AlienAsian or Alien Asians. The "Southern redneck" incarnate Long and the "motha killa" on lifetime parole Elliot displace their self-alienation onto the perennial alien, their sense of victimization onto the scapegoat deemed not from these parts.

This psychic transference is America's repetition compulsion. We have, alas, seen this horror movie many times before. Déjà vu, all over again, as it replays the Chinese Exclusion Act (1882–1943), the only time when a race was barred from entering the United States, until it metastasized into Trump's Muslim ban from 2017 to 2021. Allied with China against Japan during World War II, the US interned Japanese Americans in the wake of Pearl Harbor. Because the US was unable to avenge itself against the stealth attack, President Roosevelt, Congress and the American people decided to round up the usual suspects, including US-born Americans of Japanese descent, and put them in concentration camps en masse across the West Coast. Ironically, to prove their patriotism, Japanese American volunteers from these camps bid farewell to their families and joined the 442nd Infantry Regiment, the most decorated unit for its size in US military history. These soldiers strove to prove their allegiance, which was cast in doubt, but they might have also wished to ensure, at least subconsciously, the safety of their family still held "hostage" by the US government. The 442nd Infantry Regiment was sent to fight Nazis in Italy rather than Japan's Imperial Army in the Asian theater, conceivably, for suspicion of mixed loyalty. Did the Pentagon have the same concern over sending German or Italian Americans to fight the Axis?

Fast forward to Vincent Chin, who was bludgeoned to death in Highland Park, Detroit, in 1982 by two White unemployed automobile workers mistaking him for Japanese. Rendered "out of work" by what they called "Japanese imports [import cars]," Ronald Ebens and his stepson Michael Nitz got into a brawl with Chin at Fancy Pants, a nude bar, where Chin was celebrating his upcoming wedding in a stag party with three friends, one of whom, Jimmy Choi, was also Asian American. The erotic dancer Racine Colwell testified that Ebens blamed the "little mother fucker" for having made them "lose their jobs." This pointed to one of the ceaseless waves of Asia-bashing, this one directed against Japan in the 1980s, to be continued with the present wave against "CHY-NA" orchestrated by Trump. That Chin at five years old had been adopted from Guangzhou, China, by White parents and was apparently so Americanized that he hosted his stag party at a nude bar did not mitigate White resentment. On the contrary, the Asian-looking man enjoying himself with sex workers might have incensed the disgruntled ex-workers.

At the bar, Ebens was cited as calling Chin a "Chink," a "Nip," a "Boy." While driving around the block to stalk Chin and his friend Jimmy Choi, the father and the stepson picked up a Jimmy Perry, to whom US$20 was offered to solicit his assistance in "catching a 'Chinese guy' and busting his head." In his own testimony, Ebens admitted that he told Perry that he "was looking for two orientals [sic]." Incontrovertibly, race contributed to, if not caused, the deadly clash. Likewise, race played a role in the two dancers' testimonies; the prosecution witness Racine Colwell, White, pitted against the defense witness Starlene, Black. Defense attorneys raised doubt about Colwell who had known Chin from another establishment; Starlene appeared unreliable as well. Starlene claimed to have been such a rookie that she shied away from Chin's largesse of inserting bills into her wardrobe while allowing Ebens to "go down" on her to perform fellatio.

The legal wrangling resulted in Ebens's acquittal in 1987. No public outrage or riot broke out afterwards, like what happened on the heels of the Rodney King acquittal in 1992. Although it was White police officers who stood trial, Korean-owned businesses bore the brunt of black and brown rage in South Central LA. The similarity of how race and gender intersected is striking in these violent crimes perpetrated by, in the order of appearance, Ronald Ebens along with Michael Nitz, Robert Aaron Long, Brandon Elliot and more. Men preyed upon women in a Detroit bar, Atlanta spas and New York City. Femininity was either sexploited to gratify male desire in the first two cases or stomped on for its undesirability, for not "belong[ing] here" in the Elliot case. Desirability is a will-o'-the-wisp, shining bright if possessed with youth and glamor, darkening if without. "Possessed" is the modus operandi; males are obsessed with possessing female bodies, even if it means dispossessing them of dignity and life. Such male drivenness is driven by biological impulses out of control, or the will to power unleashed by alcohol, delusion of grandeur and sheer hate.

The exception appeared to be Vincent Chin. Vincent Chin availed himself of an extreme form of masculine pastime at Fancy Pants, only to find himself becoming the hunted due to race, his head bashed in by Ebens's baseball bat, American male's other pastime (Ma 2000). Marked by their Asianness or alienness, Vincent Chin and his fellow victims in Atlanta, New York and elsewhere arise as the New Jew. The historical scapegoat in Christendom is joined by Asians in this "Chinese Century." The ascent of China in the 21st century elicits jealousy and fear, sentiments most unbecoming to American exceptionalism. With China breathing down America's neck in the race for supremacy, the US reaction would only intensify. Trump's inflammatory "Chinese virus" had lit the fire of Sinophobia. As WHO investigators were thwarted in their probe into the source of COVID-19, as the viral wildfire continued to spread with no end in sight, we shall witness more Anti-Asian Anonymous flare-ups across America, a bit swampier after the stoking by Trump.

Any intersection of race and gender must not forget the third rail of socio-economic class, which returns us to New York, where the haves and the have-nots co-inhabit uneasily. Brandon Elliot and the upscale apartment staff who stood idly by at 360 West 43rd Street seemed to be all Black. The as yet unidentified New York hammerer against two Asian women with masks on 2 May 2021 was also Black. These belonged to the string of Black-on-Asian violence, whereby homeless or economically deprived African Americans assaulted Asian passersby. Should a Black elderly person be attacked by Elliot, would the security guard and others simply shut the front door and turn their back? Would an upper-class White, Black and even Asian elderly person dressed to the nines inflame Elliot as much, yet also intimidate and inhibit him? Should an Asian resident of the luxury apartments be the victim, would the staff feel duty-bound to intervene and lend a hand? There were at least four of them against one Elliot, for goodness' sake. Was the Filipino woman picked out on account of her physical frailty as well as plain, unremarkable clothing? Or was she simply in the wrong place at the wrong time, a self-comforting excuse we have all used to explain away killings and crimes? Should one blame this on the depraved Sin City of New York, on its lower-rung Black citizenry or simply on those individual culprits and accomplices with no larger significance whatsoever?

Let us disabuse ourselves of the last scenario of wishful thinking and self-delusion ill-fitting our time of #MeToo, racial reckoning and socioeconomic equity. A bottom feeder in an affluent New York, Elliot apparently blamed whatever he was experiencing on an Asian stranger weaker and more powerless than himself. Elliot's taking it out on an alien was acquiesced to by the complicit apartment staff entrusted with maintaining order inside and around the building, surely including its "storefront." Cowards they all were – men with guns and fists, in uniforms with badges and no guts. The investigation may yet reveal the truth behind the action of Elliot and the inaction of the security guard and bystanders, behind Long's bullets and Baker's official and unofficial, public and Facebook, statements. Satiated with Asian blood, bipolar America turns to water and life.

Minari, an Invasive Species?

Receiving six Oscar nominations and awarded Best Supporting Actress for Yuh-Jung Youn's role as the grandmother, *Minari* tells the story of a Korean immigrant family in the 1980s Arkansas. The parents Jacob Yi and Monica, along with their children Anne and David, relocated from California where they had eked out a living as chicken sexers. David suffers from a heart condition that prevents him from overexerting himself. A normal child's activities such as running and capering are forbidden. David's weakened heart harkens back to immigrants' warped lives. What used to be the immigrant's assets and capabilities – the Korean language, cultural literacy and much of their professional skills – become moot, irrelevant in a new place as though they now lapse into liabilities and disabilities, robbing the immigrant of the power of speech, of comprehension and of action. Typical of immigrants from a farming background, Jacob dreams of owning and harvesting his own land instead of scrutinizing "chicken butts" for the past ten years. Upward mobility from the bottom of society and from chicken's bottoms drives Jacob.

What Jacob plans to plant, however, reflects the immigrant paradox; one leaves home to replicate the lost home. Jacob grows Korean vegetables in Arkansas' fertile yet parched soil for California's massive immigrant population. The supplier and the consumer engage in a transaction of Koreanness outside of Korea; growing, partaking Koreanness because they have parted from it. A local religious fanatic Paul is Jacob's trusted help. Paul, on occasion, bursts out praising the Lord. Every Sunday without fail, Paul slogs along the country road, carrying Christ's wooden cross on his shoulder. Although Monica is a devout Christian, Paul, unlike his apostolic namesake who proselytized in Asia Minor, does not seem to have any effect on Jacob. Much to Jacob's dismay, Korean wholesalers back out of their deal at the last minute. A furious Jacob is left with a whole shed of vegetables and fruits wilting under the southern sun. Class resentment erupts as Jacob curses sly, untrustworthy Korean compatriots in the cities. This remains, however, the formula to minority success in businesses; milking one's own kind for cheap labor to stay competitive in the majority market. Filmmaker Chung chooses to feature intra-racial antagonism, and only briefly for that matter, rather than inter-racial tension. Local Ozark residents appear to accept the immigrant family; no significant racial rancor and conflict arise between the poor country folks and the new arrivals. Playing safe in his melodrama, Chung refrains from ruffling White self-image and mainstream sensibility.

No Ozark bigotry rears its ugly head, except an innocent enough remark from a White boy Johnnie: "How come your face is so flat?", countered by David's matter-of-fact "It's not." David and Johnnie later become fast friends. Unfavorable first impressions give way to harmony and bonding. What troubles David more, akin to Jacob's troubles with metropolitan Koreans, is the coming of his grandmother, foul-mouthed, ill-behaved, a downright stereotypical alien that is an idée fixe out of White representations of Asians. David's narrative perspective is key to the relative success with mainstream media. In between White and Korean cultures, speaking predominantly in English with the feel of an American bildungsroman, David is the perfect conduit for the alien universe and, particularly, the alien grandmother to reach the screen without ever alienating White sensibility. David's exasperation over a grandmother who shares his room, eats disgusting food and blasphemes approximates how an American would react to an unknown transplant. From the centrality of the Americanized Korean boy, the grandmother is polarized into the hated intruder and the mythical savior. Savior indeed, even David's heart is strengthened as the grandmother urges him to run wild outdoors, contrary to the parents' warning. While the first, immigrant generation, such as Jacob and Monica, struggles to raise a family, the second or third generation, such as David, enjoys the luxury of romanticizing ancestral heritage, albeit in a problematic, self-contradictory way.

David's pivotal role is beyond dispute. On the one hand, White resistance resonates with the boy's frustration over the grandmother's bizarre and incomprehensible behavior. On the other, White audience identifies with David, including his affiliation and "blood" ties with the grandmother, a familial, spiritual succor in life's struggle. That the grandmother is, simultaneously, the destroyer and the savior comes through most vividly in the wake of Jacob's grocery debacle. Incapacitated by a stroke, the grandmother seeks to help the family but accidentally torches the shed stacked with vegetables. After the grandmother passes, the bereft father and son revisit the riverbank where she had sowed minari seeds brought from Korea, seeds that would be deemed contraband smuggled in nowadays, if not in the 1980s. Jacob and David squat, a Korean body language considered uncouth in the West, to gather minari flourishing in patches near the water, the sole surviving vegetables, the gift of life from the dead, after a fire caused by the grandmother. The grandmother is the fire that incinerates and the water that inspirits. A loop of familial and cultural ecosystem, she drinks the grandson's urine by accident and gives herself back in water celery from Korea by design, the filmmaker's design, that is.

Rather than a simple, feel-good happy ending, this finale reveals an unwitting irony. For Asian Americans, just like their fellow Americans, the alien grandmother is mythologized only in death. She is redeemed as a redeemer *after* she is killed narratologically. No good alive, she is worth a million in death. Such is the course of life for this nation's minorities. Early settlers' "The only good Indian is a dead Indian" alchemizes into the "noble savage" for settlers' children, through a Midas White Touch that transubstantiates a genocide into golden memory. Beyond retiring the grandmother from life, Chung retires, likewise, the stereotype of the raging immigrant patriarch taking it out on his family for a lifetime of disillusionment, a stock character prevalent in Asian American literature and film. Jacob, fortunately, never rises to the occasion, so to speak. David's nasty trick of having the grandmother drink a coke bottle of his urine infuriates Jacob, not only morally but subconsciously. What the grandson does to the grandmother with his urine echoes what society has done to Jacob the chicken sexer, whose profession hinges on the cloaca, the posterior orifice for feces and repro-duction. The immigrant family eat because Jacob and Monica have been "eating (chicken) shit."

In his towering rage, Jacob follows, supposedly, the Korean tradition, dis-patching David to fetch a switch for his own punishment, possibly a lashing on the calves. This is already a "downgrade" from the weapon of choice in Korean historical dramas, which favor wooden clubs in the shape of police truncheons. The protagonist Chunhyang in Im Kwon-Taek's *Chunhyang* (2000), for exam-ple, is treated to a savage beating after she rejects the advances of the lecherous local magistrate, the father figure for villagers. By having the camera pan up, away from the "crime scene," to the tune of Chunhyang's non-stop *pansori* sing-ing amidst smacking of flesh and cracking of shin bones, Im aestheticizes and insulates the beating that would cripple anyone tied to the chair. In place of Im's shift to the musical to avert violence, Chung elects a pseudo-realistic twist. The father's fury dissipates when David returns with a single blade of Arkansas long grass to stroke gently, lovingly the grandmother's cheeks. A family trauma is forestalled with David's stroke of genius in using what is practically a light feather to move and remove Jacob's mountain of wrath, a fusion of Korean flam-ing sword of forbiddance and American prairie grass of forgiveness. A melodra-matic wish-fulfillment for the boy to flee from the shadow cast by the father! For the boyish Hollywood, *Minari* exits the shadow of anti-Asian hate crimes perpetrated by the bottom of America – Atlanta crazies and New York homeless and more – under the command from the very top of Trump's White House and the Trumpian horde in Congress, in states and in localities.

Minari concludes with a local Arkansas diviner locating underground water with a forked divining rod, the spot subsequently marked by the heavy black rock Jacob carries, a tradition from Korea with its rocky landscape and rock art. The coming together of the local and the exotic portends life, as water is, one hopes, to ooze from below that rock. Bipolar America evinces a contrast: Half of it sheds Asian blood in assaults; the other half let flow the secret of life, all the way from Asia, subterraneously, symbolically. Half of it sacrifices Asian bodies; the other half sacralizes Asian ghosts.

References

Eng, D. (2001) *Racial Castration: Managing Masculinity in Asian America*, Durham: Duke University Press.

Fanon, F. (1967) *Black Skin, White Masks*, New York: Grove Press.

Gearan, A. (2020) "Trump Takes Direct Aim at China as Known US Infections Double and Criticism Mounts," *Washington Post*, 19 March.

Kennedy, R. (2002) *Nigger: The Strange Career of a Troublesome Word*, New York: Vintage Books.

Ma, S.-M. (2000) *The Deathly Embrace: Orientalism and Asian American Ethnicity* (Chapter 4 Vincent Chin and Baseball: Law, Racial Violence and Masculinity), Minneapolis: University of Minnesota Press.

Ma, S.-M. (2020) "Kung Flu," *America Unfiltered*, 8 May.

Ma, S.-M. (2022) *On East-West: America's Chinee & the Chinese Century*, Columbia and Taipei: University of South Carolina Press and National Taiwan University Press.

Shimizu, C.P. (2007) *The Hypersexuality of Race: Performing Asian/American Women on Screen and Scene*, Durham: Duke University Press.

20

CAPITAL ON THE MOVE

Quantico, Im/Mobile Laboring Bodies and the Hypermediation of Racial Difference

Purnima Mankekar

Quantico (2015–2018), an American thriller television series aired on the ABC, begins with the aftermath of an explosion: Grand Central Station in New York City has been razed to the ground in a terrorist attack. In the opening frames, we see a brown arm sticking out of the rubble. Enshrouded in dust and gray smoke, this arm, this body, is unmistakably foreign. It is a woman's arm, cloaked in ash, and on its wrist is a bracelet that prominently displays "Om," one of Hinduism's most important symbols. As sirens scream through the chaos, the camera pans to reveal the detritus of buildings, then zooms to focus on the face of the woman who, for all the Hindu-ness displayed by her Om bracelet, is ethnically ambiguous. She is escorted by the FBI when she emerges from the rubble and we learn that she has a decidedly un-Hindu name, Alex Parrish. With a temporal jump characteristic of *Quantico*, we are taken back nine months in time. We see Alex going for a run through the streets of Oakland. Shortly thereafter, she gets on a flight to Washington D.C. en route to Quantico, the site of the FBI's bootcamp where she trains to become a federal agent. Alex Parrish, we learn quickly, is a woman constantly on the move.

Cut to another location, a different mise-en-scene. A Business Process Outsourcing (BPO hereafter) firm in Bengaluru where hundreds of young men and women sit in cubicles conversing with overseas customers. Their voices are hushed; an electric intensity fills the room. Thanks to information technology, fiberoptic cables and a range of software, this BPO provides customer service, back-office work, transcription services, accountancy services and debt collection to multinational companies based in the Global North. These young men and women are known, in the industry, as agents. Many of them have traveled to Bengaluru from nearby villages and small towns and cities in the farthest reaches of India to work in BPOs; now they commute long distances to work, traversing the city late at night or in the early hours of the morning. Most experience

DOI: 10.4324/9781003130628-25

upward social mobility by earning far more than their parents or other members of their families. They perform affective labor while they are kept in (their) place; their race, national location and class foreclose their ability to travel overseas.

There are several points of similarity and difference between Priyanka Chopra/Alex Parrish – Brand Chopra – and BPO agents. The objective of this chapter, however, is not to engage in a comparison between them but to engage in a relational analysis by conceiving of Brand Chopra and BPO agents as examples of the hypermediation of discontinuous formations of racial and cultural difference in conjunction with transnational capitalism. This is a form of transnational capitalism enabled by digital media, information technology, and global communication networks. Rather than "adding up" to a totalizing portrait of transnational capital, these discontinuities suggest how laboring bodies circulate in contexts shaped by Mobile Asia.

Hypermediation pertains to the production, consumption and exchange of signs that occur across different media and platforms. While hypermediation typically connotes circuits of information in online media (for example, a web page that includes graphics, sound and video), I use the term to encapsulate streaming platforms, television and film, the circulation of commodities, including the star figure and information technology-enabled labor to foreground fragmentation, simultaneity and continuous movement rather than stasis, closure or completion. Thus conceptualized, hypermediation refers to the role of mass and digital media in entertainment and information technology (hardware and software) in the workplace to foreground how media *span* domains of labor and leisure, the workplace and spaces of domesticity and intimacy. As a result of the proliferation of digital platforms, Brand Chopra appears to travel deftly across transnational borders as a global icon and star. Despite the centrality of information technology and transnational communication networks to their affective labor, BPO agents are emplaced or, as some of them put it, "stuck" in place (Mankekar and Gupta 2016, 2017, 2018). My objective is to account for the "strange affinities" (Hong and Ferguson 2011) between Brand Chopra and BPO agents in Bengaluru: I am interested in how Asian bodies – those that move, do not move, or move in distinctive ways – are positioned within, navigate and reconfigure transnational capitalism.

Within the United States, the arrival and movement of Asian bodies have frequently generated ultra-nationalist and xenophobic discourses of cultural and racial difference with violent consequences for Asian American communities. This violence is exacerbated every time there is a perceived threat to national security – exemplified in the incarceration of Japanese Americans during World War II, the racial violence against South Asian Americans and those perceived as Muslim or Middle Eastern after 11 September 2001 and, more recently, the anti-AAPI (Asian Americans and Pacific Islanders) hate that resurged during the COVID pandemic. Although most BPO agents are not likely to be able to (im) migrate to the United States, they also represent a threat to the United States through their spectral indexicality of the outsourcing of jobs to the Global South and, in particular, to Asia. The threat that they purportedly embody draws affective sustenance from genealogies of xenophobic discourses about Asian immigrants and migrant workers who, allegedly, steal jobs from White Americans. They represent Asia on the move despite the fact that they are not physically mobile.

My analysis brings together media studies perspectives that decenter Euro-American theoretical frameworks, Asian American Studies scholarship on immigration, and theorizations of global capitalism in feminist anthropology. My argument proceeds from the following premises. One, I conceive of Asia in *media res*, as always in formation and, hence, constantly on the move (Mankekar and Schein 2011:14). Scholarly discourses have been crucial to the production of Asia as an epistemological category (Ludden 2003; Duara 2010) and, in the contemporary era, transnational media have been central to the production of Asia (Mankekar and Schein 2011). Digital technologies have only further accelerated the speed by which Asia and Asianness are mobilized. Instead of ascribing a fixity to Asia, I am interested in how Asia and Asianness are produced in conjunction with the hypermediation of cultural and racial difference. Second, drawing on feminist cultural analysis and cultural geography (Massey 1994; Grewal 1996; Kaplan 1996; Ahmed et al. 2003), I take as axiomatic that mobility and immobility are not dichotomous; rather, mobility is contingent on immobility and emplacement. My conceptualization of im/mobility eschews assumptions about voluntarism, autonomy and, indeed, sovereign subjectivity. Third, mobility and the production of cultural and racial difference have long been intimately related and, in contexts of contemporary capitalism, the hypermediation of difference is co-implicated with the entrenchment of neoliberal multiculturalism and late-capitalist mutations of cosmopolitanism.

Mobility, Race, and the Production of Value

Much has been made in popular discourse and in the scholarly literature of how Priyanka Chopra and BPO agents have been trained to speak in accents that may be described as Global English or "neutral accents" (Aneesh 2015). While I do not have the space to attend to the relationship between accent, race and the production of value, I focus on how *Quantico* and the affective labor of BPO agents provide us with optics to track hypermediations of race and racialization and their displacement onto difference. In *Quantico*, these discourses of difference articulate with neoliberal multiculturalism to reinforce the security state; in the case of BPO agents, they undergird the production of capitalist value on a transnational scale through the extraction of the labor of populations and communities that are devalued or less valued. Taken together, these discourses of difference consolidate the role of digital media, information technology, and global communication networks in contemporary forms of racial capitalism. As regimes of value production they do not replicate colonial modes of extraction, but rework them through biopolitical hierarchies that both draw upon and diverge from those formerly based on phenotypical differentiation (Singh 2004; Melamed 2011).

Multicultural Difference and the Security State

Quantico demonstrates how cultural and racial differences are simultaneously generated, aestheticized and domesticated through neoliberal multiculturalism to reinforce the security state. Next, I tack back and forth between Brand Chopra and Alex Parrish as they move across multiple screens and sites to illustrate the hypermediation of specific kinds of racialized, gendered and sexualized bodies resulting from the proliferation of online media, for example, content-sharing platforms like YouTube and streaming media like Netflix. In 2015, Priyanka Chopra catapulted to international fame with the ABC television series *Quantico* which ran for three seasons and drew a global audience; for instance, it was simultaneously aired in India on Star India network, a subsidiary of The Walt Disney Corporation (Singh 2020). When Chopra arrived in the United States to launch her international career, she had already scaled the dizzy heights of stardom in the Hindi film industry, one of the largest film industries in the world, but with the success of *Quantico* she became a global star. Chopra's apparently seamless mobility across national borders foregrounds the convergence of global capital and the expansion of digital content delivery platforms such as Hulu and Netflix: Brand Chopra became a globally circulating commodity consumed across heterogeneous media, texts and audiences.

Brand Chopra demonstrates the fraught relationship between the "infrastructural flexibility" offered by streaming platforms (Singh 2020: 257) on the one hand, and the hypermediation of racial and cultural difference on the other. There is a long history of South Asian actors in Hollywood – including Om Puri, Aishwarya Rai, and Irrfan Khan – whose success in traversing national borders and screens enabled them to take roles that push back against stereotypical portrayals of ethnicity and culture. The scale of Chopra's mobility across multiple screens and texts has been unprecedented and spans her appearance in morning shows and late night television, the People's Choice Award and her highly mediatized wedding to Nick Jonas, her confrontation with a Pakistani journalist on Twitter and her much-hyped support for Indian Prime Minister Modi's COVID relief campaign, her work as a UNICEF ambassador and as an entrepreneur producing films for Indian and global audiences, her investments in the dating app Bumble and in a high-end Indian restaurant in New York. Chopra has highlighted and marketed her Indianness in her media appearances. For the most part, she represents herself as a Global Indian whose mobility across national borders coexists easily with her Indianness. In multiple television interviews, she has spoken about her life as the child of doctors in the Indian Army, her fidelity to "Indian" values, and her patriotic loyalty to the Indian nation (on the nationalist underpinnings of Global Indianness, see Mankekar 2015). When Stephen Colbert interviewed her about Kamala Harris's election as vice president of the

United States, she responded archly: "Coming from a country like India, which has seen several women in governance from prime ministers to presidents, you know, welcome to the club, America, is what I'll say!" – a comment that, presumably, expanded her fan base across India and the Indian diaspora (Jain 2021).

In her memoir and in interviews on network television and multiple streaming platforms, she emphasizes that she has achieved success – as evidenced by her mobility across national borders, texts and platforms – because of her hard work and discipline. Chopra has also spoken frequently about her experiences while in high school in the United States when she was bullied because of the color of her skin and was called "Brownie" and "Curry" (YouTube 2018). She insists that she has the ability to remake herself depending on the context in which she finds herself; in fundamental ways, she exemplifies the ideal, typical flexible and entrepreneurial neoliberal subject. During the 2016 Oscars, in an interview with an Asian American journalist, she proclaimed her Asian identity thus: "I just think … represent … own who you are and own your roots and we are amazing! We come from Asia!" (Singh 2020: 266). Being *from* Asia has never constrained Brand Chopra's mobility across national and cultural borders. This mobility is apparently compatible with her ability to adopt different identities – an Indian woman from a small town, a global citizen, an entrepreneur and a transnational media star. In fundamental ways, Brand Chopra represents Mobile Asia.

Alex Parrish, like Chopra, is a woman constantly on the move. Indeed, Chopra's personal and professional mobility dovetails into her portrayal of Alex Parrish, illustrating how the subjectivities of celebrities in the entertainment industry feed into and are sustained by their on-screen personas. Like Brand Chopra, Alex is driven, tenacious, and unapologetically ambitious. Her mentors consider her the "finest" agent in her cohort. Her intelligence and, more significantly, her athletic prowess enable her to outperform other trainees. She sprints through forests and fields, jumps nimbly over hurdles, races up climbing walls – she is seldom still. Once she becomes a prime suspect in the attack on Grand Central Station, she has to run for her life through the streets of New York and to a secluded cabin on an upstate lake to seek a former classmate who, she hopes, will help her find the mastermind behind the terrorist attacks. In desperation, she enters the Dark Web to protest her innocence to the American public. At the end of Season 1, she and her lover Ryan Booth flee the United States to escape those who are trying to hunt her down. Alex Parrish can never stay in place, never stay put.

As part of a multiracial cohort at Quantico (where the director is an African American woman, no less), Alex is not the only dark-skinned agent. Nevertheless, she is *marked* as exceptional. Her exceptionality is foregrounded every time the camera zooms in on her Om bracelet or lingers on the statue of a Nataraja on her bed stand. Parrish's race and ethnicity are deployed to mark her as, at once, alluring and threatening in ways that remediate racially sexualized and sexually racialized representations of Asian women dominant in US popular culture (Marchetti 1994; Parrenas 2007). Alex Parrish is by no means a fragile lotus flower – quite the contrary, she is physically strong and sexually assertive. She owns her sexuality in ways that appear to resist stereotypical portrayals of Asian women as shy and sexually docile. At the same time, her sexuality builds on established tropes of exotic eroticism. She is mysterious, a woman with many secrets and a past that continues to haunt her present. Early in the series, we see her flirting with a stranger on her flight to Quantico; after she has had sex with him in a parked car at the airport, she refuses to give him her name, claiming that he is not her "type." He turns out to be Ryan Booth, a member of her cohort at Quantico and, when they meet there for the first time, she has no qualms about publicly admitting that they had had sex in his car. From the very beginning, Alex transgresses stereotypical tropes of South Asian American women (*desi* girls) as virginal or sexually modest. Yet, like many Asian and Asian American women in US popular culture, her allure stems from the fact that she is seductive precisely because she is inscrutable. Thus, far from transgressing racist stereotypes, Alex Parrish illustrates the eroticization of race and the racialization of eroticism in dominant representations of the sexuality of Asian women that precede but are now recharged by discourses of difference in neoliberal multiculturalism. Taken together, Alex Parrish and Brand Chopra illustrate how racial difference is commodified, exotified, and domesticated to reinforce a purportedly post-racial ethos that undergirds neoliberal multiculturalism. A successful Asian woman in Hollywood, Chopra appears to reinforce the myth of meritocracy and justify the logics of neoliberal capitalism according to which flexibility, determination, and an entrepreneurial ethic enable individuals to transcend and render irrelevant the structural violence of dominant discourses of race, gender and sexuality (Sathe 2021).

Quantico demonstrates some of the ways in which discourses of difference in neoliberal multiculturalism reinforce the security state. Parrish is part of a multiracial, multicultural ensemble of trainees, a rainbow cohort of young men and women (with two Muslim women, one of whom wears a hijab, thrown in for good measure) who are committed to protecting the sovereignty of the United States "at all costs;" by Season 2, another Asian American woman joins the multiracial ensemble of agents in Quantico. Early in the first episode, we see this cohort, with its diversity of complexions and races, swear an oath to defend the constitution of the United States. Yet, Parrish becomes a terrorist suspect because of her racial and cultural Otherness, her unassimilability.

Chopra's portrayal of Parrish is complex, even if somewhat predictable: an FBI agent who will put her life on the line for the United States, she is a brown woman who becomes a terrorist suspect. Episode 5 begins with a newscast that centers on her racial and cultural Otherness. The White news anchor intones: "They *say* she's an American. But what kind of American murders 130 innocent people?" (emphasis in original). Her Americanness is cast further into doubt when the news anchor adds: "I don't know where she was born. India? Egypt?" Despite the fact that she was born and raised in the United States, like many immigrants from the Middle East and South Asia in post-9/11 America, speculations about where she is "from" render her into a threat. Tabloids refer to her as "Jihadi Jane" – there is no question that she is a suspect because of where she is assumed to be from. Later in this episode, she explicitly addresses how her skin color and where she is deemed to be from makes her into a suspect: "They framed the brown girl. I had spent time in India and Pakistan. In this country I am an easy person to blame." Like many brown people who were deemed "jihadi" after 11 September 2001, she has to prove her loyalty to the United States, and so she adds: "I love this country and I want to protect it. That's why I became an FBI agent in the first place." The domestication and inclusion of difference is thus put to the service of a White supremacist security state.

After 9/11, neoliberal multiculturalism has provided tools for the management of risk and danger through the classification of race and gender (Grewal 2003: 538, 2017). These classifications get hypermediated across a range of texts from print media, television, and film to online platforms, gathering affective potency as they circulate within and across national borders. Within the United States, neoliberal multiculturalism participates in the marking of certain bodies as inherently risky, foregrounding processes of racialization that are both sustained by and are different from previous forms. Thus, for example, Parrish, as the seductive (and mysterious) Asian woman is inherently risky not just because she represents entrenched portrayals of Oriental women but because she *remediates* them. As a woman whose exoticism and eroticism are inextricably entangled, she is not waiting to be penetrated by the West/a Western man: she displays no hesitation in being sexually assertive. While Orientalist discourses tend to represent the femininized East, hypostasized, placed in a subservient position, and lying in wait to be conquered by an equally hypostasized, superordinate and masculine West, she anthropomorphizes an Asia that is all the more dangerous for being mobile.

Cosmopolitan Desires and Hypermediated Labor

Neoliberalism as an ethic is confined neither to Hollywood nor to the United States (Grewal 2005; Melamed 2011). Neoliberal capitalism(s) is mutually imbricated with geohistorical and geopolitical formations to reconstitute itself in response to other domains of social life. Neoliberal capitalism is never exterior to these other domains to then penetrate them from the outside but is coproduced with them through the generation of value (Bear et al. 2015). In Bengaluru's BPOs, for instance, capitalist value is generated through affective labor enabled by information technology and global communication networks. Moreover, neoliberal multiculturalism segues into transnational discourses of cosmopolitanism to produce, seize upon and manage difference to generate capitalist value; in this sense, hegemonic renditions of cosmopolitanism are not an antidote to neoliberal multiculturalism (compare with Calhoun 2008) but, instead, articulate *with* it in discourses of difference that circulate transnationally (Cheah 1998; Grewal 2005).

The formation of Asia, and its heterogeneous histories of travel, conquest, empire, trade and religious campaigns, has long been shaped by movement and forms of cosmopolitanism that emerged in pre-modern, modern and post-modern sociohistorical conjunctures (Ludden 2003; Gupta 2008; Duara 2010). Mobility and cosmopolitanism are related in fundamental ways, and I refer here not just to physical mobility as when cosmopolitanism is engendered by migration and immigration, but also imaginative mobility generated by transnational media and the circuits of capital. Information technology and global communication networks generated the ability of BPO workers to engage in virtual (Aneesh 2006) as well as imaginative travel. Their labor was hypermediated by information technology ranging from the dialer software that put them in contact with customers and algorithmic compilations of customer profiles to the fiberoptic connectivities that enabled the transmission of the products of their labor. It is for this reason that BPOs are considered part of the Information Technology Enabled Services (ITES) industry, and it is this quality of hypermediation that distinguishes the affective labor that BPO agents provided at a distance from other forms of care work offered by, for example, nannies, housekeepers, and nurses in face-to-face settings. But what does cosmopolitanism connote in contexts of hypermediated labor? If cosmopolitanism is implicated with mobility, what forms does it take when bodies remain in place?

BPO agents engage in cosmopolitan encounters on various registers and scales through their physical, virtual, and imaginative mobility. Many of our interlocutors reported to us that when they moved to Bengaluru, they encountered, for the first time, people whose cultural practices were vastly different from their own (Mankekar and Gupta 2018). As Jisha Menon insightfully argues, BPO agents' "cosmopolitan encounters register not only intercultural difference but also intracultural differences of class, gender and regional diversity, destabilized by rapidly shifting techno-finance-media-scapes of urban India" (2022: 62). Nor does their cosmopolitanism transcend the national; in many ways, their cosmopolitanism is contingent on their emplacement within the nation, as when agents are interpellated by nationalist discourses of progress or remain in place within India because their national identity, class position, and race foreclose opportunities to emigrate.

The generation of value in BPOs is dependent on agents' mobility, immobility, and emplacement. Many were the first in their families to leave their hometowns to find work. Their ability to travel to Bengaluru was thus a prerequisite to finding jobs in BPOs. They also experienced rapid class mobility because of their relatively high salaries. Even so, most of them could not afford to rent homes close to BPOs and had to commute long distances to work. In addition, their affective labor was predicated on live interactions with customers in different time zones which meant that they had to work while their families and communities were asleep. These temporal disjunctures entailed forms of travel across distinct chronotopes. But traveling and working at night came at a cost. Commuting at night was dangerous for women who were particularly vulnerable to sexual violence. Furthermore, women agents were frequently deemed sexually promiscuous because they engaged in nightwork. In contrast to those subjects of cosmopolitanism who are treated with the "grudging accept- ance of neighbors" (Calhoun 2008: 441), women agents experienced increased surveillance and stigmatization precisely because of their mobility across differ- ent chronotopes.

For most of our interlocutors, a large part of the attraction of BPO jobs was that they offered opportunities to acquire the "soft skills" of cosmopolitanism. Although BPO agents, compared to the vast majority of unemployed and under- employed youth in India, are privileged because they have relatively well-pay- ing jobs, the cosmopolitanism they acquire is neither voluntary, nor inherently empowering or pleasurable, nor reducible to lifestyle choices. Instead, the acqui- sition of cosmopolitan traits is essential for providing affective labor for custom- ers in the Global North and is imbricated in the generation of capitalist value. The acquisition of cosmopolitan traits was a major objective of the "cultural training" in which new recruits learned about the "cultures" of their customers.

Their labor was also hypermediated in how it was predicated on their con- sumption of transnational popular culture. For instance, they were encouraged to watch American sitcoms like *Friends* to learn about the "values" of customers living in the United States or were taught the finer points of "footy" to be able to make small talk with Australians. They were required to imaginatively step outside the confines of their own lives in order to develop relationships with overseas customers. In this context, cosmopolitanism is a disciplinary technol- ogy that trains and interpellates young men and women in Bengaluru as laboring subjects so they can relate to overseas customers as they make a sale or provide service. In contrast to the cosmopolitanism of elites who choose to become citi- zens of the world through the privilege of travel or consumption, for BPO agents cosmopolitanism is neither a privilege nor an escape from emplacement but is, on the contrary, predicated on their being kept in place in India, in Bengaluru and in the cubicles where they work. And when our interlocutors had to face racist or xenophobic abuse from their overseas customers, their training as cosmopolitan subjects faltered. These instances revealed the fissures and ruptures that consti- tute cosmopolitanism by exposing the racial and class asymmetries and material inequalities that exist on a transnational scale. These instances brought to the fore the limits of cosmopolitanism in a world shaped by racial capitalism.

Neoliberal Multiculturalism, Cosmopolitanism, and Racial Capitalism

Menon (2022: 17) has pointed to cosmopolitanism's "deep entrenchment within circuits of capital." I extend her argument to posit that cosmopolitanism as well as neoliberal multiculturalism are embedded in and reinforce racial capitalism through the classification of human beings in terms of regimes of social and eco- nomic value rather than solely on the basis of phenotypical differentiation (also see Melamed 2011). Brand Chopra, as a globally circulating commodity, her portrayal of Alex Parrish in the multiracial and multicultural world of Quantico, and the hypermediated labor of BPO agents in Bengaluru generate, and are products of, discourses of difference that demonstrate that transnational capitalism is not race neutral.

Alex Parrish is visibly Other; the incorporation of her Otherness appears to push against the notion of Asians as the suspect race. Her brownness is not epiphenomenal to the narrative but is central to it. Her Otherness propels her constant mobility, both at Quantico and when she becomes a fugitive. Her brown skin, the Nataraja by her bedside, her Hindu mother Sita, her passionate repudiation of accusations of being Jihadi Jane, and her Om bracelet only underscore how her difference makes her a figure of danger even as these very differences are redirected to reinforcing national security. She is committed to protecting her nation not despite her Otherness but because of it: neoliberal multiculturalism depends on the incorporation – rather than the disavowal – of difference to consolidate the security state.

Brand Chopra personifies the mobility of the star figure as a commodity that travels adroitly across national borders, platforms, and texts; her personal and professional lives converge and diverge depending on context. Brand Chopra represents the ideal typical neoliberal subject who is flexible, entrepreneurial, and has risen to the top of her career not despite being different but, like Alex Parrish, because of it. Most importantly, Brand Chopra exemplifies how discourses of racial difference structure the production of value in capitalism. Brand Chopra demonstrates the complex positionality of Asians in contemporary forms of racial capitalism. As Wendy Cheng (2013: 151) has argued in another context, in racial capitalism, the "utility of the 'figure' of Asianness depended upon its otherness or foreignness, its 'distance' or triangulation from both Black and White;" at the same time, as immigrants, Asian Americans may also collude with the violence of the settler colonial state.

In his foundational work on racial capitalism, Cedric Robinson (1983) has argued that the modern world has been shaped by the co-constitution of racialism or racial ideologies, on the one hand, and the logic of capitalism on the other; racialism, he insists, is a material force that permeates all social structures spawned by capitalism while the logic of capital continually reshapes conceptions of race. If race and racialism shape the transnational mobility of Brand Chopra/Alex Parrish, they structure the logic of capital in the BPO industry in vastly different, but related, ways. Racial capitalism, in the case of BPOs, makes structural inequality seem fair or, worse, beneficial for those who labor in them (Nadkarni 2020). Although BPO agents earned high salaries compared to members of their families and communities, they were paid considerably less than their counterparts in the Global North because of labor arbitrage, that is, the practice of paying workers in one location less than those in another location for the same work. Labor arbitrage is a prerequisite for outsourcing to be profitable for transnational and multinational companies and becomes a process of racialization when it is based on a calculus according to which the labor and time of workers in the Global South are undervalued. BPOs illustrate how, in racial capitalism, "historic repertoires and cultural and signifying systems that stigmatize and depreciate one form of humanity for the purposes of another's health, development, safety, profit or pleasure" (Singh 2004: 223). The racialization of BPO workers does not replicate the racial logics of colonialism which were predicated on the transportation of cheap labor to metropoles but, instead, compels us to rethink theories of colonial extraction by foregrounding how information technology may remediate the relationship between racial capitalism and labor.

I find it significant that, in the course of close to a decade of ethnographic fieldwork, BPO workers seldom mentioned race or described themselves as racialized. The only exception was when they described the racist abuse they would sometimes face from customers in the Global North. Even in these instances, they preferred to attribute the abuse to the fact that they were located in an "underdeveloped" country. In these narratives, the abuse stemmed from their national location rather than race. Or, they tended to attribute the abuse to asymmetries arising from cultural rather than racial difference. On their part, managers and trainers seemed to believe that providing "cultural training" to new recruits and teaching them about the "customs" and "habits" of their overseas customers would protect them from the "communication problems" that led to racist abuse.

The purportedly post-racial world of Quantico and BPOs is founded on the production – and inclusion – of difference in myriad ways, spanning neoliberal multiculturalism in the context of the security state and the disciplinary technologies of cosmopolitanism essential to the provision of hypermediated affective labor. Displaced onto multicultural difference and cosmopolitanism, inequalities of race emerge as structuring forces in the consolidation of the security state and racial capitalism.

Capital on the Move

At particular historical moments, mobility and immobility have been closely implicated with the production and management of difference; for instance, hierarchal assumptions about cultural and racial difference enabled the moral justification of colonialism and imperialism. Since mobility is about the capacity to inhabit and navigate particular chronotopes, spatialization and temporalization are co-imbricated, as when those who cannot move are variously represented as backward or lagging behind -- in contrast to the mobility of those who purportedly propel teleological narratives of nationhood or globalized capital.

At the same time, despite its mythical self-representation as a nation of immigrants (a racialist ideology that obscures its settler colonial formation), in the United States certain migrants and immigrants, as people who move, are deemed a "problem": shifting conceptions of race have been central to the ways in which some migrants are deemed more desirable than others. Asian American studies scholars have long foregrounded the fraught positionality of immigrants who are "structurally located at the contradiction between the demands of capital for socially disunited 'abstract labor' and the demands of states for culturally unified 'abstract citizens'" (Lowe 1996: 13). Like racially Other Asian immigrant workers, BPO agents are portrayed as problems in the discourses of politicians and popular culture because they allegedly steal jobs that supposedly belong to White Americans.

This chapter has demonstrated what a relational analysis of an unlikely pairing, the transnational travels of Alex Parrish/Brand Chopra in *Quantico* and the affective labor of BPO agents in Bengaluru, teaches us about the hypermediation of im/mobility and difference in contemporary forms of racial capitalism. I have focused on how *Quantico*'s depiction of racial difference, personified by Alex Parrish, articulates with the hypermediation of the affective labor of BPO agents. There are compelling parallels between the FBI agent who is suspected of being a terrorist because she is brown and BPO agents whose labor renders them threats to the US economy. In both instances, brown bodies are perceived as endangering US national security. On a transnational scale, multiculturalism segues into a form of cosmopolitanism that undergirds the affective labor of BPO agents. Terrorism and outsourcing have been deemed major threats to US national and economic sovereignty. These are "separate but linked threats": if the threat of terrorism is spectacular, that represented by BPO agents is specular (Nadkarni 2020: 221). Given that South Asia is a locus for both the international War on Terror and the outsourcing of service, these discourses accumulate affective and political potency as they travel across transnational space.

Priyanka Chopra is part of, and puts herself in the service of, racial capitalism. As Brand Chopra, she valorizes the boundary-crossing, perpetually mobile, flexible and entrepreneurial neoliberal subject who claims to transcend racial difference even as she embodies it. The affective labor of BPO agents underscores how the hypermediation of labor in the transnational service industry is structured by racial difference in ways that both draw on and diverge from colonial modes of extraction. These formations of racial capitalism underscore how hegemonic notions of race articulate in uneven and discontinuous ways in the world of *Quantico*, where nothing is as it seems, and in the hypermediated labor of BPO agents.

Acknowledgments

I wish to acknowledge that my analysis of BPO agents' mobility and emplacement builds on collaborative ethnographic fieldwork with Akhil Gupta in three BPOs in Bengaluru between 2009 and 2015 funded by the Fulbright-Hays Senior Fellowship and a grant from the American Institute of Indian Studies, respectively. I thank our interlocutors in these BPOs for generously sharing their insights and experiences, and am grateful to Derek Lu for his meticulous research assistance for this paper.

References

Ahmed, S., Castaneda, C., Fortier, A.M. and Shelter, M. (2003) *Uprootings/Regroundings*, London: Routledge.

Aneesh, A. (2006) *Virtual Migration: The Programming of Globalization*, Durham: Duke University Press.

Aneesh, A. (2015) *Neutral Accent: How Life, Labor and Language Become Global*, Durham: Duke University Press.

Bear, L., Ho, K., Tsing, A. and Yanagisako, S. (2015) "Generating Capitalism: Theorizing the Contemporary," *Fieldsights*, 30 March.

Calhoun, C. (2008) "Cosmopolitanism and Nationalism," *Nations and Nationalism*, 14(3): 427–48.

Cheah, P. (1998) "The Cosmopolitical Today," in P. Cheah and B. Robbins (eds) *Cosmopolitics: Thinking and Feeling Beyond the Nation*, Minneapolis: University of Minnesota Press.

Cheng, W. (2013) "Strategic Orientalism: Racial Capitalism and the Problem of Asianness," *African Identities*, 11(2): 148–58.

Duara, P. (2010) "Asia Redux: Conceptualizing a Region for Our Times," *Journal of Asian Studies*, 69(4): 963–83.

Grewal, I. (1996) *Home and Harem: Nation, Gender, Empire and the Cultures of Travel*, Durham: Duke University Press.

Grewal, I. (2003) "Transnational America: Race, Gender and Citizenship After 9/11," *Social Identities*, 9(4): 535–61.

Grewal, I. (2005) *Transnational America: Feminisms, Diasporas, Neoliberalisms*, Durham: Duke University Press.

Grewal, I. (2017) *Saving the Security State: Exceptional Citizens in Twenty-first Century America*, Durham: Duke University Press.

Gupta, A. (2008) "Globalization and Difference: Cosmopolitanism Before the Nation-State," *Transforming Cultures eJournal*, 3(2): 1–20.

Hong, G. and Ferguson, R. (2011) *Strange Affinities: The Gender and Sexual Politics of Comparative Racialization*, Durham: Duke University Press.

Jain, S. (2021) "What Priyanka Chopra Said about Kamala Harris Becoming Vice President of US," *NDTV*, 29 January.

Kaplan, C. (1996) *Questions of Travel: Postmodern Discourses of Displacement*, Durham: Duke University Press.

Lowe, L. (1996) *Immigrant Acts: On Asian American Cultural Politics*, Durham: Duke University Press.

Ludden, D. (2003) "Presidential Address: Maps in the Mind and the Mobility of Asia," *Journal of Asian Studies*, 62(4): 1057–78.

Mankekar, P. (2015) *Unsettling India: Affect, Temporality, Transnationality*, Durham: Duke University Press.

Mankekar, P. and Gupta, A. (2016) "Intimate Encounters: Affective Labor in Call Centers," *Positions: East Asia Critique*, 24(1): 17–43.

Mankekar, P. and Gupta, A. (2017) "Future Tense: Capital, Labor and Technology in a Service Industry," *HAU: Journal of Ethnographic Theory*, 7(3): 67–87.

Mankekar, P. and Gupta, A. (2018) "The Missed Period: Disjunctive Temporalities and the Work of Capital in an Indian BPO," *American Ethnologist*, 46(4): 417–28.

Mankekar, P. and Schein, L. (2011) *Media, Erotics and Transnational Asia*, Durham: Duke University Press.

Marchetti, G. (1994) *Romance and the Yellow Peril: Race, Sex and Discursive Strategies in Hollywood Fiction*, Berkeley: University of California Press.

Massey, D. (1994) *Space, Place and Gender*, Minneapolis: University of Minnesota Press.

Melamed, J. (2011) *Represent and Destroy: Rationalizing Violence in the New Racial Capitalism*, Minneapolis: University of Minnesota Press.

Menon, J. (2022) *Brutal Beauty: Aesthetics and Aspiration in Urban India*, Evanston: Northwestern University Press.

Nadkarni, A. (2020) "Neoliberal Multiculturalism, Outsourced," in S. Shimpach (ed) *The Routledge Companion to Global Television*, New York: Routledge.

Parrenas, C. (2007) *The Hypersexuality of Race: Performing Asian/American Women on Screen and Scene*, Durham: Duke University Press.

Robinson, C. (1983) *Black Marxism: The Making of the Black Radical Tradition*, London: Zed Books.

Sathe, N.R. (2021) "Brand Priyanka Chopra: Neoliberal Individuality, Citizenship and the Transnational Female Celebrity," *Jump Cut: A Review of Contemporary Media*, 60(Spring).

Singh, N. (2004) *Black is a Country: Race and the Unfinished Struggle for Democracy*, Cambridge: Harvard University Press.

Singh, P. (2020) "Transnational Screen Navigations: Priyanka Chopra's Televisual Mobility in Hollywood," in S. Shimpach (ed) *The Routledge Companion to Global Television*, New York: Routledge.

YouTube (2018) "Priyanka Chopra on Being Bullied at School," 4 February.

21

DIGITAL MEDIA AND DIASPORIC NATIONALISM

Japanese Migrant Women in London

Yuiko Fujita and Kaoru Takahashi

This chapter explores how digital media use influences migrants to reconstruct and negotiate their identities through a case study of Japanese female migrants in London. In the past few decades, a growing number of migrants have moved back and forth between two or more countries. They connect transnationally and construct new identities via the improved means of communication such as the Internet and mobile phones. Exploring how the diasporic media space serves as emotional comfort for migrants situated in a precarious environment, this chapter argues that even the seemingly successful settlement does not necessarily undermine migrants' national identity but rather encourages their reevaluation of national and cultural dimensions of subjectivity. The chapter intends to illuminate the mundane and integral roles of digital media that enable transnational subjects to imagine a multiple and flexible sense of home as a deterritorialized imagined community.

Since the 1990s, researchers have explored transnational migration networks and identities and defined transnationalism as the processes by which immigrants forge and sustain multistranded social relations that link together their societies of origin and settlement (Basch et al. 1994). Transnational migration is partly enacted due to the changing conditions of global capitalism, and transmigrants develop transnational networks, activities, patterns of living and ideologies that span their home and host societies. Kasinitz et al. (2009) investigated the actual attitudes and behaviors involved in transnationalism; the circular migration between the host country and the home country, bilingual language skills, social or economic remittances to the country of origin and the use of ethnic media. Itzigsohn and Saucedo (2002) identified three explanations for such transnational participation. First, transnational practices are the result of the ties and attachments that link migrants to their families and places of origin (linear transnationalism). Second, transnational practices occur as migrants try to send money to

DOI: 10.4324/9781003130628-26

their families in their country of origin (resource-dependent transnationalism). Third, transnational practices are a reaction to a negative experience of incorporation (reactive transnationalism). An important approach to transnationalism is the complexity of identity. The concept of transnational identity often refers to new identities constructed through the experience of migrants who have two or more "homes" in the home country and the host country. Migrants develop transnational identities, moving back and forth between their home and host country with identities that do not evolve from point A to point B, but rather transcend societies and nation-states in a way that changes both the individuals and their societies (Waters 1999).

One of the key aspects in the process of such identity construction is the rapid improvement in the technologies of transport and, in particular, communication, which has made it increasingly easy for migrants to maintain close links with their places of origin.

Media researchers have generally referred to Benedict Anderson's (1983) notion of "imagined community" as a theoretical basis, maintaining that the media enable migrants to imagine transnational identities. Nonetheless, Anderson himself opposed the idea of transnationalism and instead introduced the concept of "long-distance nationalism." According to Anderson (1992), migrants continue to hold a sense of belonging to their homeland. The scale and speed of modern market-driven migrations make any traditional form of gradual assimilation into new environments very difficult because migrants can easily return home by the same ships, trains or airplanes by which they originally came. Moreover, new electronic media have encouraged them to stay connected in a way that was unimaginable in earlier patterns of migration. Therefore, many migrants today dream of "circulatory migration" rather than finding a new permanent home, even if that is what they find themselves inhabiting in the end. Today's transnational migrants can experience a new paradoxical type of subjectivity, that is, long-distance nationalists. Though many migrants live in their host country for many years, or even permanently, they feel little emotional attachment to the mainstream of the host society; rather they may find it tempting to engage in identity politics by participating in their "imagined Heimat."

Appadurai (1996) maintained that the combination of electronic media and mass migration leads to a "post national" political order composed of "diasporic public spheres." Electronic capitalism can have similar and even more powerful effects as the electronic media function at the level of the nation-state, increasingly linking producers and audiences across national boundaries. Satellite television and the Internet influence migrants and their children to construct new identities that are related to a multiplicity of cultures and places. Insofar as migrants' multiple identities are bound by their media consumption, their identities are renewed and continuously reframed within the media and mediated culture (Georgiou 2006). With the advent of digital technologies and digital diasporas, migrants within and across communities can create additional online communities, and the Internet is especially important for constructing and negotiating hybrid identities (Brinkerhoff 2009). Since the 2000s, many migrants have used social networking sites such as Facebook and Twitter, and the social media have become the central means of building online diasporic communities. Digital diasporas can be defined as electronic migrant communities whose interactions and forms of support are made possible through "new" technologies of communication. Diverse websites, web forums and social networking sites can also serve as tools for community building and communication, disseminating information relative to the given diaspora, in both the host and origin country (Marino 2015). Digital diasporas differ from virtual communities and nations because, in digital diasporas, there are strong ties with real nations before creating or recreating the community (Alonso and Oiarzabal 2010).

In short, existing studies reveal that while some migrants become "long-distance nationalists," others develop transnational identities in different contexts. The recent development of advanced digital technologies and social media now plays an important role in the complex process of identity negotiation. Drawing on empirical research on Japanese women in London, this chapter explores in depth the process of identity formation intersected with the use of digital and social media in everyday life.

The Case of Japanese Migrants: Context and Method

Previous studies of Japanese migrants reveal that international migration does not necessarily weaken their sense of "Japaneseness." By 1910, there were 130,000 Japanese living in the USA, mostly on the West Coast (Goodman et al. 2003), and it was important for the first-generation migrants to maintain their sense of Japaneseness amidst severe social and racial discrimination in American society at the time. Contemporary Japanese migrants often hold onto their sense of national identity, rather than finding a new identity: A large number of Japanese men, who have been relocated by their companies, have moved to the USA and Britain with their wives and children but these families continue to have a clear sense of being Japanese and of believing Japan to be "homogeneous" and culturally "unique" (Sakai 2000; Kurotani 2005). In contrast, many single Japanese women have "voluntarily" migrated to these countries under the impression that women have more freedom in the West than in Japan. These women often attempt to find new identities that transcend Japaneseness. However, they remain ethnic "minorities" in the host country; hence their only, and thus inevitable, choice is to live according to the dominant Western image of "Japanese women" (Sakai 2000; Fujita 2009).

As for later generations of Japanese living in the USA, they have become "Japanese American" although they continue to have a strong sense of "peoplehood" as an ethnic group (Fugita and O'Brien 1994). Today, recent generations of Japanese immigrants in the USA, Canada, Brazil, Peru and other countries in the Americas have developed transnational connections while participating in organizations and holding events to rediscover their common Japanese roots.

Even if they have long been assimilated into the host country, their transnational identity as "nikkei" is not more salient than their national identity (Minamikawa 2007). Regarding digital media use, Kim (2011) argues in her study of young Asian women including Japanese women that the Internet has become a key resource, playing a crucial role in constituting the relational networks of meaning and expression in the displacement experience and paradoxes of diasporic lives; therefore, diasporic nationalism becomes more salient through transnational flows and movement, nationalizing both transnational spaces and the Internet simultaneously.

In order to explore how Japanese women's experiences of alienation in their lived reality have unexpected consequences in their media use and identity negotiation, this chapter draws on findings from in-depth interviews with 13 Japanese women, aged between 31 and 52 years, who have lived in the UK for 3–24 years. Nine women are married to British, Japanese or Korean husbands, and six of them are mothers of children aged between 12 and 18 years. Some of them first came to the UK as students and settled down after marriage, while others met their husbands in Japan and moved to London together. The four unmarried women also have a stable and documented migrant status as either students or permanent residents. In-depth interviews were conducted via Skype, Zoom, Messenger or LINE video calls during the COVID-19 pandemic. Each interview took between one and two hours, and the respondents were asked a series of open-ended questions about their everyday life in London, how they contacted their family and friends in Japan and how they accessed Japanese news and entertainment through digital media. All interviews were audiorecorded, transcribed and coded for thematic and narrative analysis. The following analysis offers insights into the diasporic experience and the role of digital and social media in transnational spaces that shape the diasporic national identity of Japanese women migrants.

Transnational Networks via Digital and Social Media

In London, there are two free Japanese papers published locally – *Journey* (since 1985) and *UK News Digest* (since 1998). Through distribution at Japanese groceries, restaurants and hair salons in the central areas of London, these ethnic media have served as vital resources for the Japanese community because of their wide range of information from general news, in both the UK and Japan, to local job opportunities and rental rooms. However, none of the respondents in this research mentioned these ethnic media when asked how they accessed Japanese-related news in daily life, highlighting the waning significance of such print sources.

> I rarely go to the center anymore. I mean, I don't pass by Japan Centre or Rice Wine for shopping often, so I don't have a chance to take them. You know, we can still access the information online [as they also have

websites], but actually, I admit that I've almost forgotten about even the presence of those papers.

(G/51 years old/22 years in the UK)

Ah, I feel nostalgic. I used to read them before. Whenever I found them at Japanese restaurants, I often took one of them with me. But now, I don't take it even if I find it, because I don't want to add extra stuff to my home.

(K/45 years old/20 years in the UK)

The ethnic print media were often described as almost forgotten and unnecessary items for their everyday life. These Japanese women relied on the print media when they arrived in the UK between the late 1990s and the early 2000s, but this has changed over the past 20 years. The ethnic print media once played a vital role for migrants upon their arrival, providing various, locally available resources and support in their native language to achieve successful settlement and integration (Budarick 2020). These Japanese women have gradually accumulated social and cultural capital in London through marriage, childcare and work experience to navigate local everyday life. For them, the ethnic print media that tend to imagine Japanese people in the UK as a monolithic community have lost their contemporary meaning. In London which attracts tourists and short-term study abroad students, the ethnic print media distributed there were signifiers of "newcomers" to the city. In this context, the indications of physical and emotional distance from such signifiers ("I rarely go to the center," "I feel nostalgic") effectively demonstrate "successful settlement" and the locally embedded identity of these women. By identifying the ethnic print media as an item for early settlers, they make an unintentional distinction from other Japanese in London. However, while the raison d'être of the ethnic print media has been undermined, the emergence of digital media technologies has enabled transnational flows of information and diversity of digital platforms that shape migrant women's complex identity in transnational spaces.

All respondents expressed that they accessed Japanese news regularly, and for most of them, it was an everyday routine. Twitter is one of their most used platforms, followed by Internet news websites such as NHK, Yahoo Japan news, MSN and BBC Japan. Rather than relying on a single media source, they combine the use of these different news sources to understand trendy topics. Some of them have installed Japanese news applications on their smartphones so that they can receive notifications for breaking news automatically. The evolution of information and communication technology has changed the way people are connected to their home country through engagement with the diverse digital media. Having the ability to know what is happening in Japan with no time lag, a sense of togetherness is easily reinforced and Japanese women in London imagine their continuing membership in their home country. For example, the respondents often shared harsh opinions about Japanese news compared to the

UK news, highlighting their awareness of the biased information produced by Japanese mass media.

> [Regarding Japanese mass media] I feel it's very domestic and there is little important news reported. I listen to BBC radio every morning, and then I find that they are at different levels ... The UK news report makes an in-depth analysis to tell us how the current news could affect the everyday lives of the audience. But when it comes to Japanese reports, it doesn't reach that level.
>
> *(H/32 years old/3 years in the UK)*

The disappointment and frustration toward Japanese mass media as well as the naïve audiences who consume them without questioning were commonly expressed. Although such strong criticism appears to be a demonstration of disrespect or a sense of aversion to Japanese society, this should not be simply understood as emotional detachment from their homeland. Rather, it may be reflections of their sense of "transnational belonging because strong critical remarks come from intense feelings for one's own nation" (Takeda 2015: 499). Especially in extraordinary circumstances of the global COVID-19 pandemic, a sense of togetherness developed through digital media, urging them to imagine their sense of belonging to a diasporic Japanese community, which heightened their frustration in this way.

Aside from a few who had no habit of watching TV in Japan, most of the respondents expressed that they consumed Japanese entertainment media culture on a daily basis in London. With the growth and expansion of streaming services such as Netflix, Amazon Prime, BBC iPlayer, Disney Channel and Crunchyroll, the respondents enjoy watching not only Japanese but also English and other language programs regularly according to the situation and particularly with whom they watch.

> I've been watching Korean dramas on Netflix these days ... But when I watch TV with my [British] husband, I'm likely to watch British dramas on BBC or Channel 4, as he is not so interested in Korean dramas.
>
> *(H/32 years old/3 years in the UK)*

> During the lockdown, I used to watch English programs. Perhaps, having worked in the English-speaking environment and also always meeting my [British] boyfriend every weekend, I still had my "British persona" at that time. In the beginning of the lockdown, I was still carrying that tension, so it was natural for me to choose English programs. But as the lockdown prolonged and I hadn't met him for a while, gradually I have come to be on my own with a "Japanese persona" in which I prefer watching Japanese programs like comedies. Whenever I watch them, I realize my Japanese identity.
>
> *(K/45 years old/20 years in the UK)*

Some women never show their refusal or reluctance to watch English programs during their family time and highlight the wider available options for media consumption. Such flexibility enables Japanese women to accommodate their partner's tastes or language barrier and demonstrates their accumulation of cultural capital in the UK. Though it is always the Japanese women who compromise for their British partner on such occasions, they are indifferent to this gendered power; rather, the compromise seems to be interpreted positively as evidence of their successful settlement in the host society. However, once they are allowed to have autonomy in their media consumption, their "Japanese persona" is easily uncovered, where they imagine their sense of belonging to a Japanese diaspora or find emotional affiliation to a wider Asian community through engagement with Korean dramas. Admittedly, many of the respondents emphasized that they preferred Japanese programs for the psychological comfort effect in their own relaxation time.

> I don't watch entertainment TV programs in English. Watching TV is a relaxing time for me and I am not willing to choose English ones.
>
> *(A/52 years old/20 years in the UK)*

> I feel Japanese TV programs suit my taste much better. I find British dramas are too cheesy, like soap operas. That makes me feel, well that's enough … When I watch Japanese comedy shows, that makes me aware of my Japanese identity as I can empathize. It's not only about comedies but can be said for anything. Through Japanese programs, I rediscover my Japanese identity that shapes my taste.
>
> *(G/51 years old/22 years in the UK)*

For the Japanese women, English TV programs are still regarded as entertainment for "them" (British) and do not belong to "us" (Japanese). Not only through language differences but also through the various cultural scripts embedded in them, watching English programs strongly functions as a signifier of difference, while an emotionally engaging experience with Japanese programs evokes their identification of cultural origin as Japanese ("that makes me aware of my Japanese identity"). Despite their long resident history in the UK, over 20 years, Japanese-language media, particularly entertainment contents, represent a special meaning for these women as a valuable source of inner peace and comfort. In addition, watching Japanese popular TV is not just for personal enjoyment; respondents often share information and comments with their friends, family members and colleagues, in both London and Japan, via social media.

> I often talk with my Japanese colleagues [in London] about dramas, asking which drama they are watching. I also talk to my sister [in Japan] too. Actually, I've got a group chat on LINE with those colleagues just to share

our comments on a particular drama every time after its latest episode is released.

(F/47 years old/23 years in the UK)

What they share is not only their thoughts and feelings inspired by the digital content but also a sense of community in which they can access the same visual and emotional experience in the same language, almost simultaneously, regardless of the countries in which they reside. The combined use of multiple digital platforms enables diasporas to sustain shared cultural experiences (Georgiou 2012), which can be understood as a process of diasporic national identity negotiation in a transnational space. While allowing them to have a temporal mental escape from the stress of living in differences, it plays a key role in offering the pleasure of building a sense of solidarity and connectivity within the digital Japanese diaspora. Japanese female migrants reconstruct and reaffirm their Japanese identity through empathetic encounters during routine engagement with the media in the language of their home country (Kim 2011).

The rise of social media has also changed the way migrants maintain relationships with their families in their homeland. While these Japanese women's experiences underpin the structural interrelationship between the advancement of digital technology and the changes of communication practice in a transnational space, they also indicate that this involves multiple dimensions at the microlevel within the personal and intimate sphere of family, along with a shifting life course.

My mother passed away three years ago. When she was alive, she called me directly to the landline or my mobile, because she couldn't use LINE. But after she died, my father started to actively learn LINE on his smartphone, and now we've established this communication style [exchanging short texts on a regular basis]. So, it [the change of communication style] was not brought by the smartphone itself, but rather by the change in our family organization.

(I/44 years old/13 years in the UK)

It used to be difficult to find time to talk with my parents when they were still working. But now they have already retired and stay most of the time at home, so I don't need to care about the timing as much as I used to before. It's easier for us to find the timing that works well for us now. Also, they should have mobiles with them even when they are outside, so I can catch them when I need to talk to them somehow.

(F/47 years old/23 years in the UK)

These migrants with elderly parents believe that frequency matters more than the richness of the content, and therefore find the development of new communication technology, which has enabled everyday contact with their family in

Japan, "epoch-making and appreciated" compared to the old-style communication methods by letters, landline phones and emails. With the use of such new technology, most of the respondents stay connected with their parents almost every day or at least once a month. A group chat with their adult siblings is another strategy adopted for the maintenance of family relationships across distance, helping the respondents feel involved with their family and meet their responsibilities for caring. The daily updates about their parents' condition via chat help them know about the dedicated support offered by their siblings. In this regard, stronger emotional bonds and deeper obligations are created in the digital space, where the transnational daughters continuously negotiate their ambiguous feelings of gratitude and guilt. Other social media, such as Facebook, Instagram and blogs, are also used as communication tools with friends although these are less active than the family network. The increased use of social media enables the women to naturally weave their social networks with their friends and family in Japan into their everyday lives in London, allowing them to feel at "home" as diasporic subjects in the transnational space.

Marginalized Experience in Everyday Life and Identity Negotiation

Studies of young Asian migrants in Western countries, such as the USA and the UK, have shown that through negative experiences of marginalization and discrimination in the host society, they tend to develop stronger attachment to their own ethnic community, both physically and virtually, reasserting their national identity (Fujita 2007; Kim 2011). The respondents in this case study, most of whom have settled in the UK for over 20 years and established extensive social networks in the local landscape, speak little about their own experience of social exclusion or sense of alienation, while being highly aware of discriminated "others" in society. However, close examination of their narratives reveals that their perception of the social world is shaped by uneven ethnic and racial power dynamics.

> I don't know how they [British colleagues] really talked about me behind my back though, yet I'm really grateful for their inclusive attitude … But [seeing the news on Brexit and deportation of undocumented migrants], that makes me realize that there are a certain number of people who are like xenophobic, trying to eliminate foreigners from their own countries. This fact makes me scared and that's why I don't like the UK as it is now.
>
> *(C/49 years old/12 years in the UK)*

> I always feel and know well that I am a minority here … But I've never had an awful experience because of this. I understand my position quite objectively [among other White middle-class mothers] because my skin color, my name, the environment I grew up and my parents' names, all of these are different from them.
>
> *(E/45 years old/20 years in the UK)*

> Actually, English people don't have such a negative image toward Japanese people, comparing with that toward Chinese people. I feel my daughters must have gotten some advantages because of their ethnic roots in Japan. Perhaps there must be some shared positive image of Japanese characteristics among the English. But it doesn't mean that they [English people] show social inclusion of us.
>
> *(F/47 years old/23 years in the UK)*

Although these Japanese women highlight that they have never been targeted by explicit discrimination or harassment, they also understand their precarious position in society as a minority, as well as how lucky they are comparatively. An awareness of racial hierarchy within society and a currently hostile environment during the pandemic give them an uncomfortable sense that they may need to be skeptical even in their daily communication ("I don't know how they really talked about me").

Researching Japanese women in Australia who denied racial discrimination in the host society, Takeda (2014) argued that it is a powerful and effective coping strategy to avoid positioning themselves as powerless subjects. In this case study in the UK, similarly, the respondents did not share their direct experiences of discrimination because they had a relational understanding of racial discrimination. They are likely to undermine their own experiences of marginalization in the host society by seeing and hearing about those who undergo "blatant racial discrimination" through the media and hearsay reports. These Japanese women demonstrate various tactics in which they highlight their own differences as minority subjects while showing their awareness of prevailing social exclusion toward minority "others" in society. By internalizing their racialized identity as vulnerable subjects who easily become targets of discrimination, they think they experience less exclusion in society which seems to offer them a relatively positive evaluation of their migration experiences and their children's ("have gotten some advantages because of their ethnic origin"). In this context, "Japaneseness" gains value as strategic cultural capital for these women to buffer negative encounters in everyday life.

However, a sense of "inferiorization and alienation at an interpersonal level" (Kim 2011: 139) caused by their English-speaking ability was articulated by half the respondents.

> There is a group of friends who are local British mothers. When they chat amusingly in English, I can understand little of them. I don't know anything about the TV programs they are talking about, the slang they use and the various topics they talk about. In such casual conversations, I feel that I'm left out. I know it's my own issue with a limited English ability.
>
> *(A/52 years old/20 years in the UK)*

At first, I had an ambition "to be like a British," but well now I feel that I'm entirely Japanese. In terms of language, having realized that I cannot reach the level of a native speaker, I come to work out the gap between ideal and reality. I've changed my goal to be "a good English speaker as a Japanese." I want to do my best as much as I can as a Japanese.

(B/31 years old/6 years in the UK)

Despite their seemingly happy multicultural daily life in which their diverse socializing practices extend to cross-ethnic networks, the language barrier has consistently appeared as a marker of their sense of alienation in everyday life. Regardless of how they are physically welcomed into the group of dominant English people amicably, their limited language proficiency and accumulation of cultural comprehension disturb their emotional inclusion, leaving a sense of inferiority ("it's my own issue"). Ironically, the more they have intimate contacts with members of the host society, the more they feel disconnected from it and emotionally oriented toward their home country ("I'm entirely Japanese"). The everyday vulnerability and frustration that the respondents intermittently feel in social spaces in the second language appear to produce a subtle but mundane sense of alienation, which leads them to seek emotional comfort in the diasporic space of home.

A previous study (Fujita 2007) revealed that young Japanese migrants, with an average age of 25, in New York and London reaffirmed their national identity through the mundane use of transnational media rather than developing a trans-national identity. Although they had the initial ambition to "be like a Westerner," having been exposed to racial discrimination and becoming aware of displaced subjectivity as ethnic minorities in the host societies, they became more oriented toward their home culture. Despite their longer migration history, deep engagement with the local community – mainly through parental care – and reduced consciousness of their own social exclusion, these older respondents in this case study also articulate their Japanese national identity immediately, without any hesitation. Why is the self-identification of these women strongly maintained as Japanese, albeit their highly mobile and transnational life trajectory? There is a common essentialist belief among these Japanese women that one's identity is developed primarily in the environment where one was born and grew up and it cannot be transformed easily.

I think I'm Japanese, all in all. I mean, no one can give an answer to the question [Do you think you are Japanese?] other than myself. I was born in Japan and I like Japan, so I am Japanese.

(I/44 years old/13 years in the UK)

If you spent your childhood in Japan, then you must undoubtedly be Japanese. When I see my sons [who have Japanese parents but were born and grew up in the UK], sometimes they show Japanese-like ways of thinking, but basically they are foreigners to me.

(A/52 years old/20 years in the UK)

Identity is articulated as their own determination and legitimation ("no one can give an answer to the question other than myself"). The same respondent (I) also mentioned that with the use of Twitter, she has been developing a stronger feeling of connectedness with people in Japan, realizing that there are similar people like her sharing common concerns over social issues such as LGBTQ rights in recent years. Habitual engagement with Japanese language media enables migrants to be aware that there is little difference between the Japanese in Japan and those overseas, which consolidates their shared national and cultural identity as diasporic Japanese in a transnational space. Social media function as a space of communication in which the identity, meaning and boundaries of the diasporic community are continually constructed, debated and reimagined (Mandeville 2001).

Empathy plays a key role in constructing such a diasporic imagination in which the meaning and constitutive elements of "being Japanese" are continuously questioned and reflected upon. A shared ethnic origin, even within the consanguine family, has little significance in this context ("they are foreigners to me"). This is because entrance into the Japanese diasporic community is admitted by shared emotional experience, and it is only possible with a high comprehension of shared language and cultural script in Japanese. Therefore, the successful settlement of migrants, particularly that achieved through child rearing by navigating one's everyday life in the local sociocultural landscape, does not necessarily undermine one's sense of diasporic national identity and belonging. Rather, the healthy growth of children who culturally assimilate into British society makes Japanese mothers more aware of their different identities, which highlights their emotional distance from the host society and simultaneously reaffirms a stronger sense of belonging to their home country.

It is important to recognize the complex formation of diasporic imagination, which is a plural, relational and dynamic process of ongoing negotiation. The meaning and value of the homeland for migrants changes along with the sociopolitical circumstances of both the host society and the country of origin, as well as their personal and familial situations over time. This affects the way in which the diasporic community and sense of belonging are imagined.

> I don't have family in this country, so I have no idea whether I'll be still here when I get old. I really don't know, cannot imagine at all. But I am also concerned that if I were to move back to Japan in my later life, where would I live? Such random thoughts about my future make me feel that I'm an "exile," belonging nowhere.
>
> *(G/51 years old/22 years in the UK)*

> I feel staying in the UK might give me less worries for my future, especially in terms of healthcare and nursing costs … If my family in Japan would have all gone, there would be little reason for me to stay in Japan. As far as I am in healthy condition, Japan is the best place for me, with fresh air, water

and food. But realistically speaking, I have too many concerns related to healthcare services and associated financial issues in Japan in my old age.

(D/36 years old/21 years in the UK)

The future anxiety predicted by different institutional welfare systems in the UK and Japan, and the possible loss of a family member in the future, often disturb one's imagined citizenship to the home nation ("I'm an 'exile,' belonging nowhere"). Identity formation always involves an ongoing reflexive assessment of the current situation and future uncertainty of one's social world "to imagine and construct the relevant transnational linkages and to construct the appropriate discourses" (Tsagarousianou 2017: 63). The narratives of Japanese women highlight that evaluation of home fluctuates over the life course ("there would be little reason for me to stay in Japan"), which nevertheless does not suggest a dilution of the diasporic nationalism of these women. Japan which used to be understood as their home "land," as a physical space to return someday, is deterritorialized from such place-bound concept, and it is reimagined and reconstructed as a diasporic community where their national and cultural identity belongs. For example, the same respondent (D) stated:

I don't feel that I'm living abroad at all. My colleagues are foreigners, and I speak in English when I'm at work. But once I come home, I watch Japanese TV programs and cook Japanese foods. So as far as when I'm in my room, it's like I'm in Japan.

(D/36 years old/21 years in the UK)

Despite her limited sociopolitical attachment to the Japanese nation, she has developed her sense of belonging to the imagined Japanese community through daily engagement with diasporic media, which seems to constitute an integral part of her emotional comfort. Diasporic media space enables migrants dispersed all over the world to experience new forms of togetherness through empathetic encounters, and thereby Japanese women translate "home" from a physical space into an imagined diasporic community along with further reinforcement of diasporic nationalism. In this regard, diasporic nationalism functions as a strategically selected identification (Kim 2011), bridging the gap between the ideal ("Japan is the best place for me") and the reality ("I have too many concerns") that migrants encounter and negotiate in daily life.

Conclusion

As this chapter has indicated, diasporic nationalism has become more salient through transnational movement and digital communication, nationalizing transnational spaces. Japanese female migrants in London in this case study do not use local ethnic newspapers often, and the ethnic print media no longer play an important role in constructing a local Japanese community in the host society. Instead, migrants today rely on new digital media and communication technologies to create a better sense of connectivity with their home country. As migrants tend to experience, explicitly or implicitly, inferiorization and alienation at an interpersonal level (Kim 2011) in everyday life, digital and social media can be strategically appropriated as a coping mechanism to deal with the everyday diasporic conditions, and diasporic nationalism can emerge as a consequence. The paradoxical formation of identity and sense of belonging revealed in this chapter supports the earlier argument that a marginalized experience in the host society becomes a main driving force of migrants' diasporic national identity (Fujita 2009; Kim 2011). Despite their seemingly successful settlement, life as migrants is always subject to living in difference, and therefore migrants keep questioning the boundary between "them" and "us" to create a relational understanding of "who I am." As Japanese female migrants come to reevaluate the meaning of Japaneseness in a transnational space, their everyday use of transnational media is far from destabilizing of national borders, but facilitates their ongoing identity negotiation, wherein their national subjectivity is reimagined and revitalized. In this self-identification process, diasporic belonging is not simply imagined in a nostalgic effort of recovering or maintaining their identity (Tsagarousianou 2017); rather, it is a future-oriented strategic practice to navigate their life in transnational spaces where uneven racial and gender hierarchies are embedded.

References

Alonso, A. and Oiarzabal, P. (2010) *Diasporas in the New Media Age*, Reno: University of Nevada Press.

Anderson, B. (1983) *Imagined Communities*, London: Verso.

Anderson, B. (1992) "The New World Disorder," *New Left Review*, 93(1): 3–13.

Appadurai, A. (1996) *Modernity at Large*, Minneapolis: University of Minnesota Press.

Basch, L., Schiller, N. and Blanc, C. (1994) *Nations Unbound*, Langhorne: Gordon and Breach.

Brinkerhoff, J. (2009) *Digital Diasporas*, New York: Cambridge University Press.

Budarick, J. (2020) "Ethnic Media and Migrant Settlement," *Global Media Journal Australian Edition*, 14(1).

Fugita, S. and O'Brien, D. (1994) *Japanese American Ethnicity*, Seattle: University of Washington Press.

Fujita, Y. (2007) "Transnational Media and National Identity," *Journal of Mass Communication Studies*, 70: 97–15.

Fujita, Y. (2009) *Cultural Migrants from Japan*, Lanham: Lexington Books.

Georgiou, M. (2006) *Diaspora, Identity and the Media*, Cresskill: Hampton Press.

Georgiou, M. (2012) "Watching Soap Opera in the Diaspora," *Ethnic and Racial Studies*, 35(5): 868–87.

Goodman, R., Peach, C., Takenaka, A. and White, P. (2003) *Global Japan*, London: Routledge.

Itzigsohn, J. and Saucedo, S. (2002) "Immigrant Incorporation and Sociocultural Transnationalism," *International Migration Review*, 36(3): 766–98.

Kasinitz, P., Mollenkopf, J., Waters, M. and Holdaway, J. (2009) *Inheriting the City*, New York: SAGE.

Kim, Y. (2011) "Diasporic Nationalism and the Media," *International Journal of Cultural Studies*, 14(2): 133–51.

Kurotani, S. (2005) *Home Away from Home*, Durham: Duke University Press.

Mandaville, P. (2001) "Reimagining Islam in Diaspora," *Gazette*, 63(2–3): 169–86.

Marino, S. (2015) "Transnational Identities and Digital Media," *JOMEC Journal*, 7(7): 1–12.

Minamikawa, F. (2007) "Futatsu No Japanese," in H. Yoneyama and N. Kawahara (eds) *Nikkeijin No Keiken To Kokusaiido*, Tokyo: Jinbunshoin.

Sakai, J. (2000) *Japanese Bankers in the City of London*, London: Routledge.

Takeda, A. (2014) "Japanese Marriage Migrants in 'Imagined' Multicultural Australia," *Crossings*, 5(2–3): 257–72.

Takeda, A. (2015) "Intensive Transnationalism amongst Japanese Migrants after the Great East Japan Earthquake," *Studies in Ethnicity and Nationalism*, 15(3): 492–507.

Tsagarousianou, R. (2017) "Rethinking the Concept of Diaspora," *Westminster Papers in Communication and Culture*, 1(1): 52–65.

Waters, M. (1999) *Black Identities*, New York: SAGE.

22

GLOCAL INTIMACIES, DIGITAL MEDIA AND THE TRANSNATIONAL LIVES OF ELITE FILIPINO MIGRANTS DURING A GLOBAL PANDEMIC

Cecilia S. Uy-Tioco

Digital media have become an essential component of the everyday lives of transnational migrants. For "elite" Filipino migrants, everyday life is characterized by their access to rich polymedia environments and their mobility to visit loved ones in the homeland regularly which allow for social relationships to flourish. The COVID-19 pandemic has forced elite migrants to reorganize their lives due to quarantines, lockdowns and border restrictions. This chapter examines the ways everyday lives of these migrants have been reconfigured by immobility and increased dependence on digital media to maintain relationships with family and friends in the homeland. Consequently, everyday life in the host society has become more oriented to local Philippine life resulting in new experiences of intimacies while simultaneously revealing unintended consequences and limitations of digitally mediated transnational life.

Drawing on the experiences of elite transnational Filipinos during the pandemic, this chapter aims to expand the concept of "glocal intimacies" (Cabañes and Uy-Tioco 2020) in a different context. "Glocal intimacies" refers to the role of digital mobile media in normalizing and intensifying the entanglement of people's relationships with each other with the always changing and persistently negotiated flows between global modernity and local everyday life. Building on Robertson's (1994: 38) concept of "glocalization" which refers to "the simultaneity and inter-penetration of what are conventionally called the global and the local – or in more general vein – the universal and the particular," glocal intimacies put into focus how this interplay of "simultaneity" and "inter-penetration" comes to bare in relationships that are mediated by digital media. For elite Filipinos, glocal intimacies are characterized by connections with friends, family and events in geographically distant places that seamlessly weave in and out of their everyday physical lives (Uy-Tioco and Cabañes 2021). They have the

DOI: 10.4324/9781003130628-27

greatest access to rich polymedia environments that provide them with an array of digital media to maintain relationships with loved ones around the globe.

This research contributes to existing studies on global cosmopolitan elites (Massey 1993; Castells 1996) and highly skilled migrants (Smith and Favell 2006), while drawing specific attention to elite migrants coming from the Global South. By focusing on elite migrant Filipinos in the United States, this work nuances our understanding of who global elite migrants are and what their varied experiences could be. In this research, the term "elite" is used to refer to overseas Filipinos who have permanently settled in the United States (as natural-ized citizens, dual citizens or permanent residents), work in white-collar jobs and came to the country as graduate students, work placements or family mem-bers. They did not leave the Philippines because of economic poverty or political situations. Rather, they tend to have higher cultural, social and economic capital in the homeland.

This study also contributes to the literature that focuses on the role of digital media in transforming people's intimate relationships (Hjorth and Lim 2012). Much of the research on migrants and ICTs has focused on the importance of digital media in orienting them to the land of settlement or residence (Lim and Pham 2016) and navigating transnational relationships with family in the home-land (Uy-Tioco 2007, 2017; Chen 2020; Uy-Tioco and Cabalquinto 2020). This chapter instead focuses on the distinct moment of the global pandemic and how this has reconfigured digital media's role in transnational everyday life and peo-ple's experiences of glocal intimacies.

The chapter argues that due to the conditions of the global pandemic, elite Filipino migrants experience changes in their transnational cosmopolitan lives. The constraints imposed by quarantines and border restrictions have led to increased dependence on digital media for glocal intimacies with loved ones in the homeland. Although they experience immobility, elite migrants have the capacity to circumvent the limitations of these media-dependent relationships because of their class position. This analysis pushes back against Turkle's (2011: 1) contention that technology "offers the illusion of companionship without the demands of friendship … Our networked life allows us to hide from each other, even as we are tethered to each other." As this chapter demonstrates, digital media have the capacity to reinforce existing bonds and enact new forms of digital intimacies for transnational migrants. Alongside these affordances, how-ever, the chapter critically recognizes the complexity of digital media use as elite migrants also experience digital fatigue and a reappearance of social obligations they had previously avoided.

Glocal Intimacies, Transnational Elite Migrants and Digital Media

The concept of glocal intimacies emphasizes the role of digital media in normal-izing and intensifying people's relationships with each other simultaneously on a global and local level. While Turkle (2011) argues that people within America increasingly live "alone together" and rely on more low-risk technologically mediated relationships, transnational research has shown the crucial importance of digital media for transnational migrants. Instead of people losing their capacity to connect with each other in depth and engage in the complexities of human relationships as Turkle contends, glocal intimacies point to the integral role of digital media in migrants' experiences of closeness going beyond mere connection. As this chapter demonstrates, these relationships are shaped by the navigation between modern global life in the United States and dynamics of local life in the Philippines. To further build on this concept, it engages with two bodies of literature. First is the growing literature on transnational elite migrants whose everyday lives consist of simultaneously navigating two worlds. Second is on how people's relationships and experiences of closeness are increasingly shaped by the ubiquity of digital media in their everyday lives.

While research on migrants and migration has tended to focus on those from lower incomes seeking better opportunities and those fleeing economic or political hardship, there has also been an increase of studies that examine a broader variety of global migrants. These migrants leave their homeland because of education, work and lifestyle preferences. On one hand, they are members of the middle class from highly industrialized countries and have become a part of the professional global workforce (Polson 2016). On the other hand, they are elites and upper class from the Global South with the ability to seek education and employment around the globe. Thus, there is a need to "resist the clichéd opposition of 'elite' and 'ethnic' migrants in a polarized global economy" (Smith and Favell 2006: 25).

The term "global elites" has many meanings. For Castells (1996: 447), it implies a group of people whose "identity is not linked to any specific society, but to membership of the managerial circles of the informational economy across a global cultural spectrum," pointing to shared cosmopolitan lifestyles in similar spaces across the globe such as airport lounges, hotels chains and trendy food. Massey (1993: 61), in talking about the diversity of human mobility and movement, points to "the jet-setters, the ones sending and receiving the faxes and the e-mail, holding the international conference calls, the ones distributing the films, controlling the news, organizing the investments and the international currency transactions" and includes Western academics in this group. Similarly, in his discussion of "exterritorial elites," Bauman (1998) describes a class living highly cosmopolitan lifestyles of first-class travel and financial excess separate from the localities they occupy, including others who are "on the move" such as businessmen, culture managers and academics.

Although the scholars above have pointed to the existence of global elites, less work has been done on specific groups of elite or professional migrants. Polson (2016) studies the formation of a new global middle class – professionals recruited and deployed in white-collar jobs such as advertising, law, finance and engineering around the world. Jung (2020) examines *kirogi* Korean transnational migrant families who choose to split their household temporarily (from six months to more than ten years) so that their children can be educated in an English-speaking country. Kang (2020) looks at upper-middle class Taiwanese women who come to the United States to engage in birth tourism so their children would have US citizenship.

Migration research on the Philippines has often centered around Overseas Filipino Workers (OFWs) who are employed with fixed contracts, often in blue-collar jobs, enduring long separation from family (Uy-Tioco 2007; Madianou and Miller 2012; Cabalquinto 2018) and have very little chance of becoming permanent residents in host countries. There is less research on immigrant Filipinos who have chosen to live abroad permanently, periodically visit the Philippines and maintain ties to the homeland. Historically called *balikbayan* (Rafael 1990), the term has colloquially come to mean any returning Filipino, regardless of their visa or citizenship. In their work on Filipinos in the UK, Ong and Cabañes (2011: 205) describe these students as "elite" migrants – highly skilled professionals who, while abroad temporarily on student visas, "have a chance to attain a life of comfort and security in their host country, to become *balikbayans*." Lorenzana (2016) examines highly skilled Filipino workers in India, employed in local and multinational companies.

Transnational elite migrants are diverse, ranging from health industry professionals, educators, lawyers and bankers to actors. The viewpoints and everyday lives of migrants are influenced by transnational practices of exchange, communication and frequent travel (Vertovec 2004). Because they are mobile and cosmopolitan, they are also "prone to articulate complex affiliations, meaningful attachments and multiple allegiances to issues, people, places and traditions that lie beyond the boundaries of their resident nation-state" (Vertovec and Cohen 2002: 2). The ability of transnational migrants to lead bifocal lives (Rouse 1992) has been intensified by digital media, making everyday a continuous navigation of two worlds. The COVID-19 pandemic has reshaped how these migrants experience glocal intimacies with loved ones in the homeland.

Mobile media have led to the further collapsing of time and space, allowing for people who are physically apart to be digitally co-present and "socially and interactionally accountable" (Ito 2003: 1). The mobile phone gives way for people to be in "perpetual contact" despite being geographically distant (Katz and Aakhus 2002). Mobile phones' capacity for text-messaging and social media apps provides users with a sense of "connected presence" where "the (physically) absent party renders himself or herself present by multiplying mediated communication gestures up to the point where copresent interactions and mediated communication seem woven in a seamless web" (Licoppe 2004: 135). Through instantaneous and real-time communication, "social relations are lifted out of immediate interactional settings and stretched over potentially vast spans of global time-space" (Moores 2000: 106). People are "always-on" (boyd 2011) and constantly available to each other, fostering intimate relationships.

Mobile intimacy refers to the ability to be intimate across distances of time and space (Raita 2007). The increasing ubiquity of digital media, particularly the widespread use of mobile devices and social media, have shaped how "various forms of *mobility* (across technological, geographic, psychological, physical and temporal differences) and *intimacy* infuse public and private spaces" (Hjorth and Lim 2012: 478). This results in the boundaries between the online and offline worlds to be blurred and reconfigured. Because social media apps allow for both synchronous and asynchronous communication, people's everyday lives include short, scattered continuous flows of messages, voice calls, videos, photographs and graphics that Licoppe (2004: 141) calls an "irregular interaction" that are ever-present and easily activated to provide a "feeling of a permanent connection." Digital media have also resulted in a reorganization of daily life and a "tighter microcoordination" of social interaction (Ling 2004: 58).

Alongside the ubiquity of digital media across the globe is the increasingly vast array of platforms and devices to choose from. Madianou and Miller (2012) examine the consequences of these polymedia on interpersonal relationships: The ways people choose digital media are always in relation to the features and limitations of other devices and platforms and the choice is also dependent on emotional, social and moral consequences. The choice of which technology to use is not merely about cost or convenience but more about affordances. Thus, the focus is on the emotional intent of users and how they use technology to manage relationships, generating new intimate socialities, relationships and affective experiences.

The significance of digital media in maintaining transnational relationships for migrants cannot be underestimated. They have been crucial in sustaining family ties through the restaging of family rituals (Cabalquinto 2018), the development of new routines (Uy-Tioco 2017; Uy-Tioco and Cabalquinto 2020) and the reconfiguring of family dynamics (Jung 2020). This is especially noteworthy for overseas domestic workers separated from their children for long periods of time and must "mother" from afar via the mobile phone (Uy-Tioco 2007; Waruwu 2021). Left-behind children also use mobile media to both challenge and affirm the communicative regimes set by their parents (Chen 2020). For left-behind husbands of migrant worker women, digital media, while facilitating intimacies, also alter the balance of conjugal power because wives have become the breadwinner (Cabañes and Acedera 2012). These studies demonstrate the "asymmetrical communication" (Lim 2016) present in families as different members make use of digital technologies for their personal needs and their family's shared ideals, practices and values. As the social intimacies of everyday life within a transnational context are no longer place-bound, digital media have become essential for migrants and their families' glocal intimacies, particularly during the COVID-19 pandemic where the negotiation between global and local lives is amplified.

Methodology

This study emerged from a longitudinal ethnographic research project that explores elite Filipino transnational migrants and their use of digital media in sustaining ties with the homeland. The ethnographic approach to studying migrants' use of digital media allows researchers to better understand the meanings of the digital in the specific context of everyday situations and life histories (Lorenzana 2016); the nuanced ways in which migrants navigate the environment of polymedia and how this is shaped by relational dynamics (Madianou 2015). Researchers should point their ethnographic eye up to people who wield power (Nader 1972). Studying "elite" migrants enables a more comprehensive view of the diversity of Filipino migrant experiences (Ong and Cabañes 2011).

Over a period of six years, I conducted research with 15 participants that focused on their use of digital and mobile media to maintain transnational ties with their families and homeland, including during the COVID-19 pandemic. Data were collected through multiple 45-90 minutes semi-structured in-depth interviews and online participant observation with Filipinos who are members of the alumni associations of what are considered the top three Philippine universities based in Metropolitan Washington DC. These migrants work in professions such as law, medicine, business, education and research. They have permanently settled in the United States as citizens, dual citizens or permanent residents or hold a G visa (employed long-term in international organizations such as the World Bank and IMF). Interviews were conducted primarily in English, with participants also responding in Taglish – a mix of Tagalog and English. Names have been changed to preserve the anonymity of participants and protect their privacy.

Mediated Transnational Intimacies during a Pandemic

Like everyone around the world, the everyday lives of transnational migrants have been upended due to the pandemic. The ability to travel at a moment's notice, which elite migrants took for granted as always available, was halted due to quarantines and border restrictions. As such, elite migrants increasingly turned to digital media to maintain their transnational cosmopolitan lives. This section examines the ways everyday transnational life has been reconfigured through the increased use of digital media and new experiences of glocal intimacies.

Keeping in Touch and Discovering New Ways to Connect

One of the most discussed shifts for transnational migrants during the pandemic was changes in the ways they used digital media to keep in touch and discovering new platforms. Digital technologies provide people with a "connected presence" to those in their social circles (Licoppe 2004). Elite migrants found themselves reconfiguring their media use, connecting to others and "going places" (Moores

1993) while staying home. Because of their easy access to rich polymedia environments, these migrants are able to enact glocal intimacies despite prolonged physical separation. Andrea, a 42-year-old lawyer, regularly used Facebook Messenger and FaceTime to connect with family in the Philippines and Canada, which provided them with a "feeling of a permanent connection" (Licoppe 2004: 141).

> There's no travel, you can't go home or even meet up for vacation in another country, so now you talk more through apps because we're not seeing each other … At the start of the pandemic, I set up Zoom meetings with all my friend groups … Wherever in the world you are you can jump in on Zoom.

Similarly, Sandy, a 46-year-old researcher and her childhood friends living around the world always communicated through a group chat on WhatsApp, but started to get together on video calls during the pandemic.

> It's so weird, the technology has always been there, but now for some reason everyone wants to video. We always just used to text in the group text but not video chat. And then, during the COVID, we were doing Zooms … especially for birthdays. It was great, but hard to arrange with time zones.

Marga also pointed out that she and her best friend in the Philippines rarely made voice calls to each other. They would text message often, but not make voice or video calls because they saw each other once or twice a year, either when she would travel home or when her friend would visit the United States. Since they were unable to see each other during the pandemic, Marga noticed they were doing more voice and video calls on Viber.

> I feel like if I don't reach out, I'm short-changing her with the friendship. I feel like I have to extend myself a little more, because I haven't seen her the whole year. We text a lot, but text is nothing, you have to add that layer, we have to see and hear each other. I think it's the need for connection, and the time apart is longer than before because we can't travel.

To replace a long-planned family reunion canceled due to the pandemic, Matt, a 48-year-old IT specialist, and his numerous cousins around the globe instead formed a group chat on the app Viber which included all their spouses. Through messages in the group chat, the cousins got closer.

> Now we're sharing small things like somebody sending a video of somebody playing a game or someone's kid dancing … all the mundane stuff … Now everyone is commenting, and it's become a regular thing.

Migrant experiences in this research and elsewhere (Madianou and Miller 2012) reveal that in rich polymedia environments, migrants choose platforms and apps based on affordances, focusing on their emotional intent. The need to experience deeper connections during the pandemic has led migrants to use new platforms and apps for their glocal intimacies. Because everyday life became confined to the home, transnational migrants found themselves shifting social activities they would typically do in person to online, but with social networks across the globe. Ronna, a 55-year-old widow, found ways to engage in social activities with friends through digital media:

> We watch the same movies together. Or, let's say someone is out for a walk, so you schedule the same time that you guys are both out for a walk. Same activity, but in different parts of the world … even eating together. It could be breakfast for them, dinner for me. Through Zoom, whenever, say Pope Francis had those special masses, we would attend together; regardless of your time [zone] you're all there.

Likewise, Matt and his wife were able to watch their favorite Filipino band and take part in an online fundraising concert in the Philippines from their home in Washington DC.

These narratives and experiences indicate that despite the restrictions on mobility due to the pandemic, elite Filipino migrants discovered new ways to connect with each other as well as with the homeland and other parts of the world, enabling glocal intimacies. From the confines of the home, media technologies transport people to distant places, what Williams (1974) called "mobile privatization." As digital technologies sustain the "everyday worlds of families and households" of transnational migrants, they also connect them with "various spheres of information and entertainment at a regional, national or transnational level" (Moores 1993: 365).

Navigating Traditions and Social Obligations

While digital media have allowed for transnational social relationships to be maintained and provided opportunities for new kinds of intimacies, they have also brought about changes in practices of closeness. Migration to the United States had freed elite transnational Filipinos from the myriad of social obligations they would otherwise have to attend in the homeland. But with social gatherings moving to online platforms, Filipinos in the United States found themselves once again subject to social expectations in the Philippines, leading to complex navigations between the two worlds. Their experiences reveal a heightening of their glocal intimacies where the persistence of local Philippine life encroaches daily life in the United States. Filipino traditions and rituals, particularly those surrounding death and mourning, have had to be reconfigured and conducted in online spaces. In the early days of the pandemic and lockdowns, Ronna's brother and best friend both passed away in the Philippines.

> There was no funeral mass, there were none of the traditions and trappings that people do to say our goodbyes, to pay our respects. As Filipinos and as Catholics, we thrive in the togetherness when good things and bad things happen to your life and with the COVID that's not there. We all met online on Zoom every day to pray but it's not the same. Better than nothing, but not the same.

Twenty-fifth high school reunions are grand events in the Philippines and those abroad often fly home to attend. Rose, a 44-year-old analyst, not having many sentimental feelings about her high school class, had no plans of being there. Since the pandemic forced the events to move online, Rose ended up attending some events:

> I wasn't planning to fly home [for the reunion] … but going online was low investment on my part. I still didn't need to participate fully or talk to people I didn't care to see. But I had no excuse to not join since it was virtual.

Sandy was able to take part in a cousin's wedding because it was being live streamed on the church's Facebook page. However, she also felt obligated to "be there" and "had no excuse to miss it." While digital platforms have allowed her to "attend" weddings, birthdays and funerals, at times, it felt like a burden. For Sandy, being a migrant meant missing out on a lot of events at home, "but now that everything is on Zoom, I have to show my face."

Moving social activities onto digital platforms has provided migrants living apart from loved ones and social groups new ways to take part in events previously unavailable to them. Rituals and traditions were reconfigured on digital platforms allowing those far away to participate. At the same time, this has caused additional burdens and tensions to an already stressful everyday life during the pandemic. This kind of "asymmetrical mobile intimacy" (Cabalquinto 2018) arises from the diverse and contradictory experiences of intimacy at a distance. While digital media enable connections and reconfigurations of intimacies that migrants desire, they also lead to conflicted feelings, as navigating bifocal lives is heightened and local Philippine life intrudes more into everyday life for elite migrants in the United States.

Increasing Digital Fatigue

Although the ubiquity of the digital has resulted in "always-on" (boyd 2011) lives where people are constantly available to others, the pandemic shifted *all* aspects of daily life onto digital platforms. Because work, leisure, entertainment and social lives were being conducted through screens, people experience "digital fatigue – a fatigue for constantly being required to be online and plugged in" (Alevizou 2020: 3). The same platforms that allow people available to foster glocal intimacies also have become a new source of anxiety and exhaustion. Marga, a 52-year-old mother of two college-aged children, used to call her parents in the Philippines daily as she drove to work, and was surprised to realize that she was calling her mom less frequently during the pandemic.

> I think it's because I'm just online all the time, so I need a break. But I am working [regular work hours] ... she's retired and everything merges into each other, so there's no time difference; people are watching Netflix until 2am ... There's no day and night, for them there's no routine, but for me I have a work routine.

Sandy shared similar experiences:

> I'm on Zoom so much for work and feel Zoomed-out, so sometimes I just have to say no when people invite me for happy hour on Zoom. It becomes too much, and you need a break. And then there's the time difference that they forget, so it's inconvenient for me sometimes.

In some cases, people needed to unplug from digital platforms. Although FaceTime and Zoom were rare lifelines during the wakes and funerals for family members, Andrea needed to step away from her laptop and iPhone to take a walk or go hiking, even if it meant disconnecting from her family who were deeply mourning their loved ones. Constant messages and calls would become too much and too overwhelming, giving "a sense of overload" (Alevizou 2020: 3) from digital spaces. Andrea points out, "I am feeling the fatigue but what else can we do? Everyone's on the same boat, so I feel like that kind of mitigates it because you know you're not suffering by yourself."

As each part of daily life became conducted and performed on digital spaces, transnational migrants sometimes had to disconnect from the same technologies that enabled them to keep in touch with loved ones in the homeland. The feeling of digital fatigue underscores the limitations of digitally mediated intimacies. While essential for glocal intimacies, constant digital use causes burdens for transnational migrants highlighting the importance of face-to-face interaction.

Feeling Stuck, Living with Fear and Circumventing Restrictions

Being unable to travel home to the Philippines is one of the challenges elite migrants have encountered. The global pandemic has taken away the mobility that elites have taken for granted. As discussed earlier, both Andrea and Ronna were unable to return to the Philippines when family members passed away because the pandemic brought new fears and travel issues. Andrea points out, "there are deterrents to going home, the rules keep changing, you don't want to get stuck midflight. It's complicated and I don't want to get sick, I don't want to get the COVID on the flight." Rose expresses that being unable to travel, if something happens to her parents, is one of her greatest fears:

> It was a security blanket for me to always have enough money to fly home anytime for any emergency. And now it's not even a matter of if you have the money; it's a matter of can you fly home, will you be allowed to fly home … You are faced with factors that are out of your hands, out of your control.

This narrative underscores the privilege and mobility that elite migrants used to have, compared to underprivileged Filipino migrants, especially OFWs who are constrained by labor contracts and travel costs. For Andrea and Ronna, the fear of immobility became a reality under the pandemic when loved ones in the homeland died.

The unexpected feeling of being immobile is heightened for elite migrants used to always being able to travel. Sandy was unable to fly home to the Philippines for holidays – an annual trip she had taken for granted. Because of the inability to travel, Andrea notes:

> You really feel like an OFW because you're stuck … Unlike OFWs we could go home or meet family and friends in another country for vacation. OFWs don't travel with their families; their relationship is so tied to income, to providing [for those back home].

According to Rose:

> Whether you come here [to the USA] as a domestic helper or you come here for a white-collar job, you're still starting over, period. Now there's another level that is equalizing; whoever you are you don't have a say with the current [pandemic] situation.

But of course, elite migrants have the benefit of financial security, ease of building networks and social and economic capital back home that help in the migration process. In addition, Rose acknowledges that her parents could fly to the United States, "not that they would go on a plane at this time … but OFWs can't do that." Nonetheless, travel continues to exist for elite migrants who are willing to take the risk of having aging parents take the transpacific flight to the United States. Because an annual trip to home had to be canceled, Emma, a 59-year-old businesswoman, instead invited her mother to fly in from the Philippines. Going to the Philippines would have been more burdensome because of the tough border restrictions, mandatory quarantine and the overwhelmed healthcare system.

While advanced communication technologies resulted in elite migrants reconfiguring their mundane digital use to keep in touch with loved ones in the homeland, this did not make up for the immobility caused by the pandemic. Because regular travel, a feature of transnational cosmopolitan lifestyle, was curtailed, Filipino elite migrants were subject to the similar constraints OFWs face daily. However, these unusual feelings of similarity or solidarity in the diaspora are temporary as elite migrants in a privileged class position have the ability to circumvent travel restrictions in other possible ways.

Conclusion

This chapter has discussed the ways everyday lives of elite transnational Filipino migrants have been reconfigured by the global COVID-19 pandemic, resulting in physical immobility and increased dependence on digital media platforms to maintain relationships with family and friends in the homeland and across the globe. Drawing on the concept of glocal intimacies (Cabañes and Uy-Tioco 2020), it has shown how the increased digital use by transnational migrants during the pandemic is intertwined in the negotiated flows between global conditions, connections and local everyday lives. While the pandemic has restricted physical movement, transnational migrants with access to polymedia have continued to keep in touch with loved ones, discovering new ways to connect through new apps and new online social activities. Such digital connections have also led to the establishment of new routines and traditions, as well as a resurfacing of social obligations in the homeland. Despite the feelings of closeness digital media afford, the increased dependence also results in digital fatigue as all aspects of life have become digitally mediated. Nonetheless, the digital fatigue brought about by constant mediation does not necessarily mean a loosening of bonds. This chapter has recognized the complex role of digital media in negotiating existing social intimacies among transnational migrants.

As elite Filipino migrants reorganize transnational life during the global pandemic, the role of digital media in glocal intimacies is amplified. While previous research noted that for elite Filipino migrants, glocal intimacies are less dependent on technological mediation (Uy-Tioco and Cabañes 2021), this chapter has shown that this tendency has shifted in the COVID-19 context. Migrants' concern for loved ones in the homeland has led to local Philippine life becoming more central to their daily life in the United States. While mobile carework has always been a feature of transnational life (Uy-Tioco and Cabalquinto 2020), this has been more reinforced during the pandemic for a developing nation like the Philippines. Although the greater dependence on digital media has maintained glocal intimacies, complex feelings have arisen because migrants are more worried about significant others in the homeland while simultaneously they must also navigate the health risk and uncertainty in the host society. This chapter has recognized the limitations of transnational life – even for highly mobile and privileged elite migrants. Despite leading seemingly successful bifocal lives and having greater access to polymedia choices, their social intimacies during the pandemic reveal that elite migrants are more rooted with the homeland than previously thought. Both the global health crisis and the greater dependence on digital media for glocal intimacies have resulted in a reorientation of everyday life toward the homeland – similar to the situation of labor migrants such as OFWs. Digitally mediated intimacies, while welcomed, do not replace the need for face-to-face intimacies via physical travel. Elite migrants continue to need unmediated intimacies and experience the feelings of immobility akin to OFWs, indicating the limitations of digital media use regardless of class privilege. Indeed, the pandemic has prevented elite transnational Filipinos from taken-for-granted travel to the homeland during holidays, emergencies or family milestones. It has opened up new mediated ways of transnational living, the ability to take part in social events in the homeland such as weddings, funerals and Filipino church services. Digital media use during the pandemic has pushed elite migrants to orient their everyday toward local Philippine life; as glocal intimacies flourish in this context, so do new tensions and unintended consequences.

Acknowledgments

The author would like to thank Jason Cabañes for his valuable feedback and comments.

References

Alevizou, G. (2020) "Virtual Schooling, Covid-Gogy and Digital Fatigue," *Media@ LSE*, 3 April.

Bauman, Z. (1998) *Globalization*, Cambridge: Polity.

Boyd, D. (2011) "Participating in the Always-On Lifestyle," in M. Mandiberg (ed) *The Social Media Reader*, New York: New York University Press.

Cabalquinto, E. (2018) "We're Not Only Here But We're There in Spirit," *Mobile Media & Communication*, 6(1): 37–52.

Cabañes, J. and Acedera, K. (2012) "Of Mobile Phones and Mother-Fathers," *New Media & Society*, 14(6): 916–30.

Cabañes, J. and Uy-Tioco, C.S. (2020) *Mobile Media and Social Intimacies in Asia: Reconfiguring the Local and Reenacting the Global*, Dordrecht: Springer.

Castells, M. (1996) *The Rise of the Network Society*, Oxford: Blackwell.

Chen, H. (2020) "Left-Behind Children as Agents," in J. Cabañes and C.S. Uy-Tioco (eds) *Mobile Media and Social Intimacies in Asia: Reconfiguring the Local and Reenacting the Global*, Dordrecht: Springer.

Hjorth, L. and Lim S.S. (2012) "Mobile Intimacy in an Age of Affective Mobile Media," *Feminist Media Studies*, 12(4): 477–84.

Ito, M. (2003) "Mobiles and the Appropriation of Place," *Receiver Magazine*, 8: 1–3.

Jung, Y.A. (2020) "Mobile Media and *Kirogi* Mothers," in J. Cabañes and C.S. Uy-Tioco (eds) *Mobile Media and Social Intimacies in Asia: Reconfiguring the Local and Reenacting the Global,* Dordrecht: Springer.

Kang, T. (2020) "Visualizing Birth Tourism on Social Media," in J. Cabañes and C.S. Uy-Tioco (eds) *Mobile Media and Social Intimacies in Asia: Reconfiguring the Local and Reenacting the Global,* Dordrecht: Springer.

Katz, J. and Aakhus, M. (2002) *Perpetual Contact,* Cambridge: Cambridge University Press.

Licoppe, C. (2004) "Connected Presence," *Environment and Planning D: Society and Space,* 22(1): 135–56.

Lim, S.S. (2016) *Mobile Communication and the Family,* Dordrecht: Springer.

Lim, S.S. and Pham, B. (2016) "If You are a Foreigner in a Foreign Country, You Stick Together," *New Media & Society,* 18(10): 2171–88.

Ling, R. (2004) *The Mobile Connection,* Amsterdam: Elsevier.

Lorenzana, J. (2016) "Mediated Recognition," *New Media & Society,* 18(10): 2189–206.

Madianou, M. (2015) "Polymedia and Ethnography," *Social Media+Society,* 11 (May).

Madianou, M. and Miller, D. (2012) *Migration and New Media: Transnational Families and Polymedia,* London: Routledge.

Massey, D. (1993) "Power-Geometry and a Progressive Sense of Place," in J. Bird, B. Curtis, T. Putnam and L. Tickner (eds) *Mapping the Future,* London: Routledge.

Moores, S. (1993) "Television, Geography and Mobile Privatization," *European Journal of Communication,* 8: 365–79.

Moores, S. (2000) *Media and Everyday Life in Modern Society,* Edinburgh: Edinburgh University Press.

Nader, L. (1972) "Up the Anthropologist," in D. Hymes (ed) *Reinventing Anthropology,* New York: Pantheon.

Ong, J. and Cabañes, J. (2011) "Engaged, But Not Immersed," *South East Asia Research,* 19(2): 197–224.

Polson, E. (2016) *Privileged Mobilities,* New York: Peter Lang.

Rafael, V. (1990) "Nationalism, Imagery and the Filipino Intelligentsia in the Nineteenth Century," *Critical Inquiry,* 16(3): 591–611.

Raiti, G. (2007) "Mobile Intimacy," *M/C Journal,* 10(1).

Robertson, R. (1994) "Globalisation or Glocalisation?," *Journal of International Communication,* 1(1): 33–52.

Rouse, R. (1992) "Making Sense of Settlement," *Annals of the New York Academy of Sciences,* 645: 25–52.

Smith, M. and Favell, A. (2006) *The Human Face of Global Mobility,* New Brunswick: Transaction.

Turkle, S. (2011) *Alone Together,* New York: Basic Books.

Uy-Tioco, C.S. (2007) "Overseas Filipino Workers & Text Messaging," *Continuum: Journal of Media & Cultural Studies,* 21(2): 253–65.

Uy-Tioco, C.S. (2017) "Transnational Ties," in L. Lopez and V. Pham (eds) *The Routledge Companion to Asian American Media,* London: Routledge.

Uy-Tioco, C.S. (2019) "Good Enough Access," *Journal of Communication Research & Practice,* 5(2): 156–71.

Uy-Tioco, C.S. and Cabalquinto, E. (2020) "Transnational Mobile Carework," in J. Cabañes and C.S. Uy-Tioco (eds) *Mobile Media and Social Intimacies in Asia: Reconfiguring the Local and Reenacting the Global,* Dordrecht: Springer.

Uy-Tioco, C.S. and Cabañes, J. (2021) "Glocal Intimacies and the Contradictions of Mobile Media Access in the Philippines," *Media International Australia,* 179(1): 9–22.

Vertovec, S. (2004) "Migrant Transnationalism and Modes of Transformation," *International Migration Review*, 38(3): 970–1001.

Vertovec, S. and Cohen, R. (2002) *Conceiving Cosmopolitanism*, Oxford: Oxford University Press.

Waruwu, B. (2021) "Smartphone Mothering and Mediated Family Display," *Mobile Media & Communication*, 9 March.

Williams, R. (1974) *Television: Technology and Cultural Form*, Hanover: Wesleyan University Press.

23

RECONSTITUTING SEXUALITY AND HOME IN A PLATFORM AGE

Asian Australian and Asian New Zealand LGBTQ Web Series

Olivia Khoo

Web series are short videos or episodes available on the Internet that can be viewed on devices including laptops and mobile phones. Not simply "television made for the Internet," web series are a format with their own history, tied to the development of mobile devices themselves, and within that format there is much diversity. Web series encapsulate the paradoxical mobility of the Internet. On the one hand, they are highly mobile and can circulate across borders (on YouTube and Vimeo, for example). On the other hand, language, local accents and humor can impede accessibility, while more significant barriers to mobility exist through geoblocking and regional filters, in addition to more politically motivated forms of censorship. Through their content, web series have also facilitated the visibility and mobility of particular kinds of identities, especially those of marginalized groups. While there is a growing visibility of diasporic Asian identities in popular crossover cinema such as *Crazy Rich Asians* (John M. Chu, 2018), *Always Be My Maybe* (Nahnatchka Khan, 2019) and *The Farewell* (Lulu Wang, 2019), feature filmmaking has not proved the most accessible or successful of media for diasporic Asian producers, especially women and LGBTQ creatives. Asian couples are now happily (and unhappily) seen in relationships with a partner of the same race and the opposite sex, but when it comes to nonheteronormative sexualities, progress remains slow in traditional media (cinema and broadcast television). On series made for the web, however, LGBTQ stories and characters have flourished. Often created by and about the marginalized communities they speak to (Monaghan 2017), lesbian and gay characters in web series are not just token figures but appear as embodied characters through a serialized format offering ongoing engagement and narrative development.

The web series as a platform have grown exponentially in Australia, from 107 episodes in 2012 to 3248 in 2016 (ABS 2016). In Australia and New Zealand, where cultural and linguistic diversity is still under-represented on traditional

DOI: 10.4324/9781003130628-28

screen media (*Screen Australia* 2016; *NZ on Air* 2018), the web series have opened up a space for more complex diasporic Asian characters, such as in the five-part Asian Australian comedy series, *Phi and Me*, about 16-year-old Phi Nguyen and her mother Kim Huong, a refugee from Vietnam. LGBTQ stories and characters have also been embraced. There is a growing body of Australian and New Zealand web series that feature characters of marginalized races/ethnicities and sexualities. Indigenous Australians are also receiving more visibility via this medium: *Jade of Death* (2018), written and directed by Erin Good, is a supernatural web series with an indigenous lesbian protagonist, Jade (played by Bernie Van Tiel). One of the most successful Australian LGBTQ web series, Julie Kalceff's *Starting From … Now!* (2014–2016), is a drama revolving around the lives of a group of lesbians living in Sydney, featuring Asian Australian actress Rosie Lourde in a lead role. *Starting From … Now!* has received over 35 million views and has been watched in 230 countries. It screened as a web series for the first three seasons and was picked up for television for seasons 4 and 5. Also set in Sydney is another lesbian-themed web series, *Newtown Girls* (2012), written and directed by Natalie Krikowa and starring Asian Australian actress Renee Lim. *Flunk* is a teen LGBTQ drama web series set in Melbourne with Jessica Li playing Ingrid, an Asian Australian high school student who falls in love with her female best friend. Other web series featuring Asian Australian actors include *After Nightfall*, a murder mystery involving the killing of a gay young man from a small country town, written and directed by Wayne Tunks and starring Jasper Lee-Lindsay and Andrew Wang in key roles. *Ding Dong I'm Gay*, directed by Sarah Bishop, features comedienne Alex Lee as eccentric Chinese housemate Sweetie. Tim Spencer, writer for *Ding Dong I'm Gay*, observes of this trend, "it feels like gay content is at home on the web" (Leighton-Dore 2018). More specifically, as this chapter observes, diasporic Asian and queer contents have found new visibility online through the format of the web series.

This chapter examines one Asian Australian and one Asian New Zealand web series that redefine notions of home, kinship and belonging: *Homecoming Queens* (2018, Australia), written by Michelle Law and Chloe Reeson and directed by Corrie Chen, and *Flat3* (2013–2014, New Zealand), written and directed by Roseanne Liang. The chapter will argue that the serialized and collaborative nature of the web series provides a form of representation for diasporic Asian and LGBTQ identities that is not currently seen in any other media format. The highly mobile nature of the web series, able to circulate and be shared on the Internet, also engenders a form of mobility to these identities by allowing connections and networks to be made by audiences (and producers) across the region. However, this mobility is often stymied by censorship or other forms of political, economic and technical barriers, such as geoblocking. As a result, the web series as a platform enabling a mobile concept of "home" for diasporic Asian and LGBTQ identities remain to some degree a potentiality waiting to be fulfilled. Nevertheless, this chapter will argue that despite the limited (in the sense of usually short and finite) nature of web series, the ephemerality of the web series still has a lasting impact on the community it engages and that engages with it, however briefly.

Web Series as a Platform for Affective Connections

Related to the rise of the web series is the "platformization" of the Internet. Anne Helmond (2015: 5) uses this term to refer to "the rise of the platform as the dominant infrastructural and economic model of the social web." Tarleton Gillespie (2010: 349–50) has outlined four meanings of the term platform – computational, architectural, figurative and political – noting a more conceptual meaning of the term that combines all four semantic connotations. Platforms suggest "a progressive and egalitarian arrangement, promising to support those who stand upon [them]" in the contemporary global society (ibid.: 350). Reinforcing this notion of the platform in relation to web series specifically, Sue Swinburne and Richard Fabb (2017) have commented that the "explosion in web series is fostering a far more democratic platform than TV or cinema." In particular, the web series is a particular kind of platform (which is itself distributed on other platforms such as YouTube) that can facilitate affective connections between members of a community. Web series participate in, and even assert some control over, the flow and mobility of particular (marginalized) images and identities they are part of forming. In the case of diasporic Asian and queer web series, there is a broader trans-Tasman and Southeast Asian regional community to which they belong. Web series can enable a form of regional mobility that (perhaps somewhat paradoxically) provides a sense of community, or kinship, for viewers. For diasporic and queer identities online, regional mobility and community go hand in hand.

This chapter approaches the analyses of the web series to follow through the notion of "platformativity" developed by Thomas Lamarre (2017). Platformativity considers our various interactions with platforms, from the material to the affective. Lamarre notes that society and culture provide the context from which platform creators "draw ideas and to which they may in turn contribute" (ibid.: 286). This model of contextualization results, however, in a divide between individual and society, and separates platforms from their users and creators, what Lamarre refers to as a form of "methodological individualism" (ibid.: 301). Platformativity acknowledges users and user practices in a way that accounts for social relations between technical individuals (platforms), human individuals (viewers and consumers) and screen life (characters), regarding these as existing on "the same level in ontological terms" (ibid.: 302). By considering platforms and users in this way, it is possible to explore how platforms (in this case, web series) operate as "not only an infrastructure or architecture, but also a promise of a voice, of visibility" (Steinberg and Li 2017: 302). Platformativity enables an exploration of how the web series are facilitating the circulation of newly visible forms of mobile cultural identity across an Asian and queer diaspora that has arguably found its home online.

Through the two case studies to follow, the chapter explores how the web series as a platform creates a space for affective connection, visibility and voice that feels like "home" for diasporic Asian and queer audiences. Both *Homecoming Queens* and *Flat3* employ diasporic Asian talent both in front of and behind the camera. In the case of *Homecoming Queens*, the sexuality of one of the two protagonists is also centralized in the storyline. Both series are examples of diasporic media made intentionally for the web and achieving success through that platform.

Homecoming Queens: Diasporic Intimacy and Queer Kinship

Homecoming Queens is a semi-autobiographical seven-part series that marks the first commission for the Special Broadcasting Service (SBS)'s online streaming service, SBS On Demand. SBS is one of Australia's two main public broadcasters, tasked in its charter to champion multiculturalism and on-screen diversity. The series follows two best friends in their twenties, one of whom has cancer, and the other, alopecia. It is directed and produced by Corrie Chen, a young Asian Australian creative, and based partly on the life story of Asian Australian writer Michelle Law and her friend Chloe Reeson (Law plays herself in the series and Reeson is played by Liv Hewson).

Homecoming Queens was conceived as a web series from its inception in 2015, which, as Caris Bizzaca (2018) notes, was a "bold statement" at the time given that Netflix and Stan had just launched locally. Funded by SBS, Screen Australia, Screen Queensland and Film Victoria, the web series was considered the ideal platform for *Homecoming Queens* in order to appeal to its target audience of young adult viewers (Bizzaca 2018). With episodes ranging from 9 minutes to 16 minutes, the brevity of the format caters to distracted and mobile modes of viewing. Marshall Heald, SBS Director of TV and Online Content, suggests that a web series like *Homecoming Queens* meets two key goals:

> Firstly, to develop new creative voices from under-represented communities to make Australian storytelling more truly representative of the society we live in — a rich and vibrant multicultural society. Secondly, to deliver our innovation aspirations — to take big creative risks in the stories we tell and the ways in which they're told and to enable digital audiences to find and experience those shows at a time that suits them.
>
> *(Williams 2019)*

The unconventional format of the web series, with short bite-sized episodes of variable lengths, is arguably better suited to telling stories about "unconventional" characters, meaning those who are marginalized and not as visible on traditional media. Michelle Law comments, "[web series are] a very fresh form. And I think they do get a bad rap and are seen as a bit of a stepping stone to longer form series, but I think they need to be respected in their own right" (Bizzaca

2018). There are particular production constraints (as well as opportunities) specific to web series that mean they tend to focus on individual and small group stories. There is an intimacy (and immediacy) to the web series that captures the intimacy of the small screen formats on which they are usually viewed. A predominance of close-ups, a focus on individual or community stories, and viewing practices associated with small screen formats impact our affective relationship to the characters in a web series, literally bringing us closer to their stories and inviting engagement.

Discussing the notion of diasporic intimacy in Tony Ayres' *The Home Song Stories*, Audrey Yue (2008: 230) notes that while there are no overtly gay characters or homosexual subtext in the film, its narrative format is itself non-normative and unconventional for a feature film. Yue posits that queer Asian Australian migration is manifest in *The Home Song Stories* both through the minor transnationalism of its co-production and through the queer mobility of diasporic intimacy. She writes, "Diasporic intimacy disrupts the regulation of queer migration and shows how the private domains of memory, family and sexuality are reconstituted in the transnational Chinese diaspora" (ibid.: 231). Yue (2011: 135) adds, "Recent studies in queer diaspora provide an innovative approach to further consider the politics of mobility. They shift the focus away from identity and cultural hybridity by mobilizing queer as an affective site to question the broader narratives of re-nationalism and neo-liberalism." As best friends in *Homecoming Queens*, Chloe and Michelle create their own family, while their "biological" families are nowhere to be seen, and where characters like themselves do not exist in the broader national narrative.

In Episode 1 ("Backyard"), Michelle takes refuge at Chloe's house after she learns of her alopecia diagnosis. The series quickly establishes its setting in the quintessential Australian backyard with a Hills Hoist clothesline. Chloe, whose hair is just growing back after chemotherapy, converses with an elderly neighbor over the fence who asks if Michelle is "one of [her] cancer friends" and jokes that they can start a "baldy club." While the first episode sets up a typically Australian suburban scene, its circuits of mobility are transnational and also queer. Chloe is gay and does not want to waste any more time after her cancer diagnosis; this results in her conviction to work her way through her bucket list, including experiencing a gay relationship and trying some "lady sex." Writer and executive producer, Corrie Chen, is an out lesbian; and Michelle Law's brother, Benjamin, is celebrated for his autobiographical book and series, *The Family Law*, which tells his life story growing up as a young gay Asian Australian man. These references would be well known to many of the web series' audience. The mobility of *Homecoming Queens* is thus manifest not in its search for expanded resources – greater funding or audiences – but rather its participation in a regional queer diaspora that gives LGBTQ Asian Australian identities visibility beyond traditional media and in major national film and television industries.

In the case of *Homecoming Queens*, it is illness and disability (cancer and alopecia) that are at the heart of redefining notions of feminine beauty, desirability and belonging. In Episode 1, Chloe tells Michelle, "You've got a good noggin for alopecia. When my hair fell out [from chemotherapy], my skull looked like a bag of rocks." Kylie Maslen (2018) notes that Chloe and Michelle's shared experiences of illness during youth provide the narrative opportunities to add humor, allowing the audience to bond with the characters as they too bond with each other over laughter and self-acceptance. Maslen (2018: 57) writes:

> Perhaps it's the freedom that comes from creating for the web rather than television – and the growing audiences drawn to the former – that gives networks and funding bodies greater willingness to commit to projects like this. By taking risks and allowing us to depict real experiences, real bodies, real illnesses and real friendships, what these platforms are doing is empowering us to show our real selves.

Chloe and Michelle form a queer family with kinship based on affinity and shared experiences. This reconstitution of the notion of "home" and family moves away from race/ethnicity as a marker of belonging and closer to David Eng's (2010) concept of the queer diaspora conceived not in relation to nation-states but formed through new configurations of kinship, family and affect. Writing about queer Chinese cultures and mobilities, John Wei (2020) suggests that kinship, migration and the middle classes are key issues preoccupying post-2008 queer Chinese cultures. Wei (2020: 11) conceptualizes queer mobilities through three related lenses – geographical (the horizontal, geographical relocation of people), cultural (the multidimensional cultural flows and counter-flows) and social (the vertical upward social class migration). Queer kinship functions as an alternative kinship system whereby co-tenancy, for example, enables queer people to experience intimacy and the security of a family-like relationship (ibid.: 43). Queer kinship involves "an imbricated process of *home-leaving, homemaking* and *homecoming*" (ibid.: 29). In *Homecoming Queens*, disability and illness intersect with race and sexuality, allowing queer and Asian Australian characters a platform to be their real selves and to be visible. Indeed, it is the intersectionality of marginal identities that becomes the primary site through which experiences of intimacy and kinship are developed and conveyed in *Homecoming Queens*.

Flat3: Community and Collaboration

Flat3, a comedy web series written and directed by Roseanne Liang, also reconfigures traditional notions of home and the diasporic Asian family through co-tenancy as the foundation for an alternative form of kinship. Although less visible in the media than their Asian American or even Asian Australian counterparts, Asian New Zealanders have been well represented in diasporic media, not least in Roseanne Liang's earlier documentary and feature films, *Banana in a Nutshell* (2005) and *My Wedding and Other Secrets* (2011).

The first episode of *Flat3* (titled "Lee") introduces us to the three young Asian New Zealand protagonists – Lee (Ally Xue), Jessica (J.J. Fong) and Perlina (Perlina Lau). Jessica and Perlina are looking for someone to share their apartment and Lee, seeking escape from familial pressures, decides to move in with them, thus launching the premise of the web series. The first season, which premiered on YouTube and Vimeo in February 2013, was self-funded. The third and final seasons received NZ$100,000 from NZ on Air, a New Zealand government commission providing funding support for broadcasting and creative works, in 2014. The episodes range from 9 to 12 minutes in length (three series with six episodes each) with an average of 12,000 views per episode (and close to 10,000 subscribers). The first episode received over 48,000 views.

The title, *Flat3*, refers to the friendships, love lives, career aspirations and everyday escapades of these three friends, who create their own version of family in this shared apartment. However, the title also plays on the stereotype of Asian women being "flat-chested," and jokes are made throughout the series about the breast size of the women. The three leads stand in for different comic archetypes of the Asian woman: Lee is the awkward overachiever, Perlina is the opinionated "dragon lady" and Jessica is the over-sexed seductress. The series reproduces these stereotypes for comedic effect while it (only occasionally) subverts them. In Season 1, Episode 1, Lee is torn between following her passion to be an artist and having a financially stable career as an accountant. Lee visits a careers counselor who asks her, "If you could choose to be anything, have any job at all what would it be?" Lee replies, "Artist." Each response by Lee is rejected by the counselor: "You can't be that, let's try taking your expectations down one notch … How about accountancy? I bet you're good at maths." To boost Lee's chances at a job interview, the career counselor gifts her a set of breast implants, describing them as her "secret weapon." Lee asks, "What happens if I get a girl [female interviewer]?" He replies, "Let's hope she's a lesbian, because you will be looking *employable*." While this exchange between Lee and the careers counselor stretches the boundaries of what could be considered a humorous take on stereotypes, the format of the web series, and comedy in particular, allows these liberties to be taken. There is a further expectation that the anticipated target audience of a web series like *Flat3* will predominantly be the diasporic Asian New Zealand community, who can laugh at stereotypes of Asians being good at maths (and therefore over-represented in careers such as accountancy), as well as Asian women as flat-chested. An "in-joke" produced by a member of the diasporic Asian community, for this community, can provoke humor where it might otherwise create discomfort or cause offense if externally generated. Creating comedic diasporic media involves a balance between raising issues that are socially and politically relevant to the diasporic community, while packaging these in a format that is light-hearted, entertaining and humorous.

Because web series are not primarily commercially driven, producers are able to take more creative risks. As Roseanne Liang notes, "The absolute best thing about making web series, for me, is creative freedom. The budgets are so low, and the viewership so niche that you can take risks that no network or studio would usually allow you to" (Group Think 2017). The characters joke that to have one "diverse" character in a production is progressive and represents diversity, but to have *three* Asian female leads, as is the case in *Flat3*, would be a disaster in a commercial enterprise (Xue et al. 2016).

J.J. Fong, Perlina Lau and Ally Xue were inspired to create this comedy web series after experiencing a lack of roles for Asian actresses in New Zealand. Roseanne Liang, an Asian New Zealand filmmaker, joined as writer and director and the series was formed. In an interview with Arezou Zalipour, Liang recalls that she found it difficult to receive funding for her projects after making the film *My Wedding and Other Secrets* (2011), hence she was willing to explore the format of the (self-funded) web series. Zalipour (2016: 103) notes that when it comes to film production, diasporic communities may play "the role of funding agencies and resources for diasporic filmmaking. In this sense, the collective mode of production in diasporic filmmaking also refers to the various forms of ties and collaboration that relate the diasporic filmmakers to their communities."

While the bite-sized nature of the episodes may appear too minor to take on significant issues, and stereotypes are played for comedic effect, the series also tackles serious issues, from race relations and sexual harassment to non-normative sexualities. One of the most interesting episodes in the series is Season 3, Episode 17, "The White Album," which replaces the three Asian actors with White actors who play their roles. This switch is presented without explanation and without foregrounding or explicitly referring to the change in any way. Roseanne Liang recalls, "In the middle of Season 3 ... without warning, we swapped out our all Kiwi–Chinese core cast for White girls. We called the episode THE WHITE ALBUM. It was one of our most hated episodes. I loved it" (Group Think 2017). Liang's glee in creating an episode that polarized her audiences speaks to the potentially powerful and subversive nature of web series when used to question existing assumptions about ethnicity or race.

New Zealand is predominantly bicultural, with Māori (the indigenous people) and Pākehā (European settlers) as the two major groups, although it is also culturally diverse with a large Asian migrant population (Zalipour 2016: 96–7). Intercultural relationships across these groups are explored in a number of episodes in the series. Season 1, Episode 18, "Girlfight," features a rap battle between Asian New Zealanders and Polynesian/Māori, exposing the forms of racism that can exist between groups that are themselves marginalized on the basis of race/ethnicity. In Season 1, Episode 7, "Beyond Youth," the series plays with the science fiction genre. A sinister wealthy White woman attempts to harvest the blood of Asian and Black women to provide her with eternal youth. Season 2, Episode 7, "I'm Coming to Dinner," references Stanley Kramer's landmark film about inter-racial relationships, *Guess Who's Coming to Dinner?* (1967). Most of the relationships the protagonists pursue are with White men, although Perlina has a Māori ex-boyfriend and in the final episodes Jessica, who usually dates White men, falls for her Asian New Zealand landlord. There is one lesbian character who has a crush on Perlina.

Continuing the science fiction theme to explore non-normative sexualities, in a spin off series entitled *Unboxed* (2017, six episodes), the women are paid to test an "anatomically exceptional" AI robot named J (played by Peter Sudarso). While not overtly queer, the series is also not quite "straight," exploring the possibility of post-human relationships and non-normative sexualities. After three seasons, the *Flat3* team moved onto *Friday Night Bites*, a series of even shorter episodes centered around the lives of the same *Flat3* characters and taking place over 26 different Friday nights. As a weekly comedy web series, the serialization of *Friday Night Bites* allows the web series to build momentum with an audience and provide more depth to characterization than a short web series might otherwise allow. The *Flat3* team, led by director Roseanne Liang, has reconvened for their latest production entitled *Creamerie* (2021). *Creamerie* consists of 6 × 22 minute episodes and is a dystopian series set in the near future where a viral plague has killed off 99% of the Earth's men. The three original *Flat3* actresses play dairy farmers who uncover one of these rare creatures, a man. In a world essentially without men, and where pregnancy is achieved via a "re-population lottery," the world of *Creamerie* is fundamentally queer, with queer characters featuring implicitly and explicitly in the series. Tony Ayres serves as executive producer on this series principally funded by New Zealand on Air.

The ongoing nature of the collaboration between Roseanne Liang, J.J. Fong, Perlina Lau and Ally Xue on short episodes for the web consolidates and expands the audience for their continued productions. Bringing in a collaboration with well-known Asian Australian director and producer Tony Ayres, *Creamerie* also bridges Asian Australian and Asian New Zealand audiences and talent. Making connections and networks across diasporic Asian communities is vitally important with diasporic media still marginalized within national contexts.

Platform Politics: Regional Networks

The Australian and New Zealand examples discussed in this chapter are part of a proliferating body of web series circulating regionally and internationally, which give marginalized characters a voice that they are otherwise denied on traditional media. For Australian producers, there has been quite a palpable sense of finding a "home" for Asian diasporic and LGBTQ identities online, while at the same time providing opportunities for other forms of mobility to emerge. For example, the writer and producer of *Homecoming Queens*, Corrie Chen, is now in co-production with Chinese investors for a feature film being shot in China entitled *New Gold Mountain*. Roseanne Liang's new film, *Shadow in the Cloud* (2020), is a New Zealand–United States collaboration that had its world premiere at the Toronto International Film Festival in September 2020. As mentioned, Liang and *Flat3* productions are also collaborating with Tony Ayres on the new series *Creamerie*.

Given the relatively small pool of available web series, audiences often seek out regional counterparts. While the web series discussed in this chapter have been made by and about women in Australia and New Zealand, within Southeast Asia, the more visible examples throughout the region are produced by and about gay men. Censorship remains a serious concern in relation to the regulation of LGBTQ content online in Asia and several web series have been removed from the Internet since their release. Indonesia's *Conq* (the title is a slang term for gay men) could originally be found on YouTube but was removed after the Indonesian government censored LGBTQ web series and online content (Murtagh 2015). Other web series from Southeast Asia that can still be found on YouTube include *Hanging Out*, touted as the first gay Filipino web series; *Ur Tadhana*, a five-episode web series created by Fifth Solomon centered on a young Filipino vlogger named Yosef (also known as Yosefina Fierce); *My Best Gay Friends*, described as the first gay sitcom in Vietnam, a highly successful web series with each of the 13 episodes (running from 2012 to 2016) receiving millions of view on YouTube; *That's Why*, created by Huynh Nguyen Dang Khoa (and featuring a lesbian wedding); *People Like Us* (PLU), which follows the lives of four gay men in Singapore; and China's *Rainbow Family*, a gay sitcom available only online.

Rachel Syme's (2013) comments on the format of the web series – that its brevity and ephemerality best suit the distracted viewing habits of today's youth – are also applicable to its mobility and thus, its ability to facilitate community: "What a web series can do, if it deploys itself correctly, is create a pause, a visual coffee break, a moment of communion in an open tab." The mobility of the web series allows a viewer to feel locally grounded in the here and now, as well as regionally mobile and connected to a wider LGBTQ and diasporic Asian online community throughout Asia and elsewhere.

As Jennifer Brundidge (2010) notes, the Internet is both "accessible" and "traversable," with viewers of web series traversing between the entertainment space of the web series and the more social or political side of online viewership. This can take place, for instance, in the comments section of a platform, but it can also occur on outside platforms. Faithe Day (2018) has conducted a study of Black web series, examining the role that Black queer web series play in the lives of Black queer women by analyzing "commenting communities" on YouTube "as spaces which are complex in their ability to support and affirm these women, as well as reflecting the oppositional views of those from outside of Black queer communities" (ibid.: 12). In the case of the two web series discussed in this chapter, there have been only limited online comments among viewers of both series in terms of providing details about their viewing practices or experiences. This could be because the size of the diasporic communities in Australia and New Zealand is relatively small, compared to their US counterparts for instance, or because the web series is still a relatively new form. In the lack of significant online comments from (Asian Australian and Asian New Zealand) viewers, this study revisits the notion of platformativity to consider how affective relationships and connections can be possibly facilitated between viewers across the region.

Marc Steinberg and Jinying Li (2017: 174) suggest that platforms can be understood as regional entities: "Along with platforms comes a form of regionalization, a localization to a particular milieu, country, or region, through a deliberate exclusion of other countries and regions." Platforms produce not only geographical regions, as in geoblocking, but also geocultural regions (ibid.: 179).

> Every platform defines and delimits a region, whether subcultural or geographical or an amalgam of the two. This also means that counterhegemonic platforms can also emerge and, indeed, do emerge, sometimes in the cracks between the platform superpowers and sometimes before their arrival.
>
> *(ibid.: 175)*

Asian Australian and Asian New Zealand web series circulate in the form of these counterhegemonic platforms, remediating earlier forms of diasporic Asian cultural production, in particular short films and documentary features, now on social media platforms that allow users to engage with the content and each other in new ways. In exploring *Homecoming Queens* and *Flat3* through a framework of platformativity, the aim has been to consider to what extent the format of the web series has the potential to provide an online space for community formation and participation. The global flows of technology and culture are marked by differentials in power. Dal Yong Jin (2015: 11–2) has used the term "platform imperialism" to refer to "an asymmetrical relationship of interdependence in platform technologies and political culture between the West, primarily the US, and many developing countries." Platforms are shaped by government policy and flows of videos are restricted across national borders through geoblocking. New opportunities for mobility and visibility become a tactical necessity to get around these blockages, requiring a form of (regional) mobility that the web series afford. This chapter has described regional mobility and queer mobility as imbricated. Beyond technological forms of restriction and blocking, if we return to the conceptual meaning of platforms to enable (or at least provide the potential for) other forms of cultural circulation to take place, then web series allow us to move away from a consideration of platforms as tied to media imperialism (Jin 2015), and closer to a notion of platform communism (Hands 2013).

Given that digital platforms are now the dominant infrastructure of distribution, the distribution of diasporic Asian and LGBTQ content on web series can "produce a feeling of regional affinity, intimacy and proximity" (Steinberg and Li 2017: 179–80). This regional media network of web series featuring Asian or diasporic Asian characters with LGBTQ themes and characters establishes a new mobile "home" for marginalized identities on the Internet through a platform-based media regionalism in Asia. It is this form of platform connectivity and regional connectivity that Thomas Lamarre (2017) refers to in the concept of "platformativity" – in this case, a connectivity that goes beyond a national level to a trans-Tasman, and more broadly Southeast Asian regional connection.

While the examples from Australia and New Zealand discussed in this chapter are not co-produced with Asian partners, they circulate as part of a global network of LGBTQ web series and series made by women that has had to find its home online, shunned by the commercial imperatives of traditional media. Because of the tactical nature of web series (low budgets and stories of marginalized identities for niche audiences), creators do not look toward co-production for the usual reasons of expanding budgets and reaching wider audiences. Rather, the web series are a vocal and vocational platform, allowing the voicing of stories, identities and themes that are not able to be easily aired elsewhere. Australia and New Zealand have produced a number of successful web series that have achieved regional mobility and respectable audience numbers, while still remaining true to their vision. In Asia, web series featuring LGBTQ themes and characters have had to deploy alternative forms of mobility and nimbleness in order to elude online censorship. Yet the fact that they do or have existed, even when forced to go underground or elsewhere, creates ongoing and lasting effects, including the creation of an archive, however ephemeral, of a precarious state of existence. As Faithe Day (2018: 35) argues, web series provide a home for misfits, outsiders and queers. Web series are achieving prominence as an important platform that has created new spaces and forums for interaction for individuals, including an affective connection based on shared recognition of race, diaspora and sexuality.

References

ABS (Australian Bureau of Statistics) (2016) "Film, Television and Digital Games Survey," *Screen Australia*, 15 June.

Bizzaca, C. (2018) "Homecoming Queens: Why You'll Find Them Online," *Screen Australia*, 11 April.

Brundidge, J. (2010) "Political Discussion and News Use in the Contemporary Public Sphere," *Javnost-The Public*, 17(2): 63–82.

Day, F. (2018) *Quaring YouTube Comments and Creations: An Analysis of Black Web Series through the Politics of Production, Performance and Pleasure*, Ph.D. Thesis, Ann Arbor: University of Michigan.

Gillespie, T. (2010) "The 'Politics' of Platforms," *New Media & Society*, 12(3): 347–64.

Group Think (2017) "The Search for the Greatest Episode of a New Zealand Web Series Ever Made," *The Spinoff*, 13 June.

Hands, J. (2013) "Platform Communism," *Culture Machine*, 14: 1–24.

Helmond, A. (2015) "The Platformization of the Web," *Social Media+Society*, July-December: 1–11.

Jin, D.Y. (2015) *Digital Platforms, Imperialism and Political Culture*, London: Routledge.

Lamarre, T. (2017) "Platformativity: Media Studies, Area Studies," *Asiascape: Digital Asia*, 4: 285–305.

Leighton-Dore, S. (2018) "New Aussie Web Series Offers Queer Look at Comedy," *SBS*, 17 May.

Maslen, K. (2018) "Mirth and Malady: *Homecoming Queens* and Depicting Chronic Illness," *Metro Magazine*, 197: 54–7.

Monaghan, W. (2017) "*Starting From… Now!* and the Web Series to Television Crossover," *Media International Australia*, 164(1): 82–91.

Murtagh, B. (2015) "LGBT Indonesians Bring Entertainment and Activism Together Online," *Inside Indonesia*, 21 September.

NZ on Air (2018) "Diversity Report," 14 May.

Screen Australia (2016) "Seeing Ourselves: Reflections on Diversity in Australian TV Drama," 24 August.

Steinberg, M. and Li, J. (2017) "Introduction: Regional Platforms," *Asiascape: Digital Asia*, 4: 173–83.

Swinburne, S. and Fabb, R. (2017) "How Web Series are Shaking Up Australia's Screen Industry," *The Conversation*, 30 June.

Syme, R. (2013) "Why Web TV Series Are Worth Watching," *New Yorker*, 9 September.

Wei, J. (2020) *Queer Chinese Cultures and Mobilities*, Hong Kong: Hong Kong University Press.

Williams, C. (2019) "Australian TV Might Upend Reality Television's Reign with Series like *Bluey*, *The Heights* and *Robbie Hood*," *ABC News*, 24 August.

Xue, A., Fong, J. and Lau, P. (2016) "Why We Wrote Friday Night Bites," *Metro*, 12 September.

Yue, A. (2008) "Queer Asian Australian Migration: Creative Film Coproduction and Diasporic Intimacy in *The Home Song Stories*," *Studies in Australasian Cinema*, 2(3): 229–43.

Yue, A. (2011) "Critical Regionalities in Inter-Asia and the Queer Diaspora," *Feminist Media Studies*, 11(1): 131–38.

Zalipour, A. (2016) "Interstitial and Collective Filmmaking in New Zealand," *Transnational Cinemas*, 7(1): 96–110.

24

CITIZENSHIP, NATIONALISM AND THE POLITICS OF MULTICULTURALISM

Digital Networks of Indian Diasporas in Germany

Jayana Jain

Since the last decade, digital media have acted as both a channel and a repository of diasporas' collective outrage and individual discontent. They have been serving as a "socially and politically relevant tool" (Ponzanesi 2020: 986) for the diasporas' digital networks and the mediation of their collective angst in relation to conflicts in both the homeland and the hostland. It is necessary to examine the formation, nature and role of their digital congregations considering their seemingly cosmopolitan, creative, informational, motivational and provocative tendencies in bringing about major legal and political turns across borders. It is equally necessary to consider how different diasporic networks respond to a national issue in different or similar ways to foreground their transnational experiences of "locality, mobility and diasporic digitality" (ibid.: 988). This chapter explores one such transnational digital congregation that emerged in the latter half of 2019 but faded in the wake of the COVID-19 pandemic in 2020. By conducting a digital ethnography and network analysis, it sheds light on the social media networks of support and dissent of Indian diasporas and Non-Resident Indian (NRI) students residing in Germany in relation to the policy of the National Register of Citizens (NRC) and the Citizenship Amendment Act (CAA) 2019 in India.

The chapter begins by underlining how the introduction of the NRC and CAA is a corollary of the Modi-led BJP government's Hindutva nationalist politics central to the New India narrative and the definition of its desirable citizens. It then responds to why the discussion of CAA-related digital support and protest activities of Indian diasporas in Germany is worthy of attention in the global crisis of multiculturalism today. It argues that a spotlight on the Indian diasporas' digital politics enables the decoding of those affective and identarian tactics that have shaped and are shaped by the anti-immigrant and Islamophobic sentiment embedded within the far-right populist discourses on nation, nationalism,

DOI: 10.4324/9781003130628-29

citizenship and belonging in both India and a "multicultural Europe" (Chin 2017: 24).

Citizenship Amendment Act, Hindu Nationalist Politics and European Multiculturalism

> It has been said that genuine thinking begins with a scream – not of fear, but of outrage. (And if you're not outraged, so another saying goes, you're simply not paying attention). If thinking does begin with a scream of outrage – outrage at all that is intolerable in this world – then there is plenty to scream about.
>
> *(Holland 2011: ix)*

In *Nomad Citizenship*, while expressing the need for public outrage against the state politics of "populist ultranationalism," and practices of citizenship, Holland (2011: xi) calls for "thinking through the outrage philosophically, rather than simply taking sides for one State-form against the other." His call for a "slow-motion general strike" or developing alternative public practices and institutions outside the monopoly of state and capital has influenced this chapter's contours of "genuine thinking" about public outrage and citizenship laws. Although Holland's study emphasizes the need for transformation of citizenship laws based on the post-9/11 militarization and Islamophobic policies of the Bush presidency, this chapter argues for shifting the focus to the migrants' struggles and their collective outrage within the discourse on state citizenship. As an access point to "historical legacies of culture, land, livelihood and resources" (Roy 2019: 34), citizenship rights and the need for a homeland or a place of settlement are some of the most pressing issues today. When millions of Muslim refugees, migrants and stateless diasporas across geopolitical borders are confronting the dire consequences of racial/ethnic and cultural discrimination, ecological displacement and heightened forms of precarity, there arises an urgent need to think through their online and offline expressions of individual and collective discontent. Such a study is necessary to challenge the state's biopolitics of citizenship laws that blatantly exclude or privilege some communities over others, and foreground the migrants' discussions about their cultural, religious, economic and social struggles.

In the context of the migrants' struggles in Germany and India today, there is also the need to question the idealized project of neoliberal multiculturalism and its frames of recognizing and differentiating migrant subjectivities based on Eurocentric values that are purported to be "universalistic" (Ahmed, quoted in Jain 2021a: 73): Given that the core of the European multicultural politics of immigration is the demand for "fixated" recognition of the Other, it is important to underline that often at the heart of this recognition lies the Muslim migrant subject. Such a subject is framed based on specific colonial and Western historical imaginaries about "natural rights" and "age-old stereotypes" that justify their Othering (Dusche 2010: xiii, 64). Immigration policies and citizenship laws in India and Germany demonstrate varying degrees of multiculturalism that emerged in distinct historical contexts and indicate different starting points of approaching immigrant issues (Chin 2017). However, they indicate a mutual false perception of threat emanating from nation-states with a Muslim majority and a hesitancy toward the integration of Muslim migrants (Dusche 2010). Within the European multicultural context, the case of Germany's "foreigner policy" since 2010 has been termed as a policy of "willful neglect" exhibiting the nation's "threshold of tolerance" (Chin 2017: 124, 136). In the South Asian multicultural context, India's 2019 citizenship law denotes a straightforward and willful exclusion of Muslim migrants, a stance that "could trigger the largest statelessness crisis in the world" (Jay 2020).

In 2016, the Citizenship Amendment Bill (CAB) was introduced by the BJP government as an act of amendment to the earlier 1955 Citizenship Act of India. The CAB was eventually passed as a law or the Citizenship Amendment Act (CAA) in December 2019 (Ministry of Law and Justice 2019): The CAA states that migrants belonging to Hindu, Sikh, Parsi, Christian, Buddhist and Jain communities from the neighboring countries of Pakistan, Afghanistan or Bangladesh, and who fear religious persecution, are eligible for Indian citizenship if they arrived in India on or before 31 December 2014. Evidently, the law selectively excludes persecuted Muslim minorities from the neighboring countries of India such as the Ahmadiyya Muslims in Pakistan, Hazaras in Afghanistan, the Rohingya Muslims in Myanmar and the Uyghur Muslims in China (Chapparban 2020): Four months before the CAA was passed, the National Register for Citizens (NRC) in Assam was revised and as a result, "around 2 million people were listed as 'illegal' failing to provide proper documentation to prove their citizenship." Thus, the NRC combined with the CAA ensures that while the undocumented non-Muslim citizens who were excluded by the NRC can apply for Indian citizenship based on the CAA, the persecuted Muslims from neighboring countries will remain excluded irrespective of their length of residence in India.

Since the Act grants citizenship based on anti-secular sentiments and violates the democratic rubric of the Indian constitution, it caused an uproar and led to nationwide protests. During the protest movements in India, episodes of police brutality on the students of Jawaharlal Nehru University, Jamia Millia Islamia and Aligarh Muslim University intensified (Nigam 2020). Such forms of policing through repressive state apparatuses on matters of public outrage are symptomatic of the "politics of immobility" of an authoritarian state that demonstrate themselves as "filters" who can control the "penetration power of the migratory packs" (Deleuze and Guattari 2010: 51). In response to the policing of student voices and the BJP's politics of immobility perceptible in the CAA, the NRI alumni of many universities in India began to show their long-distance solidarity and staged anti-CAA protests through Twitter. Since studies on Indian diasporas in Germany tend to focus on their migratory patterns and their diasporic, cultural and gendered practices (Subrahmanian 2015; Butsch 2018), it is important to explore how digital platforms have been utilized by young Indian diasporas as they navigate the changing nationalistic and global imaginaries concerning citizenship laws.

Long-Distance Hindu Nationalisms, Digital Media and Indian Diasporas

As an integral part of election campaigns and foreign policy, the BJP leaders have been making extensive efforts to interpellate Indian diasporas as tools for "soft-power diplomacy" and "facilitators" of the "Great Indian Family" who may upscale and consolidate Hindutva perspectives at a global scale (Mahalingam 2013). By deploying young Internet-savvy volunteers across India and diaspora locations, the BJP has been amplifying its Hindu nationalist soundscape on digital media (Udupa 2019). Through websites such as the Global Hindu Electronic Network and Hindu Unity established in the 1990s, the BJP and its affiliates have been using "'a-political' lures" to code and mediate transnational Hindutva in varying degrees with the help of young Hindu students' councils based in the USA and UK (Sud 2008). The BJP has been holding sway over the young Indian Hindu diasporas and NRI professional communities by tapping on not only their "diasporic dollars" (ibid.: 63) but also their digital networks and technological skills while staging the prospect of promoting the welfare of one's "matrobhoomi" (homeland).

In the "new millennium India," Udupa (2019: 3148) suggests that "the right-wing Hindu nationalist mobilization gained momentum as a composite ideological space" concurrently with the rise in the number of the online Hindu nationalist volunteers who are "far from a homogenous group of indoctrinated foot soldiers." Even if some of the online volunteers of Hindu nationalism in the Indian diasporas appear to be uncomfortable with the anti-secular and absolutist ideas of Hindu majoritarianism, what entices them into supporting Modi-led BJP's Hindutva operations are the promises of "acche din" (good days) based on neoliberal economic reforms and the vision of a "tech blitzkrieg" in "New India" (Sharma 2013). Alongside, there is the lingering "unarticulated desire among many diasporic Hindus to be differentiated from stigmatized and often low-income Muslims" (Sud 2008: 58) especially in the post-9/11 and post-26/11 context of heightened xenophobia. This is another reason why the BJP's Hindutva desires have nested and consolidated in the social, cultural, educational and digital networks of young non-Muslim Indian diasporas (Leidig 2019). The identification with or disbelief in such techno-fascist impulses and Hindutva perspectives within the BJP narrative of "New India" have fostered new variants of "long-distance nationalism(s)" among Indian diasporic communities (Jain 2021a: 157).

While "diasporic guilt" of "deserting the motherland" for an affluent life abroad has led many Hindu nationalist diasporas to enter the arena of long-distance nationalism and contribute monetarily to the BJP and its affiliates (Sud 2008: 58), the diaspora's "nostalgic desire" to recreate one's place of birth or ancestral home in the place of settlement has been another stimulating factor to practice long-distance nationalisms (Anderson 1998). Diasporas' long-distance nationalisms may also be interpreted as "a discourse whereby people frame their aspiration by identifying with a nation" or "a project that consists of social movements and state policies through which people seek to act in terms of the nation with which they identify" (Glick Schiller 2005: 571). In today's digital era, the diasporas' long-distance nationalisms have metamorphosed as real-time nationalisms. They demonstrate supersonic impulses that travel seamlessly despite the geographical distance or different time zones across nation-states. Although the "longing" for the homeland fundamental to the long-distance nationalisms of the diasporas remains intact, paradoxically, there is also no time for yearning as their expressions of loyalty and nationalisms masquerade as "hot," "banal" or "everyday nationalism" on social media networks (Udupa 2019: 3150; Mihelj and Jiménez-Martínez 2021). The constant updates in the participatory features of digital technologies and their informative and communicative capacities demand the investment of human sensory capacities on an everyday basis, thereby generating new forms of affective encounters with national and transnational digital spaces. This study of the digital nationalist practices of Indian diasporas offers vital perspectives on how the affective intricacies within and between the personal, local and global are mediated while engaging in the debates on nation, citizenship and belonging.

Since the beginning of the 21st century, the digital Hindu nationalist space is so profoundly imbricated in the global discourses on terrorists, terrorism and counterterrorism. Its spread beyond the geopolitical borders of India and the confluence with far-right White nationalist extremisms in the USA, UK and other parts of Europe reveals the "mutual complementarity" that exists between the local and global xenophobic constructions and Islamophobic acts (Thobani 2018; Jain 2021a). In a study of Indian diaspora supporters for Brexit and Trump presidency on Twitter, Leidig (2019) argues that non-Muslim Indian diasporas attempt to distinguish a boundary against the Muslim "other," thereby escalating the Islamophobic and anti-Muslim immigrant anxiety that has culminated in various forms of state-sponsored violence in the global post-2001 context.

Similarly, this chapter suggests that there is an anxiety toward the Muslim migrants' arrival from neighboring countries and the simultaneous dominance of irrational ideas about radicalization, terrorism and terrorists. It is equally important to recognize the "heterogeneous" nature of Indian diasporas in Germany and the significance of their sociopolitical role in digitally supporting or challenging the Hindutva ideology and the anti-Muslim immigrant sentiment embedded in the CAA and NRC. In November 2019, after a meeting with the German Chancellor Angela Merkel in New Delhi, Prime Minister Modi expressed that Germany's expertise will be useful for building "New India," and sustainable bilateral ties through an exchange of teachers that may bring about new developments in education and scientific research (*Scroll* 2019). A month later, the introduction of the CAA triggered the Indian diasporas and young NRIs in Germany to enact a sociopolitical role much beyond their homogenous representation. Their attempts to create glocal pathways and opposition to the Indian diaspora supporters for the CAA and NRC become an interesting case study to explore.

Context and Method

On 24 December 2019, *The Hindu* (2019) reported that a German student on an exchange program at IIT-Madras was given an oral notice by the Indian Bureau of Immigration officials: The notice asked him to leave India for participating in the anti-CAA street protests as it implied a violation of his visa regulations. His image of carrying a placard that said "1933–1945 We have been there" was circulated widely on the Internet, attracting instant comparison between the anti-Muslim sentiment of the CAA and NRC and the anti-Semitic and racist sentiments of the Nuremberg Laws (1935) of the Third Reich in Germany (*The Hindu* 2019). The emphasis on this Indo-German entanglement exposed the historical relationship between political Hinduism and Nazism that cannot be reduced to "committed racial or religious hatred" (Visana 2021). Instead, it is important to scrutinize their logics of unification, national sovereignty and "passionate political solidarity" that demand the replacement of secularism and liberalism of a democratic system with a "palingenetic nationalist" leader (Griffin 2012; Visana 2021). Today, the rise of the Alternative für Deutschland (AfD), the far-right political party in Germany and Hindutva politics in India is partly explained through their shared Islamophobic and anti-Muslim sentiments that have led to new forms of vulnerabilities and heightened forms of anti-immigrant and exclusionary nationalism. Even if the evolutionary trajectory, the spread and the political operations of Hindutva in India have their specificities, it is useful to examine their entwined relations with Nazism in Germany, Fascism in Italy and White extremist nationalisms in the USA and a "multicultural" Europe today (Chin 2017; Leidig 2020): By situating Hindutva perspectives in relation to other nationalist contexts, it becomes possible to recognize the "transnational nature" of the right-wing extremist ideology in a digitally networked world.

In Castells's (2012: 315) *Networks of Outrage and Hope*, networked social movements are conceptualized as "human projection of multiple expressions of needs and desires," the expressions of human will and affect that contain traces of dominant political discourses and an independent individual discontent. This chapter underlines how the diasporic networks of online CAA supporters and protesters distinguish between the desirable and the undesirable state of Hindutva politics, using digital spaces and an ethical and legal rationale. In tandem with studies that incorporate both a quantitative and a qualitative approach to social media data collection and analysis (Leidig 2019; Udupa 2019; Roy et al. 2021), it discusses the digital activism of young Indian diasporas and NRIs by adopting a content analysis of their social media activities and conducting interviews to understand their online lives in relation to their offline lives.

To retrieve and collect the tweets from December 2019 until June 2020, I used Mozdeh and later AntConc to analyze the data sets. By using Tweet Binder, I was able to secure a complete historical user report of ten selected Twitter accounts (those which appeared to be the most active in terms of their CAA-related tweets) to trace the nature of their online activities since their inception. These include five pro-CAA and five anti-CAA accounts that were operated by diasporic Indian users residing in major German cities. Given that this research investigates a recently evolving and real-time phenomenon and adopts a digital tool due to the global pandemic and lockdown, it remains provisional but offers insights into the differences within, and the shifting political perspectives of, the networks of support and dissent. It further stimulates a debate on the social, cultural, legal and political implications of CAA–NRC, as well as the role of diasporic Indians in Germany within this evolving narrative.

Anti-Muslim Migrant Nationalisms and "Modi" Mania

The presence of nearly 35,000 tweets and retweets about pro-CAA and anti-CAA protests, hashtags and social media accounts – all within the four weeks of the passing of the CAA – are proof of interest in the online discussions of the CAA issue among NRIs in Germany. Hashtags include #germanindianssupportcaa, #diasporagainstfascisminindia, #nrisagainstcaa_nrc_npr, #berlinforindia, #frankfurtforindia and #indiaresists_hamburgprotests. Subject-specific Twitter accounts such as @antiCAAD, @IAFHamburg, @IndiaSolNW and @OfbjpM have been initiated. Such an uproar by the Indian diasporas was also audible in other European nation-states, evident through the launching of Twitter accounts such as @SolidarityBelg (Belgium), @NliberalIndians (Netherlands), @nlagainstcaa (Netherlands), @INSolidarityFI (Finland) and @CAAvoices (Italy).

   With regard to the lexical variations or the use of different words within the total words used in the corpus text of the pro- and anti-CAA tweets of Indians in Germany, the "type-token ratio" (TTR) was calculated with the help of AntConc. This was done separately for pro- and anti-CAA tweets of the ten most active users' accounts of Indian diasporas in Germany. The corpus of the pro-CAA tweets has 26% TTR indicating a low score as compared with the 43% score of anti-CAA tweets. Considering that a "high TTR indicates a high degree of lexical variation while a low TTR indicates the opposite" (Thomax, quoted in Vashishata and Arya 2020: 189), the high TTR score of the anti-CAA tweets is suggestive of a rich corpus text connoting a more comprehensive discourse on the CAA issue as compared to the pro-CAA tweets. The interviews with the selected users also attest to this result. While the diaspora protesters against the CAA discussed multiple issues within the Indian legal and geopolitical discourse such as the threats to democracy, secularism, free speech and student protests, the diaspora supporters for CAA repeatedly revolved around the topic of Modi, Hindutva project and the problems of the "anti-national" forces.

In the pro-CAA corpus of tweets of the five most active Twitter accounts, the words with a relatively high frequency (more than 100 times) include "indiasupportscaa," "narendra modi," "indian," "india," "bjp," "should," "amit shah," "namo," "ji" (a suffix in Hindi that is added for respect), "sir," "support," "hindus," "citizen," "Kashmir," "urbannaxals" and "caaexplained." The frequent collocates (more than five times) for the word CAA include "Germany," "isupportcab," "ofbjp," "sewaks," "sahinbagh" (Shaheen Bagh), "jamiamilliauniversity," "gathering," "uninformed," "uneducated," "Pakistanis," "muslims," "venom," "bug," "violence" and "communistvirus." The collocates for the word CAA also include names of Bollywood celebrities such as "anuragkashyap," "sonamkapoor," "sonakshisinha," "javedakhtarjadu" and the names of BJP members such as "swamy," "jagdishshetty" and "vijai." All these results point to the political and religious sentiments of the pro-CAA diasporic groups and are denotative of the insecurities and anxieties embedded within the Hindu nationalist discourse on Indian nationalism. They indicate an affective inclination of hate or support through the act of tagging people and mandate certain qualifications required to be labeled as true patriots or nationalist citizens. An attitude of nationalist territorialization is apparent in their discourse on citizenship as India is no longer an abstract imagined community but one that has geopolitical physical borders which need to be protected from the "infiltrators." What also needs attention in their online discourse is the unabashed juxtaposition of words such as "muslims," "Pakistanis," "venom," "violence," "communistvirus," "urbannaxals," "uneducated" and "uninformed" – a rhetorical trend of Othering the Muslims that has been palpable among Hindutva supporters since the 1947 Partition and that has only reinvigorated on digital platforms since the Modi-led BJP government has been elected to power. In a threatened state, enemies in the 21st century are represented as transnational "viruses" or the "immunological Other in the system, which it infiltrates and destroys" (Baudrillard, quoted in Han 2018: 76). In the post-9/11 global context and post-2014 Indian political context, Muslim migrants and refugees are represented as the "ideal enemy" (Kundnani 2014: 59) or the terrorizing Other: Such a representation is mediated, based on rescue narratives about the Hindu sovereignty of India that is overburdened by a large diverse population and "fractured by multiple antagonisms." Likewise, the representation of migrants as "viruses," "bugs" or "pests" that transmit disease and against which the nation needs to sanitize and do a "pest control" (Anand 2019) becomes extremely problematic, especially in the COVID-19 pandemic context as it further reinforces the migrants' dehumanization, mistreatment and exclusion.

Since there was a clear discomfort and rift between opinions of Indian Hindu and Indian Muslim diasporas, evident in their pro- and anti-CAA tweets, the frequent collocates for the word "Muslim" and "Hindu" were analyzed. In the case of pro-CAA tweets, frequent collocates for "Muslim" include "university," "religion," "virodhi" (opponent) and "fight," whereas for "Hindu," they are "main" (meaning "I"), "Hindu," "protected" and "Kashmiripandits." N-grams with high frequency (more than five times) in the pro-CAA tweets include "caa_nrc," "caa gathering," "caa support," "caa-germany," "caa protest" and "caa #amit shah." These results point out the users' participation in the online discourse and support for the CAA in tandem with the BJP member and Home Minister Amit Shah's political views.

To further dissect the pro-CAA group members' offline ideological justifications for the CAA, interviews were conducted and they attest to the findings excavated from the content of tweets and posts as seen on Facebook pages "German Indians Support CAA," "Overseas Friends of BJP Germany" and Twitter accounts @OFBJP_Germany, @OFBJP_Berlin, @OFBJP_Munich and @OfbjpH. Not only do they indicate a form of "Modi mania" where his image is "morally" respected and hailed as a savior, but his party politics are considered rational and democratic solely based on a large number of his Hindu supporters. Supporting Modi-led BJP government's politics and his followers digitally becomes an expression of both national duty and a mode of practicing long-distance nationalism. In an interview, when asked about the feelings of national belonging and longing, a young Hindu nationalist volunteer in Berlin expressed: "What is long-distance these days, it is not like before; as soon as we see a message from Modi on Twitter, we get started. Our online national duty goes on."

In a January 2020 post on the Facebook page "German Indians Support CAA," the Citizenship Amendment Act was called the "Citizenship Modification Act," reiterating the "Modi" mania (Jain 2021b). On YouTube, most of the pro-CAA rally videos of Germany were compiled into one long video by a Berlin-based Indian journalist who uploaded it with the hyperbolic title "Huge support for CAA by Indians in Germany," thereby attracting and misleading viewers into believing that massive support of the Indian diasporas prevailed. However, a closer investigation of the video makes the viewer wonder if a small group of people in the support rallies could be considered as "huge support" (Sukun 2020). While the reliance on hyperbole, naturalism, logic, simple narratives, bullet points and facts remains a common strategy for the Indian diaspora supporters for CAA evident through the content of their tweets and interviews, there is a sense of discomfort to elaborate discussions and opposing views. This discomfort often materializes as a verbal threat, troll or meme. Some users threatened anti-CAA group members by warning them about "bad posts" and "reporting to German cyberteam," thereby indicating intolerance of any form of criticism or elaborate discussions (Indians Europe Group 2020; Vengurlekar 2020). Another study (Udupa 2019) has observed that Hindu nationalist volunteers often rely on memes and viral trolls to consolidate perpetual attention that has been "fun"damental in turning their Hindu nationalist and targeted "individual" politics into "palpable pleasure."

On Facebook, the cover photos of the pro-CAA online Indian diasporic groups connoted a patriarchal narrative of rescue and integration of the persecuted minorities such as Christians, Parsis, Sikhs, Buddhists and Jains from Pakistan, Afghanistan and Bangladesh (German Indians Support CAA 2020): Although they demonstrated solidarity with Kashmiri pandits in their cover photos and pro-CAA rallies, they indicated anxieties against the dominance of Muslim communities in Kashmir, other parts of India and the neighboring nation-states. Such anxieties were rationalized by uploading explanatory videos of Modi and other BJP members such as Tejasvi Surya, who, on being invited as a speaker of a conference in Hamburg, had even faced opposition from other Indian diaspora groups in Germany (*Scroll* 2020). As the common theme of moral validation of BJP-led Hindutva nationalism runs through the tweets and posts of the pro-CAA groups, a sharp critique of its anti-secular and undemocratic nature underlines the digital activities of the anti-CAA groups. Despite the differences between both groups, digital proactiveness and visibility appear to be crucial for bringing about a collective change across borders while participating in social and political campaigns in India.

Diasporas' Online Politics of Dissent

While most diasporas and NRIs who associated with pro-CAA Twitter handles and Facebook groups were male Hindu students or professionals and aligned themselves with the BJP government's Hindutva agendas, the anti-CAA Twitter handles and Facebook groups tended to be more diverse in terms of users' religious background, gender and profession. Interviews found that most of the diaspora protesters against the CAA are young Hindu, Muslim, Sikh, Jain or Christian NRI professionals (aged between 20 and 45) and based in major German cities such as Berlin, Munich, Hamburg, Frankfurt and Cologne. Most of them had an educational background in Indian universities emphasizing decolonization philosophy. The interviewees gave access to their political and social networks and their Twitter accounts were anonymous or pseudonyms. They feared visibility, the possibility of exclusion from other online groups of Indians in Germany and threats from diplomatic offices or political extremists.

In the anti-CAA corpus of tweets of the five most active Twitter accounts, the words with high frequency (more than 100 times) include "india," "against," "caa," "Germany," "people," "please," "protest," "indian," "stopfundinghate," "govt," "modi," "justice," "solidarity," "women," "democracy," "muslims," "fascism" and "shaheenbaghzindahai" (Shaheen Bagh is alive). The frequent collocates (more than five times) for the word CAA include "against," "reject," "Indians," "protests," "alliance," "citizenship," "Germany," "world," "resolution," "gegen" (against), "facebook," "indien" (Indian), "elections" and "embassy." The collocates in the anti-CAA tweets for CAA also include names of major European and Indian cities, local and international media corporations, as well as words such as "shame," "exclusion," "dissent," "detention centres," "disenfranchisement," "fraternity," "liberty," "equality" and "azaadi." The most frequent N-grams include "anti-caa protests," "caa activists," "caa protesters," "caa+nrc+npr," "caa law" and "caa playbook." These results demonstrate that for the users of anti-CAA Twitter handles such as @AnticaaD, @IndiaSolNW and @IAFHamburg, there is no hailing of Modi or any political leader in their protest activities against the CAA; instead, the law-and-order situation in India and the violence against students of their alma mater in Shaheen Bagh protests in Delhi were the most alarming factors.

The collocates for CAA and the cover photos on their Twitter accounts and Facebook pages establish the preoccupation with the Indian constitution and demonstrate their multilingual efforts to underline the systematic breakdown of Indian democracy into electoral autocracy (Jain 2021b). As they demand citizenship for the persecuted Muslim minorities and uphold the secular values of the Indian constitution, their online discussions on the CAA stare at the moral and political abyss of the BJP government's political machinery and the tattered state of the secular fabric of India. In the anti-CAA tweets, frequent collocates for Muslim include "young," "violence," "towards," "alliance," "sikh," "racism," "burning," "women" and "tolerance." The collocates for Hindu include "nationalist," "india," "rss," "paramilitary," "volunteer," "sangh," "swayamsevak," "rashtra," "radical" and "pluralistic." These findings highlight that the marginalization of the left-liberal student voices in India was relatable at many levels for the young Indian Muslim and Sikh diasporic and migrant students as alienated minority communities in Germany. Their online discourse on CAA and interviews foreground the potential problems that Indians with OCI (Overseas Citizenship of India) status might face, considering that the CAA clause states, "if OCI-holders voice opposition to any government policy, they risk being accused of violating of an odd law, and losing their registration" (Almeida 2020).

As immigrants in Germany, with or without the OCI status, it is "not that easy" to organize protest rallies (Acharjee 2020); thus, social media platforms are particularly useful for the diaspora protesters to not only announce the schedule and itinerary of street protest but also reach out to influential global personalities. It is noteworthy that the anti-CAA street protests (live-streamed, recorded and uploaded on Facebook and YouTube) were held at historically significant spaces in Germany such as the Brandenburg Gate in Berlin, Rote Flora in Hamburg and White Rose Memorial in Munich (Jain 2021b). As many German and other international students joined the protest rallies (nearly 300 participants in Berlin) and chanted multilingual slogans (at least in 15 languages), it resulted in the constellation of several nation-states' histories of resisting state brutality and fascist laws (Imam 2019). At the same time, on the digital space, the linking of contemporary urgent issues, through the circulation of hashtags such as #allrefugeesarewelcome, #policebrutality, #alllivesmatter and #queerresistance led to the co-creation of pathways necessary for staging glocal resistance with large-scale sociopolitical movements such as #blacklivesmatter (Jain 2021b).

Conclusion

In 2020, due to the beginning of the COVID-19 pandemic and the introduction of nationwide stringent lockdown measures, the anti-CAA protest movement lost its momentum on streets and digital spaces. Importantly, the interviews revealed intertwining reasons that have made the networked resistance against the discriminatory CAA weak and more challenging – heightened economic precarity as job-seeking students in the EU with or without temporary work contracts; insecurities related to stringent domicile conditions for immigrants in a multicultural Europe including Germany; and the lack of unity and polarities within the different Indian diasporic groups and the expanding hold of the disrupting Hindutva narrative in online and offline lives.

The Indian diasporas' online networks of CAA support and dissent in Germany indicate a spatiotemporal and material shift in the site of citizenship practices. Their practices have relocated territorially from India to Germany and digitally from comparatively local networks (WhatsApp) to wider global platforms (Twitter, Facebook and YouTube). However, in the case of anti-CAA groups, their practices have shifted to encrypted platforms such as Telegram. The diasporas' deviating and polarized online debates on CAA have also acted as a catalyst in their socialization and integration process in which they have become either more nationalistic or cosmopolitan in their thoughts about citizenship and belonging. As they continue to articulate their discontent or collective outrage through social media, they provide insights into their diasporic experiences of navigating the interlaced networks of the personal, local, national and global.

Acknowledgments

This research has received funding from the European Research Council (ERC) Starting Grant under the European Union's Horizon 2020 research and innovation programme (Grant Agreement Number 714285).

References

Acharjee, S. (2020) "England, Germany, Switzerland: Anti-CAA Protests Break Barriers, Shake the World," *India Today*, 16 January.

Almeida, A. (2020) "The CAA's Provision for Cancelling OCI is Aimed at Punishing Dissenters," *The Wire*, 25 April.

Anand, R. (2019) "After Using the Pesticides, If the Bugs are Coming Out It Means that the Product is Good and Effective. It's Time to Do Some Pest Control in #india, #ISupportCAA, #ISupportCAA_NRC, #IndiaWithModi," *Twitter*, 22 December.

Anderson, B. (1998) "Long-Distance Nationalism," in B. Anderson (ed) *The Spectre of Comparisons: Nationalism, Southeast Asia and the World*, New York: Verso.

Butsch, C. (2018) "The Indian Diaspora in Germany," *Diaspora Studies*, 11(1): 79–100.

Castells, M. (2012) *Networks of Outrage and Hope*, Cambridge: Polity.

Chapparban, S.N. (2020) "Religious Identity and Politics of Citizenship in South Asia," *Development*, 63: 52–9.

Chin, R. (2017) *The Crisis of Multiculturalism in Europe*, New Jersey: Princeton University Press.

Deleuze, G. and Guattari, F. (2010) *Nomadology: The War Machine*, Seattle: Wormwood.

Dusche, M. (2010) *Identity Politics in India and Europe*, Delhi: SAGE.

Glick Schiller, N. (2005) "Long Distance Nationalism," in R. Ember and I. Skoggar (eds) *Encyclopedia of Diasporas: Immigrant and Refugee Cultures Around the World*, New York: Kluwer Academic/Plenum.

Griffin, R. (2012) "Studying Fascism in a Postfascist Age?," *Fascism*, 1(1): 1–17.

Han, B.C. (2018) *The Topology of Violence*, Cambridge: MIT Press.

Holland, E. (2011) *Nomad Citizenship: Free-Market Communism and the Slow-Motion General Strike*, Minneapolis: University of Minnesota Press.

Imam, S. (2019) "Anti-CAA Protests Go Global: Chants of 'Azaadi' Echo in Berlin," *The Quint*, 24 December.

Indians Europe Group (2020) "For Anti-CAA People Please Beware, If You Join Then & Write Bad Posts in the Group, Then We Will Send the Same to the Germany Cyber Team on the Violent Post & They Would Track You Down," *Facebook*, 7 January.

Jain, J. (2021a) *Thinking Past 'Post-9/11': Home, Nation and Transnational Desires in Pakistani English Novels and Hindi Films*, London: Routledge.

Jain, J. (2021b) "Error '370' Democracy is Missing or Corrupted! Digital Politics of Indian Diasporic Youth in Germany," *South Asia Journal: Covering Policy Issues from South Asia*, 34 (Spring).

Jay, M. (2020) "154 European Union Lawmakers Draft Stunning Anti-CAA Resolution," *National Herald*, 25 January.

Kundnani, A. (2014) *The Muslims Are Coming! Islamophobia, Extremism and the Domestic War on Terror*, New York: Verso.

Leidig, E. (2019) "Immigrant, Nationalist and Proud," *Media and Communication*, 7(1): 77–89.

Leidig, E. (2020) "Hindutva as a Variant of Right-Wing Extremism," *Patterns of Prejudice*, 54(3): 215–37.

Mahalingam, M. (2013) "India's Diaspora Policy and Foreign Policy," *Global Research Forum on Diaspora and Transnationalism*.

Mihelj, S. and Jiménez-Martínez, C. (2021) "Digital Nationalism," *Nations and Nationalism*, 27: 331–46.

Ministry of Law and Justice (2019) "Citizenship Amendment Act 2019 (No. 47 of 2019)," *The Gazette of India Extraordinary*, Delhi: Government of India Press.

Nigam, S. (2020) "Many Dimensions of Shaheen Bagh Movement in India," *SSRN Electronic Journal*.

Ponzanesi, S. (2020) "Digital Diasporas," *Interventions*, 22(8): 977–93.

Roy, A. (2019) "The Citizenship (Amendment) Bill, 2016 and the Aporia of Citizenship," *Economic and Political Weekly*, 54(49): 28–34.

Roy, S., Mukherjee, M., Sinha, P., Das, S., Bandopadhyay, S. and Mukherjee, A. (2021) "Exploring the Dynamics of Protest Against National Register of Citizens & Citizenship Amendment Act through Online Social Media: The Indian Experience," *ArXiv.org*, 21 February.

Scroll (2019) "Germany's Expertise will be Useful for Building 'New India,' Says PM after Meeting Chancellor Merkel," 1 November.

Scroll (2020) "Indian Diaspora Opposes BJP MP Tejasvi Surya as Speaker at Germany Conference, Call Him 'Bigoted'," 5 October.

Sharma, P. (2013) "BJP Unleashes Tech Blitzkrieg to Reach the Magic Figure of 272," *New Indian Express*, 29 September.

Subrahmanian, M. (2015) *Changing Perspectives among Indian Diaspora in Germany: Culture and Gender*, Ph.D. Thesis, Freiburg: Albert-Ludwigs-Universität.

Sud, N. (2008) "Tracing the Links between Hindu Nationalism and the Indian Diaspora," *St Antony's International Review*, 3(2): 50–65.

Sukun, V.R. (2020) "Huge Support for CAA by Indians in Germany | Citizenship Amendment Act 2019," YouTube, 23 January.

The Hindu (2019) "German Student Who Took Part in Anti-CAA Protests Told to Leave India," 24 December.

Thobani, S. (2018) "Alt-Right with the Hindu-Right," *Ethnic and Racial Studies*, 42(5): 745–62.

Udupa, S. (2019) "Nationalism in the Digital Age: Fun as a Metapractice of Extreme Speech," *International Journal of Communication*, 13: 3143–63.

Vashishata, G. and Arya, U. (2020) "Citizenship Amendment Act," *Journal of Content, Community & Communication*, 12(6): 184–97.

Vengurlekar, P. (2020) "This Man Manish Kumar Who is Admin of a Facebook Group in Germany has been Spewing Venom Against the Hindu Religion Day in and Day out and Poisoning the Minds of Indian Students. Will @CGIFrankfurt, @MEAIndia Please Take Note. Many Indians are Very Agitated Against Him," *Twitter*, 20 February.

Visana, V. (2021) "Nazism and Hindu Nationalism," Holocaust Exhibition and Learning Centre, 19 April.

INDEX